deviant behavior and social process

deviant behavior and social process

WILLIAM A. RUSHING
Editor

Vanderbilt University

Rand McNally College Publishing Company

ND M^cNALLY SOCIOLOGY SERIES

Edgar F. Borgatta, Advisory Editor

Current printing (last digit)
15   14   13   12   11   10   9   8   7   6   5   4   3   2

To Todd

PREFACE

This book is designed to be used in undergraduate sociology courses on *deviant behavior, social problems, social disorganization,* and *social control.* Its objective is to give the student a general perspective on the sociology of deviance by providing examples of particular theories about deviant behavior and examples of research on deviance. In the introductory chapter the basic framework for the analysis of deviant behavior is presented and concepts are illustrated with examples of research on industrial work groups.

Nine different types of deviant behavior are considered: juvenile delinquency, adult crime, homicide, prison subcultures, homosexuality, alcoholism, drug addiction, mental illness, and suicide.

This book does not treat aspects of deviance which are purely biological, psychological, psychiatric, or economic. All articles are concerned with social aspects of deviant behavior.

Deviant behavior is viewed as a process consisting of three dimensions: antecedents and determinants; social relations and a process of action; and a series of consequences. Most books on deviant behavior concentrate on the first dimension. From a sociological standpoint, however, analyses of the other two dimensions are equally important. Sociologists are just as interested, for example, in the effects of the social response on an individual after he commits a deviant act as they are in the factors that drove him to commit the act in the first place.

Needless to say, not all sociological questions and topics concerning deviant behavior are exhausted here. However, the student is offered some specific hypotheses and concrete research findings regarding the origins, courses, and consequences of several types of deviant behavior. By reading this material his understanding of the sociological perspective on deviant behavior should be considerably broadened.

Acknowledgement is gratefully made to the authors and publishers who have permitted the reprinting of the works in this volume. To Professors Jack P. Gibbs and James F. Short, Jr., I am especially indebted for the intellectual stimulation given me prior to the first edition in numerous discussions on deviance.

I also want to thank Kay F. Rushing for her editorial and clerical assistance, as well as for other matters that go beyond the call of wifely duty, and Cindy Miller for typing assistance.

Most of all, I want to thank the students at the University of Wisconsin, Washington State University, and Vanderbilt University who have given me the pleasure of teaching them the sociology of deviance and, as a result, helped me to sustain my interest in deviance.

William A. Rushing

CONTENTS

CHAPTER ONE

DEVIANT BEHAVIOR AND SOCIAL PROCESS

Since sociology is the study of society, and deviant behavior is a significant aspect of society, the relevance of this study needs little comment. Almost any day in the United States, one can read in the newspaper, hear over the radio, and see on television, accounts of antisocial behavior such as organized crime, prison riots, sex crimes, juvenile delinquency, and murder.

Communities have created special committees and agencies to combat deviant conduct at the local level. Congress has established "Crime Prevention Week," and juvenile delinquency, organized crime, narcotic traffic, and other forms of deviance have been investigated by congressional committees. Large federal agencies have been established to support research, treatment, and prevention programs in mental illness, alcoholism, drug abuse, and suicide. "Crime and violence," "law and order," and "crime in the streets" are campaign issues for presidential and other political candidates. Congress has passed legislation designed to aid states and cities in preventing crime. Deviant behavior is indeed a significant feature of American society.

Sociologists have been concerned with deviance for a long time. Following the early investigations and writings of Emile Durkheim, Gabriel Tarde, and W. I. Thomas, sociologists have conducted many investigations of numerous types of deviant behavior. Other disciplines are also concerned with deviance; psychologists and psychiatrists, in particular, have studied it. Consequently, the study of deviant behavior is a meeting ground for several disciplines. Nonetheless, each discipline has its own point of view or perspective. In this chapter, the sociological perspective will be outlined and distinguished from other points of view. This perspective and the basic concepts of deviance will be illustrated with two studies of deviant behavior in industrial work groups.

Definition of Deviant Behavior

Despite the amount of attention given to the subject, there is no universally accepted definition of what constitutes deviant behavior. Before discussing various definitions, I will outline the characteristics of *social norms,* since definitions of deviant behavior usually include some aspect of these phenomena.

Social norms have three properties. First, they involve *patterns of behavior,* that is, behavior and attitudes that are characteristic of most people of a population. Most Americans, for example, believe in God and go to church (at least some of the time) so that belief in God and church-going are social norms. In this sense, social norms are *statistical* concepts.

Another property is a *normative* or *moral quality.* Norms are not just patterns of behavior; they are also morally prescribed behavior. Most Americans are religious and think that people should believe in God and go to church; they may feel guilty if they have doubts about God's existence or if they fail to go to church. Sometimes norms are stated formally and expressed in writing, as in law; in other instances, as in religious belief and church-going, they are informal understandings between members of a group or society. Informal norms are the more numerous.

Third, all viable norms have *sanctions* or coercive reactions associated with them. In general, persons who violate norms are punished by the group or society. For this reason, many persons who are atheists do not make their beliefs known to others.

The above three characteristics, of course, exist in varying degrees. Some behaviors are more universal than others so that the pattern of these behaviors is clearer than that of others; driving on the right-hand side of the road is more universal than going to church on Sunday. Everyone does not go to church but everyone who drives does so on the right-hand side of the road. Similarly, norms vary in moral quality; this difference is reflected in the distinctions sociologists sometimes make between folkways, which are merely expected ways of doing things, and mores, which are expectations with moral connotations.

Disagreements on the definition of deviant behavior can be traced to the different properties of social norms—statistical, normative, and reactive.

The statistical concept, or being different.   A number of years ago, Floyd Allport[1] conducted a study of behavioral regularities in various situations. He found that for a variety of behaviors, most individuals behave alike. For example, most people stop when a stop-and-go-light is red, some slow down but do not stop, and virtually no one speeds up. The visual description of this pattern of behavior has come to be known as the "J-curve" of conforming behavior, with conforming behavior defined as the most frequently occurring type. Actually, conformity and its opposite, deviance, are viewed in terms of degree, which in turn is re-

---

[1] Floyd Allport, "The J-Curve Hypothesis of Conforming Behavior," *Journal of Social Psychology* 5 (December, 1934), pp. 1414–83.

lated to the frequency of the behavior. The pattern is illustrated in Figure 1. The most frequently occurring behavior is the most conforming and the least frequently occurring is the most deviant. In some instances, however, the distribution of individuals' behavior may conform more closely to a "bell-shaped curve." In this case, the most frequently occurring behavior is toward the middle of the distribution with the least frequently occurring behavior at *either* extreme. On many tests the most frequently occurring performance is the average for all individuals with extremely good and extremely poor performance occurring infrequently. The pattern is illustrated in Figure 2. But regardless of the precise shape of the distribution, individuals who do not act like the majority are in a minority. They are therefore different. Some theorists consider this the basis for designating an individual a deviant.[2] Hence to be different from the majority is to be deviant.

FIGURE 1. "J-SHAPED CURVE" OF CONFORMING BEHAVIOR

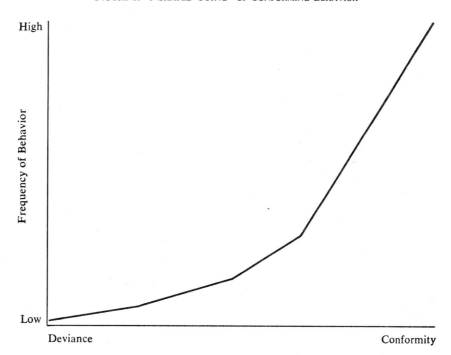

Although this may appear to be a useful definition at first glance, there are several problems with it. First, as noted, different types of behavior manifest different distributions. Consequently, how one is different from others will vary. For example, in a J-curve distribution, all deviants deviate from the majority behavior in one way, but in a bell-shaped

[2] Jonathan L. Freeman and Anthony N. Dood, *Deviancy: The Psychology of Being Different* (New York: Academic Press, 1965).

FIGURE 2. "BELL-SHAPED CURVE"

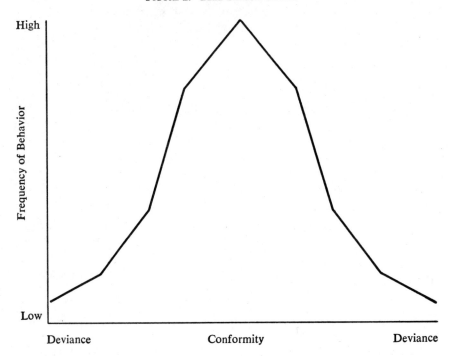

distribution, deviants differ from the majority in two opposite directions, for example, persons who score very high or very low on a test. Second, according to the "being different" criterion, persons who register as members of a minority political party (e.g., Republican) would be deviants; or persons who achieve a social status above or below that of their parents would be deviant because most persons have about the same status as their parents.[3]

Problems also arise with this conception because *statistical* deviance may be socially approved behavior (for example, social and economic improvement), which is valued and *normatively* expected by most members of society. The conception may also lead to some rather ridiculous and fruitless conclusions, such as that all noncoffee drinking adults in the United States are deviants. In general, to sociologists statistical deviance itself does not *necessarily* point to aspects of behavior that are sociologically significant. To sociologists the violation of normative expectations and the reactions and sanctions of others are the crucial phenomena in deviant behavior.

Deviance as norm violation.   To most sociologists, deviant behavior is behavior that violates group conceptions of proper conduct—rules and codes of conduct which group members are expected and obliged to obey.

---

[3] See Seymour Martin Lipset and Reinhard Bendix, *Social Mobility in Industrial Society* (Berkeley: University of California Press, 1959), p. 88.

Cohen, for example, refers to deviant behavior "as behavior which violates institutionalized expectations—that is, expectations which are shared and recognized as legitimate within a social system."[4] Merton refers to "conduct that departs significantly from norms that are socially defined as appropriate and morally binding. . . ."[5] As noted earlier, norms may be formal or informal; in either case, individuals usually follow them for two primary reasons.

One is *desire*. Through a socialization process, individuals are taught group norms. Socialization is complete when the individual has accepted or internalized the norms to the extent that they constitute his conscience. In this state, he is motivated to conform.

The other reason is *fear*, which stems from the fact that sanctions are associated with norms and deviations from them. Sanctions are group reactions to and punishments for individuals who violate socially accepted codes of conduct. Although norms vary in the extent of societal reaction to transgression, most viable norms are accompanied by punitive responses. Indeed, some consider this an essential aspect of the definition of deviant behavior. Clinard refers to situations "in which behavior is in a disapproved direction, and of significant degree to exceed the tolerance limit of the community . . .,"[6] and Erikson considers deviant behavior to be "conduct which is generally thought to acquire the attention of social control agencies—that is, conduct about which 'something should be done.' "[7] There are three general types of sanctions. Some are physical, such as imprisonment; others are economic, as when individuals are fined by the court; many, however, are social, including ostracism, ridicule, and rejection.[8] Most groups use a mixture of all three. In any case, variations in social sanction are the focal points of some sociological definitions of deviance.

Deviance defined by the social reaction.   Focus on social reaction in the definition of deviance derives partly from the fact that norm violators are not always punished. The female college coed who is known to be having sexual relations is seldom severely ostracized (unless, of course, she is promiscuous or becomes pregnant); students who demonstrate against university and government policy as well as against other issues on university premises, creating disruption and violating university rules, are rarely punished; females and whites in the United States are more apt to escape arrest and conviction of committed crimes than are males and blacks.

---

[4] Albert K. Cohen, "The Study of Social Disorganization and Deviant Behavior," in Robert K. Merton, Leonard Bloom, and Leonard S. Cottrell, Jr., *Sociology Today: Problems and Prospects* (New York: Basic Books, 1959), p. 462.

[5] Robert K. Merton, "Epilogue" in Robert K. Merton and Robert S. Nisbet, *Contemporary Social Problems*, 2nd ed. (New York: Harcourt, Brace and World, 1966), p. 805.

[6] Marshall B. Clinard, *Sociology of Deviant Behavior*, 3rd ed. (New York: Holt, Rinehart and Winston, 1968), p. 28.

[7] Kai T. Erikson, *Wayward Puritans: A Study in the Sociology of Deviance* (New York: John Wiley, 1966), pp. 10–11.

[8] For a detailed discussion of these three types of sanctions, see Amatai Etzioni, *A Comparative Analysis of Complex Organization* (New York: The Free Press of Glencoe, 1961).

Turning the matter around, many persons are punished who have committed no deviant act. Victims of jury mistakes are obvious examples, as are individuals who are held in jail until their trial in court, at which time they are found to be innocent of the charges against them. The public conception of such persons as deviant may never be eliminated; stigma is associated with the accusation and arrest and not the violation per se.

There is not necessarily a one-to-one relationship between the nature of the act and the group reaction.[9] Some deviants are neither defined as deviants nor punished as such, whereas others are defined and punished as deviants even though they have committed no deviant act. For this reason, some sociologists have argued that deviant behavior can only be defined in terms of the social reaction to it.[10] This perspective, often referred to as the "labelling approach" to deviance, points out processes that may be ignored when deviance is defined as norm violation. It makes explicit the notion that deviance is not an inherent quality of the act itself and that deviance must be viewed from the perspective of persons other than the actor himself. Furthermore, it shows, as W. I. Thomas observed a number of years ago, that if people define something as true it is apt to become true consequently; specifically, if people define a person as deviant, he is a deviant as a consequence—he is defined and treated as such, and as far as society and social reality are concerned, he *is* a deviant. Moreover, given the fact that an individual tends to view himself in terms of the way others treat and view him, a person may come to view himself as a deviant when in fact he may not have committed a deviant act. In Lemert's terms, he may become a "secondary deviant," a person who has a picture of himself as a deviant integrated into his self-image without ever being a "primary deviant." A "primary deviant" is a person who commits deviant actions without integrating such actions into his self-image; this, according to Lemert, is usually the first stage in deviance.[11] And, of course, the treatment of an individual as a deviant—for example, imprisonment—may itself have consequences that lead the individual into a deviant career. In this approach, deviance is defined by "moral entrepreneurs," that is, by individuals and groups with particular interests and the necessary resources to define persons as deviant and to prosecute them accordingly.[12]

There is much truth in this approach, but the general idea would appear to be more true of some societies than of others. In particular, "moral entrepreneurs" have greater leeway in societies where the definition of deviance is controlled by a few powerful persons and where the

[9] Howard S. Becker, *Outsiders: Studies in the Sociology of Deviance* (New York: The Free Press, 1963).

[10] See esp. Becker, *Outsiders*. See also Edwin Lemert, *Social Pathology* (New York: McGraw-Hill Book Company, 1951); John I. Kitsuse, "Societal Reaction to Deviant Behavior," *Social Problems* 9 (Winter, 1962), pp. 247–57; and Erikson, *Wayward Puritans*.

[11] Edwin M. Lemert, *Human Deviance, Social Problems and Social Control*, 2nd ed. (Englewood Cliffs: Prentice-Hall, 1973), pp. 62–63.

[12] Becker, *Outsiders*, pp. 147–63.

dominant norms of society are so general, as in the case of political and religious norms, that they pervade many specific aspects of our lives. Under these conditions it becomes much easier for a few individuals to act as "moral entrepreneurs"; this is exemplified in the religious purges of the Inquisition and the political purge in the Soviet Union during the thirties. During the period of the Inquisition, great authority was vested in the leaders of the Catholic Church and religion was so central in society that Church leaders could define almost any form of behavior in terms of religious conformity or heresy. Thus, for example, Galileo was prosecuted not because he rejected Christian beliefs but because he advocated beliefs, such as the idea that the earth moves around the sun, that Church leaders interpreted as contrary to the implications of Christian beliefs. Similarly, in the Soviet Union during the thirties, great power was centralized in Stalin, and many types of behavior were regarded as crimes against the state (this is still true today). Consequently, anyone who appeared to be lacking in loyalty to the Stalin regime could be prosecuted for a political crime.[13] Such examples suggest, indeed, that the significance of societal reaction and reactions of "moral entrepreneurs" varies depending on the centralization of power and the scope of those norms that persons in power are most concerned with enforcing.

In addition, this approach is limited in a very basic way since it assumes that reality exists only in terms of what is defined by members of society as real. This would seem to restrict too severely the range of behaviors subsumed under the title of deviance. The crime rate may increase (or decrease) dramatically but the arrest and conviction rate (the reaction rate) may remain stable. We would still want to know why there is variation in the level of criminal behavior regardless of the societal reaction; but such a question could not be asked if deviant behavior were defined only in terms of the societal reaction. Social reaction theorists themselves have difficulty in so limiting the definition of deviance and must incorporate the idea of "secret deviance."[14] But to the extent that deviance is defined in terms of reactions, secret deviance is a contradiction in terms. In any case, one would still want to know what the *causes* of secret deviance are.[15]

In addition, as Ned Polsky notes, this approach fails to consider the

---

[13] See Walter D. Connor, "The Manufacture of Deviance: The Case of the Soviet Purge, 1936–1938," *American Sociological Review* 37 (August, 1972), pp. 403–13. In addition, the success of "moral entrepreneurs" is probably greater in societies which have repressive control systems than in societies with restrained control systems. In the former there are few restraints placed on the control system whereas in the latter there are many. See Connor's comments, *"The Manufacture of Deviance,* and pp. 156–67 below. For the distinction between these two types of control systems, see Elliott P. Currie, "Crime without Criminals: Witchcraft and its Control in Renaissance Europe," *Law and Society Review* 3 (October, 1968), pp. 7–12.

[14] Becker, *Outsiders,* p. 13.

[15] For this and other criticisms of the "labelling perspective," see Jack P. Gibbs, "Conceptions of Deviant Behavior: The Old and the New," *Pacific Sociological Review,* Spring, 1966, pp. 9–14. For a response to the criticisms, see Howard S. Becker, *Outsiders: Studies in the Sociology of Deviance,* 2nd ed. (New York: Free Press, 1973), pp. 177–208. Becker's subsequent comments indicate that his position is not that deviant acts exist only in terms of the societal reaction. Instead, by emphasizing the societal reaction, the "labelling perspectives" draws attention to a dimension of deviant behavior that has not received the research attention that it deserves.

important *functions* deviant behavior may perform for society. To illustrate, a functional consequence of prostitution and pornography is the preservation of the "double institutionalization of legitimate sex," that is, to restrict the legitimate use of sex to within marriage and its scope within the marital relationship to a specified few of the possible sex acts.[16] Prostitution and pornography have these consequences for society even if the participants are not identified and punished. Polsky argues, therefore, that the insight of Thomas—that situations are real in terms of social definition—

> is true, but only half the truth. The other half is that social life, though profoundly affected by the participants' linguistic interpretation of it, is not identical with or completely determined by such interpretation. In other words, a real situation has some real consequences even if people *don't* define it as real. The fact is often lost sight of by those who take a "labelling" stance [to deviant behavior].[17]

Definitions are not right or wrong, of course, only more or less useful. A definition is superior to another to the extent that it has greater utility in helping to generate researchable ideas about a particular phenomenon. Consequently, whether the definition of deviant behavior should be in terms of norm violation or social reaction must, in the final analysis, depend on the types and number of researchable statements that can be generated by frameworks using the different definitions. On balance, I believe that deviance as norm violation holds greatest promise as a definition. But, to avoid the danger of reifying deviant behavior—that is, of associating deviant behavior with the definition and thereby assuming that the definition *is* deviant behavior (which, incidentally, we believe has occurred too frequently in the debate over the *definition* of deviant behavior)—note that my definition of deviant behavior as norm violation is *only* a definition and does not preclude the possibility of alternative definitions.

But, granting the acceptance of this definition, there is still a problem. Behavior that is deviant in one society may not be deviant in another society, as the social reaction theorists emphasize. Deviant behavior is not an absolute; it is not an inherent quality of an act or an inherent quality of the desire and motivation that are involved in an act. The point is well stated by Daniel Bell: "Illicit desires may always exist, but the definition of what is licit or illicit changes with the moral temper and practices of a society."[18] Moreover, within society, the same behavior that is considered deviant by one group may not be considered deviant when viewed from the perspectives of other groups. For example, de-

---

[16] Ned Polsky, *Hustlers, Beats and Others* (Chicago: Aldine Publishing Company, 1967), p. 196.

[17] *Ibid.* (Author's emphasis.)

[18] Daniel Bell, "The Myth of Crime Waves: The Actual Decline of Crime in the United States," in Daniel Bell, *The End of Ideology: On the Exhaustion of Political Ideas in the Fifties,* rev. ed. (New York: The Macmillan Company, 1960), p. 170.

linquent gangs may encourage forms of behavior that are viewed as deviant and negatively sanctioned by the rest of society. The social acceptance of behavior may also vary depending on one's position and status in society: "Deviant behavior cannot be described in the abstract but must be related to the norms that are socially defined as appropriate and morally binding for people occupying various statuses."[19] The social acceptability of certain types of behavior is clearly different for males and females, and there is evidence that what is acceptable as conforming behavior varies depending on one's class.[20] There is, then, a *relativity principle* in deviant behavior. Deviant behavior may also vary for the same group or position at different times in history; for example, much behavior is now permitted and encouraged for females that was considered improper conduct only a few years ago. (The same is true of some male behavior, such as letting one's hair grow long.) When referring to deviant behavior, therefore, one must indicate *whose* norms are being violated. The relativity principle of deviant behavior is an especially useful idea when considering *deviant subcultures.*

When a group's norms deviate from the norms of the dominant group, a deviant subculture is formed. Sociologists have not yet developed a fully rounded theory of deviant subcultures, but several characteristics can be identified.

First, deviant subcultures may emerge simply because deviants are attracted to each other. Homosexual subcultures[21] appear to develop this way.

Other deviant subcultures develop because of a shared experience in a particular area of behavior. The development of beliefs and expectations about the effects of various drugs occurs only after a history of drug use in society. Such shared beliefs and expectations constitute aspects of a drug subculture.[22]

In other instances deviant subcultures may originate because members of a group are unable or do not care to achieve the standards imposed by the dominant group or broader society. The reaction may be so extreme that the subcultural norms are exactly opposite to those of the dominant group; conduct is defined as good precisely because the dominant group defines it as bad. Some say that delinquent gangs originate this way.[23] In this particular case, opposition to the dominant group (middle-class society) is the basis for the original subcultural development.

Finally, groups may exist for some non-deviant reason and develop deviant norms only as their opposition to an outside group develops. This is illustrated in the following article by George C. Homans, "Output Restriction and Social Sanctions." The article also illuminates other concepts and ideas mentioned above.

---

[19] Merton, "Epilogue," p. 805.
[20] See pp. 51–54 of this volume.
[21] See Maurice Leznoff and William A. Westley, "The Homosexual Community," pp. 269–74 of this volume.
[22] See Howard S. Becker, "History, Culture, and Subjective Experience: An Exploration of the Social Bases of Drug-Induced Experiences," pp. 342–54 of this volume.
[23] See Albert K. Cohen's interpretation, pp. 48–51 of this volume.

OUTPUT RESTRICTION NORMS AND SOCIAL SANCTIONS
GEORGE C. HOMANS

The investigators discovered, in the course of the regular interviews, evidence here and there in the plant of a type of behavior which strongly suggested that the workers were banding together informally in order to protect themselves against practices which they interpreted as a menace to their welfare. This type of behavior manifested itself in (1) "straight-line" output, that is, the operators had adopted a standard [norm] of what they felt to be a proper day's work and none of them exceeded it by very much; (2) a resentment of the wage incentive system under which they worked—in most cases, some form of group piecework; (3) expressions which implied that group piecework as a wage incentive plan was not working satisfactorily; (4) informal practices by which persons who exceeded the accepted standard, that is, "rate killers," could be punished and "brought into line"; (5) informal leadership on the part of individuals who undertook to keep the working group together and enforce its rules; (6) preoccupations of futility with regard to promotion; and (7) extreme likes and dislikes toward immediate superiors, according to their attitude toward the behavior of the operators. The investigators felt that this complex of behavior deserved further study.

In view of these considerations, the decision was taken in May, 1931, to assign selected interviewers to particular groups of employees and allow them to interview the employees as often as they felt was necessary. The story of one of these groups is characteristic of the findings reached by this new form of interviewing. The work of the employees was the adjustment of small parts which went into the construction of telephone equipment. The management thought that the adjustment was a complicated piece of work. The interviewer found that it was really quite simple. He felt that anyone could learn it, but that the operators had conspired to put a

fence around the job. They took pride in telling how apparatus which no one could make work properly was sent in from the field for adjustment. Then telephone engineers would come in to find out from the operators how the repairs were made. The latter would fool around, doing all sorts of wrong things and taking about two hours to adjust apparatus, and in this way prevented people on the outside from finding out what they really did. They delighted in telling the interviewer how they were pulling the wool over everybody's eyes. It followed that they were keeping the management in ignorance as to the amount of work they could do. The output of the group, when plotted, was practically a straight line.

Obviously this result could not have been gained without some informal organization, and such organization in fact there was. The group had developed leadership. Whenever an outsider —engineer, inspector, or supervisor—came into the room, one man always dealt with him. Whenever any technical question was raised about the work, this employee answered it. For other purposes, the group had developed a second leader. Whenever a new man came into the group or a member of the group boosted output beyond what was considered the proper level, this second leader took charge of the situation. The group had, so to speak, one leader for dealing with foreign and one for dealing with domestic affairs. The different supervisors were largely aware of the situation which had developed, but they did not try to do anything about it because in fact they were powerless. Whenever necessary, they themselves dealt with the recognized leaders of the group. . . .

In order to study this kind of problem further, to make a more detailed investigation of social relations in a working group, and to supplement interview material with direct observation of the behavior of employees, the Division of Industrial Research decided to set up a new test room. The investigators . . . tried to devise an experiment which would not be radically altered by the process of experimentation itself. They chose a group of men—nine wiremen, three soldermen,

Extracted from "The Western Electric Researches" by George C. Homans, in Schuyler Dean, *Human Factors in Management*, pp. 230–41, with the permission of Reinhold Publishing Corporation and the author.

and two inspectors—engaged in the assembly of terminal banks for use in telephone exchanges, took them out of their regular department and placed them in a special room. Otherwise no change was made in their conditions of work, except that an investigator was installed in the room, whose duty was simply to observe the behavior of the men. In the Relay Assembly Test Room [name of a previous study] a log had been kept of the principal events of the test. At the beginning it consisted largely of comments made by the workers in answer to questions about their physical condition. Later it came to include a much wider range of entries, which were found to be extremely useful in interpreting the changes in the output rate of the different workers. The work of the observer in the new test room was in effect an expansion of the work of keeping the log in the old one. Finally an interviewer was assigned to the test room; he was not, however, one of the population of the room but remained outside and interviewed the employees from time to time in the usual manner. No effort was made to get output records other than the ones ordinarily kept in the department from which the group came, since the investigators felt that such a procedure would introduce too large a change from a regular shop situation. In this way the experiment was set up which is referred to as the Bank Wiring Observation Room. It was in existence seven months, from November, 1931, to May, 1932.

The method of payment is the first aspect of this group which must be described. It was a complicated form of group piecework. The department of which the workers in the observation room were a part was credited with a fixed sum of every unit of equipment it assembled. The amount thus earned on paper by the department every week made up the sum of which the wages of all the men in the department were paid. Each individual was then assigned an hourly rate of pay, and he was guaranteed this amount in case he did not make at least as much on a piecework basis. The rate was based on a number of factors, including the nature of the job a worker was doing, his efficiency, and his length of service with the Company. Records of the output of every worker were kept, and every six months there was a rate revision, the purpose of which was to make the hourly rates of the different workers correspond to their relative efficiency.

The hourly rate of a given employee, multiplied by the number of hours worked by him during the week, was spoken of as the daywork value of the work done by the employee. The daywork values of the work done by all the employees in the department were then added together, and the total thus obtained was subtracted from the total earnings credited to the department for the number of units of equipment assembled. The surplus, divided by the total daywork value, was expressed as a percentage. Each individual's hourly rate was then increased by this percentage, and the resulting hourly earnings figure, multiplied by the number of hours worked, constituted that person's weekly earnings.

Another feature of the system should be mentioned here. Sometimes a stoppage which was beyond the control of the workers took place in the work. For such stoppages the workers were entitled to claim time out, being paid at their regular hourly rates for this time. This was called the "daywork allowance claim." The reason why the employees were paid their hourly rate for such time and not their average hourly wages was a simple one. The system was supposed to prevent stalling. The employees could earn more by working than they could by taking time out. As a matter of fact, there was no good definition of what constituted a stoppage which was beyond the control of the workers. All stoppages were more or less within their control. But this circumstance was supposed to make no difference in the working of the system, since the assumption was that in any case the workers, pursuing their economic interests, would be anxious to keep stoppages at a minimum.

This system of payment was a complicated one, but it is obvious that there was a logical reason for every one of its features. An individual's earnings would be affected by changes in his rate or in his output and by changes in the output of the group as a whole. The only way in which the group as a whole could increase its earnings was by increasing its total output. It is obvious also that the experts who designed the system made certain implicit assumptions about the behavior of human beings, or at least the behavior of workers in a large American factory.

They assumed that every employee would pursue his economic interest by trying to increase not only his own output but the output of every other person in the group. The group as a whole would act to prevent slacking by any of its members. One possibility, for instance, was that by a few weeks' hard work an employee could establish a high rate for himself. Then he could slack up and be paid out of all proportion to the amount he actually contributed to the wages of the group. Under these circumstances, the other employees were expected to bring pressure to bear to make him work harder.

Such was the way in which the wage incentive scheme ought to have worked. The next question is how it actually did work. . . . Among the employees in the observation room there was a notion of a proper day's work. They felt that if they had wired two equipments a day they had done about the right amount. Most of the work was done in the morning. As soon as the employees felt sure of being able to finish what they considered enough for the day, they slacked off. This slacking off was naturally more marked among the faster than among the slower workmen.

As a result, the output graph from week to week tended to be a straight line. The employees resorted to two further practices in order to make sure that it remained so. They reported more or less output than they performed and they claimed more daywork allowances than they were entitled to. At the end of the day, the observer would make an actual count of the number of connections wired—something which was not done by the supervisors—and he found that the men would report to the group chief sometimes more and sometimes less work than they actually had accomplished. At the end of the period of observation, two men had completed more than they ever had reported, but on the whole the error was in the opposite direction. The theory of the employees was that excess work produced on one day should be saved and applied to a deficiency on another day. The other way of keeping the output steady was to claim excessive daywork allowance. The employees saw that the more daywork they were allowed, the less output they would have to maintain in order to keep the average hourly output rate steady. The claims for daywork allowance

were reported by the men to their group chief, and he, as will be seen, was in no position to make any check. These practices had two results. In the first place, the departmental efficiency records did not represent true efficiency, and therefore decisions as to grading were subject to errors of considerable importance. In the second place, the group chief was placed in a distinctly awkward position.

The findings of the observer were confirmed by tests which were made as a part of the investigation. Tests of intelligence, finger dexterity, and other skills were given to the workers in the room, and the results of the tests were studied in order to discover whether there was any correlation between output, on the one hand, and earnings, intelligence, or finger dexterity, on the other. The studies showed that there was not. The output was apparently not reflecting the native intelligence or dexterity of the members of the group.

Obviously the wage incentive scheme was not working in the way it was expected to work. The next question is why it was not working. In this connection, the observer reported that the group had developed an informal social organization, such as had been revealed by earlier investigations. The foreman who selected the employees taking part in the Bank Wiring Observation Room was cooperative and had worked with the investigators before. They asked him to produce a normal group. The men he chose all came out of the same regular shop department, but they had not been closely associated in their work there. Nevertheless, as soon as they were thrown together in the observation room, friendships sprang up and soon two well-defined cliques were formed. The division into cliques showed itself in a number of ways: in mutual exclusiveness, in differences in the games played off-hours, and so forth.

What is important here is not what divided the men in the observation room but what they had in common. They shared a common body of sentiments. A person should not turn out too much work. If he did, he was a "rate-buster." The theory was that if an excessive amount of work was turned out, the management would lower the piecework rate so that the employees would be in the position of doing more work for approximately the same pay. On the other hand, a person should not turn out too little work. If he did, he was a "chiseler," that is, he was getting paid for work he did not do. A person should say nothing which would injure a fellow member of the group. If he did, he was a "squealer." Finally, no member of the group should act officiously.

The working group had also developed methods of enforcing respect for its attitudes [norm]. The experts who devised the wage incentive scheme assumed that the group would bring pressure to bear upon the slower workers to make them work faster and so increase the earnings of the group. In point of fact, something like the opposite occurred. The employees brought pressure to bear not upon the slower workers but upon the faster ones, the very ones who contributed most of the earnings of the group. The pressure was brought to bear in various ways. One of them was "binging." If one of the employees did something which was not considered quite proper, one of his fellow workers had the right to "bing" him. Binging consisted of hitting him a stiff blow on the upper arm. The person who was struck usually took the blow without protest and did not strike back. Obviously the virtue of binging as punishment did not lie in the physical hurt given to the worker but in the mental hurt that came from knowing that the group disapproved of what he had done. Other practices which naturally served the same end were sarcasm and the use of invectives. If a person turned out too much work, he was called names, such as "Speed King" or "The Slave."

It is worthwhile pointing out that the output of the group was not considered low. If it had been, some action might have been taken, but in point of fact it was perfectly satisfactory to the management. It was simply not so high as it would have been if fatigue and skill had been the only limiting factors.

In the matter of wage incentives, the actual situation was quite different from the assumptions made by the experts. Other activities were out of line in the same way. The wiremen and the soldermen did not stick to their jobs; they frequently traded them. This was forbidden, on the theory that each employee ought to do his own work because he was more skilled in that work. There was also much informal helping of

one man by others. In fact, the observation of this practice was one means of determining the cliques into which the group was divided. A great many things, in short, were going on in the observation room which ought not to have been going on. For this reason it was important that no one should "squeal" on the men. . . .

Restriction of output is a common phenomenon of industrial plants. It is usually explained as a highly logical reaction of the workers. They have increased their output, whereupon their wage rates for piecework have been reduced. They are doing more work for the same pay. They restrict their output in order to avoid a repetition of this experience. Perhaps this explanation holds good in some cases, but the findings of the Bank Wiring Observation Room suggest that it is too simple. The workers in the room were obsessed with the idea that they ought to hold their production level "even" from week to week, but they were vague as to what would happen if they did not. They said that "someone" would "get them." If they turned out an unusually high output one week, that record would be taken thereafter as an example of what they could do if they tried, and they would be "bawled out" if they did not keep up to it. As a matter of fact, none of the men in the room had ever experienced a reduction of wage rates. What is more, as Roethlisberger and Dickson point out, "changes in piece rates occur most frequently where there is a change in manufacturing process, and changes in manufacturing process are made by engineers whose chief function is to reduce unit cost wherever the saving will justify the change. In some instances, changes occur irrespective of direct labor cost. Moreover, where labor is a substantial element, reduction of output tends to increase unit costs and instead of warding off a change in the piece rate many actually induce one."

What happened in the observation room could not be described as a logical reaction of the employees to the experience of rate reduction. They had in fact no such experience. On the other hand, the investigators found that it could be described as a conflict between the technical organization of the plant and its social organization. By technical organization the investigators meant the plan, written or unwritten, according to which the Hawthorne plant was supposed to operate, and the agencies which gave effect to that plan. The plan included explicit rules as to how the men were to be paid, how they were to do their work, what their relations with their supervisors ought to be. It included also implicit assumptions on which the rules were based, one of the assumptions being that men working in the plant would on the whole act so as to further their economic interests. It is worthwhile pointing out that this assumption was in fact implicit, that the experts who devised the technical organization acted upon the assumption without ever stating it in so many words.

There existed also an actual social situation within the plant: groups of men, who were associated with one another, held common sentiments and had certain relations with other groups and other men. To some extent this social organization was identical with the technical plan and to some extent it was not. For instance, the employees were paid according to group payment plans, but the groups concerned did not behave as the planners expected them to behave.

The investigators considered the relations between the technical organization and the social. A certain type of behavior is expected of the higher levels of management. Their success is dependent on their being able to devise and institute rapid changes. Roethlisberger and Dickson describe what happens in the following terms: "Management is constantly making mechanical improvements and instituting changes designed to reduce costs or improve the quality of the product. It is constantly seeking new ways and new combinations for increasing efficiency, whether in designing a new machine, instituting a new method of control, or logically organizing itself in a new way." The assumption has often been made that these changes are designed to force the employee to do more work for less money. As a matter of fact, many of them have just the opposite purpose: to improve the conditions of work and enable the employee to earn higher wages. The important point here, however, is not the purpose of the changes but the way in which they are carried out and accepted.

Once the responsible officer has decided that a certain change ought to be made, he gives an order, and this order is transmitted "down the line," appropriate action being taken at every level. The question in which the investigators

were interested was this: what happens when the order reaches the men who are actually doing the manual work? Roethlisberger and Dickson make the following observations: "The worker occupies a unique position in the social organization. He is at the bottom of a highly stratified organization. He is always in the position of having to accommodate himself to changes which he does not originate. Although he participates least in the technical organization, he bears the brunt of most of its activities." It is he, more than anyone, who is affected by the decisions of management, yet in the nature of things he is unable to share management's preoccupations, and management does little to convince him that what he considers important is being treated as important at the top—a fact which is not surprising since there is no adequate way of transmitting to management an understanding of the considerations which seem important at the work level. There is something like a failure of communication in both directions—upward and downward.

The worker is not only "asked to accommodate himself to changes which he does not initiate, but also many of the changes deprive him of those very things which give meaning and significance to his work." The modern industrial worker is not the handicraftsman of the medieval guild. Nevertheless, the two have much in common. The industrial worker develops his own ways of doing his job, his own traditions of skill, his own satisfactions in living up to his standards. The spirit in which he adopts his own innovations is quite different from that in which he adopts those of management. Furthermore, he does not do his work as an isolated human being, but always as a member of a group, united either through actual cooperation on the job or through association in friendship. One of the most important general findings of the Western Electric researches is the fact that such groups are continually being formed among industrial workers, and that the groups develop codes and loyalties which govern the relations of the members to one another. Though these codes can be quickly destroyed, they are not formed in a moment. They are the product of continued, routine interaction between men. "Constant interference with such codes is bound to lead to feelings of frustration, to an irrational exasperation with technical change in any form, and ultimately to the formation of a type of employee organization such as we have described—a system of practices and beliefs in opposition to the technical organization."

The Bank Wiring Observation Room seemed to show that action taken in accordance with the technical organization tended to break up, through continual change, the routines and human associations which gave work its value. The behavior of the employees could be described as an effort to protect themselves against such changes, to give management the least possible opportunity of interfering with them. When they said that if they increase their output, "something" was likely to happen, a process of this sort was going on in their minds. But the process was not a conscious one. It is important to point out that the protective function of informal organization was not a product of deliberate planning. It was more in the nature of an automatic response. The curious thing is that . . . these informal organizations much resemble formally organized labor unions, although the employees would not have recognized the fact.

Roethlisberger and Dickson summarize as follows the results of the intensive study of small groups of employees: "According to our analysis the uniformity of behavior manifested by these groups was the outcome of a disparity in the rates of change possible in the technical organization, on the one hand, and in the social organization, on the other. The social sentiments and customs of work of the employees were unable to accommodate themselves to the rapid technical innovations introduced. The result was to incite a blind resistance to all innovations and to provoke the formation of a social organization at a lower level in opposition to the technical organization."

Approaches to Deviant Behavior and the Issue of Causation

From one perspective, the cause of deviant behavior is always sociological. This stems from the relativity principle of deviant behavior—all behavior is judged in relation to the violation of social norms and to the evaluation of other persons. "Crime exists only when society has defined a certain action as criminal: without a social system there can be no crime . . ."[24] The types of behavior that are considered deviant depend on the types of norms which exist, and these in turn depend on the dominant values of a group. For example, the dominant values of the Puritan community of Salem, Massachusetts, revolved around religion. Consequently, deviant behavior existed largely in terms of religious norms—most deviants were persons who strayed from the commands of the early New England Puritan religion.[25] Similarly, the dominant values of Soviet Russia are largely political in nature and the dominant modes of deviance tend to be defined according to political norms. "The U.S.S.R. has been, and is, a politicized society, attaching political relevance to a whole range of behaviors not so regarded in many other nations, placing a high premium on political orthodoxy, and fearing subversion and disloyalty. As such, it has tended to beget political deviance."[26] In modern United States, major values revolve around the acquisition and protection of wealth and private property, and a complex maze of laws and government regulations has evolved which define the means by which property and wealth may be legally acquired as well as the ways in which it can be used and disposed

---

[24] Terence Morris, "The Sociology of Crime," *New Society* 5 (April, 1965), p. 7.
[25] Erikson, *Wayward Puritans.*
[26] Connor, "Manufacture of Deviance."

of. Fraud, theft and other forms of property crime may be high in the United States because of the value placed on material acquisition in this country. Thus, behavior is deviant only in relation to the norms and values of a society.[27] In this sense, society is a cause of deviant behavior.

Beyond this point, there is little agreement on the causes of deviant behavior. Disagreements are apt to follow disciplinary lines. Biological approaches emphasize the causal significance of heredity, congenital defects, mental deficiency, and other physiological and organic factors. Criminals, drug addicts, juvenile delinquents, and other deviants are attributed with biological defects or predispositions toward deviant behavior.[28] Some psychologists maintain that deviants and nondeviants differ in their psychological makeup.[29] Others contend that deviance results from psychopathology, that is, neurotic and psychotic behavior trends; this position is often taken by psychiatrists. An economic basis for deviance is sometimes inferred from the observation that deviance and poverty are frequently associated. In many instances such as prostitution and theft, motives appear to be purely economic. Therefore, according to this position, any program to correct large-scale deviance must ensure the chances of the economically deprived to improve their standard of living.

In general, sociologists tend to reject these positions. They point out that investigations fail to reveal systematic biological and psychological differences between most types of deviants and nondeviants.[30] Studies do show, however, that the relative frequency of most forms of deviant behavior is disproportionately higher among low socioeconomic groups, ethnic minorities, and urban populations. Until studies show that these populations have biological or psychological attributes that distinguish them from other groups, their high deviant behavior rates must be attributed to a social or group origin. Furthermore, as behavior that is

---

[27] The way an individual defends himself against the societal reaction to his (alleged) deviant act is also shaped by society's dominant values. In the United States, for example, two values are free economic enterprise and individual rights and liberties. Significantly, two of the major aspects of a successful defense in court are the ability to purchase good legal counsel and the ability to show that investigating officers violated the rights of the defendant as they accumulated evidence against him.

[28] The Italian Criminologist, Cesare Lombroso, remains the most famous biological determinist. See Gina Lombroso Ferrero, *Lombroso's Criminal Man* (New York: Putnam's Sons, 1911) and Cesare Lombroso, *Crime, Its Causes and Remedies* (Boston: Little, Brown, 1912). The best known contemporary who emphasizes biological and physiological factors in deviant behavior is William H. Sheldon; see his *Varieties of Delinquent Youth* (New York: Harper and Row, 1949). For two recent studies of biological factors and deviant behavior see: Sheldon Glueck and Eleanor Glueck, *Physique and Delinquency* (New York: Harper and Row, 1956); and Raymond J. Corsini, "Appearance and Criminality," *American Journal of Sociology* 65 (July, 1959), pp. 49–51.

[29] See the following examples: August Aichorn, *Wayward Youth* (New York: Viking Press, 1925); Kurt E. Eissler, ed., *Searchlights on Delinquency* (New York: International Universities Press, 1949); William Healy and Augusta Bronner, *New Light on Delinquency* (New Haven: Yale University Press, 1936); Fritz Redl and David Wineman, *Children Who Hate* (Glencoe: The Free Press, 1951); and Starke Hathaway and Elio D. Monachesi, *Analyzing and Predicting Juvenile Delinquency with the MMPI* (Minneapolis: University of Minnesota Press, 1953).

[30] For an overall assessment of the biological approach to deviant behavior, see Marshall B. Clinard, *Sociology of Deviant Behavior*, pp. 55–60, 167–74. For assessments of the psychological approach, see Karl F. Schuessler and Donald Cressey, "Personality Characteristics of Criminals," *American Journal of Sociology* 55 (March, 1950), pp. 476–87; John W. McDavid and Boyd R. McCandless, "Psychological Theory, Research, and Juvenile Delinquency," *Journal of Criminal Law, Criminology and Police Science* 52 (March, 1962), pp. 1–14; Leonard Lymes, "Personality Characteristics and the Alcoholic: A Critique of Current Studies," *Quarterly Journal of Studies on Alcohol* 17 (June, 1957), pp. 228–302; and Clinard, *Sociology of Deviant Behavior*, pp. 174–97, *et. passim.*

deviant to one group may be positively valued by another, attributing the cause of deviant behavior to biological and psychological defects and maladjustments may simply reflect the ethnocentric view of those groups for whom the conduct is deviant.

As for the poverty hypothesis, the frequency of occurrence of deviant behavior is likely to vary with sex, age, and residence, even when economic level is constant.[31] Also, poverty appears to have decreased over time, while many forms of deviance may have increased. Frustration and the resulting deviant behavior does not stem from economic deprivation itself, but from relative deprivation,[32] that is, the perception of one's economic condition as low relative to that of others. The crucial determinant of deviant behavior is not poverty per se, but the socially induced motives generated by a value system which encourages men with unequal opportunities to aspire to the same lofty economic goals.[33]

The overriding issue in the above arguments is clearly the causal priority of social factors. Although sociologists may disagree among themselves on the precise explanation of deviant behavior, they tend to agree that its significant antecedents and determinants are social in nature.

There are generally two procedures by which one attempts to demonstrate that a condition "causes" a particular form of behavior. One way is experimental, in which all variables are controlled except one. This one variable is experimentally manipulated to see whether it can effect variation in behavior. Although there have been some experimental studies of deviant behavior,[34] most attempts to demonstrate causes of deviant behavior have been statistical in nature. This may always be the case since society is unlikely ever to condone experimental programs designed to make some persons criminals, homosexuals, prostitutes, psychotics, suicides, etc., and some noncriminals, heterosexuals, etc. Consequently, I agree with Hirschi and Selvin that "the fruitful way toward better causal analyses in [deviant behavior] is to concentrate on improving the statistical approach."[35]

A number of philosophical and metaphysical problems are, of course, associated with the term *cause*. Nevertheless, a condition may be con-

---

[31] Donald R. Cressey, "Crime," in Merton and Nisbet, *Contemporary Social Problems,* p. 159.

[32] On the concept of relative deprivation, see James A. Davis, "A Formal Interpretation of the Theory of Relative Deprivation," *Sociometry* 22 (September, 1959), pp. 280–96.

[33] The widest read theory that emphasizes this point of view is Robert K. Merton's "Social Structure and Anomie" in Merton, *Social Theory and Social Structure,* rev. and enlr. ed. (Glencoe: The Free Press, 1957). This theory is discussed below, pp. 19–23.

[34] For probably the most famous of these studies, see Stanley Schachter, "Deviation, Rejection and Communication," *Journal of Abnormal and Social Psychology* 46 (March, 1951), pp. 190–207.

[35] Travis Hirshi and Hanen C. Selvin, "False Criteria of Causality in Delinquency Research," *Social Problems* 13 (1966), p. 254. This is an excellent discussion of the problems of establishing causality in delinquency research. Our discussion is also indebted to Hyman's discussion of variable manipulation and data analysis in seeking the "cause" of variables (See Herbert H. Hyman, *Survey Design and Analysis* [Glencoe: The Free Press, 1955], esp. pp. 242–329) and to the more recent discussion of the analysis of statistical interaction by Hubert M. Blalock. See his early statement in Hubert M. Blalock, "Theory Building and the Statistical Concept of Interaction," *American Sociological Review* 30 (June, 1965), pp. 374–80. This is not to say that studies of a nonstatistical nature (e.g., studies based on participant observation and the intensive analysis of a very few cases) are of no value. Such studies may provide data that allow for the identification of causal factors that may be investigated more systematically and extensively in studies that permit the statistical expression of results. A number of such studies are included in this volume.

sidered causal only if it meets two criteria, one temporal and one statistical. Temporally, the condition must be *antecedent* to deviant behavior; it must have existed or taken place prior to the deviant action (that is, there must be a "causal *order*"). In some instances this is easy to establish; for example, any condition or event in a person's life must be antecedent to suicide. In other instances, the causal order may not be as obvious. Much evidence indicates that individuals with low socioeconomic status are more apt to be mentally ill and to be juvenile delinquents than individuals with high socioeconomic status. Generally, sociologists consider socioeconomic status to be causally prior to, or a generating condition of, mental illness and juvenile delinquency. There is some reason to believe, however, that a low-status person who is mentally ill may be a low-status person because he is mentally ill, not that his low status and its accompanying stress, denial, and frustration led to his distraught and mental state. It would seem that there would be very little question about the causal order for the relationship between socioeconomic status and juvenile delinquency, since children and adolescents do not choose the socioeconomic status of their parents, although it is conceivable that the antisocial behavior of offspring may contribute to parental hardship and hence a lowered parental socioeconomic status. However, Robins views juvenile delinquency in generational terms and provides evidence that delinquent behavior in childhood and adolescence may be antecedent to the socioeconomic status of that person when he becomes an adult.[36] Therefore, although the causal ordering of variables may appear self-evident, in a large number of cases closer inspection may reveal that the matter is not at all obvious, and in fact may be the reverse of what it originally appeared to be. In any case, it is necessary in establishing the cause of deviant behavior to identify the causal order.

A second criterion of causality is implied in the above; there must be a statistical *association* or *relationship* between the causal condition in question and deviant behavior, and the relationship must not be *spurious*. A spurious relationship exists when (1) control of some third variable causes the relationship between the two original variables to "disappear" or "wash out," and (2) there is no plausible reason for assuming that the variable whose effects "disappear" is causally ordered with reference to deviant behavior. For example, a relationship probably exists between the wildlife density of a community (the number of wild animals per unit of area) and the rate of juvenile delinquency for the community (the ratio of children and adolescents in trouble with the law to the number not in trouble). One reason for the relationship is that *human* population density (the number of persons per unit of area) is related both to the rate of juvenile delinquency[37] and to the density of wildlife. Therefore, if we "controlled" population density, examining the density

---

[36] Lee N. Robins, *Deviant Children Grown Up* (Baltimore: The Williams and Wilkins Company, 1966).

[37] Omer R. Galle, Walter R. Gove, and J. Miller McPherson, "Population Density and Pathology: What are the Relations for Man?" *Science* 176 (April, 1972), pp. 23–30.

of wildlife and delinquency rates for communities of similar population density, we would probably find that the original relationship between density of wildlife and the delinquency rate would disappear. Discussion of the possible reasons for the association between population density and juvenile delinquency need not detain us here, but it is clear that there is no plausible reason why the density of wild animals would be a causal factor in juvenile delinquency. Consequently, we would consider the correlation between wildlife density and juvenile delinquency to be spurious.

Another reason for introducing additional variables, such as population density, is to determine whether a relationship exists under certain social and cultural conditions but not under others. This is referred to as the "specification" of relationships. If the effect of a variable X on a variable Y varies depending on certain conditions, the variable X *interacts* with those conditions.[38] It is clear from what we have said previously that deviant behavior does not exist in a social and cultural vacuum, and in fact exists only in terms of societal norms and reactions. The same is true for the relationships between deviant behavior and specific variables. Such relationships are influenced by a broad field of forces. For example poverty may play a different causal role depending on the social and cultural context in which poverty exists. Moreover, although sociologists tend to focus on social conditions as determinants of deviant behavior, most realize that nonsocial causes may be involved in many if not all types of deviance though even these factors will vary depending on the particular social and cultural context.

To investigate the effect of this broader social context on a relationship between two variables, sociologists introduce a third variable (a statistical control), examining the original relationship under different conditions. When the relationship exists in some contexts but not others (or if the strength of the relationship is significantly different in different contexts), the relationship is specified with respect to the social and cultural context. This permits the conclusion that the cause of deviant behavior is different under different social and cultural conditions. The procedure can be illustrated by one of the most well-known theories of deviant behavior, Robert K. Merton's theory of "Social Structure and Anomie."[39]

Specification of Relationships and Identification of Causes: An Illustration

In open-class societies, such as the United States, there is a strong emphasis on equal opportunity for individuals to achieve prized cultural and material goals. The cultural ideology argues that each individual, regard-

---

[38] Other outcomes are possible, of course. Results may indicate that the control variable is an *intervening* variable (sometimes referred to as an "interpretation") or an *explanatory* variable; as such it is the cause of both of the original variables (and sometimes called an "explanation"). For an original statement, see Hyman, *Survey Design and Analysis.*

[39] Merton, *Social Theory and Social Structure.*

less of class background, has the right, indeed the obligation, to strive for these goals, which are symbolic of individual success. Although equality of opportunity is emphasized as a right, differences in class status create differences in opportunity; the opportunities of persons in the lower class are less than those of persons higher in the class structure. Because of this, lower-class individuals may resort to illegitimate or deviant means to achieve those goals that they have been taught are so important and so accessible to anyone who wishes to achieve them.

Note that the formulation stipulates a relationship between blocked opportunity and deviance under particular cultural conditions, in which the drive for material success is encouraged and where equal opportunity is said to exist. These conditions are more descriptive of American society than most other societies, since "aspirations for place, recognition, wealth and socially prized accomplishments are culturally held to be appropriate for all, whatever their origin or present condition." Indeed, "American society comes as close to any in history to arguing that going up in the world is an absolute value." At the same time, "in this same society that proclaims the right, and even the duty of lofty aspirations for all, men do not have equal access to the opportunity structure." Consequently, when lower-class persons are "confronted with this contradiction in experience [between the ideal and the reality], appreciable numbers of people become estranged from a society that promises them in principle what they are denied in reality."[40] Thus, in a society like the United States, a relationship between the experience or perception of blocked opportunity and normative estrangement or deviance would be expected. In societies which do not emphasize equal opportunity and high aspirations for all regardless of class background, no such relationship would be anticipated.

According to accounts of anthropologists, there is no such emphasis in the cultures of Latin American societies. John Gillin states that, in contrast to the United States where "the individual merits respect because he has the right to be considered 'just as good as the next person,' or at least because he has the right to 'an equal chance' or opportunity with other persons," in Latin American countries equality of opportunity is not so important. The Latin American realizes that "he is *not* equal with everyone else, either in position or opportunity" but this is of no great significance to him. He "does not have to pay much attention to the unfair distribution of rights and privileges which the social system imposes upon him. . . ." Although he may rise in the social scale, not to do so does not represent a contradiction in experience because he "recognizes and accepts . . . his position in society. He has no right to expect more."[41]

---

[40] Robert K. Merton, "Anomie, Anomia, and Social Interaction: Contexts of Deviant Behavior," in Marshall Clinard, ed., *Anomie and Deviant Behavior: A Discussion and Critique* (New York: Free Press, 1964), p. 218.

[41] John Gillin, "Ethos Components in Modern Latin American Culture," in Dwight B. Heath and Richard Adams, *Contemporary Cultures and Societies of Latin America* (New York: Random House, 1965), pp. 511, 513.

Consequently, for individuals from societies with these cultural expectations we would not expect to find the relationship posited in Merton's theory.

The hypothesis for cultural differences in the relationship between perceived opportunity and deviance may be tested with data from a study of farm workers in the Northwestern part of the United States.[42] Three groups of farm workers with different cultural backgrounds were included in the study. The first group included individuals of Mexican origin who could not speak the English language and are called non-English speakers. Members of the second group were of similar cultural background but they could speak English and are called bilinguals. The third group consisted of English-speaking individuals with no Mexican heritage and are called Anglos. Given the differences in cultural ideology between the United States and Latin American countries, including Mexico, a difference between Anglos and Mexican-Americans in the relationship between perceived opportunity and deviance would be expected. And under the assumption that facility with the language of a culture is an index of cultural assimilation, bilinguals should be more assimilated into the culture of the United States and therefore more influenced by the cultural ideology about equal opportunity than non-English speakers. Consequently, we would expect the relationship between perceived opportunity and deviance to vary directly with level of assimilation, being strongest for Anglos and weakest for non-English speakers.

Measures of perceived opportunity were based on how good respondents think their children's chances are to realize a college education and to obtain some line of work besides farm work. For their children to receive a college education or to pursue an occupational career besides farm work represents a form of upward striving for farm workers, or at least for their children, since, if the children realized these goals, they would be higher on the social scale than their parents. None of the farm workers had a college education, and, based on annual income, farm work is at the bottom of the class structure. Almost any job besides farm work would be an improvement.[43] Respondents were asked if they thought their children would end up in farm work, with an affirmative response indicating poor perceived opportunity and a negative response good perceived opportunity. They were also asked how good they thought the chances were that their children would receive a college education—"very good," "fairly good," or "not good at all."

Although deviant behavior among the three groups was not studied, members of all three groups were asked six questions. The answers to these questions provide an index to the normative estrangement ("normlessness") that Merton refers to. For example, individuals were asked: "Is a person justified in doing almost anything if the reward is high enough?"

---

[42] William A. Rushing, "Class, Culture and 'Social Structure and Anomie,'" *The American Journal of Sociology* 76 (March, 1971), pp. 857–72. See also, *Class Culture and Alienation: A Study of Farmers and Farm Workers* (Lexington, Mass.: D. C. Heath, 1972).

[43] On the low status of farm workers, see Rushing, *Class Culture and Alienation.*

An affirmative response would indicate greater estrangement than a negative response. Answers to the six questions were summed; total scores range from 0 to 6, with 6 representing a strong normless attitude.[44] The average normlessness score by perceived occupational opportunity is given for the three groups in Table 1. For both Anglos and bilinguals, re-

TABLE 1. AVERAGE NORMLESSNESS SCORE BY PERCEIVED OCCUPATIONAL OPPORTUNITY FOR DIFFERENT ETHNIC GROUPS

	Perceived Opportunity		
Group	Good	Poor	P*
Anglos	0.96 (121)	1.46 (30)	.01
Bilinguals	1.21 (77)	1.96 (51)	.02
Non-English speakers	2.21 (73)	1.63 (24)	.10†

Note: Figures in parentheses are N's.
* Probability that the difference could have occured by chance based on Student t-test (one-tail test).
† Opposite direction to prediction.

spondents who perceived their children's opportunities as poor are more apt to score high on normlessness than those who perceive opportunities as good, whereas the reverse holds for non-English speakers. The difference between non-English speakers and the other two groups is consistent with Merton's theory. Somewhat different results are obtained with respect to perceived educational opportunity, however (see Table 2). While the average normless score for Anglos consistently increases from "very good" perceived opportunity to "not good at all," no consistent pattern exists for either of the two Mexican-American groups.

TABLE 2. AVERAGE NORMLESSNESS SCORES BY PERCEIVED EDUCATIONAL OPPORTUNITY FOR DIFFERENT ETHNIC GROUPS

	Perceived Opportunity			
Group	Very Good	Fairly Good	Not Good At All	P
Anglos	0.82 (22)	1.03 (65)	1.37 (31)	*
Bilinguals	1.75 (16)	1.52 (63)	1.94 (18)	†
Non-English speakers	1.65 (17)	2.14 (22)	1.82 (22)	†

Note: Figures in parentheses are N's.
* Mean for "not good at all" category is significantly different from "very good" (p < .10).
† No differences are statistically significant.

Results thus indicate that a negative relationship between perceived opportunity and normative estrangement clearly exists for Anglos as it

---

[44] Questions composing the normlessness scale are as follows:
  In your opinion, is the honest life the best regardless of the hardships it may cause?
  Do you think a person is justified in doing almost anything if the reward is high enough?
  In order to get ahead in the world today, some say you are almost forced to do some things that are not right. What do you think?
  In your opinion, should a man obey the law no matter how much it interferes with his personal ambitions?
  Would you say that the main reasons for obeying the law is the punishment that comes if one is caught?
  Some people say that to be a success in this country it is usually necessary to be dishonest. Do you think this is true?

exists for both perceived occupational and educational opportunities; exists less clearly for bilinguals since the relationship holds for perceived occupational but not educational opportunity; and does not exist at all for non-English speakers. Therefore, the relationship between perceived opportunity and normlessness varies directly with level of assimilation in a culture which places heavy emphasis on the existence of equal opportunity. Stated differently, the effect of perceived opportunity interacts with the broader cultural context and leads to normative estrangement only when the values of achieved status and equal opportunity are extolled by a culture.

In the sociological approach to causes of deviant behavior, a major objective is to identify how one factor has a different causal effect under different social and cultural conditions. A number of papers in this volume are based on this idea. For example, although several theorists view gang membership as an important causal factor of juvenile delinquency, Stanfield observes that the influence of gang membership on delinquent conduct depends on characteristics of the juvenile's family.[45] Also, Cloward and Ohlin contend that lower-class delinquent gangs that are organized around economic pursuits exist only under certain conditions of community or neighborhood organization. Denied access to legitimate opportunity (e.g., education), adolescents are more apt to engage in economic crimes when their neighborhood is characterized by organized crime than when it isn't.[46] The relationship between blocked opportunity and gang activity is, then, specific to type of neighborhood. Gibbs also shows that the apparent influence of blocked opportunity (unemployment) on adult crime is relative to the social context; it differs for different age groups and depends on the cultural expectations associated with different age groups.[47] Other studies also reveal that the causal influence of factors in homosexuality,[48] expression of aggression,[49] drug experience,[50] and suicide[51] depend on the situational context in which the factors exist.

By showing how an apparent causal relationship varies depending on the social situation, sociologists are able to show the connection between causes of deviance and the broader social and cultural context. The specification of relationships in this way also allows us to deal empirically with the contention that certain characteristics of individuals are inherently pathological, always inclining the individual toward deviant conduct. If certain variables, such as personality dispositions, poverty status, or being

---

[45] See Robert H. Hardt and Sandra J. Peterson, "Arrests of Self and Friends as Indicators of Delinquency Involvement," pp. 40–45 of this volume.

[46] See David J. Bordua, "A Critique of Sociological Interpretations of Gang Delinquency," pp. 45–58 of this volume.

[47] See Jack P. Gibbs, "Crime, Unemployment and Status Integration," pp. 96–102 of this volume.

[48] See Mary McIntosh, "The Homosexual Role," pp. 233–40 of this volume.

[49] Martin Gold, "Suicide, Homicide and the Socialization of Aggression," pp. 169–78 of this volume.

[50] Howard S. Becker, "History, Culture and Subjective Experience: An Exploration of the Social Bases of Drug-Induced Experiences," pp. 342–54 of this volume.

[51] See William A. Rushing, "Situational Contexts and the Relationship of Alcoholism and Mental Illness to Suicide," pp. 474–80 of this volume.

reared in a broken home can be shown to be *conditionally* related to deviant behavior, results support the sociological assumption that there are no intrinsic factors predisposing toward deviant behavior, but only factors that predispose toward deviant behavior under certain social and cultural conditions.[52]

To summarize, in approaching the issue of causation in deviant behavior, sociologists tend to focus on: (1) the identification of factors that are associated with deviant behavior which are distinctively social rather than biological, psychological, or economic in nature, and (2) the discovery of differences in relationships between such factors and deviant behavior depending on the broader social and cultural context.

An Additional Issue: Causes of Individual Deviance and Causes of Deviance Rates

Sociological investigations of the causes of deviant behavior revolve around two questions: (1) Why do some *groups* or *populations* of society have higher *rates* of deviance (that is, a higher proportion of their members who are deviants) than other groups, sectors or populations? (2) Why do some *individuals* in some groups or populations become deviant while other individuals do not? Answers to the first question may be involved with such things as social disorganization, urbanization, population density, socially induced aspirations, and unequal opportunities. Answers to the second may involve roles, attitudes, social motives, and other characteristics of individuals which may predispose them in deviant directions.

The difference between the two questions is that in the first, populations (groups, societies, occupations, races, etc.) are the units of analysis while in the second, individuals are the units of analysis. In the first case, generalizations about causes refer to properties of populations while in the second, generalizations refer to properties of individuals. In either case, causal statements emphasize social factors. This is clear in the question concerning population rates of deviance, and it is also true of studies which investigate the causes of deviance among individuals. By way of illustration, consider those studies that have found that a greater proportion of alcoholics commit suicide than nonalcoholics. A sociological explanation of this phenomenon might focus on the societal reaction, a social factor, to individual alcoholics.[53] So even when observing the individual, causal statements may include social as well as, or sometimes instead of, psychological processes.

Note, however, that correlations between population variables never lead directly to conclusions about individual behavior. Consider, for example, the relationship between the alcoholism *rate* and the suicide *rate*

---

[52] For a related discussion, see Hirschi and Selvin, "False Criteria of Causality," p. 267.
[53] See William A. Rushing, "Deviance, Disrupted Social Relations and Suicide," pp. 464–73 of this volume.

for occupations.[54] Some occupations may have high rates of both because factors associated with these occupations may cause some incumbents to drink to excess and *other* incumbents to kill themselves. That is to say, *individuals* who are alcoholic are not *necessarily* the *same* individuals who commit suicide. Consequently, unless relationships between population rates are explained in terms of properties of populations rather than of individuals, interpretations may be erroneous. An error of this kind is known as an "ecological fallacy," where a correlation between population variables is interpreted as though it were a correlation between properties of individuals.[55]

To take another example, consider the inverse relationship between social class and crime in the United States, which is the subject of Merton's theory. The high crime *rate* of the lower class may indeed result from an institutionalized value system that encourages all individuals to aspire to the same lofty materialistic goals combined with socially structured class barriers that prevent equal opportunity to realize those goals. However, unless we know that lower-class individuals who commit crimes are those who experience the greatest sense of denied opportunity, this interpretation of lower-class crime in terms of individuals may be erroneous.

This is not to say that causal statements about individual deviance and rates of deviance for populations necessarily contradict each other; in some instances they may be identical. For example, the high crime rate in the lower class may result because a high proportion of lower-class members aspire to cultural goals which their opportunities prevent them from achieving; at the individual level, lower-class individuals who become criminal may be those who feel most deprived of opportunities to realize culturally approved goals and ambitions. Thus, in this instance, explanations at the group and individual levels are the same. There are some sociologists, however, who argue that the causes of deviant behavior rates of groups are always different from the causes of deviant behavior among individuals.[56]

The Approach of the Book

While the study of causal conditions, the use of statistical techniques to identify these conditions, and the distinction between causes of individual behavior and population rates are important, a sociological approach is not limited to causal analysis. Two other kinds of studies are central. One investigates the social processes—social action, social interaction, and social relations—through which deviance is learned and performed. Such

---

[54] Pp. 465–66 of this volume.

[55] See William S. Robinson, "Ecological Correlations and the Behavior of Individuals," *American Sociological Review* 15 (June, 1950), pp. 351–57. See also Herbert Menzel, "Comments on Robinson's 'Ecological Correlations and the Behavior of Individuals,'" *American Sociological Review* 15 (October, 1950), p. 674.

[56] Accordingly, some contend that only rates of deviance in populations should be the focus in the sociological analysis of deviance. Cf. LeRoy C. Gould, "Crime and Its Impact in an Affluent Society," in Jack D. Douglas, ed., *Crime and Justice in American Society* (Indianapolis: Bobbs-Merrill, 1971), p. 100.

studies are just as significant as investigations which focus on the causal and antecedent conditions of these processes. Examples include studies of the interaction and relations between homosexuals and their nonhomosexual partners,[57] alcoholics and their wives,[58] and mental patients and hospital personnel.[59] Included also are studies of the processes of learning and performing deviant behavior, such as learning about a criminal subculture[60] and how armed robbery and burglary are organized.[61]

Since social relations and social learning processes are often necessary conditions for the occurrence of deviant behavior, some might classify the investigation of such relations and processes as causal studies. A leading theory on crime takes this position. This theory, originally formulated by Edwin H. Sutherland, argues that individuals become criminal because of their differential associations—associations with criminals and criminal behavior patterns and isolation from noncriminal and law-abiding patterns.[62] Criminal patterns would thus be transmitted to individuals through a pattern of social interaction. This theory is a socialization theory of crime. Although the theory may contain a generally correct conception of the social process through which much deviant behavior is learned, it is an inadequate causal explanation of important aspects of such behavior. It fails to explain why criminal behavior patterns exist in the first place and why there are differences in crime rates, that is, why criminals are unequally distributed in different groups and sectors of society. For example, the theory may be a plausible account of the process through which many lower-class persons learn criminal behavior, but it fails to explain why there are so many criminals in the lower class from whom criminal behavior can be learned. Second, at the individual level, the theory fails to explain why individuals have the associates they have.[63]

Considering differential associations as dependent on the deviant behavior rate is more fruitful than considering it as causing the deviant behavior rate. The crime rate is one of the determinants of criminal associations; a high crime rate increases the probability of the individual's interacting with criminal persons. Stated another way, a group's crime rate provides the structure within which the criminogenic social learning process[64] may take place. Consequently, studies of differential associations, and the corresponding socialization process of deviants, are properly classified as processual and relational studies.

---

[57] See Albert J. Reiss, Jr., "The Social Integration of Queers and Peers," pp. 254–67 of this volume.

[58] See Thelma Whalen, "Wives of Alcoholics," pp. 311–15 of this volume.

[59] See Ivan Belknap, "The Mental Patient in the Hospital Ward System," pp. 422–32 of this volume.

[60] See Stanton Wheeler, "Socialization in Correctional Communities," pp. 211–23 of this volume.

[61] See Werner J. Einstadter, "The Social Organization of Armed Robbery," and Neal Shover, "External Social Relations of Burglars," pp. 113–23 and 123–30 of this volume.

[62] Edwin H. Sutherland, *Principles of Criminology*, 5th ed. (New York: Lippincott, 1955), pp. 77–80.

[63] A point which the formulator of "differential association theory" recognized. See *ibid.*, p. 79.

[64] As several have pointed out, however, differential association does not itself constitute a theory of the learning process. For a formulation of differential association theory in terms of the principles of learning, see Robert L. Burgess and Ronald L. Akers, "A Differential Association-Reinforcement Theory of Criminal Behavior," *Social Problems* 14 (Fall, 1966), pp. 128–47.

Other sociological studies investigate the consequences of deviant behavior. Particularly important are studies of social reactions to deviance. Reactions to deviant individuals vary in severity[65] and may generate additional consequences. A series of problems for the individual deviant[66] as well as for others who are associated with the deviant[67] may arise. The development of deviant subcultures is another possible consequence of deviant behavior.[68] The consequences of one type of deviance may be causal factors for another type.[69] Moreover, reactions of society may decrease the rate of deviance, as Ferdinand shows for the crime rate,[70] or they may encourage further deviance, as Kobler and Stotland contend in the case of suicide.[71] The consequences of deviant behavior vary depending on the broader social and cultural context in which they occur.[72]

The consequences of deviant behavior are diverse and as yet there is no general classification scheme for them. *Anticipated, unanticipated, positive,* and *negative* consequences are the distinctions most frequently recognized.[73] Such distinctions are quite general, however, and have yet to be employed systematically in many investigations of deviant behavior. Even granting the relevance of these distinctions, a meaningful classification scheme must await detailed, empirical analyses of various consequences as well as the identification of the variables with which such consequences are associated.

As noted earlier, some sociologists argue that deviance only exists in terms of its consequences; deviance is viewed as existing only if accomplished acts are perceived and defined as deviant by others.[74] My position is that the consequences of deviance constitute one dimension of deviant behavior, but only one dimension. The deviant quality of an act does not depend upon its consequences. An act is considered deviant when a rule is violated, regardless of how it is subsequently perceived and defined by others. To be sure, perception and definition of deviant acts are often influenced by conditions other than the nature of the act. The rela-

---

[65] See Irving Piliavin and Scott Briar, "Police Encounters with Juveniles," pp. 80–87 of this volume.

[66] See Lucy Jane King et al., "Alcohol Abuse: Crucial Factor in the Social Problems of Negro Men," pp. 326–34 of this volume.

[67] See Paul W. Haberman, "Childhood Symptoms in Children of Alcoholics and Comparison Group Parents," and Albert C. Cain and Irene Fast, "Children's Disturbed Reactions to Parent Suicide," pp. 334–36 and 500–5 of this volume.

[68] For examples, see Maurice Leznoff and William A. Westley, "The Homosexual Community," Patrick H. Hughes et al., "The Social Structure of a Heroin Copping Community," and Howard S. Becker, "History, Culture and Subjective Experience: An Exploration of the Social Bases of Drug-Induced Experiences," pp. 269–74, 364–70, and 347–54 of this volume.

[69] See William R. Rushing, "Deviance, Disrupted Social Relations and Suicide," pp. 464–73 of this volume.

[70] Theodore N. Ferdinand, "Politics, the Police and Arresting Policies in Salem, Massachusetts Since the Civil War," pp. 144–57 of this volume.

[71] See Arthur L. Kobler and Ezra Stotland, "Suicide Attempts and the Social Response," pp. 491–500 of this volume.

[72] James R. Greenley, "The Psychiatric Patient's Family and Length of Hospitalization" and William A. Rushing and Jack Escoe, "The Status Resource Hypothesis and Length of Hospitalization," pp. 433–44 and 445–55 of this volume.

[73] Robert K. Merton, "Manifest and Latent Functions," in Robert K. Merton, *Social Theory and Social Structure,* pp. 19–84.

[74] Cf. Becker, *Outsiders.*

tionship between the nature of the act and the societal reaction to it may be specific to certain social and cultural conditions. This is perhaps the central postulate of the labelling perspective. But the question of what these conditions are must be answered through empirical research.[75] Studies of societal reactions are needed, such as studies which show that the way people are committed to mental hospitals varies with conditions of social class and social isolation.[76] Only through such studies will we be able to specify reactions to various types of deviants with respect to the social and cultural contexts.

However, as was noted earlier, the societal reaction perspective is unable to ask questions about deviants who are not identified by others as deviants and thus fails to account for differences in norm violation. Also, since the perspective tends to view deviant behavior only in terms of socially defined reality, it fails to recognize that deviant behavior may have unrecognized consequences that are just as important as those that are recognized.[77]

Moreover, useful studies of deviant behavior may be conducted without studying societal reaction at all. Witness Durkheim's study of suicide over half a century ago.[78] Durkheim was not particularly concerned with the consequences of suicide, yet his investigation of the social causes of suicide is a seminal contribution and has generated much subsequent research on the subject.

The approach of this book, therefore, concentrates on deviant behavior as a whole process. This process includes causes or antecedent conditions, a series of actions and interactions conducted within a matrix of social relations, and a set of consequences—particularly the reaction of others. Studies of all three parts of the process are useful. The study of one is not necessarily dependent on the study of the other two; for example, studies of causes may be pursued independently of studies of processes and consequences, and vice versa. This reveals that sociological studies may be pursued even if the causes of deviant behavior are nonsociological in nature. The analysis of social action, interaction, and relational processes, as well as the consequences of deviant behavior, may be pursued from a sociological perspective even when the causes of deviance may have been psychological and biological forces. Note, however, that the three types of studies are not incompatible. In fact, the study of one dimension may facilitate the study of another. As suggested previously, investigations may show that the consequences of one type of deviance are contributing factors for another.

Also, observe that although the study of each dimension of the process of deviant behavior is usually pursued in separate investigations,

---

[75] Thomas J. Scheff presents a series of propositions in *Being Mentally Ill* (Chicago: Aldine Publishing Company, 1966).

[76] William A. Rushing, "Status Resources, Societal Reactions and Mental Hospitalization," pp. 403–11 of this volume.

[77] See pp. 8–9 above.

[78] Emile Durkheim, *Suicide*, trans. John A. Spaulding and George Simpson (Glencoe: The Free Press, 1951). See also pp. 461–63 of this volume.

all three may be studied simultaneously because they all three exist simultaneously. True, the dimensions are linked in a temporal sequence, but the ongoing social process is such that where one dimension begins and another ends is not always easy to determine. They may be so interwoven that they can be viewed as separate phenomena only for purposes of analysis. This is apparent in the following example of deviance in an industrial factory.

The Deviant Behavior Process: An Illustration from Industry

In "Crime and Punishment in the Factory: The Function of Deviancy in Maintaining the Social System," Joseph Bensman and Israel Gerver analyze the use of an illegal tool (tap) in the manufacture of airplanes. The three dimensions of the deviant behavior process are clearly seen in the analysis.

According to the authors, the determining or causal factors of the use of the tool lay in the fact that the ends and means of various groups (workers, foremen, inspectors, and management) within the factory are in conflict. In this instance, then, the cause of deviance is located in the social system itself. Concerning social process and social relations, workers are socialized in the use of the tap by other workers, including their superiors (foremen and inspectors). This is not to say that superiors publicly condone the tool's use; in fact, they publicly warn workers not to use it and threaten to punish those who do. Such behavior is largely ceremonial, however, and deviant behavior is expected and approved. As for consequences (functions), the authors indicate that unless workers occasionally use the tap, and use it in collusion with their superiors, production would suffer. A consequence of deviance, therefore, is the continued survival of the system. The point here is not that this is always a consequence of deviance. However, notice that consequences are not always negative nor always intended and anticipated.

On the surface Bensman and Gerver's analysis resembles Merton's theory of "Social Structure and Anomie," which we reviewed above. Like Merton, Bensman and Gerver view deviant behavior as stemming from strains generated by characteristics of the social (factory) system. There is an important difference, however, between the two theories. Bensman and Gerver view deviance as not only *caused* by the system in which it occurs but also as being essential for the system to *survive* and to continue to operate. Their analysis focuses on the *social system* functions and consequences as well as social system causes.[79]

---

[79] The same general idea is present in Ivan Belknap's analysis of hospital wards in a state mental hospital: see his, "The Mental Patient in the Hospital Ward System," pp. 422–32 of this volume. This is not to say, of course, that Merton is unconcerned with the social system consequences of social action, as his writings contain some of the most penetrating theoretical analyses of this topic; see "Manifest and Latent Functions." Our comments here are limited to a comparison of his theory of "social structure and anomie" with the analysis and framework presented by Bensman and Gerver.

CRIME AND PUNISHMENT IN THE FACTORY
The Function of Deviancy in Maintaining the Social System
JOSEPH BENSMAN AND ISRAEL GERVER

This paper is a case study in the internal law of [an airplane factory]. The social functions of the violation of one "law" are treated in detail. . . . The violation of "law" is specifically a rule of workmanship. For the sake of simplicity, the rules and their violations relevant to one instrument—the tap—are the subject of study. This is because the study of the tap summarizes an entire area of rules of workmanship and their violations. One could also have selected other violations of workmanship rules such as countersinking dimples, rolling of edges in fairing, stretching of metal skins, or greasing and waxing screw threads. The tap was selected as a major example because of its frequent usage, and because it is the most serious violation of rules of workmanship.

While suggesting the engineering complexity of the data, our theoretical interest is in the social function of crime, particularly violations of private organizational law.

The research was carried out in an airplane factory employing 26,000 people in the New York metropolitan area. One of the authors was a participant observer from September 1953 through September 1954. He gathered his data in the daily course of work while working as an assembler on the aileron crew of the final wing line. No special research instruments were used; the ordinary activities of workers along the line were observed and noted as they occurred, and recorded daily. All aspects involved in the use of the tap were discussed in the context of the work situation when they were relevant and salient to the personnel involved, and without their realizing that they were objects of study.

Reprinted with permission of author and publisher from the *American Sociological Review* 28 (August, 1963), pp. 588–98 as abridged. Revised version of a paper originally presented at the annual meetings of the American Sociological Association, Washington, D.C., September, 1955. A somewhat shorter and different version of this paper appears in Alvin Gouldner and Helen Gouldner, *Modern Sociology* (New York: Harcourt Brace, 1963), pp. 589–96.

THE TAP AND ITS FUNCTIONS

The tap is a tool, an extremely hard steel screw, whose threads are slotted to allow for the disposal of the waste metal which it cuts away. It is sufficiently hard so that when it is inserted into a nut it can cut new threads over the original threads of the nut.

In wing assembly work, bolts or screws must be inserted in recessed nuts which are anchored to the wing in earlier processes of assembly. The bolt or screw must pass through a wing plate before reaching the nut. In the nature of the mass production process, alignments between nuts and plate-openings become distorted. Original allowable tolerances become magnified in later stages of assembly as the number of alignments which must be coordinated with each other increase with the increasing complexity of the assemblage. When the nut is not aligned with the hole, the tap can be used to cut, at a new angle, new threads in the nut for the purpose of bringing the nut and bolt into a new but not true alignment. If the tap is not used and the bolt is forced, the wing plate itself may be bent. Such new alignments, however, deviate from the specifications of the blueprint which is based upon true alignments at every state of the assembly process. On the basis of engineering standards, true alignments are necessary at every stage in order to achieve maximum strength and a proper equilibrium of strains and stresses.

The use of the tap is the most serious crime of workmanship conceivable in the plant. A worker can be summarily fired for merely possessing a tap. Nevertheless, at least one-half of the work force in a position to use a tap owns at least one. Every well-equipped senior mechanic owns four or five of different sizes and every mechanic has access to and, if need be, uses them. In fact, the mass use of the tap represents a wide-spread violation of this most serious rule of workmanship.

The tap is defined as a criminal instrument,

primarily because it destroys the effectiveness of stop nuts. Aviation nuts are specifically designed, so that, once tightened, a screw or bolt cannot back out of the nut under the impact of vibration in flight. Once a nut is tapped, however, it loses its holding power and at any time, after sufficient vibration, the screw or bolt can fall out and weaken the part it holds to the wing and the wing itself.

In addition, the use of a tap is an illegal method of concealing a structural defect. If the holes, for example, were properly drilled and the nuts were properly installed, the use of the tap would be unnecessary, since specifications calling for alignment would be fulfilled. Whenever a tap is used, there are indications of deviations from standards. Furthermore, such deviations make subsequent maintenance of the airplane difficult since maintenance mechanics have no records of such illegal deviations from specifications. Taps can be used in certain cases by special mechanics when such usage is authorized by engineers and when proper paper work supports such use. But such authorization usually requires one to three days for approval.

The tap, then, is an illegal tool, the use or possession of which carries extreme sanctions in private organizational law, but which is simultaneously widely possessed and used despite its illegal status. The problem of such a pattern for the meaning of private organizational law is to account for the wide acceptance of a crime as a means of fulfilling work requirements within a private organization, the aircraft plant.

THE SOCIALIZATION OF THE WORKER

To most workers entering an aircraft plant the tap is an unknown instrument. Dies which thread bolts, i.e., the process opposite to tapping, are relatively well-known and are standard equipment of the plumbing trade. The new worker does not come into this contact with the tap until he finds it impossible to align the holes in two skins. In desperation and somewhat guiltily as if he had made a mistake, he turns to his partner (a more experienced worker) and states his problem. The experienced worker will try every legitimate technique of lining up the holes,

but if these do not succeed, he resorts to the tap. He taps the new thread himself, not permitting the novice to use the tap. While tapping it, he gives the novice a lecture on the dangers of getting caught and of breaking a tap in the hole, thereby leaving telltale evidence of its use.

For several weeks the older worker will not permit his inexperienced partner to use a tap when its use is required. He leaves his own work in order to do the required tapping and finishes the job before returning to his own work. If the novice demonstrates sufficient ability and care in other aspects of his work he will be allowed to tap the hole under the supervision of a veteran worker. When the veteran partner is absent, and the now initiated worker can use the tap at his own discretion he feels a sense of pride. In order to enjoy his new found facility, he frequently uses the tap when it is not necessary. He may be careless in properly aligning perfectly good components and then compensate for his own carelessness by using the tap.

He may forego the easier illegal methods (which are also viewed as less serious crimes) of greasing and waxing bolts or enlarging the misaligned holes and indulge himself in the more pleasurable, challenging and dangerous use of the tap. Sooner or later he inevitably runs into difficulties which he is technically unprepared to cope with. When his partner and mentor is not available, he is forced to call upon the assistant foreman. If the situation requires it, the foreman will recommend the tap. If he has doubts about the worker's abilities, he may even tap the hole himself. In doing this, he risks censure of the union, because as a foreman he is not permitted to handle tools.

While the foreman taps the hole, he also lectures on the proper and technically workmanlike ways of using the tap: "The tap is turned only at quarter turns . . . never force the tap . . . it has to go in easy or it's likely to snap . . . if it snaps, your ass is in a sling and I won't be able to get you out of it."

The foreman warns the worker to make sure "not to get caught, to see that the coast is clear, to keep the tap well hidden when not in use, and to watch out for inspectors while using it." He always ends by cautioning the worker, "It's your own ass if you're caught."

When the worker feels that he is experienced and can use the tap with complete confidence, he usually buys his own, frequently displaying it to other workers and magnanimously lending it to those in need of it. He feels himself fully arrived when a foreman borrows his tap or asks him to perform the tapping. The worker has now established his identity and is known as an individual by the higher ups.

Once the right to use the tap is thus established, the indiscriminate use of it is frowned upon. A worker who uses a tap too often is considered to be a careless "botcher." A worker who can get his work done without frequently using a tap is a "mechanic," but one who doesn't use the tap when it is necessary does not get his own work done on time. Proper use of the tap requires judgement and etiquette. The tap addict is likely to become the object of jokes and to get a bad work reputation among workers, foremen and inspectors.

AGENCIES OF LAW ENFORCEMENT

The enforcement of the plant rules of workmanship devolves upon three groups: foremen, plant quality control and Air Force quality control. The ultimate and supreme authority resides in the latter group. The Air Force not only sets the blueprint specifications, but also and more importantly, can reject a finished airplane as not meeting specifications.

Furthermore, the Air Force inspectors reinspect installations which have been previously "bought," by plant quality control. If these installations do not meet Air Force standards they are "crabbed," i.e., rejected. When this happens, the plant inspectors who bought the installations are subject to "being written up," i.e., disciplinary action for unintentional negligence which may lead to suspensions, demotions or in extreme cases loss of jobs. The Air Force inspector has the absolute right to demand that any man be fired for violating work rules.

There were only two Air Force inspectors to a shop at the time of these observations, so that it was almost impossible for Air Force inspectors to police an entire shop of over 2,000 men. As an Air Force inspector walks up the line, it is standard procedure for workers to nudge other workers to inform them of the approach of the "Gestapo." When tapping is essential and when it is known that Air Force inspectors are too near, guards of workers are posted to convey advance notice of this approach to anyone who is actively tapping. This is especially true when there are plant drives against the use of the tap.

In all instances, when the Air Force inspector is in the vicinity, workers who have a reputation for open or promiscuous use of the tap are instructed by the assistant foreman to "disappear." Such types can return to work when the "coast is clear."

Despite the Air Force inspectors' high authority and the severity of their standards, they are not sufficiently numerous to be considered the major policing agency for detecting and apprehending violators of the rules of workmanship. Plant quality control is the actual law enforcement agency in terms of the daily operations of surveillance. There are approximately 150 plant inspectors to a 2,000 man shop. They work along the assembly line along with the workers. In this system a call book which guarantees the equal rotation of inspections is kept. When a worker has completed a job and requests an inspection, he enters his wing number and the requested inspection in the call book. The inspector, after completing an inspection, marks the job as completed and takes the next open inspection.

A result is the free and intimate intermingling of inspectors and workers. In off moments, inspectors and workers gather together to "shoot the breeze and kill time." Inspectors, unlike workers, may have long waiting periods before their next assignment. During such periods, out of boredom and monotony, they tend to fraternize with workers. This causes conflict between the role of "good egg" and the role of policeman. A cause of leniency on the part of inspectors is intrinsic to the relationship between mechanics and themselves in circumstances not involving the tap. There is a sufficient amount of mechanical work which is not easily and immediately accessible to inspectors. This is particularly true if the inspector does not want to spend several hours on a fairly simple inspection. In order for the inspector to complete his work and make sure that the work he "buys" will be acceptable to later inspectors, he must rely on the workmanship of the mechanic. In brief he must have faith not only in the mechanic's workmanship but also in his willingness not to "louse him up." If the inspector gets the reputation of being a "bastard," the mechanic is under no obligation to do a good job and thus protect the inspector. Since the penalties for the use of the tap are so severe, no inspector feels comfortable about reporting a violation. A number of subterfuges are resorted to in an effort to diminish the potential conflict.

There is a general understanding that workers are not supposed to use a tap in the presence of plant inspectors. At various times this understanding is made explicit. The inspector frequently tells the workers of his crew: "Now fellas, there's a big drive now on taps. The Air Force just issued a special memo. For God's sakes, don't use a tap when I'm around. If somebody sees it while I'm in the area, it'll be my ass. Look around first. Make sure I'm gone."

At other times the verbalization comes from the worker. If a worker has to use a tap and the inspector is present, he will usually wait until the inspector leaves. If the inspector shows no signs of leaving, the worker will tell him to "Get the hell outa here. I got work to do and can't do it while you're around."

If the worker knows the inspector he may take out the tap, permitting the inspector to see it. The wise inspector responds to the gesture by leaving. Of course, a worker has already "sized up" the inspector and knows whether or not he can rely upon him to respond as desired.

When there is an Air Force–inspired drive against the tap, the inspectors will make the rounds and "lay the law down": "I want no more tapping around here. The next guy caught gets turned in. I can't cover you guys any more. I'm not kidding you bastards. If you can't do a decent job, don't do it at all. If that s.o.b. foreman of yours insists on you doing it, tell him to do it himself. He can't make you do it. If you're caught, it's your ass not his. When the chips are down, he's got to cover himself and he'll leave you holding the bag!"

For about three or four days thereafter taps disappear from public view. The work slows down, and ultimately the inspectors forget to be zealous. A state of normal haphazard equilibrium is restored.

Other types of social relations and situations between workers and inspectors help maintain this state of equilibrium. An inspector will often see a tap in the top of a worker's tool box. He will pick it up and drop it into the bottom of the box where it cannot be seen easily. Perhaps he will tell the worker that he is a "damned fool for being so careless." The inspector thus hopes to establish his dependability for the worker, and creates a supply of good will credit, which the worker must repay in the form of protecting the inspector.

Another typical worker-inspector situation occurs when a mechanic is caught in the act of tapping, and the inspector does not look away. The inspector severely reprimands the mechanic, "throws the fear of God into him," holds him in suspense as to whether he will turn him in, and then lets him go with a warning. This, generally, only happens to new workers. Occasionally when a worker has a new inspector and no previously established trust relationship, the same situation may arise. In both cases they are an integral part of the socialization of the worker to the plant or, rather, to a specific phase of its operation.

THE ROLE OF THE FOREMAN

Another type of ceremonial escape from law enforcement through pseudo–law enforcement involves the foreman. In rare cases an inspector will catch a worker using the tap, reprimand him and turn him over to his foreman. The foreman then is forced to go through the procedure of reprimanding the errant worker. The foreman becomes serious and indignant, primarily because the worker let himself get caught. He gives the worker a genuine tongue lashing, and he reminds him once again that he, as foreman, has to go to bat to save the worker's neck. He stresses that it is only because of *his* intervention that the worker will not lose his job. He states, "Next time be careful. I won't stick my neck out for you again. For God's sakes don't use a tap, *unless it's absolutely necessary.*"

The worker is obliged to accept the reprimand and to assume the countenance of true penitence, even to the extent of promising that it won't happen again. He will say, "Awright, awright. So I got caught this time. Next time I won't get caught." Both the foreman and worker play these roles even though the worker tapped the hole at the specific request of the foreman. The most blatant violation of the mores in such a situation is when the worker grins and treats the whole thing as a comic interlude. When this happens, the foreman becomes truly enraged, "That's the trouble with you. You don't take your job seriously. You don't give a dam about nothing. How long do I have to put up with your not giving a dam!"

The public ritual therefore conceals an entirely different dimension of social functions involved in the use of the tap. It is inconceivable that the tap could be used without the active or passive collusion of the foreman. As noted, the foreman instructs the worker in its use, indicates when he wants it used, assists the worker in evading the plant rules, and when the worker is caught, goes through the ritual of punishment. These role contradictions are intrinsic to the position of the foreman. His major responsibility is to keep production going. At the same time he is a representative of supervision, and is supposed to encourage respect for company law. He is not primarily responsible for quality since this is the province of plant quality control, i.e., inspection. He resolves the various conflicts in terms of the strongest and most persistent forms of pressures and rewards.

The work requirements of a particular foreman and his crew are determined by the Production Analysis Section, another staff organization. Workers call it Time Study although this is only one part of its function. Production Analysis determines on the basis of time studies, the amount of men to be assigned to a specific crew, the locations of crews on the line, and the cutting-off points for work controlled by a particular foreman. Having done this, they determine the work load required of a foreman and keep production charts on completed work. These charts are the report cards of the foreman. At a moment's glance, top supervision can single out foremen who are not pulling their weight. In aviation assembly, since the work cycle for a particular team is relatively long (four to eight hours) and since a foreman has relatively few teams (usually three) all doing the same job, any slowdown which delays one team damages the foreman's

production record in the immediate perceivable terms of the report card. Moreover, delay caused by the inability of one crew to complete its task prevents other crews from working on that wing.

As a result of these considerations, the pressures "to get work out" are paramount for the foreman. There is a relatively high turnover among foremen. In the last analysis, production records are the major consideration in supervisory mobility. All other considerations, e.g., sociability, work knowledge, personality, etc., are assumed to be measured by the production chart.

In this context the foreman, vis á vis the ticklish question of the tap, is compelled to violate some of the most important laws of the company and the Air Force. Crucial instances occur at times when the Air Force institutes stringent anti-tap enforcement measures. When key holes do not line up it may be necessary, as an alternative to using the tap, to disassemble previous installations. The disassembling and reassembling may take a full eight hours before the previously reached work stage is again reached. The production chart for that eight-hour period will indicate that no work has been done. In such a situation the worker may refuse to tap a hole since he risks endangering his job. The foreman also may be reluctant to request directly that the worker tap a hole. To get the work done he therefore employs a whole rhetoric of veiled requests such as "Hell, that's easy ... you know what to do ... you've done it before." "Maybe you can clean out the threads," or "Well, see what you can do."

If the worker is adamant, the foreman will practically beg him to do the *right* thing. He will remind him of past favors, he will complain about his chart rating and of how "top brass doesn't give a dam about anything but what's on the chart." He usually ends his plea with: "Once you get this done, you can take it easy. You know I don't work you guys too hard most of the time."

If the veiled requests and pitiful pleadings don't produce results, the foreman may take the ultimate step of tapping the hole himself. He compounds the felony, because he not only violates the rules of workmanship but also violates union rules which specifically state that no foreman can use a tool. To add insult to injury, the foreman further has to borrow the tap in the midst of an anti-tap drive when taps are scarce.

From the viewpoint of production the use of the tap is imperative to the functioning of the production organization, even though it is one of the most serious work crimes. This is recognized even at official levels, although only in indirect ways.

Taps, being made of hard steel, have the disadvantage of being brittle. If not handled carefully, they may break within the nut. This not only makes further work impossible, but makes for easier detection of the crime. To cope with such a problem, the tool crib is well equipped with a supply of tap extractors. Any worker can draw an appropriately sized tap extractor from the tool crib. All these are official company property. He can do this even amidst the most severe anti-tap drives without fear or the danger of punishment.

CRIME AND THE SOCIAL SYSTEM

Deviancy, in the sense that it implies a rejection of the norms of a social system or behavior outside of the system, is not a useful concept for analyzing this type of crime. Rather, the use of the tap is literally a major crime which is intrinsic to the system. . . . Crime as defined by the use of the tap (and the other crimes of workmanship subsumed under our discussion of the tap) supports in its own way the continuance of the system, just as the avoidance of the use of the tap contributes to the perfection of the system. . . . If one considers the actions called "deviant behavior" as intrinsic to the system, deviant behavior contributes to and supports the system just as does conformity, simply because the system is composed of its interrelated parts. . . .

Obviously profit-making through production is the major end of the company, i.e., its stockholders, board of directors, officers, and supervisory staff. . . .

For the Air Force the major end is a high rate of production of high quality planes at low cost. Reducing costs and maintaining quality are secondary ends, or if one wishes to so describe it, means to the primary end of producing efficient aircraft. For the individual foreman, maintaining

his job, gaining a promotion or staying out of trouble may be his primary private ends. The maintaining or exceeding of his production quota, while a major end for the "company" as a whole and as defined by the executives, are the means of attaining the private goals of the foreman.

Similarly the primary ends of plant inspectors are to get along with workers, to avoid buying jobs which will be rejected in later inspection, and in some cases to achieve a supervisory position. Again, the actions of inspectors in developing a mutual trust situation, and in protecting themselves and workers in the tap situation, represents a compromise between different private ends. Similarly the ends of workers are to get their work done with a minimum of effort, to get along at least minimally with foremen and inspectors, to stay out of trouble and to avoid being fired. The semi-secret use of the tap, then, represents a compromise between these complexes of ends.

Taking these means-ends situations together, we find that what are means for one group are ends for another. In all cases, means and ends can be defined as either public or private attributes. Public ends are means to private ends, and private ends are in some cases limited by "public," i.e., organizationally sanctioned, ends and means. . . .

In terms of the specific problem of the tap as an instrument, and its relationship to means-and-ends relationships within the organization, we find that use of tap is a private means to publicly stated ends. But those ends to which the use of tap is oriented are, from both the standpoint of that abstraction "the company" and from the standpoint of its members, only one of a number of possible ends. It is the plurality of ends that accounts for "deviant behavior" rather than the conflict between means and ends. Production is a major end, and quality is a necessary condition for the attainment of that end. Moreover, as individuals are distributed at different levels and in different lines of the status hierarchy, different ends become more salient to individuals occupying different positions. The relationship of means to ends at both the public and private levels is different (in fact is sometimes reversed) for individuals in different positions in the organization. The statement of "public ends" attached to the organization or the social system describes the ends of a limited number of particular and publicly accessible or visible positions in the system.

Thus any theoretical model which accepts as an initial postulate the dominance of an ultimate end, and which conceptualizes disorganization as a conflict between means and ends, overlooks the possibility that conflicting means and ends are actually conflicts between the means to one end with the means to another end.

Moreover, in any complex organization where plural ends are distributed in different ways among office holders, the conflict of ends and the conflicts between means and ends, are institutionalized as conflicts between various departments of segments in the organization. Thus from the point of view of production supervision, quality control is a major obstacle to the achievement of its ends. From the standpoint of quality control, sloppy workmanship is a major crime which may result in sanctions to the inspector. The tolerance of the tap is a means by which workers, inspectors and production supervisors attempt to achieve their respective ends in a mutually tolerable manner in a situation where they are forced to work together according to directives, which if closely followed would result in mutual frustration. For the worker, the inspector and the foreman, the development of a satisfactory social environment, the minimization of conflict, and the development of tolerable social relations become a major end. Crime, and the toleration of crime within the limits of avoiding extreme sanctions, becomes a means of these social ends, as well as means to the publicly recognized ends of the organization.

In sum, a large part of behavior, visible to an insider or to a sophisticated observer, is "criminal," i.e., it violates publicly stated norms. But since such behavior is accepted—in fact often stimulated, aided and abetted by the effective on-the-spot authorities—the criminality of such behavior has limited consequences.

CONCLUSION

The resolution of the "means-end conflict" results in crime. But such crime often becomes

fairly acceptable behavior and is stabilized as a permanent aspect of the organization. Crime becomes one of the major operational devices of the organization ... (Tap use) is a crime only in that there is an official ruling against its use, and that there are a wide range of ceremonial forms of law-enforcement and punishment. With respect to the Air Force, use of the tap still remains a serious crime. But in this area the wide range of cooperative behavior between workers, foremen, and plant inspectors combines to reduce the importance of Air Force law-enforcement as a significant factor in this situation.

The ceremonial aspects of law-enforcement are, however, of importance. These include secrecy in the use of the tap to avoid embarrassing the inspector, the reporting of tap violations by the inspector to the foreman who initially requested the use of the tap, the rhetoric used by the foreman in requesting the use of the tap, the mock severity of the foreman in reprimanding the reported violator, and the penitence of the apprehended criminal before his judge, the foreman.

All of these are serious social accompaniments to the use of the tap. They enable the personnel involved to maintain the public values, while performing those actions necessary to attain the public or private ends appropriate to their evaluations of their positions. Thus a form of institutional schizophrenia is the major result of the conflict of ends and the conflict of means and ends. Individuals act and think on at least two planes, the plane of the public ideology and the plane of action. They shift from plane to plane, as required by their positions, their situations, and their means-ends estimations. In a sense, it is a form of double-think, and double-think is the major result of means-ends conflict.

From the point of view of the actors involved, and in the light of the double-think mechanism, the major definition of "deviancy" takes on another dimension. The major crime for the actors involved, is the lack of respect for the social ceremonialism surrounding the tap. The worker who allows an inspector to see him possessing or using a tap, threatens the defenses of the inspector and is likely to be reprimanded for not being careful. He is likely to find it harder to "sell" his work to that inspector. He gets a bad reputation and is thought of as a "character."

Similarly in talking to an inspector the worker who casually mentions illegal workmanship is told by this inspector not to mention it. Finally, a worker who grins while being reprimanded for the use of the tap, is likely to be bawled out for lack of awareness of the seriousness of his act and his flippant attitude. The foreman is likely to threaten him with a withdrawal from the circle of protection given by the foreman to apprehended criminals.

Thus, lack of seriousness in adhering to the ceremonial forms of law violation is defined as a case of inappropriateness of affect and lack of reality orientation to which serious forms of informal social control are addressed. The major crime, then, is the violation of the *rules* of criminal behavior.

The fact that tapping is a crime, a violation of an inoperative public ideology, does not mean that it is uncontrolled anomalous behavior. On the contrary, the very pervasiveness of the use of tap and its functional indispensability result in a relatively close control of tapping by supervisory authority.

The worker is taught the proper techniques of tapping, and he is taught the situations for which use of the tap is appropriate. Misuse of the tap (using the tap as a substitute for lining up holes and for careless workmanship) is frowned upon by supervisors. Using the tap as a substitute for less severely defined illegal techniques of workmanship is also frowned upon.

The worker who uses the tap promiscuously is subject to a wide variety of informal controls. He is kidded and teased by other workers. Inspectors become sensitive to his action and when he is caught, he is reported and bawled out, primarily because of his reputation and not so much for the use of the tap in a specific situation. The foreman rides him unmercifully and tends to become more sensitive to all his faults of workmanship. If he persists in abusing the use of the tap, he ultimately gets transferred to another foreman who is short of men. The floating worker is presumed to be a botcher by the very fact of his being transferred.

In no case, however, are formal actions, which involve the possibility of dismissal, taken against the worker. This is because, in writing up a worker for abusing the tap, the foreman would risk the danger of bringing into the open and into official and public channels the whole issue of the use of the tap. In punishing promiscuous tappers by official means, the foreman might risk losing opportunities to have the tap used in situations which are advantageous to him. Moreover, in bringing serious charges against the deviant tapper, the foreman might find that workers necessarily would be hesitant to use the tap in situations the foreman regards as necessary.

For these reasons, foremen and inspectors do not use the formal channels of law enforcement, but rely instead on informal controls. The informal controls tend to limit the use of the tap to necessary situations. In addition, the use of such controls results in a new definition of crime and its function at the behavioral level. A "crime" is not a crime so long as its commission is controlled and directed by those in authority toward goals which they define as socially constructive. A violation of law is treated as a crime when it is not directed and controlled by those in authority or when it is used for exclusively personal ends.

The kind, type and frequency of crime are functions of the system of authority. The ranges of "socially permissible crime" and the degree and severity of punishment are determined by the ends and interests of those who are responsible for law enforcement. Severe law enforcement limits the freedom of leadership groups in attainment of their own ends. Loosening the fabric of law enforcement enables these groups to have greater freedom of action in the attainment of their ends, but also permits a greater amount of crime at lower levels.

CHAPTER TWO

JUVENILE DELINQUENCY

Official statistics based on arrests and court dispositions indicate that juvenile delinquency is increasing rapidly.[1] Caution should be taken while examining these statistics, however. Variation in official statistics may depend as much, or more, on variation in the behavior of officials (police, judges, etc.) and their interpretation of particular acts than on variation in the actual extent of delinquency itself. There are wide differences between jurisdictions (city, county, or state), and within the same jurisdiction over time concerning the definition of juvenile delinquency, as well as in the accuracy with which acts defined as delinquent are actually recorded. Moreover, official statistics include only delinquent acts known to the police and courts. Consequently, variation in official statistics may not be an accurate gauge of variation in actual delinquency at all. The problems associated with measuring juvenile delinquency,[2] therefore, leave any generalization about its increase (or decrease) open to question.

Evidence indicates that juvenile delinquency is predominantly social in nature. Adolescent crimes frequently involve more than one participant; in fact, estimates based on official statistics indicate that somewhere between 70 and 90 percent of adolescent crimes occur with companions.[3] Such statistics have led many to view juvenile delinquency almost exclusively in social terms. The following quote concerning the relevance of psychopathology to delinquent behavior is illustrative:

> The importance of group formations in socially undesirable behaviors by youth almost precludes greater importance to individual pathology as a causative factor (in delinquent conduct). Being a responsible, reliable

---

[1] See Albert K. Cohen and James F. Short, Jr., "Juvenile Delinquency," in Robert K. Merton and Robert A. Nisbet, eds., *Contemporary Social Problems*, rev. ed. (New York: Harcourt, Brace and World, 1966), pp. 91–93.

[2] For an early discussion of problems involved in interpreting official statistics on juvenile delinquency, see Sophia M. Robinson, *Can Delinquency Be Measured?* (New York: Columbia University Press, 1936). For a comprehensive survey of attempts to measure juvenile delinquency, see Thorsten Sellin and Marvin Wolfgang, *The Measurement of Delinquency* (New York: John Wiley, 1964).

[3] For a review of the evidence, see Maynard L. Erickson, "The Group Context of Delinquent Behavior," *Social Problems* 19 (Summer, 1971), p. 113.

member of a group, who can be counted upon by others even in secret and dangerous activities, is simply not possible for any period of time if one is severely disturbed emotionally, subject to acute anxieties, depression, persecution or other such symptoms. If one persistently fails to follow what his fellows feel is "right" and does what they denounce as "wrong," his presence will not be tolerated by other members.[4]

Thus, much juvenile delinquency is viewed as having a social basis and as being integrated into a set of ongoing group activities. It is not the result of uncontrolled, impulsive psychopathological behavior. The selections under "Antecedants and Determinants" emphasizes this conception of delinquency behavior.

A. ANTECEDENTS AND DETERMINANTS

In the first selection we present a study of the social basis of *delinquent commitment,* specifically of the extent to which an individual adolescent's commitment to delinquent behavior is influenced by the delinquent behavior of his friends as much evidence based on arrest records would indicate. On the basis of a study of self-reported delinquency of junior high school students, Robert H. Hardt and Sandra J. Peterson, in "Arrests of Self and Friends as Indicators of Delinquency Involvement," report that the involvement of a student is indeed associated with the delinquent behavior of his friends. The relationship is independent of the arrest record of the individual himself. In addition, the use of "neutralization techniques"—beliefs which rationalize or justify delinquent behavior (e.g., "most of the people who get robbed can afford to lose a little money")—tends to have a social basis; the endorsement of such beliefs is directly related to the arrest record of friends. The results of Hardt and Peterson clearly show, therefore, that the delinquency tendencies of individual juveniles are closely associated with the behavior patterns (and, by inference, the normative standards) of their juvenile associates.

Hardt and Peterson's results are consistent with gang theories of delinquent behavior. Such theories stress the significance of gang relationships and subcultural norms as determinants of delinquent conduct. Gang members become delinquents because they are socialized in the gang subculture and are sensitive to the evaluations of other gang members. While this may be correct (although Yablonsky's analysis below questions it), it still leaves unanswered the question of what causes adolescent groups to have delinquent norms. In "A Critique of Sociological Interpretations of Gang Delinquency," David Bordua reviews the position of four theories of gang delinquency on this issue. While all four of the theories view

---

[4] Muzafer Sherif and Carolyn W. Sherif, *Reference Groups: Explorations into Conformity and Deviation of Adolescents* (New York: Harper and Row, 1964), p. 279.

delinquency as a subcultural phenomenon, each attributes its cause to a set of specific factors, such as city growth, status deprivation, differential opportunity, and lower class subculture.

An alternative interpretation of juvenile delinquency, common among psychologists and psychiatrists, focusses on parent-child relationships, especially parental discipline. In "The Interaction of Family Variables and Gang Variables in the Aetiology of Delinquency," Robert Everett Stanfield shows that a father's discipline (whether consistent or eratic-lax) is important but that its effects differ depending on the socioeconomic status of the family and the youth's participation in gang activity; the father's discipline interacts with socioeconomic status and gang participation. At the same time, Stanfield data also show that the effect of gang participation varies depending on the father's discipline.

ARRESTS OF SELF AND FRIENDS AS INDICATORS OF DELINQUENCY INVOLVEMENT

ROBERT H. HARDT AND SANDRA J. PETERSON

In a recent investigation of the effect of school adjustment on delinquency involvement, Toby and Toby rejected the use of arrest and court appearances of a juvenile as a satisfactory index of "commitment to a delinquent style of life"[1] and proposed, instead, that the arrest histories of his *friends* are a more valid index of the boy's commitment than his *own* arrest record.

They were critical of arrests as an indication of commitment to a delinquent role since such a source includes "cases that should not be included" and excludes, of necessity, "offenders who were not caught."[2] In the first group, which might be considered "false positives," youngsters would be included who were mentally ill, involved in family conflict, or impulsive pranksters. The second group, the "false negatives," would include participants in group delinquency who have not been apprehended. Although other alternatives to the use of official records for the identification of delinquents have been developed, such as the techniques of self-report[3] and observation,[4] frequently they are not feasible because of cost or administrative restrictions.

We tested the Toby approach in a different community. In addition, we examined some characteristics of the deviant cases (the false positives and the false negatives) by drawing upon data collected in an opinion survey of a junior high school population. This examination helped clarify whether the Toby assumptions about these deviant cases are tenable.[5]

PROCEDURES

The present analysis is based on one segment of data collected within a community embarking

---

Reprinted with the permission of the authors and the National Council on Crime and Delinquency, from *Journal of Research in Crime and Delinquency* 5 (January, 1968), pp. 44–51.

[1] Jackson Toby and Marcia L. Toby, "Low School Status as Predisposing Factor in Subcultural Delinquency," mimeographed (Report of a Cooperative Research Project of the U.S. Office of Education and Rutgers University, n.d.), p. 7.

[2] *Ibid.*

[3] Several recent studies using the self-report technique are reviewed in Robert H. Hardt and George E. Bodine, *Development of Self-Report Instruments in Delinquency Research: A Conference Report* (New York: Syracuse University Youth Development Center, 1965).

[4] Two studies using observational approaches are Muzafer Sherif and Carolyn Sherif, *Reference Groups: Explorations into Conformity and Deviation of Adolescents* (New York: Harper and Row, 1964); James F. Short, Jr., and Fred L. Strodtbeck, *Group and Gang Delinquency* (Chicago: University of Chicago Press, 1965).

[5] The "Toby approach" has received considerable attention in criminological circles, but the Tobys' original study has never been published. Thus, the publication of this paper serves a dual purpose.

upon the development of a neighborhood-based delinquency prevention program.[6] The city has a population of slightly under 250,000 and is the center of a major metropolitan area in New York State.

Initially, those sections of the city were selected for intensive study which, during a recent period, showed consistently the highest delinquency and school-dropout rates. This procedure identified three contiguous low-income areas: a predominantly Negro section adjacent to the center of the city (NLC) and two predominantly white areas which differed from each other in ethnic composition. In the present paper, data from the two white low-income areas (WLC) have been combined. For purposes of comparison, a middle-income section of the community (WMC) which has had low delinquency and dropout rates was selected.

Questionnaires were administered to seventh-, eighth-, and ninth-grade pupils attending one parochial and four public junior high schools in the study areas. A special team of test monitors, consisting of college graduate students, provided the pupils with standard explanations and instructions. In almost all classes, teachers left the room after introductions were completed. Pupils were assured about the confidentiality of their answers and were asked not to sign their names. They were allotted approximately an hour and two-thirds (two classroom periods) to complete the questionnaire. In addition to a section on reported delinquent behavior, the questionnaire provided information on a variety of other topics, such as the pupil's educational and occupational aspirations and his perception of the school, the neighborhood, police, and agencies.

---

[6] This paper is fourth in a series reporting on the distribution of self-reported delinquency of juveniles. The first and second were concerned with substantive issues, while the third placed greater emphasis on methodological problems involved in the use of self-report approaches. See Robert H. Hardt and Sandra J. Peterson, "Neighborhood Status and Delinquent Activity as Indexed by Police Records and a Self-Report Survey," mimeographed (Paper presented at the 1964 meeting of the Eastern Sociological Society, Boston, Syracuse University Youth Development Center); Robert H. Hardt, "Delinquency and Social Class: Bad Kids or Good Cops?" in *Among the People: Studies of the Urban Poor*, Irwin Deutscher and Elizabeth Thompson, eds. (New York: Basic Books, forthcoming); Robert H. Hardt and Sandra J. Peterson, "How Valid are Self-Report Measures of Delinquent Behavior?" mimeographed (Paper presented at the 1966 meeting of the Eastern Sociological Society, Philadelphia, Syracuse University Youth Development Center.)

While responses were obtained from both boys and girls, this report is restricted to findings based on the male sample.

Official data on the arrest or ticketing history of pupils in the five schools were obtained from the county's central registry of juvenile offenders, which contains standard reports of police contacts with juveniles obtained from nineteen police agencies serving the county. These data are believed to be virtually complete since January, 1957.

The data on friendship choices were obtained very early in the questionnaire. Pupils were asked to "print the names of your four best friends in this school. These are the boys and girls whom you hang around with most after school."

The nineteen items included in the general self-report scale are reproduced in the Appendix, along with the introductory statement that preceded the scale. Fourteen items deal with delinquent or disapproved activities. Some were selected from previous inventories; others were developed to represent delinquent acts of local concern. Two items were designed as "good boy" items to help break the tendency to a particular response set. Three items deal with reports of contact with the police and courts.

In response to each self-report item, pupils were asked to check "the last time that you did each of the following things," with four alternatives listed: (1) in the last seven days, (2) in the last twelve months, (3) over a year ago, or (4) never.

FINDINGS

The Toby findings are based on a five-year longitudinal study of seventh-grade boys attending the only public junior high school in a New Jersey community of forty thousand. The interviews, which were conducted each year, focused mostly on questions of a sociometric type. The answers were used to establish an alphabetic friendship file, which was checked against a delinquency file established from the records of several police, court, and probation agencies serving the community.

As seen in Table 1, the Toby study discovered that "while many boys without a delinquency record themselves had delinquent friends, vir-

TABLE 1. RELATIONSHIP BETWEEN ARREST RECORDS OF CHOOSERS AND THEIR FRIENDS (NEW JERSEY SAMPLE)

Status of Chooser	Arrest Records of Friends			
	None Arrested	A Few Arrested	Many Arrested	Total
Has record	9	24	84	117
No record	70	95	38	203
Total	79	119	122	320

Note: Calculated from data presented by Toby and Toby, "Low School Status as a Predisposing Factor in Subcultural Delinquency," mimeographed (Report of a Cooperative Research Project of the U.S. Office of Education and Rutgers University, n.d.), Table 2, p 9

TABLE 2. THE RELATIONSHIP BETWEEN ARREST RECORDS OF CHOOSERS AND THEIR FRIENDS (NEW JERSEY AND NEW YORK SAMPLES)

Status of Chooser	Percentage Having at Least One Delinquent Friend											
	New Jersey		New York									
			NLC		WLC		WMC		Total			
	Percent	N	Percent	N	Percent	N	Percent	N	Percent	N		
Has record	92%	(117)	89%	(72)	77%	(48)	62%	(24)	81%	(144)		
No record	65	(203)	64	(114)	40	(216)	23	(226)	37	(556)		
Total	75	(320)	74	(186)	47	(264)	27	(250)	47	(700)		
Percent with record	37%		39%		18%		10%		21%			

Note: Abbreviations: NLC—School predominantly Negro lower class; WLC—school predominantly white lower class; WMC—school predominantly white middle class; N—the number of cases on which the percentages are based.

tually none with a delinquency record lacked delinquent friends."[7] Of the 117 boys with a delinquency record, only nine failed to name at least one delinquent friend. By the Toby index, these nine boys would not be classified as showing a commitment to a delinquent role.

In the current study, an almost identical pattern is revealed in the school which had a delinquency rate most similar to the New Jersey school. Table 2 shows that, in the Negro lower-class school (NLC), nine out of ten boys (89%) with a delinquency record have at least one friend with a record. A somewhat different pattern is revealed in the white middle-class school (WMC). In this school, only six out of ten boys (62%) with a record have a friend who has a record.[8] Thus, the Toby index would miss or exclude a larger proportion of arrested boys in those schools in which pupils had a lower arrest rate. The Toby study defends the exclusion of

such cases on the ground that they are likely to be psychopathological delinquents rather than subcultural delinquents.

Again, as in the Toby study, we find that a large proportion of boys with no arrest history have at least one friend with an arrest. In the NLC school, nearly two out of three boys with an unblemished record have at least one friend with a record. In contrast, in the WMC school, less than one out of four boys with an unblemished record has a friend with a record. Thus, using the Toby procedure, we find that a relatively large proportion of unticketed boys from high-delinquency neighborhoods would be categorized as having some commitment to a delinquent role. The Tobys justify such a classification on the assumption that these boys are largely unapprehended delinquents.[9]

To what extent are the assumptions the Tobys use to justify the inclusion of "deviant cases" supported by the characteristics of such cases as revealed in our opinion survey? The findings in

---

[7] Toby and Toby, "Low School Status as a Predisposing Factor," p. 8.

[8] The difference between schools WMC and NLC is not a result of variations in a tendency toward differential association in the two schools, but a reflection of the differences in the proportion of delinquents in each school.

[9] Toby and Toby, "Low School Status as a Predisposing Factor" p. 10.

Table 3 are based on the responses to an eleven-item omnibus self-report delinquency scale presented in the Appendix.[10] In this analysis, a score was derived for lifetime incidence by totaling the number of items on which a student admitted involvement anytime during his life. These scores range from 0 to 11, with a mean of 3.51 and a standard deviation of 2.85.

Table 3 reveals that self-report delinquency scores tend to be higher both for boys who have a record and for boys whose friends have a record. (Since the number of cases in some of the cells is relatively small, the data for all three types of neighborhoods have been combined here and in the subsequent tables.) Indeed, both categorizations appear to have an independent and additive effect on violation scores. Thus, the lowest mean violation score (2.7) is obtained by boys without a record who have no friends with a record; the highest mean score (5.2) is obtained by boys with a record who have two or more friends with a record.

TABLE 3. MEANS OF SELF-REPORTED DELINQUENCY VIOLATION SCORES BY ARREST STATUS OF SELF AND OF FRIENDS

Status of Chooser	Number of Officially Delinquent Friends			
	0	1	2+	Total
Has record	4.2	4.9	5.2	4.9
No record	2.7	3.2	3.9	3.0
Total	2.8	3.7	4.5	3.4

Among the boys without an official record, there is a positive relationship between the number of friends with an official record and the boy's own self-reported violation score. This finding lends support to the assumption the Tobys made for classifying the boys with delinquent peers as having some delinquent commitment.

However, what about the cases that Toby excludes as "false positives"—boys with an official record who do not have friends who are officially delinquent? This particular group has a mean violation score (4.2) higher than any group of

unarrested boys, including unarrested boys with two or more delinquent friends. Thus, it appears that the Toby procedure would exclude a group of arrested boys who have an admitted violation history higher than average.

In addition to the measure of self-reported delinquent behavior, an attitudinal measure of delinquent commitment was also obtained in the survey. Sykes and Matza[11] and Matza[12] have suggested that techniques of neutralization (justifications of deviant behavior) serve to facilitate as well as rationalize the commission of delinquent acts. A six-item neutralization scale (e.g., "Most of the people who get robbed can afford to lose a little money") was included in the opinion questionnaire. Mean scores on this measure in relation to arrest of self and friends are presented in Table 4.

TABLE 4. MEAN NUMBER OF NEUTRALIZATION ITEMS ENDORSED BY ARREST STATUS OF SELF AND OF FRIENDS

Status of Chooser	Number of Officially Delinquent Friends			
	0	1	2+	Total
Has record	1.4	2.0	2.1	1.9
No record	.8	1.1	1.7	1.0
Total	.8	1.4	2.0	1.2

Neutralization scores are linked both to the boy's own arrest record and that of friends. Boys without an official record have lower neutralization scores (1.0) than those with a record (1.9). Boys with no delinquent friends have much lower neutralization scores (0.8) than those with two or more officially delinquent friends (2.0). Independently, the arrest records of the boy and his friends are related to neutralization scores so that the two variables tend to have an additive effect on neutralization scores. The Tobys' first assumption dealing with "false negatives" again receives support: boys with no record but with two or more delinquent friends tend to have higher than average neutralization scores. However, the assumption dealing with false positives is again rendered subject to ques-

---

[10] For further description of the characteristics of the scale, see Hardt and Peterson, "Neighborhood Status and Delinquent Activity."

[11] Gresham Sykes and David Matza, "Techniques of Neutralization: A Theory of Delinquency," *American Sociological Review*, December, 1957, pp. 664–70.

[12] David Matza, *Delinquency and Drift* (New York: John Wiley, 1964).

tion. Boys who have a record but have no officially delinquent friends have a neutralization score higher than average.

While these two sets of findings suggest that the Toby procedure would tend to exclude from a delinquent categorization those boys with a moderately high delinquency involvement, are these excluded boys solitary or psychopathological delinquents? We do not have direct information on the extent of each boy's involvement in group delinquency, but we do have reports on the types of peer groups in which boys are involved.

The opinion poll included an item dealing with the typical pattern of peer association in which the boy participated. The question was, "Do you usually go around with a bunch of other kids or by yourself?" The response options were the following: (1) with a group having its own name; (2) with a bunch of others; (3) with one or two others; (4) by myself.

Table 5 presents findings on the percentage of boys responding either "with a group" or "with a bunch" in relation to the arrest status of the boy and his friends. Regardless of their own arrest history, boys with two or more delinquent friends are somewhat more likely to travel in these larger groups. However, there is little indication that arrested boys with no officially delinquent friends are a particularly solitary group. Over a third of them travel in these larger groups, and only 10 percent of them report that they generally "go around by myself."

TABLE 5. PERCENTAGE OF BOYS WHO REPORT THEY USUALLY SPEND TIME WITH GANG OR IN BUNCH BY ARREST STATUS OF SELF AND OF FRIENDS

Status of Chooser	Number of Officially Delinquent Friends			
	0	1	2+	Total
Has record	34.5	28.9	52.9	35.4
No record	27.0	31.3	39.2	29.8
Total	27.6	30.5	44.2	30.4

SUMMARY AND CONCLUSIONS

In many delinquency investigations, the researcher wishes to identify juveniles in the community who represent extremes in the extent of delinquency involvement. In some of these cases, the objective may be to develop special demonstration programs; in other instances, the goal may be to identify groups for more detailed and intensive study. Often, the investigator cannot mount a large-scale research effort for the case-identifying phase of the project and must rely on the official records of arrest to identify his delinquent and nondelinquent sample. The Tobys have suggested that, if the investigator can obtain sociometric information, the arrest record of friends may be a more valid indicator of delinquency commitment than the arrest record of the juvenile himself.

In the present study, the authors have collated data on official arrests, sociometric choices, and self-reports of behavior and opinions to examine the Toby proposal more critically. In general, we have found that arrests of the boy himself and of his friends are independently linked to a number of indicators of delinquency involvement. Boys who have not been arrested but have friends with arrest records are more likely to have a delinquency commitment than nonarrested boys whose friends also have an unblemished record. Thus, we suggest that this latter categorization identifies a particularly nondelinquent group of boys.

The Toby index contained an acknowledged "paradoxical feature: A boy who himself had a long delinquency record would not be categorized as committed to a delinquent role unless he had delinquent friends."[13] Our data suggest that while this boy may not be as heavily committed as the arrested boy with several delinquent friends, he is likely to have a higher than average delinquency commitment. Our findings provide no support for the Tobys' suggestion that such a boy represents a solitary or psychopathological delinquent. Thus, in identifying a low delinquent group, it would not be desirable to exclude any boy with a record even if he has no delinquent friends. The use of arrest records of the boy himself and of his friends in combination promises to provide a much better discrimination of boys with differential delinquency involvement than the use of either measure alone.

---

[13] Toby and Toby, "Low School Status as a Predisposing Factor," p. 8.

APPENDIX

Reported Behavior

Young people do lots of things that are good but once in a while they break some rules. Some of our most famous people said they broke quite a few rules when they were growing up.

We want to get a clear picture of the things young people do. The way you can help is by giving a true picture of how young people act.

Don't worry about looking good—or looking bad.

When was the last time that you did each of the following things? (——in the last 7 days; ——in the last 12 months; ——over a year ago; ——never).

Check only the *last time* this happened:

1.* I smoked a cigarette.

2.* I broke street lights or windows in a building.

3. I was sent to court.

4.* I took something worth more than 50¢ from a store.

5. I helped my parents around the house.

6.* I damaged or messed up something in a school or some other building.

7.* I stayed out all night and didn't tell my parents where I was.

8.* I broke into a parking meter.

9.* I drank some beer, wine, or liquor without my parents knowing about it.

10. I was warned or questioned by a policeman.

11.* I took part in a fight where our group of kids fought a different group.

12.* I helped to jump somebody and beat him up.

13. I tried to get kicks from smoking reefer cigarettes, taking pep pills, or sniffing glue.

14. I ran around with some kids who had a bad reputation.

15. I took something which didn't belong to me which was worth more than $2.

16.* I took part in a fight where knives or other weapons were used.

17. I was given a ticket or was arrested by the police.

18.* I went for a ride in a car taken without the owner's permission.

19. I let a friend borrow a little of my own money.

* Item included in eleven-item omnibus scale.

* Item included in eleven-item omnibus scale.

A CRITIQUE OF SOCIOLOGICAL INTERPRETATIONS OF GANG DELINQUENCY

DAVID J. BORDUA

The problem of group delinquency has been a subject of theoretical interest for American sociologists and other social observers for well over a half century. In the course of that period, the group nature of delinquency has come to be a central starting point for many theories of delinquency, and delinquency causation has been seen by some sociologists as preeminently a process whereby the individual becomes associated with a group which devotes some or all of its time to planning, committing, or celebrating delinquencies and which has elaborated a set of lifeways—a subculture—which encourages and justifies behavior defined as delinquent by the larger society.

In addition to the processes whereby an individual takes on the beliefs and norms of a preexisting group and thereby becomes delinquent —a process mysterious enough in itself in many cases—there is the more basic, and in many re-

Reprinted with permission of author and publisher from the *Annals of the American Academy of Political and Social Science* 338 (November, 1961), pp. 120–36.

spects more complex, problem of how such groups begin in the first place. What are the social conditions that facilitate or cause the rise of delinquency-carrying groups? What processes of planned social control might be usable in preventing the rise of such groups or in redirecting the behavior and moral systems of groups already in existence? All these questions and many others have been asked for at least two generations. Within the limits of this brief paper, it is impossible to present and analyze in detail the many answers to these questions which have been put forward by social scientists. What I can do is single out a few of the major viewpoints and concentrate on them.

In its more well-developed and extreme forms, gang or subcultural delinquency has been heavily concentrated in the low status areas of our large cities. The theoretical interpretations I will discuss all confine themselves to gang delinquency of this sort.

THE CLASSICAL VIEW

Still the best book on gangs, gang delinquency, and—though he did not use the term—delinquent subcultures is *The Gang* by Frederick M. Thrasher, and his formulations are the ones that I have labeled "the classical view." Not that he originated the basic interpretative framework, far from it, but his application of the theoretical materials available at the time plus his sensitivity to the effects of social environment and his willingness to consider processes at all behavioral levels from the basic needs of the child to the significance of the saloon, from the nature of city government to the crucial importance of the junk dealer, from the consequence of poverty to the nature of leadership in the gang still distinguish his book.[1]

Briefly, Thrasher's analysis may be characterized as operating on the following levels. The ecological processes which determine the structure of the city create the interstitial area characterized by a variety of indices of conflict, disorganization, weak family and neighborhood

controls, and so on. In these interstitial areas, in response to universal childhood needs, spontaneous play groups develop. Because of the relatively uncontrolled nature of these groups—or of many of them at least—and because of the presence of many attractive and exciting opportunities for fun and adventure, these groups engage in a variety of activities, legal and illegal, which are determined, defined, and directed by the play group itself rather than by conventional adult supervision.

The crowded, exciting slum streets teem with such groups. Inevitably, in a situation of high population density, limited resources, and weak social control, they come into conflict with each other for space, playground facilities, and reputation. Since many of their activities, even at an early age, are illegal, although often not feloniously so—they swipe fruit from peddlers, turn over garbage cans, stay away from home all night and steal milk and cakes for breakfast, play truant from school—they also come into conflict with adult authority. Parents, teachers, merchants, police, and others become natural enemies of this kind of group and attempt to control it or to convert it to more conventional activities. With some groups they succeed, with some they do not.

If the group continues, it becomes part of a network of similar groups, increasingly freed from adult restraint, increasingly involved in intergroup conflict and fighting, increasingly engaged in illegal activities to support itself and to continue to receive the satisfactions of the "free" life of the streets. Conflict, especially with other groups, transforms the play group into the gang. Its illegal activities become more serious, its values hardened, its structure more determined by the necessity to maintain eternal vigilance in a hostile government.

By middle adolescence, the group is a gang, often with a name, usually identified with a particular ethnic or racial group, and usually with an elaborate technology of theft and other means of self-support. Gradually, the gang may move in the direction of adult crime, armed robbery, perhaps, or other serious crimes.

Prior to that time, however, it is likely to have engaged in much stealing from stores, railroad cars, empty houses, parents, drunks, almost anywhere money or goods are available. The ready

---

[1] Frederick M. Thrasher, *The Gang* (Chicago: University of Chicago Press, 1927).

access to outlets for stolen goods is of major importance here. The junk dealer, especially the junk wagon peddler, the convenient no-questions-asked attitudes of large numbers of local adults who buy "hot" merchandise, and the early knowledge that customers are available all help to make theft easy and profitable as well as morally acceptable.[2]

Nonutilitarian?

It is appropriate at this point to deal with a matter that has become important in the discussion of more recent theories of group delinquency. This is Albert K. Cohen's famous characterization of the delinquent subculture as nonutilitarian, by which he seems to mean that activities, especially theft, are not oriented to calculated economic ends.[3]

Thrasher makes a great point of the play and adventure quality of many illegal acts, especially in the pregang stages of a group's development, but he also describes many cases where theft has a quite rational and instrumental nature, even at a fairly early age.

The theft activities and the disposition of the loot make instrumental sense in the context of Thrasher's description of the nature of the group or gang. Much theft is essentially for the purpose of maintaining the group in a state of freedom from adult authority. If a group of boys lives days or weeks away from home, then the theft of food or of things which are sold to buy food is hardly nonutilitarian. If such a group steals from freight cars, peddles the merchandise to the neighbors for movie money, and so on, this can hardly be considered nonutilitarian. The behavior makes sense as instrumental behavior, however, only after one has a picture of the general life led by the group. Boys who feed themselves by duplicating keys to bakery delivery boxes, creep out of their club rooms right after

delivery, steal the pastry, pick up a quart of milk from a doorstep, and then have breakfast may not have a highly developed sense of nutritional values, but this is not nonutilitarian.

Such youngsters may, of course, spend the two dollars gained from selling stolen goods entirely on doughnuts and gorge themselves and throw much of the food away. I think this largely indicates that they are children, not that they are nonutilitarian.[4]

Let us look a little more systematically at the Thrasher formulations, however, since such an examination can be instructive in dealing with the more recent theories. The analysis proceeds at several levels, as I have mentioned.

Levels of Analysis

At the level of the local adult community, we may say that the social structure is permissive, attractive, facilitative, morally supportive of the gang development process.

It is permissive because control over children is weak; attractive because many enjoyable activities are available, some of which are illegal, like stealing fruit, but all of which can be enjoyed only if the child manages to evade whatever conventional controls do exist.

In another sense, the local environment is attractive because of the presence of adult crime of a variety of kinds ranging from organized vice to older adolescents and adults making a living by theft. The attraction lies, of course, in

---

[2] One of the charms of Thrasher's old-time sociology is the fashion in which fact intrudes itself upon theorizing. For example, he tells us that there were an estimated 1,700 to 1,800 junk wagon men in Chicago, most of whom were suspected of being less than rigid in inquiring about the source of "junk." *Ibid.*, p. 148. He also does some other things that seem to have gone out of style, such as presenting information on the age and ethnic composition of as many of the 1,313 gangs as possible. *Ibid.*, pp. 73, 74, 191–93.

[3] Albert K. Cohen, *Delinquent Boys: The Culture of the Gang* (Glencoe: The Free Press, 1955), pp. 25, 26.

[4] The examples cited above are all in Thrasher along with many others of a similar nature. In general, views of the nature of gang activity have shifted quite fundamentally toward a more irrationalist position. Thus, the gang's behavior seems to make no sense. Underlying this shift is a tendency to deal almost entirely with the gang's subculture, its values, beliefs, and the like, to deal with the relationships between this subculture and presumed motivational states which exist in the potential gang members before the gang or protogang is formed, and to deal very little with the developmental processes involved in the formation of gangs. Things which make no sense without consideration of the motivational consequences of gang membership are not necessarily so mysterious given Thrasher's highly sensitive analysis of the ways in which the nature of the gang as a group led to the development—in relation to the local environment—of the gang subculture. Current theory focuses so heavily on motive and culture to the exclusion of group process that some essential points are underemphasized. It would not be too much of a distortion to say that Thrasher saw the delinquent subculture as the way of life that would be developed by a group becoming a gang and that some recent theorists look at the gang as the kind of group that would develop if boys set about creating a delinquent subculture.

the fact that these adults may have a lot of money and live the carefree life and have high status in the neighborhood.

The local environment is facilitative in a number of ways. There are things readily available to steal, people to buy them, and places to hide without adult supervision.

The environment is morally supportive because of the presence of adult crime, as previously mentioned, but also for several additional reasons. One is the readiness of conventional adults to buy stolen goods. Even parents were discovered at this occasionally. The prevalence of political pull, which not only objectively protected adult crime but tended to undercut the norms against crime, must be mentioned then as now. The often bitter poverty which turned many situations into matters of desperate competition also contributed.

Additionally, many gang activities, especially in the protogang stage, are not seriously delinquent and receive adult approval. These activities include such things as playing baseball for "side money" and much minor gambling such as penny pitching. Within limits, fighting lies well within the local community's zone of tolerance, especially when it is directed against members of another ethnic group.

At the level of the adolescent and preadolescent groups themselves, the environment is essentially coercive of gang formation. The presence of large numbers of groups competing for limited resources leads to conflict, and the full-fledged adolescent gang is preeminently a conflict group with a high valuation of fighting skill, courage, and similar qualities. Thus, the transition from spontaneous group to gang is largely a matter of participating in the struggle for life of the adolescent world under the peculiar conditions of the slum.

At the level of the individual, Thrasher assumes a set of basic needs common to all children. He leans heavily on the famous four wishes of W. I. Thomas, security, response, recognition, and new experiences, especially the last two. Gang boys and boys in gang areas are, in this sense, no different from other boys. They come to choose different ways of satisfying these needs. What determines which boys form gangs is the differential success of the agencies of socialization and social control in channeling these needs into conventional paths. Thus, due to family in-

adequacy or breakdown or school difficulties, coupled with the ever present temptations of the exciting, adventurous street as compared to the drab, dull, and unsatisfying family and school, some boys are more available for street life than others.

Finally, it should be pointed out that the gang engages in many activities of a quite ordinary sort. Athletics are very common and highly regarded at all age levels. Much time is spent simply talking and being with the gang. The gang's repertory is diverse—baseball, football, dice, poker, holding dances, shooting the breeze, shoplifting, rolling drunks, stealing cars.

This is more than enough to give the tenor of Thrasher's formulations. I have purposely attempted to convey the distinctive flavor of essentially healthy boys satisfying universal needs in a weakly controlled and highly seductive environment. Compared to the deprived and driven boys of more recent formulations with their status problems, blocked opportunities (or psychopathologies if one takes a more psychiatric view), Thrasher describes an age of innocence indeed.

This is, perhaps, the most important single difference between Thrasher and some—not all—of the recent views. Delinquency and crime were attractive, being a "good boy" was dull. They were attractive because they were fun and were profitable and because one could be a hero in a fight. Fun, profit, glory, and freedom is a combination hard to beat, particularly for the inadequate conventional institutions that formed the competition.

WORKING CLASS BOY AND MIDDLE CLASS MEASURING ROD

If Thrasher saw the gang as being formed over time through the attractiveness of the free street life and the unattractiveness and moral weakness of the agencies of social control, Albert K. Cohen sees many working class boys as being driven to develop the delinquent subculture as a way of recouping the self-esteem destroyed by middle-class–dominated institutions.

Rather than focusing on the gang and its development over time, Cohen's theory focuses on the way of life of the gang—the delinquent subculture. A collective way of life, a subculture, develops when a number of people with a common problem of adjustment are in effective interaction, according to Cohen. The bulk of his basic viewpoint is the attempted demonstration that the common problem of adjustment of the lower-class gang boys who are the carriers of the delinquent subculture derives from their socialization in lower class families and their consequent lack of preparation to function successfully in middle class institutions such as the school.

The institutions within which the working class boy must function reward and punish him for acceptable or unacceptable performance according to the child-assessing version of middle class values. The middle class value pattern places great emphasis on ambition as a cardinal virtue, individual responsibility (as opposed to extreme emphasis on shared kin obligations, for example), the cultivation and possession of skills, the ability to postpone gratification, rationality, the rational cultivation of manners, the control of physical aggressions and violence, the wholesome and constructive use of leisure, and respect for property (especially respect for the abstract rules defining rights of access to material things).[5]

The application of these values adapted to the judgment of children constitutes the "middle class measuring rod" by which all children are judged in institutions run by middle class personnel—the school, the settlement house, and the like. The fact that working class children must compete according to these standards is a consequence of what Cohen, in a most felicitous phrase, refers to as the "domestic status universe" characteristic of American society. Everyone is expected to strive, and everyone is measured against the same standard. Not everyone is equally prepared, however, and the working class boy is, with greater statistical frequency than the middle-class boy, ill-prepared through previous socialization.

Cultural Setting

Social class for Cohen is not simply economic position but, much more importantly, a set of more or less vertically layered cultural settings which differ in the likelihood that boys will be taught the aspirations, ambitions, and psychological skills necessary to adjust to the demands of the larger institutions.

Cohen goes on to describe this predominantly lower working class cultural setting as more likely to show restricted aspirations, a live-for-today orientation toward consumption, a moral view which emphasizes reciprocity within the kin and other primary groups and correlatively less concern with abstract rules which apply across or outside of such particularistic circumstances. In addition, the working class child is less likely to be surrounded with educational toys, less likely to be trained in a family regimen of order, neatness, and punctuality. Of particular importance is the fact that physical aggression is more prevalent and more valued in the working class milieu.

When a working class boy thus equipped for life's struggle begins to function in the school, the settlement, and other middle-class–controlled institutions, and encounters the middle class measuring rod, he inevitably receives a great deal of disapproval, rejection, and punishment. In short, in the eyes of the middle class evaluator, he does not measure up. This is what Cohen refers to as the problem of status deprivation which constitutes the fundamental problem of adjustment to which the delinquent subculture is a solution.

Self-Derogation

But this deprivation derives not only from the negative evaluations of others but also from self-derogation. The working class boy shares in this evaluation of himself to some degree for a variety of reasons.[6] The first of these is the previously mentioned democratic status universe wherein the dominant culture requires everyone to compete against all comers. Second, the parents of working class boys, no matter how adjusted they seem to be to their low status position, are

---

[5] Albert K. Cohen, *Delinquent Boys*, pp. 88–93.

[6] In presenting the theoretical work of someone else, it is often the case that the views of the original author are simplified to his disadvantage. I have tried to guard against this. At this point in Cohen's formulation, however, I may be oversimplifying to his benefit. In view of the considerable struggle over the matter of just what the working class boy is sensitive to, I should point out that Cohen is less than absolutely clear. He is not as unclear, however, as some of his critics have maintained. For the best statement in Cohen's work, see *Delinquent Boys*, pp. 121–28.

likely to project their frustrated aspirations onto their children. They may do little effective socialization to aid the child, but they are, nevertheless, likely at least to want their children to be better off than they are. Third, there is the effect of the mass media which spread the middle class life style. And, of course, there is the effect of the fact of upward mobility as visible evidence that at least some people can make the grade.

In short, the working class boy is subjected to many social influences which emphasize the fact that the way to respect, status, and success lies in conforming to the demands of middle class society. Even more importantly, he very likely has partly accepted the middle class measuring rod as a legitimate, even superior, set of values. The profound ambivalence that this may lead to in the individual is simply a reflection of the fact that the larger culture penetrates the lower working class world in many ways.

Thus, to the external status problem posed by devaluations by middle class functionaries is added the internal status problem of low self-esteem.

This, then, is the common problem of adjustment. Given the availability of many boys similarly situated, a collective solution evolves, the delinquent subculture. This subculture is characterized by Cohen as nonutilitarian, malicious, and negativistic, characterized by versatility, short-run hedonism, and an emphasis on group autonomy, that is, freedom from adult restraint.

These are, of course, the direct antitheses of the components of the middle class measuring rod. The delinquent subculture functions simultaneously to combat the enemy without and the enemy within, both the hated agents of the middle class and the gnawing internal sense of inadequacy and low self-esteem. It does so by erecting a counterculture, an alternative set of status criteria.

Guilt

This subculture must do more than deal with the middle-class–dominated institutions on the one hand and the feelings of low self-esteem on the other. It must also deal with the feelings of guilt, overagression, theft, and the like that will inevitably arise. It must deal with the fact that the collective solution to the common problem of adjustment is an illicit one in the eyes of the larger society and, certainly, also in the eyes of the law-abiding elements of the local area.

It must deal, also, with the increasing opposition which the solution arouses in the police and other agencies of the conventional order. Over time, the subculture comes to contain a variety of definitions of these agents of conventionality which see them as the aggressors, thus legitimating the group's deviant activities.

Because of this requirement that the delinquent subculture constitute a solution to internal, psychological problems of self-esteem and guilt, Cohen sees the group behavior pattern as being overdetermined in the psychological sense and as linking up with the mechanism of reaction formation.

Thus, the reason for the seeming irrationality of the delinquent subculture lies in the deeply rooted fears and anxieties of the status-deprived boy. I have already discussed the shift from Thrasher's view of delinquency as attractive in a situation of weak social control to the views of it as more reactive held by some modern theorists. Cohen, of course, is prominent among these latter, the irrationalists. It is extremely difficult to bring these viewpoints together at all well except to point out that Cohen's position accords well with much research on school failure and its consequences in damaged self-esteem. It does seem unlikely, as I will point out later in another connection, that the failure of family, school, and neighborhood to control the behavior of Thrasher's boys would result in their simple withdrawal from such conventional contexts without hostility and loss of self-regard.

Cohen emphasizes that not all members of an ongoing delinquent group are motivated by this same problem of adjustment. Like any other protest movement, the motives which draw new members at different phases of its development will vary. It is sufficient that a core of members share the problem.

The analysis of the delinquent subculture of urban working class boys set forth in *Delinquent Boys* has been elaborated and supplemented in a later article by Cohen and James F. Short.[7]

---

[7] Albert K. Cohen and James F. Short, Jr., "Research in Delinquent Sub-Cultures," *Journal of Social Issues* 14 (1958), pp. 20–36.

Other Delinquent Subcultures

Responding to the criticism that there seemed a variety of kinds of delinquent subcultures, even among lower class urban youths, Cohen and Short distinguish the parent-male subculture, the conflict-oriented subculture, the drug addict subculture, and a subculture focused around semiprofessional theft.[8]

The parent subculture is the now familiar subculture described in *Delinquent Boys*. Cohen and Short describe it as the most common form.[9]

> We refer to it as the parent subculture because it is probably the most common variety in this country—indeed, it might be called the "garden variety" of delinquent subculture—and because the characteristics listed above seem to constitute a common core shared by other important variants.

In discussing the conditions under which these different subcultures arise, Cohen and Short rely on a pivotal paper published in 1951 by Solomon Kobrin.[10] Dealing with the differential location of the conflict-oriented versus the semiprofessional theft subculture, Kobrin pointed out that delinquency areas vary in the degree to which conventional and criminal value systems are mutually integrated. In the integrated area, adult criminal activity is stable and organized, and adult criminals are integral parts of the local social structure—active in politics, fraternal orders, providers of employment. Here delinquency can form a kind of apprenticeship for adult criminal careers with such careers being relatively indistinct from conventional careers. More importantly, the interests of organized criminal groups in order and a lack of police attention would lead to attempts to prevent the wilder and more untrammeled forms of juvenile violence. This would mean, of course, that crime in these areas was largely of the stable, profitable sort ordinarily associated with the rackets.

LOWER-CLASS BOY AND LOWER-CLASS CULTURE

The interpretation of the delinquent subculture associated with Albert Cohen that I have just described contrasts sharply in its main features with what has come to be called the lower class culture view associated with Walter B. Miller.[11] Miller disagrees with the Cohen position concerning the reactive nature of lower class gang culture.[12]

> In the case of "gang" delinquency, the cultural system which exerts the most direct influences on behavior is that of the lower class community itself—a long-established, distinctively patterned tradition with an integrity of its own—rather than a so-called delinquent subculture which has arisen through conflict with middle class culture and is oriented to the deliberate violation of middle class norms.

What, then, is the lower class culture Miller speaks of and where is it located? Essentially, Miller describes a culture which he sees as emerging from the shaking-down processes of immigration, internal migration, and vertical mobility. Several population and cultural streams feed this process, but, primarily, lower class culture represents the emerging common adaptation of unsuccessful immigrants and Negroes.

> It is the thesis of this paper that from these extremely diverse and heterogeneous origins (with, however, certain common features), there is emerging a relatively homogeneous and stabilized native-American lower class culture; however, in many communities the process of fusion is as yet in its earlier phases, and evidences of the original ethnic or locality culture are still strong.[13]

[8] For criticism in this vein as well as for the most searching general analysis of material from *Delinquent Boys*, see Harold L. Wilensky and Charles N. Lebeaux, *Industrial Society and Social Welfare* (New York: Russell Sage Foundation, 1958), Chap. 9.

[9] Cohen and Short, "Delinquent Sub-Cultures," 24. The characteristics are those of maliciousness and so on that I have listed previously.

[10] Solomon Kobrin, "The Conflict of Values in Delinquency Areas," *American Sociological Review* 16 (October, 1951), pp. 653–61.

[11] See the following papers, all by Walter B. Miller: "Lower Class Culture, as a Generating Milieu of Gang Delinquency," *Journal of Social Issues* 14 (1958), pp. 5–19; "Preventive Work with Street Corner Groups: Boston Delinquency Project," *The Annals of the American Academy of Political and Social Science* 322 (March, 1959), pp. 97–106; "Implications of Urban Lower Class Culture for Social Work," *The Social Service Review* 33 (September, 1959), pp. 219–36.

[12] Walter B. Miller, "Lower Class Culture as a Generating Milieu of Gang Delinquency," pp. 5, 6.

[13] Walter B. Miller, "Implications of Urban Lower Class Culture for Social Work," p. 225. Miller seems to be saying that the processes of sorting and segregating which characterized American industrial cities in the period referred to by Thrasher are beginning to show a product at the lower end of the status order. In this, as in several other ways, Miller is much more the inheritor of the classical view, as I have called it, than are Cohen or Cloward and Ohlin. Miller shows much the same concern for relatively wholistic

In his analysis, Miller is primarily concerned with what he calls the hard core group in the lower class—the same very bottom group referred to by Cohen as the lower–lower class. The properties of this emerging lower class culture as described by Miller may be divided into a series of social structural elements and a complex pattern of what Miller calls focal concerns.

Focal Concerns

The first of the structural elements is what Miller calls the female-based household, that is, a family form wherein the key relationships are those among mature females (especially those of different generations but, perhaps, also sisters or cousins) and between these females and their children. The children may be by different men, and the biological fathers may play a very inconsistent and unpredictable role in the family. Most essentially, the family is not organized around the expectation of stable economic support provided by an adult male.

The relationship between adult females and males is characterized as one of serial mating, with the female finding it necessary repeatedly to go through a cycle of roles of mate-seeker, mother, and employee.

Closely related to and supportive of this form of household is the elaboration of a system of one-sex peer groups which, according to Miller, become emotional havens and major sources of psychic investment and support for both sexes and for both adolescents and adults. The family, then, is not the central focus of primary, intimate ties that it is in middle class circles.

In what is surely a masterpiece of cogent description, Miller presents the focal concerns of lower class culture as trouble, toughness, smartness, excitement, fate and autonomy. His description of the complexly interwoven patterns assumed by these focal concerns cannot be repeated here, but a brief discussion seems appropriate.[14]

Trouble is what life gets you into—especially trouble with the agents of the larger society. The central aspect of this focal concern is the distinction between law-abiding and law-violating behavior, and where an individual stands along the implied dimension either by behavior, reputation, or commitment is crucial in the evaluation of him by others. Toughness refers to physical prowess, skill, masculinity, fearlessness, bravery, daring. It includes an almost compulsive opposition to things seen as soft and feminine, including much middle class behavior, and is related, on the one hand, to sex-role identification problems which flow from the young boy's growing up in the female-based household and, on the other hand, to the occupational demands of the lower class world. Toughness, along with the emphasis on excitement and autonomy, is one of the ways one gets into trouble.

Smartness refers to the ability to "con," outwit, dupe, that is, to manipulate things and people to one's own advantage with a minimum of conventional work. Excitement, both as an activity and as an ambivalently held goal, is best manifested in the patterned cycle of the week end night-on-the-town complete with much drink and sexual escapades, thereby creating the risk of fighting and trouble. Between week ends, life is dull and passive. Fate refers to the perception by many lower class individuals that their lives are determined by events and forces over which they have little or no control. It manifests itself in widespread gambling and fantasies of "when things break for me." Gambling serves multiple functions in the areas of fate, toughness, smartness, and excitement.

The last focal concern described by Miller is that of autonomy—concern over the amount, source, and severity of control by others. Miller describes the carrier of lower class culture as being highly ambivalent about such control by others. Overtly, he may protest bitterly about restraint and arbitrary interference while, covertly, he tends to equate coercion with care and unconsciously to seek situations where strong controls will satisfy nurturance needs.

Growing Up

What is it like to grow up in lower class culture? A boys spends the major part of the first twelve years in the company of and under the domina-

---

description of the local community setting and much the same sensitivity to group process over time. Whether his tendency to see lower class culture in terms of a relatively closed system derives from differences in fact due to historical change or primarily to differences in theoretical perspective is hard to say.

[14] This description of the focal concern is taken from Walter B. Miller, "Lower Class Culture as a Generating Milieu of Gang Delinquency," especially Charts 1, 7. In this case especially, the original should be read.

tion of women. He learns during that time that women are the people who count, that men are despicable, dangerous, and desirable. He also learns that a "real man" is hated for his irresponsibility and considered very attractive on Saturday night. He learns, too, that, if he really loves his mother, he will not grow up to be "just like all men" but that, despite her best efforts, his mother's pride and joy will very likely turn out to be as much a "rogue male" as the rest. In short, he has sex-role problems.

The adolescent street group is the social mechanism which enables the maturing boy to cope with a basic problem of feminine identification coupled with the necessity of somehow growing up to be an appropriately hated and admired male in a culture which maximizes the necessity to fit into all male society as an adult. The seeking of adult status during adolescence, then, has a particular intensity, so that manifestations of the adult culture's focal concerns tend to be overdone. In addition, the street group displays an exaggerated concern with status and belongingness which is common in all adolescent groups but becomes unusually severe for the lower class boy.

The street group, then, is an essential transition mechanism and training ground for the lower class boy. Some of the behavior involved is delinquent, but the degree to which the group engages in specifically delinquent acts, that is, constructs its internal status criteria around the law-violating end of the trouble continuum, may vary greatly depending on local circumstances. These include such things as the presence and salience of police, professional criminals, clergy, functioning recreational and settlement programs, and the like.

Like Thrasher, Miller emphasizes the wide range of activities of a nondelinquent nature that the gang members engage in, although, unlike Thrasher's boys, they do not do so because of poor social control, but because of the desire to be "real men."

Participation in the lower class street group may produce delinquency in several ways:[15]

1. Following cultural practices which comprise essential elements of the total pattern of lower class culture automatically violates certain legal norms.
2. In instances where alternative avenues to similar objectives are available, the non-law-abiding avenue frequently provides a greater and more immediate return for a relatively smaller investment of energy.
3. The "demanded" response to certain situations recurrently engendered within lower class culture involves the commission of illegal acts.

Impact of Middle Class Values

Miller's approach, like the approaches of Thrasher and Cohen, has its strengths and weaknesses. Miller has not been very successful in refuting Cohen's insistence on the clash between middle class and lower class standards as it affects the sources of self-esteem. To be sure, Cohen's own presentation of just what the lower class boy has or has not internalized is considerably confused. As I have remarked elsewhere, Cohen seems to be saying that a little internalization is a dangerous thing.[16] Miller seems to be saying that the involvements in lower class culture are so deep and exclusive that contacts with agents of middle-class–dominated institutions, especially the schools, have no impact.

Actually, resolution of this problem does not seem so terribly difficult. In handling Cohen's formulations, I would suggest that previous internalization of middle class values is not particularly necessary, because the lower class boys will be told about them at the very time they are being status deprived by their teachers and others. They will likely hate it and them (teachers and values), and the process is started. On the other hand, it seems unlikely that Miller's lower class boys can spend ten years in school without some serious outcomes. They should either come to accept middle class values or become even more antagonistic or both, and this should drive them further into the arms of lower class culture.

This would be especially the case because of the prevailing definition of school work as girlish, an attitude not at all limited to Miller's lower class culture. With the sex-role identification problems Miller quite reasonably poses for his boys, the demands of the middle class school teacher that he be neat and clean and well-be-

---

[15] Walter B. Miller, "Lower Class Culture as a Generating Milieu of Gang Delinquency," p. 18.

[16] David J. Bordua, *Sociological Theories and Their Implications for Juvenile Delinquency* (Children's Bureau, Juvenile Delinquency: Facts and Facets, No. 2; Washington, D.C.: U.S. Government Printing Office, 1960), pp. 9–11.

haved must be especially galling.[17] In short, it seems to me inconceivable that the objective conflict between the boys and the school, as the most crucial example, could end in a simple turning away.

Miller also seems to be weak when he insists upon seeing what he calls the hard core of lower class culture as a distinctive form and, at the same time, must posit varieties of lower class culture to account for variations in behavior and values. This is not necessarily a factually untrue position, but it would seem to underemphasize the fluidity and variability of American urban life. It is necessary for him to point out that objectively low status urban groups vary in the degree to which they display the core features of lower class culture, with Negroes and Irish groups among those he has studied displaying it more and Italians less.

Validity of Female Base

Miller seems so concerned that the features of lower class culture, especially the female-based household, not be seen as the disorganization of the more conventional system or as signs of social pathology that he seems to overdo it rather drastically. He is very concerned to show that lower class culture is of ancient lineage and is or was functional in American society. Yet, at the same time, he says that lower class culture is only now emerging at the bottom of the urban heap. He also forgets that none of the low status groups in the society, with the possible exception of low status Negroes, has any history of his female-based household, at least not in the extreme form that he describes.[18]

A closely related problem is posed by Miller's citation of cross-cultural evidence, for example, "The female-based household is a stabilized form in many societies—frequently associated with polygamy—and is found in 21 percent of

world societies."[19] I do not doubt the figure, but I question the implication that the female-based household as the household form, legitimated and normatively supported in societies practicing polygamy, can be very directly equated with a superficially similar system existing on the margins of a larger society and clearly seen as deviant by that larger society. Surely, in primitive societies, the household can count on the stable economic and judicial base provided by an adult male. The very fact that such a household in the United States is under continuous and heavy pressure from the law, the Aid to Dependent Children worker, and nearly all other agents of the conventional order must make for a very different situation than in societies where it is the accepted form. In such societies, would mothers generally regard men as "unreliable and untrustworthy" and would the statement "all men are no good" be common?[20] Surely, such an attitude implies some awareness that things should be otherwise.

All this is not to argue that tendencies of the sort Miller describes are not present nor to underestimate the value of his insistence that we look at this way of life in its own terms—a valuable contribution indeed—but only to ask for somewhat greater awareness of the larger social dynamics that produce his lower class culture.

Danger of Tautology

Finally, a last criticism of Miller's formulations aims at the use of the focal concerns material. There seems more than a little danger of tautology here if the focal concerns are derived from observing behavior and then used to explain the same behavior. One would be on much safer ground to deal in much greater detail with the structural roots and reality situations to which lower class culture may be a response. Thus, for example, Miller makes no real use of the vast literature on the consequences of prolonged instability of employment, which seems to be the root of the matter.

These criticisms should not blind us to very real contributions in Miller's position. Most im-

---

[17] For evidence that lower class Negro girls seem to do much better than boys in adjusting to at least one middle class institution, see Martin Deutsch, *Minority Group and Class Status as Related to Social and Personality Factors in School Achievement* (Monograph No. 2, The Society for Applied Anthropology; Ithaca, New York: The Society, 1960).

[18] E. Franklin Frazier, *The Negro Family in the United States* (Chicago: University of Chicago Press, 1939).

[19] Walter B. Miller, "Implications of Urban Lower Class Culture for Social Work," p. 225, fn.

[20] *Ibid.*, p. 226.

portantly, he tells us what the lower class street boys are for, rather than just what they are against. In addition, he deals provocatively and originally with the nature of the adult culture which serves as the context for adolescent behavior. Finally, he alerts us to a possible historical development that has received relatively little attention—the emergence of something like a stable American lower class. This possibility seems to have been largely neglected in studies of our increasingly middle class society.

SUCCESS GOALS AND OPPORTUNITY STRUCTURES

The last of the major approaches to the problem of lower class group delinquency to be considered here is associated with Richard A. Cloward and Lloyd E. Ohlin.[21] Stated in its briefest form, the theory is as follows: American culture makes morally mandatory the seeking of success goals but differentially distributes the morally acceptable means to these success goals, the legitimate opportunities that loom so large in the approach.[22]

This gap between culturally universalized goals and structurally limited means creates strain among lower class youths who aspire to economic advancement. Such strain and alienation leads to the formation of delinquent subcultures, that is, normative and belief systems that specifically support and legitimate delinquency, among those boys who blame the system rather than themselves for their impending or actual failure. The particular form of delinquent subculture—conflict, criminal, or retreatist (drug-using)—which results depends on the nature of the local neighborhood and, especially, on the availability of illegitimate opportunities, such as stable crime careers as models and training grounds.

The criminal subculture develops in stable neighborhoods with much regularized crime present; the conflict form develops in really disorganized neighborhoods where not even illegitimate opportunities are available; the retreatist, or drug-use, subculture develops among persons who are double failures due either to internalized prohibitions against violence or theft or to the objective unavailability of these solutions.

Intervening between the stress due to blocked aspirations and the creation of the full-fledged subculture of whatever type is a process of collectively supported "withdrawal of attributions of legitimacy from established social norms."

This process, coupled with the collective development of the relevant delinquent norms, serves to allay whatever guilt might have been felt over the illegal acts involved in following the delinquent norms.

Since the argument in *Delinquency and Opportunity* is, in many ways, even more complicated than those associated with Cohen, Short, and Miller, I will discuss only a few highlights.[23]

Potential Delinquents

On the question of who aspires to what, which is so involved in the disagreements between Cohen and Miller, Cloward and Ohlin take the position that it is not the boys who aspire to middle class status—and, therefore, have presumably partially internalized the middle class measuring rod—who form the raw material for delinquent subculture, but those who wish only to improve their economic status without any change in class membership. Thus, it is appropriate in their argument to say that the genitors of the delinquent subcultures are not dealing so much with an internal problem of self-esteem as with an external problem of injustice. Cohen says, in effect, that the delinquent subculture prevents self-blame for failure from breaking through, the reaction formation function of the delinquent subculture. Cloward and Ohlin say that

---

[21] The full statement of the approach is in Richard A. Cloward and Lloyd E. Ohlin, *Delinquency and Opportunity* (Glencoe: The Free Press, 1960); see also Richard A. Cloward, "Illegitimate Means, Anomie and Deviant Behavior," *American Sociological Review* 24 (April, 1959), pp. 164–76.

[22] For the original version of this formulation, see Robert K. Merton, *Social Theory and Social Structure*, rev. and enlr. ed., (Glencoe: The Free Press, 1951), Chaps. 4, 5.

[23] Large segments of *Delinquency and Opportunity* are devoted to refutations of others' positions, especially those of Cohen and Miller. I felt that, at least for the present paper, criticizing in detail other people's refutations of third parties might be carrying the matter too far. It should be pointed out, however, that the tendency to take extreme positions as a consequence of involvement in a polemic which is apparent in Miller's work seems even more apparent in the Cloward and Ohlin book.

the delinquent norm systems are generated by boys who have already determined that their failures, actual or impending, are the fault of the larger social order.[24]

This insistence that it is the "system blamers" who form the grist for the subcultural mill leads Cloward and Ohlin into something of an impasse, it seems to me. They must, of course, then deal with the determinants of the two types of blame and choose to say that two factors are primarily relevant. First, the larger culture engenders expectations, not just aspirations, of success which are not met, and, second, there exist highly visible barriers to the fulfillment of these expectations, such as racial prejudice, which are defined as unjust.

These do not seem unreasonable, and, in fact, in the case of Negro youth, perhaps, largely fit the case. Cloward and Ohlin, however, are forced for what seems overwhelmingly polemical reasons into a position that the feeling of injustice must be objectively correct. Therefore, they say (1) that it is among those actually fitted for success where the sense of injustice will flourish and (2) that delinquent subcultures are formed by boys who do not essentially differ in their capacity to cope with the larger institutions from other boys. This point deserves some attention since it is so diametrically opposed to the Cohen position which states that some working class boys, especially lower working class boys, are unable to meet the demands of middle-class–dominated institutions.

> It is our impression that a sense of being unjustly deprived of access to opportunities to which one is entitled is common among those who become participants in delinquent subcultures. Delinquents tend to be persons who have been led to expect opportunities because of their potential ability to meet the formal, institutionally-established criteria of evaluation. Their sense of injustice arises from the failure of the system to fulfill these expectations.

Their criticism is not directed inward since they regard themselves in comparison with their fellows as capable of meeting the formal require-

ments of the system. It has frequently been noted that delinquents take special delight in discovering hypocrisy in the operation of the established social order. They like to point out that it's "who you know, not what you know" that enables one to advance or gain coveted social rewards. They become convinced that bribery, blackmail, fear-inspiring pressure, special influence, and similar factors are more important than the publicly avowed criteria of merit.[25]

Delinquents and Nondelinquent Peers

On the same page in a footnote, the authors go on to say that the research evidence indicates "the basic endowments of delinquents, such as intelligence, physical strength, and agility, are the equal of or greater than those of their nondelinquent peers."

The material in these quotations is so riddled with ambiguities it is difficult to know where to begin criticism, but we can at least point out the following. First, Cloward and Ohlin seem to be confusing the justificatory function of delinquent subcultures with their causation. All of these beliefs on the part of gang delinquents have been repeatedly reported in the literature, but by the very argument of *Delinquency and Opportunity,* it is impossible to tell whether they constitute compensatory ideology or descriptions of objective reality.

Second, Cloward and Ohlin seem to be victims of their very general tendency to ignore the life histories of their delinquents.[26] Thus, there is no way of knowing really what these subcultural beliefs may reflect in the experience of the boys. Third, and closely related to the ignoring of life history material, is the problem of assessing the degree to which these gang boys are in fact prepared to meet the formal criteria for success. To say they are intelligent, strong, and agile is to parody the criteria for advancement. Perhaps Cohen would point out that intelligent,

---

[24] Richard A. Cloward and Lloyd E. Ohlin, *Delinquency and Opportunity.* For the problem of types of aspiration and their consequences, see, especially, pp. 86–97. For the matter of self-blame and their system blame for failure, see pp. 110–26.

[25] *Ibid.,* p. 117.

[26] This is the most fundamental weakness in the book. The delinquents in Thrasher, Cohen, and Miller were, in varying degrees, once recognizably children. Cloward and Ohlin's delinquents seem suddenly to appear on the scene sometime in adolescence, to look at the world, and to discover, "Man, there's no opportunity in my structure." It is instructive in this connection to note that the index to *Delinquency and Opportunity* contains only two references to the family. One says that the family no longer conducts occupational training; the other criticizes Miller's ideas on female-based household.

agile, strong boys who begin the first grade using foul language, fighting among themselves, and using the school property as arts and crafts materials do not meet the criteria for advancement.

It is quite true that members of highly sophisticated delinquent gangs often find themselves blocked from whatever occupational opportunities there are, but this seems, often, the end product of a long history of their progressively cutting off opportunity and destroying their own capacities which may begin in the lower class family, as described by either Cohen or Miller, and continue through school failure and similar events. By the age of eighteen, many gang boys are, for all practical purposes, unemployable or need the support, instruction, and sponsorship of trained street-gang workers. Participation in gang delinquency in itself diminishes the fitness of many boys for effective functioning in the conventional world.[27]

If, indeed, Cloward and Ohlin mean to include the more attitudinal and characterological criteria for advancement, then it seems highly unlikely that any large number of boys trained and prepared to meet these demands of the occupational world could interpret failure exclusively in terms which blame the system. They would have been too well socialized, and, if they did form a delinquent subculture, it would have to perform the psychological function of mitigating the sense of internal blame. This, of course, would make them look much like Cohen's boys.

In short, Cloward and Ohlin run the risk of confusing justification and causation and of equating the end with the beginning.

All of this is not to deny that there are real obstacles to opportunity for lower class boys. There are. These blocks on both the performance and learning sides, are a major structural feature in accounting for much of the adaption of lower class populations. But they do not operate solely or even primarily on the level of the adolescent. They create a social world in which he comes of age, and, by the time he reaches adolescence, he may find himself cut off from the larger society. Much of the Cloward and Ohlin approach seems better as a theory of the origins of Miller's lower class culture. Each generation does not meet and solve anew the problems of class structure barriers to opportunity but begins with the solution of its forebears.[28] This is why reform efforts can be so slow to succeed.

Some Insights

The positive contributions of the Cloward-Ohlin approach seem to me to lie less on the side of the motivational sources of subcultural delinquency, where I feel their attempts to clarify the ambiguities in Cohen have merely led to new ambiguities, but more on the side of the factors in local social structure that determine the type of subcultural delinquency.

The major innovation here is the concept of illegitimate opportunities which serves to augment Kobrin's almost exclusive emphasis on the differentially controlling impact of different slum environments. I do think that Cloward and Ohlin may make too much of the necessity for systematic, organized criminal careers in order for the illegitimate opportunity structure to have an effect, but the general argument has great merit.

In addition to the concept of illegitimate opportunities and closely related to it is the description, or speculation, concerning historical changes in the social organization of slums. Changes in urban life in the United States may have truly produced the disorganized slum devoid of the social links between young and old, between children and older adolescents which characterized the slums described by Thrasher. Certainly, the new conditions of life seem to

[27] Here, again, Thrasher seems superior to some of the modern theorists. He stressed the fact that long-term involvement in the "free, undisciplined" street life with money at hand from petty theft and with the days devoted to play was not exactly ideal preparation for the humdrum life of the job. Again, Thrasher's sensitivity to the attitudinal and subcultural consequences of the gang formation and maintenance process truly needs reintroduction.

[28] Parenthetically, the Cloward and Ohlin position has great difficulty in accounting for the fact that lower class delinquent subculture carriers do not avail themselves of opportunities that do exist. The mixed success of vocational school training, for example, indicates that some fairly clear avenues of opportunity are foregone by many delinquent boys. For Negro boys, where avenues to the skilled trades may indeed be blocked, their argument seems reasonable. For white boys, I have serious question. In fact, the one really convincing case they make on the aspiration-blockage, system-blame side is for Negroes.

have created new problems of growing up, though our knowledge of their precise impact leaves much to be desired.

CONCLUSION

This paper should not, I hope, give the impression that current theoretical interpretations of lower class, urban, male subcultural delinquency are without value. Such is far from the case. Many of my comments have been negative since each of the theorists quite ably presents his own defense, which should be read in any case. In fact, I think that this problem has led to some of the most exciting and provocative intellectual interchange in all sociology in recent years. I do believe, however, that this interchange has often been marred by unnecessary polemic and, even more, by a lack of relevant data.

As I have indicated, there have been some profound changes in the way social theorists view the processes of gang formation and persistence. These, I believe, derive only partially, perhaps even unimportantly, from changes in the facts to be explained. Indeed, we must wait for a study of gangs which will approach Thrasher's in thoroughness before we can know if there are new facts to be explained. Nor do I

believe that the changes in viewpoint have come about entirely because old theories were shown to be inadequate to old facts. Both Cohen and Cloward and Ohlin feel that older theorists did not deal with the problem of the origins of delinquent subcultures, but only with the transmission of subculture once developed.[29] A careful reading of Thrasher indicates that such is not the case.

All in all, though, it does not seem like much fun any more to be a gang delinquent. Thrasher's boys enjoyed themselves being chased by the police, shooting dice, skipping school, rolling drunks. It was fun. Miller's boys do have a little fun, with their excitement focal concern, but it seems so desperate somehow. Cohen's boys and Cloward and Ohlin's boys are driven by grim economic and psychic necessity into rebellion. It seems peculiar that modern analysts have stopped assuming that "evil" can be fun and see gang delinquency as arising only when boys are driven away from "good."[30]

---

[29] Albert K. Cohen, *Delinquent Boys,* p. 18; Richard A. Cloward and Lloyd E. Ohlin, *Delinquency and Opportunity,* p. 42.

[30] For a more thorough commentary on changes in the view of human nature, which, I think, partly underlie the decline of fun in theories of the gang, see Dennis Wrong, "The Oversocialized View of Man," *American Sociological Review* 26 (April, 1961), pp. 183–93.

THE INTERACTION OF FAMILY VARIABLES AND GANG VARIABLES IN THE AETIOLOGY OF DELINQUENCY

ROBERT EVERETT STANFIELD

A sociologist has recently written that "[w]herever one can develop a rationale for predicting interaction, one should make a conscious effort to construct and test theories that explicitly take advantage of interactive effects."[1] In empirical research on opportunity theory in delinquency,

some evidence has been presented showing interactive relationships between variables representing availability of both legitimate and illegitimate opportunities.[2] This article is a further effort to press for theory building and testing through the use of statistical interaction in empirical studies.

Over the past decades, two major traditions

Reprinted with permission of the author and the Society for the Study of Social Problems, from *Social Problems,* 13 (1966), pp. 414–17.

[1] Hubert M. Blalock, Jr., "Theory Building and the Statistical Concept of Interaction," *American Sociological Review* 30 (June, 1965), p. 374, also pp. 374–80.

[2] Erdman Palmore and Phillip E. Hammond, "Interacting Factors in Juvenile Delinquency," *American Sociological Review* 29 (December, 1964), pp. 848–54.

have emerged in the aetiology of delinquency. These have been variously called the psychogenic and the sociogenic,[3] the psychiatric-psychoanalytic and the sociological,[4] the individual and the collective.[5] The first has traced delinquency to the development of a personality with a disposition toward the violation of law. The second has regarded delinquency as a phenomenon of cultural areas that lack social controls over the violation of law or that have positive supports for delinquent behavior.

Proponents of these traditions have argued whether the family or the gang has the greater importance in determining delinquent behavior. Supporters of the psychogenic tradition have tended to emphasize the association between juvenile crime and certain aspects of family life: rejection or lack of affection by a parent; the laxity, inconsistency, or severity of discipline; the absence or inappropriateness of a parent as a role model.[6] Those that hold the sociogenic view have maintained that delinquent behavior is learned in a gang as a system of preferred behavior that is either a consequence of a dissociation in the social structure between culturally prescribed goals and culturally approved means[7] or a result of a conflict of values and norms among the social classes of society.[8]

Theory and research in delinquency have benefited from activity along independent lines of development within these two traditions, but further progress in the field might be achieved by investigating the relationship between the family and the gang in the aetiology of delinquency.

THEORY BUILDING WITH EXPECTATIONS OF STATISTICAL INTERACTION

Some efforts at integrating the two traditions already exist in the literature of social science. Shaw and McKay[9] asserted that delinquent behavior occurs when an individual, disposed toward delinquency by a particular family situation, learns such behavior from a group of peers in a neighborhood that has traditional and positive influences acting in support of such behavior. Tannenbaum[10] described delinquency as the consequence of the gang replacing the family as an individual's primary reference group due to the "inadequacy" of the family. Weinberg[11] proposed that boys become delinquent "when, for individualized purposes of emotional security, self-enhancement, or conflict-resolution, they seek and select accessible associates from whom they learn, accept, and express criminal attitudes." He suggested an empirical test that would utilize, as independent variables, certain aspects of family relations, the capacity for peer relations, and the accessibility of delinquent or nondelinquent peers. Haskell[12] identified the family as a reference group aligned with the dominant cultural system and the peer group as a reference group aligned with a deviant subcultural system. The delinquent boy was an individual who had taken the gang as his primary reference group. Haskell explained the negative case of the nondelinquent gang boy by arguing that satisfying experiences in the family as a normative reference group could overcome the effect of the gang as a delinquent reference group.

There seems implicit in all these attempts at integration an extension of Sutherland's theory of differential association,[13] with the family and

[3] Albert K. Cohen, *Delinquent Boys: The Culture of The Gang* (Glencoe, Ill.: The Free Press, 1955), pp. 11–19.

[4] Marshall B. Clinard, "The Sociology of Delinquency and Crime," in Joseph B. Gittler, ed., *Review of Sociology: Analysis of a Decade* (New York: John Wiley, 1957), pp. 465–99.

[5] S. Kirson Weinberg, "Theories of Criminality and Problems of Prediction," *Journal of Criminal Law, Criminology and Police Science* 45 (1954), pp. 412–24.

[6] For example, see: Sheldon Glueck and Eleanor Glueck, *Unraveling Juvenile Delinquency* (New York: Commonwealth Fund, 1950); William McCord and Joan McCord, with Irving Kenneth Zola, *Origins of Crime: A New Evaluation of the Cambridge-Somerville Youth Study* (New York: Columbia University Press, 1958).

[7] For example see: Cohen, *Delinquent Boys;* Richard A. Cloward and Lloyd E. Ohlin, *Delinquency and Opportunity: A Theory of Delinquent Gangs* (Glencoe, Ill.: The Free Press, 1960).

[8] Walter B. Miller, "Lower Class Culture as a Generating Milieu of Gang Delinquency," *Journal of Social Issues* 14, No. 3 (1958), pp. 5–18.

[9] Clifford R. Shaw and Henry D. McKay, *Social Factors in Juvenile Delinquency: A Study of the Community, the Family, and the Gang in Relation to Delinquent Behavior* (Washington, D.C.: United States Government Printing Office, 1931), esp. pp. 383–93.

[10] Frank Tannenbaum, *Crime and the Community* (New York: Columbia University Press, 1951 [originally published 1938]), pp. 12–13. Italics are omitted.

[11] Weinberg, "Theories of Criminality."

[12] Martin Roy Haskell, "Toward a Reference Group Theory of Juvenile Delinquency," *Social Problems* 8 (1960), pp. 219–30.

[13] Edwin H. Sutherland, *Principles of Criminology*, 5th ed., revised by Donald R. Cressey (Philadelphia: Lippincott, 1955 [originally published 1927]), pp. 74–81.

the gang regarded as competing groups within which the individual may encounter definitions favorable or unfavorable to the violation of law. The differential frequency, duration, priority, and intensity of interpersonal associations within these groups affect the extent to which the values of the group are accepted by the individual. All these views seem to assume that the family is on the side of conformity with law, that the gang favors violation of law, and that a breakdown of associations within the family virtually assures the victory of a gang.

These assumptions, however, may be questioned. It might be appropriate to leave the culture of the family and the culture of the gang (that is, the values and norms regarding conformity to or violation of law) to be determined empirically. Not all families may favor conformity to law; not all gangs may support violation of law. Further, the consequences of a breakdown of interpersonal associations within the family should be more precisely conceptualized.

Although satisfying experiences may increase receptivity to the culture of the group, dissatisfying experiences do not necessarily result in the adoption of an opposing or conflicting culture. Nonacceptance of the family culture renders an individual more receptive to the culture of other groups within his experience. It is possible that dissatisfying experiences in the home will make a boy more receptive to a gang culture that is not greatly different from his family culture. An encounter with a variant cultural pattern is most likely to occur when the socioeconomic status of the family differs from the socioeconomic status of the area in which it resides.

Satisfying experiences in the home do not diminish to a zero point the influence of the gang, but the boy is likely to select a peer group that has a culture compatible with that of the family. In contrast to Tannenbaum's view of the gang as a substitute for the family, one may see the gang as a group reinforcing the cultural pattern learned from the family. Thus, one may say that satisfying or pleasant experiences in a family increase the intensity of relationships within the family, leading to a greater probability of accepting the cultural pattern of the family. Acceptance of the family culture then tends to produce greater selectivity toward peers, leading toward the choice of a gang that supports the cultural pattern of the family. Unsatisfying or unpleasant experiences in a family, however, reduce the intensity of family relationships, leading to reduced receptivity toward family cultural patterns and susceptibility to outside (though not necessarily conflicting or opposing) cultural influences such as a gang.

These considerations suggest that explanation only in terms of direct causal relationships oversimplifies the situation. Family experiences and gang activity are related to delinquency only when such experiences and such activity occur in a cultural context that supports delinquent behavior. Unsatisfying family experiences are likely to result in delinquency to the degree that there exist in the neighborhood environment cultural definitions favorable to the violation of law. Gang activity is less likely to produce delinquent behavior when the gang does not have a culture providing support for criminal activity.

Confirmation of this view would depend on the empirical demonstration of interactive effects that can be adequately accounted for by these considerations. One may approach data with certain expectations of interactive effects. The effect of family experiences may vary according to the socioeconomic status of the family. Similarly, gang activity may be more strongly related to delinquency at one level of socioeconomic status than at another. Further, the impact of frequent peer activity may depend on the nature of family experiences.

THEORY TESTING WITH OBSERVATIONS OF STATISTICAL INTERACTION

Appearances in a court for one or more juvenile offenses as a dependent variable show in the Cambridge-Somerville Youth Study[14] a direct relationship with each of the three independent variables being examined here. (See Table 1).

[11] For background on this study, see: Edwin Powers and Helen Witmer, *An Experiment in the Prevention of Delinquency: The Cambridge-Somerville Youth Study* (New York: Columbia University Press, 1951); McCord and McCord, *Origins of Crime.*

TABLE 1. DIRECT RELATIONSHIPS BETWEEN DELINQUENCY AND DISCIPLINE, SOCIOECONOMIC STATUS, AND PEER INVOLVEMENT

Father's Occupational Status	Percentage Convicted of Delinquency
Low	29% (n = 154)
High	18 (n = 99)
	Diff. = 11%
	$\chi^2 = 3.52$ p < .10
Father's Discipline	
Erratic or lax	33% (n = 120)
Consistent	15 (n = 86)
	Diff. = 18%
	$\chi^2 = 7.13$ p < .01
Peer Activity	
Frequent	30% (n = 132)
Occasional	19 (n = 118)
	Diff. = 11%
	$\chi^2 = 3.94$ p < .05

The lower the occupational status[15] of the father, the greater the percentage of boys appearing in court as juveniles for theft, assault, or sex offenses. A greater percentage of delinquent boys had fathers who were erratic or lax in discipline rather than consistent in discipline. A greater percentage of those active in gangs were delinquent than were those not active in gangs. In addition to these three direct relationships, one can find three meaningful instances of interaction among these variables.[16]

First, the impact of paternal discipline seems clearly to be stronger among families of low socioeconomic status. (See Table 2.) The difference in the delinquent proportion between those with erratic or lax fathers, and those with consistent fathers, is about twice as great among those from low status families as among those from high-status families.

Among families of low socioeconomic status, there is probably greater opportunity for a boy to encounter a cultural pattern outside the family that supports behavior that violates law. If family experiences are of the kind that reduce receptivity to the family culture, the boy from a low-status family is more likely to come into contact with a delinquency-supporting culture than is a boy from a high-status family. Unpleasant family experiences are more likely to produce delinquency in circumstances where there is an alternative cultural pattern that is favorable to the violation of law.

Second, delinquency is more strongly related to the frequency of peer activity among boys from high-status families than among those from low-status families. (See Table 3.) Frequent peer activity produces about the same delinquent proportion at both status levels in this study, but infrequent peer activity produces a much smaller proportion of juvenile offenders among those from high-status families. The frequency of peer activity makes less difference in low-status families.

The opportunities for learning delinquent behavior are less common for boys from high-status families unless they spend a considerable amount of time on the street with friends. An individual from a low-status family who associates rarely or only occasionally with peers still manages to learn delinquent behavior. The family itself may be the source of such learning. On the other hand, support for delinquency may so pervade the lower status levels that learning such a cultural pattern can be accomplished without frequent interaction with peers.

Third, the difference in the proportion of juvenile offenders between those active with peers and those not active with peers is greater among those with erratic or lax paternal discipline than among those with consistent paternal discipline. (See Table 4.) Where paternal supervision is

---

[15] Measured by a scale of occupational status described in Albert J. Reiss, Jr., with Otis Dudley Duncan, Paul K. Hatt, and Cecil C. North, *Occupations and Social Status* (New York: The Free Press of Glencoe, 1961), pp. 109–61, 263–75.

[16] Although theoretically meaningful, these instances of interaction cannot be tested for the statistical significance of the differences in proportions. The Dorn-Stouffer-Tibbitts technique and its modification by Goodman are applicable for statistical tests of this sort when the data are derived from a large, random sample. The sample used here is neither large nor random. See Leo Goodman, "Modifications of the Dorn-Stouffer-Tibbitts Method for 'Testing the Significance of Comparisons in Sociological Data,'" *American Journal of Sociology* 66 (January, 1961), pp. 355–63. A test for second-order interaction proposed by Goodman produces a statistically significant result in only the second of the three examples of interaction that follow. See Leo Goodman, "On the Multivariate Analysis of Three Dichotomous Variables," *American Journal of Sociology* 71 (November, 1965), pp. 290–301. In Table 2, $W^2 = 0.40$ (n.s.); in Table 3, $W^2 = 4.25$ (p < .05); in Table 4, $W^2 = 1.23$ (n.s.). These data, then, should be treated merely as examples rather than as confirmations of hypotheses.

TABLE 2. DELINQUENCY, SOCIOECONOMIC STATUS, AND DISCIPLINE

| | Percentage with Convictions for Delinquency | |
| | Father's Occupation | |
	Low Status	High Status
Father's discipline		
Erratic or lax	39% (n = 77)	21% (n = 43)
Consistent	17 (n = 46)	13 (n = 40)
	Diff. = 22%	Diff. = 20%
	$X^2 = 5.31$ p $< .05$	$X^2 = 0.54$ p $> .60$

TABLE 3. DELINQUENCY, SOCIOECONOMIC STATUS, AND PEER INVOLVEMENT

| | Percentage with Convictions for Delinquency | |
| | Father's Occupation | |
	Low Status	High Status
Peer activity		
Frequent	31% (n = 83)	28% (n = 47)
Occasional	27 (n = 67)	8 (n = 51)
	Diff. = 4%	Diff. = 20%
	$X^2 = 0.17$ p $> .60$	$X^2 = 5.39$ p $< .05$

weak, frequent activity with peers tends to be associated with delinquency. Consistent discipline by the father keeps the probability of delinquency low, whether or not the boy is actively involved in a gang. Similarly, frequency of peer activity has a stronger effect when the father rejects the son.

TABLE 4. DELINQUENCY, DISCIPLINE, AND PEER INVOLVEMENT

| | Percentage with Convictions for Delinquency | |
| | Father's Discipline | |
	Erratic or Lax	Consistent
Peer activity		
Frequent	43% (n = 60)	16% (n = 44)
Occasional	23 (n = 57)	14 (n = 42)
	Diff. = 20%	Diff. = 2%
	$\chi^2 = 4.66$ p $< .05$	$\chi^2 = 0.01$ p $> .80$

The evidence in regard to the father's discipline suggests that the influence of the gang in producing delinquency is stronger when experiences within the family limit the degree to which an individual learns the family's cultural pattern. Lax or erratic discipline by the father obscures the distinction between approved and disapproved behavior. Paternal rejection leads a boy to seek warmer interpersonal relationships in another context, and, thereby, increases the boy's susceptibility to learning a cultural pattern that supports violation of law.

Although the number of cases in each cell drops rather low, some interesting findings consistent with expectations of interaction emerge when one examines the interrelationships among the dependent variables and the three independent variables. (See Table 5.) Assuming only additive effects, one would expect outcomes of the sort suggested by the column headed "Expectation of Delinquent Outcome Based on Additive Effects." The actual outcomes are somewhat consistent with those expected outcomes, but two of the outcomes seem somewhat lower than might have been anticipated. The combination of consistent discipline, low socioeconomic status, and active gang participation might have been expected to produce a proportion of delinquents in the thirty to forty percent range, consistent with the other combinations that have two of the three variables tending toward delinquency; it is, however, only fourteen percent. Similarly, the combination of erratic or lax discipline, high socioeconomic status, and lack of active gang participation might have been expected to have a percentage greater than nine percent. These low percentages are consistent with expectations based on the idea of interactive effects.

TABLE 5. DELINQUENCY, DISCIPLINE, SOCIOECONOMIC STATUS, AND PEER INVOLVEMENT

Father's Discipline	Father's Occupation	Peer Activity	Expectation of Delinquent Outcome Based on Additive Effects	Percentage Convicted of Delinquency
Erratic or lax (1)	Low status (1)	Frequent (1)	3 Very high	46% (n = 41)
		Occasional (0)	2 High	32 (n = 34)
	High status (0)	Frequent (1)	2 High	37% (n = 19)
		Occasional (0)	1 Low	9 (n = 23)
Consistent (0)	Low status (1)	Frequent (1)	2 High	14% (n = 22)
		Occasional (0)	1 Low	21 (n = 24)
	High status (0)	Frequent (1)	1 Low	18% (n = 22)
		Occasional (0)	0 Very low	6 (n = 18)

The low percentage of delinquents among those with consistent discipline, low father's occupational status, and gang activity may demonstrate the efficacy of consistent discipline in forestalling delinquency when the surrounding culture and the extent of peer group participation would suggest a high likelihood of delinquent behavior. The low percentage among those with erratic or lax paternal discipline, high father's occupational status, and infrequent gang activity, similarly, would demonstrate the efficacy of higher socioeconomic status and lack of peer group participation in forestalling delinquency despite the influence of bad discipline.

B. SOCIAL RELATIONS AND PROCESS

The first two selections in this section focus on two fundamental aspects of delinquents and delinquent gangs as portrayed in most gang theories of delinquency. First, the theories outlined by Bordua view gangs as well-organized, cohesive groups. New members are socialized and learn delinquent norms through older members and social relations, and activities are tightly structured and organized around such norms. However, in "The Delinquent Gang as a Near-Group," Lewis Yablonsky argues that this conception of most delinquent gangs is false. According to Yablonsky, gangs have a minimum of consensus on norms and group objectives. They are not well organized. Except for the few psychologically disturbed leaders, gang membership is temporary; in most instances, membership is precipitated by temporary emotional needs or situational contingencies. Gang relations, therefore, are amorphous, unstable, and fluid, not tightly structured, durable, and cohesive. Consequently, Yablonsky calls delinquent gangs "near-groups" rather than "true groups."

Second, gang theories describe the norms of delinquent gangs as being in opposition to the norms of the wider society, and they view individual members of delinquent gangs as being strongly committed to gang norms and as having little attachment to the conventional norms of middle-class society. Another theory argues,[1] however, that delinquents and non-delinquents are not really very different in their normative orientations. According to this theory, delinquents are believed to resemble nondelinquents in their moral inhibitions to delinquent conduct. The primary difference is that the occasional release from moral restraints ("drift") leads some to engage in delinquent behavior.

Theories, therefore, focus on three phenomena: socially accepted norms of society in general, peer norms, and the individual's relative attachment to the two types of norms. In the second selection in this section, Buffalo and Rodgers, in "Behavioral Norms, Moral Norms and Attachment: Problems of Deviance and Conformity," show that delinquents do deviate from socially accepted behavior but are not as committed to delinquent patterns as they think their peers are. Hence, delinquents are oriented to the norms of the wider society as well as to the deviant norms of their peers, suggesting that gang theories and the "drift" theory may both be valid.

Most theory and research on juvenile delinquency focus on urban patterns. In the final selection, Jerry J. Tobias in "The Affluent Suburban Male Delinquent," describes differences between a group of affluent suburban delinquents and a group of urban delinquents. His emphasis is not the relative frequency of delinquency among the different groups but differences in the type of delinquencies committed. His results indicate that the pattern and the nature of delinquency for the two groups differ depending on the social context.

---

[1] See David Matza and Gresham M. Sykes, "Juvenile Delinquency and Subterranean Values," *American Sociological Review* 26 (October, 1961), pp. 712–19; David Matza, *Delinquency and Drift* (New York: John Wiley, 1964); and Gresham M. Sykes and David Matza, "Techniques of Neutralization: A Theory of Delinquency," *American Sociological Review* 26 (December, 1957), pp. 664–70.

THE DELINQUENT GANG AS A NEAR-GROUP
LEWIS YABLONSKY

This paper is based on four years of research and direct work with some thirty delinquent gangs in New York City. During this period I directed a crime prevention program on the upper West Side of Manhattan for Morningside Heights, Inc., a community social agency sponsored by fourteen major institutions including Columbia University, Barnard Teacher's College, Union Theological Seminary, and Riverside Church.

Approaches used in data gathering included field study methods, participant observation, role-playing, group interaction analysis, and sociometry. The data were obtained through close daily interaction with gang boys over the four-year period during which I was the director of the project.

Reprinted with permission of author and publisher from *Social Problems* 7 (Fall, 1959), pp. 108–17 as abridged. Footnotes have been renumbered. This is a revised version of a paper delivered at The Eastern Sociological Meetings in New York City, April 11, 1959. The theory of near-groups and gang data presented in this paper is part of a volume by the author entitled *The Violent Gang* (New York: Macmillan Company, 1962).

Although data were obtained on 30 gangs, the study focused on two, the Balkans and the Egyptian Kings. It was the latter which committed the brutal killing of a polio victim, Michael Farmer, in an upper west side park of New York City. The trial lasted over three months and received nationwide attention. These two groups were intensively interviewed and contributed heavily to the formulation of a theory of near-groups. In addition to the analysis of the gang's structure, a number of delinquent gang war events produced vital case material.

There is a paucity of available theory based on empirical evidence about the structure of delinquent gangs. Two landmarks in the field are Thrasher's *The Gang* and Whyte's *Street Corner Society*. Some recent publications and controversy focus on the emergence of gangs and their function for gang members. Professor Cohen deals with gangs as subcultures organized by working-class boys as a reaction to middle-class values.[1] In a recent publication Block and Nederhoffer discuss gangs as organizations designed to satisfy the adolescent's striving for the attainment of adult status.[2]

Although partial group structuring has been extensively discussed in sociological literature on "groups," "crowds," and "mobs," my gang research revealed that these collectivity constructs did not seem to adequately describe and properly abstract the underlying structural characteristics of the delinquent gang. Consequently, I have attempted here to construct a formulation which would draw together various described social dimensions of the gang under one conceptual scheme. I call this formulation Near-Group Theory.

NEAR-GROUP THEORY

One way of viewing human collectivities is on a continuum of organization characteristics. At one extreme, we have a highly organized, cohesive, functioning collection of individuals as members of a sociological group. At the other

extreme, we have a mob of individuals characterized by anonymity, disturbed leadership, motivated by emotion, and in some cases representing a destructive collectivity within the inclusive social system. When these structures are observed in extreme, their form is apparent to the observer. However, in viewing these social structures on a continuum, those formations which tend to be neither quite a cohesive integrated group nor a disturbed malfunctioning mob or crowd are often distorted by observers in one or the other direction.

A central thesis of this paper is that midway on the group-mob continuum are collectivities which are neither groups nor mobs. These are structures prevalent enough in a social system to command attention in their own right as constructs for sociological analysis. Near-groups are characterized by some of the following factors: (1) diffuse role definition, (2) limited cohesion, (3) impermanence, (4) minimal consensus of norms, (5) shifting membership, (6) disturbed leadership, and (7) limited definition of membership expectations. These factors characterize the near-group's "normal" structure.

True groups may manifest near-group structure under stress, in transition, or when temporarily disorganized; however, at these times they are moving toward or away from their normative, permanent structure. The near-group manifests its homeostasis in accord with the factors indicated. It never fully becomes a *group* or a *mob*.

THE GANG AS A NEAR-GROUP PATTERN

Some recent sociological theory and discourse on gangs suffers from distortions of gang structure to fit a group rather than a near-group conception. Most gang theorizing begins with an automatic assumption that gangs are defined sociological groups. Many of these misconceived theories about gangs in sociological treatises are derived from the popular and traditional image of gangs held by the general public as reported in the press, rather than as based upon empirical scientific investigation. The following case material reveals the disparities between popular reports of gang war behavior and their organization as revealed by more systematic study.

[1] Albert K. Cohen, *Delinquent Boys* (Glencoe: The Free Press, 1955).

[2] Herbert Block and Arthur Nederhoffer, *The Gang* (New York: The Philosophical Library, 1958).

The official report of a gang fight which made headlines in New York papers as the biggest in the city's history, detailed a gang war between six gangs over a territorial dispute.[3] The police, social workers, the press, and the public accepted a defined version of groups meeting in battle over territory. Research into this gang war incident, utilizing a near-group concept of gangs, indicates another picture of the situation.

N.Y. Daily News
NIP 200—PUNK FIGHT NEAR COLUMBIA CAMPUS
by Grover Ryder and Jack Smee
A flying squad of 25 cops, alerted by a civilian's tip, broke up the makings of one of the biggest gang rumbles in the city's turbulent teen history last night at the edge of Columbia University campus on Morningside Heights.

N.Y. Herald Tribune
POLICE SEIZE 38, AVERT GANG BATTLE—RIVERSIDE PARK RULE WAS GOAL
Police broke up what they said might have been "a very serious" battle between two juvenile factions last night as they intercepted thirty-eight youths.

N.Y. Times
GANG WAR OVER PARK BROKEN BY POLICE
The West Side police broke up an impending gang fight near Columbia University last night as 200 teen-agers were massing for battle over exclusive rights to the use of Riverside Park.

N.Y. Journal-American
6-GANG BATTLE FOR PARK AVERTED NEAR GRANT'S TOMB COPS PATROL TROUBLE SPOT
Police reinforcements today patrolled Morningside Heights to prevent a teen-aged gang war for "control" of Riverside Park.

World-Telegram and Sun
HOODLUM WAR AVERTED AS COPS ACT FAST
38 to 200 Seized near Columbia
by Richard Graf
Fast police action averted what threatened to be one of the biggest street gang fights in the city's history as some 200 hoodlums massed last night on the upper West Side to battle over "exclusive rights" to Riverside Park.

In depth interviews with 40 gang boys, most of whom had been arrested at the scene of the gang fight, revealed a variety of reasons for attendance at the battle. There were also varied perceptions of the event and the gangs involved reported simply in the press as "gangs battling over territory." Some of the following recurring themes were revealed in the gang boys' responses.

Estimates of number of gang boys present varied from 80 to 5,000.

Gang boys interviewed explained their presence at the "battle" as follows:

I didn't have anything to do that night and wanted to see what was going to happen.

Those guys called me a Spic and I was going to get even. [He made this comment even though the "rival" gangs were mostly Puerto Ricans.]

They always picked on us. [The "they" is usually a vague reference.]

I always like a fight; it keeps up my rep.

My father threw me out of the house: I wanted to get somebody and heard about the fight.

The youth who was responsible for "calling on" the gang war—the reputed Balkan Gang leader—presented this version of the event:

That night I was out walkin' my dog about 7:30. Then I saw these guys coming from different directions. I couldn't figure out what was happening. Then I saw some of the guys I know and I remembered we had called it on for that night.

I never really figured the Politicians [a supposed "brother Gang" he had called] would show.

Another boy added another dimension to "gang war organization":

How did we get our name? Well, when we were in the police station, the cops kept askin' us who we were. Jay was studying history in school—so he said how about The Balkans. Let's call ourselves Balkans. So we told the cops—we're the Balkans—and that was it.

Extensive data revealed this was not a case of two organized groups meeting in battle. The press, public, police, social workers, and others projected group conceptions onto a near-group activity. Most of the youths at the scene of the gang war were, in fact, participating in a kind of mob action. Most had no real concept of belonging to any gang or group; however, they were in-

---

[3] New York Newspaper Headlines—June 11, 1955.

terested in a situation which might be exciting and possibly a channel for expressing some of their aggressions and hostilities. Although it was not necessarily a defined war, the possibilities of a stabbing or even a killing were high—with a few hundred disturbed and fearful youths milling around in the undefined situation. The gang war was not a social situation of two structured teen-aged armies meeting on a battlefield to act out a defined situation; it was a case of two near-groups in action.

Another boy's participation in this gang war further reveals its structure. The evening of the fight he had nothing to do, heard about this event and decided that he would wander up to see what was going to happen. On his way to the scene of the rumored gang fight he thought it might be a good idea to invite a few friends "just to be on the safe side." This swelled the final number of youths arriving at the scene of the gang fight, since other boys did the same. He denied (and I had no reason to disbelieve him) belonging to either of the gangs and the same applied to his friends. He was arrested at the scene of "battle" for disorderly conduct and weapon-carrying.

I asked him why he had carried a knife and a zip gun on his person when he went to the gang fight if he did not belong to either of the reputed gangs and intended to be merely a "peaceful observer." His response: "Man, I'm not going to a rumble without packin'." The boy took along weapons for self-defense in the event he was attacked. The possibilities of his being attacked in an hysterical situation involving hundreds of youths who had no clear idea of what they were doing at the scene of a gang fight was, of course, great. Therefore, he was correct (within his social framework) in taking along a weapon for self-protection.

These characteristic responses to the situation when multiplied by the numbers of others present characterizes the problem. What may be a confused situation involving many aggressive youths (belonging to near-groups) is often defined as a case of two highly mechanized and organized gang groups battling each other with definition to their activities.

In another "gang war case" which made headlines, a psychotic youth acted out his syndrome by stabbing another youth. When arrested and questioned about committing the offense, the

youth stated that he was a member of a gang carrying out retaliation against another gang, which was out to get him. He attributed his assault to gang affiliation.

The psychotic youth used the malleable near-group, the gang, *as his psychotic syndrome*. Napoleon, God, Christ and other psychotic syndromes, so popular over the years, may have been replaced on city streets by gang membership. Not only is it a convenient syndrome, but some disturbed youths find their behavior as rational, accepted, and even aggrandized by many representatives of society. Officials such as police officers and social workers, in their interpretation of the incident, often amplify this individual behavior by a youth into a group gang war condition because it is a seemingly more logical explanation of a senseless act.

In the case of the Balkans, the societal response of viewing them as a group rather than a near-group solidified their structure. After the incident, as one leader stated it, "lots more kids wanted to join."

Another gang war event further reveals the near-group structure of the gang. On the night of July 30, 1957, a polio victim named Michael Farmer was beaten and stabbed to death by a gang varyingly known as the Egyptian Kings and the Dragons. The boys who participated in this homicide came from the upper West Side of Manhattan. I had contact with many of these boys prior to the event and was known to others through the community program I directed. Because of this prior relationship the boys cooperated and responded openly when I interviewed them in the institutions where they were being held in custody.[4]

Responses to my interviews indicated the near-group nature of the gang. Some of the pertinent responses which reveal this characteristic of the Egyptian King gang structure are somewhat demonstrated by the following comments made by five of the participants in the killing. (These are representative comments selected from over ten hours of recorded interviews.)

---

[4] The research and interviewing at this time was combined with my role as consultant to the Columbia Broadcasting System. I assisted in the production of a gangwar documentary narrated by Edward R. Murrow, entitled "Who Killed Michael Farmer?" The documentary tells the story of the killing through the actual voices of the boys who committed the act.

I was walking uptown with a couple of friends and we ran into Magician [one of the Egyptian King gang leaders] and them there. They asked us if we wanted to go to a fight, and we said yes. When he asked me if I want to go to a fight, I couldn't say no. I mean, I could say no, but for old time's sake, I said yes.

Everyone was pushin' and I pulled out my knife. I saw this face—I never seen it before, so I stabbed it.

He was laying on the ground lookin' up at us. Everyone was kicking, punching, stabbing. I kicked him on the jaw or someplace; then I kicked him in the stomach. That was the least I could do was kick 'im.

They have guys watching you and if you don't stab or hit somebody, they get you later. I hit him over the head with a bat. [Gang youths are unable to articulate specific individuals of the vague "they" who watch over them.]

I don't know how many guys are in the gang. They tell me maybe a hundred or a thousand. I don't know them all. [Each boy interviewed had a different image of the gang.]

These comments and others revealed the gang youths' somewhat different perceptions and rationale of gang war activity. There is a limited consensus of participants as to the nature of gang war situations because the gang structure—the collectivity which defines gang war behavior—is amorphous, diffuse, and malleable.

Despite the fact of gang phenomena taking a diffuse form, theoreticians, social workers, the police, the press, and the public autistically distort gangs and gang behavior toward a gestalt of clarity. The rigid frame of perceiving gangs as groups should shift to the fact of gangs as near-groups. This basic redefinition is necessary if progress is to be made in sociological diagnosis as a foundation for delinquent gang prevention and correction.

THE DETACHED GANG WORKER

The detached-worker approach to dealing with gangs on the action level is increasingly employed in large cities and urban areas throughout the country. Simply stated, a professional, usually a social worker, contacts a gang in their milieu on the street corner and attempts to re-

direct their delinquent patterns into constructive behavior.

Because of the absence of an adequate perceptual framework, such as the near-group concept, detached gang workers deal with gang collectivities as if they were organized like other groups and social organizations. The following principle stated in a New York City Youth Board manual on the detached gang worker approach reveals this point of view:

Participation in a street gang or club, like participation in any natural group, is a part of the growing-up process of adolescence. Such primary group associations possess potentialities for positive growth and development. Through such a group, the individual can gain security and develop positive ways of living with other individuals. Within the structure of his group the individual can develop such characteristics as loyalty, leadership, and community responsibility.[5]

This basic misconception not only produces inaccurate reports and theories about gang structure but causes ineffectual work with gangs on the action level. This problem of projecting group structure onto gangs may be further illuminated by a cursory examination of detached gang-worker projects.

Approaching the gang as a group, when it is not, tends to project onto it a structure which formerly did not exist. The gang worker's usual set of notions about gangs as groups includes some of the following distortions: (1) the gang has a measurable number of members, (2) membership is defined, (3) the role of members is specified, (4) there is a consensus of understood gang norms among gang members, and (5) gang leadership is clear and entails a flow of authority and direction of action.

These expectations often result in a group-fulfilling prophecy. A group may form as a consequence of the gang worker's view. In one case a gang worker approached two reputed gang leaders and told them he would have a bus to take their gang on a trip to the country. This gang had limited organization; however, by travel-time there were 32 gang members ready to go on the trip. The near-group became more

---

[5] Sylvan S. Furman, *Reaching the Unreached* (New York: Youth Board, 1952), p. 107.

organized as a result of the gang worker's misconception.

This gang from a near-group point of view was in reality comprised of a few disturbed youths with rich delusional systems who had need to view themselves as leaders controlling hordes of other gang boys in their fantasy. Other youths reinforce this ill-defined collectivity for a variety of personal reasons and needs. The gang, in fact, had a shifting membership, no clarity as to what membership entailed, and individualized member images of gang size and function.

The detached worker, as an agent of the formal social system, may thus move in on a gang and give a formerly amorphous collectivity structure and purpose through the projection of group structure onto a near-group.

NEAR-GROUP STRUCTURE

Research into the structure of 30 groups revealed three characteristic levels of membership organization. In the center of the gang, on the first level, are the most psychologically disturbed members—the leaders. It is these youths who require and need the gang most of all. This core of disturbed youths provides the gang's most cohesive force. In a gang of some 30 boys there may be five or six who are central or core members because they desperately need the gang in order to deal with their personal problems of inadequacy. These are youths always working to keep the gang together and in action, always drafting, plotting, and talking gang warfare. They are the center of the near-group activity.

At a second level of near-group organization in the gang, we have youths who claim affiliation to the gang but only participate in it according to their emotional needs at given times. For example, one of the Egyptian Kings reported that if his father had not given him a "bad time" and kicked him out of the house the night of the homicide, he would not have gone to the corner and become involved in the Michael Farmer killing. This second-level gang member's participation in the gang killing was a function of his disturbance on that particular evening. This temporal gang need is a usual occurrence.

At a third level of gang participation, we have peripheral members who will join in with gang activity on occasion, although they seldom identify themselves as members of the gang at times. This type of gang member is illustrated by the youth who went along with the Egyptian Kings on the night of the Farmer killing, as he put it, "for old time's sake." He just happened to be around on that particular evening and went along due to a situational condition. He never really "belonged" to the gang nor was he defined by himself or others as a gang member.

The size of gangs is determined in great measure by the emotional needs of its members at any given point. It is not a measure of actual and live membership. Many of the members exist only on the thought level. In the gang, if the boys feel particularly hemmed in (for paranoid reasons), they will expand the number of their near-group. On the other hand, at other times when they feel secure, the gang's size is reduced to include only those youths known on a face-to-face basis. The research revealed that, unlike an actual group, no member of a near-group can accurately determine the number of its membership at a particular point in time.

For example, most any university department member will tell you the number of other individuals who comprise the faculty of their department. It is apparent that if there are eight member in a department of psychology, each member will know each other member, his role, and the total number of members of the department. In contrast, in examining the size of gangs or near-group participation, the size increases in almost direct relationship to the lack of membership clarity. That is, the second- and third-level members are modified numerically with greater ease than the central members. Third-level members are distorted at times to an almost infinite number.

In one interview, a gang leader distorted the size and affiliations of the gang as his emotional state shifted. In an hour interview, the size of his gang varied from 100 members to 4,000 from five brother gangs or alliances to 60, from about ten square blocks of territorial control to include jurisdiction over the five boroughs of New York City, New Jersey, and part of Philadelphia.

Another characteristic of the gang is its lack of role definition. Gang boys exhibit considerable difficulty and contradiction in their roles in the gang. They may say that the gang is organized for protection and that one role of a gang is to fight. How, when, whom, and for what reason he is to fight are seldom clear. The right duties and obligations associated with the gang members' role in the gang varies from gang boy to gang boy.

One gang boy may define himself as a protector of the younger boys in the neighborhood. Another defines his role in the gang as "We are going to get all those guys who call us Spics." Still other gang boys define their participation in the gang as involuntarily forced upon them, through their being "drafted." Moreover, few gang members maintain a consistent function or role within the gang organization.

Definition of membership is vague and indefinite. A youth will say he belongs one day and will quit the next without necessarily telling any other gang member. I would ask one gang boy who came into my office daily whether he was a Balkan. This was comparable to asking him, "How do you feel today?"

Because of limited social ability to assume rights, duties, and obligations in constructive solidified groups, the gang boy attaches himself to a structure which requires limited social ability and can itself be modified to fit his monetary needs. This malleability factor is characteristic of the near-group membership. As roles are building blocks of a group, diffuse role definitions fit in adequately to the near-group which itself has diverse and diffuse objectives and goals. The near-group, unlike a true group, has norms, roles, functions, cohesion, size, and goals which are shaped by the emotional needs of its members.

GANG LEADERSHIP CHARACTERISTICS

Another aspect of near-groups is the factor of self-appointed leadership, usually of a dictatorial, authoritarian type. In interviewing hundreds of gang members one finds that many of them give themselves some role of leadership. For example, in the Egyptian Kings, approximately five boys defined themselves as "war counsellors." It is equally apparent that, except on specific occasions, no one will argue with this self-defined role. Consequently, leadership in the gang may be assumed by practically any member of the

gang if he so determines and emotionally needs the power of being a leader at the time. It is not necessary to have his leadership role ratified by his constituents.

Another aspect of leadership in the gang is the procedure of "drafting" or enlisting new members. In many instances, this pattern of coercion to get another youth to join or belong to the gang becomes an end in itself, rather than a means to an end. In short, the process of inducing, coercing, and threatening violence upon another youth, under the guise of getting him to join, is an important gang leader activity. The gang boy is not truly concerned with acquiring another gang member, since the meaning of membership is vague at best; however, acting the power role of a leader forcing another youth to do something against his will becomes meaningful to the "drafter."

GANG FUNCTIONS

In most groups some function is performed or believed to be performed. The function which it performs may be a constructive one, as in an industrial organization, a P.T.A. group, or a political party. On the other hand, it may be a socially destructive group, such as a drug syndicate, a group of bookies, or a subversive political party. There is usually a consensus of objectives and goals shared by the membership, and their behavior tends to be essentially organized group action.

The structure of a near-group is such that its functions not only vary greatly and shift considerably from time to time, but its primary function is unclear. The gang may on one occasion be organized to protect the neighborhood; on another occasion, to take over a particular territory; and on still another, it may be organized in response to or for the purpose of racial discrimination.

The function of near-groups, moreover, is not one which is clearly understood, known, and communicated among all of its members. There is no consensus in this near-group of goals, objectives, or functions of the collectivity—much near-group behavior is individualistic and flows from emotional disturbance.

A prime function of the gang is to provide a

channel to act out hostility and aggression to satisfy the continuing and momentary emotional needs of its members. The gang is a convenient and malleable structure quickly adaptable to the needs of emotionally disturbed youths, who are unable to fulfill the responsibility and demands required for participation in constructive groups. He belongs to the gang because he lacks the social ability to relate to others and to assume responsibility for the relationship, not because the gang gives him a "feeling of belonging."

Because of the gang youth's limited "social ability," he constructs a social organization which enables him to relate and to function at his limited level of performance. In this structure norms are adjusted so that the gang youth can function and achieve despite his limited ability to relate to others.

An example of this is the function of violence in the near-group of the gang. Violence in the gang is highly valued as a means for the achievement of reputation or "rep." This inversion of societal norms is a means for quick upward social mobility in the gang. He can acquire and maintain a position in the gang through establishing a violent reputation.

The following comments by members of the Egyptian Kings illustrate this point:

If I would of got the knife, I would have stabbed him. That would have gave me more of a build-up. People would have respected me for what I've done and things like that. They would say, "There goes a cold killer."

It makes you feel like a big shot. You know some guys think they're big shots and all that. They think, you know, they got the power to do everything they feel like doing.

They say, like, "I wanna stab a guy," and the other guy says, "Oh, I wouldn't dare to do that." You know he thinks I'm acting like a big shot. That's the way he feels. He probably thinks in his mind, "Oh, he probably won't do that." Then, when we go to a fight, you know, he finds out what I do.

Momentarily, I started to thinking about it inside: den I have my mind made up I'm not going to be in no gang. Then I go on inside. Something comes up den here come all my friends coming to me. Like I said before, I'm intelligent and so forth. They be coming to me—then they talk to me about what they gonna do. Like, "Man, we'll go out here and kill this guy." I say, "Yeah." They kept on talkin', and talkin'. I said, "Man, I just gotta go with you." Myself, I don't want to go, but when they start talkin' about what they gonna do, I say, "So, he isn't gonna take over my rap. I ain't gonna let him be known more than me." And I go ahead just for selfishness.

The near-group of the gang, with its diffuse and malleable structure, can function as a convenient vehicle for the acting out of varied individual needs and problems. For the gang leader it can be a superpowered organization through which (in his phantasy) he dominates and controls "divisions" of thousands of members. For gang members, unable to achieve in more demanding social organizations, swift and sudden violence is a means for quick upward social mobility and the achievement of a reputation. For less disturbed youths, the gang may function as a convenient temporary escape from the dull and rigid requirements of a difficult and demanding society. These are only some of the functions the near-group of the gang performs for its membership.

BEHAVIORAL NORMS, MORAL NORMS, AND ATTACHMENT
Problems of Deviance and Conformity

M. D. BUFFALO AND JOSEPH W. RODGERS

Questions of considerable import to delinquency theory concern the degree of delinquent attachment or commitment to conventional behavior patterns. Cohen and Short[1] claim a strong covert attachment but a low overt attachment due to reaction formations. Cloward and Ohlin[2] assert the delinquent has completely withdrawn all sentiments of legitimacy from the conventional normative structure. Matza and Sykes[3] suggest the greatest degree of attachment to the normative structure. They maintain that a large portion of delinquents are not committed to their delinquencies, but transmit miscues to their delinquent peers which suggest commitment. These miscues result in a set of "shared misunderstandings" regarding commitment within the delinquent group.

Attempting to resolve at least part of this controversy, Empey[4] suggested that research should center around two questions: "(1) the extent to which adolescents legitimate official conventional patterns and (2) the extent to which they simultaneously participate in, or espouse in some way, deviant patterns." These, of course, are essential but would leave the question of peer norm perception unanswered. If Matza and Sykes are correct, we would expect the delinquent's perception of peer norms to be an important consideration in understanding the attachment pattern of delinquents.

PROCEDURE

Following Empey's suggestion, we shall distinguish between two types of norms: moral norms and behavioral norms.[5] Moral norms will refer to standards of conduct that are believed to be "right," "just," or "ideal" forms of behavior. Behavioral norms, on the other hand, refer to standards of conduct that are deemed the "real patterns," i.e., what people actually do, irrespective of what they are ideally supposed to do, or what they themselves believe they should do. The distinction between the two norms is one of the ideal (moral) vs. the real (behavioral) as perceived by the delinquent. Along with this distinction between the two norms, we will consider additionally the delinquents' self-asserted behavior, comparing this attachment either to his moral norms or to his perception of peer behavioral norms.

The research setting was the Kansas Boys Industrial School in Topeka, Kansas, where 170 boys were given self-administered questionnaires. Six of the original number did not possess sufficient reading skills to complete the questionnaire and were subsequently excluded from the study. The boys ranged from 13 to 18 years of age and all had been committed to the school as the result of delinquent behavior.

Each boy was presented five hypothetical problem situations, each situation designed to portray a realistic problem of adjustment dilemma for a teen-aged boy.[6] One situation dealt with cheating in school, three dealt with problems of stealing, and one with a problem of courtesy in boy-girl relationships. Each situation was given three alternative solutions; one solution being the socially accepted norm, another solution involving only a partial violation of the

Adapted with permission of the authors and The Society for the Study of Social Problems, from *Social Problems* 19 (Summer 1971), pp. 101–107. Footnotes have been renumbered.

[1] Albert K. Cohen and James F. Short, Jr., "Research in Delinquent Subcultures," *Journal of Social Issues* 14, No. 3 (1958), pp. 20–37.

[2] Richard A. Cloward and Lloyd E. Ohlin, *Delinquency and Opportunity* (New York: The Free Press, 1960).

[3] David Matza and Gresham M. Sykes, "Juvenile Delinquency and Subterranean Values," *American Sociological Review* 26 (October, 1961), pp. 712–19; David Matza, *Delinquency and Drift* (New York: John Wiley, 1964); and Gresham M. Sykes and David Matza, "Techniques of Neutralization: A Theory of Delinquency," *American Sociological Review* 26 (December, 1957), pp. 664–70.

[4] Lamar T. Empey, "Delinquency Theory and Recent Research," *Journal of Research in Crime and Delinquency* 4 (January, 1967), p. 38.

[5] Elliott suggested this distinction; however, he did not include the concept of Moral Norms in his own research. Delbert S. Elliott, *Opportunity and Patterns of Orientation* (unpublished Ph.D. thesis. University of Washington).

[6] The basic form of the scale was adapted from Elliott, *ibid.*

socially accepted norm, and the third solution representing a clear violation of the socially approved norm.

Each boy was asked to indicate: (1) what he *thought most boys his age would do,* (2) what *he would do,* and (3) what *he thought he should do.* The first answer indicates his perception of peer behavioral norms; the second answer provides his behavioral attachment; and the third, his moral norms.

FINDINGS

Our data shown in Table 1, demonstrate with considerable clarity that most delinquents claim or perceive moral norms that are in conformity with the socially approved norm. This seems to indicate that delinquents, for the most part, do recognize the socially approved norm and that their moral norms are *not* in contradiction to those of the dominant society. However, we should also observe that a small group of boys (11.2 percent to 3.8 percent) do claim moral norms which are in total opposition to the dominant ideal norms of society. This finding reflects, perhaps, a small but nevertheless existent contra-culture.

The data also reveal that the behavioral norms of peers as perceived by the delinquent are clearly deviant.[7]

When behavioral norms are compared to moral norms, the difference is most striking. While the trend of behavioral norms is clearly deviant, the trend of moral norms is in conformity with traditional behavioral patterns. This finding would substantiate Matza's ideas regarding the situation of company, in which the delinquent holds private attitudes conforming with traditional standards while perceiving his peers as deviant.

Further, it was found that the majority of our sample are not behaviorally committed either to

the socially acceptable solution or to their moral norms. No more than 37.2 percent and as few as 23.4 percent indicated that their own behavior would conform to the socially acceptable norm. We believe the behavioral attachment of the respondents was deviant for at least two reasons. First, the respondents were defined as delinquent by society. The boy's solution to the problem situations may have reflected the actions which resulted in being so defined. Second, their perception of their peers' behavioral norms would also suggest that their attachment, insofar as they accept peer behavioral norms as their own, would be deviant.

A comparison of the attachment of delinquents with their perception of behavioral norms also reveals that from society's viewpoint, attachment patterns of the delinquent are less deviant than their perception of peer behavioral norms. This finding also lends empirical support to the assertion of Matza and Sykes that delinquents view themselves as less deviant than their delinquent peers, that they perceive their peers as committed to their misdeeds while they, themselves, are not so committed.

In his study of student deviance, Heise[8] found that moral norms provide an inadequate guide to behavior patterns. Our data lend support for his findings. Heise[9] suggests that situational milieu may be involved in the deviancy pattern. What he failed to consider was the students' perception of their peers' norms, which may well represent a reflection of age-specific pressures as well as the institutional milieu (or in the delinquents' case, the situation of company). While our data do not show that delinquents conform to their perception of behavioral norms, their reported attachment does seem to be closer to these perceived behavioral norms than to their moral norms. Furthermore, behavioral norms provide another standard from which to measure deviant and conforming behavior. Of course, our findings do indicate that delinquents deviate from both their moral norms and their behavioral norms, and the direction of this non-conformity is an important consideration.

---

[7] While we are unable to know if the respondents answered as if most boys their age were their delinquent peers or a generalized other, the distinction here may be of minor importance. That is, it is not important, in so far as we now know that delinquents perceive one set of norms as clearly deviant from the socially acceptable norms. Data in Table 1 indicate that as few as 14.5 and as many as 30.1 percent of the delinquents perceive peer behavioral norms in conformity with the socially approved norm.

[8] David R. Heise, "Norms and Individual Patterns in Student Deviancy," *Social Problems* 16 (Summer, 1968), pp. 78–92.

[9] *Ibid.,* p. 90.

TABLE 1. MORAL NORMS, BEHAVIORAL NORMS, AND ATTACHMENTS

Solutions*	Situation I				Situation II			
	1	2	3	N	1	2	3	N
Moral norms	87.4%	7.5%	5.1%	159	77.5%	11.3%	11.2%	160
Behavioral norms	15.2	15.8	69.0	158	18.4	36.7	44.9	158
Attachment	35.4	17.1	47.5	158	36.3	31.9	31.9	160

$$
\begin{array}{llcc}
\text{B.N. \& M.N.:} & \chi^2 = & 172.89 & 111.51 \\
& C = & .59 & .51 \\
\text{A. \& B.N.:} & \chi^2 = & 19.16 & 13.38 \\
& C = & .24 & .20 \\
\text{A. \& M.N.:} & \chi^2 = & 95.18 & 55.50 \\
& C = & .48 & .38 \\
& & p < .05 & p < .05
\end{array}
$$

	Situation III				Situation IV			
	1	2	3	N	1	2	3	N
Moral norms	88.6%	8.2%	3.8%	159	73.4%	19.0%	7.6%	158
Behavioral norms	15.7	8.2	76.1	159	14.5	13.9	71.5	158
Attachment	30.2	14.5	55.3	159	23.4	21.5	55.1	158

$$
\begin{array}{llcc}
\text{B.N. \& M.N.:} & \chi^2 = & 184.28 & 145.06 \\
& C = & .61 & .56 \\
\text{A. \& B.N.:} & \chi^2 = & 15.23 & 9.22 \\
& C = & .21 & .17 \\
\text{A. \& M.N.:} & \chi^2 = & 119.33 & 97.86 \\
& C = & .52 & .49 \\
& & p < .05 & p < .05
\end{array}
$$

	Situation V			
	1	2	3	N
Moral norms	76.4%	14.6%	8.9%	157
Behavioral norms	30.1	38.5	31.4	156
Attachment	37.2	39.7	23.1	156

$$
\begin{array}{llc}
\text{B.N. \& M.N.:} & \chi^2 = & 67.84 \\
& C = & .42 \\
\dagger\text{A. \& B.N.:} & \chi^2 = & 3.17 \\
& C = & .10 \\
\text{A. \& M.N.:} & \chi^2 = & 49.17 \\
& C = & .37 \\
& & p < .05
\end{array}
$$

* Solution 1 refers to the solution closest to the socially approved norm, and Solution 3 to the solution most distant or deviant from that norm

† Situation V, Attachment and Behavioral norms is the only case in which the chi square is not significant at the .05 level

TYPE OF DEVIANCE

Figure 1 is a graphic summation of the findings thus far presented for all boys and is intended to portray graphically the difference between the delinquent's moral norms, his perception of peer behavioral norms, and his own attachment relative to the accepted social norm. The differences are reflected by the distance between percentage points as expressed below the base line in each situation. Complete agreement with the accepted social norm is indicated by 100 percent. The points on the base line correspond to the percent of conformity with the accepted social norm.

Figure 1 reveals at least one important point. While the exact position of the three variables in relation to the accepted social norm varies in each situation, the position of each variable never changes in its basic relationship to the other two variables. In other words, while the delinquent's own behavioral attachment is deviant and his perception of peer behavioral norms is also deviant, the delinquent's attachment when compared to his perception of peer behavioral norms is always closer to the accepted social norm than to his moral norms. This, of course, means that the delinquent is doubly deviant: deviant from his moral norms and deviant from his peer behavioral norms.

DISCUSSION

These findings suggest that delinquents recognize what is expected of them by society in terms of behavior. They also believe that the ideal patterns of behavior are not the actual or real patterns of behavior as expressed by their perception of peer behavioral norms. Accordingly, delinquents may claim, as Matza and Sykes suggest, that their behavior is not deviant, but somewhat conforming behavior or at least comparatively less deviant than most boys their age.

FIGURE 1. CONFORMITY WITH ACCEPTED SOCIAL NORM BY MORAL NORMS, BEHAVIORAL NORMS, AND ATTACHMENT

Situation		BN		A			MN	
I	0%		25%		50%		75%	100%
Situation			BN	A			MN	
II	0%		25%		50%		75%	100%
Situation		BN		A				MN
III	0%		25%		50%		75%	100%
Situation		BN	A			MN		
IV	0%		25%		50%		75%	100%
Situation			BN	A			MN	
V	0%		25%		50%		75%	100%

Legend: MN—moral norms—standards of conduct believed to be "right," "just" or "ideal" forms of behavior
BN—peer behavioral norms—perception of the "real" behavior patterns of peers
A—attachment—the behavior pattern the delinquent maintains he would follow

THE AFFLUENT SUBURBAN MALE DELINQUENT

JERRY J. TOBIAS

Since World War II the rate of delinquency in suburban areas has increased enormously,[1] and recent statistics suggest that the largest increase in the delinquency rate is no longer in the slum, but in suburban America.[2] This rise in antisocial

Adapted with the permission of the author and the National Council on Crime and Delinquency, from "The Affluent Suburban Male Delinquent," *Crime and Delinquency* 16 (July, 1970), pp. 272–79.
[1] S. Kirson Weinberg, *Social Problems in Our Time* (Englewood Cliffs, N.J.: Prentice Hall, 1960), p. 121.

[2] "The Explosion in Teen-Age Crimes," *U.S. News & World Report* Oct. 9, 1967, p. 74; J. Robert Moskin, "Suburbs Made to Order for Crime," *Look*, May 31, 1955, pp. 21–27.

behavior, chiefly manifested in increased suburban property damage, not only is a cause for concern among the individual families involved, the schools, and the police, but also has led to general public alarm.

It further appears that available data on suburban delinquency is neither adequate nor conclusive as to the nature of the delinquency within such areas. No subject is more difficult to analyze or even to investigate than the extent and nature of antisocial activity by the children of white-collar families, the "better families," the families that make up 90 percent of the population of so many suburbs and residential developments.[3]

Thus, the ingredients of a major social problem are clearly evident:[4]

1. A noticeable breakdown in suburban middle- and upper-middle-class adolescent social behavior exists.

2. The situation involves a considerable number of suburban youth.

3. The condition is of serious concern to many segments of the community.

Since the scarcity of current data compounds the seriousness of the situation, there is an obvious need for research into this suburban social pathology. A study was therefore undertaken attempting to describe (1) the specific antisocial behavior patterns of suburban middle- and upper-middle-class delinquent boys, and (2) the causal factors associated with this antisocial behavior.

THE RESEARCH SETTING

The study area, a suburban community located in the midwestern United States, had a population of slightly more than 35,000 in 1967 and has its own governmental unit, police and fire departments, school system, churches, and library. The average family consists of a middle- to upper-middle-class husband and wife and their two children. They have two cars and are in the process of purchasing a new, spacious suburban home costing at least $35,000. The head of the family is college-educated and earns well over $10,000 a year. He is likely to be employed in a professional, executive, or managerial position in the city. Although living twenty miles from the central city creates some inconvenience, apparently it cannot overshadow such positive benefits as freedom from urban congestion.

Police records indicate that in 1967, when the study was conducted, there was a substantial increase in antisocial behavior among the juvenile population in the area.

METHODOLOGY

In order to fulfill the goals of this study, two groups of suburban subjects, all residents of the community, were selected. One group consisted of one hundred white male delinquent juveniles; the other was a comparison group of one hundred white male nondelinquent juveniles. Both groups were predominantly Christian; in both the majority were Protestant. Although ages range from ten through sixteen, 80 percent of the delinquents and 85 percent of the nondelinquents were from fourteen to sixteen years old. Each subject was from a middle- or upper-middle-class family in terms of parental occupation, income, and residence. In addition, the records of the local urban youth bureau for 1967 were utilized in order to contrast the behavior of the suburban delinquent with that of the urban delinquent.

Three formal interview questionnaires provided the most valuable information; official records were used to determine supplemental data.

FINDINGS

1. *The specific antisocial behavior patterns of suburban middle- and upper-middle-class delinquent boys.*

The affluent suburban offenders are predominantly represented in Class II types of crimes.[5]

---

[3] Harrison Salisbury, *The Shook-Up Generation* (New York: Harper & Row, 1958), p. 86.

[4] See Robert K. Merton and Robert A. Nesbit, *Contemporary Social Problems* (New York: Harcourt, Brace & World, 1961), p. 11 (a Social Problem defined).

[5] The 1966 Annual Report of the local urban police department separates juvenile crimes into the following two-class categories: Class I—criminal homicide, rape, robbery, aggravated assaults, burglary (breaking and entering), larceny (theft), auto theft; Class II—other assaults, forgery

[See Table 1.] They may be further categorized in terms of their specific type of crime involvement.

TABLE 1. SPECIFIC OFFENSE INVOLVEMENT OF AFFLUENT SUBURBAN MALE DELINQUENTS

Class I Offenses	Percentage of Youth Participating in Offense	
Criminal homicide	0%	
Rape	0	
Robbery	0	
Aggravated assault	0	
Burglary (breaking and entering)	0	
Larceny	16	
Auto theft	4	
	20	20%
Class II Offenses		
Other assaults	1%	
Forgery and counterfeiting	0	
Embezzlement and fraud	0	
Stolen property (buying, selling, receiving, and possessing)	0	
Weapons (carrying or possessing)	3	
Sex offenses (indecent exposure)	1	
Narcotic drugs (possessing or using)	2	
Disorderly conduct	15	
Vagrancy	0	
Traffic violations	2	
Arson	0	
Careless use of firearms (gun violations—usually BB and pellet guns)	5	
Extortion	0	
Malicious destruction of property	31	
Unlawfully taking or using a motor vehicle	5	
Running away	15	
	80	80%
Total		100%

For purposes of comparison, the urban offenders were also categorized according to the class and specific type of offense. In contrast to his suburban counterpart, the urban delinquent is more likely to involve himself in Class I offenses.

Tables 2 and 3 show that most suburban de-

linquents involve themselves in such offenses as malicious destruction of property, running away from home, disorderly conduct, and larceny, while most urban delinquents participate in such offenses as burglary, breaking and entering, larceny, and auto theft. These differences become

TABLE 2. SPECIFIC OFFENSE INVOLVEMENT OF URBAN MALE DELINQUENTS

Class I Offenses	Percentage of Youth Participating in Offense	
Criminal homicide	0%	
Rape	0	
Robbery	7	
Aggravated assault	8	
Burglary (breaking and entering)	26	
Larceny	10	
Auto Theft	21	
	72	72%
Class II Offenses		
Other assaults	5%	
Forgery and counterfeiting	0	
Stolen property (buying, selling, receiving, or possessing)	2	
Weapons (carrying or possessing)	5	
Sex offenses	3	
Narcotic drugs (possessing or using)	2	
Disorderly conduct	1	
Vagrancy	0	
Traffic violations	0	
Arson	0	
Careless use of firearms	0	
Extortion	0	
Malicious destruction of property	1	
Unlawfully taking or using a motor vehicle	0	
Trespassing	1	
Truant from home	8	
	28	28%
Total		100%

more significant when a comparative analysis of the crime classifications is made between the two youth groups in Table 3.

Several slang terms describe some of the most popular types of antisocial behavior among today's affluent suburban male delinquents:

Mooning—exposing one's bare bottom through a car window to a passing motorist.

---

and counterfeiting, embezzlement and fraud, buying or receiving or possessing stolen property, carrying concealed weapons, sex offenses, violation of narcotic laws, disorderly conduct, drinking, vagrancy, loitering, arson, malicious destruction of property, unlawfully taking and using a motor vehicle, trespassing, truancy from home, truancy from school, running away.

Grasser—a beer party held in an open area or grassy field.

Jungle Patching—driving a car across suburban lawns or golf courses and spinning the tires, thus leaving bare patches in the grass.

Patching—starting from a traffic light or other dead stop in a car at a high rate of speed, thus leaving long black rubber tire marks on the roadway.

Drag Racing—racing a car down a roadway from a dead stop or a cruising speed.

Making a Doughnut—spinning a car in a complete circle on a gravel or dirt road so as to make circular marks on the roadway.

Garaging—entering a garage to steal the personal property of another.

Mobile Party—having a party in a rented "U-Haul" truck while cruising through the suburban community.

Bombing or Blasting—placing an M-80 firecracker or some other explosive device in a mailbox, thus as a rule totally destroying the receptacle.

Partying in an Empty Palace—having a party in an affluent suburban home when the parents are away.

Keeping a Score—recording the amount of alcoholic beverages one drinks during the course of a week in order to see who can consume the most.

Other terminology often used includes the following:

Making the Rounds—cruising the local drive-in restaurants in an attempt to pick up a female companion.

Making Out—necking or petting with a member of the opposite sex.

Beer Muscles—an unusual amount of bravado or strength brought on by overindulgence in beer or alcohol.

In the Wheat—has been drinking.

Suds—beer.

Bombed or Smashed—drunk.

The specific offense pattern of the affluent suburban delinquent is further illustrated by more detailed descriptions of three of the most frequently reported antisocial incidents (malicious destruction of property, larceny, and disorderly conduct):

A. Malicious destruction of property.
1. Blowing up or pulling down mail boxes.
2. Breaking windows.
3. Throwing beer bottles through car windows.

TABLE 3. A COMPARISON OF SUBURBAN AND URBAN OFFENSES WITH REGARD TO CRIME CLASSIFICATIONS

Offense	Total	Number		Percentage	
		Suburban Delinquents	Urban Delinquents	Suburban Delinquents	Urban Delinquents
Class I	92	20	72	20	72
Class II	108	80	28	80	28
Total	200	100	100	100	100

$\chi^2 = 54.43$ Degrees of freedom = 1
Probability is less than .01

4. Destroying lawns or golf greens.
5. Dumping pool furniture into pools.
6. Chipping or chiseling pools.
7. Chopping down trees or wrecking gardens.
8. Egging, painting, or shooting at houses.
9. Damaging new houses under construction.
10. Breaking fences.
11. Killing pets.
12. Despoking bicycles.
13. Shooting out lights.
14. Painting cars.
15. Twisting off car aerials and shattering windshields with BB's and pellets.
16. Painting streets and bridge overpasses.
17. Painting street and subdivision signs.
18. Cutting garden hoses.
19. Bending flag poles.
20. Destroying children's outdoor toys—swings, cars, and teeter-totters.
21. Dumping over garbage cans.

B. Larceny.
1. Garaging.
2. Taking trees and shrubbery.
3. Stealing street, real estate, speed, warning, and subdivision signs.
4. Taking bicycles, mini-bikes, gocarts, motorcycles, and snowmobiles.
5. Stealing outdoor decorations such as statues and driveway markers.
6. Stealing lawn mowers and garden tools.
7. Carrying away microphones and trays from drive-in restaurants and drive-in movies.

8. Pilfering outdoor Christmas tree lights and decorations.

9. Stealing outdoor furniture, pool hardware, and children's play sets.

10. Taking sporting equipment such as bowling balls, golf clubs, and baseball and football gear.

11. Shoplifting candy, comic books, cigarettes, gum, and clothing from local stores.

C. Disorderly conduct.

1. Drinking or possessing alcoholic beverages.

2. Using abusive language in school, at home, or in a public place.

3. Fighting or roughing it up in the local drive-in restaurant.

4. Loitering and refusing to order food in the local restaurant.

5. Crashing a party.

6. Refusing to leave a party upon request.

7. Refusing to quiet down at local pool or beach parties.

8. Window peeping.

9. Ringing doorbells and knocking on windows.

10. Roughing it up in local stores and other public places.

SUMMARY

The general purpose of the study was to investigate and describe the affluent suburban male delinquent. More specifically, it attempted to describe the behavior patterns of the suburban middle- and upper-middle-class male delinquent. The findings indicate that the middle- and upper-middle-class suburban affluent male offender is overrepresented in Class II offenses and appears to be developing a type of antisocial involvement that reflects his affluent style of life.

C. CONSEQUENCES

One of the possible consequences of committing delinquent acts is, of course, encountering the police and court authorities. The outcome of this encounter (e.g., release or confinement) may vary depending on a number of factors that are extraneous to the act itself. Piliavin and Briar, in "Police Encounters with Juveniles," show that the outcome is significantly related to a youth's demeanor. Officers have a conception of the typical demeanor associated with "true" delinquent boys, and when such demeanor is manifest during the youth's encounter with the authorities, the probability of a more severe sanction increases.

In the next selection, "Delinquency as a Stable Role," William P. Lentz contends that a youth's development of a delinquent self-image and his adoption of a delinquent *role* depends on the way he is treated by others. If he is apprehended and officially labelled a delinquent and responded to as such by official agencies, he is more apt to assume such a role. According to Lentz, this creates a dilemma even for those agencies designed to help the youth: in treating him as a delinquent, they reinforce and validate the role. Therefore, rather than encouraging the delinquent to relinquish the delinquent role, the helping agent may actually stabilize the individual's activities around such a role.

One of the most consistent findings in criminological and delinquency research is the high recidivism rate among criminals and delinquents. In our final selection, however, Kelly and Baer, in "Age of Male Delinquents

When Father Left Home and Recidivism," show that the probability of recidivism among a group of males varies depending on aspects of the family situation to which the delinquent returns. The consequence of delinquent behavior may vary depending on the situation.

POLICE ENCOUNTERS WITH JUVENILES
IRVING PILIAVIN AND SCOTT BRIAR

As the first of a series of decisions made in the channeling of youthful offenders through the agencies concerned with juvenile justice and corrections, the disposition decisions made by police officers have potentially profound consequences for apprehended juveniles. Thus arrest, the most severe of the dispositions available to police, may not only lead to confinement of the suspected offender but also bring him loss of social status, restriction of educational and employment opportunities, and future harassment by law-enforcement personnel.[1] According to some criminologists, the stigmatization resulting from police apprehension, arrest, and detention actually reinforces deviant behavior.[2] Other authorities have suggested, in fact, that this stigmatization serves as the catalytic agent initiating delinquent careers.[3] Despite their presumed significance, however, little empirical analysis has been reported regarding the factors influencing, or consequences resulting from, police actions with juvenile offenders. Furthermore, while some studies of police encounters with adult offenders

have been reported, the extent to which the findings of these investigations pertain to law-enforcement practices with youthful offenders is not known.[4]

The above considerations have led the writers to undertake a longitudinal study of the conditions influencing, and consequences flowing from, police actions with juveniles. In the present paper findings will be presented indicating the influence of certain factors on police actions. Research data consist primarily of notes and records based on nine months' observation of all juvenile officers in one police department.[5] The officers were observed in the course of their regular tours of duty.[6] While these data do not lend themselves to quantitative assessments of reliability and validity, the candor shown by the officers in their interviews with the investigators and their use of officially frowned-upon practices while under observation provide some assurance that the materials presented below accurately reflect the typical operations and attitudes of the law-enforcement personnel studied.

Reprinted with permission of the authors and the University of Chicago Press, from *The American Journal of Sociology* 70 (September, 1964), 206–14.

[1] Richard D. Schwartz and Jerome H. Skolnick, "Two Studies of Legal Stigma," *Social Problems* X (April, 1962), pp. 133–42; Sol Rubin, *Crime and Juvenile Delinquency* (New York: Oceana Publications, 1958); B. F. McSally, "Finding Jobs for Released Offenders," *Federal Probation* XXIV (June, 1960), pp. 12–17; Harold D. Lasswell and Richard C. Donnelly, "The Continuing Debate over Responsibility: An Introduction to Isolating the Condemnation Sanction," *Yale Law Journal* LXVIII (April, 1959), pp. 869–99.

[2] Richard A. Cloward and Lloyd E. Ohlin, *Delinquency and Opportunity* (Glencoe, Ill.: Free Press, 1960), pp. 124–50.

[3] Frank Tannebaum, *Crime and the Community* (New York: Columbia University Press, 1936), pp. 17–20; Howard S. Becker, *Outsiders: Studies in the Sociology of Deviance* (New York: Free Press of Glencoe, 1963), chaps. i and ii.

[4] For a detailed accounting of police discretionary practices, see Joseph Goldstein, "Police Discretion Not to Invoke the Criminal Process: Low Visibility Decisions in the Administration of Justice," *Yale Law Journal* LXIX (1960), pp. 543–94; Wayne R. LaFave, "The Police and Non-enforcement of the Law—Part I," *Wisconsin Law Review*, January, 1962, pp. 104–37; S. H. Kadish, "Legal Norms and Discretion in the Police and Sentencing Processes," *Harvard Law Review* LXXV (March, 1962), pp. 904–31.

[5] Approximately thirty officers were assigned to the Juvenile Bureau in the department studied. While we had an opportunity to observe all officers in the Bureau during the study, our observations were concentrated on those who had been working the Bureau for one or two years at least. Although two of the officers in the Juvenile Bureau were Negro, we observed these officers on only a few occasions.

[6] Although observations were not confined to specific days or work shifts, more observations were made during evenings and weekends because police activity was greatest during these periods.

The setting for the research, a metropolitan police department serving an industrial city with approximately 450,000 inhabitants, was noted within the community it served and among law-enforcement officials elsewhere for the honesty and superior quality of its personnel. Incidents involving criminal activity or brutality by members of the department had been extremely rare during the ten years preceding this study; personnel standards were comparatively high; and an extensive training program was provided to both new and experienced personnel. Juvenile Bureau members, the primary subjects of this investigation, differed somewhat from other members of the department in that they were responsible for delinquency prevention as well as law enforcement, that is, juvenile officers were expected to be knowledgeable about conditions leading to crime and delinquency and to be able to work with community agencies serving known or potential juvenile offenders. Accordingly, in the assignment of personnel to the Juvenile Bureau, consideration was given not only to an officer's devotion to and reliability in law enforcement but also to his commitment to delinquency prevention. Assignment to the Bureau was of advantage to policemen seeking promotions. Consequently, many officers requested transfer to this unit, and its personnel comprised a highly select group of officers.

In the field, juvenile officers operated essentially as patrol officers. They cruised assigned beats and, although concerned primarily with juvenile offenders, frequently had occasion to apprehend and arrest adults. Confrontations between the officers and juveniles occurred in one of the following three ways, in order of increasing frequency: (1) encounters resulting from officers' spotting officially "wanted" youths; (2) encounters taking place at or near the scene of offenses reported to police headquarters; and (3) encounters occurring as the result of officers' directly observing youths either committing offenses or in "suspicious circumstances." However, the probability that a confrontation would take place between officer and juvenile, or that a particular disposition of an identified offender would be made, was only in part determined by the knowledge that an offense had occurred or that a particular juvenile had committed an offense. The bases for and utilization of non-offenses related criteria by police in accosting and disposing of juveniles are the focuses of the following discussion.

SANCTIONS FOR DISCRETION

In each encounter with juveniles, with the minor exception of officially "wanted" youths,[7] a central task confronting the officers was to decide what official action to take against the boys involved. In making these disposition decisions, officers could select any one of five discrete alternatives:

1. outright release
2. release and submission of a "field interrogation report" briefly describing the circumstances initiating the police-juvenile confrontation
3. "official reprimand" and release to parents or guardian
4. citation to juvenile court
5. arrest and confinement in juvenile hall.

Dispositions 3, 4, and 5 differed from the others in two basic respects. First, with rare exceptions, when an officer chose to reprimand, cite, or arrest a boy, he took the youth to the police station. Second, the reprimanded, cited, or arrested boy acquired an official police "record," that is, his name was officially recorded in Bureau files as a juvenile violator.

Analysis of the distribution of police disposition decisions about juveniles revealed that in virtually every category of offense the full range of official disposition alternatives available to officers was employed. This wide range of discretion resulted primarily from two conditions. First, it reflected the reluctance of officers to expose certain youths to the stigmatization presumed to be associated with official police action. Few juvenile officers believed that correctional agencies serving the community could effectively help delinquents. For some officers this attitude reflected a lack of confidence in rehabilitation techniques; for others, a belief that high case loads and lack of professional training among

---

[7] "Wanted" juveniles usually were placed under arrest or in protective custody, a practice which in effect relieved officers of the responsibility for deciding what to do with these youths.

correctional workers vitiated their efforts at treatment. All officers were agreed, however, that juvenile justice and correctional processes were essentially concerned with apprehension and punishment rather than treatment. Furthermore, all officers believed that some aspects of these processes (e.g., judicial definition of youths as delinquents and removal of delinquents from the community), as well as some of the possible consequences of these processes (e.g., intimate institutional contact with "hard-core" delinquents, as well as parental, school, and conventional peer disapproval or rejection), could reinforce what previously might have been only a tentative proclivity toward delinquent values and behavior. Consequently, when officers found reason to doubt that a youth being confronted was highly committed toward deviance, they were inclined to treat him with leniency.

Second, and more important, the practice of discretion was sanctioned by police-department policy. Training manuals and departmental bulletins stressed that the disposition of each juvenile offender was not to be based solely on the type of infraction he committed. Thus, while it was departmental policy to "arrest and confine all juveniles who have committed a felony or misdemeanor involving theft, sex offense, battery, possession of dangerous weapons, prowling, peeping, intoxication, incorrigibility, and disturbance of the peace," it was acknowledged that "such considerations as age, attitude, and prior criminal record might indicate that a different disposition would be more appropriate."[8] The official justification for discretion in processing juvenile offenders, based on the preventive aims of the Juvenile Bureau, was that each juvenile violator should be dealt with solely on the basis of what was best for him.[9] Unofficially, administrative legitimation of discretion was further justified on the grounds that strict enforcement practices would overcrowd court calendars and detention facilities, as well as dramatically increase juvenile crime rates—consequences to be avoided because they would expose the police department to community criticism.[10]

In practice, the official policy justifying use of discretion served as a demand that discretion be exercised. As such, it posed three problems for juvenile officers. First, it represented a departure from the traditional police practice with which the juvenile officers themselves were identified, in the sense that they were expected to justify their juvenile disposition decisions not simply by evidence proving a youth had committed a crime —grounds on which police were officially expected to base their dispositions of nonjuvenile offenders[11]—but in the *character* of the youth. Second, in disposing of juvenile offenders, officers were expected, in effect, to make judicial rather than ministerial decisions.[12] Third, the shift from the offense to the offender as the basis for determining the appropriate disposition substantially increased the uncertainty and ambiguity for officers in the situation of apprehension because no explicit rules existed for determining which disposition different types of youths should receive. Despite these problems, officers were constrained to base disposition decisions on the character of the apprehended youth, not only because they wanted to be fair, but because persistent failure to do so could result in judicial criticism, departmental censure, and, they believed, loss of authority with juveniles.[13]

DISPOSITION CRITERIA

Assessing the character of apprehended offenders posed relatively few difficulties for officers in the case of youths who had committed serious crimes such as robbery, homicide, aggravated assault, grand theft, auto theft, rape, and arson. Officials generally regarded these juveniles as

---

[8] Quoted from a training manual issued by the police department studied in this research.

[9] Presumably this also implied that police action with juveniles was to be determined partly by the offenders' need for correctional services.

[10] This was reported by beat officers as well as supervisory and administrative personnel of the juvenile bureau.

[11] In actual practice, of course, disposition decisions regarding adult offenders also were influenced by many factors extraneous to the offense per se.

[12] For example, in dealing with adult violators, officers had no disposition alternative comparable to the reprimand-and-release category, a disposition which contained elements of punishment but did not involve mediation by the court.

[13] The concern of officers over possible loss of authority stemmed from their belief that court failure to support arrests by appropriate action would cause policemen to "lose face" in the eyes of juveniles.

confirmed delinquents simply by virtue of their involvement in offenses of this magnitude.[14] However, the infraction committed did not always suffice to determine the appropriate disposition for some serious offenders;[15] and, in the case of minor offenders, who comprised over 90 percent of the youths against whom police took action, the violation per se generally played an insignificant role in the choice of disposition. While a number of minor offenders were seen as serious delinquents deserving arrest, many others were perceived either as "good" boys whose offenses were atypical of their customary behavior, as pawns of undesirable associates or, in any case, as boys for whom arrest was regarded as an unwarranted and possibly harmful punishment. Thus, for nearly all minor violators and for some serious delinquents, the assessment of character—the distinction between serious delinquents, "good" boys, misguided youths, and so on—and the dispositions which followed from these assessments were based on youths' personal characteristics and not their offenses.

Despite this dependence of disposition decisions on the personal characteristics of these youths, however, police officers actually had access only to very limited information about boys at the time they had to decide what to do with them. In the field, officers typically had no data concerning the past offense records, school performance, family situation, or personal adjustment of apprehended youths.[16] Furthermore, files at police headquarters provided data only about each boy's prior offense record. Thus both the decision made in the field—whether or not to bring the boy in—and the decision made at the station—which disposition to invoke—were based largely on cues which emerged from the interaction between the officer and the youth, cues from which the officer inferred the youth's character. These cues included the youth's group affiliations, age, race, grooming, dress, and demeanor. Older juveniles, members of known delinquent gangs, Negroes, youths with well-oiled hair, black jackets, and soiled denims or jeans

TABLE 1. SEVERITY OF POLICE DISPOSITION BY YOUTH'S DEMEANOR

Severity of Police Disposition	Youth's Demeanor		Total
	Cooperative	Uncooperative	
Arrest (most severe)	2	14	16
Citation or official reprimand	4	5	9
Informal reprimand	15	1	16
Admonish and release (least severe)	24	1	25
Total	45	21	66

(the presumed uniform of "tough" boys), and boys who in their interactions with officers did not manifest what were considered to be appropriate signs of respect tended to receive the more severe dispositions.

Other than prior record, the most important of the above clues was a youth's *demeanor*. In the opinion of juvenile patrolmen themselves the demeanor of apprehended juveniles was a major determinant of their decisions for 50–60 percent of the juvenile cases they processed.[17] A less subjective indication of the association between a youth's demeanor and police disposition is provided by Table 1, which presents the police dispositions for sixty-six youths whose encounters with police were observed in the course of this study.[18] For purposes of this analysis, each

---

[14] It is also likely that the possibility of negative publicity resulting from the failure to arrest such violators—particularly if they became involved in further serious crime—brought about strong administrative pressure for their arrest

[15] For example, in the year preceding this research, over 30 percent of the juveniles involved in burglaries and 12 percent of the juveniles committing auto theft received dispositions other than arrest.

[16] On occasion, officers apprehended youths whom they personally knew to be prior offenders. This did not occur frequently, however, for several reasons. First, approximately 75 percent of apprehended youths had no prior official records; second, officers periodically exchanged patrol areas, thus limiting their exposure to, and knowledge about, these areas; and third, patrolmen seldom spent more than three or four years in the juvenile division.

[17] While reliable subgroup estimates were impossible to obtain through observation because of the relatively small number of incidents observed, the importance of demeanor in disposition decisions appeared to be much less significant with known prior offenders.

[18] Systematic data were collected on police encounters with seventy-six juveniles. In ten of these encounters the police concluded that their suspicions were groundless, and consequently the juveniles involved were exonerated; these ten cases were eliminated from this analysis of demeanor. (The total number of encounters observed was considerably more than seventy-six, but systematic data-collection procedures were not instituted until several months after observations began.)

youth's demeanor in the encounter was classified as either cooperative or uncooperative.[19] The results clearly reveal a marked association between youth demeanor and the severity of police dispositions.

The cues used by police to assess demeanor were fairly simple. Juveniles who were contrite about their infractions, respectful to officers, and fearful of the sanctions that might be employed against them tended to be viewed by patrolmen as basically law-abiding or at least "salvagable." For these youths it was usually assumed that informal or formal reprimand would suffice to guarantee their future conformity. In contrast, youthful offenders who were fractious, obdurate, or who appeared nonchalant in their encounters with patrolmen were likely to be viewed as "would-be tough guys" or "punks" who fully deserved the most severe sanction: arrest. The following excerpts from observation notes illustrate the importance attached to demeanor by police in making disposition decisions.

1. The interrogation of "A" (an 18-year-old upper-lower-class white male accused of statutory rape) was assigned to a police sergeant with long experience on the force. As I sat in his office while we waited for the youth to arrive for questioning, the sergeant expressed his uncertainty as to what he should do with this young man. On the one hand, he could not ignore the fact that an offense had been committed; he had been informed, in fact, that the youth was prepared to confess to the offense. Nor could he overlook the continued pressure from the girl's father (an important political figure) for the police to take severe action against the youth. On the other hand, the sergeant had formed a low opinion of the girl's moral character, and he considered it unfair to charge "A" with statutory rape when the girl was a willing partner to the offense and might even have been the instigator of it. However, his sense of injustice concerning "A" was tempered by his image of the youth as a "punk," based, he explained, on information he had received that the youth belonged to a certain gang, the members of which were well known to, and

disliked by, the police. Nevertheless, as we prepared to leave his office to interview "A," the sergeant was still in doubt as to what he should do with him.

As we walked down the corridor to the interrogation room, the sergeant was stopped by a reporter from the local newspaper. In an excited tone of voice, the reporter explained that his editor was pressing him to get further information about this case. The newspaper had printed some of the facts about the girl's disappearance, and as a consequence the girl's father was threatening suit against the paper for defamation of the girl's character. It would strengthen the newspaper's position, the reporter explained, if the police had information indicating that the girl's associates, particularly the youth the sergeant was about to interrogate, were persons of disreputable character. This stimulus seemed to resolve the sergeant's uncertainty. He told the reporter, "unofficially," that the youth was known to be an undesirable person, citing as evidence his membership in the delinquent gang. Furthermore, the sergeant added that he had evidence that this youth had been intimate with the girl over a period of many months. When the reporter asked if the police were planning to do anything to the youth, the sergeant answered that he intended to charge the youth with statutory rape.

In the interrogation, however, three points quickly emerged which profoundly affected the sergeant's judgment of the youth. First, the youth was polite and cooperative; he consistently addressed the officer as "sir," answered all questions quietly, and signed a statement implicating himself in numerous counts of statutory rape. Second, the youth's intentions toward the girl appeared to have been honorable; for example, he said that he wanted to marry her eventually. Third, the youth was not in fact a member of the gang in question. The sergeant's attitude became increasingly sympathetic, and after we left the interrogation room he announced his intention to "get 'A' off the hook," meaning that he wanted to have the charges against "A" reduced or, if possible, dropped.

2. Officers "X" and "Y" brought into the police station a seventeen-year-old white boy who, along with two older companions, had been found in a home having sex relations with a fifteen-year-old girl. The boy responded to police officers' queries slowly and with obvious disregard. It was apparent that his lack of deference toward the officers and his failure to evidence concern about his situation were irritating his questioners. Finally, one of the officers turned to me and, obviously angry, commented that in his view the boy was simply a "stud" interested only in sex, eating, and sleeping. The policemen conjectured

19 The data used for the classification of demeanor were the written records of observations made by the authors. The classifications were made by an independent judge not associated with this study. In classifying a youth's demeanor as cooperative or uncooperative, particular attention was paid to: (1) the youth's responses to police officers' questions and requests; (2) the respect and deference—or lack of these qualities—shown by the youth toward police officers; and (3) police officers' assessments of the youth's demeanor.

that the boy "probably already had knocked up half a dozen girls." The boy ignored these remarks, except for an occasional impassive stare at the patrolmen. Turning to the boy, the officer remarked, "What the hell am I going to do with you?" And again the boy simply returned the officer's gaze. The latter then said, "Well, I guess we'll just have to put you away for a while." An arrest report was then made out and the boy was taken to Juvenile Hall.

Although anger and disgust frequently characterized officers' attitudes toward recalcitrant and impassive juvenile offenders, their manner while processing these youths was typically routine, restrained, and without rancor. While the officers' restraint may have been due in part to their desire to avoid accusation and censure, it also seemed to reflect their inurement to a frequent experience. By and large, only their occasional "needling" or insulting of a boy gave any hint of the underlying resentment and dislike they felt toward many of these youths.[20]

PREJUDICE IN APPREHENSION AND DISPOSITION DECISIONS

Compared to other youths, Negroes and boys whose appearance matched the delinquent stereotype were more frequently stopped and interrogated by patrolmen—often even in the absence of evidence that an offense had been committed[21]—and usually were given more severe disposi-

tions for the same violations. Our data suggest, however, that these selective apprehension and disposition practices resulted not only from the intrusion of long-held prejudices of individual police officers but also from certain job-related experiences of law-enforcement personnel. First, the tendency for police to give more severe dispositions to Negroes and to youths whose appearance corresponded to that which police associated with delinquents partly reflected the fact, observed in this study, that these youths also were much more likely than were other types of boys to exhibit the sort of recalcitrant demeanor which police construed as a sign of the confirmed delinquent. Further, officers assumed, partly on the basis of departmental statistics, that Negroes and juveniles who "look tough" (e.g., who wear chinos, leather jackets, boots, etc.) commit crimes more frequently than do other types of youths.[22] In this sense, the police justified their selective treatment of these youths along epidemiological lines: that is, they were concentrating their attention on those youths who they believed were most likely to commit delinquent acts. In the words of one highly placed official in the department:

If you know that the bulk of your delinquent problem comes from kids who, say, are from 12 to 14 years of age, when you're out on patrol you are much more likely to be sensitive to the activities of juveniles in this age bracket than older or younger groups. This would be good law enforcement practice. The logic in our case is the same except that our delinquency problem is largely found in the Negro community and it is these youths toward whom we are sensitized.

As regards prejudice per se, eighteen of twenty-seven officers interviewed openly admitted a dislike for Negroes. However, they attributed their dislike to experiences they had, as policemen, with youths from this minority group. The officers reported that Negro boys were much

[20] Officers' animosity toward recalcitrant or aloof offenders appeared to stem from two sources: moral indignation that these juveniles were self-righteous and indifferent about their transgressions, and resentment that these youths failed to accord police the respect they believed they deserved. Since the patrolmen perceived themselves as honestly and impartially performing a vital community function warranting respect and deference from the community at large, they attributed the lack of respect shown them by these juveniles to the latters' immorality.

[21] The clearest evidence for this assertion is provided by the overrepresentation of Negroes among "innocent" juveniles accosted by the police. As noted, of the seventy-six juveniles on whom systematic data were collected, ten were exonerated and released without suspicion. Seven, or two-thirds of these ten "innocent" juveniles were Negro, in contrast to the allegedly "guilty" youths, less than one-third of whom were Negro. The following incident illustrates the operation of this bias: One officer, observing a youth walking along the street, commented that the youth "looks suspicious" and promptly stopped and questioned him. Asked later to explain what aroused his suspicion, the officer explained, "He was a Negro wearing dark glasses at midnight."

[22] While police statistics did not permit an analysis of crime rates by appearance, they strongly supported officers' contentions concerning the delinquency rate among Negroes. Of all male juveniles processed by the police department in 1961, for example, 40.2 percent were Negro and 33.9 percent were white. These two groups comprised at that time, respectively, about 22.7 percent and 73.6 percent of the population in the community studied.

more likely than non-Negroes to "give us a hard time," be uncooperative, and show no remorse for their transgressions. Recurrent exposure to such attitudes among Negro youth, the officers claimed, generated their antipathy toward Negroes. The following excerpt is typical of the views expressed by these officers:

> They (Negroes) have no regard for the law or for the police. They just don't seem to give a damn. Few of them are interested in school or getting ahead. The girls start having illegitimate kids before they are 16 years old and the boys are always "out for kicks." Furthermore, many of these kids try to run you down. They say the damnedest things to you and they seem to have absolutely no respect for you as an adult. I admit I am prejudiced now, but frankly I don't think I was when I began police work.

IMPLICATIONS

It is apparent from the findings presented above that the police officers studied in this research were permitted and even encouraged to exercise immense latitude in disposing of the juveniles they encountered. That is, it was within the officers' discretionary authority, except in extreme limiting cases, to decide which juveniles were to come to the attention of the courts and correctional agencies and thereby be identified officially as delinquents. In exercising this discretion policemen were strongly guided by the demeanor of those who were apprehended, a practice which ultimately led, as seen above, to certain youths, (particularly Negroes[23] and boys dressed in the style of "toughs") being treated more severely than other juveniles for comparable offenses.

But the relevance of demeanor was not limited only to police disposition practices. Thus, for example, in conjunction with police crime statistics the criterion of demeanor led police to concentrate their surveillance activities in areas frequented or inhabited by Negroes. Furthermore, these youths were accosted more often than others by officers on patrol simply because their

skin color identified them as potential troublemakers. These discriminatory practices—and it is important to note that they are discriminatory, even if based on accurate statistical information —may well have self-fulfilling consequences. Thus it is not unlikely that frequent encounters with police, particularly those involving youths innocent of wrongdoing, will increase the hostility of these juveniles toward law-enforcement personnel. It is also not unlikely that the frequency of such encounters will in time reduce their significance in the eyes of apprehended juveniles, thereby leading these youths to regard them as "routine." Such responses to police encounters, however, are those which law-enforcement personnel perceive as indicators of the serious delinquent. They thus serve to vindicate and reinforce officers' prejudices, leading to closer surveillance of Negro districts, more frequent encounters with Negro youths, and so on in a vicious circle. Moreover, the consequences of this chain of events are reflected in police statistics showing a disproportionately high percentage of Negroes among juvenile offenders, thereby providing "objective" justification for concentrating police attention on Negro youths.

To a substantial extent, as we have implied earlier, the discretion practiced by juvenile officers is simply an extension of the juvenile-court philosophy, which holds that in making legal decisions regarding juveniles, more weight should be given to the juvenile's character and life-situation than to his actual offending behavior. The juvenile officer's disposition decisions—and the information he uses as a basis for them—are more akin to the discriminations made by probation officers and other correctional workers than they are to decisions of police officers dealing with non-juvenile offenders. The problem is that such clinical-type decisions are not restrained by mechanisms comparable to the principles of due process and the rules of procedure governing police decisions regarding adult offenders. Consequently, prejudicial practices by police officers can escape notice more easily in their dealings with juveniles than with adults.

The observations made in this study serve to underscore the fact that the official delinquent, as distinguished from the juvenile who simply commits a delinquent act, is the product of a

---

[23] An uncooperative demeanor was presented by more than one-third of the Negro youths but by only one-sixth of the white youths encountered by the police in the course of our observations.

social judgment, in this case a judgment made by the police. He is a delinquent because someone in authority has defined him as one, often on the basis of the public face he has presented to officials rather than of the kind of offense he has committed.

DELINQUENCY AS A STABLE ROLE
WILLIAM P. LENTZ

Studies of the use of the casework method with delinquents generally have been disappointing. Casework procedures as reported in *Girls at Vocational High* did not produce noteworthy results.[1] Also, the services studied by Tait and Hodges did not furnish evidence of success for such methods and one of the pioneer works in the field—the Cambridge-Somerville study—indicated that over two-thirds of the boys who were involved in the experiment failed to benefit from the services offered.[2] There is sufficient evidence to warrant the conclusion that the efficacy of preventive casework was not demonstrated in these projects.

There are those, however, who have attacked these experiments and questioned the validity of the methods and procedures used. The criteria used to determine success and failure have frequently evoked philosophical discussions regarding the measurement of effectiveness in social work. Although the debate goes on, one cannot escape some of the questions that have been raised by the studies. As Cottrell points out, such results indicate the need for a reassessment of the conceptualizations of social work and social science as they relate to delinquency.[3]

How does one account for the results obtained? It is suggested that it may be worthwhile to examine the phenomenon of delinquency in the light of the knowledge of social roles. More specifically, if delinquency is viewed as a stable role, an additional perspective of the problem may be obtained.

SOCIAL ROLE

The social situation, according to Mead, is of the utmost importance for an individual in determining who he is and how he acts.[4] The social role he plays, Shibutani points out, not only includes specific behavior and his concept of self, but also reflects the roles that are acted out by others in response to it as well as the individual's evaluation of those activities.[5] Therefore, it follows that the mere commission of delinquent acts will not guarantee the assumption of a delinquent role. The evidence of Wallerstein and Wylie supports this contention.[6] Their study showed that many persons committed offenses, some of which could be considered felonies, but which were not officially known or punished. Therefore, one must look to another group to identify those who are role-playing delinquents.

The individual who assumes a delinquent role must be known to be such by others or be officially acknowledged—the essentials of the role are found only in such an individual. The so-called "official" delinquent is recognized by agencies and his subsequent activities are identified with his deviant behavior. The actions of these "others" in treating the person as a delinquent

Reprinted with permission of the author and the National Association of Social Workers, from *Social Work* 11 (October, 1966), pp. 66–70.

[1] Henry J. Meyer, Edgar F. Borgatta, and Wyatt C. Jones, *Girls at Vocational High: An Experiment in Social Work Intervention* (New York: Russell Sage Foundation, 1965).

[2] C. Downing Tait, Jr., and Emory F. Hodges, Jr., *Delinquents, Their Families, and the Community* (Springfield, Ill.: Charles C. Thomas, 1962); Edwin Powers and Helen Witmer, *An Experiment in the Prevention of Delinquency* (New York: Columbia University Press, 1951), p. 449.

[3] Leonard S. Cottrell, Foreword to *Girls at Vocational High*, by Meyer, Borgatta, and Jones, pp. 3–5.

[4] George Herbert Mead, *Mind, Self, and Society* (Chicago: University of Chicago Press, 1934), pp. 153–54.

[5] Tomatsu Shibutani, *Society and Personality* (Englewood Cliffs, N.J.: Prentice Hall, 1961), pp. 118–21.

[6] James S. Wallerstein and Clement J. Wylie, "Our Law-abiding Lawbreakers," *Probation* Vol. 25, No. 4 (April, 1947), pp. 107–12.

are necessary components of the social situation that gives rise to the delinquent role. For it is the delinquent's evaluation of these activities that may lead to confirmation of his status. Only when all of these aspects of the self and others are manifest may one say that a delinquent role has been assumed.

STABLE ROLE

A stable role may be considered as one that is firmly established and resistant to change. The degree of role stability assumed by the official delinquent will depend on how strongly he thinks of himself as a delinquent as well as how others react to his role. Hence, the extent to which a delinquent is recognized by others becomes a crucial element in the development of a stable role.

The distinction between a transitory delinquent role and one that is stable is intimately related to the labeling process. If peers, parents, schools, police, and social agencies single out and describe a person as different or delinquent, role stability is enhanced. When others overtly or covertly consistently treat an individual as a delinquent, stability is assured. Whether the behavior of these persons reflects a stereotyped conception of delinquency or is motivated by the finest humanitarian impulses to help him, the results may be the same. It does not matter whether sympathy and understanding, reproach and disapproval, or a nonjudgmental attitude are reflected in the worker's contacts with the delinquent; the crucial ingredient in role stability is his continuous identification as a deviant person.

AGENCY'S DILEMMA

One may then recognize the existence of an anachronism. The agency, whose aim it is to help or treat the delinquent through its activities, may actually reinforce and lend stability to his role. There are several reasons why this is possible.

1. The teenager becomes a client of such an agency because he has been identified officially as a delinquent; it is in this status that he associates with the agency.

2. Moreover, the delinquent is treated as a person with a special problem, which may become a unique feature of his delinquent status.

3. The agency's work with the individual is primarily concerned with his status as a delinquent. The official title of the agency and the rules its clients must follow provide constant reaffirmation of this focus.

4. The agency is also aware of other forces. The effects of the law and public opinion place the agency in a position where it must—at least nominally—be recognized as protecting society from the offender.

Two conflicting philosophies may contribute to role stability. If an agency adopts a punitive policy or one calculated to provide maximum security for the public, the labeling of the delinquent cannot be avoided. However, if a treatment policy is adopted, a paradox is created. The more the worker attempts to treat the delinquent and the greater the emphasis placed on the problem, the more likely it is that labeling will occur. Agency policy may be at either pole of a treatment-punishment continuum, but labeling will still occur.

DELINQUENT'S VIEWPOINT

The attitudes the delinquent has of the activities of others in a situation may reinforce and stabilize his role as a delinquent. How does he feel about the police, the court, and the caseworker? There is considerable evidence that role stability is enhanced by the delinquent's interpretation of the actions of these others.

Police. The gang boy described by Thrasher in 1927 regarded the police as corrupt individuals.[7] Although since then the situation may have improved, enough corruption probably still exists to maintain a tarnished image of the police.[8] The city-dwelling gang delinquent may consider the policeman to be a representative of the larger society who is not only an enemy but a person who cannot be trusted. He conceives of the law-enforcement effort as being selective and directed principally at himself and his lower-class counterparts. Also, because the police must

---

[7] Frederic Thrasher, *The Gang* (Chicago: University of Chicago Press, 1927), p. 453.
[8] Estes Kefauver, *Crime in America* (New York: Doubleday & Co., 1951), pp. 175–76.

do a great deal of investigating and screening, the delinquent may have frequent contacts with them. These contacts, coupled with his existent attitudes toward the police, are likely to lend stability to his delinquent role.

Juvenile court. The delinquent may consider the individualized justice characteristic of the juvenile courts as a form of injustice. He need only compare the fact that adults are granted all due process with the treatment he witnesses in his hearing before the juvenile court.[9] Moreover, the court's informality and lack of rules may be construed by him to be contributing to a situation in which he has been prejudged.[10] If the court is overloaded with work, the effect may be heightened. To a juvenile who has been subjected to the barriers to opportunity described by Cloward and Ohlin, the court may be viewed as heaping legal injustice on top of social injustice.[11] Therefore, the individualized handling by the juvenile court may sustain the delinquent's sense of injustice, as has been suggested by Matza.[12]

Caseworker. The delinquent who is assigned a caseworker may have ambivalent feelings toward the caseworker. The worker appears to be a representative of the court and an extension of the system of individualized justice.[13] Furthermore, the delinquent may regard the worker as a marginal professional who represents a socially ineffective system for dealing with delinquency. This rationalization may be strengthened by his court experience and his knowledge of the many persons who have violated the law but who have not been prosecuted.

Not only is the worker viewed as a representative of officialdom, but frequently he may be considered an intruder—a member of a higher-class group who has nothing in common with the lower class. This outsider, as an enforcer of rules and regulations, may also be seen as usurping at least a portion of the parental role. He is an adult and, therefore, to be regarded with distrust since his goal is to bring about a change in the delinquent's behavior. The delinquent may question the worker's sincerity because he does not see *himself* as a person to be trusted. Instead, he may think that the worker is someone who is attempting to manipulate his activities. In short, there appear to be many factors over which the worker has practically no control that are likely to alienate the client rather than bring him into a positive relationship.

CLIENT-WORKER RELATIONSHIP

In view of the enormous odds against the development of a positive client-worker relationship, this crucial aspect of casework merits further examination. The need for the caseworker to establish a positive relationship has been well described in the literature. It is widely recognized that such a relationship is basic to the accomplishment of the worker's goals.[14] The delinquent's perception of the social system and of the worker as a representative of officialdom could tend to block the development of a favorable climate. There is considerable evidence from the previously cited experiments that the client-worker relationship is not a productive medium for client change. In *Girls at Vocational High* it was reported that 47 percent of the subjects were hardly involved or not at all involved in a treatment relationship and that 26 percent were slightly involved. Moreover, 38 percent of the clients initially were observed to be negative or hostile toward the worker.[15] Tait and Hodges also noted that limited cooperation was one of the factors that contributed to their project's lack of success.[16]

If there is an apparent failure in many situations to develop a client-worker relationship, what is the effect on the delinquent? Regardless of the worker's motives, the absence of rapport may have far-reaching consequences. The lack of a favorable setting and the development of

[9] Lewis Diana, "The Rights of Juvenile Delinquents: An Appraisal of Juvenile Court Procedures," *Journal of Criminal Law, Criminology and Political Science* 47, No. 5 (January–February, 1957), pp. 561–69.

[10] Robert G. Caldwell, "The Juvenile Court: Its Development and Some Major Problems," *Journal of Criminal Law, Criminology, and Political Science* 51, No. 5 (January–February, 1961), p. 505.

[11] Richard A. Cloward and Lloyd E. Ohlin, *Delinquency and Opportunity: A Theory of Delinquent Gangs* (Glencoe, Ill.: Free Press, 1960), pp. 97–103.

[12] David Matza, *Delinquency and Drift* (New York: John Wiley, 1964), pp. 111–37.

[13] *Ibid.,* pp. 131–47.

[14] Helen Harris Perlman, *Social Casework* (Chicago: University of Chicago Press, 1957), pp. 64–83.

[15] Meyer, Borgatta, and Jones, *Girls at Vocational High,* pp. 149–150.

[16] Tait and Hodges, *Delinquents,* pp. 72–73.

hostility in the delinquent become crucial barriers to resolving problems. It is probable, in many situations, that there are more factors present that encourage the delinquent's stable role than those that may serve to break it down.

CONCLUSION

The foregoing discussion indicates that, at least for some delinquents, there is a preponderance of factors favoring the development of a stable role. Changing the role or enabling the delinquent to abandon it may be extremely difficult to accomplish. Without some changes the individual will become a young adult criminal. The development of criminal careers as well as the abandonment of delinquent activities as one matures have been well described by the Gluecks.[17] The stable delinquent role may probably be shed when sufficiently attractive options are presented. Undoubtedly, with maturation adult role responsibilities become the preferred alternative to delinquency.

The assumption of the delinquent role and its

subsequent stability may be considered a process that seriously hinders goal attainment on the part of social control agencies. Work with individuals on a one-to-one basis would appear to be an unfruitful task within the social system that presently handles the problem of delinquency. It may also be concluded that the hostile or resistive client develops within the context of this social system.

Acceptance of this frame of reference may have some utility in indicating those directions that must be taken to prevent delinquent role stability. Unless there are widespread modifications of the social matrix that produces the problem, its elimination is patently impossible. Sweeping changes or adjustments would have to be made in the agencies of delinquency control. From a pragmatic point of view there is no evidence that the social system that now provides care for delinquents will be radically revised. It can only be concluded that the problem of role stability will continue to thwart the efforts of agencies. Workers and agencies, through an awareness of the problem, may, however, attempt to minimize those situations that contribute to the development of the stable role and may lend their support to those proposals that will lead to change.

---

[17] Sheldon Glueck and Eleanor Glueck, *Five Hundred Criminal Careers* (New York: Knopf, 1930).

AGE OF MALE DELINQUENTS WHEN FATHER LEFT HOME AND RECIDIVISM

FRANCIS J. KELLY AND DANIEL J. BAER

Numerous studies have supported the conclusion that the absence of father in the home may adversely affect the personality development of the children. As part of a larger study[1] concerning the effects of a short-term program involving severe physical challenge on the subsequent recidivism of male adolescent delinquents, the family constellation was examined. Consistent with ex-

pectations, delinquents coming from families where both parents were present had significantly lower recidivism rates (7 percent) than those from broken homes (33 percent). Since the father's absence is most frequently the case in broken homes, the age of the child when the father left the home was then examined. In Table 1 it may be seen that only 12 percent of the delinquents coming from homes where the father had not left subsequently recidivated, while 39 percent of those delinquents whose fathers had left home prior to the age of 7 were returned to institutions. On the other hand, if the father's ab-

---

Reprinted with permission of the author and the publisher, from *Psychological Reports* 25 (1969), p. 1010.
[1] F. J. Kelly and D. J. Baer, *Outward Bound Schools as an Alternative to Institutionalization for Adolescent Delinquent Boys* (Boston: Fandel Press, 1968).

TABLE 1. AGE OF MALE DELINQUENT WHEN FATHER LEFT HOME AND RECIDIVISM

Age When Father Left Home	Recidivism			
	Return		Not Return	
	N	%	N	%
Not leave	4	12	28	88
Birth to 6 yr.	7	39	11	61
7 yr. or over	1	10	9	90
	$\chi^2 = 5.76, df = 2, p = .05$			

sence occurred after the age of 6, only 10 percent recidivated. This significant association ($x^2 = 5.76$, $p = .05$) lends support to the "critical period hypothesis," which suggests that the absence of the father in early childhood contributes to a more profound deficiency in char-acter formation in the delinquent child than if the condition occurs at a later age. Thus, individuals concerned with parole prediction and after-care of delinquents should consider this background factor in their own planning and research.

CHAPTER THREE

CRIME

One of the biggest contemporary issues in the United States, usually symbolized in the political context as "law and order," "breakdown of law and order," and "crime in the streets," is the issue of crime. Although the political significance of the issue is not new in American society—it has been an issue in state and local politics as well as the subject of numerous congressional investigating committees for many years—its emphasis at the national level in presidential elections in recent years has been unusually strong. It was an explicit part of the 1964 election, was important in the 1968 election, and, to a somewhat lesser extent, was a focus in the 1972 election. Political issues aside, it is generally assumed that there is a heightened concern about crime in society today. There is evidence for this. For example, in 1966 the National Opinion Research Center (NORC) found that crime was second to race relations in the amount of attention respondents paid to it.[1] In addition, several surveys have shown that a high proportion of the population express worry about being victimized; for example, in a NORC survey over 65 percent worried about being victims of burglary alone.[2] In surveys of high crime districts in Boston and Chicago, 5 out of 8 persons interviewed indicated at least one major change in behavior (e.g., staying off the streets at night) because of their fear of crime.[3] Given this evidence, it is easy to assume that concern about "crime taking over" has reached a new peak in modern society.

Other evidence raises certain questions about whether the fear of crime is unusually high today. Only a small percentage of persons, even persons living in areas characterized by high crime rates, believe that their own neighborhoods present a greater danger than other areas.[4] Moreover, while the crime rate may have increased in recent years, the increase in absolute numbers has been mostly in property crimes; yet according to evi-

---

[1] Robert W. Winslow, *Crime in a Free Society: Selections from the President's Commission on Law Enforcement and Administration of Justice* (Belmont, California: Dickenson Publishing Co. (1968), p. 17.
[2] *Ibid.*, pp. 18–20.
[3] *Ibid.*, pp. 21–22.
[4] *Ibid.*, pp. 19–20.

dence summarized by the President's Commission on Law Enforcement and Administration of Justice, the "core of public anxiety about the crime problem involves a concern about personal safety" and the fear of physical assault and to "a somewhat lesser extent, the fear that personal property will be taken."[5] This suggests that in a large proportion of cases concern about crime stems from what people believe is happening to others and not from having been personal victims of crime.[6] This is largely due, no doubt, to mass media and to the political rhetoric that is expressed through the media and that may cause people to be concerned about their personal safety regardless of their experience. Also to be considered is that groups that manifest a heightened sense of anxiety and fear, such as ghetto blacks,[7] are counterbalanced by groups that manifest a reduced sense of anxiety, such as southern blacks who are influenced by changes that have taken place in their region during the past several years. (The same may be true for other regions of the country since civil rights legislation, while largely directed toward the South, had consequences for other regions as well. Southern blacks were not the only blacks in the United States whose civil rights were jeopardized although blacks were more apt to meet with violence in the South.)

Daniel Bell writes that public alarm about crime is not new and has been a recurring theme in American society for many years. Over a hundred years ago there were many areas in San Francisco where, according to historical account, "no decent man was in safety to walk the street after dark; while at all hours, both night and day, his property was jeopardized by incendiarism and burglary." And during the same period in New York City, a leading chronicler declared that because of the crime problem "municipal law is a failure" and that "we must soon fall back on the law of self preservation."[8] So it is not at all clear that the public's concern about crime, either as a general social problem or a source of personal anxiety and fear, is any greater today than in the past. As the President's Commission stated: "Virtually every generation since the founding of the Nation and before has felt itself threatened by the spectre of rising crime and violence."[9]

Aside from the question of public opinion, there is the question of whether there has in fact been an increase in the crime rate over time. Is the crime rate higher today than in the past? The source of almost all statistics on crime for the entire country is the F.B.I.'s *Crime in the United States, Uniform Crime Reports.* This is an annual report and includes the number of offenses for 28 different crimes, seven of which (homicide, forcible rape, robbery, aggravated assault, burglary, larceny of $50 and over, and motor vehicle theft) compose the Bureau's "Crime Index."

---

[5] *Ibid.,* p. 20.
[6] *Ibid.,* pp. 17–20.
[7] See "Fear and Trembling in Black Streets," *New York Magazine,* November 20, 1972.
[8] Daniel Bell, "The Myth of Crime Waves," in Daniel Bell, *The End of Ideology: On the Exhaustion of Political Ideas in the Fifties,* rev. ed. (New York: The Free Press, 1962), pp. 171, 172.
[9] Winslow, *Crime in a Free Society,* p. 44.

Since 1930 when the Bureau's efforts began, the index has shown a rather steady increase. On this basis, one would conclude that the rate is higher today than in the past.

These statistics have been criticized because the agencies that report them—law enforcement departments from communities across the nation—have become more professional and efficient. Not only have they become more efficient at detection and apprehension, but they have become more careful and thorough at keeping records; all of which tends to increase the number of crimes reported and recorded. That there is a greater emphasis on record keeping is indicated by the fact that the percentage of police employees whose work is clerical and statistical in nature has increased over the years.[10]

On the other hand, the "Crime Index" underestimates the amount of crime at any one point in time, since it is based on crimes known to the police; the actual crime rate is probably much higher than the index would indicate. For example, a survey conducted in 1965–66 by the NORC for the President's Commission revealed that over 20 percent of the population had been a victim of one of six crimes which are included in the "Crime Index" (homicide is excluded).[11] It should be noted, however, that very few of the incidents in which individuals report being victimized "were of such great significance in their lives as to be readily remembered for any length of time."[12] When individuals report incidents of personal victimization, most of the incidents have occurred in recent months, which suggests that most cases are too minor to remember for longer than a short period of time.

But in any case, we have no comparable data from previous years by which to assess the 20 percent figure as higher or lower than in the past. As with questions about public concern, questions about whether the crime rate is higher today than in the past cannot be conclusively answered.

Less difficult to answer are questions concerning the rates of increase (or decrease) for different types of crime. The Crime Index consists of two types of crime—crimes of violence and crimes against property. Although the F.B.I.'s reports indicate that rates of both types have increased over time, the rate for property crimes has increased much more sharply.[13] In our section on antecedents and determinants, we will deal with factors that are believed to be causal in *property* crime.

A. ANTECEDENTS AND DETERMINANTS

Although different sociologists emphasize different factors as crucial in the causation of crime, the perspectives of all are similar. Causes are

---

[10] *Ibid.*, p. 50
[11] *Ibid.*, p. 9.
[12] *Ibid.*, p. 18.
[13] *Ibid.*, p. 46.

conceived as social forces that are independent of individual personalities and motives. Thus an increase in the *rate* of property crime, if in fact there has been an increase, is due to changes in the structure of society, not in the character of individual personalities and basic motivational processes. Even when motivational processes are implied, as in Merton's framework of "Social Structure and Anomie," which is the most well-known sociological theory of economic crime, motives are viewed as deriving from the social and cultural order. Both of our selections on causal processes in crime have implications for Merton's theory.

We recall from the first chapter that the crucial relationship postulated in Merton's theory is a relationship between blocked opportunity and deviant behavior. We also noted that this particular relationship may be specific to the cultural context, being true for people of a culture which emphasizes equal opportunity but not for people of a culture where this is not emphasized. In another study, Glaser and Rice also find that the relationship in the United States is specific with respect to age status. They find that the relationship between the unemployment rate (which they use as an index of blocked mobility) and the crime rate over time varies according to age; it is negative for young and old populations but positive for middle-age categories.[14] For example, the relationship is negative for persons under nineteen but positive for persons in the 25 to 34-year-old age range. Jack P. Gibbs, in "Crime, Unemployment and Status Integration," uses the same data and shows that the correlation between unemployment and crime rates for age groups varies with the *status integration* of the age group. Specifically, Gibbs' hypothesis is that the crime rate for a specific age group is not only a function of its unemployment rate, but also is influenced by the *cultural employment expectations* for members of that age group. For example, persons under nineteen are not expected to be employed, and most of them are actually not in the employed labor force; for this group, age and employment statuses are integrated under conditions of unemployment. Consequently, we would not expect a positive correlation between unemployment and crime for this age group; unemployment is not a barrier to the achievement of the cultural goals that most members of this age range are likely to pursue. However, cultural goals and social expectations are different for persons in the 25 to 34-year-old category, for most of whom unemployment constitutes blocked opportunity. In Gibbs' terminology, age and employment statuses are not integrated when members of this age group are unemployed. As is consistent with our analysis in the first chapter, the relationship postulated by Merton between blocked opportunity and deviant behavior is culturally specific.

Note that Merton's theory emphasizes economic *scarcity* in the sense that certain sectors of society (e.g., the lower-class sector) are denied opportunities to achieve wealth. However, LeRoy C. Gould, in "The Changing Structure of Property Crime in an Affluent Society," shows that

---

[14] Daniel Glaser and Kent Rice, "Crime, Age, and Employment," *American Sociological Review* 24 (October, 1959), pp. 679–86.

property crime may increase in society as the *availability* of property and wealth increases. He contends that this is the case because scarce wealth tends to be tightly guarded and, also, because people in general feel less deprived and as a result are less disposed toward stealing it. During periods of greater availability, wealth is less tightly guarded and general deprivation is more apparent so that more persons are disposed to obtaining it by illegal means. In addition, Gould contends that the relative availability-scarcity of wealth is associated with the type of thievery that prevails, professional or amateur. When wealth is closely guarded, as in periods of scarcity, professional thievery is the dominant style, whereas during periods of abundance relatively fewer professionals and more amateurs are involved. Thus, both the magnitude and structure of property crime are influenced by the general availability of wealth in a society. This, of course, has its origin in broad social and economic factors of the social and economic order of society, not in the characteristics of individuals.

CRIME, UNEMPLOYMENT AND STATUS INTEGRATION

JACK P. GIBBS

There is evidence of a growing sophistication in the study of crime. Rather than be content to lay waste outmoded theories, such as the habitual trouncing of Lombroso, criminologists appear to be adopting more constructive views, particularly with regard to the exploitation of old ideas in such a way as to gain new insights. This is clearly the case in Glaser and Rice's treatment[1] of the relation between unemployment and crime rates in the United States. Rather than carry on the ancient and now sterile debate on economic determinism, the authors suggest that the behavioural consequences of unemployment are relative to the social context. This suggestion is consistent with the fact that observed correlations between economic variables and crime rates vary so much, as to both direction and magnitude, that no definite conclusions can be drawn.[2] The point is, however, that Glaser and Rice's findings provide a basis

for a reconsideration of economic factors. They have demonstrated that in the United States over the years 1932–50 the relation between arrest rates for *property* offences and unemployment varies from one age group to the next. Their findings on this point are summarized in the first column of Table 1.

Note that the relation between unemployment and *relative* crime rates (arrests in an age group as a proportion of total arrests) changes from inverse to direct and then from direct to inverse with increasing age. This pattern indicates that the consequences of unemployment are, at least as far as crime is concerned, relative to social status (in this case, age).

STATUS INTEGRATION AND THE RELATIONSHIP BETWEEN CRIME AND UNEMPLOYMENT

Although Glaser and Rice's research has great theoretical import, their analysis is deficient in one particular respect. The authors do not present an adequate rationale for either anticipating or explaining the results. True, they follow the widespread practice of invoking the concept

Reprinted with permission of the author and the Institute for the Study and Treatment of Delinquency, from *British Journal of Criminology*, January, 1966, pp. 49–58.

[1] D. Glaser and K. Rice, "Crime, Age, and Employment," *American Sociological Review* 24 (1959), pp. 679–86.

[2] G. B. Vold, *Theoretical Criminology* (New York: Oxford University Press, 1958).

TABLE 1. LABOUR FORCE STATISTICS, 1940, AND COEFFICIENTS OF CORRELATION (r) BETWEEN TRENDS IN ARREST RATES AND UNEMPLOYMENT RATES, 1932–50, FOR U.S. MALES BY AGE GROUPS

Age Groups	1 Coefficients of Correlation Between Trends in Unemployment and Arrest Rates, 1932–50[a]	2 Proportion in Labour Force and Employed, 1940	3 Proportion Unemployed or not in Labour Force, 1940	4 Measure of Integration of Labour Force Status with Age, 1940 (Σx^2)[b]
0–17[c] (14–19)[d] [14–15][e]	—.62	.070	.930	.870
18[c] (14–19)[d] [16–17][e]	—.43	.214	.785	.662
19–20[c] (20–24)[d] [18–19][e]	.41	.505	.495	.500
21–24[c] (20–24)[d] [20–24][e]	.51	.753	.247	.628
25–34[c] (25+)[d] [25–34][e]	.72	.876	.124	.783
34–44[c] (25+)[d] [35–44][e]	—.26	.882	.118	.792
45+[c] (25+)[d] [45+][e]	—.64	.706	.294	.585

Sources: Labor force statistics in *Sixteenth Census of the United States: 1940*, Vol. III, Part I, Table 5; coefficients of correlations in Glaser and Rice, *American Sociological Review*, Vol 24, p 682

[a] Property offence arrests (larceny, burglary, robbery, and auto theft) for each age group as a percentage of property offence arrests for all ages

[b] Sum of the squares of the proportions in columns 2 and 3.

Age groups:

[c] For arrests data;

[d] For unemployment rates;

[e] For 1940 labor force data.

anomie, in this case, to interpret changes in the relation between crime rates and unemployment from one age group to the next; but the interpretation is *ex post facto* and purely verbal. Specifically, they do not relate any measure or indicator of anomie to variation in the coefficients of correlation from one age group to the next.

The obvious need in this case is to link the findings of Glaser and Rice with concepts that have specific empirical reference. Only in this way can the findings be interpreted in such a way as to generate testable propositions (as opposed to *ad hoc* explanations) concerning the relationship between economic conditions and crime rates.

There is at least one sociological theory[3] that provides a basis for extending Glaser and Rice's findings to an empirical generalisation. The theory is based on the concept status integration and a series of related assumptions. Status integration refers to the degree to which status occupancy in a population conforms to a particular pattern. In a population where status integration is at a maximum, knowledge of all but one of a person's statuses makes it possible

to predict correctly the remaining unknown status. Table 2 provides an illustration of status integration and its measurement, in this case the integration of marital status with each of all occupied status configurations in a hypothetical society. Status integration is less than maximum in Table 2. To illustrate, given knowledge of all of the statuses of a person *except* marital status, it would not be possible to predict marital status correctly in all cases. On the other hand, if all persons in each status configuration had the same marital status, one could make a correct prediction in each case, which is to say that marital integration would be at a maximum.

One measure of the degree of status integration is the proportion in each cell of a status integration table.[4] These proportions indicate, in a strictly statistical sense, the degree of integration between the status in question and the other statuses in the configuration. The assumption is made in the theory that status occupancy is indicative of the amount of role conflict between

---

[3] J. P. Gibbs and W. T. Martin, *Status Integration and Suicide: A Sociological Study* (Eugene, Oreg.: University of Oregon Books, 1964).

---

[4] Two other measures can be derived from a status integration table: (1) a measure which describes the degree of status integration for a column (see the $\Sigma\chi^2$ in Table 2) and (2) a composite measure which describes the degree of status integration for the table as a whole ($\Sigma\Sigma\chi^2$). Note that only achieved statuses enter into the rows of a status integration table.

TABLE 2. THE INTEGRATION OF MARITAL STATUS WITH SELECTED STATUS CONFIGURATION IN A HYPOTHETICAL SOCIETY WHERE MARITAL INTEGRATION IS LESS THAN MAXIMUM

Marital Status	All Occupied Status Configurations*				
	R1–A1– Re1–O1– S1–P1	R2–A2– Re3–O2– S2–P2	R1–A3– Re3–O3– S1–P1	R1–A4– Re1–O4– S1–P1	R2–A5– Re3–O5– S2–P2
Single	.15	.05	.00	.35	.05
Married	.05	.75	.05	.25	.90
Widowed	.60	.15	.25	.20	.05
Divorced	.20	.05	.70	.20	.00
$\Sigma\chi$	1.00	1.00	1.00	1.00	1.00
$\Sigma\chi^2$	.4250	.5900	.5550	.2650	.8150

* Each letter in the column headings represents a family of statuses and each number a particular status within the family of statuses. Thus, *e.g.* R1 is a particular race, A1 a particular age, Re1 a particular religion, O1 a particular occupation, S1 a male, and P1 a particular parental status.

the statuses in a configuration. Thus, in the case of the first column of Table 2, the least amount of role conflict would be found among widowed persons, while the greatest amount of role conflict would prevail among the married. In other words, within each column the proportion in a cell is indicative of the relative amount of role conflict.

The figures in Table 2 also serve to illustrate how a change from one status to the next influences the degree of integration ($\Sigma\chi^2$) for the column total. Thus, in the second column of Table 2 an increase in the proportion of married persons would increase the amount of integration within the column, while an increase in the proportion of single persons in the fourth column would increase status integration in that column.

Status integration, as described above, is particularly relevant in an analysis of unemployment. When the proportion in a given age group who are not employed is high, an increase in unemployment actually increases integration of age with labour force status, i.e., results in an increase in *the proportion not in the labour force, including unemployed.*[5] This can be seen

to be the case by inspection of columns 2, 3 and 4 of Table 1. There we see that in certain age groups an increase in unemployment would actually increase the degree of integration between labour force status and age (see column 4). If the influence of unemployment on the crime rate depends on how it changes status integration, then we should find that an increase in unemployment is associated with an absolute or relative decline in the crime rate of those age groups where a large proportion of the persons are not employed.[6] Stated in the way of an empirical proposition: *Unemployment in an age group varies inversely over time with the property crime rate to the extent that members of the age group are not employed.*[7]

The rationale for the above proposition is derived from the observations on anomie by Merton[8] and the theory of status integration. If it is true that some crimes, particularly crimes against property, represent the use of illegal means to obtain culturally approved goals, then unemployment is a possible factor in the etiology of crime, because it may deprive a person of access to culturally approved means for achieving culturally approved goals. However, whether or not a person is pursuing goals that typically require employment as a means is

[5] Labour forces statistics generally recognize two major classes: (1) persons in the labour force, including those actually employed and the unemployed; and (2) persons not in the labour force. The practice of including the unemployed as members of the labour force may be justified for certain purposes, but for other purposes it is obvious that the unemployed can be considered as not in the labour force because, like persons not in the labour forces and not seeking employment, they are not actually working. For the purpose of this study, the fact that the "unemployed" are potential workers is secondary to the fact that they are not working and are therefore deprived of the economic benefits of employment.

[6] The category "not employed" for the purpose of this study includes persons unemployed and persons not in the labour force. See note 5, above.

[7] An alternative expression of this empirical proposition is: unemployment rates in an age group vary directly over time with the crime rate to the extent that members of the age group are employed.

[8] R. K. Merton, *Social Theory and Social Structure*, rev. ed. (Glencoe, Ill.: The Free Press, 1957).

largely a matter of his age. Thus, the young person typically is neither employed nor expected to be employed. As a consequence, if he is employed and later becomes unemployed, this status change does not deprive him of means of achieving goals appropriate for his age. In fact, since the majority of his peers are not employed, the young person who becomes unemployed is not forced into an alien situation; he actually has greater status integration as a consequence of his unemployment. On the whole, this is also true for elderly persons, who are not expected to pursue goals that are usually achieved only through employment. However, what is true of the old and the young is not true for the person in the intervening years. He is expected to pursue goals (marriage, children, a home, a car, etc.) that usually are achieved only by employment. Faced with unemployment, he can no longer achieve these goals by legal means; but there is no doubt that he continues to be motivated to achieve them, and he may resort to illegal means to obtain what otherwise cannot be achieved without employment.

The notion of status integration enables one to go beyond the general assertion that the influence of unemployment on criminality is relative to the social context. The specific social context is that of status. If unemployment operates to decrease status integration (as it does in the mature adult years), the unemployed can no longer achieve culturally approved goals which usually are achieved through employment. On the other hand, if the majority of persons in an age group are not employed (i.e., not in the labour force), as in the case of the old and young, then unemployment does not deprive the individual of a means to achieve the culturally approved goals peculiar to that age group. Indeed, when employment is not typical in an age group, the employed person of that age is less subject to customary means of social control (supervision by parents and teachers in the case of the young and isolation from peers in the case of the elderly person).

An explanation of certain aspects of the relation between unemployment and criminality in terms of status integration is particularly relevant in considering crime trends in economic depressions. A strictly economic perspective leads to the prediction that crime would increase sharply in a period of widespread unemployment, but Sellin's study of crime trends[9] in the last great depression found no conclusive evidence of a marked increase in the general crime rate. In the context of the present theory, this finding is neither surprising nor inexplicable, and for reasons apart from the possibility that unemployment may not affect the incidence of all types of crime the same way. If it is true that unemployment may increase crime rate in some age groups but lower it in others, then the net effect may be no substantial change in the total rate. Further, to cite another anomaly which is consistent with the present theory, in England the crime rate of persons over twenty-one decreased along with a decline in unemployment after 1932, but the rate for persons under twenty-one increased.[10]

What has been said of crime during economic depressions applies also to periods of war, with the difference that employment may increase in all age groups during a war. Accordingly, it is not surprising that in some countries the crime rate during a war has not changed uniformly in all age groups. Nor is it surprising that in some countries the crime or delinquency rate during a war has increased most among the young, because status integration in this segment of the population is lowered by an increase in employment.

As an additional consideration, observe that unemployment and labour force participation rates by age groups vary from one society to the next and from time to time. Consequently, if the above observations on status integration are valid, there is a basis for anticipating that the relation between unemployment and crime by age is not the same for all societies and historical periods. Thus, to illustrate, if persons remain employed throughout most of their lives, the relation between crime and unemployment will continue to be direct up the age scale, rather than becoming inverse as it does in the United States, a country characterized by early retirement. Further, since the labour force status of

[9] Thorsten Sellin, *Research Memorandum on Crime in the Depression* (New York: Social Science Research Council, 1937).

[10] H. Mannheim, *Social Aspects of Crime in England between the Wars* (London: George Allen and Unwin Ltd., 1940).

women varies a great deal from place to place and time to time, there is a basis for anticipating a differential influence of unemployment on the female crime rate.

Since the theory of status integration applies only to the differential relation between unemployment and crime by age groups, it cannot be construed as a general theory of crime, or even of variation in crime rates. In other words, the idea has a limited scope. For one thing, it applies only to crimes against property, and even here it may be much more applicable to one type of a property crime than another (e.g., burglary as opposed to vandalism). Further, the theory does not purport to explain why the crime rate varies from one population to the next, not even variation by age groups. Again, it applies only to the differential relation between unemployment and crime rates by age groups.

TEST OF THE PROPOSITION

The proposition stated above has been tested in the way of the following operational hypothesis: there will be an inverse relationship between the values in column 1 and in column 3 of Table 1. The coefficient of correlation (*rho*) in this instance is $-.54$ ($N = 7$), indicating that as the proportion of an age group not employed increases, there is an increasingly inverse relationship between the unemployment rate and the crime rate. As Figure 1 reveals, the relation between the two variables is actually much closer than is suggested by the coefficient of correlation. With only one exception, an increase or decrease in the coefficient of correlation between arrest and unemployment rates from one age group to the next is associated with a corresponding increase or decrease in the percentage not employed (unemployed or not in the labour force).

In evaluating the relationship between the values in columns 1 and 3 in Table 1, due recognition should be given to the fact that there are certain deficiencies in the data employed by Glaser and Rice. For example, it was necessary for them to use the age group twenty-five and older in computing annual unemployment rates over the years 1932–50, rather than rates for

each age group over twenty-five (25–34, 35–44, and 45 + in Table 1). This is clearly a source of possible error, since unemployment may not have changed uniformly in each age group over the 1932–50 period. Accordingly, it is not surprising to find that, when we exclude all age groups above twenty-four years of age and recompute the coefficient of correlation reported above, we find it to be -1.00 ($N = 4$ in this instance).

Certain other deficiencies in Glaser and Rice's data may also have influenced the result. The statistics on arrest are at best only fairly reliable and, even if reliable, they may not have a close relation to the actual incidence of crime.[11] The statistical problem is further complicated by the fact that Glaser and Rice found it necessary to use the percentage of total arrests in an age group as an arrest rate for the age group, and they were not able to exclude female arrests (this is a minor problem since males account for approximately 92 percent of property offences). In view of the extensive deficiencies in Glaser and Rice's data, it is remarkable that their findings show such clear-cut differences among age groups with regard to the temporal relation between unemployment and crime rates, and it is all the more remarkable that these differences are so closely associated with the integration of labour force status with age.

SUMMARY AND CONCLUSIONS

Despite some obvious deficiencies in the data, the findings of the present study clearly suggest that the relation between crime and unemployment depends on the social context. At least one specific component of the social context can be identified—age as a social status. Specifically, to the extent that persons in an age group are not employed, unemployment in that age group varies inversely over time with the *relative* crime rate of the age group.

This generalisation not only receives empirical

---

11 E. H. Sutherland and D. R. Cressey, *Principles of Criminology*, 6th ed. (Chicago: Lippincott, 1960); and L. T. Wilkins, "The Measurement of Crime," *British Journal of Criminology* 3 (1963), pp. 321–41.

FIGURE 1. PERCENTAGE NOT IN LABOUR FORCE OR UNEMPLOYED, 1940, AND COEFFICIENTS OF CORRELATION BETWEEN TRENDS IN PROPERTY OFFENCE ARREST RATES* AND UNEMPLOYMENT RATES, 1932–50, FOR U.S. MALES BY AGE GROUPS

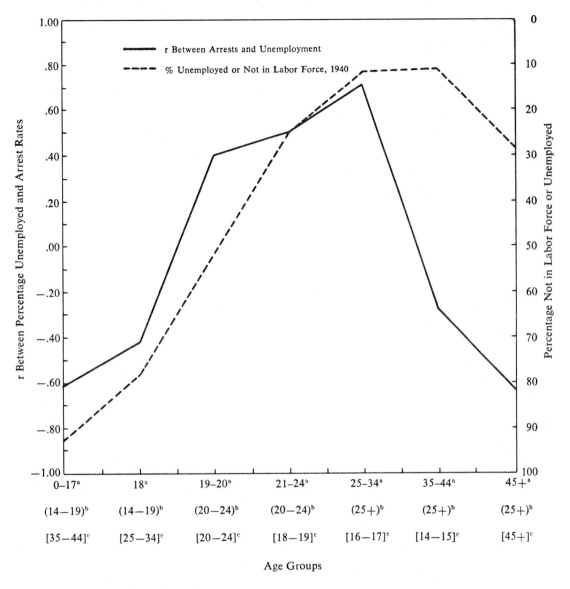

Age Groups

* Arrests for the age group as a percentage of all arrests.
a Age group for arrest rates.
b Age group for unemployment rate.
c Age group for 1940 percentage not in labour force or unemployed.

support but is also closely linked to two theories. The theory of status integration provides a basis for anticipating a differential influence of unemployment, and Merton's observations on anomie suggest the mechanism by which the differential influence of unemployment is manifested in crime. However, in contrast to Glaser and Rice's use of the concept, observations on anomie in this instance are employed to generate testable empirical propositions rather than *ad hoc* interpretations.

As the quality of statistics on crime improves,

it will be possible to undertake further tests of the empirical proposition in question. Even now two series of additional tests can be made. First, the procedure followed in the present investigation can be applied to several other countries. Secondly, to explore certain unanswered questions concerning individual versus ecological correlations, comparisons of rates of crime by labour force status and age should be undertaken. Since published statistics are not available for the second kind of investigation, tests will have to be restricted to those cities and countries in which the police keep reliable information on arrests by labour force status.

THE CHANGING STRUCTURE OF PROPERTY CRIME IN AN AFFLUENT SOCIETY

LEROY C. GOULD

The study of deviance a decade ago was almost exclusively the study of deviants. Why do people commit crimes? Why do people become mentally ill? Why do people become alcoholics, or drug addicts? These were the types of questions most often asked.

Today, a much broader range of questions is being asked about deviance: How do people get assigned to the role of deviant?[1] What are the processes by which norms or laws come into existence, and what are the processes by which they are applied to the conduct of individuals?[2] How do agents of social control, like the police, enforce the rules of society?[3] What is the impact of deviance on the structure of society?[4]

These questions seem to reflect a growing awareness that deviance probably cannot be understood well by studying only the actions and past histories of deviants. Indeed, they seem to reflect an awareness that deviance, in its broadest sense, is not an individual matter, but a process which involves the interaction between many social units. Deviance involves not only a person who commits a deviant act, but the institutions in society which define certain activities as being deviant. Deviance also involves the people and institutions which detect the act and apply sanctions or treatment to the offending party.

Criminal deviance, as others have noted,[5] involves all of these elements and more: it also involves a victim.[6] Recognition of this involvement is not new, but the meaning of the involvement is. Historically, the victim's role in crime was considered primarily a legal, rather than an etiological, matter.[7] That is, much more attention was given to the victim's rights and obligations as a victim than to any role he might have played in causing the crime to occur in the first place.

Some criminologists, to be sure,[8] have been concerned with this etiological issue, but so far little victimological research has been conducted and that research which does exist involves

Reprinted with permission of the author and the University of North Carolina Press, from *Social Forces* 48 (September, 1969), pp. 50–59. Footnotes have been renumbered.

[1] Howard S. Becker, Outsiders (Glencoe, Ill.: Free Press, 1963).

[2] *Ibid.*

[3] Jerome H. Skolnick, *Justice Without Trial* (New York: John Wiley, 1967).

[4] Kai T. Erikson, *Wayward Puritans* (New York: John Wiley, 1966).

[5] George M. Camp, "Nothing to Lose: A Study of Bank Robbery in America" (Unpublished Ph.D. dissertation, Yale University, 1967).

[6] Crimes of vice might be an exception since no one (except possibly society itself) has been victimized in the usual sense of the word. Even in this case, however, there is still usually a second party to the crime, even if the second party is a willing participant.

[7] Stephen Schafer, *The Victim and His Criminal* (New York: Random House, 1968).

[8] Cf. Hans von Hentig, *The Criminal and His Victim, Studies in the Sociology of Crime* (New Haven: Yale University Press, 1948); and Marvin Wolfgang, *Patterns in Criminal Homicide* (Philadelphia: University of Pennsylvania Press, 1958).

almost exclusively crimes of violence,[9] or sexual abuse.[10] Little has been done to examine the role of property victims in the etiology of property crime.[11]

There are some obvious reasons for this omission; crimes of violence and sexual abuse are more interesting and their victims more likely to be an active party in the crime. But, there may be a less noticeable reason as well. Sex crimes and crimes of violence have a human victim, a victim which can play a willful role in the criminal process. Property is not a willful agent, and for that reason, it may have been overlooked as an agent in the etiology of crime.

While it is not customary to think of property as the victim of a crime there is no reason, aside from legal tradition, for not doing so. It is property, after all, not the owner of property (who is technically the victim), in which the thief is usually most interested. And, characteristics of this property, rather than characteristics of its owner, are likely to have the greater influence on whether or not someone will try to steal it. Is it a kind of property that someone would want to steal for himself? Is it a kind of property that can be easily disposed of through a "fence"? Is the risk of capture great in trying to steal it, or the potential sentence long if caught? These, and other similar considerations involving the property itself, are what a potential thief is probably most concerned about, and they are thereby considerations which should play an important part in determining the rate of crime against different kinds of property.

The central concern of this paper is the impact on theft of just one characteristic of property: its abundance. While other characteristics of property, like its value on the legitimate or illegitimate market and the ease with which it may be stolen, are no doubt closely related to its abundance, the assumption of this paper is that abundance alone may explain a sizable portion of the variation in rates of property crime.

SOURCES OF DATA

Although the concern of this paper is all crimes in which the victim is a form of property, appropriate national data are readily available on only two kinds of property crime: motor vehicle theft and bank robbery and bank burglary.[12] While these two property crimes are by no means a sample of all kinds of property crime, they are at least sufficiently different to form a useful base for analysis. One crime involves cash, the other a commodity which either has to be used for its own sake or has to be transformed into money on the illegitimate market. One crime is against property owned by an institution (a bank); the other crime is primarily a crime against property owned by individuals. One crime, bank robbery (but not necessarily burglary), involves the threat of violence, while the other, motor vehicle theft, usually does not. And finally, motor vehicle theft, at least in recent years, is primarily a crime of juveniles, while bank robbery and burglary is a crime most often committed by adults.

National estimates of the number of motor vehicle thefts come from the *Uniform Crime Reports* of the International Association of Chiefs of Police and the Federal Bureau of Investigation since 1936, and estimates back to 1933 come from the President's Commission on Law Enforcement and Administration of Justice, *Crime and its Impact—An Assessment*.[13] The actual number of completed bank robberies and burglaries from 1921 through 1929 and the number of both completed and attempted bank robberies and burglaries from 1930 through 1965 come from the American Bankers Association (unpublished, but available in Camp, 1967: 144–145). While there no doubt is error in the national estimates of the number of motor

---

[9] Cf. von Hentig, *The Criminal and His Victim*; and Schafer, *The Victim and His Criminal*.

[10] Cf. John H. Gagnon, "Female Child Victims of Sex Offenses," *Social Problems* 13 (Fall, 1965), pp. 176–93.

[11] That research which has been conducted to date is summarized by Schafer, *The Victim and His Criminal*. In all cases, however, the research has been concerned with characteristics of the owners of the property, rather than characteristics of the property itself.

[12] Since bank robbery and bank burglary are crimes against the same property, cash and coin in banks, they have been combined for the purposes of this analysis.

[13] Actual figures are not given in this source; interpolations were made from a graph.

vehicle thefts, this error is probably less than that in any other crime listed in the *Uniform Crime Reports*.[14] The data on number of bank robberies and burglaries is probably extremely accurate.[15]

Figures for the number of registered motor vehicles and the amount of cash and coin in banks,[16] the two properties under consideration in this analysis, come from *Historical Statistics of the United States* (U.S. Department of Commerce, 1957 and continuaton to 1962) and *Statistical Abstracts of the United States* (U.S. Department of Commerce, 1941–1966). There is only one major problem in these data, and this involves cash and coin in banks. The data contained in *Historical Abstracts of the United States,* although continuous until 1962, are entered as of July 1 of each year; data on the number of bank robberies and burglaries are calculated as of the end of each year. While this is a small discrepancy, involving only six months, it turns out to be an important discrepancy, as the later analysis will show.

In order to overcome this discrepancy, I have employed the data from the *Statistical Abstracts of the United States,* which list cash and coin in banks for the end of each year from 1940–65, computing the regression equation for the

two sets of data for the years in which they overlap (1940–62) where y equals the year-end figures and x the July figures.[17] The missing y values (1921–39) are then estimated from this formula.[18] What results is two series of data, one the amount of cash and coin in banks as of July 1 and the other the amount of cash and coin in banks as of December 31 (with actual figures for 1940–65 and estimates for 1921–39). Whenever the six-month discrepancy in the data is not crucial to the analysis, I have used the July 1 series, which is the most complete, plus three years (1963–65) from the December 31 series. When the six-month discrepancy is crucial, I have used both the July 1 and December 31 data.

PROPERTY CRIME AND THE AVAILABILITY OF PROPERTY

Figures 1 and 2 compare the availability of property, that is the number of registered motor vehicles and the amount of cash and coin in banks, with the number of thefts against that property from 1933 and 1921 through 1965. Inspection of these figures indicates that a simple linear relationship between the two variables over this time period does not exist, but there do seem to be fairly strong relationships in certain periods of time. Specifically, it appears that the correlations during the 1930s and early 1940s are negative, while the correlations in the later period are positive.

This observation holds true when the actual correlations are computed. The correlation between the number of registered motor vehicles and motor vehicle theft is —.73 for the years 1933 through 1949 and .97 for the years 1950 through 1965. In the case of bank robbery and burglary, the correlations with cash and coin in banks for the period 1930 through 1943 is —.81 while the correlation during the period

---

[14] This is the only F.B.I. Index crime which showed rates in 1967 which were comparable to the rates found by the President's Commission on Law Enforcement and Administration of Justice in its national survey of victims. See *The Challenge of Crime in a Free Society* (Washington D.C.: U.S. Government Printing Office, 1950), p. 21.

[15] Since banks have to report these crimes in order to collect their insurance, and since there would be no particular reason to hide the crimes, these figures are probably very accurate.

[16] Using the number of registered motor vehicles as the property base for motor vehicle theft seems straightforward. It is not so clear however that the amount of cash and coin in banks is the most appropriate property base for bank robbery and burglary; should the base, for example, not be the number of banking offices? I have used the number of banking offices, as well as the amount of cash and coin per banking office, in earlier analyses but have reported the results only for total amount of cash and coin. The analysis using cash and coin per bank gives essentially the same results as those reported here; the analysis employing number of banking offices does not. This latter index of availability is complicated, however, because the trends in number of banking offices reflect changes in both the number of central banking offices and branch banking offices. Given that branch banks are probably robbed more easily than central banking offices and that the growth in branch banking has not paralleled that of central banks (at times, for example, one was expanding while the other contracting) it seems inappropriate to use this as a simple index of availability.

[17] The correlation coefficient for the years 1940 through 1962 is .88. While this coefficient is not as strong as would be desirable, a better estimating procedure does not seem to be available.

[18] Similar regression estimates for the missing July 1 values (1964 through 1965) could also be computed, but this seems unnecessary since so few years are missing from that series of data.

1944 through 1965 is .98.[19] During the period 1921 through 1929 the correlation is —.42.[20]

FIGURE 1. MOTOR VEHICLE REGISTRATIONS AND MOTOR VEHICLE THEFTS—1933 TO 1965

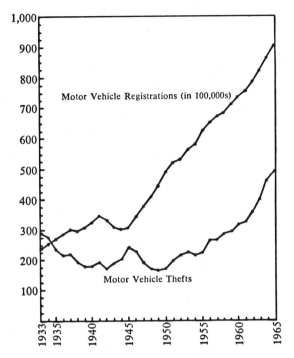

The amount of property available to be stolen, then, is related to the amount of theft, but this relationship has changed. In the 1930s and early 1940s, increases in the amount of property are associated with decreases in the amount of theft; in the later period, increases in the amount of property are associated with increases in the amount of theft.

These correlations are striking for two reasons: first, they are strong, explaining up to 96 percent of the variance in amount of crime (as in the case of bank robbery and burglary from 1944 through 1965), and second, they change

direction very abruptly at a single point in time; about 1943–44 for bank robbery and burglary and about 1949–50 for motor vehicle theft.

FIGURE 2. CASH AND COIN IN BANKS AND BANK ROBBERY AND BURGLARY—1921 TO 1965

While it is difficult to show the abruptness of this change statistically, it can be shown graphically. The most conventional way would be to plot the scatter diagram of x and y intercepts. While this procedure clearly shows the abrupt change in direction of the relationships, it loses the dimension of time. In order to retain the time dimension I have employed a somewhat less conventional procedure which consists of plotting the correlations between theft and property for successive ten-year intervals.[21] The resulting graph (Figure 3) begins with the years 1930 through 1939 for bank robbery and burglary and the years 1933 through 1942 for motor vehicle theft and ends with the years 1956 through 1965 for both series of data. Each successive ten-year interval overlaps nine years with the preceding interval. In other words, the second point on the graph for bank robbery and

[19] Using cash and coin per banking office as the index of availability, the correlations are—.86 for the years 1930 through 1943 and .64 for the years 1944 through 1965. The correlation between bank robbery and burglary and number of banking offices is .53 for the earlier period and .98 for the latter period.

[20] The years 1921 through 1929 cannot be combined with later years because attempted, but unsuccessful, robberies and burglaries were not recorded in those years.

[21] J. Zvi Namenwirth, "Some Long and Short Term Trends in One American Political Value: a Computer Analysis of Concern with Wealth in 62 Party Platforms." Unpublished paper presented before the National Conference on Content Analysis, Annenberg School of Communications, University of Pennsylvania; Phyllis Dean and W. A. Cole, *British Economic Growth, 1688–1959* (Cambridge, England: Cambridge University Press, 1964).

burglary is the correlation with cash and coin in banks for the years 1931 through 1940, the third point covers the years 1932 through 1941, and so on to 1956 through 1965.

The correlation between cash and coin in banks and bank robbery and burglary is strongly negative from the first ten-year period, 1930–39, through the period 1937–46, after which it quickly becomes strongly positive. The correlations between number of registered motor vehicles and motor vehicle thefts is also strongly

FIGURE 3. TIME TRENDS IN CORRELATIONS BETWEEN CASH AND COIN IN BANKS AND BANK ROBBERY AND BURGLARY AND BETWEEN REGISTERED MOTOR VEHICLES AND MOTOR VEHICLE THEFTS

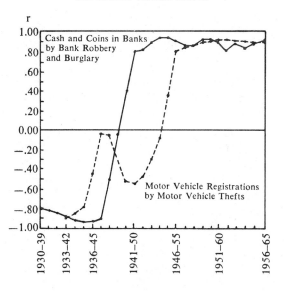

negative in the first period, 1933–42, but this relationship immediately becomes weaker in successive ten-year intervals (although it never quite becomes positive) until the time period 1937–46. After that time the correlation again becomes more strongly negative for a few years, not becoming positive until the period 1945–54. The relationship is strongly positive for the remaining time periods.

Noting, however, that both availability of property and theft show rather consistent trends over time, the correlations between the two, over time, may reflect nothing more than these time trends, there being no real causal linkage between the two. In order to check this possibility

it is necessary to remove the long-term trends from the theft and property data and recompute the correlations between each.

Since the time trends are not linear, it is not possible to remove them by the conventional method of a linear regression. Instead, I have used the technique of moving averages. The long-term time trends are estimated by computing averages for successive, overlapping five-year intervals (analogous to the procedures used for computing moving correlations), and the short-term trends consist of the yearly deviations from these averages.

The correlation between these short-term deviations from the five-year moving averages are in the same direction as the overall correlations. The strength of the correlations, however, is not uniformly high. While the correlation between bank robbery and burglary and cash and coin in banks is —.42 for the period 1930 through 1943 and —.42 for the period 1944 through 1965,[22] the correlation between motor vehicle theft and registered motor vehicles is only —.13 for the period 1933 through 1949 and .12 for the years thereafter.

That these latter correlations are so weak does not negate the causal argument. If it is the case that the availability of property influences the amount of theft against it, it is unlikely that this relationship would be instantaneous. Therefore, the correlation between these two variables at the same points in time would not truly reflect the relationship involved since no allowance is made for this time lag in the causal sequence.

Such a lag can be approximated statistically by correlating the amount of theft with the amount of property available at prior points of time. Table 1 presents the results of such an analysis. For motor vehicle theft, one-year time-lag intervals are used. That is, motor vehicle thefts are first correlated with the number of registered motor vehicles for the same year, for one year preceding, and for two years preceding.

In the case of bank robbery and bank burglary, a six-month time lag has already been built into the data since the figures on the

---

[22] Since five-year moving averages remove two years from the beginning and end of a time series, the long-term trends and deviations for the years 1921 through 1929 would consist of only five points, too few for reliable correlations.

amount of cash and coin in banks is calculated as of July 1 of each year, while the number of bank robberies and burglaries are listed as of the end of each year. In order to overcome this time lag, estimates were made, as discussed in the preceding section of this paper, for the amount of cash and coin in banks as of the end of each year. These estimates along with the July 1 figures allow six-month time-lag intervals for the analysis of bank robbery and bank burglary.

The data in Table 1 are consistent with the argument that the availability of property influences theft against that property. Allowing a six-month or one-year time lag, the correlations between theft and property, controlling for time, are all in the same direction as the overall correlations (i.e., when not controlling for time), and they are reasonably strong, explaining between 17 and 27 percent of the variance in amount of theft. What is more important, allowing a time lag increases the strength of all of the short-term trend relationships and strengthens all but two of the correlations where the long-term trends have not been removed.

Although this analysis has dealt specifically with only two kinds of property crime and with only one of a number of possible indexes of the availability of property to be stolen, it nevertheless shows two important things. First of all it

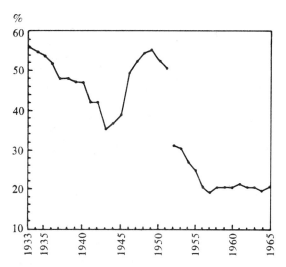

FIGURE 4. PERCENT OF THOSE ARRESTED FOR MOTOR VEHICLE THEFT IN THE U.S. WHO ARE TWENTY-ONE YEARS OLD OR OLDER

Note: Figures for this graph come from the *Uniform Crime Reports* of the International Association of Chiefs of Police and the Federal Bureau of Investigation, 1933–65.

shows that the amount of property available for two quite different kinds of property crime is related to the amount of crime against that property. Secondly, it shows that these relationships have changed direction over time. This suggests that there has been a fundamental

TABLE 1. TIME-LAG CORRELATIONS BETWEEN MOTOR VEHICLE THEFT AND MOTOR VEHICLE REGISTRATIONS AND BETWEEN BANK ROBBERY AND BURGLARY AND CASH AND COIN IN BANKS

Motor Vehicle Thefts and Registrations	No Time Lag	One-year Time Lag	Two-year Time Lag
Overall correlations:			
1933–49	—.74	—.80	—.73
1950–65	.97	.96	.95
Correlation of short-term trends:			
1933–49	—.12	—.52	—.42
1950–65	.13	.41	.30

Bank Robbery and Burglary and Cash and Coin in Banks	No Time Lag	Six-month Time Lag	One-year Time Lag
Overall correlations:			
1930–43	.85	—.81	—.73
1944–62	.90	.95	.83
Correlation of short-term trends:			
1930–43	—.28	—.42	.32
1944–62	—.48	.42	.08

change in the social structuring of these two kinds of property crime (if not of all kinds of property crime) during recent years. What is this change, and what accounts for it?

PROPERTY CRIME IN TIMES OF SCARCITY AND ABUNDANCE

The most immediately discernible difference between the period of the 1930s and the early 1940s and the period to follow is that the former period was a period of economic scarcity while the latter period was marked by abundance. The former period encompassed the Great Depression and World War II while the latter period has seen almost uninterrupted prosperity. This suggests, then, that property crime is not only related to the availability of property, but that this relationship itself is structured by the relative scarcity or abundance of the property being stolen.

That this should be true becomes even more plausible in view of the fact that the relationship between motor vehicle theft and registered motor vehicles switches to positive some five or six years later than the relationship between cash and coin in banks and bank robbery and burglary. Because no motor vehicles were produced for the public market during the years of World War II, this form of property, which was becoming relatively abundant immediately prior to the war, again became scarce and did not reach a point of abundance until late in the 1940s. It was not until 1947, for example, that the per capita rate of motor vehicle registrations regained the level which it had reached in 1941, and the rate continued to grow very rapidly until 1950 at which point the rate of growth leveled off. The rate of growth of the availability of money started upward much earlier, coinciding more or less with the beginning of World War II. The amount of cash and coin in banks, for example, remained almost constant from 1920 through 1940 but then increased sharply in 1941 and in general, has been increasing steadily ever since.

These changes in the relationship between theft and the availability of property are also paralleled by changes in the populations of thieves who prey on these kinds of property.

The most striking change in the population of motor vehicle thieves is the extent to which this population has become dominated by youths. While there are no data which will show this precisely, because many motor vehicle thieves are never caught and thus their age remains unknown, the data on arrests for motor vehicle theft, as shown in Figure 4, indicate that most car thieves today are probably juveniles. While there were evidently also many youths in this population before and during World War II, the proportion of adults was evidently larger in those years and, what is even more important, the proportion of adults varied inversely with the availability of motor vehicles. In the years 1933–41, while motor vehicle registrations were rising, the proportion of adults arrested for motor vehicle theft declined. This proportion continued to decline for two more years and then increased dramatically during the war years when motor vehicle registrations were on the decline. The proportion of adults remained high during the postwar years and then, beginning in 1950, the proportion declined steadily until 1957 and has remained at about that level ever since. In other words, motor vehicle theft has apparently changed from being a crime which is influenced primarily by matters of economic gain to being simply "joy-riding."

The case for bank robbery is somewhat different. (There has been no systematic study of bank burglars.) While the nature of this population of thieves has also changed, bank robbery has not become, as in the case of auto theft, a crime of youth. It has become what might be called a crime of desperation.

A recent and extensive study of bank robbery in the United States, which included interviews with a random national sample of bank robbers incarcerated in Federal Prisons,[23] revealed two important things about the population of bank robbers. First of all, there is evidence that most bank robbers prior to 1940 were professional, full-time criminals who robbed banks for financial gain. Bank robbery like other forms of crime was a means of livelihood. Since about 1945 or so a new, essentially nonprofessional, criminal element has entered the ranks of bank

---

[23] Camp, "Nothing to Lose."

robbers. Forty-five percent of bank robbers presently incarcerated were not pursuing a criminal career prior to robbing a bank. (Since approximately 90 percent of all bank robbers are caught, these figures are fairly representative of all bank robbers.) In addition, even the habitual or professional criminals presently incarcerated for bank robbery did not rob banks simply as a means of livelihood.

What today characterizes both the habitual criminals who rob banks and those who rob banks who are not habitual criminals is the desperation which motivates the act. In approximately one-fourth of the cases this desperation results from some threat to the individual's person or his livelihood (e.g., pending business failure, financial foreclosure, or unpaid gambling debts). In the rest of the cases the desperation results from an inability to get ahead in one's profession (either legitimate or illegitimate profession). What is important in this latter category is that bank robbery is not viewed as a normal means of livelihood even by the long-time criminals who turn to bank robbery but as a source of ready cash, albeit a risky one, which could serve to improve one's position in his more usual economic pursuits.

What is more important about both of these types of crime, then, is that they have moved from being crimes of economic gain to being crimes which reflect an abundant economy. Auto theft is committed primarily by youths who, as part of this rich society, presumably share in the general admiration of automobiles and in the assumption that everyone has the right to share in their enjoyment. Bank robbers are people who have gotten themselves into difficulty because of economic overextension or who are not advancing economically as rapidly as they think is their due.

One final characteristic of motor vehicle theft and bank robbery and burglary which has changed in recent years should be mentioned: that is, the ease with which these crimes can be committed. When cars were scarce and money not plentiful, it was harder to steal these commodities than it is today. Not only were there not as many cars around to be stolen in the 1930s but those who had cars then probably watched them more carefully and locked them more diligently than people do today. In addi-

tion, it is easier to drive automobiles today because of the introduction of automatic transmissions in the late 1940s and early 1950s. This may be of particular importance since automobiles today are often stolen by youths who are likely to be inexperienced drivers. (Many young people today could not even drive a stolen car away if they had to know how to manipulate a clutch and gearshift.)

The ease of bank robbery today is even more striking. Unlike the banks of thirty or forty years ago which separated tellers and customers (and robbers) by iron bars and which were likely to have armed guards on the premises, banks today are open (and, therefore, easily "cased"), often isolated (and, therefore, easy to get away from), poorly protected institutions.[24] Banks seldom employ armed guards any more and over half of the banking offices in this country do not even have adequate alarm systems (that is alarms which sound in a police station or in the office of a protection agency).

CONCLUSIONS

While the information about the changes in the nation's populations of motor vehicle thieves and bank robbers is fragmentary, it is nonetheless consistent with the changes which have occurred in the relationship between the amount of cash and coin in banks and bank robbery and the number of registered motor vehicles and the number of motor vehicle thefts. Even more important, these apparent changes in the population of criminals point to a mechanism which would help explain the relationship between the availability of property and thefts against that property and the fact that this relationship has changed from negative to positive.

When property is scarce, and therefore expensive, there are a number of reasons why theft against that property should be dominated by what might be called professional thieves,[25] that is people who have developed some skill at thievery and who treat theft as a means of

---

[24] *Ibid.* Fifty-four percent of all banking offices in 1965 were branch banks. In 1943 the figure was 21 percent; in 1930, 13 percent; and in 1921, 4 percent.
[25] Edwin H. Sutherland, *The Professional Thief* (Chicago: University of Chicago Press, 1937).

economic gain. First of all, if property is scarce and expensive, it is also likely to be well guarded, thus demanding the skills of a professional in order to steal it. Secondly, if professionals are at all interested in theft against some form of property, they will themselves try to keep amateurs out of their domain.[26] And finally, when a form of property is relatively scarce, people in general will probably feel less deprived if they do not have that property and thus be less likely to try to steal it for their own use.

As the availability of property increases, however, it probably becomes less attractive to professional thieves. While increased availability would probably make the property easier to steal (there would be more of it and it probably would be less well guarded), it would also be less worth stealing, first because its value relative to other forms of property would have declined, and secondly because the demand for stolen property would probably also have declined. Therefore, during a period of relative scarcity, when the population of criminals is predominantly professional, increases in the availability of property would be followed by decreases in amount of theft against that particular property, while decreases in availability would be followed by increases in the rate of theft against it.

Once a form of property reaches a certain point of abundance, however, thefts against it will probably no longer be dominated by professional thieves. First of all, professional thieves will be less interested in it, either in stealing it or in protecting themselves from amateur thieves, and at the same time the owners of the property will probably have relaxed their protective measures to a point where amateurs can successfully steal the property. Maybe even more important, however, once property becomes generally available, but for one reason or another is not enjoyed by everyone in society, the conditions are set for a whole new group of criminals to enter the criminal marketplace, that is those who are not sharing in the abundance of the economy but who have come to feel that they have

a right to do so. These are the people, it would seem, who could legitimately be called amateur thieves, that is thieves with little or no commitment to theft as a livelihood, with little or no skill at thievery, who steal goods primarily for their own use or money primarily as a means to get themselves out of a financial crisis.

During a period dominated by amateur thieves, increases in the amount of property would serve to increase the relative deprivation of those who were still not sharing in the ownership of the property, while at the same time making it easier for these people to steal the property for their own use. Therefore, during a period of abundance, increases in the availability of property would be followed by increases in the rate of theft against that property, while decreases in availability would be followed by decreases in the crime rate.

Although this analysis has covered only two specific kinds of property crime—the only two kinds for which data were immediately available regarding the availability of the property being stolen—there is no apparent reason why the hypotheses derived from the analysis should not also apply to other forms of property theft.[27] The fact that motor vehicle theft and bank robbery and burglary are quite different kinds of crime involving very different kinds of property, would seem to make the uniformities found between them important and worthy of further investigation. At the very least, the analysis has shown how one simple characteristic of two specific victims of crime, in this case property victims, seems to explain a rather sizable proportion of the amount of crime committed against that victim.

---

[26] Ibid.

[27] The other property crimes listed in the *Uniform Crime Reports* show a cycle from the early 1930's to 1965 similar to that of motor vehicle theft and bank robbery and burglary. While per capita rates of burglary are now twice what they were in 1933, they are three times what they were in 1942. Per capita rates of robbery (listed in the *Uniform Crime Reports* as a crime against the person—because of the threat of violence involved—but for purposes of this paper better thought of as a crime against property) were, in 1965, only two-thirds what they were in 1933, but in 1944 they were only about half as high (President's Commission, *Challenge of Crime* pp. 22–23). Rates of larceny of $50 and over, the one remaining *Uniform Crime Reports* indexed as property crime, are not comparable over time because of monetary inflation which has continually lowered the level of seriousness necessary for including crimes in this category.

B. SOCIAL RELATIONS AND PROCESS

The analysis of the social relations and processes involved in crime is as significant for understanding crime as the analysis of causal factors. This is true even if we assume that the causes of crime can be attributed to universal tendencies embedded in human nature, such as an inherent human drive to resist all forms of social control or the tendency to seek reward and avoid punishment. Such universal tendencies would still not explain the different ways in which crime is organized. As Bell notes, "the problem of economic crime does not rest upon truisms about human nature, but on the way methods of securing gain are organized."[1] And the ways methods are organized depend in turn on the broader societal context of crime, just as the causal factors of crime will depend on the broader context.

Traditionally, sociological conceptions of social relations in criminal activity have been strongly influenced by the "principle of differential association," which was first systematically presented by Edwin H. Sutherland. This principle asserts that individuals become criminals when they are isolated from noncriminal persons and exposed to persons who have criminalistic attitudes and a knowledge of criminal techniques. Moreover, many forms of criminal behavior, such as professional theft, evolve into fully developed roles in which the individual himself is integrated in a network of criminal social relations. These relations, which may involve co-operation among criminals, are always controlled by a set of social norms, or a subculture that includes criminalistic techniques as well as attitudes. It is through a network of social relations regulated by such a subculture that an individual becomes a criminal. Various criminal roles and the skills and values associated with these roles are transmitted to the neophyte. Like all learned social activities, criminal behavior normally is organized, involves relationships with others, and is taught by the experienced to the inexperienced. The evidence most often cited to support this picture is Sutherland's case study of *The Professional Thief*.[2]

Evidence indicates that this is not a valid picture of all types of criminals. For example, Roebuck and Johnson[3] study what they call the "jack-of-all trades" offender, who does not specialize in any form of crime and has only limited contact with other criminals. Most of his crimes are petty in nature and require neither cooperation of others nor exposure to more experienced criminals in order to learn specific techniques and attitudes. The lack of developed skills makes them "losers"; they

[1] Daniel Bell, "The Myth of Crime Waves," in Daniel Bell, *The End of Ideology: On the Exhaustion of Political Ideas in the Fifties* (New York: The Free Press, 1962), p. 170.

[2] Edwin R. Sutherland, *The Professional Thief* (Chicago: The University of Chicago Press, 1937).

[3] Julian Roebuck and Ronald Johnson, "The Jack-of-All-Trades Offender," *Crime and Delinquency* 8 (1962), pp. 172—81.

have long arrest records. Probably as a consequence of this they are avoided by other criminals and are thus excluded from a network of stable social relationships. Consequently, once they are caught they do not have the advantages of professional thieves, who, according to Sutherland, are able to arrange for bail, court counsel, and, in some instances, a "fix" (getting the charge deleted from the record).

In our first selection in this section, Werner J. Einstadter, in "The Social Organization of Armed Robbery," compares his examination of career robbers with Sutherland's description of professional thieves. Little correspondence is found. In general, Einstadter observes that the career robber is more like the businessman than Sutherland's professional thief who resembles the legitimate professional by cultivating and refining a set of specific skills and by earning status before his peers in accordance with his skills. The career robber is more concerned with seeking a quick profit and less concerned with maintaining enduring social relationships with other robbers. He is less concerned with how he appears before his peers. Although Einstadter notes that the differences between Sutherland's description of the professional thief and his own description of the career robber may be due to the fact that different types of crime require different styles and different types of organization, he also wonders if there hasn't been an historical change in the roles of career criminals stemming from changes in the structure of the broader society (see also Gould's comments, pp. 108–9 above, and Irwin and Yablonsky's analysis below).

In the next selection, "External Social Relations of Burglars," Neal Shover describes the types of relationships which burglars establish and maintain with persons who live on the margin of legitimate society (the tipster and the fence) and with persons who occupy positions in legitimate society (bondsmen and attorneys). Although these persons do not aid or participate in the act of burglary, burglary would be far more risky and less lucrative without them. Unless there were persons to find goods in legitimate society that were worth stealing, to dispose of those goods to legitimate society, and to protect the burglar from legitimate society, many forms of burglary would not be worth the effort. Although burglars are enemies of legitimate society, they are also very much dependent on legitimate society for their existence.

The hypothesis of an historical change in criminal career roles alluded to above is explored in detail in the next selection by John Irwin and Lewis Yablonsky, "The New Criminal: A View of the Contemporary Offender." The authors' specific hypothesis is that the style and character of the individual criminal has changed largely as a result of changes in urban slums. Slums have become more internally disorganized with a concomitant loss of a visible neighborhood criminal hierarchy. As a consequence of this, visible role-models for adolescents have disappeared, and the neighborhood is less a training ground for recruitment in professional crime. In addition, the deterioration of the criminal subculture associated with the slum may have been hastened by the development of modern police technology. Just as the causation of criminal behavior must be viewed in terms of a broader social, cultural, and economic context, so the relationships typical of criminals at a particular point in time must be viewed in terms of a broader context.

THE SOCIAL ORGANIZATION OF ARMED ROBBERY

WERNER J. EINSTADTER

In most criminological studies, when the group life of adult professional criminals is discussed a single theoretical model is employed. It is usually assumed that the adult professional criminal operates within the structural context of the *mob*. The model of the mob has been variously described in the literature but was most clearly formulated by Sutherland.[1]

A body of literature on professional crime has centered largely on an extension or modification of Sutherland's conception of the essential social characteristics of professional theft and his unifying theoretical statement of differential association.[2] As Clinard and Quinney have pointed out, however, empirical research concerning various types of professional crime has been sparse; this is especially true with regard to the social organization of various professional criminal groups.[3] No studies appear to have been concerned specifically with a reexamination of Sutherland's conception of the social organization of the professional criminal.

The concept of the mob implies that professional criminal collectivities operate according to a number of common understandings, rules of conduct, or working relationships which are considered binding on all its members. These modes of conduct found among groups of professional thieves are presumed to have universal applicability to all professional criminal groups.

The purpose of this paper is twofold; first, it is an attempt to relate Sutherland's conception of the mob to professional robbery and to reassess its utility and relevance as a generic explanatory model; secondly, it is an effort to describe a specific type of criminal behavior system.

Methodology

Twenty-five convicted robbers on parole in California were studied. In addition to interview material, data gathered over several years from an equal number of convicted robbers who were confined were used. Official records were employed as supplementary material, to check the official criminal record, prior commitments, and offense statements.

The respondents selected represent robbers who were considered to be professional or career robbers in that they all met the following criteria:

(1) Each subject in company with others committed more than a single robbery prior to detection. Each subject either committed a series of robberies or several series of robberies separated by prison terms. In a number of instances there were robberies unknown to officials.

(2) All were armed robbers. All employed weapons that were operative. None simulated weapons. Each instance of robbery was calculated and the subject fully intended to carry the act to its completion.

(3) Each subject considered himself a robber and for various periods had spent considerable portion of his time in the engagement of robbery.

(4) In all instances the subject's sole stated interest was robbery. In no case was the robbery

Excerpted with permission of the author and the Society for the Study of Social Problems, from *Social Problems* 17 (Summer, 1969), pp. 64–78.

[1] Edwin H. Sutherland, *The Professional Thief* (Chicago: University of Chicago Press, 1937), pp. 27–42.

[2] Edwin H. Sutherland and Donald R. Cressey, *Principles of Criminology*, 7th ed. (Philadelphia: Lippincott, 1966).

[3] Marshall B. Clinard and Richard Quinney, *Criminal Behavior Systems—A Typology* (New York: Holt, Rinehart and Winston, 1967), p. 429. See their listing of the few representative studies in this area.

incidental to some other form of crime (e.g., rape, drug addiction).

The subjects, therefore, may be considered as representing more than just casual robbers, but individuals who engaged in this form of criminal conduct on a purposive, rational and sustained basis over various periods of time.

Findings

Sutherland describes a number of significant features that emerge in the group life of professional thieves which he considers the binding rules of the mob. As such, these rules develop into a formal code of ethics subscribed to by the professional thief much like other codes of conduct among legitimate professional groups.[4]

A comparison of the type of organization that develops among professional robbers with the type of organization that develops among professional thieves reveals little similarity as the following discussion will make clear. Whereas the professional thief finds his organizational counterpart in the legitimate professions, the professional or career robber may be compared more accurately with the legitimate businessman in the organizational form of the partnership.

Sutherland's thief is quite explicit in his description of the norms that develop in the mob. A review of the rules of the mob should prove revealing in highlighting the differences between the type of structure that is characteristic of groups of professional thieves and that of groups of armed robbers:

1. Gains are equally shared. A percentage is given to outsiders who assist the mob.

In general, robbers share equally with their associates whatever is taken. However, there is no sharing with outsiders as they do not exist for the robber. If someone has helpful knowledge about sites to rob or assist in some way in the robbery even if only tangentially, from the robber's point of view, he is not an outsider, but a member of the group and receives his share of the gain. Once robbery is discussed by a group with any amount of seriousness all become full partners and all consider themselves equally

involved and have a stake in the success of the planned enterprise. Planning need not be extensive in order for this involvement to occur; there merely needs to be some discussion of robbery amongst a group that intends to carry it to completion.[5] Hence no one is ever considered an outsider to the group after preliminary discussions have taken place. The statement of one robber is illustrative:

(If) you compare notes with somebody, you are going to join them. In other words, my crime partner and I were talking to you and another fellow, and we were comparing notes, eventually the four of us are going to do something together, whether it be tonight, tomorrow night or the next night, regardless. By openly admitting to one another our situation, I think we find a binding point, where we, you say, I know a spot over there, let's go get it. And you say let's go get it, why, the four of you go instead of one or two.

2. Expenses of the mob come off the top.

The robber's expenses are minimal and are usually paid out of pocket by the individual concerned. Such outlays are in the nature of small business expenses and are managed quite informally from one robbery to the next. One respondent stated it simply:

I paid the gas and oil on the first job, the second time around somebody else got it. Usually it was just a couple of bucks and nobody expected anything back....

Large expenses, such as the purchase of an automobile or the purchase of weapons are usually paid on a share-and-share-alike basis. Each contributes his amount to the total. In some instances, expenses are taken off the top, but this is not by any means a regular procedure. There is nothing formal about any of these arrangements, rather like any other informal group undertaking where there are expenses, there is a tacit agreement that each member contributes his share.

3. All loans are repaid out of the first sum of stolen money.

---

[4] Sutherland, *The Professional Thief*, pp. 35–42, 215ff.

[5] For a fuller discussion of the process of commitment involved in becoming a professional robber see W. J. Einstadter, *Armed Robbery—A Career Study in Perspective*, unpublished doctoral dissertation (University of California, Berkeley, 1966).

A number of robbers who were asked about this provision seemed perplexed and had no knowledge regarding this type of arrangement. These loans refer to an organized mob that needs capital to carry out its illegal enterprises. This rarely occurs in the sense that there are financial backers for the robber. When large sums of monetary outlays are necessary that can not readily be managed by the group, other methods than seeking a backer are employed. A group that generally commits the more sophisticated variety of robbery—e.g., banks, large grocery chains—where such outlays sometimes become necessary, may commit a number of small preliminary minor robberies before venturing to tackle a more formidable victim. Often such a group may rob a few smaller establishments to fund a contemplated large robbery which may require some additional equipment. Frequently such items are stolen directly.

4. A fourth rule described by Sutherland is concerned with a number of general understandings about the mob's action when a member is arrested. Basically, the understanding is that the mob helps the apprehended member by sharing the expenses of court costs if he is arrested "on business." Furthermore, a share of the *take* is saved for him and money is regularly set aside for bail to be used by any member.

The reply of one informant when queried about this procedure is graphically illustrative and provides a good summary:

> Hell, no, the guy went into this with his eyes wide open, oh, sure, we'd feel sorry for the guy, but, hell, he'd be on his own. If he were arrested we'd split to save our own necks. He'd be expected to keep his mouth shut, but that can only last for a little while. Whatever dough there was would be split amongst the guys out; if we get caught we'd come to an understanding later, but if he ratted he'd have nothing coming.

Robbers give little thought to being arrested while actively engaging in robbery. That such occurrence is an eventuality is recognized, but is given little weight. Should an arrest be made, the arrestee expects no assistance from his partners. Conversely, the group expects the member arrested to remain silent but is realistic enough to realize that this cannot be a permanent situation; nevertheless, it may apply sanctions if the arrested member gives information too readily.[6] In view of the seriousness of the offense, robbers are rarely released on bail once arrested. When bail is set, it is usually a high amount which the arrested member has difficulty in obtaining. Were a fund established by a robbery group to meet this need it would have to be a considerable sum, something prohibitive for most groups of robbers. Both the nature of the robbery venture and the type of group that emerges preclude this kind of foresight.

Hence there is little evidence in the social organization of robbers of group cohesion during periods of stress in the manner described by Sutherland. The robber's organization is a more fluid arrangement taking into account existing conditions; it is not conceived by those involved as a permanent group but more or less a loose confederation of individuals joined together for a specific purpose on a short-term basis. Among certain types of robbers specific role relationships do develop; however, these always are assumed to be temporary by the robbery participants even though the association is of some duration. When this type of social organization exists no provision need be made for incapacitated members; each member considers himself on his own.

5. Members of the mob are to deal honestly with each other.

This rule generally applies to armed robber groups. As was pointed out under rule one, participants are expected to make even division of the stolen money, and are required to deal honestly in matters of robbery. But this expectation applies only to matters of the immediate present; hence robbers are not expected, for example, to reveal all their background or even be completely honest when they do. Most robbers anticipate that their partners will exaggerate about their

---

[6] An interesting parallel is found in military life. During war time, a soldier is expected to give only his name, rank, and serial number if captured. It is recognized that he might "break" due to "brainwashing" and torture but he is still considered a traitor by his side if he does and is sanctioned accordingly. As one informer put it, "He should do his own time and number."

Sanctions may be applied in prison to the informing robber in the form of ostracism or violence. But often a curious reversal of intentions occurs. Since prison authorities usually are aware of the informing robber's "enemies," those who intend harm are placed in the ironic position of having to protect the informer since they would receive the blame in case any injury befalls him.

past exploits as robbers, other criminal activities, prison experiences, dealings with women, etc., and openly tolerate a certain amount of these exaggerations when such information is supplied. Furthermore, robbers, as a rule, do not reveal too much about themselves to each other with the exception of current pressing problems, the stated reasons, which bring them into robbery. This lack of candor is respected. But there are "understandings" and cues which reveal much to the robber about his associates.

> And, well, I don't know it's just kind of a thing, you meet some guy and you say, I like him, and he likes you, and so you start horsing around, well, you don't know each other, really, you don't know anything about each other, but eventually, it comes out, you know. You let it slip you ask him about something—how do you like what you're doing—and he says—it's whole lot better than doing time. Then I knew, and I told him yeah, and you finally out on your backgrounds. So, we got to talking and talking about an easier way to make money.... He says 'I know a couple of guys, and we all got guns, and we can go out and hit a few places now, and then. If we don't hit it heavy, we won't get caught.' So, we started doing this stuff.

> ...You are not exactly hanging around in a place for a long period of time, which we were. We were there, oh hell, six out of the seven nights a week. And, quite naturally, you learn to know somebody by their conversation, at least outwardly, you know them. And eventually, the money is going to drain out then a suggestion is going to come up, provided you feel that the person you are talking to is of your same caliber, and evidently when I met him at this particular time I felt that I could trust him, and I think there was, at my suggestion, if I remember correctly, that he come in with me. And between the two of us, why, we did a series of robberies.

Unless the robbers are acquaintances of long standing or are related and aware of each other's backgrounds, these understandings play a significant part in the trust relationship that becomes established.

6. Members voluntarily leaving the mob may ask to be taken back in, but it would not be proper for the leader of the mob to request they return.

This is another rule which is not applicable to armed robbers; indeed, there is serious question as to leadership in the first place. Any member is privileged to leave the group any time. He may also "sit one out" if he feels a particular robbery will be too dangerous for him, although this is not a frequent practice. Leaving robbery voluntarily is a rare occurrence; when it does occur it is temporary and returning presents no problems. There are no particular rules of etiquette that govern robbery group conduct as the group is not a tightly knit organization with fixed personnel and standards of behavior. The needs of the moment dictate the method of operation; there are few subtleties or niceties among robbers, and in this respect also, a group of robbers bears little resemblance to the mob described by Sutherland's thief.[7]

7. Members of the mob are not held responsible for events which they cannot control.

This is the only rule that seems relevant; robbers as well as thieves do not appreciably blame each other too severely for certain blunders that are made.

> We planned to get around $30,000 to $40,000 or $80,000 out of this bank; as it turned out, this one who was spending the money, he's quite a nervous fellow, anyhow, he went into the vault, had the assistant manager go into the vault, and there was a big sack. It must have been as big as a mail sack, and he picked it up and said, "What's in this?" It was locked, and the guy said it was non-negotiable securities, so the kid let it down. Turned out it was $40,000.... Anyhow he went out and cleaned out two or three of the cages and he got $10,000 out of that but... he thought he had more... we found out we had missed $40,000 so we were kinda grumbling at him for overlooking it but we figured he didn't have any experience and he wouldn't know how much paper would weigh anyhow....

Here a loss of $40,000 was rationalized away as insufficient experience. At a later time this same individual again made a costly error and again he was excused:

> So that time we got $16,500 and $17,000... again we passed up $80,000, I think it was, I forget the reason why they missed it. But again it was the same guy who goofed it up....

The fates enter heavily into robbers' lives in general, and this is merely an instance of the com-

---

[7] This has been recognized for criminal relationships in general. "The social relationships of criminals are quite tenuous and much more likely to take the form of transient combination...." See Edwin M. Lemert, *Social Pathology* (New York: McGraw-Hill, 1951), p. 48.

mon tendency among robbers to use "fate" as a rationale of life. It's the "breaks" that count; you either have them or not. Fate is deemed to control the robber's destiny;[8] when the cards are right, when the dice are right, when the *setup* is perfect, nothing can go wrong but if luck is against you, "you haven't got a chance." It, therefore, becomes easy to excuse what would under ordinary circumstances be considered an unforgivable error. Also with this rationale the occasional violence that occurs may be explained away as an accidental twist of fate. The fate motif is probably more responsible for the group attitude of not holding members responsible for uncontrollable events than any other aspect in the robber's group life. This seeming reversion to magic on the part of the robber is difficult to explain. One would expect a lessening of this motif as the robber becomes more proficient, i.e., as he has learned to reduce the hazards and is more in control of the situation; however, such is not the case.[9] The fate motif is discernible in all levels of robbers' groups. It may be that robbery, no matter how well planned, in view of its direct personal interaction, always presents the possibility of uncontrollable hazards and hence uncertainty.

8. No member of a mob should cut in on another member. This is another etiquette rule which forbids any mob member from "cramping the style" of another. The exception being an emergency or an inexperienced member who has only been given a minor role to perform.

Robbers, when necessary, help each other out in the performance of a robbery in the event of an "emergency." The rule appears to refer to mobs of pickpockets or shoplifters, and only in a very general way would be applicable to a group of robbers.[10]

9. The last mob maxim refers to the mob member's responsibility to do everything possible to fix a case for any other member of the mob who may have been arrested as a result of mob activities.

This raises the entire question regarding the practice of "fixing" cases, bribes, etc., as it exists today and would go beyond the confines of this paper. It is quite clear that the *fix* as described by Sutherland with reference to thieves is not practiced by contemporary armed robbers.

Arrest Strategy

If arrested, the strategy is to obtain the best "deal" with the prosecutor on the basis of the amount of information and evidence known to him. The "fixer" as described in the *Professional Thief* is unknown to the informants. Members of robber troupes also express no feelings of obligation to help out a member arrested; the main concern is with maintaining their own individual anonymity.

The practice of obtaining the best "bargain" possible often requires the revelation of the crime partners' identities in exchange for a more favorable disposition; knowledge of the possibility of this occurrence creates considerable anxiety on the part of a group when one of its members is arrested. The result, therefore, is for all members to "split" and attempt to "ride it out" if possible, but it is a well-known fact among robbers that the arrest of one usually spells the end for all. Hence, under present circumstances, the last thing a robber would think about is to attempt a "fix" even were it possible, for not only would he reveal his identity and suffer the likelihood of arrest, but he would also defeat a possible bargaining position of his associates.

DISCUSSION

From the foregoing comparison it becomes obvious that the group of careerist robbers seems to bear only slight resemblance to the mob that Sutherland describes. How can one account for this difference? One obvious answer is simply that times have changed and so has the complexity of relationships in society. What was possible during the first quarter or more of this cen-

[8] See Walter B. Miller, "Lower Class Culture as a Generating Milieu of Gang Delinquency," *Journal of Social Issues* XIV (1958), pp. 5–19. Fate is discussed as one of the focal concerns of the lower class. [See p. 52 of this volume.]
[9] Primitive practices at least follow this pattern. Malinowski has noted in his study of Trobrianders that when they fished using the reliable method of poisoning and a rich catch was a certainty, magic was not practiced. On the other hand, when they fished in the open sea with its dangers, magical rituals were abundantly employed. See Robert K. Merton, *Social Theory and Social Structure*, 2d ed., rev. (New York: Free Press of Glencoe, 1957), p. 108.
[10] A recent study of department store shoplifting would indicate that this form of theft is no longer primarily a group phenomenon. See Mary Owen Cameron, *The Booster and the Snitch* (New York: Free Press of Glencoe, 1964), p. 58.

tury is no longer feasible under present circumstances. The entire scope and function of law enforcement has changed, making certain criminal styles obsolete. One need only mention the revolutionary developments in systems of identification of criminals, modern communication, transportation methods, and methods of scientific investigation to stress the point.

The mob as an organized form of criminal activity must be related to a particular point in historical experience, a point where it served a purpose—a point where it was functional. During the first few decades of this century the "mob style" was particularly adapted to the social conditions of the day; the "fix" was possible because personal relationships were simpler and more direct.[11] Criminals, as well as others, knew each other personally with the resultant development of congeniality and rules of behavioral etiquette which guided the criminal mob both in its relationship among its own members and with outsiders. With the increasing complexity of society, these relationships were no longer possible and the mob was due to change. To paraphrase Bell, as the style of society changed, so did, in lagging fashion, its style of crime.[12]

There is, however, another reason why the robber's group differs from the mob. The mob, in general, referred to the organization of professional theft, which Sutherland distinguishes from robbery on the basis of style. Whereas the thief relies chiefly on wits, front, and talking ability Sutherland declares, ". . . robbers, kidnappers and others who engage in the 'heavy rackets' are generally not regarded as professional thieves for they depend primarily on *manual dexterity or force*."[13] However, there are those robbers who "use their wits, 'front,' and talking ability, and these are regarded by the professional thieves as belonging to the profession."[14] The robber's group also reflects the peculiar

style of the robber; the elements of robbery require a different type of organization in order for the crime to be carried to completion. Furthermore, the robber's group reflects the life style of persons not concerned with the etiquette of relationships, nor the reciprocals inherent in group life, but chiefly concerned with accomplishing a specific goal—the rapid accumulation of money.

The armed robber's entire engagement in robbery differs from the professional thief's engagement in theft, even when the former possesses "wit, front, and talking ability." Both the quality and the nature of the commitment itself differ, with the robber being more compelled in his action in the sense of feeling restricted as to the alternative courses of action open to him.[15] He is in a "get-rich-quick enterprise" and as such needs to move quickly and strike swiftly when the opportunity presents itself. In his scheme of action, he simply does not have time for the amenities of the professional thief, nor can he appreciate the latter's moderate approach to profit.[16] The formal relationships of the mob are not functional for his needs; more adaptable to the style necessary for the accomplishment of his goal is the social organization represented by the partnership.[17] Much as the professional thief resembled other professionals, the careerist robber resembles the businessman who conducts his business through the tutelage of a partnership. The robber similarly works through a group of partners with whom he shares equally in what risks there are and invests his services to the total enterprise. As a partner he shares in the profits and losses of the operation. The partnership also provides opportunity for differentiation of various tasks necessary to carry out a robbery

---

[11] The fix still seems to be pervasive and widespread but in subtler form in relationship to organized crime. See Report by the President's Commission on Law Enforcement and Administration of Justice. "The Challenge of Crime in a Free Society 1967," Chapter 7 *passim*.

[12] Daniel Bell, "Crime as an American Way of Life," *Antioch Review* XIII (Summer, 1953), pp. 131–57.

[13] Sutherland, *Professional Thief*, p. 198 (emphasis supplied).

[14] *Ibid.*

---

[15] Einstadter, *Armed Robbery*, Chapter 12 *passim*.

[16] It is perhaps also imprecise to refer to the robber who engages in robbery on a persistent basis as professional in the sense that Sutherland refers to a thief as professional. More descriptive are the terms career robber or careerist. Others have found difficulty in applying Sutherland's professional criteria to criminal groups other than thieves. Cf. Edwin M. Lemert "The Behavior of the Systematic Check Forger," in *The Other Side*, Howard S. Becker, ed. (New York: Free Press of Glencoe, 1963), pp. 211–24.

[17] Webster defines partnership as "a relationship . . . involving close cooperation between parties having specified and joint rights and responsibilities (as in a common enterprise)." Robbers tend to refer to their associates as crime partners.

and to plan its strategy. Career robbery is conducted in and through partnerships; the lone systematic robber is rare.[18]

Armed career robbers then develop a form of social organization that is essentially dissimilar to the model originally proposed by Sutherland for professional thieves, which by extension has been applied to all professional criminal activities. A closer examination of career armed robbery will serve to further distinguish this form of deviant action from other criminal behavior systems.

Functional Differentiation and Group Structure in Career Robbery

From the beginning the strategy or engineering of a *job* is a group product and must be viewed in an interaction context. An individual may present a solid robbery plan to his associates which is eventually acted upon; however, there is always deliberation by the group. Thus, partnership consensus must be reached prior to the commission of any act of robbery.

Although there is little discernible evidence of distinctive leadership roles, previous experiences of members are given due recognition. Where leaders are recognizable, they become most apparent in adroit partnerships, in the less definitive form of what might more appropriately be titled *planning consultants*. The role behavior is one of guiding rather than directing and in this sense fully meets the role expectations of the members of the partnership. Some members may become more persuasive than others, but dicta from partners are frowned upon and do not con-

stitute the basis of action. When there is divergence of opinion, there is majority rule of sorts, but as has been implied, there is no enforcement of majority rule on dissident members; rather the partners make accommodations.

It may be argued that in terms of the explicit goals of the partnership these types of arrangements are functional since to force an unwilling or dissident member to join in a robbery would only endanger the whole group. The success of the partnership depends on cooperative effort. The group then is a partnership of equals, each with a voice; what leadership arises comes out of mutual recognition of the expertise of an individual member which serves the group's goals.

These deliberations are informally structured, vary in duration of time, and are likely to occur anywhere the potential participants happen to be congregated—an automobile, a bar, a motel room—throughout, it is a rational and deliberative, albeit at times haphazard process of decision making. Once the decision is reached that a particular robbery or series of robberies is to be performed, there does not appear to exist a specific pattern of planning the robbery encounter. The planning of a robbery may vary from a simple drive around a neighborhood to "case a joint" to a series of complex maneuvers; the strategy employed depends on the type of robbery and the sophistication of those involved.

Prior to any robbery, however, no matter what the level of potential complexity, assignments are made as to the role each partner is to play in the encounter. In this effort the strengths and weaknesses of various members may be assessed and conclusions reached as to the roles best fitted to each participant.[19] Again this decision is reached through group interaction; no single individual gives orders or assigns positions without group and individual consensus.

---

[18] Although robberies may be performed by a single person, careerists feel that a profitable robbery is rarely completed successfully alone. Groups have also been found to have greater probability of accuracy in solving problems, since groups of individuals have greater resources for ideas and capacity for dealing with error—hence the possibility for the robber to better plan his crimes. See generally D. C. Barnlund, "A Comparative Study of Individual, Majority and Group Judgment," *Journal of Abnormal and Social Psychology* LVIII (January, 1959), pp. 55–60; J. F. Dashiell, "Experimental Studies of the Influence of Social Situations on the Behavior of Individual Human Adults," *A Handbook of Social Psychology*, C. Murchinson, ed. (Worcester: Clark University Press, 1935), pp. 1097–1158; H. V. Perlmutter and Germaine de Montmollin, "Group Learning of Nonsense Syllables," *Journal of Abnormal and Social Psychology* XLVII (October, 1952), pp. 762–69; R. C. Ziller, "Group Size: A Determinant of the Quality and Stability of Group Decisions," *Sociometry* XX (June, 1957), pp. 165–73.

[19] Robber partnerships confirm previous findings about group structure. Thus, for example, the fact that individuals vary in the ability to assume a given role has been shown by T. R. Sarbin and D. S. Jones, "An Experimental Analysis of Role Behavior," *Journal of Abnormal and Social Psychology* LI (September, 1955), pp. 236–41, and that particular traits are needed to meet certain role expectations as shown by, E. F. Borgatta, "Role-Playing Specification, Personality, and Performance, *Sociometry* XXIV (September, 1961), pp. 218–33; R. Rapoport and I. Rosow, "An Approach to Family Relationships and Role Performance," *Human Relations* X (September, 1957), pp. 209–221.

The account of one respondent who preferred not to participate directly in holdups but was a competent driver describes the process of how one such decision was reached.

> For one reason, I wasn't going in, that was the first reason. I told them that, but they wanted me to go in. Then they got talking about that he (another partner) was going to drive the car because one of them couldn't see good, and the second one, he's so damn nervous he'd probably take the key out and put it in his pocket and then couldn't find the key. We didn't think he would keep his head cool enough to stay in the car listening to the radio calls come in, especially if one came in that said there was a robbery in progress. Then we didn't know how to trust the fourth guy that just came in; we didn't know whether he might run off and leave all of us, if all three of us went in. He probably wasn't going to do it, but they were considering it. Well, anyway, it all boiled down to that I should be driving the car because I don't get excited and I drive well.

At other times a more flexible arrangement is used with assignments shifting from robbery to robbery. The functional differentiation depends chiefly on what talents are available; however, the temperament of individual partners also may enter as a determinant.

> We switched around one time I went in with —at other times—went in. We sorta decided on the spur of the moment. All of us were pretty good, so it didn't matter. It sorta depended on how we felt at the time, you know, the mood we were in so we usually sorta decided beforehand; we agreed on who would go in . . .

A loose type of specialization results which is flexible and adaptable according to circumstances. In this way partnerships conform to fluctuations of members' moods and the possible eccentricities of various individuals. Individuality is never completely relinquished by the careerist. He cooperates but he is never subjugated. He fits himself into the allocated roles of the partnership to accomplish certain purposes but tries whenever possible to carry them out on his own terms. In so doing, he attempts to use the partnership as a vehicle to reach his goal—nothing more.

The Minimum Essentials—The Actor's Role

The successful completion of a robbery depends mainly on the coordination of various tasks that must be completed. Through coordination and specialization of roles of participants in the robbery, the robbery group not only assures more protection to itself but adds a measure of efficiency and shock in quickly overtaking the victim by a show of disciplined force. A well operating partnership need only have three men and successfully carry out profitable robberies. Sometimes the same results may be obtained by a dyad, but generally a group of three men appears to be the most tactically effective unit.[20]

The typical career robbery triad consists of two men who enter the establishment armed; the third remains outside in the vicinity in an automobile, is usually armed but need not be.[21] Of the two men who perform the actual robbery, one is considered the "backup." It is his function to watch any customers in the establishment, prevent any from leaving, and "cover" those that might enter while his partner gathers the cash. At times he assists also in gathering the *take* if there are no customers or other conditions that need his attention. The "wheel" or "wheelman" in addition to driving the get-away-car also acts as lookout or "pointman," and at times is given added responsibilities of a variety of sorts.

An example of a wheelman's role in a series of bank robberies is informative both of his role obligation and the rather sophisticated planning that may take place in some partnerships. Not all robberies committed by the careerist robber are this well planned and executed, but the interview excerpt describes the extent to which the systematic robber may go to assure his goal:

> I. So then you had the place cased and then did you commit the robbery?
> S. No. We decided against it for some reason. I think we might have kept refining our plans as we went along and what we had done was decided, well we found that there were a number of characteristics the bank had to have before it was acceptable into our situation; one, it had to have a nice getaway, so we could abandon one

---

[20] Hare has pointed out that "in general, when the size of the group decreases, the strength of the affectional ties between members increases, with the dyad allowing the possibilities for the greatest degree of intimacy," A. Paul Hare, "Interpersonal Relations in the Small Group," *Handbook of Modern Sociology*, Robert E. L. Faris, ed. (Chicago: Rand McNally, 1964), p. 252. When a dyad exists the partners as a rule are either close friends or are related.

[21] It has also been shown that where there is a need for fine coordination there is a tendency to restrict the size of the group. *Ibid.,* p. 253.

car if a police car or some citizen chased us; we didn't want to shoot anyone, you know, or shoot at them or be shot at, so we could leave this car and either jump over a fence or go through a culvert or through a walkway so no car could follow us and report it. Then we could go over and pick up another car and then take off. So not all banks would fit into this sort of category. . . . Anyhow, my job was to go up the telephone pole and cut the telephone wires so they couldn't call the cops. And then as soon as I cut the wires then these two walk in the bank and then I would go down the pole and get in the car. We had a police radio so we could tell if the cops got a signal, I could drive up to the bank and honk; otherwise I could get into the car and give them one minute exactly to go clean out the bank.

I. How did you decide on the one minute?

S. Well, we figured how long it would take, if everybody cooperated, and we decided that one minute would probably be safe. So anyway they went in. They had the stocking caps up under these men's hats, snap brim hats, and then they had masks that dropped down, I think one of them had a stocking cap that pulled over and the other one had a mask that just dropped down. So as soon as they walked in the door they just dropped it; customers walked in and noticed it; they just walked out; they didn't believe there was a bank robbery going on. So I sat there and watched all of that. I was just sitting there listening to the radio and watching my watch. So anyhow, as soon as one minute was up, I left the parking place, looking carefully to see that there were no cops, and I drove up to the bank and just as I did, the guy inside, one was holding at bay and the other was getting the money, he got nervous or something. Anyway, he gathered up all he could and ran out the door just at the very minute I got to the door, just as we had rehearsed it, and I had the doors open for him. They jumped in the car and off we went. And all the customers and people out on the sidewalk just going like this and I don't think anybody chased us, although later we heard somebody did. It was some three blocks back. So we got about $10,000 out of that. We pulled the car up near a school and went down a little ravine and jumped into another car, drove it to one of the fellow's house and drove it right into his garage, pulled the garage door down, went out the back door and went into his cottage and got in there and stayed in there listening to the police radio. . . .

Additional men may be added depending on the size of the robbery and its felt complexity; however, these men perform no different roles from the basic triad. They assist those engaged in the holdup, that is, they become extra personnel.

The "wheelman" does not have assistants but often has additional responsibilities such as planning the escape route, obtaining the getaway car, arranging lodging, and acting as lookout. There is general agreement among career robbers that the "wheel" has the greatest responsibility at the critical period of escape; as such, he is required to be the most "mature" of the group.

No matter how many robbers participate in a robbery and no matter how functionally differentiated the partnership might be, the element of surprise and momentary domination of the scene must be maximized if the robbery is to be successfully completed.

Robberies are foiled if either (1) the victim is not surprised, (2) the coordination of the partnership is poor, (3) the robbers do not completely dominate the scene. Violence is also likely to occur if any one or combinations of these conditions exist. The aim, therefore, is to so structure the situation that the victim is rendered helpless to resist and "cooperates" toward the successful completion of the crime. In the words of one robber, "It has to be a smooth operation or else someone is likely to get hurt." To accomplish this goal, robbers employ a number of tactics or styles with varying degrees of "smoothness" which reveal different levels of planning and proficiency depending in part on the type of partnership and in part on the situation.

Styles of Career Robbery

These robbery tactics may for purposes of discussion be divided into three categories and labeled according to style of approach.

1. *The Ambush.* This type of robbery is the least planned of all and depends almost entirely on the element of surprise. All participants literally attack an establishment guerrilla fashion and attempt to obtain whatever might be found in cash or other items of value. There is no sophistication in this style of robbery and it is considered the *lowest* form of robbery from the viewpoint of the careerist. There is almost randomness in the selection of the victim, with no thought as to what conditions might be present in the situation that may affect the outcome of the robbery. It is also the type of robbery where the chances of violence are high. As a rule it is a style employed by less systematic robbers.

2. *The Selective Raid.* In this form there is

a minimum of planning. Sites are tentatively selected and *cased* even though very briefly. Site conditions are analyzed to some degree before the robbery is attempted. There is a tentative plan of approach; however, the planning may be accomplished very casually and several robberies may be committed in rapid succession.

3. *The Planned Operation.* Robberies that fall into this category are well planned and well structured crimes where all aspects are carefully delineated in the group and each partner knows his part well. At times there may be rehearsals or "dry runs" so that all possible conditions are taken into account. Risks are held at a minimum.

It would be ideal, for purposes of analysis, if partnerships practiced one style during the life of the group. Such, however, is not the case. Each individual partnership practices different styles of robbery during its existence. Thus, for example, one partnership that is in the planning stages of a *planned operation* may commit a few *selective raids* to finance what is thought to be a more lucrative robbery. On the other hand, certain groups may practice only one style and become quite proficient in it. Generally, however, the *ambush* is a desperation measure for careerists and is resorted to only when an emergency occurs such as the threatened capture of the group where money for flight must be raised quickly.

Robbery Skills

This raises the issue of skills required to engage in robbery. Obviously the three robbery styles require different levels of planning ability and creative potential. A *planned operation* may be a highly sophisticated crime requiring unique creative capacities, whereas an *ambush* can be attempted by anyone. A number of skills, therefore, are necessary to plan the more resourceful types of robberies that are committed by the careerist. In order to engage in robberies other than the ambush, the robber must have a sense of organization, timing, ability to take into account unforeseen events, etc. But these are skills or capacities of planning which bring structure to the robbery; the robbery itself requires little skill or ability. The synthesizing of robbery requires talent; its commission does not. This is not the case with certain other professional crimes, the variety of which Sutherland speaks. Compare the pickpocket, who must learn intricate sets of muscular movements, learn to perfect the art of misdirection in order to become successful in his endeavor, or the booster who must learn techniques of concealment and misdirection to avoid detection as a shoplifter. The confidence man has to develop a high degree of front, wit, and talking ability, before he can carry out his swindle. All the robber needs, in the final analysis, is a revolver. This one attribute can make him the master of the situation. The skill involved in robbery pertains to the style employed and to the amount of planning of which the individual partnership is capable. These skills may be brought to robbery and need not necessarily be learned exclusively through interaction with other robbers.[22] They may, however, be modified and shaped to meet the conditions of the robbery situation. Noncriminal learning structures may provide the necessary qualifications which may easily be converted to robbery.

Military experience of a certain variety, for example, lends itself readily to robbery:

And I thought, well, with four of us—I can start running out squad training techniques—another of those I learned in the military and that possibly we could start ... doing some fairly large things—One thing I had sort of in mind—I thought of taking ... the golf prizes from the ... Lodge which usually involves a couple hundred thousand dollars—and—doing it around the point by water—and we had actually run an intelligence project on this ... My partner had made it a point to become acquainted with and questioned fairly thoroughly, if indirectly, a fellow that worked in the office there—the assistant to the accountant—and so we actually knew much of the scheduling around the handling of this money

---

[22] These findings are at variance with the "differential association tradition" which purports that criminal techniques are learned in association with other criminals. See Edwin H. Sutherland and Donald R. Cressey, *Principles of Criminology*, 5th edition rev. (New York: Lippincott, 1955), pp. 74–81. What is being maintained here is that the planning skills required in robbery are generic skills which are adaptable from a variety of noncriminal experiences and need not necessarily be learned only in association with other robbers. These capacities may be brought into the partnership from the outside. They may, however, be modified to meet specific requirements of robbery. See also Cressey's critique in Donald R. Cressey, *Other People's Money* (New York: The Free Press of Glencoe, 1953), and his review of the theory and criticism of literature in Donald R. Cressey, "Epidemiology and Individual Conduct: A Case from Criminology," *The Pacific Sociological Review* III (Fall, 1960), pp. 47–54.

and the operation of the Lodge and we were going to make our approach by water—and with four of us operating as a commando unit, it would have gone quite smoothly. I approached the thing as I would approach a military problem. I ran general intelligence rather than just the sort of thing that usually in the criminal profession is called 'casing.' I had hoped to train my men to the—disguise that didn't bear the earmarks of camouflage—whistles and so forth.

Business acumen may also be turned to robbery:

I planned it just like I've seen businesses operate and what I did in my own 'front' business. We checked out details just like anybody running a firm. I didn't want anybody getting hurt or getting too excited, so I checked to see whether anybody had heart trouble in the bank through channels I knew about, that are open to employers. . . .

These planning capacities may, of course, come from previous criminal experiences or indeed through association with robbers, but need not be limited to these sources.

The skills of robbery, therefore, center mainly around planning ability. The greater the organization aptitudes of the members of the partnership, the greater the number of *planned operations* in the career of the partnership. The greater the number of *planned operations*, the more successful the partnership becomes, the more likely the pattern will continue.

It is a consequence of planning ability being brought to robbery that relatively newly formed partnerships may adopt more sophisticated styles from the beginning and are thus able to prolong their careers because of their expertise. Furthermore during the initial period they may be unknown robbers, a characteristic which tends to lessen the probability of detection.[23] Thus one bank robber states:

It was really a well planned job and we knew exactly what to do. It was perfect. . . . Now I'm known. I've been mugged and printed. I wouldn't think of trying anything. Hell, every time somebody pulls something around here and even faintly resembles me, I better have a good alibi.

[23] This is also contrary to the professional thief whose professionalism depended on being accepted, tutored, and recognized by other thieves. To the careerist robber, planning ability combined with anonymity are important factors in a successful career. See Sutherland, *Professional Thief*, p. 207.

EXTERNAL RELATIONS OF BURGLARS
NEAL SHOVER

One of the contributions of American sociologists to the analysis of crime was the early recognition that certain types of criminal pursuits could, like legitimate occupations, be studied as structured and collective activity.[1] It was recognized that these structures, or *behavior systems,* commonly consist of distinctive argot, an ideology of defense and legitimation, esoteric knowledge, behavioral norms, and more or less stable relationships between the occupational practitioners and a host of others on whom they are dependent for their successful work performance. Sutherland[2] applied this sensitizing and organizing concept of the behavior system to theft, insightfully tracing the structure of *professional theft* and the crucial contingencies without which a career as a professional thief could not be realized. This analysis is intended as a continuation in the same tradition. It explicates some of the characteristics of the social relationships which enable one type of burglary offender, the "good burglar," to carry on his activities. The nature of the social relationships

Excerpted with permission of author and The Society for the Study of Social Problems, from "The Social Organization of Burglary," *Social Problems* 20 (1973), pp. 499–513.
[1] Edwin Sutherland, *The Professional Thief* (Chicago: University of Chicago Press, 1937); A. B. Hollingshead, "Behavior Systems as a Field for Research," *American Sociological Review* 4 (October, 1939), pp. 816–22; and Jerome Hall, *Theft, Law and Society*, rev. ed. (Indianapolis: Bobbs-Merrill, 1952).

[2] Sutherland, *The Professional Thief.*

between working ... burglars and quasi-legitimate members of the host society are sketched.

METHODS

Four different sources of materials were used for this study. First, I read 34 autobiographies of thieves—primarily, though not exclusively, burglars—in their entirety. In addition, 12 novels or journalistic accounts of crime and the activities of criminals were read.[3] Second, a total of 47 interviews were conducted with men incarcerated in the various branches of the Illinois State Penitentiary system. Third, on the basis of these interviews, a lengthy questionnaire was constructed and administered to an additional 88 inmates, in small groups of from three to 12 men at a time. And fourth, interviews were conducted with seven unincarcerated burglars or former burglars, one former fence, and one very peripheral associate of a gang of former bank burglars. All nine of these men were contacted and interviewed without the assistance or cooperation of law enforcement or correctional agencies. Table 1 contains limited demographic data on the three different samples. All materials were collected by the author personally.

The collection of data by prison interview and questionnaire proceeded in two steps. First, interviews were conducted with 25 inmates in various Illinois penal institutions; a topical guide was used to provide minimal structure for these interviews. (The same guide was used to abstract and classify material from the autobiographies.) These interviews each lasted approximately one hour. Following the completion of these initial interviews, the questionnaire was constructed, pretested, and revised. Questionnaire respondents all were new admissions to the Illinois State Penitentiary system for burglary or some related offense (e.g., possession of burglary tools) during the period of the study. Only those men were asked to fill out the questionnaire who were shown by routine testing to be reading at or above a seventh grade level. The questionnaire was usually administered during the first month in the institution, usually in groups of from three to 12 men at a time. Thirteen men declined to complete the questionnaire, in most cases because of suspicion of the author's motives, and in the remaining cases because of feelings of extreme naivete about burglary.

Prison interview respondents were purposively selected, primarily from new admissions to the various institutions. At all times in the selection of interview respondents, I sought to maximize differences in criminal sophistication for comparative purposes. Those respondents who were more criminally sophisticated were all selected by snowballing, after I had made an initial contact with one good burglar. Several of these men were at that time serving sentences for some offense other than burglary; however, each of them had at some time in his life been a skilled burglar. Interviews with 13 men were tape recorded and several of the men were interviewed two or more times. Participation by all respondents was completely voluntary. I repeatedly informed those who participated that "there is no way that you can either be helped or hurt by this."

The use of the questionnaire, autobiographies, and free-world interviews were intended to provide a crude triangulation of methods,[4] which

---

[3] E.g., Clyde B. Davis, *The Rebellion of Leo McGuire* (New York: Farrar and Rinehart, 1944). A copy of the list of sources is available upon request from the author.

[4] Norman K. Denzin, *The Research Act* (Chicago: Aldine, 1970).

TABLE 1. DEMOGRAPHIC CHARACTERISTICS OF THE SAMPLES

	Mean (X̄) Age	Race		N
		White	Black	
Prison interview sample	23.4	38	9	47
Prison questionnaire sample	24.6	71	16	87*
Free world interview sample	31.6	9	0	9
Total	24.6	118	25	143

* Does not include one case for which no records were available.

was considered especially important in view of the understandable controversy surrounding the use of captive samples.[5] It was recognized, however, that each of the varied methods and research settings contains its own often unique threats to validity. Through the use of a combination of methods and settings, an attempt was made to deal with these validity problems. A more extended discussion of these issues and the methodology can be found in an earlier report.[6]

FINDINGS

. . . By the external social organization of burglary, I refer to the relationships between burglars and those outside of their crews with whom they tend to maintain symbiotic social relationships. It is first necessary, however, to discuss the meaning of the concept *good burglar,* since the materials presented here are intended to apply to this type of offender.

The designation "good thief" or "good burglar" is one which is applied selectively by thieves themselves to those who (1) are technically competent, (2) have a reputation for personal integrity, (3) tend to specialize in burglary, and (4) have been at least relatively successful at crime; success in turn is determined by (1) how much money one has made stealing, and (2) how much time, if any, he has done. The good burglar, then, is the man who generally confines his stealing activities to burglary, has been relatively successful, has a reputation as "good people," and is technically competent. At times such a person would be referred to by the more generic designation as a good thief. But in either case the qualitative distinction is most important.[7]

Of the total number of respondents interviewed for this study, only ten men were considered to be good burglars. These determinations were made on the basis of peer evaluations and material elicited during the interview which indicated past success and sophistication in burglary. All of these men had, at some time, supported themselves solely by criminal activities, the shortest for one year and the longest for approximately 20 years—without incarceration. Of the total questionnaire sample (88), only 20 men were classified as good thieves. This was done on the basis of an arbitrary scoring system applied to (1) the largest sum of money ever received from a single score, and (2) the kind of techniques used to enter places and/or open safes. . . .[8]

External Social Organization

The most important of the social relationships which the good burglar maintains with persons outside his group are closely related to the problems he faces in this work. Collectively these social relationships are known as one's "connections"; the person who is "well connected" has been fortunate in establishing and maintaining a particularly profitable set of such relationships. Systematic burglars face several problems in their work; and their connections are particularly important in helping them to cope with these problems.

First, the good burglar must know before burglarizing a place that it would be worth his while to do so. He wants, above all, to avoid unnecessary exposure to the "bitch of chance";[9] so he tries, if possible, to assure himself in advance that a score will be rewarding. Second, if he steals a quantity of merchandise—or anything else that he cannot sell directly—he must have a safe outlet for it; he must be able to sell it without risk to himself of detection. And third, in the event of his arrest, he must be able to so thwart the criminal justice system, so that he either goes free or else receives an extremely

[5] Cf. Ned Polsky, *Hustlers, Beats and Others* (Chicago: Aldine, 1967); and Edwin Lemert, "The Behavior of the Systematic Check Forger," *Social Problems* 6 (Fall, 1958), pp. 141–49.

[6] Neal Shover, "Burglary as an Occupation" (Ph.D. dissertation, University of Illinois, Urbana, 1971).

[7] Cf. James (Big Jim) Morton, (with D. Wittels), "I Was King of the Thieves," *Saturday Evening Post* (August 2, 12, and 19, 1950), pp. 17–19, 78–81; 28, 92, 94–96; 30, 126, 130–32. An extended discussion of how the social organization of contemporary systematic burglars compares to the behavior system of professional theft as sketched by Sutherland is beyond the scope and space limitations of this paper.

[8] In order to be considered a good burglar a respondent must have (1) received $4,000 or more on his largest score, and either (2) opened a safe at some time by drilling or burning, or (3) entered a place at some time by cutting a hole in the roof or wall. For a more extended discussion of the scoring system used to categorize the sample, see Shover, "Burglary as an Occupation."

[9] Malcolm Braly, *On the Yard* (Boston: Little, Brown, 1967), p. 233.

light sentence for his crime(s). The first of these problems, the informational one, is handled by connections with "tipsters"; the second problem, the merchandising problem, is handled by relationships with the "fence"; the third is handled by attorneys, bondsmen, and occasionally, the "fix."[10]

The Tipster

A tipster (also known as a "spotter" or "finger-man") is a person who conveys information to a burglar about some premises or its occupants which is intended to aid in burglarizing those premises. Among even moderately successful burglars, tipsters represent an important connection and source of information.

> Your professional burglars depend on information. Any time you read about a darn good burglary, they didn't just happen to be walking along the street and say, Here's a good looking house, let's go in there. They depend upon information from strictly legitimate fellas.[11]

Tipsters are of several types. Many of them (perhaps the majority) are fences who convey tips to thieves as a way of controlling their inventory. Another type is the ex-thief who holds legitimate employment but still maintains friendships with his old associates. A third type is the active thief who learns about some potentially lucrative score but cannot make it himself because the finger of suspicion would immediately be pointed at him. And finally, another type of tipster is what Hapgood[12] referred to as the "sure thing grafter." This is a person, usually an older thief, who has become extremely selective in his scores. Whenever he hears about a score but does not want to make it himself, he may pass on the tip to some other thief of his acquaintance.

Tipsters of all four types are aware of the value of good information to the burglar; and should they ever receive such information, they are ready to pass it along to someone who can use it. Besides receiving tips from such individuals, the good burglar will, however, occasionally receive information from persons who are not so well informed on burglary and the role of the tipster. This may involve purchasing information from a person who is known to have it; while at other times it may involve the utilization of the knowledge of a personal friend —who may be employed on the premises or may have learned about it some other way.

> In all walks of life you've got people who are morally dishonest. They won't go and steal something themselves. But they'll buy something stolen if they get the right price and they'll give you a little information too. As long as they don't get hurt. Those people are usually legitimate businessmen. They're in a position to give you a lot of information that you couldn't get otherwise. About the protection of different places. About the assets of different places. And the different security measures of different business houses.[13]

Or the burglar may take a more active part in the search for information.

> This particular place was here in town. I knew a girl that knew a girl that worked there. So I approached this girl and said "Hey I'd like some information about this place. Why don't you ask her and see what she says 'cause I'll pay her for it?" ... So this girl came back and said, "Yeah, the 15th and 31st there's money there 'cause they cash company payroll checks..." Then I sent back for some specific information, what kind of safe it was and how the alarm was tied in... We got the place and then I gave this other girl $500 and I never heard anymore about it (Free world interview, March 30, 1971).

Having briefly considered the activities of the tipster, we might now inquire as to just who he is; what kinds of legitimate occupational roles do tipsters occupy? It must be emphasized at the outset that tipsters are not confined to any particular social strata. They are found at all levels of the social structure. As one thief has remarked: "There are some amazing people

---

[10] In many cities gamblers and loan-sharks are also important sources of support for working thieves. Because of their contacts in diverse social circles they are often instrumental in the integration of criminal networks, and in the integration of criminals with quasi-legitimate business and professional men.

[11] John Bartlow Martin, *My Life In Crime* (New York: Signet Books, 1953), p. 68.

[12] Hutchins Hapgood, *Autobiography of a Thief* (New York: Fox, Duffield, 1903), p. 262.

---

[13] Martin, *My Life in Crime*, p. 65.

who come to you with information—people you just wouldn't believe could do such things."[14]

The following specific examples of the legitimate occupations of tipsters are mentioned in the autobiographical literature: night watchman,[15] window cleaner,[16] prostitute,[17] attorney,[18] coal deliveryman,[19] catering service employee,[20] jeweler, gambler, detective, and used car dealer.[21] In addition, the questionnaire sample was asked if they had "ever received a tip on a place to burglarize." Of the total sample of 88 men, 61 percent replied in the affirmative. These men were then asked to indicate the legitimate occupation of one such person. Responses were given by 26 men, as shown in Table 2. The data presented in this table should not be interpreted as a representative picture of the larger population of tipsters. It is presented here only as a means of emphasizing the diversity of backgrounds of tipsters.

TABLE 2. LEGITIMATE OCCUPATIONS REPORTED FOR 26 TIPSTERS

Occupation	N
Tavern owner or bartender	7
Owner or employee of victimized place	5
Repairman or deliveryman	3
Beautician	2
Businessman (unspecified)	2
Other (e.g., police officer, janitor, shipping clerk)	7
Total	26

There is reason to believe that the success of a burglar is directly related to the size of the geographical area over which he maintains connections such as relationships with tipsters (and fences). Some men scarcely know anyone outside of their own city, while others can count on receiving information and assistance from persons in widely separated parts of the United States—or even nearby countries such as Canada and Mexico. The following is a typical account of how these far flung connections are established:

Q: How did you get connected as well as you were?
A: Well, first I was thrown in jail with a man who was pretty well respected throughout the country. I made three or four trips across the country with him, meeting friends of his. And then it just more or less snowballed. It developed that a person in one city [would] say. "If you're going to Miami stop and see so-and-so, tell him I sent you. [There] may be something laying around you can pick up" ... (Free World interview, May 27, 1971).

The value of connections such as these can be appreciated.

Q: You've seen a lot of men, then, who never really amounted to anything stealing. Why was it that they never progressed or became more proficient?
A: Well, one reason is lack of intelligence. [Others are] a lack of connections, a lack of integrity—nobody would trust them—and possibly just no ambition.
Q: You mentioned connections. Do you think they're important.
A: Highly important—well, it depends. Some people are born, raised, steal, and die in the same town. They never get out of the state. They might get out of the city to go to the county jail or penitentiary, then back home. Every policeman in the city knows who they are after they've fallen a couple of times on petty stuff. ... They don't travel far and fast enough.
Q: In what way were connections important to you?
A: They're what I just said in an indirect manner. Because if you're far enough away and fast enough away—through connections—then the local heat don't even bother you. If somebody robbed a safe for $50,000 on westhill today, who would get the blame for it? Where would they start sweeping? All the known safecrackers in this area. Certainly no farther away than Toledo. But suppose someone flew in here from Los Angeles and flew out. He's just about as safe as he can be. Because nobody knows he was here, he don't know anybody in the town except the man who sent for him [tipster]. So he does his little piece of work and goes. The cops are running around picking up everybody in town. But they're not

[14] Peter Crookston, *Villain* (London: Jonathan Cape, 1967), p. 127.
[15] Jean Genet, *The Thief's Journal*, trans. by Bernard Frechtman, (New York: Grove Press, 1964), p. 58.
[16] Sir Leo Page, *The Young Lag* (London: Faber and Faber, n.d.), pp. 76–77.
[17] Brian Wilson, *Nor Iron Bars a Cage* (London: William Kimber and Company, 1964), p. 57.
[18] Jack Black, *You Can't Win* (New York: A. L. Burt, 1926), p. 141; Crookston, *Villain*, p. 128; and Bruce Jackson, *A Thief's Primer* (New York: Macmillan, 1969), pp. 121–22.
[19] Martin, *My Life in Crime*, p. 65.
[20] Malcolm X (with the assistance of Alex Haley), *The Autobiography of Malcolm X* (New York: Grove Press, 1964), p. 140.
[21] Robert Earl Barnes, *Are You Safe from Burglars?* (Garden City, New York: Doubleday, 1971), pp. 51–68.

bothering him. You couldn't do that without connections (Free World interview, June 9, 1971).

The Fence

A fence is a person who buys stolen merchandise, or some other type of commodities (e.g., a coin collection), generally for purposes of resale, which he knows or strongly suspects are stolen. As in the case of tipsters, fences are stratified such that some are better able than others to dispose of a more diversified line of products, a larger quantity of products, and to handle more frequent purchases of products. Additionally, fences can be ordered hierarchically on the basis of how deeply and heavily involved they are in the purchase of stolen goods.[22] The lowest level of fence would be the "square john," who purchases an occasional item from a thief for his own use; the highest level fence would be the person who is able to dispose of nearly any type and quantity of merchandise on the shortest of notices. If it were not for the existence of fences, thieves would have great difficulty disposing of the merchandise they steal. Indeed, systematic theft would be a quite different sort of enterprise without them.

Fences, as already suggested, are one of the most common sources of tips for good burglars. The reason for this is related to the fence's need to exercise some control over the nature and quantity of his inventory. "Giving up scores" (tips) to burglars is one tested and proven technique for doing so. Evidence indicates that this is a very common practice on the part of fences.[23] In fact, it is this practice which seems to be largely responsible for the fence's having a ready buyer for his products before the thief even "takes off" the score. Giving up scores works, then, to the advantage of both the burglar and the fence. The latter must be seen as occupying a dual role in the behavior system of theft; he purchases stolen goods and simultaneously gathers information about future scores to which the good burglar can be tipped off. By searching out the kinds of merchandise he wants, and then giving the score to burglars, he is able to control his inventory.

But leaving aside the fence's role as a buyer of stolen merchandise, we find that sometimes their relationship with burglars is considerably more complex. Frequently, for example, the fence will be in a position to provide the burglar with several social services.[24] For example:

> I had . . . this one fence I was doing a lot of business with and he was giving me scores, too. . . . He wasn't a juice man [loan shark] but if you needed $500 and you did a lot of business with him, if you sold to him regularly, there was no problem. . . . If you had any problem and you needed money quick, say to go out of town to look at something, or if you got sort of short, he could come up with a G-note (Prison interview, March 13, 1970).

Moreover, because of their business contacts, fences occasionally learn about legitimate businessmen or business employees who have gotten themselves into some potentially embarrassing problem. For many of them, this is the kind of problem which could be solved by a contracted "burglary."[25] The fence can put the businessman in touch with a burglar; and the two of them can reach an agreement which works to the benefit of each. Still another service which the fence can provide for the burglar is the introduction of solitary burglars to established crews or gangs, thus helping to link together disparate elements in the thief category.

With few exceptions fences maintain some sort of role in the legitimate business world. Most of them do appear, in fact, to be businessmen of one kind or another. According to burglars, there are primarily three reasons for this. First, it is usually only the businessman who has on hand at any given time the ready cash required in dealings with thieves. Second, businessmen can utilize the contacts and knowledge acquired in their legitimate business activities to evaluate and dispose of illicit merchandise.[26] And third, the fence can use his legitimate business transactions to mask his illicit dealings, thereby making it more difficult for law enforcement officials to build a case against him.[27]

---

[22] Cf. Hall, *Theft, Law, and Society*, pp. 155–64, 218–19.
[23] Malcolm X, *Autobiography of Malcom X*, p. 144.

[24] Martin, *My Life in Crime*, pp. 98–99.
[25] Cf. Crookston, *Villain*, pp. 143–44.
[26] Cf. Hall, *Theft, Law, and Society*, pp. 156–57.
[27] Cf. Robert M. Yoder, "The Best Friend a Thief Ever Had," *Saturday Evening Post* 227 (December 25, 1954), pp. 18–19, 72–73.

Again, the members of the prison questionnaire sample were asked to indicate the legitimate occupations of "two persons you have personally known who bought stolen merchandise." A total of 61 replies were received and are listed in Table 3. There is strong support here for the assertion that most fences are persons who are engaged in some kind of legitimate business. As in the case of Table 2, which listed the occupations of tipsters, these data are not presented

TABLE 3. LEGITIMATE OCCUPATIONS REPORTED FOR 61 FENCES

Occupation		Frequency
Tavern owner or bartender		14
Store owner or business owner (unspecified)		9
Other business owner		14
service station	4	
restaurant	3	
automobile dealer	3	
pawn shop	2	
barbershop	2	
Policeman		3
Insurance broker		2
Automobile mechanic		2
Television repairman		2
Other (e.g., alderman, jewelry salesman, auctioneer)		15
Total		61

as representative of the total population of fences, rather they are presented only to give some idea of the types of legitimate occupations found among fences. Actually we would probably be justified in assuming that the data in Table 3 are representative of the smaller scale, and less successful, fences.

Bondsmen and Attorneys

Bondsmen and attorneys occupy positions in legitimate society which carry with them the socially sanctioned approval to associate, at least to some extent, with persons who are known to be criminals. That some of them are corrupted in the process is common knowledge;[28]

of much more fundamental consequence, however, for the stability and perpetuation of the activities of professional criminals—and this includes the good burglar—are the routinized working relationships and understandings which have emerged out of this socially sanctioned link between the underworld and quasi-representatives of the criminal justice system.

For both the attorney and the bondsman there are two extremely important consequences of prolonged contact with members of the underworld. The first of these is a knowledge of the differences in personal integrity which exist among some of the criminal offenders with whom they have contact. The second is a recognition that there are constraints which operate so as to reduce the risks which are run by anyone, who in doing business with thieves, crosses the line of unethical or illegal behavior. Both the attorney and the bondsman learn rather quickly that some members of the underworld are more trustworthy than others. One result of this is recognition that they need not fear the consequences of unethical or illegal transactions so long as they are selective in the types of clients with whom they have potentially embarrassing dealings. Moreover, they learn that members of the underworld usually cannot divulge their guilty knowledge anyway because they themselves would stand to lose much by doing so. They would be sufficiently stigmatized by such disclosures as to make it difficult to acquire competent legal counsel and the services of bondsmen on any subsequent criminal charges. This sets the stage for the emergence and flowering of a number of quasi-ethical practices and working relationships.

It must be noted that these practices are further stimulated, and possibly even generated, by certain characteristics of the problems faced by criminal lawyers and bondsmen generally in their work. The former, for example, unlike his corporate counterpart, routinely deals with clients who have little ready cash with which to compensate him for his services.

Now a criminal lawyer has to give credit, and the main reason for this is that burglars and armed robbers, if they had any money, they wouldn't be out stealing, they'd be partying. It's as simple as that. If they have money, they're partying, and when they're broke, they start to stealing again.

[28] Ronald Goldfarb, *Ransom* (New York: Harper and Row, 1965).

If they get caught while they're stealing, they're broke.[29]

One result of this is likely to be the attempt by his clients to obtain his services by offering other types of consideration.[30] Among these other kinds of consideration are such things as the sexual favors of wives or girl-friends, and property, both real and personal, some of which is almost certainly stolen. The good thief's ability to manipulate the criminal justice system cannot be comprehended unless it is recognized that he differs greatly from the petty thief and first time offender in his knowledge of the workings of the system. Unlike them, he has had a great deal of contact with the various actors which comprise it.

When the good burglar is arrested—as he frequently is—he can count upon receiving the services of both a bondsman and an attorney, even if he has virtually no ready cash. In lieu of a cash down payment the thief will be able to gain his release from confinement, and also preliminary legal representation, on the basis of his reputation and a promise to deliver the needed cash at a later date. He will then search for one or more suitable burglaries (or some other type of crime) which holds out the promise of a quick and substantial reward—so that he can pay his attorney and bondsman. On occasion he will resort to high interest loan sharks ("juice loans") in order to quickly acquire the sums of cash which his attorney and bondsman demand for their services. This period of time when the thief is trying to acquire the cash which he so desperately needs is a particularly stressful one for him. Often he will resort to high risk scores which he would under normal circumstances have passed up. One consequence of this high risk stealing is likely to be another arrest, sometimes in a distant jurisdiction, thus only intensifying his problems.

The principal strategy which the good thief's attorneys use appears to be delay, in the hope that some kind of unforeseen contingency will arise which permits him to gain his client's release or, failing that, to strike a particularly

favorable bargain. The fix, which once was relatively common in many American jurisdictions,[31] has become a much less predictable and available option for the good thief.[32] Admittedly, however, this is an area in which there has never been any thorough research. Nevertheless, if it is true that the fix has become less available for the good thief—as some have contended[33]—this could account in part for the alleged decline in the ethical standards of thieves in their dealings with one another;[34] in a situation in which the probability of serving some time in prison has increased, it would be expected that the willingness of thieves to "cooperate" would similarly increase. And this could lead to a number of working relationships between thieves and the police.[35] This also is an area in which more empirical research is needed.

In addition to what has already been noted about the relationships between good burglars and bondsmen and attorneys, other matters should be briefly mentioned. The latter have been known on occasion to provide tips to burglars on places to burglarize. In addition, some of them are alleged occasionally to purchase stolen property from burglars. Finally, in those unusual cases in which the fix can be arranged, attorneys, of course, act as the go-between in working out the details.

CONCLUSION

It should be clear on the basis of what has been said here that an understanding of the activities of the systematic burglar must take into account the social matrix in which he carries on his work, indeed on which he is dependent. . . .

---

[29] Jackson, A Thief's Primer, p. 136.
[30] Jerome Carlin, Lawyer's Ethics (New York: Russell Sage Foundation, 1966).
[31] Cf. Thomas Byrnes, Professional Criminals of America (New York: Chelsea House, 1969 [originally published in 1886]).
[32] Space precludes a discussion of the fix as it exists today; however, there is no doubt that the fix is still used in criminal cases. But there is real doubt about how often it is available to the burglar. My own views on the contemporary availability of the fix are quite similar to those expressed by Gould, et al. and Jackson. See LeRoy Gould, Egon Bittner, Sol Chaneles, Sheldon Messinger, Kriss Novak, and Fred Powledge, Crime As a Profession (Washington, D.C.: U.S. Department of Justice, Office of Law Enforcement Assistance, 1968); and Jacksin, A Thief's Primer.
[33] Gould, et al., Crime As a Profession.
[34] Ibid.
[35] William Chambliss and Robert B. Seidman, Law, Order, and Power (Reading, Mass.: Addison-Wesley, 1971), pp. 486–88.

THE NEW CRIMINAL: A VIEW OF THE CONTEMPORARY OFFENDER

JOHN IRWIN AND LEWIS YABLONSKY

This paper will attempt to delineate the "basic character" of the new criminal, in contrast with the basic criminal type of the past. These conclusions about the new criminal are not based on any special study but upon the author's close association with various offenders and the structure of the crime problem over the past ten years. The development of the theme of the new addict is taken from perceptions and studies of New York violent gangs, ex-addicts, and ex-criminals currently living in an anticriminal society at Synanon House (Santa Monica, California).[1] Incorporated is one author's experience in running group psychotherapy sessions with offenders in custody in various institutions over the past ten years. Much valuable material was collected by John Irwin directly in over fifty depth interviews with various "old" and "new" criminals in and out of prison.

On the basis of varied evidence we would contend that the basic personality of the majority of criminals has shifted from the well-trained, resourceful, "ethical" offender of the past to a new, unskilled and reckless deviant type. Here reference is made to an overall shift of the basic personality and behavior of the modern criminal. Old criminal types are still around, however, they represent a dying breed.

The new criminal's crimes tend to be more violent and "senseless." He lacks the skill in his profession that older criminals had. He is more apt to be involved with "kicks" or "thrills" and emotional gratification, and less with the material profit of his crimes. His training as a "good criminal" is sketchy and ill-defined, unlike the "breaking-in" process of the criminal of the past. Not all criminals of today fit this new mold; however, the pendulum has swung in this direction. It is important to diagnose correctly the modal quality of the problem which we attempt

to correct. In the treatment of social problems, there is often a cultural lag between correct diagnosis of the problem and the development of treatment approach. By the time correct treatment is constructed it is often no longer appropriate to the problem at hand—since it has shifted. We would contend this is true of the current crime problem. This fact accentuates the need to speculate on the gross qualities of our social problems, in this case, the criminal.

The old criminal codes of "honor among thieves," "thou shalt not squeal," and standing up for one's "crime partner" are fast becoming criminal slogans of the past. The new criminal is more apt to turn in his partners, cheat on them and make technical errors in his crimes. He is also younger and more apt to be some type of addict (e.g., in California over 40 percent of the prison population has had some type of narcotics experience). The dimensions of the problem to be described are more hypothetical than hard research results; yet they seem to be confirmed by considerable evidence.

THE "NEW" AND "OLD" CRIMINAL[2]

Sutherland's conception of the criminal remains as our current sociological model of the offender. This paper contends that, although the criminal type described by Sutherland still exists in some measure, in terms of numbers and character the old criminal is decreasing and is being increasingly replaced by a new breed of sociopathic offenders.

Sutherland's classic theory of "differential association," grossly oversimplified, states that criminals learn to become criminal from association with other offenders. They are trained in-

---

Reprinted with permission of author and the Institute for the Study and Treatment of Delinquency, from *British Journal of Criminology* 5 (April, 1965), pp. 183–90.
[1] See Lewis Yablonsky, *The Tunnel Back: Synanon* (New York: The Macmillan Co., 1965), p. 403.

[2] "New" and "old" refer to the basic mode of behavior rather than age. Although most "new criminals" are young—and "old criminals" old—this reference is to style of criminal pattern. Offenders use the terms "old school" and "new school" with reference to this phenomenon. In prison our "new criminal" is often referred to as a "bonnarue" offender.

to criminal patterns at an early age in a school of criminal *modus operandi,* which specifies certain criminal values and behavior patterns. Sutherland[3] cites the "professional thief" as a primary case example.

> "Professional thieves make a regular business of theft. They use techniques which have been developed over a period of centuries and transmitted to them through traditions and personal association. They have codes of behavior, *esprit de corps,* and consensus. They have a high status among other thieves and in the political and criminal underworld in general. They have differential association in the sense that they associate with each other and not, on the same basis, with outsiders, and also in the sense that they select their colleagues.
>
> "Because of this differential association they develop a common language or argot which is relatively unknown to persons not in the profession, and they have organization. A thief is a professional when he has these six characteristics: regular work at theft, technical skill, consensus, status, differential association, and organization.
>
> "Professional thieves have their group ways of behavior for the principal situations which confront them in their criminal activities. Consequently professional theft is a behavior system and a sociological entity."

This modal image of the criminal characterizes him as a resourceful, well-trained and effective felon—a member of a profession (albeit illegal) with certain ethics and values which dictate his conduct. In criminal jargon, the "professional thief" had "class" or "character." He would not "give his buddies up" and even certain victims were proscribed. Assault and violence were used as means to an end, not as ends in themselves.

> "When I was 16 or 17 I used to hang around a pool hall in our neighborhood a lot. I got so I could shoot pool pretty good and once in a while I would make a couple of bucks. But there were older guys there who were really doing good. They had 'good reputations' in the neighborhood and they always had money, cars and broads. Me and some kids my age were doing a lot of petty stealing at this time, cars and things from cars, but we didn't know how to make any real money. What we wanted to do is get in with the older guys so we could learn something and

make some money. One day, I remember, I had just got out of jail for some petty beef and one of the older thieves, a guy that was supposed to be one of the slickest safe men then, come over to me and talked to me for a while. This made me feel pretty good. Later one of his friends asked me if I wanted to help him carry a safe out of some office. We worked half a night on that safe and never did get it out of the place. But from then on I was in with the older bunch. Every once in a while one of them would get me to do some little job for him, like standing point (look out) or driving a car or something like that, and once in a while when they had snatched a safe, I would get to help them open it. I was learning pretty fast.

> "By the time I was 19 or 20, me and a couple of my buddies had real solid names with the older thieves. We were beating a lot of places on our own and we handled ourselves pretty well. But we were still willing to learn more. We used to sit around some coffee shop half the night or ride around in a car listening to a couple of the old hoodlums cut up different scores. We would talk about different scores other guys had pulled or scores we had pulled, and we would also talk about how you were supposed to act in other situations; how to spend your money, how to act when you got arrested. We discussed different trials we knew about, we even talked about San Quentin and Folsom and prisons in other states, because usually the older thieves had done time before. We talked about how much time each beef carried, how much time the parole board would give you for each beef. I guess we talked about everything that had anything to do with stealing. Of course we didn't talk about it all the time. Lots of the time we just shot the bull like anyone else. But by the time I was 21 I had a pretty good education in crime."

This well-trained type of offender is in sharp contrast with a young modern violent gang offender who commented as follows after being involved in a brutal homicide:

> "Momentarily, I started thinking about it inside; I have my mind made up I'm not going to be in no gang. Then I go on inside. Something comes up, then here all my friends coming to me. Like I said before, I'm intelligent and so forth. They be coming to me—then they talk to me about what they gonna do. Like, 'Man, we'll go out here and kill this cat.' I say, 'Yeah.' They kept on talkin'. I said, 'Man, I just gotta go with you.' Myself, I don't want to go, but when they start talkin' about what they gonna do, I say, 'So, he isn't gonna take over my rep. I ain't gonna let him be known more than me.' And I go ahead, just for selfishness . . ."

---

[3] E. Sutherland, *Principles of Criminology* (New York: Lippincott, 1947).

This type of offender at the moment is indeterminable. He is at the time, and is apt to remain, a new criminal. However, since he is young and not formed, he might become a more skilled offender with proper criminal training. However, as will be pointed out, since this type of offender generally grows up in a disorganized slum which contains few well-developed old criminal role-models, he is more apt to continue as a here-and-now new criminal.[4]

The described senseless "other-directed" violence of the larger proportion of modern offenders is perpetrated for ego-status—for "kicks" or "thrills." The "kicks" involve and produce a type of emotional euphoria which, the new criminal maintains, "makes me feel good." He does it for "selfishness." The goals of the crime are self-oriented in a primary fashion with material gain as a very secondary consideration. The old criminal could never be induced to place himself in jeopardy for this type of senseless offense. He used violence as an instrument for material gain, rather than for an emotional charge.

If the tight, cohesive criminal gang involved in burglary and robbery represented the "professional" model criminal behavior patterns of the past,[5] the modern violent gang in many respects represents the prototype structure for the incipient new criminal.[6] This is not to say that criminal gangs do not exist today or that violent gangs were not active in the past; but it is to say that the dominant emphasis has shifted to the wilder criminal and hence to the wilder gang organization.

These violent gang structures as a modern criminal group prototype are characterized more specifically by many or all of the following factors: (1) there are no evidences of prior contact or interaction between the assailant(s) and his (their) victim; (2) the act occurs in an unpremeditated, generally spontaneous and impulsive manner; (3) in some cases (particularly, for example, in violent gang assault) there is a degree of prior build-up to the act; however, the final consequence (often homicide) is not really anticipated; (4) the violent assailant or collectivity has indicated by prior behavior or personality factors for some period of time a potentiality for the commission of violence; (5) the postrationale expressed by the offender(s) for the violent behavior is usually without regret or inappropriate to the act which has been committed. The "old criminals'" rationales and motives in their gangs were at the opposite pole.

Refocusing on the individual offender, the pendulum of criminal prototype or "basic personality type" has swung towards the "new criminal." In an ideal-type fashion he may be classified as follows. He has a persistent pattern of deviant behavior characterized by an almost total disregard for the rights and feelings of others. A listing of overt personality and behavior traits of this brand of sociopath would include most, if not all, of the following factors: (a) limited social conscience; (b) egocentrism dominating most interaction, "instrumental manipulation" of others for self-advantage (rather than affective relating); (c) inability to forgo immediate pleasure for future goals; (d) a habit of pathological lying to achieve personal advantage (according to Hervey Cleckley in *The Mask of Sanity*, the sociopath's feelings and emotions are "word deep"); and (e) persistent violent physical and emotional outbursts when blocked from achieving momentary goals.

THE "INNER-DIRECTED" (OLD CRIMINAL) AND THE "OTHER-DIRECTED" (NEW CRIMINAL)

Taking a leaf from Riesman's *Lonely Crowd*,[7] another observed characteristic of the new criminal basic personality involves a shift from "inner-direction" to "other-direction." With this reference in mind we would speculate that the change in the basic personality which has taken place in the middle-class person in the United States (as described by Riesman) may be equat-

[4] Richard Cloward and Lloyd Ohlin, *Delinquency and Opportunity* (New York: The Free Press, 1959), pp. 174–75.
[5] See especially Shaw and McKay's writing on Delinquency in Chicago in the 1930s.
[6] Lewis Yablonsky, *The Violent Gang* (New York: The Macmillan Co., 1962). [See Yablonsky's "The Delinquent Gang as a Near-Group, pp. 64–71 of this volume.]

[7] David Reisman, *The Lonely Crowd* (New Haven: Yale University Press, 1950).

ed with this shift in the basic personality of the criminal. The overall shift of societal forces which form the causal context of this change in the middle-class man also appears to correspond to changes in the participant in criminal culture. In particular, there is a striking similarity between the inner-directed middle-class man and the old type criminal.

The "inner-directed" person (old criminal) was more concerned with concrete material gain and less with psychic emotional gratification characteristic of "other-directed" individuals (new criminals). The business of the criminal of the past was making money, and to make money took skill. Highly skilled professionals thus emerged within the criminal subcultures. As in the legitimate society, the skills were those that allowed the person to manipulate the material world. Burglary, robbery, hi-jacking, forgery, counterfeiting methods and other professional skills became highly developed. The criminal was more secure in himself and developed his professional craft. The "inner-directed" old criminal not only knew how to "pull a caper," but how to do it in the "cleanest" way possible. This implied a knowledge of law, of court proceedings, of police methods, and many other aspects of the "caper." Unlike the current flimsy relationships characteristic of the new criminal, the old criminal had to make contacts with trusted people whom he needed in the pursuit of his criminal work. He had to trust others to cooperate with his criminal venture. This often meant using a steady "fence" when he was dealing in merchandise. He often made contracts with lawyers whom he could trust, who were "right." Such a lawyer would afford him legal advice before a crime, and would be ready to go to bat for him if he was caught. There was even a right way to "do time" when he was caught and couldn't "beat the rap." This training entailed doing "easy time" and getting out with a minimum sentence. It also prescribed the correct behavior in relation to other criminals and officials while "in stir."

THE "COOL," VIOLENT, AND ADDICTED

There are several traits or styles of criminal action on the part of the new criminal. Since he has no strong "inner-direction" the new criminal will seize on "the scene" or behavior pattern which is popular at the time. These entail being "cool" or "hip," as well as violence and drugs. Sometimes all of these behavior patterns fit the offender, or he has several of these traits which shift.

Among New York delinquents the following symptomatic pattern change has been observed. The violent gang youth, utilizing violence for "kicks" decides that being "hip or cool is the scene" and that "gang fights are for kids." He shifts to dressing and being sharp. This involves some "blowing pot" (smoking marijuana) and "short con" (petty hustling). If heroin drug addiction is the style, he shifts to it. Of course, after he becomes a heroin addict, the dictatorship of king heroin pushes him into other reckless petty theft directions. This sequence has been observed to occur in the evolution of the new criminal.[8]

The new criminal style of being cool or "hip" (the "manipulative" principle of relating) has perhaps filtered down from the middle-class competitive system. For the new criminal, "how to win friends and influence people" becomes interpreted and related to how to beat a "mark" (victim). This new definition of how to earn money has a different emphasis from the former definition. The old thief was out to make money in the cleanest, quickest, fastest way. The new hip-criminal is out to make money but equally important is the process of beating someone, by manipulating them and looking sharp to "others." Here the emphasis is often on the sharpness, not on making money. The important thing is the "cat's" ability, through his conversation or his keenness to manipulate others. The means for theft becomes a "kicks"-oriented end in itself.

A central theme in hipsterism is "having a ball" or getting "kicks." "The main purpose of life for the 'cat' is to experience the 'kick.' A 'kick' may be any act tabooed by 'squares' which heightens and intensifies the present movement of experience and differentiates it as much as possible from the humdrum routine of daily life."[9] "Kicks" may grossly be viewed as a meth-

---

[8] Yablonsky, *The Violent Gang.*
[9] Harold Finestone, "Cats, Kicks and Color," *Social Problems* (July, 1957). (See pp. 355–63 of this volume.)

od of existential validation. The bored-dull person on a death-life continuum is closer to being nonexistent or the "death side." He seeks some means of self-feeling validation. This need requires some intense emotional experience—"kicks." Senseless violence or drugs can produce this change of feeling state. The "kicks" experience of intense "dyonisian" gratification may thus validate the individual feeling of *being* or *existing*.

In addition violence as a form of "kicks" provides status in the delinquent subculture. As a young gang-killer commented:

> "If I would of got the knife, I would have stabbed him. That would of gave me more of a build-up. People would have respected me for what I've done and things like that. They would say, 'There goes a cold killer.'"

Addiction is another adaptable pattern for the new criminal. If one views hipsterism, "coolness" and "kicks" as overt symptom patterns of an underdeveloped self, it is logical to anticipate how the drug addiction symptom could also take over. In many ways, addiction is a new fad which the "other-directed" new criminal has gravitated toward.

The basic personality of the "other-directed" new criminal makes him very susceptible to drug addiction. All that he requires to start using drugs is to come into contact with a drug-using collectivity. He is seeking "kicks," trying to keep up with the trends of *his* culture, trying to be "hip"; so if drugs are "the scene," the "other-directed" new criminal will "make it." Also drug addiction is a neat, problem-solving complex. As one "hip" new criminal stated: "Man, getting on drugs is like putting all your little bills in one easy package. When you become hooked, you only got one problem getting stuff."

In summary, the new criminal is "kicks"-oriented, be it violence, drugs or being a hipster. As an "other-directed" personality, he is amenable and susceptible to criminal fads or new scenes. As a sociopath, he is not totally disoriented to the larger society. However, he characteristically has a limited social conscience or concern for "others." He is under-socialized to the legal society and his own criminal subculture has few clear and binding rules or demands. This is in marked contrast with the well-trained

old criminal who assumed the responsibility of relating positively to his cohorts in their criminal activities. He had "character" or "ethics" in his criminal pursuits. The new criminal in contrast would literally give his crime partner up for a "fix" or a pill, and does.

THE NEW CRIMINAL IN SOCIETY

For speculative purposes we would divide the criminal hierarchy into upper, middle and lower-class offenders. At the top we would place the skilled syndicated criminal form, greatly controlled by old mobsters. Their criminal tentacles enter into labor unions and some big businesses. These criminals are intelligent and highly skilled professionals. The middle class would be comprised essentially of the professional thief or the "old criminal" as described here. In the lower class, we would place the unskilled grifter, sometimes addict or, as described, the "new criminal." In this context it is our contention that the middle-class old criminal is the category on the demise and that there is some increase in the described upper and lower-class criminals, with a limited bridge between the upper and lower world of crime.

The causal context of this shift of criminal modal personality may very well be connected to some of the following factors:

1. The shift from a stable slum condition of the past to a disorganized slum. The high delinquency areas of the past had a stable population. A criminal hierarchy could develop. There was room at the top for an enterprising "hood" if he trained with an older criminal and had vision. The modern scene emphasises "kicks" and achievement in the "here and now," partly because there is no criminal ladder to climb in the shifting slum. With the demise of the middle-class criminal, the bridge to the top, the new deviant is restricted to his bottom position.

2. Because of the current limited neighbourhood criminal hierarchy, there is a concomitant limited training or recruitment system for the youth personally predisposed towards a life of professional crime. As a corollary of this fact, good professional criminal role-models and educators are disappearing from the crime scene.

3. The downfall of the old criminal culture of

the past may also partially be related to improved police methods. In the big cities police methods seem to have won the technological race with the professional criminal. New safes, new detection methods, fingerprint systems, etc. make it difficult for the old type professional criminal to operate effectively.

These, of course, are only partial explanations of the backdrop to the ascendancy of the new offender. The world picture of potential total destruction and manipulation of instruments of violence, although difficult to prove as a causal force, no doubt filters down to affect the problem. The acceleration of great social change currently affecting our society also plays an important role in producing the changed sociocultural context which spawns the new criminal. There may be a close association between the rate of social change and the type of criminal a society produces. It would be our contention that rapid social change correlates with the proportion of "new criminals."

C. CONSEQUENCES

The consequences of crime have been approached from several levels. Many studies have focussed on court proceedings and dispositions and have shown that these proceedings differ depending on the racial and socioeconomic characteristics of individuals involved.[1] Even the provision of legal counsel at no charge to the accused does not guarantee adequate representation to those unable to afford legal counsel.[2] Other studies have focussed on different consequences in terms of continued stigma beyond the courts and prisons. For example, Schwartz and Skolnick[3] find that offenders of medical malpractice, unlike offenders of more common crimes, are not the object of continued stigma and status degradation. They do not even suffer any negative economic consequences (such as loss of patients, since fellow physicians continue to make referrals to them). Still other studies have focussed on the reaction of the police. The two selections in this section deal with police reactions.

The use of brutality by the police has been a focus of the attention of the public, the press and the Supreme Court. The next selection, "Violence and the Police," examines such police actions. William A. Westley outlines several sources of police brutality, such as community pressure for the capture and conviction of law violators, the desire for prestige and promotion, and the preservation of self-esteem. Westley's analysis reveals that, despite the fact that police brutality is illegal, the *police* consider it legitimate, at least on occasion. While Westley does not deal systematically with the question of brutality, police brutality is probably more frequent for some offenses than for others.

The analysis of the police reaction to crime need not be limited to brutality or to the differences in the reaction depending on characteristics

[1] Theodore G. Chiricos, Phillip D. Jackson, and Gordon P. Waldo, "Inequality in the Imposition of a Criminal Label," *Social Problems* 19 (Spring, 1972), pp. 553–71.

[2] David Sudnow, "Normal Crimes: Sociological Features of the Penal Code in a Public Defender Office," *Social Problems* 12 (Winter, 1965), pp. 255–74.

[3] Richard D. Schwartz and Jerome H. Skolnick, "Two Studies of Legal Stigma," *Social Problems* 10 (Fall, 1962), pp. 133–42.

of the offender. Police reactions may also be examined in terms of collective properties and their relationship to other collective properties. For example, Currie's study makes a distinction between repressive and restrained social control systems.[4] The basic difference is that in the former there are few internal restraints within the control system (e.g., belief and values regarding due process) and few external restraints from institutions outside the control system itself (e.g., legal representation of the accused). It is probable, given a constant rate of criminal behavior, that reactions to crime will differ depending on types of control systems involved. Specifically, we would expect greater fluctuations in official reactions over time in repressive systems; with few restraints on those who operate the control system, reactions are dependent on the inclinations of those in power. We have little evidence regarding the causes of reaction variation for repressive systems although several investigations have been made of variation in restrained controlled systems, which is the dominant system in the United States.

Note Kai Erikson's hypothesis that the amount of deviance tends to remain fairly constant over time largely because the capacity of a society's reactive system, which deals with and processes deviants, changes slowly (e.g., jail and prison capacities are relatively fixed, changing very slowly).[5] If the number of recognized deviants remains fairly constant from one time to another, little difference in the reaction of the police, as reflected in the arrest rate, would be expected over time.

There is probably much truth to Erikson's hypothesis, and he produces evidence of its validity for Salem, Massachusetts during the Puritan period. At the same time, however, investigations have shown rather consistent declines in the arrest rate for several cities in northeastern United States and parts of Europe beginning shortly after the Civil War. In the next selection, Theodore N. Ferdinand shows the same pattern for Salem during this period.

Two explanations have generally been given for variations in the arrest rate under conditions of a constant crime rate. One explanation is that industrialization led to the domination of politics by businessmen. This led, in turn, to more conservative tax policies, reducing tax rates and hence the number and quality of personnel in the police system, and bringing about a lower arrest rate. The other explanation argues that police effectiveness and the arrest rate are reduced when there is political conflict and struggle for control within local government. Police departments become too concerned with internal political matters and the patronage system. This increases the likelihood of internal corruption and decreases effectiveness. Ferdinand provides evidence that both hypotheses are correct for Salem.

---

[4] Elliott P. Currie, "Crime without Criminals: Witchcraft and Its Control in Renaissance Europe," *Law and Society Review* 3 (October, 1968), pp. 7–12.

[5] Kai T. Erikson, *Wayward Puritans: A Study in the Sociology of Deviance* (New York: John Wiley, 1966).

VIOLENCE AND THE POLICE

WILLIAM A. WESTLEY

Brutality and the third degree have been identified with the municipal police of the United States since their inauguration in 1844. These aspects of police activity have been subject to exaggeration, repeated exposure, and virulent criticism. Since they are a breach of the law by the law-enforcement agents, they constitute a serious social, but intriguing sociological, problem. Yet there is little information about or understanding of the process through which such activity arises or of the purposes which it serves.

This paper is concerned with the genesis and function of the illegal use of violence by the police. . . . It shows that (1) the police accept and morally justify their illegal use of violence; (2) such acceptance and justification arise through their occupational experience; and (3) its use is functionally related to the collective occupational, as well as to the legal, ends of the police. . . .

The technical demands of a man's work tend to specify the kinds of social relationships in which he will be involved and to select the groups with whom these relationships are to be maintained. The social definition of the occupation invests its members with a common prestige position. Thus, a man's occupation is a major determining factor of his conduct and social identity. This being so, it involves more than man's work, and one must go beyond the technical in the explanation of work behavior. One must discover the occupationally derived definitions of self and conduct which arise in the involvements of technical demands, social relationships between colleagues and with the public, status, and self-conception. To understand these definitions, one must track them back to the occupational problems in which they have their genesis.[1]

The policeman finds his most pressing problems in his relationships to the public. His is a service occupation but of an incongruous kind, since he must discipline those whom he serves. He is regarded as corrupt and inefficient by, and meets with hostility and criticism from, the public. He regards the public as his enemy, feels his occupation to be in conflict with the community, and regards himself to be a pariah. The experience and the feeling give rise to a collective emphasis on secrecy, an attempt to coerce respect from the public, and a belief that almost any means are legitimate in completing an important arrest. These are for the policeman basic occupational values. They arise from his experience, take precedence over his legal responsibilities, are central to an understanding of his conduct, and form the occupational contexts within which violence gains its meaning. This then is the background for our analysis.[2]

The materials which follow are drawn from a case study of a municipal police department in an industrial city of approximately one hundred and fifty thousand inhabitants. This study included participation in all types of police activities, ranging from walking the beat and cruising with policemen in a squad car to the observation of raids, interrogations, and the police school. It included intensive interviews with over half the men in the department who were representative as to rank, time in service, race, religion, and specific type of police job.

Reprinted from *The American Journal of Sociology* 49 (July, 1953), pp. 34–42. "Violence and the Police" by William A. Westley as abridged by permission of the University of Chicago Press. Footnotes have been renumbered. The writer is indebted to Joseph D. Lohman for his assistance in making contact with the police and for many excellent suggestions as to research procedure and insights into the organization of the police. This paper presents part of a larger study of the police by the writer. For the complete study see William A. Westley, "The Police: A Sociological Study of Law, Custom, and Morality" (unpublished doctoral dissertation, University of Chicago, Department of Sociology, 1951).

[1] The ideas are not original. I am indebted for many of them to Everett C. Hughes, although he is in no way responsible for their present formulation (see E. C. Hughes, "Work and the Self," in Rohrer and Sherif, *Social Psychology at the Crossroads* [New York: Harper and Brothers, 1951]).

[2] The background material will be developed in subsequent papers which will analyze the occupational experience of the police and give a full description of police norms.

DUTY AND VIOLENCE

In the United States the use of violence by the police is both an occupational prerogative and a necessity. Police powers include the use of violence, for to them, within civil society, has been delegated the monopoly of the legitimate means of violence possessed by the state. Police are obliged by their duties to use violence as the only measure adequate to control and apprehension in the presence of counterviolence.

Violence in the form of the club and the gun is for the police a means of persuasion. Violence from the criminal, the drunk, the quarreling family, and the rioter arises in the course of police duty. The fighting drunk who is damaging property or assailing his fellows and who looks upon the policeman as a malicious intruder justifies for the policeman his use of force in restoring order. The armed criminal who has demonstrated a casual regard for the lives of others and a general hatred of the policeman forces the use of violence by the police in the pursuit of duty. Every policeman has some such experiences, and they proliferate in police lore. They constitute a common-sense and legal justification for the use of violence by the police and for training policemen in the skills of violence. Thus, from experience in the pursuit of their legally prescribed duties, the police develop a justification for the use of violence. They come to see it as good, as useful, and as their own. Furthermore, although legally their use of violence is limited to the requirements of the arrest and the protection of themselves and the community, the contingencies of their occupation lead them to enlarge the area in which violence may be used. Two kinds of experience—that with respect to the conviction of the felon and that with respect to the control of sexual conduct—will illustrate how and why the illegal use of violence arises.

1. *The conviction of the felon.* The apprehension and conviction of the felon is, for the policeman, the essence of police work. It is the source of prestige both within and outside police circles, it has career implications, and it is a major source of justification for the existence of the police before a critical and often hostile public. Out of these conditions a legitimation for the illegal use of violence is wrought.

The career and prestige implication of the "good pinch"[3] elevate it to a major end in the conduct of the policeman. It is an end which is justified both legally and through public opinion as one which should be of great concern to the police. Therefore it takes precedence over other duties and tends to justify strong means. Both trickery and violence are such means. The "third degree" has been criticized for many years, and extensive administrative controls have been devised in an effort to eliminate it. Police persistence in the face of that attitude suggests that the illegal use of violence is regarded as functional to their work. It also indicates a tendency to regard the third degree as a legitimate means for obtaining the conviction of the felon. However, to understand the strength of this legitimation, one must include other factors: the competition between patrolman and detectives and the publicity value of convictions for the police department.

The patrolman has less access to cases that might result in the "good pinch" than the detective. Such cases are assigned to the detective, and for their solution he will reap the credit. Even where the patrolman first detects the crime, or actually apprehends the possible offender, the case is likely to be turned over to the detective. Therefore patrolmen are eager to obtain evidence and make the arrest before the arrival of the detectives. Intimidation and actual violence frequently come into play under these conditions. This is illustrated in the following case recounted by a young patrolman when he was questioned as to the situations in which he felt that the use of force was necessary:

> One time Joe and I found three guys in a car, and we found that they had a gun down between the seats. We wanted to find out who owned that gun before the dicks arrived so that we could make a good pinch. They told us.

Patrolmen feel that little credit is forthcoming from a clean beat (a crimeless beat), while a number of good arrests really stands out on the

---

[3] Policemen, in the case studied, use this term to mean an arrest which (1) is politically clear and (2) likely to bring them esteem. Generally it refers to felonies, but in the case of a real vice drive it may include the arrest and *conviction* of an important bookie.

record. To a great extent this is actually the case, since a good arrest results in good newspaper publicity, and the policeman who has made many "good pinches" has prestige among his colleagues.

A further justification for the illegal use of violence arises from the fact that almost every police department is under continuous criticism from the community, which tends to assign its own moral responsibilities to the police. The police are therefore faced with the task of justifying themselves to the public, both as individuals and as a group. They feel that the solution of major criminal cases serves this function. This is illustrated in the following statement:

There is a case I remember of four Negroes who held up a filling station. We got a description of them and picked them up. Then we took them down to the station and really worked them over. I guess that everybody that came into the station that night had a hand in it, and they were in pretty bad shape. Do you think that sounds cruel? Well, you know what we got out of it? We broke a big case in ————. There was a mob of twenty guys, burglars and stick-up men, and eighteen of them are in the pen now. Sometimes you have to get rough with them, see. The way I figure it is, if you can get a clue that a man is a pro and if he won't cooperate, tell you what you want to know, it is justified to rough him up a little, up to a point. You know how it is. You feel that the end justifies the means.

It is easier for the police to justify themselves to the community through the dramatic solution of big crimes than through orderly and responsible completion of their routine duties. Although they may be criticized for failures in routine areas, the criticism for the failure to solve big crimes is more intense and sets off a criticism of their work in noncriminal areas. The pressure to solve important cases therefore becomes strong. The following statement, made in reference to the use of violence in interrogations, demonstrates the point:

If it's a big case and there is a lot of pressure on you and they tell you you can't go home until the case is finished, then naturally you are going to lose patience.

The policeman's response to this pressure is to extend the use of violence to its illegal utilization in interrogations. The apprehension of the felon or the "good pinch" thus constitutes a basis for justifying the illegal use of violence.

2. *Control of sexual conduct.* The police are responsible for the enforcement of laws regulating sexual conduct. This includes the suppression of sexual deviation and the protection of the public from advances and attacks of persons of deviant sexual tendencies. Here the police face a difficult task. The victims of such deviants are notoriously unwilling to cooperate, since popular curiosity and gossip about sexual crimes and the sanctions against the open discussion of sexual activities make it embarrassing for the victim to admit or describe a deviant sexual advance or attack and cause him to feel that he gains a kind of guilt by association from such admissions. Thus the police find that frequently the victims will refuse to identify or testify against the deviant.

These difficulties are intensified by the fact that, once the community becomes aware of sexual depredations, the reports of such activity multiply well beyond reasonable expectations. Since the bulk of these reports will be false, they add to the confusion of the police and consequently to the elusiveness of the offender.

The difficulties of the police are further aggravated by extreme public demand for the apprehension of the offender. The hysteria and alarm generated by reports of a peeping Tom, a rapist, or an exhibitionist result in great public pressure on the police; and, should the activities continue, the public becomes violently critical of police efficiency. The police, who feel insecure in their relationship to the public, are extremely sensitive to this criticism and feel that they must act in response to the demands made by the political and moral leaders of the community.

Thus the police find themselves caught in a dilemma. Apprehension is extremely difficult because of the confusion created by public hysteria and the scarcity of witnesses, but the police are compelled to action by extremely public demands. They dissolve this dilemma through the illegal utilization of violence.

A statement of this "misuse" of police powers is represented in the remarks of a patrolman:

Now in my own case when I catch a guy like that I just pick him up and take him into the woods and beat him until he can't crawl. I have had seventeen cases like that in the last couple of years.

I tell that guy that if I catch him doing that again I will take him out to those woods and I will shoot him. I tell him that I carry a second gun on me just in case I find guys like him and that I will plant it in his hand and say that he tried to kill and that no jury will convict me.

This statement is extreme and is not representative of policemen in general. In many instances the policeman is likely to act in a different fashion. This is illustrated in the following statement of a rookie who described what happened when he and his partner investigated a parked car which had aroused their suspicions:

He [the partner] went up there and pretty soon he called me, and there were a couple of fellows in the car with their pants open. I couldn't understand it. I kept looking around for where the woman would be. They were both pretty plastered. One was a young kid about eighteen years old, and the other was an older man. We decided, with the kid so drunk, that bringing him in would only really ruin his reputation, and we told him to go home. Otherwise we would have pinched them. During the time we were talking to them they offered us twenty-eight dollars, and I was going to pinch them when they showed the money, but my partner said, "Never mind, let them go."

Nevertheless, most policemen would apply no sanctions against a colleague who took the more extreme view of the right to use violence and would openly support some milder form of illegal coercion. This is illustrated in the statement of another rookie:

They feel that it's okay to rough a man up in the case of sex crimes. One of the older men advised me that if the courts didn't punish a man we should. He told me about a sex crime, the story about it, and then said that the law says the policeman has the right to use the amount of force necessary to make an arrest and that in that kind of a crime you can use just a little more force. They feel definitely, for example, in extreme cases like rape, that if a man was guilty he ought to be punished even if you could not get any evidence on him. My feeling is that all the men on the force feel that way, at least from what they have told me.

Furthermore, the police believe, and with some justification it seems, that the community supports their definition of the situation and that they are operating in terms of an implicit directive.

The point of this discussion is that the control of sexual conduct is so difficult and the demand for it so incessant that the police come to sanction the illegal use of violence in obtaining that control. This does not imply that all policemen treat all sex deviants brutally, for, as the above quotations indicate, such is not the case. Rather, it indicates that this use of violence is permitted and condoned by the police and that they come to think of it as a resource more extensive than is included in the legal definition.

LEGITIMATION OF VIOLENCE

The preceding discussion has indicated two ways in which the experience of the police encourages them to use violence as a general resource in the achievement of their occupational ends and thus to sanction its illegal use. The experience, thus, makes violence acceptable to the policeman as a generalized means. We now wish to indicate the particular basis on which this general resource is legitimated. In particular we wish to point out the extent to which the policeman tends to transfer violence from a legal resource to a personal resource, one which he uses to further his own ends.

Seventy-three policemen, drawn from all ranks and constituting approximately 50 percent of the patrolmen, were asked, "When do you think a policeman is justified in roughing a man up?" The intent of the question was to get them to legitimate the use of violence. Their replies are summarized in Table 1.

TABLE 1. BASES FOR THE USE OF FORCE NAMED BY 73 POLICEMEN

Type of Response	Frequency	Percentage
(A) Disrespect for police	27	37
(B) When impossible to avoid	17	23
(C) To obtain information	14	19
(D) To make an arrest	6	8
(E) For the hardened criminal	5	7
(F) When you know man is guilty	2	3
(G) For sex criminals	2	3
Total	73	100

Note: Many respondents described more than one type of situation which they felt called for the use of violence. The "reason" which was either (1) given most heatedly and at greatest length and/or (2) given first was used to characterize the respondent's answer. However, this table is exhaustive of the types of replies which were given.

An inspection of the types and distribution of the responses indicates (1) that violence is legitimated by illegal ends (A, C, E, F, G) in 69 percent of the cases; (2) that violence is legitimated in terms of purely personal or group ends (A) in 37 percent of the cases (this is important, since it is the largest single reason for the use of violence given); and (3) that legal ends are the bases for legitimation in 31 percent of the cases (B and D). However, this probably represents a distortion of the true feelings of some of these men, since both the police chief and the community had been severely critical of the use of violence by the men, and the respondents had a tendency to be very cautious with the interviewer, whom some of them never fully trusted. Furthermore, since all the men were conscious of the chief's policy and of public criticism, it seems likely that those who did justify the use of violence for illegal and personal ends no longer recognized the illegality involved. They probably believed that such ends fully represented a moral legitimation for their use of violence

The most significant finding is that at least 37 percent of the men believed that it was legitimate to use violence to coerce respect. This suggests that policemen use the resource of violence to persuade their audience (the public) to respect their occupational status. In terms of the policeman's definition of the situation, the individual who lacks respect for the police, the "wise guy" who talks back, or any individual who acts or talks in a disrespectful way, deserves brutality. This idea is epitomized in admonitions given to the rookies such as, "You gotta make them respect you" and "You gotta act tough." Examples of some of the responses to the preceding question that fall into the "disrespect for the police" category follow:

Well, there are cases. For example, when you stop a fellow for a routine questioning, say a wise guy, and he starts talking back to you and telling you you are no good and that sort of thing. You know you can take a man in on a disorderly conduct charge, but you can practically never make it stick. So what you do in a case like that is to egg the guy on until he makes a remark where you can justifiably slap him and, then, if he fights back, you can call it resisting arrest.

Well, it varies in different cases. Most of the police use punishment if the fellow gives them

any trouble. Usually you can judge a man who will give you trouble though. *If there is any slight resistance,* you can go all out on him. You shouldn't do it in the street though. Wait until you are in the squad car, because, even if you are in the right and a guy takes a poke at you, just when you are hitting back somebody's just likely to come around the corner, and what he will say is that you are beating the guy with your club.

Well, a prisoner deserves to be hit when he goes to the point where he tries to put you below him.

You gotta get rough when a man's language becomes very bad, when he is trying to make a fool of you in front of everybody else. I think most policemen try to treat people in a nice way, but usually you have to talk pretty rough. That's the only way to set a man down, to make him show a little respect.

If a fellow called a policeman a filthy name, a slap in the mouth would be a good thing, especially if it was out in the public where calling a policeman a bad name would look bad for the police.

There was the incident of a fellow I picked up. I was on the beat, and I was taking him down to the station. There were people following us. He kept saying that I wasn't in the army. Well, he kept going on like that, and I finally had to bust him one. I had to do it. The people would have thought I was afraid otherwise.

These results suggest (1) that the police believe that these private or group ends constitute a moral legitimation for violence which is equal *or superior* to the legitimation derived from the law and (2) that the monopoly of violence delegated to the police, by the state, to enforce the ends of the state has been appropriated by the police as a personal resource to be used for personal and group ends.

THE USE OF VIOLENCE

The sanctions for the use of violence arising from occupational experience and the fact that policemen morally justify even its illegal use may suggest that violence is employed with great frequency and little provocation. Such an impression would be erroneous, for the actual use of violence is limited by other considerations, such as individual inclinations, the threat of detection, and a sensitivity to public reactions.

Individual policemen vary of course in psychological disposition and past experience. All have been drawn from the larger community which tends to condemn the use of violence and therefore have internalized with varying degrees of intensity this other definition of violence. Their experience as policemen creates a new dimension to their self-conceptions and gives them a new perspective on the use of violence. But individual men vary in the degree to which they assimilate this new conception of self. Therefore, the amount of violence which is used and the frequency with which it is employed will vary among policemen according to their individual propensities. However, policemen cannot and do not employ sanctions against their colleagues for using violence,[4] and individual men who personally condemn the use of violence and avoid it whenever possible[5] refuse openly to condemn acts of violence by other men on the force. Thus, the collective sanction for the use of violence permits those men who are inclined to its use to employ it without fear.

All policemen, however, are conscious of the dangers of the illegal use of violence. If detected, they may be subject to a lawsuit and possibly dismissal from the force. Therefore, they limit its use to what they think they can get away with. Thus, they recognize that, if a man is guilty of a serious crime, it is easy to "cover up" for their brutality by accusing him of resisting arrest, and the extent to which they believe a man guilty tends to act as a precondition to the use of violence.[6]

The policeman, in common with members of other occupations, is sensitive to the evaluation of his occupation by the public. A man's work is an important aspect of his status, and to the extent that he is identified with his work (by himself and/or the community) he finds that his self-esteem requires the justification and social elevation of his work. Since policemen are low in the occupational prestige scale, subject to continuous criticism, and in constant contact with this criticizing and evaluating public, they are profoundly involved in justifying their work and its tactics to the public and to themselves.

The way in which the police emphasize the solution of big crimes and their violent solution to the problem of the control of sexual conduct illustrate this concern. However, different portions of the public have differing definitions of conduct and are of differential importance to the policeman, and the way in which the police define different portions of the public has an effect on whether or not they will use violence.

The police believe that certain groups of persons will respond only to fear and rough treatment. In the city studied they defined both Negroes and slum dwellers in this category. The following statements, each by a different man, typify the manner in which they discriminate the public:

> In the good districts you appeal to people's judgment and explain the law to them. In the South Side the only way is to appear like you are the boss.

> You can't ask them a question and get an answer that is not a lie. In the South Side the only way to walk into a tavern is to walk in swaggering as if you own the place and if somebody is standing in your way give him an elbow and push him aside.

> The colored people understand one thing. The policeman is the law, and he is going to treat you rough and that's the way you have to treat them. Personally, I don't think the colored are trying to help themselves one bit. If you don't treat them rough, they will sit right on top of your head.

Discriminations with respect to the public are largely based on the political power of the group, the degree to which the police believe that the group is potentially criminal, and the type of treatment which the police believe will elicit respect from it.

Variations in the administration and community setting of the police will introduce variations in their use of violence. Thus, a thoroughly corrupt police department will use violence in supporting the ends of this corruption, while a carefully administered nonpolitical department can go a long way toward reducing the illegal use of violence. However, wherever the basic conditions here described are present, it will be very difficult to eradicate the illegal use of violence.

Given these conditions, violence will be used when necessary to the pursuit of duty or when basic occupational values are threatened. Thus a threat to the respect with which the policeman

---

[4] The emphasis on secrecy among the police prevents them from using legal sanctions against their colleagues.

[5] Many men who held jobs in the police station rather than on beats indicated to the interviewer that their reason for choosing a desk job was to avoid the use of violence.

[6] In addition, the policeman is aware that the courts are highly critical of confessions obtained by violence and that, if violence is detected, it will "spoil his case."

believes his occupation should be regarded or the opportunity to make a "good pinch" will tend to evoke its use.

CONCLUSIONS

The policeman uses violence illegally because such usage is seen as just, acceptable, and, at times, expected by his colleague group and because it constitutes an effective means for solving problems in obtaining status and self-esteem which policemen as policemen have in common. Since the ends for which violence is illegally used are conceived to be both just and important, they function to justify, to the policeman, the illegal use of violence as a general means. Since "brutality" is strongly criticized by the larger community, the policeman must devise a defense of his brutality to himself and the community, and the defense in turn gives a deeper and more lasting justification to the "misuse of violence." This process then results in a transfer in property from the state to the colleague group. The means of violence which were originally a property of the state, in loan to its law-enforcement agent, the police, are in a psychological

sense confiscated by the police, to be conceived of as a personal property to be used at their discretion. This, then, is the explanation of the illegal use of violence by the police which results from viewing it in terms of the police as an occupational group.

The explanation of the illegal use of violence by the police offers an illuminating perspective on the social nature of their occupation. The analysis of their use of brutality in dealing with sexual deviants and felons shows that it is a result of their desire to defend and improve their social status in the absence of effective legal means. This desire in turn is directly related to and makes sense in terms of the low status of the police in the community, which results in a driving need on the part of policemen to assert and improve their status. Their general legitimation of the use of violence *primarily* in terms of coercing respect and making a "good pinch" clearly points out the existence of occupational goals, which are independent of and take precedence over their legal mandate. The existence of such goals and patterns of conduct indicates that the policeman has made of his occupation a preoccupation and invested in it a large aspect of his self.

POLITICS, THE POLICE, AND ARRESTING POLICIES IN SALEM, MASSACHUSETTS SINCE THE CIVIL WAR
THEODORE N. FERDINAND

There is little question that the overall level of arrests for serious crime has declined in many American cities since the latter part of the 19th century. Long-term studies of arrests in Boston,[1] Buffalo,[2] and New Haven[3] have consistently

found sizable declines in arrest rates of the order of 80 to 90 percent between the 1870s and the modern era. In the present study arrests for major crimes (murder through assault) in Salem, Massachusetts, dropped from a rate of 1,231 per 100,000 in 1877–79 to a rate of 177 in 1964–66, a decline of nearly 86 percent. Interestingly enough, similar declines have also been reported for Sardinia[4] and France[5] over the same period.

Reprinted with permission of the author and Society for the Study of Social Problems, from *Social Problems* 19 (Spring, 1972), pp. 572–88.

Thanks are due to Mark Haller, Ruth Cavan, and James Banovetz for many useful suggestions regarding an earlier version of this essay and to Robin Berger who helped in collecting the data.

[1] Theodore N. Ferdinand, "The Criminal Patterns of Boston Since 1846," *American Journal of Sociology* 73 (July, 1967), pp. 84–99.

[2] Elwin H. Powell, "Crime as a Function of Anomie," *Journal of Criminal Law, Criminology, and Police Science* 67 (June, 1966), pp. 161–71.

[3] Theodore N. Ferdinand, "The Criminal Patterns of New Haven Since 1861" (unpublished manuscript, 1967).

[4] Franco, Ferracuti, et al., *Violence in Sardinia* (Rome: The Institution of Psychology, University of Rome, 1970).

[5] Abdul Quaiyum Lodhi and Charles Tilly, "Urbanization, Criminality, and Collective Violence in Nineteenth Century France" (paper presented at the American Society of Criminology meetings, Pennsylvania State University, 1970).

The steepness of these declines (in Salem, for example, the arrest rate for major crime dropped by 75 percent in less than 20 years) suggests quite strongly that something other than changes in the actual rate of crime was responsible; and the generality of the declines (Boston, New Haven, Salem, and Buffalo) suggests that broad, regional pressures or conditions were at work and not local factors.

TWO THEORIES OF MUNICIPAL DECLINE

There are two explanations that might be used to account for such widespread changes in arrest practices. First, we might suggest that the elected officials in these cities adopted rather conservative fiscal policies in the 1870's with the result that city departments generally and the police in particular were substantially hampered in achieving their usual levels of effectiveness. Dahl[6] has argued that industrialization, as it swept through the cities of the Northeast, shattered the composure of the patrician class and paved the way for a new class of entrepreneures with a different governing philosophy. Frisch[7] has extended Dahl's thesis in a study of Springfield, Mass., by suggesting that these entrepreneurial city officials, when confronted with the severe depression of 1873–1878, assumed that their first responsibility to the electorate was to defend tax rates against upward pressures.

But if conservative fiscal policies were typical of businessmen in government, especially after the depression of 1873–78, we would expect a decline in the effectiveness of city government generally as these policies took hold. And, therefore, as businessmen became the dominant occupational group in city government in the 19th century, we should also find a persistent decline in the effectiveness of the police.

A second thesis that might also explain a general decline in police effectiveness emphasizes the impact of factionalism and political conflict upon city government. Wilson[8] has argued that factionalism in city politics has a profound effect upon the style and organization of the police. As entrenched factions contend for control of City Hall, they typically use every weapon at their command, including the use of patronage to insure the loyalty of their followers. But the patronage system tends to draw city departments into the conflict; and it tends to encourage the heads of these departments to keep political considerations in mind as they form administrative policies. In other words, sharp changes in the arresting practices of the police may reflect the intrusion of politics into the day-to-day operations of the department. According to Wilson,[9] such departments tend to assume the watchman form of organization. In addition to their involvement in community politics, such departments tend to be slow in adopting new methods and technologies; they tend to promote men more in terms of political reliability than performance in police work; and they are likely to exhibit some corruption if commercialized vice flourishes in the community.

Factionalism came to many of the cities of the Northeast (Buffalo is probably an exception) in an extremely virulent form when the Irish immigrants of the 1840s, 50s, and 60s began to seek their fortunes in city politics in the 1880s and the 90s. Thus, as they challenged Yankee politicians, intense political skirmishes were fought in many cities; and it is common knowledge that the police became pawns in many of these battles. The sharp changes in arresting practices noted above, therefore, may also represent an adjustment by police to the eruption of bitter struggles in their immediate political environment.

Both arguments might be used to explain changes in the level of arrests among the police departments of the Northeast, because both identify broad, regional changes as the initial stimulus to change. Most of the communities of the Northeast encountered the effects of industrialization at about the same time, and all of them experienced the depression of 1873–78 almost simultaneously. Hence, all the cities of the Northeast developed business-oriented city

[6] Robert A. Dahl, *Who Governs?* (New Haven: Yale University Press, 1961).

[7] Michael H. Frisch, "The Community Elite and the Emergence of Urban Politics: Springfield, Massachusetts, 1840–1880," in Stephen Thernstrom and Richard Sennett, eds., *Nineteenth-Century Cities* (New Haven: Yale University Press, 1969).

[8] James W. Wilson, *Varieties of Police Behavior* (Cambridge: Harvard University Press, 1968).

[9] *Ibid.*, Chapter 5.

officials and conservative fiscal policies at about the same time. All of these cities, therefore, should display similar changes in arrest practices during the latter part of the 19th century.

By the same token, intense political struggles also developed in the major cities of the Northeast at about the same time when Irish leaders began to enter city politics in the 1880s and 1890s. There was probably some variation among the cities as to the precise date when Irish politicians became a force to reckon with, but, in general, their activity became quite prominent in many cities in the last decades of the 19th century. Thus, the effects of their battles with Yankee politicians should have become noticeable generally around the turn of the century.

Both arguments appear quite reasonable in that they depend upon premises that are known to be valid, and they suggest a plausible series of events to explain the decline in police effectiveness. Moreover, since they postulate quite distinct initial conditions, it is entirely possible that both are relevant to the same city at the same time. In the analysis that follows, therefore, I shall attempt to show that the arrest rates of the Salem police over the last century reacted sharply *both* to the conservative policies of business-oriented city officials and to a growing Irish-Yankee conflict as the city moved into the 20th century.

METHOD

In order to test this thesis, two types of information were needed: descriptions of the changing character of politics in the late 19th and early 20th centuries in Salem; and data describing the adjustments of the police department to these changes. Since there are no careful histories of Salem of this period, it was necessary to use the daily reports of the *Salem Evening News* to reconstruct the course of politics in Salem. The *Evening News* began publishing in the 1880's and continued uninterrupted throughout the period in question.

To assess the changes that the Salem police department underwent after the 1870s, the annual reports of the department, which are collected in the State House Library in Boston,

were consulted. These reports have been issued annually since the establishment of the department in 1852 with the exception of 1862, 1946, 1947, and 1948. In addition to a breakdown of arrests according to offense, they present a roster of the department from which the ethnic composition and the size of the department was determined. This information, together with budgetary data from the annual report of the town's auditor, provided the basis for a long-term description of the Salem police department and its adjustment to a changing political environment.

The city of Salem was selected for this research because it presented a long history going back to the 17th century. Since others have already studied its early period,[10] through the cumulation of individual efforts a complete history of Salem's criminality and mechanisms of social control might eventually be written. It was selected also because Salem is relatively small. In a city of 30–40,000, the newspaper can be depended upon to report the intimate details of events in the city; the counter-balancing currents of larger cities would be more likely to confound the analysis of its politics or its criminality.

BUSINESSMEN IN SALEM POLITICS

In the waning years of the 19th century, Salem was a slowly growing city of about 30,000. It had reached 20,000 in 1850; 30,000 in 1890; and by 1910 its population had edged up to 43,000. Its elections before the turn of the century were notable for their tranquility and the absence of issues. According to the *Salem Evening News,* for example, the election of 1891 was an exceedingly dull affair. "Salem is a city entirely without issues upon which to make parties. Personal popularity is the only test of a candidate's fitness . . ." (editorial page, Nov. 17, 1891); and there were several reports during the months and weeks before the campaign of prominent individuals who refused to run.

The *Evening News* was usually neutral in local politics, but it was distinctly Republican

---

[10] Kai T. Erikson, *Wayward Puritans* (New York: John Wiley, 1966).

and conservative in its editorial policies. It opposed, for example, permissive naturalization laws (Oct. 12, 1891); it supported the temperance movement (Dec. 1, 3, 7, 10, 1891); it favored the poll tax (Nov. 11, 1891); and it kept a critical eye on machine politics in other cities (Oct. 20, 22, and 24 and Nov. 18, 1891). At the same time, it was proud of Salem's politicians and the manner in which they usually conducted themselves (Oct. 13, 1891). There can be little doubt, moreover, that most of them were businessmen before entering politics and that businessmen in politics enjoyed considerable esteem among the town's people. A careful inspection of the candidates' campaign advertisements reveals that an early career as a small businessman was almost routine among Salem's politicians, and at one point the *Evening News* commented editorially on a slate of candidates as follows: "All are solid businessmen and there is no doubt of their ability. . . ." (Nov. 14, 1908).

This was also a period of declining city budgets. The city budget decreased every year but one between 1888 to 1895, and it fluctuated between $1,000,000 and $1,230,000 from 1896 to 1903. At the same time there was an active interest in police matters. The *Evening News* routinely reported police raids (July 18, 23, 24, 1891); and it was quick to report improprieties by the police in other cities (July 15 and Sept. 10, 1891). Moreover, on at least one occasion the City Council intervened to sanction a delinquent patrolman (Dec. 23, 1891).

As viewed through the eyes of the *Evening News,* Salem was a united city before the turn of the century, with few issues to divide its citizens into antagonistic camps. Its politicians were drawn mainly from business, and they pursued a policy of fiscal caution and restraint. The police were under careful scrutiny by both the *Evening News* and city officials, with the latter playing an active role in internal police matters. What effect did this rather placid but critical environment have upon the Salem police?

THE SALEM POLICE IN THE 19TH CENTURY

From 1876 to the end of the century, there is clear evidence of declining support for the po-

lice. Although their budget throughout this period was relatively stable (in 1876 it was $36,408 and in 1902 it was still only $38,866), their share of the city budget dropped from 6.9 percent in 1874–76 to 3.2 percent in 1901–03; and the number of officers per 1,000 population (see Figure 1) declined from 1.42 in 1871–73 to 0.97 in 1901–03, primarily because of population increase. In 1871–73 there was an average of 35 men on the force, and 30 years later in 1901–03 there was still an average of only 36. Clearly, during this period of fiscal caution, the Salem police were forced to accept a dwindling portion of the city's resources and to police a slowly growing city with essentially an unchanged complement of men.

What impact did these changes in budgetary support have upon the ways in which the Salem police performed their duties? They almost certainly had a damaging effect. Arrests per officer are also graphed in Figure 1, and it would appear that as budgetary support declined so did the vigilance of the men. Arrests per man dropped from 42.0 in 1871–73 to 23.4 in 1898–1900, *even though* there was a relatively smaller force to police the city.

But did declining vigilance affect the several functions of the police differently, or was the decline in effectiveness general? Wilson[11] draws a relevant distinction between law enforcement and order maintenance. In law enforcement the patrolman exercises somewhat less discretion than in maintaining order, since there is usually an angry citizen who demands action in some specific offense. In maintaining order, however, it is often only the patrolman who determines whether a crime has been committed; there is generally no one pushing him to make an arrest.

If the Salem police were demoralized by the city's lack of support, it should show most clearly in their order maintenance functions, since this is where arrests depend most heavily on police vigilance. Thus, the sharpest declines might be expected among crimes like vagrancy, drunkenness, and sex offenses, where arrests depend basically upon the initiative of the police; and the smallest declines should occur among those crimes like murder, manslaughter, rape,

---

[11] Wilson, *Varieties of Police Behavior,* Chapter 2.

FIGURE 1. POLICE PER 1,000 POPULATION AND ARRESTS PER OFFICER IN SALEM, 1862–1966

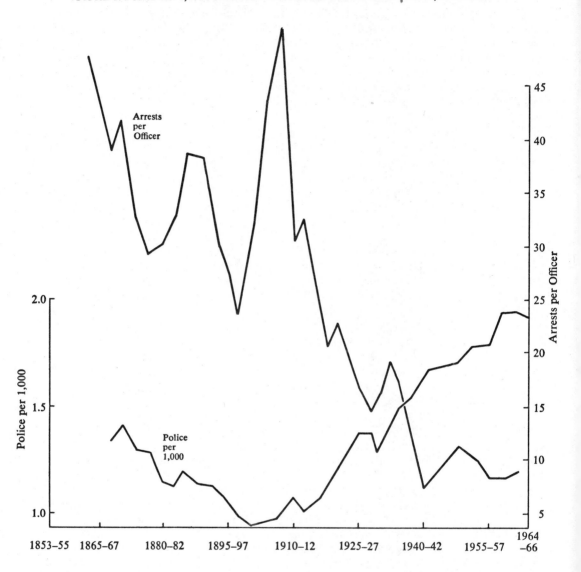

robbery, and aggravated assault, which tend to create considerable public pressure for arrests.

Inspection of Figure 2 suggests that this expectation was not precisely fulfilled. It is clear that arrests for vagrancy and sex offenses did decline substantially between 1874–76 and 1901–03. But the curve for drunkenness shows no obvious downward tendency during this period. Moreover, although arrests for murder, manslaughter, burglary, and rape (see Table 1) also fail to show any obvious declines during

this period—as they should—both arrests for aggravated assault and robbery do (see Table 1).

One reason that arrests for drunkenness show little evidence of declining police effectiveness may be that the sale of liquor in Salem was a subject of intense political debate throughout this period. In virtually every election, the question of whether to licence the sale of liquor in Salem was voted upon; and periodically no sale of liquor, i.e., prohibition, was endorsed by the citizens. During no-licence years, the number of arrests for drunkenness might be expected to decline; and according to the *Evening News* that is exactly what happened (Nov. 20, 1911, p. 10). Moreover, every raid of an illegal still was noted with approval in the *Evening News*. Since the activities of the police in arresting drunks and raiding illegal stills attracted attention, it may be that the police had little chance to relax their efforts in this area. In short, for reasons peculiar to Salem and the 19th century, arrests for drunkenness may not be a very good indicator of police vigilance.

To clarify this picture somewhat, we might also look at two additional crimes, i.e., simple assault and larceny, that stand midway between the most serious crimes that tend to spur even the most phlegmatic police departments into action and those public nuisance crimes that basically await police initiative for an arrest. These crimes generally have a victim who is interested in seeing an arrest, but they are so common and such minor crimes that arrests depend to a large extent upon the initiative and perseverance of the police. Moreover, they are crimes

FIGURE 2. ARRESTS FOR VAGRANCY, SEX OFFENSES AND DRUNKENNESS IN SALEM, 1853–1966

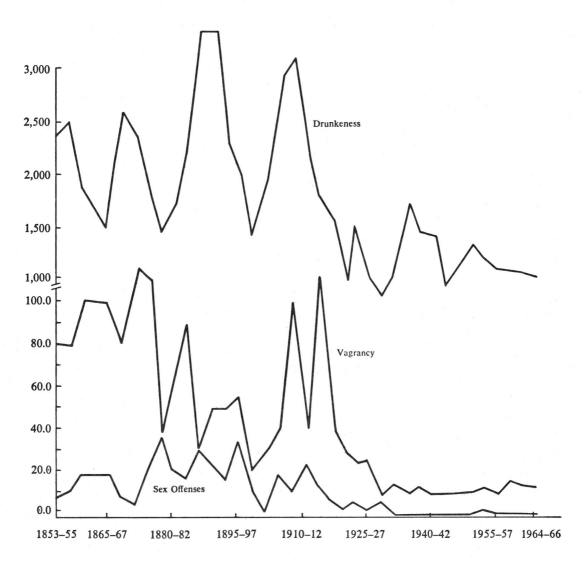

TABLE 1. ARRESTS PER 100,000 FOR MURDER, MANSLAUGHTER, RAPE, AGGRAVATED ASSAULT, ROBBERY, AND BURGLARY IN SALEM, MASSACHUSETTS

Year	Murder	Manslaughter	Rape	Agg. Assault	Robbery	Burglary
1966–64	0.8	0.8	2.5	5.0	8.3	44.0
1963–61	0.0	1.7	5.9	1.7	3.4	37.9
1960–58	0.8	0.0	5.1	8.4	11.0	50.6
1957–55	0.0	0.8	4.7	0.8	0.8	18.7
1954–52	3.2	0.8	4.1	4.1	4.9	17.1
1951–49	0.0	0.0	0.0	1.6	17.6	11.2
1948–46	—	—	—	—	—	—
1945–43	0.8	0.8	2.4	1.6	0.0	10.4
1942–40	0.0	0.0	4.0	0.0	1.6	13.7
1939–37	0.0	1.6	1.6	4.0	16.0	21.6
1936–34	0.0	0.8	3.2	3.9	7.9	43.4
1933–31	0.0	2.3	4.7	7.0	23.3	55.2
1930–28	0.0	3.8	2.3	6.2	3.1	39.3
1927–25	0.0	3.1	5.4	6.2	11.6	50.3
1924–22	0.0	10.1	7.0	7.1	13.2	50.6
1921–19	1.6	7.8	5.5	7.8	7.0	47.0
1918–16	3.1	7.8	2.3	19.4	1.6	48.2
1915–13	0.0	5.4	5.4	15.4	3.8	38.5
1912–10	0.0	2.3	3.8	16.1	0.0	47.4
1909–07	0.0	1.6	2.4	8.7	0.0	63.3
1906–04	0.0	0.8	0.8	2.5	0.0	51.9
1903–01	0.0	2.7	0.9	0.0	0.9	27.5
1900–98	0.0	0.0	1.9	0.0	0.0	41.4
1897–95	0.0	1.0	3.0	1.0	3.9	24.6
1894–92	0.0	0.0	2.2	3.1	4.1	29.9
1891–89	2.2	0.0	4.3	6.5	5.4	27.0
1888–86	0.0	0.0	1.8	7.8	0.0	23.4
1885–83	1.2	1.2	0.0	2.3	3.5	72.8
1882–80	0.0	0.0	4.8	9.6	13.1	53.8
1879–77	0.0	0.0	1.2	17.4	6.2	74.4
1876–74	0.0	1.3	3.9	29.7	14.2	74.8
1873–71	0.0	0.0	1.3	8.1	8.1	43.0
1870–68	0.0	0.0	0.0	2.8	12.6	32.1
1867–65	4.3	0.0	0.0	0.0	7.1	38.5
1864–62	—	—	—	—	—	—
1861–59	0.0	0.0	4.5	1.5	6.0	21.0
1858–56	0.0	0.0	6.2	3.1	7.7	23.1
1855–53	0.0	0.0	3.2	0.0	0.0	44.4

that excite little or no indignation among the general population.

Figure 3 reveals that, indeed, arrests for both crimes show remarkably sharp declines during the period under consideration. Arrests for assaults fell from a level of 882.3 per 100,000 in 1871–73 to 162.3 in 1895–97; arrests for larceny fell from 533.6 per 100,000 in 1877–79 to 114.1 in 1895–97. Thus, in the 30 years between 1870 and the turn of the century, arrests for

these two crimes dropped by about 80 percent! It would seem, then, that the Salem police did in fact relax their efforts in attempting to solve these common, but relatively innocuous crimes, even though they continued a high level of vigilance in most of the major crimes that occurred in Salem and in arrests for drunkenness.

Why did they also relax their attempts to solve robberies and aggravated assaults (see Table 1)? Robberies are especially difficult to

FIGURE 3. ARRESTS FOR LARCENY AND SIMPLE ASSAULT IN SALEM, 1853–1966

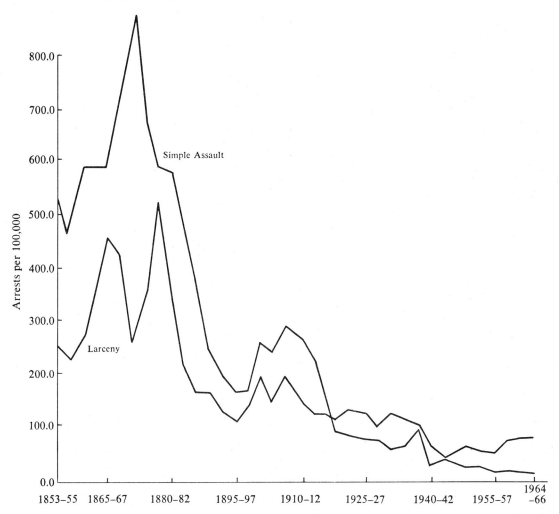

solve; unless the robber is apprehended at the scene, a solution of the crime requires very aggressive detective work. Any decline in the morale and alertness of the police, therefore, might be expected to make itself felt in the search for robbery suspects. The decline in arrests for aggravated assault may reflect a tendency around the turn of the century to regard *all* assaults as simple assaults. Aggravated assault was never a common crime in Salem; but for an eight-year period between 1896 and 1904, no arrests at all for aggravated assault were recorded! The Salem police seemingly sought to make their task easier by downgrading aggravated assaults to simple assault and ignoring a good portion of the total.

ETHNIC POLITICS COMES TO SALEM

As we have seen, before the turn of the century, politics in Salem was a relatively tame affair, with a minimum of issues and a dearth of campaign debate. Although the police department was weakened by cautious fiscal policies, it had not yet become a political pawn. Although the City Council routinely involved itself in the internal matters of the department, neither it nor the mayor regarded the department as a source of patronage. Indeed, quite the reverse. The town steadfastly refused to increase the size of the force, even though added slots would have meant additional ways of rewarding loyal supporters.

All this changed abruptly when the citizens of Salem elected John F. Hurley mayor in 1901 and 1902. Hurley was an Irishman who had come up the hard way. He had come to this country as a boy; before entering politics he had run a number of small businesses in Salem, including several taverns. He was a classic example of Dahl's ex-plebe in politics.[12]

Although his first term as mayor was rather uneventful, in his second term he instituted a number of changes in the police department that aroused much comment. First, he changed City Marshalls; and the new man, Marshall McKnight, was obviously not dedicated to the highest standards of police work. According to Hurley's critics, the City Marshall arbitrarily juggled beat assignments to punish his enemies and reward his friends; he allowed men accused of gambling to hire stand-ins to take their place in court; he failed to raid the largest illegal taverns in Salem; and when he did plan a raid, he allowed leaks to filter out to the intended target. Moreover, Mayor Hurley himself removed five patrolmen for vigorously enforcing the liquor laws, and he withheld the formal appointments of the entire force for nine months to intimidate those who might resist his permissive policy toward liquor enforcement (*Evening News*, Nov. 24 and Dec. 1, 1902, p. 1).

Whatever evaluation one may place on these actions, it is clear that under Mayor Hurley the Salem police department was drawn rather dramatically into the thick of political battle. Its role in enforcing the liquor ordinances inevitably brought it into the controversy between the wets and the dries; and in order to see *his* policy enforced, Mayor Hurley found it necessary to remove several men and to intimidate the rest.

At issue, however, was not simply the Mayor's peculiar views regarding the liquor ordinances. There was also an unmistakable overtone of

---

[12] Dahl, *Who Governs?* Chapter 4.

ethnic conflict when Mayor Hurley ran for a third term. The fact that Mayor Hurley was an Irish Catholic undoubtedly helped some make up their minds more easily in the controversy. Although the *Evening News* steadfastly denied that "sectarian considerations" played a part in its stand against Hurley (Nov. 25, 1902), his most vocal critics were the Protestant clergymen (Nov. 24, 1902, p. 1), and one of his Irish supporters publicly complained that Hurley would probably be criticized by the "ministers who use the pulpit as 'campaign stamping grounds'" for hiring a theater for a Sunday rally (Dec. 8, 1902). The Catholic priest in Salem proclaimed his neutrality in the election, even though Hurley supporters had used his church for a rally and had rumored it about town that Father Gadowry supported their leader.

The campaign of 1902 was clearly one of the most bitter ever to hit Salem. Hurley campaigned on a platform of Economy and Low Taxes; but when the votes were in, he had lost to Joseph N. Peterson 4,037 to 2,353. The result attracted considerable editorial comment around the state, with virtually all of it complimenting the people of Salem for having rid themselves of Hurley. For example, the *Lawrence Telegram* observed that:

> The people of Salem were first amused at his antics and then... disgusted. He brought no honor to the reputation of this staid old city. He was a nightmare, the result of a protest against the cut and dried methods of a ring of politicians who had run things to suit themselves so long that they fancied that they owned the city. The election of Mayor Hurley jarred the old combination and heralded the advent of a new order of things ...He has been weighed and found a trifle short measure. (Quoted in the Evening News, Dec. 11, 1902, p. 1.)

We might have expected that John F. Hurley would disappear from the political scene after such a bitter campaign and crushing defeat. But he came back as mayor in 1908, 1909, and won a three year term in 1912. In 1908 he ran against a respected businessman and Harvard graduate, Charles A. Archer, who was resolved to bring honesty back to City Hall. Archer campaigned against Hurley much as Peterson had done in 1902. He accused Hurley's City Marshall of ignoring a tavern selling illegal booze across the street from the police department; he called Hurley's administration "one of the rottenest political machines" he had ever seen (Dec. 2, 1908). Nevertheless, this time the people chose Hurley by a comfortable margin. There were no overtones of ethnic prejudice in this election sufficiently prominent to warrant a denial from the *Evening News;* but in the 1911 campaign in which Rufus D. Adams defeated William H. McSweeney, someone distributed a handout on election eve branding McSweeney as merely another Irish candidate seeking the Irish vote (Dec. 12, 1911, p. 5).

All in all, then, it would appear that ethnic conflict took a familiar course in Salem. There was a strong suspicion on the part of his Protestant critics that the Irish Mayor had used the office to further mainly his and his supporters' interests, principally by manipulating the police department; and there were indications throughout the campaign of appeals from both sides to ethnic or religious prejudice.

ETHNIC CONFLICT AND THE SALEM POLICE

In the midst of this kind of bitter political infighting we might expect that the reputation of the police would be tarnished and that their morale and effectiveness would be even further undermined. As political considerations became a determining factor in the administration of the department, the men on the force could not help but be stigmatized as political lackies by the people. Moreover, as the department's reputation plummeted, we might expect also that its budgetary support would weaken, its morale would decline, and its overall effectiveness would reach an abysmal low.

But for a variety of reasons, what actually happened was somewhat more complicated. The reputation of the department did suffer badly; its budgetary support was undercut, but its overall effectiveness *improved* considerably for a short time.

In the aftermath of the bitter political fights of 1902 and 1908, there is ample evidence that the police department was held in contempt by the people of Salem. During the campaign of 1908, the City Council itself was so divided that it was unable to pass an appropriation that would pay the full salaries of the police during the last three weeks of November; and as a result, the police were forced to go on half pay during this period (*Evening News,* Nov. 11, 1908, p. 1). The police eventually got their full salaries for November, but it is hard to imagine the police being treated today in such a cavalier fashion by their City Council.

Later, in 1911 the *Evening News* featured a front-page story describing the unwholesome conditions existing in the department's jail; it headlined the article, "Police Station a Filthy Hole" (Oct. 4, 1911). Again on November 6, 1911, the *Evening News* (p. 9) printed a letter from Charles F. W. Archer, a leading citizen of Salem, which was sharply critical of City Marshall Harris and his running of the department. The letter concluded by urging the voters to reject a proposal before the people that the City Marshall be brought under Civil Service and, thereby, placed beyond the control of the City Council and the mayor. On November 8, 1911, the *Evening News* reported that the people of Salem had rejected the proposal 3,310 to 1,619.

Two days later, on November 10, 1911, the citizens were startled to read in the *Evening News* of Marshall Harris' sudden resignation. The front page headline read, "No Politics Back of the Resignation of Marshall." But the accompanying story pointed out that the Marshall had resigned to care for his ailing wife, whose illness had been aggravated by "the constant persecution of her husband ... particularly the written attacks day after day...." The story concluded, "the opinion is current that there is room for great improvement in the local police force, and as head of the department the Marshall was forced to shoulder all the blame." Hard on the heels of Harris' resignation, Alderman Howard proposed that the salaries of the top officials in the city including the City Marshall's be cut by 25 percent (*Evening News,* Dec. 1, 1911, p. 1). The motion was carried with little debate.

Patrick J. Lehan replaced Marshall Harris on January 1, 1912, but the town's disenchantment with its police department was not dispelled. After Marshall Lehan had established himself in office, he began, predictably enough, a systematic campaign against commercialized vice in

Salem. The *Evening News* reported a series of police raids against gambling dens and illegal stills on October 5, 7, 29, and November 11, 1912.

It also reported on October 24, 1912, that the Board of Aldermen was raising a question about the police department. It seems that several pawn tickets had been confiscated from a suspect, and by the time the case was adjudicated, the tickets had disappeared. On November 14, 1912, the *Evening News* reported that the Board of Aldermen had asked for an accounting of the missing pawn tickets, and on December 4, 1912, an open hearing into the matter was held. According to a front page story in the *Evening News* on Dec. 5, 1912, the hearing was inconclusive; but the series of articles leading up to the hearing could not have helped but arouse dark suspicions among the people of Salem regarding their police department.

As far as the department's budget is concerned, after the turn of the century the police continued to receive a slowly declining portion of the city's revenues. Between 1901–03 and 1922–24 the department's share of the city budget fell from 3.2 percent to 2.7 percent of the total; and it continued to fluctuate between 3.1 and 2.7 percent until 1943–45. The actual appropriations received by the department showed moderate increases up to 1930, but these increases actually represented a slowly shrinking share of the city's overall resources. It is probably not incorrect to suggest that the tarnished reputation of the department before World War I seriously undermined its ability to inspire support from the city and its officers.

Ordinarily the morale and effectiveness of the police might be expected to deteriorate badly before such criticism and lack of budgetary support. But it is apparent from Figure 2, that its effectiveness, at least, increased sharply after the turn of the century. We have already seen that arrests per officer declined abruptly during the last 25 years of the 19th century. But in 1901–03 they started upward again; by 1907–09 they had more than doubled their 1901–03 level. In 1910–12, however, arrests per officer started a decline that has continued to the present. Nevertheless, for ten years after the turn of the century, they rose to record levels. How

might we explain this rather surprising development?

It may be that the city faced an extraordinary crime wave during this period which forced the police to make an unprecedented number of arrests. If so, it is interesting that the number of arrests increased most sharply for those crimes that depend most heavily upon police initiative and vigilance. We have already seen why arrests for larceny and assault are probably good indicators of police vigilance in Salem. As can be seen from Figure 3, these crimes, along with vagrancy (Figure 2), display marked increases in arrests between 1900 and 1910. It would be difficult to explain simultaneous increases in these offenses, none in major crimes, and only moderate increases in drunkenness and sex offenses, in terms of a highly specific crime wave.

A more acceptable explanation may be that during this period Irishmen were coming into the department in increasing numbers; and since this was also a period of rather sharp Irish-Yankee conflict, they felt obliged to prove their worth as policemen to their Yankee superiors by an extraordinary attention to their duties and responsibilities. Many black policemen today have displayed similar reactions in predominantly white departments;[13] and it is clear from Figure 4 that between 1900 and 1910 the percentage of Irish officers was climbing rapidly. In 1901–03 the department included 31.2 percent Irishmen; by 1907–09 this figure had climbed to 39.7. By 1910 several ranking officers were Irishmen; and in 1912 the first Irish City Marshall was appointed, Patrick J. Lehan.

By 1910, then, Irishmen needed no longer fear the critical scrutiny of Yankee superior officers; they could relax their vigilance in police work. Hence, when the department became substantially Irish, with Irish leadership, its level of arrests declined to levels more nearly normal. The fact that these declines were most noticeable in exactly those crimes that depend heavily upon police vigilance for their solution, i.e., larceny, assault, and vagrancy, suggests strongly that there is some substance to this argument.

After 1912 the Irish solidified their hold on

---

[13] Nicholas Alex, *Black in Blue* (New York: Appleton-Century-Crofts, 1969).

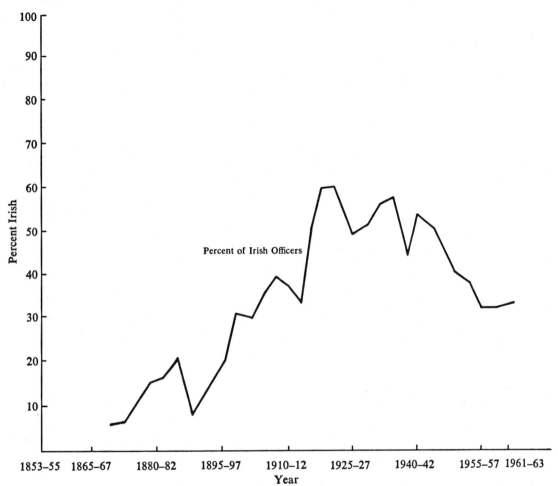

FIGURE 4. THE PERCENTAGE OF IRISH OFFICERS IN THE SALEM POLICE DEPARTMENT FROM 1868 TO 1963

the department. Although Yankee mayors have been elected periodically since 1912, leadership in the police department has consistently been Irish during this period. The declines that had set in in the late 19th century reasserted themselves after 1912 with the result that the Salem department today resembles Wilson's watchman department quite closely.[14]

As can be seen from Figures 2 and 3, the department is still quite selective in its arrest policies. Minor crimes that arouse little indignation in the community like larceny, assault, and vagrancy, are not pursued vigorously at all;

and now, reflecting a shift in the concern of the community, drunkenness and sex offenses are also included in this category.

No general drop in arrests for major crimes is apparent. True, arrests for manslaughter and aggravated assault have dropped off in the 20th century, but we have already explained that the Salem police began to regard nearly all assaults as simple assault around the turn of the century; and the decline in manslaughter arrests probably reflects a change in the manner in which deaths in auto accidents are handled in Massachusetts.[15]

As might be expected in light of these spe-

---

[14] Wilson, *Varieties of Police Behavior*, Chapter 5.

[15] Ferdinand, "The Criminal Patterns of Boston Since 1846."

cific changes, arrests per officer (see Figure 1) resumed their downward path in 1910–12 and reached in 1961–63 a level one-fifth their 1907–09 level.

The police budget tells much the same story. From 1907–09 to 1961–63 the police budget increased tenfold—from $149,368 to $1,530,233—but this absolute increase actually reflects a slight decrease in the proportion of the city budget allocated to the police, from 3.9 to 3.3 percent. The fact that during this period the relative size of the force nearly doubled (see Figure 1), from 1.0 per 1,000 population in 1907–09 to 1.9 in 1964–66, merely adds support to the thesis of a continuing deterioration.

The increasing size of the department together with the *decreasing* number of arrests per officer implies quite clearly that the increases in the force have had little positive effect upon the overall effectiveness of the department. The steady increases in relative size, which began in Mayor Hurley's administration in 1902 and have continued almost without interruption to the present, more probably reflect the politicizing of the department. Additions to the force provided a convenient means of increasing the patronage available to the mayor.

In sum, then, I have suggested that the long decline of the Salem police department from the 1870s to the present era can best be explained in terms of two quite distinct transformations in the structure of politics in Salem. First, as the city and the Northeast as a whole participated in the commercial and industrial expansion of the late 19th century, businessmen entered politics in numbers and brought with them, especially after the depression of 1873–78, a cautious, conservative philosophy in fiscal matters. During this period the police department began a long, continuing decline, during which both the budget and levels of arrests showed a steady deterioration. The police were under close scrutiny from both the City Council and the *Salem Evening News;* but as yet there was no indication that the department did not enjoy the general confidence and respect of the public.

During Mayor John F. Hurley's second term in 1902, however, Salem was transformed. Her elections—that had once been routine and almost serene—were knock-down, drag-out affairs in which issues, personalities, and ethnic slanders were inextricably intertwined. For whatever reasons, Mayor Hurley intervened drastically in the operations of the police and contributed thereby to its general deterioration. Soon the police were coming under almost constant criticism from the clergy, the *Evening News,* and the mayor's opponents on the City Council; and after the Irish had established themselves in the department, the department's long decline began again.

In essence, then, although the department was already crumbling as a result of stringent budgets during the last decades of the 19th century, it still enjoyed wide respect among the town's people. But when bitter partisan politics came to Salem in the wake of the Irish immigration, the police department was drawn into the thick of battle; and its reputation dropped to an abysmal low, never to recover. Thus it is clear from this research that the effectiveness of Salem's police department was deeply affected by both the general level of budgetary support provided by the city and its general reputation in the city. When either of these was depressed, the effectiveness of the department, as measured by differential arrest rates, was sharply affected. The theses advanced both by Dahl[16] and by Wilson[17] seem to be supported.

CONCLUSION

A legitimate question at this point (and one that is often heard) could be: "So what?" Of what value is an understanding of the circumstances behind the long deterioration of the Salem department? Apart from the fact that it is of some satisfaction finally to have answered a nagging problem, I might suggest that this knowledge provides an important perspective on events today. Many city administrations today are in the process of changing from white to black; and if the experience of Salem is any criterion, these transformations in City Hall may have profound effects upon the relevant police departments. It could be that as politics engulfs the police departments in these cities in the

16 Dahl, *Who Governs?*
17 Wilson, *Varieties of Police Behavior.*

1970s, they will undergo long declines not unlike that seen in Salem after 1902. These departments will deteriorate, that is, if we fail to learn from the past.

White mayors in cities like St. Louis, Philadelphia, Detroit, Chicago, and New York, which in the foreseeable future will have black mayors, must begin to take this probability into account when making appointments to city agencies, including the police department. If these white mayors can make the transition from white to black relatively peaceful by appointing men today who can facilitate it, they may be able to isolate these departments from politics and protect them from the worst ravages of white-black conflict. But if they refuse to accept the inevitable and to prepare their departments for black leadership, they will encourage a politicizing of these departments and pave the way for another period of demoralization and ineffectiveness.

By looking at the changing fortunes of the police in Salem, we have gained some insights into the implications of bitter factional politics for the police. Perhaps we can avoid some of the worst results of this factionalism by taking steps now to head it off. Some cities have not been prepared for these basic shifts, see Cleveland, Gary, and Newark; as a result, the incoming black mayors have had to build their administrations upon the wreckage that accompanied their coming to power.

CHAPTER FOUR

HOMICIDE

In comparison to economic crime, crimes of violence are few in number. In terms of economic impact on society, violent crimes take much less toll than white-collar crime. Yet, because of the physical violence involved, violent crimes (whether or not in connection with economic crimes, such as robbery) probably evoke greater fear among the law-abiding public. Andrew Hacker states: "A face-to-face threat of bodily harm or possibly violent death is so terrifying to most people that the $20 or so stolen in a typical mugging must be multiplied many times if comparisons with other offenses are to be made."[1] Although it may be an overstatement to assert "that a majority of city-dwellers would accept a bargain under which if they would not be mugged this year they would be willing to allow white-collar crime to take an extra ten percent of their incomes,"[2] there is most certainly an element of truth here. As we noted in the previous chapter, evidence indicates that the primary fear most people have about crime focusses on physical violence and their own physical safety.[3] The most extreme form of violence is murder, of course. This is the topic of this chapter.

In contrast to most forms of deviant behavior, there have been few empirical or theoretical analyses of homicide. Nevertheless, there are some well-established facts about this type of behavior. One is the interpersonal context of homicide. The homicide victim is usually a person well acquainted with the murderer, so that the relationship between the murderer and his victim is frequently emotional in nature. (See p. 178 below.) Homicide may occur when there is a disruption in this relationship (e.g., quarrel), so that tempers flare and violence ensues. Most homicides, therefore, are not rational and planned acts but are spontaneous outbursts of violence. A second established fact is that the weapon most frequently

---

[1] Andrew Hacker, "Street Crime: Getting Used to Mugging," *The New York Review* 20 (April 19, 1973), p. 9.

[2] *Ibid.*

[3] See Robert W. Winslow, *Crime in a Free Society: Selections from the President's Commission on Law Enforcement and Administration of Justice* (Belcourt, California: Dickerson Publishing Company, 1968), p. 17.

used in homicide is a firearm. Since it is probably impossible to eliminate disruptions in emotionally-charged relationships, one way to reduce the homicide rate would be to control the sale and possession of firearms. This, of course, is the aim of advocates of gun control legislation. The relationship between the level of firearm ownership and the homicide rate is dramatically portrayed in Detroit. A surge in ownership of guns, which began in 1967, is generally attributed to the riots and burnings that occurred in the black ghetto sections of the city in that year. In just 6 years, the rate of homicides by firearms increased eightfold.[4]

A. ANTECEDENTS AND DETERMINANTS

In developing etiological theories of homicide, sociologists have focussed on the fact that there are group differences in the homicide rate. For example, the homicide rate is much higher for males and blacks than it is for females and whites. There are two major types of sociological theories on the subject of group differences in the homicide rate. One emphasizes subcultural differences in the *expression* of violence; the other focusses on group and subcultural differences in the *channeling* of responses to frustration and contends that homicide is an alternative to suicide. An example of each theory is presented in this section.

The first type of theory is supported by Marvin Wolfgang's investigation, reported in *Patterns in Criminal Homicide.* His investigation is the most extensive empirical analysis of homicide available. In this chapter the selection by Wolfgang, "The Sociological Analysis of Homicide," is a condensed version of his book. While a number of facets of homicide are explored in the paper, of primary concern are the determinants of homicide.

One of Wolfgang's major findings is that certain social categories are overrepresented among murderers. For example, a disproportionate number of murderers are blacks and males. Wolfgang proposes a "subculture of violence" hypothesis to account for this. Physical combat to prove one's courage or to defend one's status receives more support in the value systems of blacks and males than in that of whites and females. It is also true that homicide rates are higher in southern states than in most other regions of the country; according to one author,[5] this is due to regional differences in the subculture of violence, which is considered to be stronger in the southern region than other regions. This regional difference may be a factor in the high homicide rate in Detroit. Because of its need for unskilled workers, this city attracts large numbers of unskilled rural migrants from the South. The subculture of violence hypothesis is consistent with the findings of a recent psychiatric study of individual

---

[4] *Time* (April 16, 1973), p. 17.
[5] Raymond D. Gastil, "Homicide and a Regional Culture of Violence," *American Sociological Review* 36 (April, 1971), pp. 412–27.

murders, which concludes that "the homicidal act seems 'determined' more by an environment of violence than by specific dynamic mechanisms or individual pathology."[6]

Another theory includes psychological dynamics in its causal explanation of homicide. In this theory homicide is examined in terms of the dynamics of frustration and aggression; suicide and homicide represent two alternative ways of responding aggressively to frustration. (Other similarities between suicide and homicide will be noted in Chapter 10, pp. 461–505.) One way to respond to frustration is to direct aggression inward toward the self, with suicide being the ultimate form of expression. The other way is to express aggression outward against others; in which case homicide is the ultimate form. Proponents of this type of theory observe that homicide and suicide rates are inversely related—e.g., groups with low rates of one frequently have high rates of the other.[7] This suggests that conditions that encourage one kind of aggression may tend to inhibit the other.

This position is taken by Andrew F. Henry and James F. Short, Jr., in *Suicide and Homicide.* Their theory is reviewed by Martin Gold in "Suicide, Homicide, and the Socialization of Aggression," which is reprinted in this section. In Henry and Short's theory, both suicide and homicide originate in frustration, but "external restraints" determine how frustration will be expressed. When restraints are high, aggression is more apt to take the form of homicide than suicide, whereas the reverse is likely when restraints are low. Gold contends, however, that parental discipline is also crucial. He argues that the type of punishment administered by parents is an important determinant in how aggression will be expressed later in life. Specifically, psychological punishment encourages suicide while physical punishment encourages homicide. He believes that this accounts for group differences in the ratio of homicides to suicides.

---

[6] Jordan H. Lachman and James M. Cravens, "The Murderers—Before and After," *The Psychiatric Quarterly* 43 (1969), p. 11.

[7] For cities and states in the United States, see Austin L. Porterfield, "Indices of Suicide and Homicide by States and Cities: Southern-Non-Southern Contrasts with Implications for Research," *American Sociological Review* 14 (August, 1949), p. 488.

A SOCIOLOGICAL ANALYSIS OF CRIMINAL HOMICIDE
MARVIN E. WOLFGANG

Murder and other types of criminal homicide are deviations of the most serious and visible kind in our society. Public concern, the amount

Reprinted with permission of author and publisher from *Federal Probation Quarterly* 25 (March, 1961), pp. 48–55 as abridged.

of time the police spend in detection and investigation, the ratio of the number of police to the number of these crimes, and the quantity of stories in literature and the drama that use murder as a central theme all attest to the interest we have in homicide. However, the television or literary mystery usually is concerned with the relatively rare premeditated type of killing. Most homicides have typical forms and are crimes of passion that arise from a world of violence.

The typical criminal slayer is a young man in his twenties who kills another man only slightly older. Both are of the same race; if Negro, the slaying is commonly with a knife, if white, it is a beating with fists and feet on a public street. Men kill and are killed between four and five times more frequently than women, but when a woman kills she most likely has a man as her victim and does it with a butcher knife in the kitchen. A woman killing a woman is extremely rare, for she is most commonly slain by her husband or other close friend by a beating in the bedroom.

These are some of the findings of a study more fully described in *Patterns in Criminal Homicide*.[1] Since publication of this book, a variety of requests for a summary discussion have come to my desk, partly, I imagine, because of the recent renewed interest in the sociopsychological aspects of criminal homicide reflected in Guttmacher's *The Mind of the Murderer*,[2] Palmer's *A Study of Murder*,[3] and in Bohannan's *African Homicide and Suicide*.[4] What follows, therefore, is an abbreviated analysis of my own sociological study with suggestive theoretical points of departure for additional research. For detailed information of the research methods and interpretive analysis of criminal homicide, the reader is referred to the present author's book.

WHAT IS CRIMINAL HOMICIDE?

The popular press and even some of our national, state, and municipal police officials sometimes confuse murder with other types of criminal homicide. As every capable policeman should know, homicide is the killing of another person and is divided into criminal and noncriminal homicide. The former category comprises mur-

der (commonly in the first and second degree) as well as voluntary (nonnegligent) and involuntary (negligent) manslaughter. Noncriminal homicide is excusable, or a killing in self-defense, and justifiable homicide, or homicide performed as a legal duty by a peace officer or executioner. Confusion of these terms, mixing criminal with noncriminal cases, and mislabeling murder for other types of criminal homicides, has occurred in both professional and popular studies.

In order to produce some clarity among these terms and to provide a sociological and statistical analysis of criminal homicide, research was conducted in Philadelphia, using all criminal homicides recorded by the Philadelphia Homicide Squad from January 1, 1948 through December 31, 1952. Excusable and justifiable homicides were excluded from the study and concentration was only on criminal cases listed by the police. I spent many long hours over several years collecting the data and participating in arrest and interrogation of offenders, and I have the highest respect for the police officers with whom I came into contact during that period. The homicide detectives consistently showed due respect for the constitutional rights of persons they arrested as well as an attitude of understanding rather than that of vengeance and retribution. These are, of course, qualities desirable in all police officers, for their function is to protect as well as to apprehend, to make suspects available for prosecution, but not to judge guilty.

It is almost axiomatic in criminal statistics that for purposes of determining the amount and type of crime committed in a community, police statistics yield the most valid data.[5] Too many cases are lost through court trials to use court statistics, and to use prison data means a still further reduction of cases that are highly selected to result in incarceration instead of probation or some other form of disposition. For this reason, police statistics were used to obtain

---

[1] Marvin E. Wolfgang, *Patterns in Criminal Homicide* (Philadelphia, Pennsylvania: University of Pennsylvania Press, 1958), p. 413.

[2] Manfred S. Guttmacher, *The Mind of the Murderer* (New York, N.Y.: Farrar, Strauss and Cudahy, 1960).

[3] Stuart Palmer, *A Study of Murder* (New York, N.Y.: Thomas Y. Crowell, 1960).

[4] Paul Bohannan, editor, *African Homicide and Suicide* (Princeton, N.J.: Princeton University Press, 1960).

---

[5] The advantages of police statistics and limitations of other sources of data for criminal homicide research have been discussed in: Thorsten Sellin, "The Basis of a Crime Index," *Journal of Criminal Law and Criminology* 22 (September, 1931), pp. 335–56; T. Sellin, *Crime and the Depression* (New York: Social Science Research Council Memorandum*, 1937), Chapter 4; T. Sellin, "The Measurement of Criminality in Geographic Areas," *Proceedings of the American Philosophical Society* 97 (April, 1953), pp. 163–67. For additional references, see the author's *Patterns in Criminal Homicide*, p. 12, n. 1.

the most valid picture of criminal homicides over this 5-year period.

Another important aspect of the research design was to distinguish between victims and offenders in terms of their major social characteristics. Usually this distinction is not maintained in studies of homicide, especially in those that rely only on mortality statistics published by the Office of Vital Statistics from death certifications. The Philadelphia study and review of the literature on criminal homicide reveal that much confusion of terminology pervades the field; that data about victims often are confused with data about offenders; rates per population unit are sometimes confused with reports about proportionate distributions or percentages of criminal slayings. We have emphasized constantly the invalidity of inferring characteristics about victims from criminal statistics, some of which supply data only for offenders; or of inferring characteristics about offenders from mortality statistics, which supply data only for victims.

Most previous research has examined *either* the victim *or* the offender. In the present work, analysis has been made of *both* victims and offenders, separately, as distinct units, but also as mutual participants in the homicide. A broad social approach is interested both in the active, "to kill," and in the passive, "to be killed." It is one type of analysis to consider victims as a social group and offenders as another social group; it is quite a different and more refined type of analysis to consider specific victim-offender relationships, and to find race, sex, age, and other patterns among them.

During the period from 1948 through 1952 there were 588 cases of criminal homicide in Philadelphia; i.e., there were 588 victims. Because several people were sometimes involved in killing one person, there were 621 offenders arrested by the police and taken into custody. In terms of a mean annual rate per 100,000 population in the city, the victim rate was 5.7 and the offender rate 6.0. This is neither high nor low. Compared with 18 other cities across the country, each of which had a population of a quarter of a million or more in 1950, Philadelphia ranks ninth, with the range between Miami having a victim rate of 15.1 and Milwaukee having a low of 2.3. New York's rate was only

3.7, Los Angeles 4.0, and Chicago 7.8. The rate for Pennsylvania as a whole for 1950 was only 3.5, but the most fair comparison is between cities of comparable size.[6]

The years 1948–52 were advantageous years for research purposes because the census fell exactly in the middle of this period so that the population statistics for 1950 could be used for computing a rate for any of the single 5 years or for all of them together. Moreover, it should be noted that the data collected from police files and used to analyze suggested associations and questions are expressed in numerical and percentage frequency distributions, in rates per 100,000 population in some cases, and in ratios. In order to safeguard against loose generalizations, several tests of statistical significance were employed.[7]

SOME BASIC FINDINGS: RACE, SEX, AND AGE

Research has shown that although criminal homicide is largely an unplanned act, there are nonetheless in the act regular uniformities and patterns. We have found, as previous research has noted, that there is a statistically significant association between criminal homicide and the race and sex of both victim and offender. Negroes and males involved in homicide far exceed their proportions in the general population and rates for these two groups are many times greater than for whites and females. The rate per 100,000 by race and sex of offenders reveals the following rank order of magnitude: Negro males (41.7), Negro females (9.3), white males (3.4), and white females (.4). Although Negroes of either sex, and males of either race, are positively related to criminal slayings, the associa-

---

[6] It is obvious to any student in the field that there are many criminal offenses committed that are never reported or recorded by the public authorities. This generalization is applicable to criminal homicide as it is to other offenses. But a theoretical analysis of the social visibility of crime, or the varying degrees of high and low reportability of specific offenses, leads us to suggest that there is a relatively low ratio between offenses committed and those known to the police in cases of criminal homicide.

[7] For the most part, the statistical tests involved use of the non-parametric technique of Chi-square (X^2) with corrections for continuity and a probability level of (P) less than .05.

tion between race and homicide is statistically more significant than that between sex and homicide. This relationship of Negroes and males to criminal homicide confirms reports and studies made elsewhere in this country, although the proportion of female offenders is reportedly much higher in England. It should be noted, however, that the whole of the British Isles has no more criminal homicides in a year than the city of Philadelphia alone (or about 125 annually).

Among offenders, the age group 20–24 predominates with a rate of 12.6 per 100,000, while the highest rate for victims is in the age group 25–34. In short, victims are generally older than their offenders; the median age of the former being 35.1 years and of the latter, 31.9 years. The importance of the race factor here is striking in view of the fact that the *lowest* 5-year age-specific rates for Negro males and females are similar to, or higher than the *highest* of such rates for white males and females, respectively. Although males of both races more frequently commit criminal homicide during their twenties than during any other period of life, Negro males in their early sixties kill as frequently as do white males in their early twenties.

The race factor in criminal homicide is alarming and should be the cause of both Negro and white community leaders to examine more closely the reasons for this differential. The child is not born with homicide tendencies in his genes, so that in no way can we infer a biological explanation for this difference. Negroes are a minority group that still suffer from residential and general cultural isolation from the rest of the community, despite recent advances in integration. So long as this ethnic group is socially isolated and required to live in restricted residential areas they will continue to constitute a "subcultural" area. This subculture is characterized by poor housing, high density of population, overcrowded home conditions, and by a system of values that often condones violence and physical aggression from child-rearing processes to adult interpersonal relationships that sometimes end in criminal slayings. To a lesser degree, whites in the lower socioeconomic classes as well as Negroes become part of this *subculture of violence* and participate in criminal homicide. Only by breaking up this culturally isolated group and by integrating them into the general community of morality and values can society hope to reduce violence that results in homicide.

METHODS AND TIME OF ASSAULT

We have also noted significant associations between methods of inflicting death and the race and sex of both victims and offenders. In Philadelphia 39 percent of all homicides were due to stabbings, 33 percent to shootings, 22 percent to beatings, and 6 percent to other and miscellaneous methods. There appears to be a cultural preference for particular types of methods and weapons. Males, if Negro, usually stab and are stabbed to death; and if white, beat and are beaten to death. Females generally stab their victims with a butcher knife, but are very often beaten to death.

Although homicides tend to increase during the hot summer months, there is no significant association by seasons or months of the year. But homicide is significantly associated with days of the week and hours of the day. The weekend in general, and Saturday night in particular, are related to homicide, as are the hours between 8 P.M. and 2 A.M. Between 8 P.M. Friday and midnight Sunday there were, during the 5 years under review, 380 criminal homicides; but from the beginning of Monday morning to 8 P.M. Friday, there were only 208. Thus, on the average, 65 percent of all homicides occurred during the shorter time span of 52 hours, while only 35 percent occurred during the longer time span of 116 hours.

The time between assault and death of the victim varies according to the method employed by the offender. Relatively quick death (within 10 minutes after assault) occurred for half of the victims in a shooting, for less than three-tenths in a stabbing, and for only one-sixteenth in a beating. About a third of the victims were dead within 10 minutes after assault, slightly less than three-fifths after the first hour had passed, and four-fifths within a day. Only 5 percent lived more than 10 days after being assaulted. Probably fewer persons today die from aggravated assault wounds than was true a generation ago, for data suggest that (1) improved communication with the police, (2) more rapid transportation to a hospital (usually by the police), and (3) advanced medical technology have contributed to the decreasing homicide rates in this country during the last 25 years.

We do not know, of course, just how many aggravated assaults, assaults with intent to kill, and other violent assaults are today prevented from becoming classified as criminal homicides because of these three factors, but the steady increases of other crimes of personal violence, such as aggravated assaults and rapes, regularly reported in the Uniform Crime Reports lead us to suggest that something other than a greater repugnance to commit crimes of personal violence has entered our mores. Many factors are involved in changing rates of homicide, such as the age composition, business cycles, etc. But because crimes of violence against the person, excluding homicide, appear to have increased during the past two decades, it is logical to assume that if these gross social factors affect homicide, they should affect other crimes of violence in the same way.

Research testing the hypothesis suggested by the three factors mentioned above might be useful in explaining the general decrease in criminal homicide over the past 25 years.[8] It would be valuable, for example, to know the recovery rate for those who are today greviously assaulted but who would have probably died under medical and other conditions of a generation ago. Although this type of analysis fails to account for any psychological dimensions in the phenomenon of homicide, the approach nonetheless has the virtue of measurability in testing the validity of the explanation.

PLACE WHERE CRIMES OCCUR

The place where the crime occurred is also important. The most dangerous single place is the highway (public street, alley, or field), although more slayings occur in the home than outside the home. Men kill and are killed most frequently in the street, while women kill most often in the kitchen but are killed in the bedroom. For victims and offenders of each race and sex group significant differences have been noted. Most cases of Negro males who kill Negro males involve a stabbing in a public street; most cases of white males who kill white males involve a beating in a public street. However, the high proportion of females who kill with a butcher knife in a kitchen, and of those who are killed in a bedroom by being beaten is associated with the fact that 84 percent of all female offenders slay males and 87 percent of all female victims are slain by males.

PRESENCE OF ALCOHOL

Either or both the victim and offender had been drinking immediately prior to the slaying in nearly two-thirds of the cases. The presence of alcohol in the homicide situation appears to be significantly associated with Negroes—either as victims or as offenders—and, separately, with Negro male and female victims. Particular caution[9] must be exercised in evaluating the presence of alcohol in these homicides, since drinking—particularly on Saturday night, the time of highest incidence of homicide—is an integral part of the mores of most groups involved in this crime. A significantly higher proportion of weekend homicides than of homicides occurring during the remainder of the week had alcohol present (in either the victim, the offender, or both). An association between alcohol, weekend slayings, and the payment of wages on Friday was indicated and crudely confirmed by the available data. We have, therefore, suggested that when the socioeconomic group most likely to commit homicide almost simultaneously receives its

---

[8] A recent analysis of this hypothesis has been made for Ceylon. See Cleobis Jayewardene, "Criminal Homicide: A Study in Culture Conflict," Ph.D. Thesis (University of Pennsylvania, 1960).

[9] Problems of analyzing the presence of alcohol in the victim and in the offender were particularly trying. In addition to Chapter 8 in the book, the reader is referred to the author's paper (with R. Strohm) for discussion of these problems in "The Relationship Between Alcohol and Criminal Homicide," *Quarterly Journal of Studies in Alcohol* 17 (September, 1956), pp. 411–25.

weekly wages, purchases alcohol, and meets to-gether socially, it is not unlikely that the inci-dence of homicide should also rise.

PREVIOUS POLICE RECORD AND VICTIM-OFFENDER RELATIONSHIPS

Contrary to many past impressions, an analysis of offenders in criminal homicide reveals a rela-tively high proportion who have a previous po-lice or arrest record. Of total offenders, nearly two-thirds have a previous arrest record, and of total victims, almost half have such a record. Having a previous record is also associated with males both among victims and offenders, and is obvious from the fact that more *male victims* have such a record than do *female offenders*. Moreover, when an offender has a previous rec-ord, he is more likely to have a record of of-fenses against the person than against property; and when he has a record of offenses against the person, he is more likely than not to have a record of having committed a serious assault of-fense, such as aggravated assault or assault with intent to kill. A greater proportion of Negro male and female victims have a previous arrest record than do white male and female offenders, respectively. In view of these facts, it is of in-terest to future attempts at prevention and con-trol of potential offenders in criminal homicide that *a larger proportion of offenders with an ar-rest record have a record of aggravated assault than of all types of property offenses combined.* The courts should take special care not to re-lease too hastily and without proper individual-ized treatment those persons arrested on charges of personal assault in order to prevent later homicides.

Criminal homicide usually results from a vaguely defined altercation, domestic quarrel, jealously, argument over money, and robbery. These five police-recorded "motives" are in-volved in 8 out of 10 cases. Most of the identi-fied victim-offender relationships may be clas-sified as "primary group" relations, or those that include intimate, close, frequent contacts. Close friends and relatives accounted for over half of the contacts, and the combined categories which involve primary group contacts constitute 59 per-cent of all victim-offender relationships among males, but significantly as much as 84 percent among females. Because white males were killed more frequently than Negro males during the commission of a robbery, the former were also more frequently strangers to their slayers than the latter.

Mate slayings have been given special atten-tion.[10] Of the 100 husband-wife homicides, 53 victims were wives and 47 were husbands. The number of wives killed by their husbands con-stitutes 41 percent of all women killed, whereas husbands slain by their wives make up only 11 percent of all men killed. Thus, when a woman commits homicide, she is more likely than a man to kill her mate; and when a man is killed by a woman, he is most likely to be killed by his wife. Husbands are often killed by their wives in the kitchen with a butcher knife, but nearly half of the wives are slain in the bedroom. More male than female offenders in these spouse slayings were found guilty, were convicted of more seri-ous degrees of homicide, and committed suicide.

In 94 percent of the cases, the victim and of-fender were members of the same race, but in only 64 percent they were of the same sex. Thus, the ratio of intra- to interracial homicide is 15.2 to 1; but the ratio of intra- to intersex homicide is only 1.8 to 1. In general, it may be said that victims were homicidally assaulted most fre-quently by males of their own race, and least frequently by females of another race.

In 32 cases involving 57 offenders and 6 vic-tims, a felony, in addition to the killing, was perpetrated at the time of the slaying. In most cases the other felony was robbery, and white males accounted for a larger proportion of these felony-murders than they did among all homi-cides in general.

VICTIM-PRECIPITATED HOMICIDE

The term *victim-precipitated* homicide has been introduced to refer to those cases in which the victim is a direct, positive precipitator in the

---

[10] See also the author's analysis of "Husband-Wife Homi-cides," *The Journal of Social Therapy* 2 (1956), pp. 263–71.

crime—the first to use physical force in the homicide drama. After establishing a theoretical and legal basis for analysis, the Philadelphia data reveal several factors significantly associated with the 150 victim-precipitated homicides, which is 26 percent of all homicides. These factors are: Negro victims and offenders, male victims, female offenders, stabbings, victim-offender relationships involving male victims and female offenders, mate slayings, husbands who were victims in mate slayings, alcohol, victims with a previous arrest record, particularly an arrest record of assault. Thus, in most of these cases, the role and characteristics of the victim and offender are reversed, the victim assumes the role of determinant, and the victim makes a definite contribution to the genesis of his own victimization.[11]

Recently, I have extended the meaning of victim-precipitated homicide to include a sociological and psychoanalytic discussion of these 150 victims as being bent on suicide.[12] Although it is impossible to verify an assumption of subconscious suicide wishes among these victims, empirical data from broad social factors combine with psychological and sociological data suggesting that victims in many cases present themselves as willing targets for violent aggression leading to homicide. It is hoped that the material presently being accumulated by John Macdonald at the Colorado Psychopathic Hospital on "The Murderer and His Victim"[13] will shed additional light on this area of analysis.

SUICIDE AFTER PERFORMING HOMICIDE

In 24 cases the offenders committed suicide after performing the homicide.[14] Of these, 22 were males, nearly half of whom were men who had killed their wives. Analysis and evaluation of these homicide-suicides indicate that half of the homicides would have been classified as first-degree murder had the offender experienced a court trial. As a result, even with the low amount of suicide after homicide in this country, more offenders inflict death upon themselves than are put to death by the social sanction of legal execution. Twelve persons who committed suicide appear to have committed first degree murder. Thus the number of self-inflicted "executions" is greater than the 7 offenders who were sentenced to death by a court of record. However, suicide following homicide is 5 to 6 times more frequent in England than in the United States.

UNSOLVED HOMICIDES

Of particular importance to the police are unsolved homicides. The definition used in this study was not exactly like that of offenses not cleared by arrest, which is used for uniform crime reporting purposes, but there were similarities. Comparisons of the unsolved with solved cases reveal that the former have higher proportions of: white male and female victims, victims 65 years of age and over, robbery as a prelude of the slaying, victims who were strangers to their assailants, beatings, weekend slayings, and assaults that occurred in the public street.

COURT DISPOSITIONS

Finally, analysis has been made of the tempo of legal procedures, of court disposition, designation of the degree of homicide, insanity, and sentences imposed by the court. Two-thirds of the offenders were arrested on the same day that the crime was committed, and over half appeared in court for trial within 6 months after the crime. Two-thirds of those taken into police custody, and over three-quarters of those who experienced a court trial were declared guilty. Proportionately, Negroes and males were convicted more frequently than whites and females; but previous analysis of the nature of these cases reveals that Negroes and males had in fact committed more serious offenses, and that a charge

---

[11] For more detailed treatment of this concept of victim-precipitation, which is increasingly becoming an important element in theoretical discussions of the poorly designated term, "victimology," see Chapter 14 in the book as well as "Victim-Precipitated Criminal Homicide," *Journal of Criminal Law, Criminology, and Police Science* 48 (June, 1957), pp. 1–11.

[12] "Suicide by Means of Victim-Precipitated Homicide," *Journal of Clinical and Experimental Psychopathology* 20 (Oct.–Dec., 1959), pp. 335–49.

[13] A forthcoming publication by Charles C. Thomas, Publisher.

[14] In addition to Chapter 15 in the book, see also the author's "An Analysis of Homicide-Suicide," *Journal of Clinical and Experimental Psychopathology* 19 (July–Sept., 1958), pp. 208–18.

of unjust race and sex discrimination in court would not necessarily be correct.[15] Of the 387 offenders convicted and sentenced, 30 percent were guilty of murder in the first degree, 29 percent of murder in the second degree, 36 percent of voluntary manslaughter, and 15 percent of involuntary manslaughter. Less than 3 percent of the offenders were declared insane by the courts, which is a proportion similar to that reported in other studies in this country, but considerably smaller than the 30 percent or more reported insane in England.

FURTHER RESEARCH

We have only touched on some of the highlights of this analysis of criminal homicide. There are many aspects of special importance to the police that can aid them in making investigations and particularly in working on cases in which it is difficult to determine suspects, or that are listed as unsolved cases. Each city and each police department has its own peculiar problems, of course, but studies of this sort can easily be made if proper records are kept. Other types of crime need the same kind of research attention, but ultimately all such research depends on the veracity and efficiency of the police in recording and reporting their information. The greatest service the police can make to scientific research is their cooperation with the social scientist and the maintenance of valid, efficient records of their cases.

The Baltimore Criminal Justice Commission, under the direction of Ralph Murdy, former agent of the Federal Bureau of Investigation, is presently engaged in a 5-year study (1960–65) of criminal homicides in Baltimore—a study modeled on the kind of analysis made in Philadelphia. Dr. John Macdonald, Assistant Director of the Colorado Psychopathic Hospital, intends to collect similar data for Denver over a 5-year period. Professor Franco Ferracuti, from the Institute of Criminal Anthropology at the University of Rome, has proposed simultaneous analysis of criminal homicide in San Juan, Puerto Rico, and in Rome, Italy. Ongoing research

like this that seeks to duplicate and to expand on the Philadelphia study will confirm, reject, or modify the patterns in criminal homicide that have thus far been described and analyzed. Only in this way, as Albert Morris[16] has suggested, can science produce meaningful understanding of this delimited phenomenon, leading from empirical data to a meaningful sociopsychological theory of crimes of violence.[17]

CONCLUSION

On the basis of these findings thus far, it is obvious that homicides are principally crimes of passion, or violent slayings that are not premeditated or psychotic manifestations. Emerging out of the data is a theory that suggests a conflict between the prevailing middle-class values of our society and the values of a subsocial or subcultural group. Previously we have referred to this group as constituting a "subculture of violence." If there exists a subculture of violence, then we must further propose that the greater the degree of integration of the individual into this subculture the higher the likelihood that his behavior will often be violent; or, we may assert that there is a direct relationship between rates of homicide and the degree of integration of the subculture of violence to which the individual belongs. The importance of human life in the scale of values, the kinds of expected reactions to certain types of stimuli, the perceptual differences in the evaluation of the stimuli, and the general personality structure are all factors of importance in this theory. As has been pointed out,

the significance of a jostle, a slightly derogatory remark, or the appearance of a weapon in the hands of an adversary are stimuli differentially perceived and interpreted by Negroes and whites, males and females. Social expectations of response in particular types of social interaction result in differential "definitions of the situation." A male

[16] Albert Morris, *Homicide: An Approach to the Problem of Crime* (Boston: Boston University Press, 1955).
[17] The most recent theoretical statement about criminal homicide, based on data from the Philadelphia study, has been made by the author with the collaboration of Professor Ferracuti in "Subculture of Violence: An Interpretive Analysis of Homicide," paper presented before the Annual Meeting of the American Sociological Association, Section on the Sociology of Deviation, Marshall Clinard, chairman, New York, N.Y., August 29–31, 1960.

[15] Cf. Edward Green, "An Analysis of the Sentencing Practices of Criminal Court Judges in Philadelphia," Ph.D. Thesis (University of Pennsylvania, 1959).

is usually expected to defend the name and honor of his mother, the virtue of womanhood . . . and to accept no derogation about his race (even from a member of his own race), his age, or his masculinity. Quick resort to physical combat as a measure of daring, courage, or defense of status appears to be a cultural expression, especially for lower socioeconomic class males of both races. When such a culture norm response is elicited from an individual engaged in social interplay with others who harbor the same response mechanism, physical assaults, altercations, and violent domestic quarrels that result in homicide are likely to be common. The upper-middle and upper social class value system defines and codifies behavioral norms into legal rules that often transcend subcultural mores, and considers many of the social and personal stimuli that evoke a combative reaction in the lower classes as "trivial." Thus, there exists a cultural antipathy between many folk rationalizations of the lower class, and of males of both races, on the one hand, and the middle-class legal norms under which they live, on the other.[18]

Highest rates of rape, aggravated assaults, persistency in arrests for assaults (recidivism) among these same groups with high rates of homicide are additional confirmations of the contention of a subculture of violence. Ready access to weapons may become essential for protection against others in this milieu who respond in similarly violent ways, and the carrying of knives or other protective devices becomes a common symbol of willingness to participate in and to expect violence, and to be ready for its retaliation. As in combat on the front lines during wartime where the "it-was-either-him-or-me" situation arises, there are similar attitudes and reac-

tions among participants in homicide. The Philadelphia study shows that 65 percent of the offenders and 47 percent of the victims had a previous police record of arrests. Here, then, is a situation often not unlike that of combat in which two persons committed to the value of violence come together, and in which chance often dictates the identity of the slayer and of the slain.

We have not tried to explain the causes of this subculture of violence, but such an endeavor would involve analysis of social class and race relations that would include residential, occupational, and other forms of discrimination and social isolation as important factors. Some consideration of the groups from which the individual obtains a conception of himself and an analysis of child-rearing practices that employ punishment and promote early patterns of physical aggression would aid the search for causal factors and methods of treatment.

As we have indicated, dispersing the group that shares the subculture of violence should weaken the value. Through wider economic opportunities, freedom of residential mobility, etc., integration of the group members into the larger society and its predominant value system should function to destroy or at least to reduce the subculture of violence. The work done in New York City in breaking up delinquent gangs has demonstrated the effectiveness of this approach. Similarly in correctional institutions, the treatment program, especially when using individual or group psychotherapy, should try to counterbalance or to eliminate the allegiance of the individual to the subculture of violence and his violent perception of the world.

---

[18] Wolfgang, *Patterns in Criminal Homicide*, pp. 188–89.

SUICIDE, HOMICIDE, AND THE SOCIALIZATION OF AGGRESSION
MARTIN GOLD

Our purpose is to explore the relationship between certain psychological and sociological theories and between relevant data from both disciplines which pertain to the choice of suicide or homicide as an expression of aggression. We will try to show that the choice of suicide or homicide, essentially a psychological problem, is determined in part by the individual's place in a social system. We will focus on socialization as the process by which sociological factors are translated into determinants of a psychological choice between directions of aggression.

Our research gains impetus from the work of the late Andrew F. Henry and James F. Short, Jr., reported in their book, *Suicide and Homicide*.[1] A discussion of the sociological and psychological factors leading to these two ultimate forms of aggression is only one of the several problems they discuss, but it is the one we pursue here. This paper is not intended as a critical review of their book. Rather it is a report of research which attempts to build upon and amplify a portion of the theoretical structure they presented.

We have two specific aims: one, primarily theoretical; the other, methodological.

First, Henry and Short's theory will be examined from a social-psychological point of view. Where they have dealt separately with psychological and sociological antecedents of suicide and homicide, we will suggest some child-rearing links which mediate between social structural variables and intrapersonal determinants of behavior. Second, we will examine the way in which Henry and Short tested their hypotheses about the choice of suicide or homicide. It seems to us that a more appropriate

methodology is needed, and we will suggest a possible alternative. Finally, we will use the suggested methodology to test hypotheses generated by Henry and Short and by the theory of socialization presented here. The findings will be compared.

THEORY OF EXTERNAL RESTRAINT

Henry and Short are interested in suicide and homicide as acts of aggression which originate in frustration. They theorize that degree of external restraint distinguishes individuals who choose to commit one rather than the other. An individual is externally restrained to the degree that his alternatives of behavior are limited by others. It is postulated that the more an individual is externally restrained, the more likely it is that he will regard others as legitimate targets for aggression. Hence, the greater the degree of external restraint upon an individual, the more likely that he will commit homicide rather than suicide.

It is assumed that individuals in higher-status categories . . . are less externally restrained than those in lower-status categories and are therefore more likely to prefer suicide to homicide. The authors specify the following high- and low-status segments of the American population:

High Status	Low Status
Males	Females
White	Non-white
Aged 25–34	Aged 65 or more
Army officers	Enlisted men

They hypothesize that, given frustration, members of low status are more likely than members of high-status categories to commit homicide rather than suicide. Further, they follow Durkheim in assuming that individuals involved in more intimate social relationships are more externally restrained. Hence, married people and rural dwellers, who are more subject to external restraint, are therefore more likely

Reprinted from *The American Journal of Sociology* 43 (May, 1958), pp. 651–61, "Suicide, Homicide, and the Socialization of Aggression," by Martin Gold, with permission of the University of Chicago Press and the author. Copyright 1958 by The University of Chicago Press. Footnotes have been renumbered. The author wishes to thank D. R. Miller and G. E. Swanson for their aid during the research and on the manuscript. He is also grateful to J. F. Short, Jr., for helpful comments.

[1] A. F. Henry and J. F. Short, Jr., *Suicide and Homicide* (Glencoe, Ill.: Free Press, 1954).

to prefer homicide to suicide than single or divorced people and urbanites.

A number of Henry and Short's assumptions may be questioned. It is debatable that members of higher-status categories are less restrained externally than their lower-status counterparts. For example, the behavior appropriate for an "officer and gentleman" is in many respects more limited than that allowed an enlisted man. Drunkenness off the base, for example, is apt to earn the enlisted man mild reproof but to invoke strong penalties on an officer. Similarly, eccentricities tolerated in persons over sixty-five may result in institutionalization of a twenty-five year-old. External restraints on behavior are exerted not only by persons but also by norms—norms which may apply more stringently to persons in higher-status positions. Rather than arguing directly from status positions, let us consider other sources of behavioral restraints, specifically, limits imposed on expressions of aggression.

What are the interpersonal events through which restraints over aggression are made manifest? What are the processes by which aggression is displaced from the restraining figures to other targets? Why the choice of the *self* as a legitimate target for aggression in the absence of any other legitimate target? In short, what are the socialpsychological variables mediating between the sociological conditions and the psychological event?

THE SOCIALIZATION OF AGGRESSION

A body of theory exists which helps to link sociological variables with preferences for self or others as targets for aggression. A brief presentation of the theory and some supporting data will lead us to hypotheses about preferences for suicide or homicide similar to Henry and Short's.

One of the early lessons a child must learn, if he is to continue to live among others, is to control his rages. Sigmund Freud recognized the importance of hate affect as well as love in the developing personality and marked the ego's mastery of these affects as a critical point in personality development.

An individual may control his aggression in many ways. Miller and Swanson order the modes of control in their theory of defenses.[2] An impulse, like the wish to destroy, is taken as an *action-tendency* which has four components: intended act, agent or actor, target object, and affect. Control can be established by manipulation of one or several of these components.

For example, the *intention* to destroy an object may be modulated into tongue-lashing. The aggressive *agent* may be distorted, as in projection: "He wants to destroy me; I don't want to hurt him." The impulse may be displaced to another *object* such as a socially acceptable scapegoat. The *affect* may be shifted, dislike displacing hate, or it may be distorted completely through the working of a reaction formation, hate becoming love. The action-tendency as a whole may be postponed temporarily or frustrated indefinitely.

Which mode or modes of control are selected depends to a great extent on the culture in which the individual participates. Among the Sioux, for example, an infant's tantrums were a matter of pride to his parents, and he was hurt and frustrated as a child to encourage his rage. Rages were later controlled by venting them against extratribal enemies in forays which promised social rewards.[3] Among the Alorese, on the other hand, aggression is suppressed at an early age and later finds expression in intratribal stealing.[4]

There is evidence, too, that modes of control and expression of aggression vary among the social classes in the United States. B. Allinsmith found that the TAT protocols of lower-class adolescent boys were more apt to include direct references to and direct expressions of aggression than those of middle-class boys.[5] While lower-class boys told stories of attacking or fleeing from authority, middle-class boys

[2] D. R. Miller· and G. E. Swanson, *Inner Conflict and Defense in the Child* (New York: Henry Holt & Co., 1958).

[3] E. H. Erikson, "Observations on Sioux Education," *Journal of Psychology* 7 (1937), pp. 101–56.

[4] A. Kardiner, *Psychological Frontiers of Society* (New York: Columbia University Press, 1945).

[5] B. B. Allinsmith, "Parental Discipline and Children's Aggression in Two Social Classes," (unpublished Ph.D. Dissertation, University of Michigan, Ann Arbor, 1954). Summarized in D. R. Miller and G. E. Swanson, "The Study of Conflict," *Nebraska Symposium on Motivation* (Lincoln, Neb.: University of Nebraska Press, 1956).

either told stories devoid of hate or stories in which aggression was turned against themselves.

B. J. Beardslee aroused the anger of lower- and middle-class boys halfway through a set of story-completion projectives.[6] The middle-class boys showed the greater increase in the use of defenses against aggression from the pre- to the post-arousal story endings.

How are these differences in control of aggression between the social classes established? Allinsmith suggests that one cause is the type of punishment meted out by parents to misbehaving children.[7] Lower-class mothers report that they or their husbands are likely to strike their children or threaten to strike them. Middle class mothers report that their type of punishment is psychological rather than physical. Middle-class parents are more apt to say to a naughty son, "After all I've done for you . . .," or, "You ought to be *ashamed. We* don't do that sort of thing."

Allinsmith reports that type of punishment is related to boys' TAT protocols; boys who are punished physically express aggression more directly than those who are punished psychologically. She suggests that type of punishment operates in two ways to generate this relationship. First, physical punishment clearly identifies the punisher. A son can see plainly who controls the flailing arm. The relationship between parent and child is, for the moment, that of attacker and attacked. Psychological punishment creates a more subtle relationship. It is often difficult for the son to tell where his hurt feelings are coming from. Their source is more likely to seem inside him than outside. If there is to be a target for aggression then, the physically punished child, who is more likely to be lower-class, has an external target readily available; the psychologically punished child does not have such a ready target. If he selects one, it is likely to be himself.

Second, the type of punishment a parent administers identifies for the child the approved behavior when one is hurt or angry. The punishing parent serves as a model whom the child imitates and whose behavior instructs the moral conscience—the superego.

Why is it that lower-class parents are more likely to employ physical punishment and middle-class parents psychological punishment? McNeil has gathered data which suggest that lower-class Americans generally express themselves physically, while members of the middle class express themselves conceptually.[8] He found that lower-class adolescent boys are more spontaneous and expansive in their bodily expression of emotions in a game of statues, while their middle-class peers are more facile at the symbolic task of creating abstract drawings of emotions. He interprets these results as a reflection of the values and skills dominant in the two social classes. Lower-class boys are identifying with fathers who work with their bodies; middle-class boys are identifying with fathers who work with their heads.

Beardslee lends further support to the notion that children's behavior reflects these dominant class values.[9] She finds, as others have, that middle-class boys are apt to do better on tests of verbal intelligence than lower-class boys.

Selective factors are likely to be at work here. Since a great deal of social mobility in modern America is achieved in schools, where verbal ability is a core skill, boys who have such ability have a better chance of becoming middle-class adults. Degree of verbal facility is likely to affect modes of expression, such as the parents' expression of disapproval of the misbehavior of their children.

Several factors converge in the relationship between social class and modes of aggressive expression. We have already seen how differential skills and occupations may enter into this relationship. It may also be that class ideologies concerning interpersonal relations differ. In the bureaucratic middle class, stress may be laid on "getting along" with others, for economic success rests heavily on the development of harmonious social relations. In this context di-

---

[6] "The Learning of Two Mechanisms of Defense," (unpublished Ph.D. Dissertation, University of Michigan, Ann Arbor, 1955). Summarized in Miller and Swanson, "The Study of Conflict."
[7] Allinsmith, "Parental Discipline and Children's Aggression."

[8] E. B. McNeil, "Conceptual and Motoric Expressiveness in Two Social Classes," (unpublished Ph.D. Dissertation, University of Michigan, Ann Arbor, 1953). Summarized in Miller and Swanson, "The Study of Conflict."
[9] Beardslee, "Two Mechanisms of Defense."

rect expression of aggression becomes a disruptive force.

But, in the working class, direct aggression is not so dysfunctional. If we assume less interdependency among people and less need for harmony in social relations, the forces against expressing aggression are not so strong.

In this framework, type of punishment becomes an index to the values and skills of a category. As such, it may serve, along with social class, as a predictive variable.

Let us return now to our concern with the preference for suicide or homicide as the mode of aggressive expression. The theory presented above generates predictions similar to Henry and Short's about the kinds of people who are likely to turn aggression outward compared to those who will turn it inward. The predictions are based on the assumption that type of punishment is both an index to and a factor in shaping values concerning expression of aggression. Physical punishment leads to outward expression, while children punished psychologically should turn their aggression against themselves. The derivations below make use of the relationship found between type of punishment and social class.

Of the seven comparisons made by Henry and Short, the theory of socialization of aggression makes predictions in six. There is no prediction here for the married-unmarried comparison.

Since non-whites are heavily concentrated in the working class, the theory of socialization of aggression offers the hypothesis that non-whites should show a greater preference for homicide than whites. If we accept the common assumption that army officers are recruited from the middle class and that enlisted men are more likely to be working class, especially in times of peace, we can hypothesize that army officers are more likely than enlisted men to commit suicide.

Comparing rural to urban populations, it seems safe to assume that the proportion of urban people who work in bureaucratic settings should be greater than the rural proportion. If the previous argument about the source of physical conceptual values and modes of expression is correct, urbanites should have the greater preference for suicide.

There is evidence that in America boys are more apt to be punished physically than are girls, regardless of race or social class.[10] Therefore, females should have a greater preference for suicide than males.

Were we able to compare the childhood punishments administered to people now over sixty-five with the type borne by people now between twenty-five and thirty-four, we could predict to their preferred expression of aggression. Such data might be obtained by interviewing members of these two age categories or by content-analyzing the child-rearing literature their parents read. Unfortunately, data needed to test this prediction are not available. Similarly, stratified data are not available to test the prediction that middle-class people are more likely than working-class people to destroy themselves.

When we compare the hypotheses based on the socialization theory with those based on external restraint, we find that three of the four to be tested are identical. That is, both theories predict that greater preference for suicide should occur among whites, army officers, and urbanites. On the other hand, Henry and Short expect men to show a greater preference for suicide, since they are more externally restrained, while we predict women would. For women's childhood experiences are more apt than men's to be of psychological rather than physical punishment, indicative of an ideology of appropriate behavior expected from and to women.

METHODOLOGY

Before we go about testing our hypotheses, let us examine them a little more closely. We think that careful consideration of what we mean by "choice of" or "preference for" suicide or homicide suggests a more appropriate way of handling the data than Henry and Short employed.

In part I of *Suicide and Homicide* the authors try to establish that the business cycle is a common source of frustration for all segments of the population. But they find that suicide rates do not decrease uniformly in all segments of the population in prosperous times. In addi-

---

[10] E. Douvan and S. Withey, *A Study of Adolescent Boys* (Ann Arbor: Institute for Social Research, 1955); and E. Douvan, C. Kaye, and S. Withey, *A Study of Adolescent Girls* (Ann Arbor: Institute for Social Research, 1956). I am grateful to these authors for making these data available to me.

tion, they report that homicide rates increase during prosperity. But, if homicidal aggression is an index of frustration, this suggests that prosperity may in part be frustrating. The authors explain that lower-status categories are relatively more deprived and frustrated by prosperity, since they gain less, relative to higher-status categories.

At this point Henry and Short state their crucial hypothesis: people in higher-status categories are more likely to prefer suicide to homicide; people in lower-status categories, homicide to suicide. If this hypothesis is confirmed, then higher homicide rates during prosperity and higher suicide rates during depression are explained. Part I of their work takes this hypothesis as an important assumption.

In Part II the authors test this hypothesis. They raise the question: "Why does one person react to frustration by turning the resultant aggression against someone else, while another person reacts to frustration by turning the resultant aggression against himself?"[11] They take upon themselves the responsibility of proving that members of higher-status categories are more apt to react to frustration by committing suicide and members of lower-status categories by committing homicide.

To support this, they offer absolute rates of suicide and homicide for specific years or series of years. These data show that the suicide rates presented are higher in most of the higher-status categories and that the homicide rates presented are higher in most of the lower-status categories. But it appears that Henry and Short may not really prove their point with these data.

If Henry and Short wish to demonstrate that members of higher-status categories have a greater preference for suicide than members of lower-status categories, it is not enough to demonstrate a greater suicide rate for higher-status categories. This may only indicate that they are more frustrated and hence more aggressive in general. For example, the authors' work on business cycles indicates that members of higher-status categories may at any one time be more frustrated than those in lower. If this is true, they may commit more homicide as well. Nor is it enough to demonstrate that within the

higher-status category the suicide rate is higher than the homicide rate. This does tell us that higher-status citizens prefer suicide to homicide certainly, but it does not show that the preference in this category is any greater than the preference in the lower-status category where the suicide rate may also be higher than the homicide rate.

To illustrate this point, we may consider data in chapters v and vi of *Suicide and Homicide*. The writers first present evidence that the male suicide rate is higher than the female rate and so find support for their hypothesis that the higher-status category prefers aggression against self more than the lower. In chapter vii they show that the male homicide rate is also higher than the female. We might conclude from these data only that men are either more frustrated than women or more given to both these ultimate forms of violence.

In order to demonstrate a preference on the part of a population category, it is necessary to take their total amount of suicide and homicide into account. To get an index of preference for suicide over homicide, we can divide the suicide rate by the sum of suicide rate and the comparable homicide rate: (Suicide rate/Suicide rate + Homicide rate). We may call this the Suicide-Murder Ratio, or SMR. Comparing the SMR of one category with the SMR of another, the larger ratio demonstrates the greater preference for suicide.

Whether or not this mode of data analysis yields results different from those obtained by Henry and Short remains to be seen; in any case, it appears to have two advantages. First, it seems a surer way to establish preference for suicide or homicide. Second, it enables us to test whether a difference in preference between categories is statistically significant. For SMR's are proportions, and, assuming an infinite population, tests of significance of differences between proportions may be applied to them.

RESULTS

At this point we will apply the suggested methodology to the hypotheses advanced previously. We agree with Henry and Short that whites, urbanites, and army officers will demonstrate a greater preference for suicide—have a higher

---

[11] Henry and Short, *Suicide and Homicide*, p. 65.

SMR—than nonwhites, rural dwellers, and enlisted men. But, predicting to sex differences, Henry and Short think that males should have the greater preference for suicide, while the present author expects that females should.

In order to compute an SMR for a category, it is necessary to have data on the suicide rate and the homicide rate for the same population and for the same time period. It is not too difficult to get data on the number of suicides and the size of the population, so that a suicide rate can be computed. But data on homicides committed are not so easy to come by.

According to Henry and Short, "Cause of death by homicide statistics provide our most reliable comparison of homicide rates of whites and Negroes [since] the overwhelming majority of murders are committed by members of the same race as the person murdered."[12] The same type of data is used here for the racial comparison. Similarly, on the assumption that most urban murders are committed by urbanites, and most rural murders by rural dwellers, cause of death by homicide statistics are used in the rural-urban comparison also.

Table 1 presents the data comparing the preferences of whites and non-whites. Supporting our predictions, it demonstrates that, in every year from 1930 to 1940, whites clearly chose suicide over homicide more often than did non-whites.

---

[12] *Ibid.*, p. 82.

Table 2 presents the data on the preferences of the urban compared to the rural population, controlling on race. The prediction that urbanites have the greater preference for suicide is confirmed. Although the differences in SMR's are not large, they are consistent over the three years we examined and within both race categories. It should be noted that presentation of the homicide rates alone would not have supported the hypothesis. According to the reasoning in *Suicide and Homicide,* the higher absolute homicide rates of the urban population would lead us to conclude that urban residents prefer homicide more than rural residents.

To compare army officers with enlisted men, it was necessary to use number of convictions for homicide as an estimate of the homicide rate. Inasmuch as not all murderers are caught, our data provide us with an approximation. Further, since the figures on convictions for homicide are low in the armed forces (no officers were convicted for this offense in the year for which data were available), data on convictions for assaults against persons are also included. So the homicide rate here is, strictly speaking, an index of "violence against others."

Table 3 reveals that army officers have a greater preference for aggression against the self than do enlisted men. This is as predicted. Note that the data on the suicide rates alone do not reveal the true magnitude of the difference in preferences between these two categories. But, when the suicide and the homicide (assault)

TABLE 1. SUICIDE-MURDER RATIOS OF WHITES AND NON-WHITES, 1930–40

Year	Suicide Rate		Homicide Rate*		SMR†	
	White	Non-White	White	Non-White	White	Non-White
1930	18.0	5.9	5.9	38.5	75.3	13.0
1931	19.2	6.0	6.0	41.2	76.2	12.7
1932	19.7	6.8	5.9	40.0	77.0	14.5
1933	18.0	6.1	6.1	44.6	74.7	12.0
1934	16.6	5.9	5.7	46.5	74.4	11.3
1935	15.8	5.6	4.9	40.9	76.3	12.0
1936	15.7	5.2	4.5	41.4	77.7	11.2
1937	16.3	5.5	4.3	38.6	79.1	12.5
1938	16.4	5.5	3.8	34.9	81.1	13.6
1939	15.1	4.7	3.3	35.0	82.1	11.8
1940	15.2	5.1	3.2	34.2	82.6	13.0

Source: United States Department of Health, Education, and Welfare, *Vital Statist cs*, XXX, 467; XXXI, 485.
* Adjusted by age.
† All differences within years between white and non-white SMR's are significant beyond .0001 (two-tailed).

rates are combined in the SMR's, a large difference emerges.

TABLE 2. SUICIDE-MURDER RATIOS FOR URBAN AND RURAL RESIDENTS, 1930, 1932, AND 1933, FOR WHITES AND NON-WHITES

	Suicide Rate	Homicide Rate	SMR*
1930:			
White			
Urban	19.8	6.2	76.2
Rural	14.1	4.9	74.2
Non-white			
Urban	8.0	56.4	12.4
Rural	2.9	23.8	12.2
1932:			
White			
Urban	21.3	6.0	78.0
Rural	16.2	5.4	75.0
Non-white			
Urban	8.6	56.7	13.2
Rural	3.5	24.6	12.4
1933:			
White			
Urban	19.8	6.2	76.2
Rural	15.0	5.7	72.5
Non-white			
Urban	7.4	57.7	11.4
Rural	3.2	26.5	10.8

Source: United States Bureau of the Census, *Mortality Statistics* for the years 1930, 1932, and 1933

* Differences between SMR's within the white category are all significant beyond .01 (two-tailed). Differences within the non-white category are not significant (chance probability greater than .10 [two-tailed]).

TABLE 3. SUICIDE-MURDER RATIOS OF ARMY OFFICERS AND ENLISTED MEN, JUNE, 1919–JUNE, 1920

Category	Suicide Rate	Homicide Rate*	SMR†
Officers	5.9	7.1	45.4
Enlisted men	5.4	22.7	19.2

Source: "Reports of the Adjutant General, Judge Advocate General, and the Surgeon General" *Annual Report of the Secretary of War, 1920* (Washington, D.C., 1921).

* Includes assaults on persons.

† Significance of difference in SMR's beyond .001 (two-tailed).

To test differences between preferences of males and females for one form of aggression or another, the homicide rate is computed on the basis of convictions for homicide. Reasoning in terms of external restraint, Henry and Short expect that men will show the greater preference for suicide. The present author, taking socializa-

tion processes into account, predicts that women will show the greater preference. Table 4 presents relevant data.

In every year, for both race categories, women are more likely to choose suicide over homicide than men are. These findings reflect a problem Henry and Short encountered. They found, consistent with their prediction, that males have higher suicide rates, but they also found, contrary to expectations, that males have higher homicide rates. It is just this type of problem which the use of SMR's avoids. Further, these findings suggest that socialization practices loom as important mediating conditions between sociological categories and expressions of aggression.

But Henry and Short have still a point to make. They suggest that the female has a higher status than the male among Negroes; if this is so, they would predict that the male has the higher homicide rate. And, since Negroes are disproportionately represented in the homicide statistics, this reasoning would account for the higher male homicide rate in general. They conclude that "further research should show that the ratio of male to female homicide among Negroes is higher than the male to female homicide among whites."[13]

Table 4 supports this last hypothesis. Among the non-whites, who are predominately Negroes, there are seven male murderers to one female murderer, while the ratio among whites is three to one. Even more important, a comparison of SMR's shows that there is a greater difference between the sexes in the non-white population in the preference for suicide over homicide. So Henry and Short find evidence here for their explanation of the findings.

However, the theory of socialization of aggression also explains why the difference in preference for suicide is greater between sexes among Negroes than among whites. This explanation does not seem co-ordinate with Henry and Short's. Our findings would be expected if the type of punishment received by boys and girls differs more among Negroes than among whites. Suppose the percentage of Negro boys who receive physical punishment is much great-

[13] *Ibid.*, p. 88.

TABLE 4. SUICIDE-MURDER RATIOS OF MALES AND FEMALES, WHITE AND NON-WHITE, 1930, 1932, AND 1933

Year	Suicide Rate		Homicide Rate		SMR*	
	Male	Female	Male	Female	Male	Female
1930:						
White	27.7	7.9	2.7	0.1	91.2	98.6
Non-white	9.0	2.6	8.0	1.0	52.8	71.8
1932:						
White	30.9	8.0	3.1	0.1	90.9	98.8
Non-white	10.5	2.8	21.5	2.9	32.8	49.1
1933:						
White	28.0	7.6	3.1	0.2	90.0	97.4
Non-white	9.4	2.6	22.0	2.9	29.9	47.3

Sources: United States Department of Health, Education, and Welfare, *V tal Statistics* for the years 1930, 1932, and 1933; United States Bureau of the Census, *Prisoners in State and Federal Prisons and Reformatories* for the years 1926–36. Data for 1931 were incomplete.
* All differences between male and female SMR's each year are significant beyond .001 (two-tailed).

er than the percentage of Negro girls who receive such punishment but that the percentage of white boys who receive physical punishment is only slightly larger than the percentage of white girls who receive such punishment. Then it would follow that Negro boys should have a much lower SMR than Negro girls, while white boys would show an SMR only slightly lower than white girls. Table 5 presents the relevant punishment data on a nation-wide sample of schoolboys and girls. The subjects are aged fourteen to sixteen, and race is controlled.

Table 5 clearly validates the assumption that differences in type of punishment is greater among Negro boys and girls than among white boys and girls. Furthermore, the figures here directly parallel the SMR's in Table 4: the white children are less likely than the Negroes to be punished physically and to show the lower SMR's. There is strong evidence here, then, that the manner in which children are socialized, as indicated by the way in which they are punished, is a factor in determining a later preference for suicide or homicide.

Let us raise one more issue. Henry and Short present us with a contradiction of factors affecting homicide and suicide rates in the "central disorganized sectors of cities": "From the general negative correlation between homicide and status position, we would expect the low status ethnic and Negro inhabitants of these areas to raise the homicide rate. From the suggested relation between homicide and strength of the relational system, we would expect the 'homeless men' and 'anonymous' residents of rooming houses in these areas to lower the homicide rate."[14]

This contradiction of factors becomes unimportant if socialization of aggression is recog-

_____
[14] *Ibid.,* p. 93.

TABLE 5. TYPE OF PUNISHMENT RECEIVED BY FOURTEEN-TO-SIXTEEN-YEAR-OLD MALES AND FEMALES, WHITE AND NEGRO

	Percent Physical*	Percent Other	Percent Never Punished	Percent Unknown	Number
White					
Boys	8.9	85.8	3.5	1.4	649
Girls	6.2	90.0	3.2	0.5	769
Negro:					
Boys	50.0	50.0	0.0	0.0	40
Girls	22.0	73.2	4.9	4.9	41

Source: E. Douvan and S. Withey, *A Study of Adolescent Boys* (Ann Arbor: Institute for Social Research, 1955); E. Douvan, C. Kaye, and S. Withey, *A Study of Adolescent Girls* (Ann Arbor: Institute for Social Research, 1956).
* Significance of differences in percentage of physical punishment given boys and girls: white, >.10; Negro, >.01 (two-tailed).

nized as a crucial mediating process between sociological categories and determinants of aggressive behavior. For, although there are ethnic and other differences within the central urban population, the overwhelming majority of these people, non-white or homeless, are in the working class. This fact suggests that certain socialization practices concerning aggression are generally present in the hub, which would lead to a choice of homicide rather than suicide. By considering socialization as primary, we can generate this straightforward hypothesis involving comparisons of urban centers with the periphery, which a theory of external restraint could not.

Although the necessary rates were not available to compute the appropriate SMR's, data gathered by Schmid, and cited by Henry and Short,[15] support the hypothesis. They indicate that homicides are more concentrated in the hub than are suicides—quite a different picture from that presented by other areas.

DISCUSSION

Now, Durkheim tentatively regarded the choice of anomic suicide or homicide as a purely psychological matter, unrelated to sociological variables. In *Suicide* he writes:

> Anomie, in fact, begets a state of exasperation and irritated weariness which may turn against the person himself or another according to circumstances; in the first case, we have suicide, in the second, homicide. The causes determining the direction of such over-excited forces probably depend on the agent's moral constitution. According to its greater or less resistance, it will incline one way rather than the other.[16]

Henry and Short suggest that the choice of suicide or homicide, prompted by a state of anomie, is not purely a psychological matter. While their *Suicide and Homicide* includes an insightful discussion of psychological determinants of this choice, they assert that sociological variables play an active and separate role as well,[17] that is, external restraint growing directly out of position in the social structure conditions expression of aggression.

Our own position lies somewhere between the two. We assert that, if sociological variables condition expression of aggression, it is necessary to search for the manner in which these variables are translated into those psychological determinants which lie closer to the actual individual choice. This position has led us to examine the socialization process, particularly socialization of aggression. We have cited evidence that a pivotal child-rearing variable—type of punishment—is related to position in the social structure. We have tried to show why this relationship exists: outward aggression seems to be more disturbing to the interpersonal relationships inherent to the middle class than to those of the working class; outward aggression is more consistent with the role of men than of women in our society; and verbal ability is closely related to recruitment into social classes in our society and may have a good deal to do with the way parents punish children. It is a short step from these arguments to the choice of suicide or homicide.

We have pointed out that many of the relationships derived by Henry and Short from a theory of external restraint might equally well be derived from the association of particular socialization practices with social classes in America. Further, the problem of suicide and homicide rates in central portions of large cities, unresolved by the former, may be resolved by the latter.

But this does not by any means make the concept of external restraint less useful. On the contrary, if by external restraint we mean the degree to which one's behavior is controlled by an external other, the findings emphasize its value, for the theory of socialization presented and tested here also involves external restraint as a core concept. Physical punishment operates to create a preference for homicide insofar as it represents a pattern of controls which allows expression of aggression and does not build in controls over direct expression. We have assumed that this type of punishment is consistent with a value system which manifests itself in other child-rearing practices as well.

But rather than formulate external restraints

[15] *Ibid.*, p. 92.
[16] Emile Durkheim, *Suicide*, trans. A Spaulding and G. Simpson (Glencoe, Ill.: Free Press, 1951).
[17] Ibid., pp. 106–9.

in terms of relationships between broad socio-logical categories, we have availed ourselves of the clues psychology has to offer, particularly, that the relationship between parent and child is the crucial one.

It is possible that our proposal here is not alternative to Henry and Short's. Perhaps it is in addition. Those researchers certainly make it clear that they would not ignore psychological factors. But our feeling is that we are dealing with a unity. We have attempted to bring a socialpsychological orientation to bear on the problem in order to show how sociological and psychological factors are related in one process.

B. SOCIAL RELATIONS AND PROCESS

Regardless of the etiology of group differences in homicide, few homicides appear to be premeditated; most homicides seem to be impulsive responses to anger. A number of studies, including Wolfgang's, show that the murderer and his victim are homogeneous with respect to sex and race. Other evidence reveals that a victim is apt to be a person with whom the murderer had a close, intimate relationship. These patterns are not limited to the United States; studies show the same patterns in other countries as well.[1]

The intimate relationship between murderer and victim seems rather anomalous since interaction theory, as well as considerable empirical evidence, indicates that persons who interact a lot tend to like each other a lot.[2] The contradiction occurs, however, since interaction and liking are related only as long as individuals conform to social norms. In "Interaction and Criminal Homicide in India," Edwin Driver's analysis suggests that the murder of an intimate associate tends to be precipitated by the victim's violation of important norms. It is also probable that dislike for another is most intense in relationships where interaction is frequent, particularly in those instances where it is difficult to avoid interaction, as with marital partners and relatives.

In another selection Robins explores in detail the relationship of homicide to general patterns of conduct among urban black males. She notes that the murderer and his victim tend to be similar with respect to their *behavior patterns*. She also observes that a victim's behavior patterns during childhood and adolescence are not just a precursor of death by homicide; they are a precursor of death in general. Hence, homicide seems to be one aspect of a broader pattern of deaths.

---

[1] Studies have shown the pattern in countries as diverse as Denmark and India. See Kaare Svalastoga, "Homicide and Social Contact in Denmark," *American Journal of Sociology* 62 (July, 1956), pp. 37–41.

[2] George C. Homans, *Social Behavior: Its Elementary Forms* (New York: Harcourt, Brace and World, 1961), pp. 181–204.

INTERACTION AND CRIMINAL HOMICIDE IN INDIA

EDWIN D. DRIVER

Several studies of criminal homicide in the United States and Europe have found that criminals and their victims are generally homogeneous with respect to sex and personal relations. Berg and Fox found that 66 percent of 200 male convicts in Michigan had chosen as victims persons of their own sex.[1] The study of 500 male and female murderers in Alabama by Harlan indicates that victims were of the same sex in 59.8 percent, of the same race in 92.8 percent, and of the same sex and race in 56.6 percent of the cases.[2] Approximately the same degree of homogeneity is found for Texas[3] and North Carolina cases.[4] These characteristics of homicide are also noted by Sutherland[5] and other students of criminology.[6]

Further, victims are usually kinsmen or close associates rather than strangers. In 87 percent of 489 homicides studied by Bullock, criminals and their victims had had intimate, face-to-face relations.[7] The results of Svalastoga's investigation of 172 Danish victims are similar: 57.0 percent were kinsmen; 30.8 percent were close associates; and only 12.2 percent were strangers.[8] East's study of 200 sane and 300 insane murders in England revealed that only 16.5 percent of the former and 6.5 percent of the latter chose strangers as victims.[9] According to the Royal Commission on Capital Punishment, spouses, parents, and lovers constituted 45 percent of the persons killed by the 1210 persons convicted of murder and sentenced to death in England and Wales from 1900 to 1949.[10] Of the 588 victims in Wolfgang's analysis of Philadelphia cases, 136 were kinsmen, of which 100 were wives or husbands.[11] On the basis of German statistics, von Hentig likewise shows that spouses are prominent among the victims.[12]

OBJECTIVES AND DATA

The aim of this paper is to describe the kinds of interaction which characterize homicide in India, a country that is mainly rural and which has a complex religious and caste structure. Consideration is given to the degree of homogeneity between criminals and their victims with respect to religion, caste, sex, and the extent to which they are kinsmen or close associates rather than strangers. The second objective is to describe the kinds of "motives" which, in the opinion of the judge in each trial, brought about the acts of homicide. Data for this study were obtained from the 1946–56 official records of two courts of sessions which have jurisdiction over 4,000,000 persons in Central India. The study is limited to the 144 convictions for murder during the above-named years. Approximately 34 percent of the persons charged with this act are subsequently convicted.[13] In India, murder is an act of commission or omission by a person who has the knowledge and the intent that his act will cause death or such bodily injury as will result in the death of another.[14] It is punishable by death, but if it is proved that the act was

Adapted with permission from the author and University of North Carolina Press, from *Social Forces* 40 (December, 1961), pp. 153–57.

[1] Irving A. Berg and Vernon Fox, "Factors in Homicides Committed by 200 Males," *Journal of Social Psychology* 26 (August, 1947), p. 115.

[2] Howard Harlan, "Five Hundred Homicides," *Journal of Criminal Law and Criminology* 40 (March-April, 1950), p. 744.

[3] Henry A. Bullock, "Urban Homicide in Theory and Practice," *Journal of Criminal Law, Criminology and Police Science* 45 (January-February, 1955), p. 570.

[4] Harold Garfinkel, "Research Notes on Inter- and Intra-Racial Homicides," *Social Forces* 27 (May, 1949), p. 370.

[5] Edwin H. Sutherland, *Principles of Criminology* (New York: Lippincott, 1947), p. 25.

[6] See the studies cited by Marvin E. Wolfgang, *Patterns of Criminal Homicide* (Philadelphia: University of Pennsylvania Press, 1958), pp. 222–37.

[7] Bullock, "Urban Homicide," p. 572.

[8] Kaare Svalastoga, "Homicide and Social Contact in Denmark," *American Journal of Sociology* 62 (July, 1956), p. 40.

[9] W. Norwood East, *Medical Aspects of Crime* (London: J. and A. Churchill, 1939), p. 369.

[10] Royal Commission on Capital Punishment, *1949–1953 Report* (London: H. M. Stationery Office, 1953), pp. 304–5.

[11] Wolfgang, *Patterns of Criminal Homicide*, pp. 212–13.

[12] Hans von Hentig, *The Criminal and His Victim* (New Haven: Yale University Press, 1948), p. 392.

[13] Government of Madhya Pradesh, *Report on Judicial Administration, 1953* (Nagpur, India: Government Printing Office, 1956), p. 6.

[14] Noshirvan H. Jhabvala, *The Indian Penal Code, Ninth Edition* (Bombay: C. Jamnadas, 1957), pp. 154–61.

due to sudden or grave provocation of the offender by the victim, then the sessions court may sentence the offender to life imprisonment and recommend to the Provincial Government a further reduction in the penalty.[15] Because of this circumstance, the judge, irrespective of the jury's finding of murder with or without premeditation, will carefully weigh all evidence in order to form an opinion about the offender's motive.

FINDINGS

Homogeneity and Social Relationship

Our data show a high degree of homogeneity between criminals and their victims in the matter of religion, caste, and sex. In 136 of the 144 cases (94.5 percent), as indicated by Table 1, they were of the same religion. However, the tendency of offenders to select as victims members of their own religion is more pronounced among Hindus (97.7 percent) than Muslims (66.7 percent).

In view of the fact that most of the 25 castes in our study may be found living adjacent to

---

[15] *Ibid.*

TABLE 1. RELATION OF RELIGION OF CRIMINAL TO RELIGION OF VICTIM

			Frequency	
	Criminal	Victim	Number	Percent
Homogeneity	Hindu	Hindu	127	88.2
	Muslim	Muslim	8	5.6
	Sikh	Sikh	1	0.65
Heterogeneity	Hindu	Muslim	3	2.1
	Muslim	Hindu	4	2.8
	Christian	Hindu	1	0.65
Total			144	100.0

one another, it is quite significant that 83.7 percent of murders are of an intracaste character. This percentage as well as that for religious homogeneity is, of course, in part attributable to the frequency of kinsmen among victims. For the individual castes (Table 2) the degree of homogeneity ranges from 66.7 percent in the case of Telis to 100.0 percent in the case of Brahmins, Dhimars, Lodhis, and Powars.

There is also a high degree of homogeneity (70.8 percent) between criminals and their victims with respect to sex but, as indicated by Table 3, this results from both the way that

---

TABLE 2. RELATION OF CASTE OF CRIMINAL TO CASTE OF VICTIM

Caste of Victim (1)	Brahmin (2)	Dhimar (3)	Lodhi (4)	Kosthi (5)	Kunbi (6)	Kalar (7)	Powar (8)	Teli (9)	Mahar (10)	Other* (11)	Total† (12)
1. Brahmin	2	—	—	—	—	—	—	—	—	—	2
2. Dhimar	—	3	—	—	—	—	—	—	—	—	3
3. Lodhi	—	—	5	—	—	—	—	2	—	—	7
4. Kosthi	—	—	—	15	—	—	—	—	—	2	17
5. Kunbi	—	—	—	—	9	1	—	—	—	2	12
6. Kalar	—	—	—	—	—	8	—	—	—	—	8
7. Powar	—	—	—	—	—	—	3	—	—	—	3
8. Teli	—	—	—	—	—	—	—	6	2	1	9
9. Mahar	—	—	—	1	—	—	—	—	20	—	21
10. Other*	—	—	—	—	3	—	—	1	2	16	22
11. Total†	2	3	5	16	12	9	3	9	24	21	104
12. Identical victims by number	2	3	5	15	9	8	3	6	20	16	87
13. Identical victims by percent	100.0	100.0	100.0	93.8	75.0	88.8	100.0	66.7	83.3	76.2	83.7

* Includes: Mali, Gaoli, Telanga, Maratha, Sonar, Mehtar, Gowari, Pasi, Agarwal, Thakur, Kohari, Merar, Mochi, Dhanagar, Kachi, and Gond (a tribal group).

† Of the 130 cases in which Hindus were offenders, only 104 gave the caste of both criminal and victim.

males select victims and the fact that only 6.3 percent of the murderers are female. . . .

TABLE 3. RELATION OF SEX OF CRIMINAL TO SEX OF VICTIM

	Criminal	Victim	Frequency Number	Percent
Homogeneity	Male	Male	97	67.3
	Female	Female	5	3.5
Heterogeneity	Male	Female	38	26.4
	Female	Male	4	2.8
Total			144	100.0

In general, irrespective of the sex of the criminal, victims are seldom strangers but rather kinsmen or close associates, i.e., neighbors, friends, sweethearts, or co-workers. Of the total victims, 70 were kinsmen, 61 were close associates, and only 13 were strangers. Of the strangers 10 were killed while attempting to thwart the commission of a crime, and they constitute over one-half the persons thus killed.

Motives

Our previous discussion of the kinds of victims selected by female offenders throws some light on the court's view of the motives of offenders. In our cases of male offenders homicide is likewise viewed as the product of considerable provocation rather than a sudden impulse, mental aberration, or the influence of intoxicants. Except for homicides associated with the commission of other crimes and those resulting from street brawls, the act is the culmination of growing enmity between the actor and his victim. The friendly, affectionate relationship which initially existed is transformed into a hostile one when the actor correctly or incorrectly perceives of the victim as a violator of important social norms. It is the view of the court that hostility increased and finally took the form of physical aggression after personal appeals, mediation by community leaders, legal threats, and other social devices failed to resolve the dispute.

The major situations which motivated male offenders to attack their victims were: public embarrassment; sexual infidelity, trespass or rivalry, and other transgressions of norms governing heterosexual relations; disputes over the ownership or use of property, especially agricultural land and products; abuse or neglect of a child, sister, wife, or mother; and the refusal of a wife or her kin to accept the living arrangements provided by the husband. Most frequently, homicide occurred after the victim refused to apologize for or to desist from actions which were publicly embarrassing. Of major importance in this regard were habitual disobedience or other inappropriate conduct by the wife and derogatory references to the offender, his kin, or caste by neighbors. Next in importance as a motive for homicide are transgressions against norms governing heterosexual relations. In 22 cases there was either sexual infidelity, real or suspected, on the part of a wife or paramour, or sexual trespass or rivalry by kinsmen or close associates of the offender. A distinction between infidelity and trespass may seem unnecessary because where infidelity exists, there is usually a third party (rival or trespasser). In our cases, the difference lies in the fact that in trespass the offender attacks the third party rather than his beloved. It is evident from a comparison of column 2 with column 3 (Table 4) that offenders are just as prone to kill their loved ones as rivals or trespassers. In addition to these 22 cases there are several others (column 4) where various kinds of disparity between actual and ideal heterosexual relations, as perceived by the offender, motivated the aggressive act.

Third in frequency are disputes over property. The striking feature of the 25 cases in this category is that most of them were bona fide disputes between kinsmen or neighbors in the sense that property rights were not clearly defined because of either changes in the tenancy laws or the failure to adequately demarcate land boundaries. Other disputes centered around the purchase, use, or sale of implements and produce, and the obligations of kinsmen to render financial assistance. The remaining situations which apparently motivated the homicides are distributed as follows: nine disputes over the failure of a wife to reside with her husband; six instances where the offender was aggrieved by the persistent abuse or neglect of primary kin by other kinsmen or neighbors; and 13 miscellaneous acts.

TABLE 4. STATUS OF THE VICTIM AND COURT'S JUDGMENT OF OFFENDER'S MOTIVE

Status of the Victim (1)	Sexual			Dispute over Living Arrangement (5)	Abuse or Neglect of Primary Kin (6)	Dispute over Property Use, Ownership, etc. (7)	Public Embarrassment (8)	Robbery or Other Crime (9)	Physical Assault (10)	Other (11)	Total (12)
	Infidelity (2)	Trespass or Rivalry (3)	Other (4)								
A. *Kinsmen**											
a. Primaries											
1. Wife	9	—	1	3	1	—	6	—	—	4	24
2. Husband	—	—	1	—	—	—	—	—	—	1	2
3. Father	—	—	—	—	1	2	—	—	—	—	3
4. Mother	—	—	—	1	—	1	—	—	—	—	2
5. Son	—	—	—	—	—	—	2	—	—	—	2
6. Daughter	—	—	—	—	—	—	4	—	—	1	5
7. "Bhau" (brother)	—	1	—	—	—	6	—	—	1	1	9
b. Collaterals											
8. "Culata" (father's brother)	—	—	—	—	1	4	—	—	—	—	5
9. "Mama" (mother's brother)	—	1	—	—	—	1	—	—	—	—	2
10. "Culat bhau" (father's brother's son)	—	1	2	—	—	—	—	—	—	—	3
c. Affines											
11. "Sala" (wife's brother)	—	—	—	—	—	—	2	1	—	—	3
12. "Bhauji" (sister's husband)	—	—	—	—	2	—	—	—	—	—	2
13. "Sali" (wife's sister)	—	—	1	—	—	—	—	1	—	—	2
14. Others†	—	—	—	2	1	1	1	—	—	1	6
15. Total	9	3	5	6	6	15	15	2	1	8	70
B. *Close Associates*											
16. Sweetheart, paramour	2	—	1	—	—	—	—	—	—	—	3
17. Paramour's husband	—	—	3	—	—	—	—	—	—	—	3
18. Wife's paramour	—	4	—	—	—	—	—	—	—	1	5
19. Friend	—	1	—	—	—	—	1	—	3	—	5
20. Neighbor	—	2	—	—	4	10	16	3	3	—	38
21. Employer, employee, co-worker	—	1	—	—	—	—	2	2	—	2	7
22. Total	2	8	4	..	4	10	19	5	6	3	61
C. *Strangers*											
23. Constable	—	—	—	—	—	—	—	7	—	—	7
24. Other	—	—	—	—	—	—	—	3	1	2	6
25. Total	0	0	0	0	0	0	0	10	1	2	13
26. Grand Total	11	11	9	6	10	25	34	17	8	13	144

* The terms in quotation marks are in Marathi, the major language of the area included in this study. For a complete list of kinship terms for India, see: G. S. Ghurye, *Family and K n in Indo-European Culture*, London: Oxford University Press, 1955.

† Includes one of each of the following: "bhabi" (brother's wife); "sasura" (wife's father); "sasu" (wife's mother); "sadu" (wife's sister's husband); "mausa" (wife's sister's son); and "javai" (daughter's husband).

SUMMARY

Criminal homicide in India, as in Western countries, usually involves interaction between kinsmen or close associates rather than strangers and between persons of the same sex, religion, and caste. The affectionate or friendly relationship which has existed between them may be altered by an act on the part of one which is interpreted by the other as a violation of the norms governing sexual conduct, the use or ownership of property, terms of reference, treatment of primary kin, residence of the wife, and other important matters. When the customary devices employed to resolve disputes fail, enmity increases and finally culminates in homicide.

NEGRO HOMICIDE VICTIMS—WHO WILL THEY BE?

LEE N. ROBINS

At birth, the American Negro has a life expectancy shorter than that of the newborn American white. This is also true of the Negro who is 5 years old, 15, 25, 50, or 75—he will probably die sooner than whites of the same age. The number of years of life remaining for the average Negro, at *each* of these ages, is less than the number remaining for the average white.

The usual explanations for this disparity include:

—genetic factors like sickle-cell anemia, a blood disease that occurs chiefly in Negroes;

—environmental factors, such as the unheated, unsanitary quarters many Negroes live in and that help account for their higher rates of illness; their more dangerous jobs; and the overcrowded and decaying homes that account for their higher rates of accidents;

—their poorer access, because of poverty, to medical care; and

—their skepticism toward medical-care personnel, as well as their views about illness and therapy that may keep them from using available health facilities.

But another important reason for the high Negro death rate has been almost entirely overlooked: the fact that the adult Negro's *behavior patterns* may shorten his life. Negro women, for example, may die sooner than white women because more of them have illegitimate pregnancies—and illegitimately pregnant women usually get poor prenatal care. Excessive drinking is another behavior pattern that contributes to the high Negro death rate. A man who is drunk is more likely to have an auto accident or to get into a fight. Then too, habitual heavy drinking can lead to a variety of physical illnesses.

Now, is there a way that, by looking at Negro children, we can predict which ones will eventually have behavior patterns that will serve as their death warrants? If so, then it should be possible to identify those children likely to die an early death—and to begin taking preventive measures. In this article, I will report on some recent research that indicates that we *can* identify those Negro boys most likely to die before their mid-thirties.

Negro death rates exceed white death rates for every major cause of death except suicide, but the greatest difference of all occurs with respect to homicide. (See graph 1.) The Negro homicide rate is about 10 times the white rate. For young Negro men (those between 25 and 44), the homicide rate is over 12 times the white rate. Homicide is the second leading cause of death among Negro men 15–25, the third leading cause between 25 and 44. Among Negro women 15–44, it is the fifth leading cause of death. If a Negro man is between 25 and 44, his chances of being murdered are more than 80 in 100,000—or greater than the chances that a white man will die from the number one cause of death among whites of the same age, accidents. (See Graph 1.)

Obviously, homicide is the result of behavior patterns—the murderer's act itself is criminal behavior. What is not so obvious is that Negro homicides can be accounted for almost exclusively by behavior patterns of *Negroes*. A study in Philadelphia by Martin Wolfgang showed

GRAPH 1. NEGRO MEN, COMPARED WITH WHITE MEN OF THE SAME AGE, FACE HIGH RISK OF DEATH BY HOMICIDE

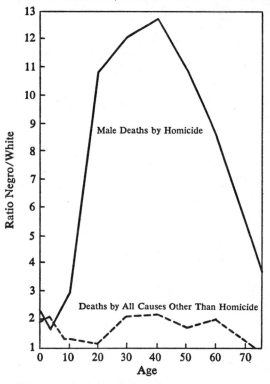 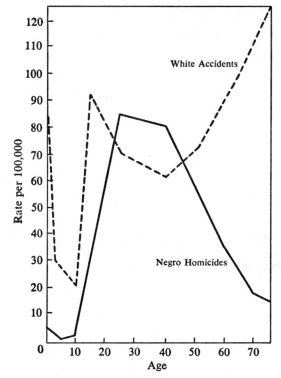

Note: At age 40, for every white murder victim, there are 12–13 Negro victims (ratio 1 to 12–13). At the same age, the white/Negro ratio of death from all other causes is only 1 to 2.

Note: Thirty is the dangerous age for Negro men. About 86 out of every 100,000 die by homicide when they are 30 years old.

that Negroes had committed 97 percent of the criminal homicides in which the victim was Negro—and only 14 percent of the criminal homicides in which the victim was white. And 75 percent of all these Negro homicides, interestingly, were committed by Negro *men*. Among male Negro murderers, 74 percent were between 15 and 40. In short, the high Negro rate of death by homicide is caused, in large part, by the high rate of violence among young Negro men.

The Victim's Contribution

It is also not so obvious that homicide is a result of the behavior pattern of the homicide *victim*, and not just of his murderer. In Philadelphia, 61 percent of the male Negro victims of murder had prior criminal records (compared with 72 percent of Negro murderers), and 54 percent of these murder victims had been arrested for "offenses against the person"—showing that victims as well as murderers have been prone to

engage in overt physical aggression. In addition, the most common relationship between the victim and his murderer was that of "close friend" (35 percent); only 10 percent were strangers to each other. This again suggests that the victim and his murderer have similar behavior patterns. Then too, as many victims as murderers (61 percent of victims, 59 percent of murderers) had been drinking at the time of the homicide. And finally, one-third of the homicides, Wolfgang says, were "victim-precipitated"—that is, the death resulted from a dispute, and it was the victim who committed the first aggressive act. In *justifiable* homicides—where the killing is done in self-defense, or in an attempt by a policeman to capture a felon—it is even clearer that the victim's behavior plays an important part.

In short, the Negro homicide victim is usually no innocent bystander. He, like his murderer, usually has behavior problems.

To find out whether it is possible to find signs

in Negro children that will indicate which ones are most likely to die, my assistants and I traced the careers of 326 Negro boys. We had obtained their records from the St. Louis public schools. All of the 326 had I.Q.s of at least 85; all were born in St. Louis between 1930 and 1934; and all had attended public schools for at least six years. When we learned that one of them had died, we ascertained the cause of death from death certificates or armed-services records.

The findings: of the boys alive at age 15 (at the end of elementary school) in 1946, 14 had died before reaching an average age of 33. The death rate in this sample, then, was 42.9 per thousand (actually, since 40 men of the 326 were unaccounted for, the rate was between 42.9 and 49.0). The expected rate for whites would have been 31.4 per thousand, or 10.2 deaths in 326 cases.

Among the 14, the chief cause of death was homicide—5 of them, or 36 percent, had died by homicide. The only other cause that accounted for more than one death was the Korean war (3 deaths, or 21 percent). Natural causes were responsible for only 5 of the 14 deaths.

Now, from their elementary-school records we had information about the childhood of the 326 boys. To find what piece of information might have been linked to their deaths, we drew up four measures:

The absence or presence of the father in the home;

The occupation of the guardian;

Academic problems—indicated by a boy's having been held back at least two quarters of the term, or his having been placed in an ungraded room for slow learners; and

Truancy or behavior problems—indicated by a boy's having been absent more than 20 percent of the time in five or more quarters, his transfer to a reform school, or both.

Confirming our hunch that whatever predicted adult behavior problems would also predict death, we found that childhood measures that predicted being found in *prison* at age 33 also predicted being found *dead* at the same age. (Two men were both—they died in prison.) We found that a male guardian's presence in the home while a boy was in elementary school was not significantly related to a boy's subsequent imprisonment. Nor was it related to a boy's subsequent death. Similarly, we found no significant relationship between the occupation of the guardian in elementary school and either a boy's eventual imprisonment or death. (Imprisonment rates *were* lower among boys whose guardians had a higher social status, but the difference was below statistical significance.)

The High Price of Truancy

Of our four measures, the best predictor of death was *truancy*. Truancy predicted *death* just as well at it predicted imprisonment—and past studies have firmly linked truancy to criminality. Among truants, the death rate was 80.8 per thousand. (See Table 1.) The rate of imprisonment among truants was exactly the same. For

TABLE 1. THE BEST WAY TO PREDICT EARLY NEGRO DEATHS

Possible Predictors	Number	Death Rates Per Thousand		
		All deaths	Homicide	Other causes
No school problems	154	13.0	0.0	13.0
Truancy	99	80.8	40.4	40.4
Truancy and failures	74	108.1	54.1	54.1
Father in the home	171	40.9	11.7	29.2
Father absent	155	45.2	19.4	25.8
High occupation for guardian	47	42.6	0.0	47.6
Low occupation for guardian	279	43.0	17.9	25.1
(Total sample)	(326)	(42.9)	(15.3)	(27.6)

Note: Negro boys with fathers at home, or fathers absent, have death rates close to the average in this sample—42.9 per thousand. The same is true of Negro boys with high-status or low-status guardians. But Negroes with no school problems have a low death rate; Negroes truant in school have a high rate; and Negroes both truant and failing in school have an extraordinarily high death rate—eight times as high as Negroes with no school problems.

boys *without* serious truancy problems, the death rate was only 26.4 out of 1000, and the rate of imprisonment was only 15.3 out of 1000.

Among boys who had not only been truant, but also had been held back in elementary school, the death rate—and the imprisonment rate—were even higher: Both rates were 108.1 out of 1000, or 11 percent. Among boys who were neither seriously truant nor held back, only 19.7/1000 (2 percent) were in prison, and only 1 percent (13.0/1000) were dead. These children *without* school problems were also *urban* Negroes; almost all were of low social status; and half of them came from broken homes. Yet their death rate was *less than half* of that expected in a sample of white men!

It should be surprising that while we found school problems strongly related to death and imprisonment, we found no such relationship between broken homes or low social status and death or imprisonment. In the real world, school problems, broken homes, and low social status all go together. But our sample was carefully chosen so that these three childhood variables were *not* correlated. The fact that we found only school problems to be an important predictor suggests that the repeated findings that low social class is related to young adult deaths may have been misinterpreted. The association may result, to a considerable degree, from the confounding of *class* and *behavior problems*. Poor young men may have a high death rate not *because* they are poor, but rather because this group includes most of the chronically antisocial youths. In young manhood, death comes largely by accident, homicide, and heart disease—three causes for which lack of medical care is less responsible than it is for deaths from infections and chronic disease, the main killers at other ages. It is no wonder then that poverty, and the inferior medical care it results in, show little independent effect on the death rates of young men.

Just how strong a linkage there was between school problems and homicide is shown by the following: four of the five men dead by homicide had been both truant and held back in elementary school. Over 5 percent of all truant, failing boys had died by homicide between 15 and 33. And none of the boys *without* school problems had been murdered.

Interestingly, school problems seemed also to predict deaths from causes other than homicide. Four times as many truant, failing boys as boys without school problems died from other causes (54.1/1000 versus 13.0/1000). This confirmed my expectation that behavior problems would be linked not only with homicide, but with deaths from other causes. Among men who had both school problems, one death was from pneumonia resulting from a long history of alcoholism, and another from meningitis contracted in prison. The only natural death among these men that was apparently *not* related to behavior problems was one from hypertension. Among men who had no severe school problems, the one death that occurred was from heat exhaustion, not seemingly related to behavior problems.

Why was there a linkage between school problems and death? Certainly truancy and academic failure among these boys were not related to any lack of intelligence on their part. All of them had I.Q.s of 85 or higher. Therefore, none had failed because of an intellectual handicap. In short, both their failures and their truancy may be regarded as evidence of childhood behavior problems. The boys' childhood behavior problems were carried on into young adulthood: they became alcoholics, drug addicts, criminals. They lived violently and died either violently or from medical complications of their drinking. Or, failing in school, the young men dropped out and, unable to find work, lied about their age to join the Army, where they died in the Korean War.

Sources of Difference

Although our findings on the high Negro death rate have confirmed the importance of Negro behavioral patterns, they do not undercut the importance of genetic or environmental factors, the Negro's lack of medical care, and his negative attitudes toward illness and therapy. The fact is that the men in our sample were selected *after* they had already passed the ages—infancy and childhood—when poor medical care and poor housing account for a high risk of death; and they had not entered the period when aging accounts for the highest percentage of total deaths.

To sum up: In our sample of urban Negro boys, almost all came from poor families. Half came from broken homes. Many had serious school problems. Yet it was school problems alone that dramatically predicted early deaths. Negro boys without school problems had a death rate even lower than the national rate for white boys.

As we had expected from the national figures on deaths of young Negro men, among these young men homicide was a very important cause of death. It is staggering to realize that over 1.5 percent of a normal sample of urban Negro boys alive at 15 had been murdered before 33. These homicides were concentrated among Negro boys with academic and behavior problems in elementary school. Among them, death by homicide was the prospect for more than one out of 20.

This vulnerable group, then, was highly visible. These Negroes could have been easily identified in childhood by their behavior in elementary school. My sample was small, but if my results are replicated in larger samples of urban Negro boys, we should be able to identify those boys who will account for the excess number of deaths among young Negro men.

It is well documented that truancy and academic failure are more common among Negro students than white students. Until we begin to cope with the sources of these differences, we will probably find that equalizing the Negro's access to medical treatment, upgrading his environment, and changing his attitudes toward illness and therapy will in themselves *not* close the gap between Negro and white death rates.

THE BRIEF LIVES OF THREE NEGRO MEN

A SHOOTING. J.H., a boy with an I.Q. of 93, lived with both parents. His father was a janitor, but his parents were on welfare by the time he entered the first grade.

In school, J.H. was often truant and did poor work from the fourth grade on. At 14 he was placed in the city reformatory, where he remained for two years. At the reformatory he was placed in an ungraded room, and managed to complete his eighth-grade education there. He entered high school upon his release, completing only one semester before being returned to the reformatory. His brother went to the same reformatory, and later accompanied him to the city workhouse.

J.H. had an illegitimate child by a Chicago prostitute, but never married. His mother and brother were arrested together for selling narcotics, and he himself was involved in the narcotics racket. At 23 he was admitted to a hospital with an injured and infected hand. At the time he had not worked in over a year. Against advice, he signed out of the hospital. Within a year he had been shot to death in a gang-style killing, linked to the sale of narcotics.

A WAR DEATH. J.B., with an I.Q. of 98, was brought up by his grandmother. He had moderate school problems. He was held back in the seventh grade, and was frequently absent in both seventh and eighth grades. He entered high school, but attended only 30 days, leaving at age 15 to enlist in the Army by falsifying his age. After a year in service (at age 16), he was court-martialed for being A.W.O.L. Five months later he was again court-martialed, this time for disobeying an officer. At the age of 17 (officially at 20), he was killed in action and received a posthumous Purple Heart.

A DEATH FROM "NATURAL CAUSES." S.L., with an I.Q. of 102, lived with his mother, who worked as a domestic. His parents had separated when he was 5.

His first year in school was marked by frequent absence, and he repeated one semester. Absences continued in his second year but decreased, and he completed the eighth grade at 14. He entered high school and in the first year attended regularly, but made poor grades, failing two courses. During his third semester he attended rarely and earned no credits. He transferred to a technical high school for a few days, then back to his original high school—and then dropped out entirely. He went to work as a binding examiner for a bookbinding company.

The family was well known to the police when S.L. was a boy. S.L. was the victim of two traffic accidents (at 5 and 8 years of age). In the second, he was knocked unconscious. His father was picked up as destitute, and his mother was known for assaulting members of the family. But the boy himself had no arrests before entering the Marine Corps at 21.

While in the Marine Corps, he was twice court-martialed (for disobeying an officer and for leaving his place of duty), but was honorably discharged. When discharged at 23, he returned to his mother's house.

At this point he had a series of arrests, beginning with speeding and progressing to suspicion of rape, theft, peace disturbance, and burglary. He was finally convicted of grand theft at 29 and placed on probation for two years. During his two years on probation he was repeatedly arrested—for peace disturbance, burglary, gambling, auto theft, and finally public drunkenness. He spent a few months in jail awaiting trial, but was not convicted of theft.

He married at 22 because the girl he was going with became pregnant. They lived together only 4 months. He remarried at 26, to a divorced woman with children. They lived together four years, then separated.

At 27, he was fired for drinking. From 29 to 31, he drank regularly and heavily. At 31, he stopped drinking for about five months, but then began again and continued drinking heavily up until his death.

At 30, he was hospitalized for an injury following a fight in a bar. At this time he had not been employed for the past year.

He finally found a job making deliveries for a printing company—a much less desirable job than his previous one as a printing-press operator. When, at 35, he died of lobar pneumonia, it was clear that S.L.'s death had resulted from complications of his alcoholism.

C. CONSEQUENCES

Society probably fears murderers more than any other criminal type. Yet the fact that the act of murder is typically impulsive and precipitated by a conflict with an intimate associate suggests that murderers are unlikely to repeat their offense; the act is more the result of situational factors than of traits of the offender. And certainly, in light of evidence reported by Wolfgang and Driver, a former murderer is not apt to murder persons with whom he is not closely acquainted. On this basis, fear of murderers should be lower than fear of other types of criminals. Indeed, John M. Stanton shows in "Murderers on Parole" that murderers have better parole records overall than other offenders. In comparison with other offenders, they have lower delinquency and new conviction rates. That parolled murderers are probably selected more carefully, serve longer sentences, and are generally older than other parollees may be factors in causing these differences. Stanton believes, however, that murderers are better parole risks because many murders are situationally determined and committed by persons who have committed no previous offenses.

MURDERERS ON PAROLE

JOHN M. STANTON

What kind of risk is the paroled murderer? An Ohio research report finds that "the 169 first-degree life-sentence murderers paroled since 1945 have compiled the highest parole success rate of any offense group." For years practitioners in the New York State Division of Parole have observed that paroled murders are relatively safe parole risks, and surveys of limited scope have corroborated this.

The purpose of this study is to make an extensive survey of paroled murderers in New York State and to compare their delinquency rates with those of paroled nonmurderers.[1]

Reprinted with permission of the author and the National Council on Crime and Delinquency, from *Crime and Delinquency* 15 (January, 1969), pp. 149–55. Footnotes have been renumbered.

[1] Detailed statistics on the findings of this study may be found in John M. Stanton, "Parole Experiences of Murderers," *Thirty-fourth Annual Report of the New York State Division of Parole*, Legislative Document 1964, No. 107, pp. 53–74.

Because most of those convicted of first-degree murder were originally sentenced to be executed, whereas those convicted of second-degree murder were not, the statistical data will be presented separately for each group. One may thereby learn what happened to those persons whose lives were spared by governors' commutations of sentence and who were later released on parole. The Revised Penal Law in New York State, effective September 1, 1967, provides for only one degree of murder, which ordinarily draws a maximum sentence of life imprisonment; in certain exceptional cases, capital punishment may be the penalty.

MURDER FIRST DEGREE

From July 1930, when the New York State Division of Parole was established, to December 31, 1961, sixty-three persons convicted of first-degree murder were released from New York State correctional institutions to original parole supervision. Fifty-five were paroled as a result of commutation by governors; eight were released after September 1960 by action of the Parole Board under Chapter 292 of the Laws of 1960, which provides that a person serving a term of natural life may be paroled as though the sentence fixed a minimum of forty years and a maximum of natural life. Before enactment of Chapter 292, only the governor could parole a person convicted of first-degree murder. Of the sixty-three paroled first-degree murderers, sixty-one had been originally sentenced to be executed, but the executions had been commuted to natural life sentences by the governors.

The sixty-three murderers consisted of fifty white males, nine Negro males, one Chinese male, one Japanese male, one white female, and one Negro female. Their mean age at the time of release was fifty-one years. Thirty had not completed the eighth grade; five had completed high school and, of these, three had attended college and one was a graduate of a university in Japan. Thirty-six were single; the marital status of one was not known; of the twenty-six who had been married, six were widowed, five were separated, and six were divorced.

Fifty-six had no prior felony conviction, six

had one, and one had three. Before their parole, nine served less than nine years in prison and seven served more than thirty years; the mean time of imprisonment for the entire group before release on parole was twenty-three years.

Three of the sixty-three murderers paroled between 1930 and 1961 became effective delinquents before December 31, 1962. One of these three was returned to prison with a new sentence after being convicted of burglary; two were returned to prison by the Board of Parole as technical parole violators.

MURDER SECOND DEGREE

From January 1945 to December 31, 1961, 514 persons convicted of second-degree murder were released from New York State correctional institutions to original parole supervision by the Board of Parole. Of this group, 343 (66.7 percent) were white males; 148 (28.8 percent), Negro males; five, males other than white or Negro; eleven, white females; and seven, Negro females. Their mean age at the time of release was forty-six years. Fourteen (2.8 percent) had graduated from high school; 295 (57.3 percent) had not completed the eighth grade. There were 272 single persons; of the 242 who had been married, fifty-six were widowed, sixty-nine were separated, and thirty-three were divorced.

Of this group, 417 (81.1 percent) had no prior felony conviction, seventy-seven (15 percent) had one, and twenty had two or three. Before their parole, five spent two years and two spent thirty-one years in prison; the mean time of imprisonment for the entire group before release on parole was fifteen years.

Of these 514 murderers released on parole from 1945 to 1961, 115 (22.4 percent) became effective delinquents before December 31, 1962. Of the 115, seventeen were convicted of felonies, thirty-three were convicted of misdemeanors or lesser offenses, and sixty-five were technical parole violators. Of the seventeen convicted of felonies, two (0.4 percent of the 514) were convicted of first-degree murder. One of these two had been paroled after spending seventeen years in prison; the other, after thirteen years. One committed two murders less than a month after his release on parole; he was executed in Sing

Sing Prison in March 1963. The other had been on parole for a little over a year when he became involved in the murder which eventually resulted in his conviction of first-degree murder; he was executed in Sing Sing in July 1955.

TWO CRITERIA

Two rates are used here to compare paroled murderers with paroled nonmurderers. One is the overall delinquency rate, based on all the effective delinquencies occurring in one year. The other is the new convictions rate, based on the number of convictions for felonies, misdemeanors, and lesser offenses occurring from the date of release to the end of the observation period. The procedures, populations, periods of observation, etc., used to arrive at these comparative rates are explained in the next two sections.

OVERALL DELINQUENCY RATES

The parolee population used for the comparative overall delinquency rate consisted of all males released from New York State correctional institutions to original parole supervision[2] during 1958 and 1959, exclusive of those released to warrants[3] and to deportation.[4] Not counting the 195 released to warrants and the sixty-one deported, the number of persons released on original parole who constituted the subjects of the overall delinquency rate comparison was 7,370.

For those released in 1958, the period of observation of delinquent parolee behavior was 1958, 1959, and 1960; for those released in 1959, the observation period was 1959, 1960, and 1961. The average length of the observation period is thirty months; it is considered an adequate period since most parolees who are de-

[2] Persons released on reparole were excluded because they would have impaired the homogeneity of the parolee populations in the study.

[3] Parolees released to warrants were eliminated because they are kept in custody in other jurisdictions for varying periods of time during which they have little opportunity to violate their parole conditions.

[4] Parolees released to deportation were not included because it is unlikely that they will be declared delinquent in a foreign country.

clared delinquent violate within thirty months of their release. (Of the 2,420 parolees declared delinquent in 1960, 2,252—93 percent—were declared delinquent within thirty months of their release.)

In this study delinquent parolee behavior is defined as any delinquency not cancelled during the same year it was declared. Most effective delinquencies, which may be divided into technical violations and arrests, result in return to the institution for parole violation.[5]

During 1958 and 1959, sixty-five murderers were paroled. (Eight of them had been convicted of first-degree murder; fifty-seven, second-degree murder.) In the same two-year period, 7,305 men were paroled who had been convicted of all offenses other than murder. During the three-year observation periods, nine (13.8 percent) of the sixty-five murderers became delinquent, compared with 2,996 (41 percent) of the 7,305 nonmurderers. In both technical violations and new arrests, as Table 1 shows, the delinquency rate for the nonmurderer group was three times greater than the rate for the murderer group, and the chi square of the difference between the two groups was found to be statistically very significant—that is, most unlikely to occur through chance.

NEW CONVICTIONS RATE

In the ten-year period of 1948–57, 28,788 persons convicted of crimes other than first- or second-degree murder were released to original parole supervision and were observed by the Division of Parole for periods that varied from a few months up to five years, the mean period being approximately four and a half years. During the same ten-year period, 336 persons convicted of first- or second-degree murder were released to original parole supervision and were similarly observed for five years. As shown in Table 2, 7.2 percent of the 336 murderers were convicted of felonies, misdemeanors, or lesser offenses during the five-year observation period

[5] Almost 90 percent of all parole violators returned to institutions in New York State are returned at the discretion of the Parole Board; the remainder are returned by the courts as new commitments.

following their release, whereas 20.3 percent of the 28,788 nonmurderers were convicted of similar crimes during the same observation periods. In brief, the paroled nonmurderers were convicted, while under parole supervision, of almost three times as many offenses as were the murderers. The chi square of the difference between the two groups was found to be statistically very significant.

Tables 1 and 2 show that, considering both the overall delinquency and new conviction rates, parolees who had been convicted of murder are better risks than parolees who had been convicted of all other offenses.

DISCUSSION OF FINDINGS

The sixty-three paroled first-degree murderers made exceptionally good parole risks. None of them was seriously assaultive while under parole supervision; by the end of 1962, only one had been returned to prison after conviction of a new felony.

Of course, first-degree murderers whose sentences are commuted and who are eventually paroled are a select group. During the period 1930 to 1961, when these sixty-three murderers were paroled, 327 others with the same conviction were executed in New York State. On December 31, 1962, New York State prisons contained over one hundred persons serving life sentences who had been convicted of first-degree murder and had not been paroled. Obviously, therefore, the sixty-three whose parole experiences were observed in this study were a select sample of all persons convicted of first-degree murder.

Prisoners convicted of second-degree murder also made good parole risks, but apparently not as good as those convicted of first-degree murder. One of the reasons for this difference is probably that they are not as select a group. Everyone convicted of second-degree murder is eventually eligible for parole, whereas anyone convicted of first-degree murder and sentenced to be executed could not be paroled unless his sentence was commuted by the governor. Other possible reasons for the disparity between rates of the two groups are the greater age and less extensive previous criminal record of the first-degree murderers, which may partially explain their better parole experiences.

Although the 514 second-degree murderers had relatively good parole records, two of them committed crimes while on parole which resulted in their being convicted of first-degree murder and later executed. One was involved in

TABLE 1. EFFECTIVE DELINQUENCIES, IN A THREE-YEAR PERIOD, OF MURDERERS AND OF PERSONS CONVICTED OF OTHER OFFENSES

Crime of Conviction	Number Released	Effective Delinquencies					
		Technical Violations		New Arrests		Total Delinquencies	
		No.	Percent	No.	Percent	No.	Percent
Murder first degree or murder second degree	65	5	7.7	4	6.1	9	13.8
All other offenses	7,305	1,667	22.8	1,329	18.2	2,996	41.0

TABLE 2. PERCENTAGE OF NEW CONVICTIONS OF TWO GROUPS OF PAROLEES

Crime of Conviction	Number Released	Percent of New Convictions		
		Felony	Misdemeanor or Lesser Offense	Total Convictions
Murder first degree or murder second degree	336	2.4	4.8	7.2
All other offenses	28,788	8.2	12.1	20.3

an armed holdup and, although he did not actually perpetrate the killing, was convicted of first-degree murder. The other killed two drinking companions during an altercation shortly after his release on parole.

WHY MURDERERS ARE BETTER RISKS

A previous study of mine[6] found that delinquency rates of parolees are at their highest in the age groups under forty-one; as the ages increase, the delinquency rates regularly decrease. The median age of all persons paroled in 1958 and 1959 was twenty-six; the median age of the paroled murderers observed in this study was forty-five. Because of this age factor alone one would expect that the paroled murderers would make better parole risks than the nonmurderers. The study also found that the lowest delinquency rate was maintained by those who had spent the longest time in prison before their parole. The median period of institutional treatment of all parolees released in 1958 and 1959 was twenty-eight months, whereas the median period of imprisonment of the paroled murderers was fifteen years. Although length of institutional treatment is probably closely related to the age factor, on the basis of their greater length of confinement, murderers would be expected to do better on parole than all other offenders.

In my opinion murderers are better parole risks than nonmurderers because a majority of them are first-felony offenders and many are occasional or situational offenders whose crime may be most aptly described as a "crime of passion." In this study fifty-six (89 percent) of the sixty-three persons convicted of first-degree murder and 417 (81 percent) of the 514 convicted of second-degree murder had no previous felony conviction. Numerous studies have demonstrated that prior criminal record is positively correlated with delinquencies on parole; multiple offenders are more likely to violate parole than first offenders. Also, another recent study of mine has shown that parolees classified as occasional or situational offenders have the lowest delinquency rates of all other categories.[7] However, this study is concerned with paroled murderers, and not all of them are first, occasional, or situational offenders. Some murderers are professional criminals or potentially so, or are psychologically abnormal. These types are recognized as being serious threats to community safety and are not usually released by the New York State Parole Board. The two murderers mentioned in this study who were paroled and again committed murders appeared, at the time of their release, to have developed positive attitudes toward society and to have been relatively safe parole risks. That they proved to be otherwise is one of the risks society must take if it follows a policy of rehabilitation based on the individualized treatment and evaluation of each offender.

OTHER HOMICIDES

This study is concerned with the parole experiences of murderers and not with persons convicted of manslaughter. Yet in New York State the majority of offenders committed to state institutions for homicides are convicted of manslaughter. For example, in 1966, of the 4,919 persons placed in New York State correctional institutions, seventy had been convicted of murder and 334 of manslaughter. To describe the legal distinctions between murder and manslaughter is unnecessary, but generally speaking, persons convicted of murder are guilty of a more serious crime against society than those convicted of manslaughter. However, a study of the descriptions of homicides would not enable one, in many instances, to determine exactly how manslaughter differs from murder. The efficiency of the police and the prosecutor, the legal sophistication of the offender and the skill of his lawyer, the willingness of the offender to plead guilty to manslaughter rather than stand trial for murder—all have considerable effect on the final legal conviction regardless of the substance of the crime itself.

---

[6] John M. Stanton, "Some Factors Associated with Delinquent Parolee Behavior," *Thirty-second Annual Report of the New York State Division of Parole,* Legislative Document 1962, No. 112, pp. 65–93.

[7] John M. Stanton, "A Suggested Typology of Male New York State Parolees for Purposes of Treatment and Supervision," *Thirty-eighth Annual Report of the New York State Division of Parole,* Legislative Document 1968.

Thus, regarding the enormity of the offense, many persons convicted of manslaughter are guilty of crimes just as serious as those committed by convicted murderers. Since they represent a greater proportion of offenders than those convicted of murder, some attention should be given to them whenever the parole experiences of murderers are discussed. Although this study does not include manslaughter cases, through observation I have found that, like those convicted of murder, they are primarily first-time felons, many of whom fit into the accidental-situational offender classification and make better parole risks than nonhomicide offenders.

CONCLUSIONS

Using both the overall delinquency rate and the new convictions rate as the criteria, this study has demonstrated that paroled murderers in New York State commit significantly fewer delinquencies on parole than other offenders.

That the excellent parole records of murderers are not confined to parolees in New York State is supported by two surveys reported in 1968. One was conducted by the National Council on Crime and Delinquency[8] and the other by the Massachusetts Department of Correction.[9] In the NCCD survey, which was based on a one-year follow-up of men and women paroled from twenty-two agencies in twenty-one states during 1965, the best parole performance (90.89 percent) was found among those convicted of offenses classified as willful homicide. In the Massachusetts survey, which reported on the experiences of 238 persons committed for murder from 1943 to 1966, the murderers were found to have much less serious criminal records than other offenders, and the recidivism rate of the murderers (10.3 percent) was significantly lower than the overall recidivism rate of other offenders (59.5 percent).

---

[8] "Uniform Parole Reporting, One Year Experience," NCCD Research Center, National Council on Crime and Delinquency, January, 1968.

[9] "An Analysis of Convicted Murderers in Massachusetts: 1943–1966," Massachusetts Departmeent of Correction, June, 1968.

CHAPTER FIVE

PRISON SUBCULTURES

As in most organizations, prisons have a system of unofficial or informal norms which regulate social relations between members of the organization. Several studies of prisons reveal that such a system regulates the relationships among prisoners and influences their relationship with prison officials. In the first selection, "The Inmate Social System," Sykes and Messinger review the evidence and conclude that this system of norms, or subculture, emphasizes strong opposition to prison officials and prison rules and policy, and strong allegiance and loyalty to fellow inmates.

A. ANTECEDENTS AND DETERMINANTS

There are two theories concerning the origin of prison subcultures. Sykes and Messinger argue that the major determinants are the pains and indignities imposed by the prison system. It should be noted that the deprivations prisoners feel are not just physical; they are also social-psychological. There are two respects in which this is true. First, many of the deprivations are relative rather than absolute. For example, prisoners are not deprived of basic nutritional, medical and clothing needs—inmates do not go "hungry, cold, or wet"; it is largely with reference to life on the outside that prisoners are deprived.[1] Second, the treatment inmates receive threatens their self-esteem and their feelings of worth, security, and autonomy. According to Sykes and Messinger, the prison subculture represents a collective attempt to mitigate the effects of these deprivations. (The dynamics are not unlike those that Cohen hypothesizes for delinquent gang subcultures.[2])

Irwin and Cressey argue in the next selection that there are *two* prison

---

[1] For a detailed analysis of the "pains of imprisonment," see Gresham M. Sykes, *The Society of Captives* (Princeton: Princeton University Press), pp. 63–83.
[2] See pp. 48–51 of this volume.

subcultures. In addition to the prison or convict subculture described by Sykes and Messinger, there is a criminal or thief subculture. The latter has its origin in society outside and is imported into prison. Also, the origin of the former is not necessarily found in depriving prison conditions, although such conditions may help to sustain it. Irwin and Cressey's theory, therefore, calls Sykes and Messinger's central hypothesis into question.

However, both analyses tend to challenge the belief that prison life helps to perpetuate criminal behavior by exposing inmates to criminal techniques and attitudes. Sykes and Messinger's analysis suggests that the subculture may be *situationally specific* to the prison, and Irwin and Cressey contend that it may be imported. Neither analysis supports the image of the prison as a "breeding ground" for crime.

THE INMATE SOCIAL SYSTEM

GRESHAM M. SYKES AND SHELDON L. MESSINGER

In recent years increased attention has been paid to the custodial institution in terms of general sociological theory rather than in terms of social problems, notably with reference to aspects of prison life commonly identified in the relevant literature as the "inmate culture," the "prisoner community," or the "inmate social system." This system of social relationships—its underlying norms, attitudes, and beliefs—as found in the American prison is examined in this paper. After summarizing the salient features of the society of prisoners as presented in the sociological literature of the last two decades, we comment briefly on the major theoretical approach that has been used in discussing prison life in the past. Then we develop a theory of the structure and functioning of the inmate social system, primarily in terms of inmate values and their related roles.

THE PRISON SOCIETY

Despite the number and diversity of prison populations, observers of such groups have reported

only one strikingly pervasive value system. This value system of prisoners commonly takes the form of an explicit code, in which brief normative imperatives are held forth as guides for the behavior of the inmate in his relations with fellow prisoners and custodians. The maxims are usually asserted with great vehemence by the inmate population, and violations call forth a diversity of sanctions ranging from ostracism to physical violence.

Examination of many descriptions of prison life[1] suggests that the chief tenets of the inmate

---

[1] The following contain relevant material:

David Abrahamson, "Evaluation of the Treatment of Criminals," in Paul H. Hoch, ed., *Failure in Psychiatric Treatment* (New York: Grune and Stratton, 1948), pp. 58–77. Holley Cantine and Dachine Rainer, eds., *Prison Etiquette* (Bearsville, N.Y.: Retort Press, 1950). Donald Clemmer, "Leadership Phenomena in a Prison Community," *Journal of Criminal Law and Criminology* 28 (March-April, 1938), pp. 861–72; *The Prison Community* (Boston: Christopher Publishing House, 1940); "Observations on Imprisonment as a Source of Criminality," *Journal of Criminal Law and Criminology* 41 (September-October, 1950), pp. 311–19.

R. J. Corsini, "A Study of Certain Attitudes of Prison Inmates," *Journal of Criminal Law and Criminology* 37 (July-August, 1946), pp. 132–40; R. J. Corsini and Kenwood Bartleme, "Attitudes of San Quentin Prisoners," *Journal of Correctional Education* 4 (October, 1952), pp. 43–46.

George Devereux and Malcolm C. Moos, "The Social Structure of Prisons, and the Organic Tensions," *Journal of Criminal Psychopathology* 4 (October, 1942), pp. 306–24.

Patrick J. Driscoll, "Factors Related to the Institutional Adjustment of Prison Inmates," *Journal of Abnormal and Social Psychology* 47 (July, 1952), pp. 593–96.

Maurice L. Farber, "Suffering and Time Perspective of the

Reprinted with permission of authors and publisher from *Theoretical Studies in Social Organization of the Prison*, Pamphlet 15 (New York: Social Science Research Council, 1960), pp. 5–19.

code can be classified roughly into five major groups:

(1) There are those maxims that caution: *Don't interfere with inmate interests,* which center of course in serving the least possible time and enjoying the greatest possible number of pleasures and privileges while in prison. The most inflexible directive in this category is concerned with betrayal of a fellow captive to the institutional officials: *Never rat on a con.* In general, no qualification or mitigating circumstance is recognized; and no grievance against another inmate—even though it is justified in the eyes of the inmate population—is to be taken to officials for settlement. Other specifics include: *Don't be nosey; don't have a loose lip; keep off a man's back; don't put a guy on the spot.* In brief and positively put: *Be loyal to your class—the cons.* Prisoners must present a unified front against their guards no matter how much this may cost in terms of personal sacrifice.

(2) There are explicit injunctions to refrain from quarrels or arguments with fellow prisoners: *Don't lose your head.* Emphasis is placed on the curtailment of affect; emotional frictions are to be minimized and the irritants of daily life ignored. Maxims often heard include: *Play it cool* and *do your own time.* As we shall see, there are important distinctions in this category, depending on whether the prisoner has been subjected to legitimate provocation; but in general a definite value is placed on curbing feuds and grudges.

(3) Prisoners assert that inmates should not take advantage of one another by means of

Prisoner," *University of Iowa Studies in Child Welfare* 20 (1944), pp. 153–227.

Joseph F. Fishman, *Sex Life in American Prisons* (New York: National Library Press, 1934).

Vernon Fox, "The Effect of Counseling on Adjustment in Prison," *Social Forces* 32 (March, 1954), pp. 285–89.

L. M. Hanks, Jr., "Preliminary for a Study of Problems of Discipline in Prisons," *Journal of Criminal Law and Criminology* 30 (March-April, 1940), pp. 879–87.

James Hargan, "The Psychology of Prison Language," *Journal of Abnormal and Social Psychology* 30 (October-December, 1935), pp. 359–65.

Ida Harper, "The Role of the 'Fringer' in a State Prison for Women," *Social Forces* 31 (October, 1952), pp. 53–60.

Frank E. Hartung and Maurice Floch, "A Social-Psychological Analysis of Prison Riots: An Hypothesis," *Journal of Criminal Law, Criminology and Police Science* 47 (May-June, 1956), pp. 51–57.

Norman S. Hayner, "Washington State Correctional Institutions as Communities," *Social Forces* 21 (March, 1943), pp. 316–22; Norman S. Hayner and Ellis Ash, "The Prisoner Community as a Social Group," *American Sociological Review* 4 (June, 1939), pp. 362–69, and "The Prison as a Community," *American Sociological Review* 5 (August, 1940), pp. 577–83.

F. E. Haynes, "The Sociological Study of the Prison Community," *Journal of Criminal Law and Criminology* 39 (November-December, 1948), pp. 432–40.

Hans von Hentig, "The Limits of Penal Treatment," *Journal of Criminal Law and Criminology* 32 (November-December, 1941), pp. 401–10.

Alfred C. Horsch and Robert A. Davis, "Personality Traits and Conduct of Institutionalized Delinquents," *Journal of Criminal Law and Criminology* 29 (July-August, 1938), pp. 241–44.

John James, "The Application of the Small Group Concept to the Study of the Prison Community," *British Journal of Delinquency* 5 (April, 1955), pp. 269–80.

Benjamin Karpman, "Sex Life in Prison," *Journal of Criminal Law and Criminology* 38 (January-February, 1948), pp. 475–86.

Robert M. Lindner, *Stone Walls and Men* (New York: Odyssey Press, 1946); "Sex in Prison," *Complex* 6 (Fall, 1951), pp. 5–20.

Walter A. Lunden, "Antagonism and Altruism Among Prisoners," in P. A. Sorokin, *Forms and Techniques of Altruistic and Spiritual Growth* (Boston: Beacon Press, 1954), pp. 447–60.

Richard McCleery, *The Strange Journey: A Demonstration Project in Adult Education in Prison,* University of North Carolina Extension Bul., Vol. 32 (1953); "Power, Communications and the Social Order: A Study of Prison Government, unpublished Doctoral Dissertation, University of North Carolina, 1956.

Lloyd W. McCorkle and Richard Korn, "Resocialization Within Walls," *The Annals* 293 (May, 1954), pp. 88–89.

Hermann Mannheim, *Group Problems in Crime and Punishment* (London: Routledge and Kegan Paul, 1955).

William R. Morrow, "Criminality and Antidemocratic Trends: A Study of Prison Inmates," in T. W. Adorno and others, *The Authoritarian Personality* (New York: Harper & Brothers, 1950), pp. 817–90.

Victor F. Nelson, *Prison Days and Nights* (Boston: Little, Brown, and Company, 1933).

Paul Nitsche and Karl Wilmanns, *The History of Prison Psychosis,* Nervous and Mental Disease Monograph Series No. 13 (1912).

Norman A. Polansky, "The Prison as an Autocracy," *Journal of Criminal Law and Criminology* 33 (May-June, 1942), pp. 16–22.

Harvey Powelson and Reinhard Bendix, "Psychiatry in Prison," *Psychiatry* 14 (February, 1951), pp. 73–86.

Donald Rasmussen, "Prisoner Opinions about Parole," *American Sociological Review* 5 (August, 1940), pp. 584–95.

Hans Riemer, "Socialization in the Prison Community," *Proceedings of the American Prison Association, 1937,* pp. 151–55.

Clarence Schrag, "Social Types in a Prison Community," unpublished Master's Thesis, University of Washington, 1944; "Crimeville: A Sociometric Study of a Prison Community," unpublished Doctoral Dissertation, University of Washington, 1950; "Leadership Among Prison Inmates," *American Sociological Review* 19 (February, 1954), pp. 37–42.

Lowell S. Selling, "The Pseudo Family," *American Journal of Sociology* 37 (September, 1931), pp. 247–53.

Gresham M. Sykes, "The Corruption of Authority and Rehabilitation," *Social Forces* 34 (March, 1956), pp. 257–62; "Men, Merchants, and Toughs: A Study of Reactions to Imprisonment," *Social Problems* 4 (October, 1956), pp. 130–38.

Donald R. Taft, "The Group and Community Organization Approach to Prison Administration," *Proceedings of the American Prison Association, 1942,* pp. 275–84.

Ruth Sherman Tolman, "Some Differences in Attitudes Between Groups of Repeating Criminals and of First Offenders," *Journal of Criminal Law and Criminology* 30 (July-August, 1939), pp. 196–203.

force, fraud, or chicanery: *Don't exploit inmates.* This sums up several directives: *Don't break your word; don't steal from the cons; don't sell favors; don't be a racketeer; don't welsh on debts.* More positively, it is argued that inmates should share scarce goods in a balanced reciprocity of "gifts" or "favors," rather than sell to the highest bidder or selfishly monopolize any amenities: *Be right.*

(4) There are rules that have as their central theme the maintenance of self: *Don't weaken.* Dignity and the ability to withstand frustration or threatening situations without complaining or resorting to subservience are widely acclaimed. The prisoner should be able to "take it" and to maintain his integrity in the face of privation. When confronted with wrongfully aggressive behavior, whether of inmates or officials, the prisoner should show courage. Although starting a fight runs counter to the inmate code, retreating from a fight started by someone else is equally reprehensible. Some of these maxims are: *Don't whine; don't cop out* (cry guilty); *don't suck around.* Prescriptively put. *Be tough; be a man.*

(5) Prisoners express a variety of maxims that forbid according prestige or respect to the custodians or the world for which they stand: *Don't be a sucker.* Guards are *hacks* or *screws* and are to be treated with constant suspicion and distrust. In any situation of conflict officials and prisoners, the former are automatically to be considered in the wrong. Furthermore, inmates should not allow themselves to become committed to the values of hard work and submission to duly constituted authority—values prescribed (if not followed) by *screws*—for thus an inmate would become a *sucker* in a world where the law-abiding are usually hypocrites and the true path to success lies in forming a "connection." The positive maxim is: *Be sharp.*

In the literature on the mores of imprisoned criminals there is no claim that these values are asserted with equal intensity by every member of a prison population; all social systems exhibit disagreements and differing emphases with respect to the values publicly professed by their members. But observers of the prison are largely agreed that the inmate code is outstanding both for the passion with which it is propounded and

the almost universal allegiance verbally accorded it.

In the light of this inmate code or system of inmate norms, we can begin to understand the patterns of inmate behavior so frequently reported; for conformity to, or deviation from, the inmate code is the major basis for classifying and describing the social relations of prisoners. As Strong has pointed out, social groups are apt to characterize individuals in terms of crucial "axes of life" (lines of interests, problems, and concerns faced by the groups) and then to attach distinctive names to the resulting roles or types.[2] This process may be discerned in the society of prisoners and its argot for the patterns of behavior or social roles exhibited by inmates; and in these roles the outlines of the prison community as a system of action[3] may be seen.

An inmate who violates the norm proscribing the betrayal of a fellow prisoner is labeled a *rat* or a *squealer* in the vocabulary of the inmate world, and his deviance elicits universal scorn and hatred.[4] Prisoners who exhibit highly aggressive behavior, who quarrel easily and fight without cause, are often referred to as *toughs.* The individual who uses violence deliberately as a means to gain his ends is called a *gorilla;* a prisoner so designated is one who has established a satrapy based on coercion in clear contravention of the rule against exploitation by force. The term *merchant,* or *peddler,* is applied to the inmate who exploits his fellow captives not by force but by manipulation and trickery, and who typically sells or trades goods that are in short supply. If a prisoner shows himself unable to withstand the general rigors of existence in the custodial institution, he may be referred to as a *weakling* or a *weak sister.* If, more specifically, an inmate is unable to endure prolonged deprivation of heterosexual relationships

---

[2] Samuel M. Strong, "Social Types in a Minority Group," *American Journal of Sociology* 48 (March, 1943), pp. 563–73. Schrag in "Social Types in a Prison Community" notes the relevance of Strong's discussion for examination of the inmate social system.

[3] See Schrag, "Social Types in a Prison Community," and Sykes, "Men, Merchants, and Toughs," for discussion of this approach to the prison as a system of action.

[4] The argot applied to a particular role varies somewhat from one prison to another, but it is not difficult to find the synonyms in the prisoners' lexicon.

and consequently enters into a homosexual liaison, he will be labeled a *wolf* or a *fag*, depending on whether his role is an active or a passive one.[5] If he continues to plead his case, he may soon be sarcastically known as a *rapo* (from "bum rap") or *innocent*. And if an inmate makes the mistake of allying himself with officialdom by taking on and expressing the values of conformity, he may be called a *square John* and ridiculed accordingly.

However, the individual who has received perhaps the greatest attention in the literature is the one who most nearly fulfills the norms of the society of prisoners, who celebrates the inmate code rather than violates it: the *right guy*, the *real con*, the *real man*—the argot varies, but the role is clear-cut. The *right guy* is the hero of the inmate social system, and his existence gives meaning to the villains, the deviants such as the *rat*, the *tough*, the *gorilla*, and the *merchant*. The *right guy* is the base line, however idealized or infrequent in reality, from which the inmate population takes its bearings. It seems worthwhile, therefore, to sketch his portrait briefly in the language of the inmates.

A *right guy* is always loyal to his fellow prisoners. He never lets you down no matter how rough things get. He keeps his promises; he's dependable and trustworthy. He isn't nosey about your business and doesn't shoot off his mouth about his own. He doesn't act stuck-up, but he doesn't fall all over himself to make friends either—he has a certain dignity. The *right guy* never interferes with other inmates who are conniving against the officials. He doesn't go around looking for a fight, but he never runs away from one when he is in the right. Anybody who starts a fight with a *right guy* has to be ready to go all the way. What he's got or can get of the extras in the prison—like cigarettes, food stolen from the mess hall, and so on—he shares with his friends. He doesn't take advantage of those who don't have much. He doesn't strong-arm other inmates into punking or fagging for him; instead, he acts like a man.

In his dealings with the prison officials, the *right guy* is unmistakably against them, but he doesn't act foolishly. When he talks about the officials with other inmates, he's sure to say that even the hacks with the best intentions are stupid, incompetent, and not to be trusted; that the worst thing a con can do is give the hacks information—they'll only use it against you when the chips are down. A *right guy* sticks up for his rights, but he doesn't ask for pity: he can take all the lousey screws can hand out and more. He doesn't suck around the officials, and the privileges that he's got are his because he deserves them. Even if the *right guy* doesn't look for trouble with the officials, he'll go to the limit if they push him too far. He realizes that there are just two kinds of people in the world, those in the know and the suckers or squares. Those who are in the know skim it off the top; suckers work.[6]

In summary then, from the studies describing the life of men in prison, two major facts emerge: (1) Inmates give strong verbal support to a system of values that has group cohesion or inmate solidarity as its basic theme. Directly or indirectly, prisoners uphold the ideal of a system of social interaction in which individuals are bound together by ties of mutual aid, loyalty, affection, and respect, and are united firmly in their opposition to the enemy out-group. The man who exemplifies this ideal is accorded high prestige. The opposite of a cohesive inmate social system—a state in which each individual seeks his own advantage without reference to the claims of solidarity—is vociferously condemned. (2) The actual behavior of prisoners ranges from full adherence to the norms of the inmate world to deviance of various types. These behavioral patterns, recognized and labeled by prisoners in the pungent argot of the dispossessed, form a collection of social roles which, with their interrelationships, constitute the inmate social system. We turn now to explanation of the inmate social system and its underlying structure of sentiments.

---

[5] The inmate population, with a keen sense of distinctions, draws a line between the *fag,* who plays a passive role in a homosexual relationship because he "likes" it or "wants" to, and a *punk,* who is coerced or bribed into a passive role.

[6] We have not attempted to discuss all the prison roles that have been identified in the literature, although we have mentioned most of the major types. Two exceptions, not discussed because they are not distinctive of the prison, are the *fish,* a novitiate, and the *ding,* an erratic behaver. The homosexual world of the prison, especially, deserves fuller treatment; various role types within it have not yet been described.

THEORETICAL APPROACH TO THE INMATE SOCIAL SYSTEM

The literature shows that few explicit attempts to develop a theory accounting for the norms and behavior of imprisoned criminals have been made. As in literature on other areas of intense public concern, polemics compete with scientific hypotheses, and descriptive anecdotes outnumber empirical generalizations. It may be of greater importance that when the inmate social system has been approached from a theoretical viewpoint, attention has usually been focussed on the induction of the individual into inmate society, i.e., the problem of "prisonization."[7] There has been little concerted effort to account for the structure and functioning of the system into which the individual becomes socialized.[8]

It is not difficult to understand why the transformation of the novitiate into a fully accredited convict has received so much emphasis. Penology in the past has been the province primarily of the moralizer and the social reformer, and the major questions have related to how current patterns of adjustment may affect the offender's *future* readjustment to the free community. Thus, the nature of the inmate social system has tended to remain a "given," something to be accepted without systematic explanation, and its functions for current behavior have tended to remain unproblematic. As suggested in the introduction, however, the prison is important as an object of study in its own right; and even from the viewpoint of interests in criminal reform, study only of the socialization process in prison is insufficient, on both theoretical and practical grounds.

On the theoretical side, study of the socialization process in prison leaves a serious hiatus: it does not illuminate the conditions determining the presence (or absence) of inmate society. Acting on the implicit assumption that an inmate behaves like an inmate because of the presence of other inmates who exhibit a distinctive culture, sociologists concerned with the prison have largely failed to provide a theory explaining the remarkable similarity of the inmate social systems found in one custodial institution after another. This fact presses for theoretical consideration at the present time; and if we are to understand the fact, more attention must be given to the social setting in which the inmate population must live and to the problems generated by this setting. We want to know why inmate society "is there," as well as how inmates sustain it.

On the practical side, the major administrative directive that may be traced to studies of socialization in the prison is to separate the "prisonized" from the "nonprisonized." Aside from the financial and administrative imponderables involved in any attempt to carry out this directive, however, we believe that in the long run it would not resolve the basic problem: the development of inmate society under the conditions of imprisonment, only one of which is the presence of formerly incarcerated inmates. Any satisfactory solution to this problem will depend on the development of an adequate theory of the social structure of the inmate world; and only as such a theory is developed will knowledge of the socialization process gain perspective.

A NEW THEORY

The loss of liberty is but one of the many deprivations or frustrations inflicted on imprisoned criminals, although it is fundamental to all the rest. As Hayner and Ash have pointed out, inmates are deprived of goods and services that are more or less taken for granted even at the lowest socioeconomic levels in the free community.[9] Inmates must live in austerity as a matter of public policy. Barnes and Teeters have discussed the constraints imposed by the mass of institutional regulations under which prisoners are required to live.[10] Clemmer, Fishman, and others have stressed the severe frustrations imposed on prisoners by the denial of heterosexual relationships.[11] Numerous other writers have de-

---

[7] Cf. Clemmer, *The Prison Community*, pp. 298 ff. on the use of this term.

[8] Albert K. Cohen in *Delinquent Boys* (Glencoe: Free Press, 1955), esp. pp. 18–19, makes a similar point relative to discussions of "delinquency."

[9] Hayner and Ash, "The Prisoner Community as a Social Group."

[10] Harry E. Barnes and Negley K. Teeters, *New Horizons in Criminology* (2nd ed.; New York: Prentice-Hall, 1951), pp. 438–39.

[11] Clemmer, *The Prison Community*, pp. 249–73.

scribed the various pains of confinement in conditions of prolonged physical and psychological compression.

Although the inmate population may no longer suffer the brutality and neglect that in the past aroused the anger of John Howard and similar critics of penal institutions, prisoners still must undergo a variety of deprivations and frustrations which flow either by accident or intent from the fact of imprisonment. Furthermore, it is of greatest significance that the rigors imposed on the inmate by the prison officials do not represent relatively minor irritants which he can somehow endure; instead, the conditions of custody involve profound attacks on the prisoner's self-image or sense of personal worth, and these psychological pains may be far more threatening than physical maltreatment.[12] Brief analysis of the nature of these attacks on the inmate's personality is necessary, for it is as a response to them that we can begin to grasp the rationale of the inmate social system.

The isolation of the prisoner from the free community means that he has been rejected by society. His rejection is underscored in some prisons by his shaven head; in almost all, by his uniform and the degradation of no longer having a name but a number. The prisoner is confronted daily with the fact that he has been stripped of his membership in society at large, and now stands condemned as an outcast, an outlaw, a deviant so dangerous that he must be kept behind closely guarded walls and watched both day and night. He has lost the privilege of being *trusted* and his every act is viewed with suspicion by the guards, the surrogates of the conforming social order. Constantly aware of lawful society's disapproval, his picture of himself challenged by frequent reminders of his moral unworthiness, the inmate must find some way to ward off these attacks and avoid their introjection.[13]

In addition, it should be remembered that the offender has been drawn from a society in which personal possessions and material achievement are closely linked with concepts of personal

worth by numerous cultural definitions. In the prison, however, the inmate finds himself reduced to a level of living near bare subsistence, and whatever physical discomforts this deprivation may entail, it apparently has deeper psychological significance as a basic attack on the prisoner's conception of his own personal adequacy.

No less important, perhaps, is the ego threat that is created by the deprivation of heterosexual relationships. In the tense atmosphere of the prison, with its perversions and constant references to the problems of sexual frustration, even those inmates who do not engage in overt homosexuality suffer acute attacks of anxiety about their own masculinity. These anxieties may arise from a prisoner's unconscious fear of latent homosexual tendencies in himself, which might be activated by his prolonged heterosexual deprivation and the importunity of others; or at a more conscious level he may feel that his masculinity is threatened because he can see himself as a man—in the full sense—only in a world that also contains women. In either case the inmate is confronted with the fact that the celibacy imposed on him by society means more than simple physiological frustration: an essential component of his self-conception, his status as male, is called into question.

Rejected, impoverished, and figuratively castrated, the prisoner must face still further indignity in the extensive social control exercised by the custodians. The many details of the inmate's life, ranging from the hours of sleeping to the route to work and the job itself, are subject to a vast number of regulations made by prison officials. The inmate is stripped of his autonomy; hence, to the other pains of imprisonment we must add the pressure to define himself as weak, helpless, and dependent. Individuals under guard are exposed to the bitter ego threat of losing their identification with the normal adult role.[14]

The remaining significant feature of the inmate's social environment is the presence of other imprisoned criminals. Murderers, rapists, thieves, confidence men, and sexual deviants are

---

[12] A. H. Maslow, "Deprivation, Threat and Frustration," *Psychological Review* 48 (July, 1941), pp. 364–66.
[13] McCorkle and Korn, "Resocialization Within Walls," p. 88.

[14] Bruno Bettelheim, "Individual and Mass Behavior in Extreme Situations," *Journal of Abnormal and Social Psychology* 38 (October, 1943), pp. 417–52.

the inmate's constant companions, and this enforced intimacy may prove to be disquieting even for the hardened recidivist. As an inmate has said, "The worst thing about prison is you have to live with other prisoners."[15] Crowded into a small area with men who have long records of physical assaults, thievery, and so on (and who may be expected to continue in the path of deviant social behavior in the future), the inmate is deprived of the sense of security that we more or less take for granted in the free community. Although the anxieties created by such a situation do not necessarily involve an attack on the individual's sense of personal worth—as we are using the concept—the problems of self-protection in a society composed exclusively of criminals constitute one of the inadvertent rigors of confinement.

In short, imprisonment "punishes" the offender in a variety of ways extending far beyond the simple fact of incarceration. However just or necessary such punishments may be, their importance for our present analysis lies in the fact that they form a set of harsh social conditions to which the population of prisoners must respond or *adapt itself*. The inmate feels that the deprivations and frustrations of prison life, with their implications for the destruction of his self-esteem, somehow must be alleviated. It is, we suggest, as an answer to this need that the functional significance of the inmate code or system of values exhibited so frequently by men in prison can best be understood.

As we have pointed out, the dominant theme of the inmate code is group cohesion, with a "war of all against all"—in which each man seeks his own gain without considering the rights or claims of others—as the theoretical antipode. But if a war of all against all is likely to make life "solitary, poor, nasty, brutish, and short" for men with freedom, as Hobbes suggested, it is doubly so for men in custody. Even those who are most successful in exploiting their fellow prisoners will find it a dangerous and nerve-wracking game, for they cannot escape the company of their victims. No man can assure the safety of either his person or his pos-

sessions, and eventually the winner is certain to lose to a more powerful or more skillful exploiter. Furthermore, the victims hold the trump card, since a word to the officials is frequently all that is required to ruin the most dominating figure in the inmate population. A large share of the "extra" goods that enter the inmate social system must do so as the result of illicit conniving against the officials, which often requires lengthy and extensive cooperation and trust; in a state of complete conflict the resources of the system will be diminished. Mutual abhorrence or indifference will feed the emotional frictions arising from interaction under compression. And as rejection by others is a fundamental problem, a state of mutual alienation is worse than useless as a solution to the threats created by the inmate's status as an outcast.

As a population of prisoners moves toward a state of mutual antagonism, then, the many problems of prison life become more acute. On the other hand, *as a population of prisoners moves in the direction of solidarity, as demanded by the inmate code, the pains of imprisonment become less severe.* They cannot be eliminated, it is true, but their consequences at least can be partially neutralized. A cohesive inmate society provides the prisoner with a meaningful social group with which he can identify himself and which will support him in his struggles against his condemners. Thus it permits him to escape at least in part the fearful isolation of the convicted offender. Inmate solidarity, in the form of toleration of the many irritants of life in confinement, helps to solve the problems of personal security posed by the involuntary intimacy of men noteworthy for their seriously antisocial behavior in the past.

Similarly, group cohesion in the form of a reciprocity of favors undermines one of the most potent sources of aggression among prisoners, the drive for personal aggrandizement through exploitation by force and fraud. Furthermore, although goods in scarce supply will remain scarce even if they are shared rather than monopolized, such goods will be distributed more equitably in a social system marked by solidarity, and this may be of profound significance in enabling the prisoner to endure better the psychological burden of impoverishment. A

---

[15] Gresham M. Sykes, *Crime and Society* (New York: Random House, 1956), p. 109.

cohesive population of prisoners has another advantage in that it supports a system of shared beliefs that explicitly deny the traditional link between merit and achievement. Material success, according to this system, is a matter of "connections" rather than skill or hard work, and thus the imprisoned criminal is partially freed from the necessity of defining his material want as a sign of personal inadequacy.

Finally, a cohesive inmate social system institutionalizes the value of "dignity" and the ability to "take it" in a number of norms and reinforces these norms with informal social controls. In effect, the prisoner is called on to endure manfully what he cannot avoid. At first glance this might seem to be simply the counsel of despair; but if the elevation of fortitude into a primary virtue is the last refuge of the powerless, it also serves to shift the criteria of the individual's worth from conditions that cannot be altered to his ability to maintain some degree of personal integration; and the latter, at least, can be partially controlled. By creating an ideal of endurance in the face of harsh social conditions, then, the society of prisoners opens a path to the restoration of self-respect and a sense of independence that can exist despite prior criminality, present subjugation, and the free community's denial of the offender's moral worthiness. Significantly, this path to virtue is recognized by the prison officials as well as the prisoners.

One further point should be noted with regard to the emphasis placed on the maintenance of self as defined by the value system of prisoners. Dignity, composure, courage, the ability to "take it" and "hand it out" when necessary—these are the traits affirmed by the inmate code. They are also traits that are commonly defined as masculine by the inmate population. As a consequence, the prisoner finds himself in a situation where he can recapture his male role, not in terms of its sexual aspects, but in terms of behavior that is accepted as a good indicator of virility.

The effectiveness of the inmate code in mitigating the pains of imprisonment depends of course on the extent to which precepts are translated into action. As we have indicated, the demands of the inmate code for loyalty, generosity, disparagement of officials, and so on are most fully exemplified in the behavior of the *right guy*. On the other hand, much noncohesive behavior

occurs on the part of the *rat,* the *tough,* the *gorilla,* the *merchant,* and the *weak sister.* The population of prisoners, then, does not exhibit perfect solidarity in practice, in spite of inmates' vehement assertions of group cohesion as a value; but neither is the population of prisoners a warring aggregate. Rather, the inmate social system typically appears to be balanced in an uneasy compromise somewhere between these two extremes. The problems confronting prisoners in the form of social rejection, material deprivation, sexual frustration, and the loss of autonomy and personal security are not completely eliminated. Indeed, even if the norms of the inmate social system were fully carried out by all, the pains of imprisonment would only be lessened; they would not disappear. But the pains of imprisonment are at least relieved by whatever degree of group cohesion is achieved in fact, and this is crucial in understanding the functional significance of the inmate code for inmates.

One further problem remains. Many of the prisoners who deviate from the maxims of the inmate code are precisely those who are most vociferous in their verbal allegiance to it. How can this discrepancy between words and behavior be explained? Much of the answer seems to lie in the fact that almost all inmates have an interest in maintaining cohesive behavior on the part of others, *regardless of the role they play themselves,* and vehement vocal support of the inmate code is a potent means to this end.

There are, of course, prisoners who "believe" in inmate cohesion both for themselves and others. These hold the unity of the group as a high personal value and are ready to demand cohesive behavior from their fellow prisoners. This collectivistic orientation may be due to a thorough identification with the criminal world in opposition to the forces of lawful society, or to a system of values that transcends such divisions. In any case, for these men the inmate code has much of the quality of a religious faith and they approach its tenets as true believers. In a second category are those prisoners who are relatively indifferent to the cohesion of the inmate population as a personal value, but who are quick to assert it as a guide to behavior because in its absence they would be likely to become chronic victims. They are committed to the ideal of inmate solidarity to the extent that they have little or no desire to take advantage of their fellow captives, but they do not go so far as to subscribe to the ideal of self-sacrifice. Their behavior is best described as passive or neutral; they are believers without passion, demanding adherence from others, but not prepared to let excessive piety interfere with more mundane considerations. Third, there are those who loudly acclaim the inmate code and actively violate its injunctions. These men suffer if their number increases, since they begin to face the difficulties of competition; and they are in particular danger if their depredations are reported to the officials. The prisoners who are thus actively alienated from other inmates and yet give lip service to inmate solidarity resemble a manipulative priesthood, savage in their expression of belief but corrupt in practice. In brief, a variety of motivational patterns underlies allegiance to the inmate code, but few inmates can avoid the need to insist publicly on its observance, whatever the discrepancies in their actions.

THIEVES, CONVICTS AND THE INMATE CULTURE

JOHN IRWIN AND DONALD R. CRESSEY

In the rapidly-growing literature on the social organization of correctional institutions, it has become common to discuss "prison culture" and "inmate culture" in terms suggesting that the behavior systems of various types of inmates stem from the conditions of imprisonment themselves. Use of a form of structural-functional analysis in research and observation of institutions has led to emphasis of the notion that internal conditions stimulate inmate behavior of various kinds, and there has been a glossing over of the older notion that inmates may bring a culture with them into the prison. Our aim is to suggest that much of the inmate behavior classified as part of the prison culture is not peculiar to the prison at all. On the contrary, it is the fine distinction between "prison culture" and "criminal subculture" which seems to make understandable the fine distinction between behavior patterns of various categories of inmates.

A number of recent publications have defended the notion that behavior patterns among inmates develop with a minimum of influence from the outside world. For example, in his general discussion of total institutions, Goffman acknowledges that inmates bring a culture with them to the institution, but he argues that upon entrance to the institution they are stripped of this support by processes of mortification and dispossession aimed at managing the daily activities of a large number of persons in a small space with a small expenditure of resources.[1] Similarly, Sykes and Messinger note that a central value system seems to pervade prison populations, and they maintain that "conformity to, or deviation from, the inmate code is the major basis for classifying and describing the social relations of prisoners."[2] The emphasis in this code is on directives such as "don't interfere with inmate interests," "don't lose your head," "don't exploit inmates," "don't weaken," and "don't be a sucker." The authors' argument, like the argument in other Sykes' publications is that the origin of these values is situational; the value system arises, out of the conditions of imprisonment. . . .[3]

It is our contention that the "functional" or

Reprinted with permission of author and the Society for the Study of Social Problems, from *Social Problems* 10 (Fall, 1962), pp. 142–55, as abridged. Footnotes have been renumbered. The authors are indebted to the following persons for suggested modifications to the original draft: Donald L. Garrity, Daniel Glaser, Erving Goffman, and Stanton Wheeler.

[1] Erving Goffman, "On the Characteristics of Total Institutions," Chapters 1 and 2 in Donald R. Cressey, editor, *The Prison: Studies in Institutional Organization and Change* (New York: Holt, Rinehart and Winston, 1961), pp. 22–47.

[2] Richard A. Cloward, Donald R. Cressey, George H. Grosser, Richard McCleery, Lloyd E. Ohlin, Gresham M. Sykes and Sheldon L. Messinger, *Theoretical Studies in Social Organization of the Prison* (New York: Social Science Research Council, 1960), p. 9.

[3] *Ibid.*, pp. 15, 19. See also Gresham M. Sykes, "Men, Merchants, and Toughs: A Study of Reactions to Imprisonment," *Social Problems* 4 (October, 1957), pp. 130–38; and Gresham M. Sykes, *The Society of Captives* (Princeton: Princeton University Press, 1958), pp. 79–82.

"indigenous origin" notion has been overemphasized and that observers have overlooked the dramatic effect that external behavior patterns have on the conduct of inmates in any given prison. Moreover, the contradictory statements made in this connection by some authors, including Cressey,[4] seem to stem from acknowledging but then ignoring the deviant subcultures which exist outside any given prison and outside prisons generally. More specifically, it seems rather obvious that the "prison code"—don't inform on or exploit another inmate, don't lose your head, be weak, or be a sucker, etc.—is also part of a *criminal* code, existing outside prisons. Further, many inmates come to any given prison with a record of many terms in correctional institutions. These men, some of whom have institutional records dating back to early childhood, bring with them a ready-made set of patterns which they apply to the new situation, just as in the case with participants in the criminal subculture. In view of these variations, a clear understanding of inmate conduct cannot be obtained simply by viewing "prison culture" or "inmate culture" as an isolated system springing solely from the conditions of imprisonment. Becker and Geer have made our point in more general terms: "The members of a group may derive their understandings from cultures other than that of the group they are at the moment participating in. To the degree that group participants share latent social identities (related to their membership in the same 'outside' social groups) they will share these understandings, so that there will be a culture which can be called *latent*, i.e., the culture has its origin and social support in a group other than the one in which the members are now participating."[5]

We have no doubt that the total set of relationships called "inmate society" is a response to problems of imprisonment. What we question is the emphasis given to the notion that solutions to these problems are found within the prison, and the lack of emphasis on "latent culture"— on external experiences as determinants of the solutions. We have found it both necessary and helpful to divide inmates into three rough categories: those oriented to a criminal subculture, those oriented to a prison subculture, and those oriented to "conventional" or "legitimate" subcultures.

THE TWO DEVIANT SUBCULTURES

When we speak of a criminal subculture we do not mean to imply that there is some national or international organization with its own judges, enforcement agencies, etc. Neither do we imply that every person convicted of a crime is a member of the subculture. Nevertheless, descriptions of the values of professional thieves, "career criminals," "sophisticated criminals," and other good crooks indicate that there is a set of values which extends to criminals across the nation with a good deal of consistency.[6] To avoid possible confusion arising from the fact that not all criminals share these values, we have arbitrarily named the system a "thief" subculture. The core values of this subculture correspond closely to the values which prison observers have ascribed to the "right guy" role. These include the important notion that criminals should not betray each other to the police, should be reliable, wily but trustworthy, cool-headed, etc. High status in this subculture is awarded to men who appear to follow these prescriptions without variance. In the thief subculture a man who is known as "right" or "solid" is one who can be trusted and relied upon. High status is also awarded to those who possess skill as thieves, but to be just a successful thief is not enough; there must be solidness as well. A solid guy is respected even if he is unskilled, and no matter how skilled in crime a stool pigeon may be, his status is low.

Despite the fact that adherence to the norms of the thief subculture is an ideal, and the fact that the behavior of the great majority of men arrested or convicted varies sharply from any

[4] Edwin H. Sutherland and Donald R. Cressey, *Principles of Criminology,* 6th ed. (New York: Lippincott, 1960), pp. 504–5.

[5] Howard S. Becker and Blanche Geer, "Latent Culture: A Note on the Theory of Latent Social Roles," *Administrative Science Quarterly* 5 (September, 1960), pp. 305–6. See also Alvin W. Gouldner, "Cosmopolitans and Locals: Toward an Analysis of Latent Social Roles," *Administrative Science Quarterly* 2 (1957), pp. 281–306 and 2 (1958), pp. 444–80.

[6] Walter C. Reckless, *The Crime Problem,* 2nd ed. (New York: Appleton-Century-Crofts, 1945), pp. 144–45; 148–50; Edwin H. Sutherland, *The Professional Thief* (Chicago: University of Chicago Press, 1937).

"criminal code" which might be identified, a proportion of the persons arrested for "real crime" such as burglary, robbery, and larceny have been in close contact with the values of the subculture. Many criminals, while not following the precepts of the subculture religiously, give lip service to its values and evaluate their own behavior and the behavior of their associates in terms relating to adherence to "rightness" and being "solid." It is probable, further, that use of these kinds of values is not even peculiarly "criminal," for policemen, prison guards, college professors, students, and almost any other category of persons evaluate behavior in terms of ingroup loyalties. Whyte noted the mutual obligations binding corner boys together and concluded that status depends upon the extent to which a boy lives up to his obligations, a form of "solidness."[7] More recently, Miller identified "toughness," "smartness," and "autonomy" among the "focal concerns" of lower class adolescent delinquent boys; these also characterize prisoners who are oriented to the thief subculture.[8] Wheeler found that half of the custody staff and sixty percent of the treatment staff in one prison approved the conduct of a hypothetical inmate who refused to name an inmate with whom he had been engaged in a knife fight.[9] A recent book has given the name "moral courage" to the behavior of persons who, like thieves, have shown extreme loyalty to their in-groups in the face of real or threatened adversity, including imprisonment.[10]

Imprisonment is one of the recurring problems with which thieves must cope. It is almost certain that a thief will be arrested from time to time, and the subculture provides members with patterns to be used in order to help solve this problem. Norms which apply to the prison situation, and information on how to undergo the prison experience—how to do time "standing on your head"—with the least suffering and in a minimum amount of time are provided. Of course, the subculture itself is both nurtured and diffused in the different jails and prisons of the country.

There also exists in prisons a subculture which is by definition a set of patterns that flourishes in the environment of incarceration. It can be found wherever men are confined, whether it be in city jails, state and federal prisons, army stockades, prisoner of war camps, concentration camps, or even mental hospitals. Such organizations are characterized by deprivations and limitations on freedom, and in them available wealth must be competed for by men supposedly on an equal footing. It is in connection with the maintenance (but not necessarily with the *origin*) of this subculture that it is appropriate to stress the notion that a minimum of outside status criteria are carried into the situation. Ideally, all status is to be achieved by the means made available in the prison, through the displayed ability to manipulate the environment, win special privileges in a certain manner, and assert influence over others. To avoid confusion with writings on "prison culture" and "inmate culture," we have arbitrarily named this system of values and behavior patterns a "convict subculture." The central value of the subculture is utilitarianism, and the most manipulative and most utilitarian individuals win the available wealth and such positions of influence as might exist.

It is not correct to conclude, however, that even these behavior patterns are a consequence of the environment of any particular prison. In the first place, such utilitarian and manipulative behavior probably is characteristic of the "hard core" lower class in the United States, and most prisoners come from this class. After discussing the importance of toughness, smartness, excitement and fate in this group, Miller makes the following significant observation:

In lower class culture a close conceptual connection is made between "authority" and "nurturance." To be restrictively or firmly controlled is to be cared for. Thus the overtly negative evaluation of superordinate authority frequently extends as well to nurturance, care, or protection. The desire for personal independence is often expressed in terms such as "I don't need *nobody* to take care of me. I can take care of myself!" Actual patterns of behavior, however, reveal a marked discrepancy between expressed sentiments

[7] William Foote Whyte, "Corner Boys: A Study of Clique Behavior," *American Journal of Sociology* 46 (March, 1941), pp. 647–63.

[8] Walter B. Miller, "Lower Class Culture as a Generating Milieu of Gang Delinquency," *Journal of Social Issues* 14 (1958), pp. 5–19. [See also pp. 51–54 of this volume.]

[9] Stanton Wheeler, "Role Conflict in Correctional Communities," Chapter 6 in Cressey, *The Prison*, p. 235.

[10] Compton Mackenzie, *Moral Courage* (London: Collins, 1962).

and what is covertly valued. Many lower class people appear to seek out highly restrictive social environments wherein stringent external controls are maintained over their behavior. Such institutions as the armed forces, the mental hospital, the disciplinary school, the prison or correctional institution, provide environments which incorporate a strict and detailed set of rules defining and limiting behavior, and enforced by an authority system which controls and applies coercive sanctions for deviance from these rules. While under the jurisdiction of such systems, the lower class person generally expresses to his peers continual resentment of the coercive, unjust, and arbitrary exercise of authority. Having been released, or having escaped from these milieux, however, he will often act in such a way as to insure recommitment, or choose recommitment voluntarily after a temporary period of "freedom."[11]

In the second place, the "hard core" members of this subculture as it exists in American prisons for adults are likely to be inmates who have a long record of confinement in institutions for juveniles. McCleery observed that, in a period of transition, reform-school graduates all but took over inmate society in one prison. These boys called themselves a "syndicate" and engaged in a concentrated campaign of argument and intimidation directed toward capturing the inmate council and the inmate craft shop which had been placed under council management. "The move of the syndicate to take over the craft shop involved elements of simple exploitation, the grasp of a status symbol, and an aspect of economic reform."[12] Persons with long histories of institutionalization, it is important to note, might have had little contact with the thief subculture. The thief subculture does not flourish in institutions for juveniles, and graduates of such institutions have not necessarily had extensive criminal experience on the outside. However, some form of the convict subculture *does* exist in institutions for juveniles, though not to the extent characterizing prisons for felons. Some of the newcomers to a prison for adults are, in short, persons who have been oriented to the convict subculture, who have found the

utilitarian nature of this subculture acceptable, and who have had little contact with the thief subculture. This makes a difference in their behavior.

The category of inmates we have characterized as oriented to "legitimate" subcultures includes men who are not members of the thief subculture upon entering prison and who reject both the thief subculture and the convict subculture while in prison. These men present few problems to prison administrators. They make up a large percentage of the population of any prison, but they isolate themselves—or are isolated—from the thief and convict subcultures. Clemmer found that forty percent of a sample of the men in his prison did not consider themselves a part of any group, and another forty percent could be considered a member of a "semi-primary group" only.[13] He referred to these men as "ungrouped," and his statistics have often been interpreted as meaning that the prison contains many men not oriented to "inmate culture" or "prison culture"—in our terms, not oriented to either the thief subculture or the convict subculture. This is not necessarily the case. There may be sociometric isolates among the thief-oriented prisoners, the convict-oriented prisoners, and the legitimately oriented prisoners. Consequently, we have used the "legitimate subcultures" terminology rather than Clemmer's term "ungrouped." Whether or not men in this category participate in cliques, athletic teams, or religious study and hobby groups, they are oriented to the problem of achieving goals through means which are legitimate outside prisons.

BEHAVIOR PATTERNS IN PRISON

On an ideal-type level, there are great differences in the prison behavior of men oriented to one or the other of the three types of subculture. The hard core member of the convict subculture finds his reference groups inside the institutions and, as indicated, he seeks status through means available in the prison environment. But it is

---

[11] *Ibid.*, pp. 12–13.
[12] Richard H. McCleery, "The Governmental Process and Informal Social Control," Chapter 4 in Cressey, *The Prison*, p. 179.

[13] Donald Clemmer, *The Prison Community*, Reissued Edition (New York: Rinehart, 1958), pp. 116–33.

important for the understanding of inmate conduct to note that the hard core member of the thief subculture seeks status in the broader criminal world of which prison is only a part. His reference groups include people both inside and outside prison, but he is committed to criminal life, not prison life. From his point of view, it is adherence to a widespread criminal code that wins him high status, not adherence to a narrower convict code. Convicts might assign him high status because they admire him as a thief, or because a good thief makes a good convict, but the thief does not play the convicts' game. Similarly, a man oriented to a legitimate subculture is by definition committed to the values of neither thieves nor convicts.

On the other hand, within any given prison, the men oriented to the convict subculture are the inmates that seek positions of power, influence, and sources of information, whether these men are called "shots," "politicians," "merchants," "hoods," "toughs," "gorillas," or something else. A job as secretary to the captain or Warden, for example, gives an aspiring prisoner information and consequent power, and enables him to influence the assignment or regulation of other inmates. In the same way, a job which allows the incumbent to participate in a racket, such as clerk in the kitchen storeroom where he can steal and sell food, is highly desirable to a man oriented to the convict subculture. With a steady income of cigarettes, ordinarily the prisoners' medium of exchange, he may assert a great deal of influence and purchase those things which are symbols of status among persons oriented to the convict subculture. Even if there is no well-developed medium of exchange, he can barter goods acquired in his position for equally desirable goods possessed by other convicts. These include information and such things as specially starched, pressed, and tailored prison clothing, fancy belts, belt buckles or billfolds, special shoes, or any other type of dress which will set him apart and will indicate that he has both the influence to get the goods and the influence necessary for keeping and displaying them despite prison rules which outlaw doing so. In California, special items of clothing, and clothing that is neatly laundered, are called "bonaroos" (a corruption of *bonnet rouge*, by means of which French prison trustees were once distinguished from the common run of prisoners), and to a lesser degree even the persons who wear such clothing are called "bonaroos."

Two inmates we observed in one prison are somewhat representative of high-status members of the convict subculture. One was the prison's top gambler, who bet the fights, baseball games, football games, ran pools, etc. His cell was always full of cigarettes, although he did not smoke. He had a job in the cell block taking care of the laundry room, and this job gave him time to conduct his gambling activities. It also allowed him to get commissions for handling the clothing of inmates who paid to have them "bonarooed," or who had friends in the laundry who did this for them free of charge, in return for some service. The "commissions" the inmate received for doing this service were not always direct; the "favors" he did gave him influence with many of the inmates in key jobs, and he reputedly could easily arrange cell changes and job changes. Shortly after he was paroled he was arrested and returned to prison for robbing a liquor store. The other inmate was the prison's most notorious "fag" or "queen." He was feminine in appearance and gestures, and wax had been injected under the skin on his chest to give the appearance of breasts. At first he was kept in a cell block isolated from the rest of the prisoners, but later he was released out into the main population. He soon went to work in a captain's office, and became a key figure in the convict subculture. He was considered a stool pigeon by the thieves, but he held high status among participants in the convict subculture. In the first place, he was the most desired fag in the prison. In the second place, he was presumed to have considerable influence with the officers who frequented the captain's office. He "married" another prisoner, who also was oriented to the convict subculture.

Since prisoners oriented either to a legitimate subculture or to a thief subculture are not seeking high status within any given prison, they do not look for the kinds of positions considered so desirable by the members of the convict subculture. Those oriented to legitimate subcultures take prison as it comes and seek status through channels provided for that purpose by prison administrators—running for election to the inmate council, to the editorship of the institutional newspaper, etc.—and by, generally, conforming to what they think administrators expect of "good prisoners." Long before the thief has come to prison, his subculture has defined proper prison conduct as behavior rationally calculated to "do time" in the easiest possible way. This means that he wants a prison life containing the best possible combination of a maximum amount of leisure time and a maximum number of privileges. Accordingly, the privileges sought by the thief are different from the privileges sought by the man oriented to prison itself. The thief wants things that will make prison life a little easier—extra food, a maximum amount of recreation time, a good radio, a little peace. One thief serving his third sentence for armed robbery was a dish washer in the officers' dining room. He liked the eating privileges, but he never sold food. Despite his "low-status" job, he was highly respected by other thieves, who described him as "right," and "solid." Members of the convict subculture, like the thieves, seek privileges. There is a difference, however, for the convict seeks privileges which he believes will enhance his position in the inmate hierarchy. He also wants to do easy time but, as compared with the thief, desirable privileges are more likely to involve freedom to amplify one's store, such as stealing rights in the kitchen, and freedom of movement around the prison. Obtaining an easy job is managed because it is easy and therefore desirable, but also is managed for the purpose of displaying the fact that it can be obtained.

In one prison, a man serving his second sentence for selling narcotics (he was not an addict) worked in the bakery during the entire term of his sentence. To him, a thief, this was a "good job," for the hours were short and the bakers ate very well. There were some rackets conducted from the bakery, such as selling cocoa, but the man never participated in these activities. He was concerned a little with learning a trade, but not very seriously. Most of all, he wanted the eating privileges which the bakery offered. A great deal of his time was spent reading psychology, philosophy, and mysticism. Before his arrest he had been a reader of tea leaves and he now was working up some plans for an illegal business involving mysticism. Other than this, his main activity was sitting with other inmates and debating.

Just as both thieves and convicts seek privileges, both seek the many kinds of contraband in a prison. But again the things the thief seeks are those that contribute to an easier life, such as mechanical gadgets for heating water for coffee and cocoa, phonographs and radios if they are contraband or not, contraband books, food, writing materials, socks, etc. He may "score" for food occasionally (unplanned theft in which advantage is taken of a momentary opportunity), but he does not have a "route" (highly organized theft of food). One who "scores" for food eats it, shares it with his friends, sometimes in return for a past or expected favors, but he does not sell it. One who has a "route" is in the illicit food selling business.[14] The inmate oriented to the convict subculture, with its emphasis on displaying ability to manipulate the environment, rather than on pleasure, is the inmate with the "route." The difference is observable in the case of an inmate assigned to the job of clerk in the dental office of one prison. This man was known to both inmates and staff long before he arrived at the institution, for his crime and arrest were highly publicized in the newspapers. It also became known that he had done time in another penitentiary for "real crime" and that his criminal exploits had frequently taken him from one side of the United States to the other. His assignment to the dental office occurred soon after he entered the prison, and some of the inmates believed that such a highly desirable job could not be achieved without "influence" and "rep." It was an ideal spot for conducting a profitable business, and a profitable business was in fact being conducted there. In order to get on the list to see the dentist, an inmate had to pay a price in cigarettes to two members of the convict subculture who were running the dental office. This practice soon changed, at least in reference to inmates who could show some contact with our man's criminal friends, in or out of prison. If a friend vouched for a man by saying he was

---

[14] See Schrag, "Some Foundations for a Theory of Correction," p. 343.

"right" or "solid," the man would be sitting in the dental chair the next day, free of charge.

Generally speaking, an inmate oriented to the thief subculture simply is not interested in gaining high status in the prison. He wants to get out. Moreover, he is likely to be quietly amused by the concern some prisoners have for symbols of status, but he publicly exhibits neither disdain nor enthusiasm for this concern. One exception to this occurred in an institution where a thief had become a fairly close friend of an inmate oriented to the prison. One day the latter showed up in a fresh set of bonaroos, and he made some remark that called attention to them. The thief looked at him, laughed, and said, "For Christ's sake, Bill, they're *Levi's* (standard prison blue denims) and they are always going to be Levi's." The thief may be accorded high status in the prison, because "rightness" is revered there as well as on the outside, but to him this is incidental to his being a "man," not to his being a prisoner.

Members of both subcultures are conservative —they want to maintain the status quo. Motivation is quite different, however. The man oriented to the convict subculture is conservative because he has great stock in the existing order of things, while the man who is thief oriented leans toward conservatism because he knows how to do time and likes things to run along smoothly with a minimum of friction. It is because of this conservatism that so many inmates are directly or indirectly in accommodation with prison officials who, generally speaking, also wish to maintain the status quo. A half dozen prison observers have recently pointed out that some prison leaders—those oriented to what we call the convict subculture—assist the officials by applying pressures that keep other inmates from causing trouble, while other prison leaders —those oriented to what we call the thief subculture—indirectly keep order by propagating the *criminal* code, including admonitions to "do your own time," "don't interfere with others' activities," "don't 'rank' another criminal." The issue is not whether the thief subculture and convict subculture are useful to, and used by, administrators; it is whether the observed behavior patterns originate in prison as a response to official administrative practices. . . .

BEHAVIOR AFTER RELEASE

If our crude typology is valid, it should be of some use for predicting the behavior of prisoners when they are released. However, it is important to note that in any given prison the two deviant subcultures are not necessarily as sharply separated as our previous discussion has implied. Most inmates are under the influence of *both* subcultures. Without realizing it, inmates who have served long prison terms are likely to move toward the middle, toward a compromise or balance between the directives coming from the two sources. A member of the convict subculture may come to see that thieves are the real men with the prestige; a member of the thief subculture or even a do-right may lose his ability to sustain his status needs by outside criteria. Criminologists seem to have had difficulty in keeping the two kinds of influence separate, and we cannot expect all inmates to be more astute than the criminologists. The fact that time has a blending effect on the participants in the two deviant subcultures suggests that the subcultures themselves tend to blend together in some prisons. We have already noted that the thief subculture scarcely exists in some institutions for juveniles. It is probable also that in army stockades and in concentration camps this subculture is almost nonexistent. In places of short-term confinement, such as city and county jails, the convict subculture is dominant, for the thief subculture involves status distinctions that are not readily observable in a short period of confinement. At the other extreme, in prisons where only prisoners with long sentences are confined, the distinctions between the two subcultures are likely to be blurred. Probably the two subcultures exist in their purest forms in institutions holding inmates in their twenties, with varying sentences for a variety of criminal offenses. Such institutions, of course, are the "typical" prisons of the United States.

Despite these differences, in any prison the men oriented to legitimate subcultures should have a low recidivism rate, while the highest recidivism rate should be found among participants in the convict subculture. The hard core members of this subculture are being trained in manipulation, duplicity and exploitation, they are not sure they can make it on the outside, and even when they are on the outside they continue to use convicts as a reference group. This sometimes means that there will be a wild spree of crime and dissipation which takes the members of the convict subculture directly back to the prison. Members of the thief subculture, to whom prison life represented a pitfall in outside life, also should have a high recidivism rate. However, the thief sometimes "reforms" and tries to succeed in some life within the law. Such behavior, contrary to popular notions, is quite acceptable to other members of the thief subculture, so long as the new job and position are not "anti-criminal" and do not involve regular, routine, "slave labor." Suckers work, but a man who, like a thief, "skims it off the top" is not a sucker. At any rate, the fact that convicts, to a greater extent than thieves, tend to evaluate things from the perspective of a prison and to look upon discharge as a short vacation from prison life suggests that their recidivism rate should be higher than that of thieves . . .

Noting that the origins of the thief subculture and the convict subculture are both external to a prison should change our expectations regarding the possible reformative effect of that prison. The recidivism rates of neither thieves nor convicts are likely to be significantly affected by incarceration in any traditional prison. This is not to say that the program of a prison with a "therapeutic milieu" like the one the Wisconsin State Reformatory is seeking, or of a prison like some of those in California, in which group counseling is being used in an attempt to change organizational structure, will not eventually affect the recidivism rates of the members of one or another, or all three, of the categories. However, in reference to the ordinary custodially oriented prison the thief says he can do his time "standing on his head"—except for long-termers, imprisonment has little effect on the thief one way or the other. Similarly, the routine of any particular custodial prison is not likely to have significant reformative effects on members of the convict subculture—they will return to prison because, in effect, they have found a home there. And the men oriented to legitimate subcultures will maintain low recidivism rates even if they never experience imprisonment. Garrity[15] has shown that it is not correct to conclude, as reformers have so often done, that prisons are the breeding ground of crime. It probably is not true either that any particular prison is the breeding ground of an inmate culture that significantly increases recidivism rates.

---

[15] Donald R. Garrity, "The Prison as a Rehabilitation Agency," Chapter 9 in Cressey, *The Prison.*

B. SOCIAL RELATIONS AND PROCESS

In "Socialization in Correctional Communities," Stanton Wheeler describes prisonization, or the process by which the antagonistic prison subculture is assimilated. Wheeler does not distinguish between different types of prison subcultures, as do Irwin and Cressey. He finds that prisonization varies with the inmate's relations with fellow inmates and his institutional career phase. Close relationships encourage participation in the subculture and social isolation accompanies the refusal to participate. Also, participation is greater during the middle phase of the inmate's sentence than just after entering prison, or just prior to release. It appears, therefore, that it is during the first and last phases that inmates are most oriented to life outside the prison. This suggests that the inmate "sheds" the prison subculture prior to release, which again questions the belief that prisons are "breeding grounds" for crime. The subculture may thus have little effect on the ex-convict after release. However, the subcultural attitudes can be reactivated on occasion. This may depend more on the nature of the social situation to which the ex-inmate returns (e.g., availability of job opportunities, continued stigma, etc.) than the extent of exposure to the subculture while in prison.

SOCIALIZATION IN CORRECTIONAL COMMUNITIES
STANTON WHEELER

This paper grows out of a tradition of sociological investigation established some twenty years ago by Donald Clemmer.[1] One of the most important of the many contributions in Clemmer's *The Prison Community* was his analysis of the changes inmates undergo during periods of confinement—changes Clemmer signified by use of the concept of *prisonization*. The present paper reviews the processes Clemmer described, provides an empirical test of some of his propositions, and attempts to relate the analysis of socialization processes to other features of correctional communities.

PRISONIZATION

Clemmer employed the concept of prisonization to describe the central impact of the prison on its inmates—the impact of an inmate society whose code, norms, dogma, and myth sustained a view of the prison and the outside world distinctly harmful to rehabilitation. The core of this view was indicated in an inmate code or system of norms requiring loyalty to other inmates and opposition to the prison staff, who served as representatives of a rejecting society beyond the walls. The consequences of exposure to the inmate society were summed up by the concept of prisonization, which Clemmer defined as "the taking on, in greater or lesser degree, of the folkways, mores, customs and general culture of the penitentiary."[2] Clemmer saw prisonization as a specific illustration of more general processes of assimilation occurring wherever persons are introduced to an unfamiliar culture. The net result of the process was the internalization of a criminal outlook, leaving the "prisonized" individual relatively immune to the influence of a conventional value system. Both Clemmer and the inmates who served as his principal informants felt that the degree of prisonization was the most important factor affecting adjustment after release from the institution.[3]

Clemmer noted that no inmate could remain completely unprisonized. Merely being an incarcerated offender exposed one to certain "universal features" of imprisonment. These included acceptance of an inferior role and recognition that nothing is owed the environment for the supplying of basic needs. Beyond these features were other conditions that he felt influenced both the speed and degree of prisonization. Thus prisonization would be lowest for those inmates who have had "positive" and "socialized" relationships during prepenal life, those who continue their positive relationships with persons outside the walls, those whose short sentences subject them to only brief exposure to the universal features of imprisonment, those who refuse or are unable to affiliate with inmate primary groups, and those who by chance are

Reprinted with permission of author and publisher from the *American Sociological Review* 26 (December, 1961), pp. 697–712 as abridged. Footnotes have been renumbered. Expanded and revised version of a paper read at the meetings of the American Sociological Association, Chicago, 1959. The author is greatly indebted to Dr. Clarence C. Schrag, University of Washington, for aid and criticism in the formulation of the research, to the inmates and staff of Western State Reformatory for their cooperation.

[1] Donald Clemmer, *The Prison Community* (New York: Rinehart and Co., 1958). (Reissue of Original 1940 edition.)

[2] *Ibid.*, p. 299.
[3] *Ibid.*, pp. 300–2, 312.

placed with other inmates not integrated into the inmate community. Clemmer felt that the most crucial of the factors was the degree of primary group affiliation.[4]

Though some twenty years have passed since Clemmer's work was first published, his account remains the most thorough and detailed description of the socialization process in prisons ... The theory is found wanting, however, because it accounts only for the process of cultural transmission and does not explain why the culture is "there" to be transmitted. It is criticized for being incomplete rather than false. But in addition to this omission and the need for more evidence concerning the process, there is a further problem in employing the concept of prisonization that requires clarification before Clemmer's propositions can be adequately tested. It concerns the temporal frame of reference within which socialization effects are studied.

The usual way of treating the time variable in studies of assimilation is to classify persons according to their length of exposure to the new social setting. This conception is usually employed in studies of prison adjustment, and was explicitly stated by Clemmer, who directed his attention to "the manner in which the attitudes of prisoners are modified as the men spend month after month in the penal milieu."[5] Throughout his work Clemmer concentrated on the process of induction into the community. He had little to say about changes that might occur as inmates neared the time for release. His proposition that prisonization is the most important determinant of parole adjustment is based on the assumption that processes observed during the early and middle phases of incarceration continue until the inmate is paroled.

It is easy to understand how this emphasis on the process of induction developed, for it grew out of the awareness that the prison is a community with its own norms and structure. The task of accounting for processes of assimilation

into the community developed as a natural concern. In addition there were no well-developed notions of what Merton has called "anticipatory socialization," the preparatory responses that frequently precede an actual change in group membership, such as the movement from prison to the broader community. The result is that we know much more about processes of socialization into the community than we do about re-adaptation to the outside world. There is evidence, however, that from the inmate's perspective the length of time *remaining* to be served may be the most crucial temporal aspect. Many inmates can repeat the precise number of months, weeks, and days until their parole date arrives, whereas few are equally accurate in reporting the length of time they have served. The inmate language system contains terms such as being "short" and having "short-time-itis" that suggest the importance of the last few weeks in the institution, just as the term "fish" denotes the new inmate's status.

These observations merely illustrate that at any given point in time the temporal frame of reference of different types of inmates may have various psychological and social meanings. So long as we restrict our analysis to the length of time since entrance into the prison, we may miss important features of the inmate's response to the institution.[6]

In order to clarify the different temporal aspects of socialization in the prison, the data reported below are divided into two sections. The first uses a definition of time similar to that implied by Clemmer, and allows for the test of his hypotheses. The second classifies inmates according to phases of their institutional career, thus enabling us to observe changes that may occur

---

[4] *Ibid.*, p. 312. Clemmer noted two other conditions that affect degree of prisonization: degree of "blind acceptance" of the dogmas and codes of the inmate population, and degree of participation in gambling and abnormal sex activity. Since these variables seem so closely tied to the concept of prisonization, they might be thought of as indicators of that concept rather than as conditions that affect it.

[5] Clemmer, *The Prison Community*, p. 294.

[6] In addition to possible differences in response depending on whether the inmate has a time orientation to the past, the present or the future, (or perhaps an orientation which encompasses all these by stressing the total expected duration of confinement) there is, of course, the important variable of indefiniteness of knowledge about the date of release. Cf. Maurice L. Farber, "Suffering and Time Perspective of the Prisoner," *University of Iowa Studies in Child Welfare* 20 (1944), pp. 153–227. The indefiniteness is probably more important in other types of total institutions, especially concentration camps, tuberculosis sanitoria, and mental hospitals. In correctional institutions the sentence and release authorities tend to develop routinized forms of administering the indeterminate sentence laws, so that most offenders know quite early in their stay about how long they will have to serve.

as inmates are preparing for release from the institution.

RESEARCH SETTING AND METHOD

The research was conducted in a western state reformatory, one of two adult penal institutions in the state. It is a walled, close custody institution receiving inmates from 16 to 30 years of age. The only felony offenders excluded by statute from sentence to the reformatory are those convicted of capital crimes. The physical plant is roughly typical of many northern state institutions designed to handle young adult offenders.

Samples of inmates were drawn from each of the housing units of the institution, using stratified random sampling procedures with a variable sampling rate designed to increase the number of inmates in the sample who were in the early and late stages of their incarceration. Of 259 men originally assigned to the sample, 95 percent completed questionnaires and 92 percent of the questionnaires were usable for research purposes. The only inmates excluded from the sample design were those screened by the clinical psychologist as psychotic or near psychotic, or too low in intelligence to understand and respond meaningfully to the questionnaire. The sample n is 237 from an inmate population of approximately 750.[7]

Hypothetical conflict situations were used to develop an index of conformity to staff role-expectations. Several conflict situations were employed in the research. The ones selected for the index were those that (1) gave evidence of normative consensus on the part of custody and treatment staff members, and (2) showed variation in inmate response. Five items adequately

met these criteria. The items, arranged in decreasing order of "conformity to staff" response, were as follows:

1. An inmate, Owens, is assigned to a work crew. Some other inmates criticize him because he does more work than anybody else on the crew. He works as hard as he can.

2. Inmate Martin goes before a committee that makes job assignments. He is given a choice between two jobs. One job would call for hard work, but it would give Martin training that might be useful to him on the outside. The other job would allow Martin to do easier time in the institution. But it provides no training for a job on the outside. Martin decides to take the easier job.

3. An inmate, without thinking, commits a minor rule infraction. He is given a "write-up" by a correctional officer who saw the violation. Later three other inmates are talking to each other about it. Two of them criticize the officer. The third inmate, Sykes, defends the officer, saying the officer was only doing his duty.

4. Inmates Smith and Long are very good friends. Smith has a five-dollar bill that was smuggled into the institution by a visitor. Smith tells Long he thinks the officers are suspicious, and asks Long to hide the money for him for a few days. Long takes the money and carefully hides it.

5. Inmates Brown and Henry are planning an escape. They threaten inmate Smith with a beating unless he steals a crowbar for them from the tool shop where he works. He thinks they mean business. While he is trying to smuggle the crowbar into the cell house, he is caught by an officer, and Smith is charged with planning to escape. If he doesn't describe the whole situation, he may lose up to a year of good time. He can avoid it by blaming Brown and Henry.

Responses to the first four items were on a four category approve-disapprove continuum. Response categories for the fifth item were:

What should inmate Smith do?

He should clear himself by telling about the escape plan of Brown and Henry.

He should keep quiet and take the punishment himself.

---

[7] The analysis below excludes from the protection and segregation units fourteen inmates for whom data were lacking on the time variable. Another eight inmates were excluded because of non-response to one of the five items in the conformity index. The resulting n is 214. Wherever the reported n's fall below that figure it is due to lack of complete information on one of the independent variables. Results from each sampling unit have been combined in the analysis but have not been weighted for differences in sampling rates. Such differences could affect the results only if r_{ab} in sampling unit x differs from r_{ab} in sampling unit y. Snedecor's test for heterogeneity showed no significant differences for ten of the most important relationships in the study. Therefore the simplification achieved by unweighted combining would seem to be justifiable.

On each of the items at least 75 percent of the custody and treatment staff members were in the modal response category: They approve the inmate's conduct in items one and three, disapprove on two and four, and feel that inmate Smith "should clear himself ..." Sixty-seven percent of the staff were in agreement on all five items, and 93 percent were in agreement on at least four items. Thus for these items there is a relatively high degree of normative consensus among staff as to proper inmate behavior. Inmates are classified into three categories, according to the number of situations in which the inmate response is the same as that of the modal staff response. The high conformity group includes inmates whose own response agreed with the staff in at least four of the five situations, the medium conformists, those who agreed in two or three situations, and the low conformists, those who agreed in none or in one situation. The relatively small number in the extreme nonconformity group has led to their inclusion with the medium conformists at several points in the analysis.[8]

RESULTS: LENGTH OF TIME SERVED AND CONFORMITY TO STAFF EXPECTATIONS

When the usual method of treating the time variable is employed, the results give strong support to Clemmer's propositions regarding prisonization. Table 1 shows the relationship between length of time served and conformity to staff norms. As expressed in this table, the effect of increased length of exposure is to reduce the proportion of men who conform to the staff's expectations. Furthermore, when analysis is made separately for first termers and recidivists (Table 2), there is evidence of a relearning process among the recidivists. Although recidivists

are more likely to be nonconformists than are the first termers, the effect of time served on their nonconformity is about the same. Instead of entering the prison already prisonized, a re-prisonization process appears to occur.

If the process of prisonization is operating effectively we should be able to observe its effects over shorter time periods. And we would expect the effect to be present particularly for offenders serving their first term in an adult penal institution. In Table 3, inmates are classified into as refined time categories as can be justified with a small number of cases. The results are presented for a period up to one year, for which period we can be almost positive that selective factors are not operating. The results again confirm Clemmer's observations, and suggest the importance of the first few months in the socialization process.[9]

A central theme in Clemmer's analysis is that the degree of prisonization will vary according to the degree of involvement in the informal life of the inmate community. In the present research, two items were used to tap the extent of inmate involvement. One item reflects the extensiveness of involvement in terms of the number of close friendships established with other inmates. A second item reflects the intensity of involvement by ascertaining the degree to which inmates spend their free time with other inmates or by themselves. The relationship of each of these indexes of involvement to conformity to staff expectations is presented in Tables 4 and 5.[10]

The results indicated in both tables lend sup-

---

[8] Staff responses were based on samples of 81 of 111 custody staff members, and 18 of 21 treatment staff members. For a fuller discussion of the methodology employed, see Stanton Wheeler, *Social Organization in a Correctional Community,* unpublished Ph.D. Dissertation (University of Washington, 1958). More recent analysis of the index suggests that the items form a Guttman scale with reproducibility = .92, only moderately high for five items. Results reported below are based, however, on the Likert scoring system used earlier. Differences are very slight and do not affect the conclusions.

[9] Richard Cloward reports a similar finding based on research in a military prison. See Helen Witmer and Ruth Kotinsky, editors, *New Perspectives for Research on Juvenile Delinquency* (Washington, D.C., U.S. Dept. of Health, Education and Welfare, Children's Bureau, 1956), pp. 80–91.

[10] The items used to measure extensiveness and intensity were: Have you developed any close friendships with other inmates since you have been in the reformatory?
.... Yes, several, (more than 5)
.... Yes, a few, (3 to 5)
.... Yes, one or two
.... No
Think back over the past month in the reformatory. How would you say you spent most of your free time?
.... Mostly with a group of inmates who are together quite a lot.
.... With one or two inmates
.... With several different inmates, but not in any one group
.... Mostly by myself
In Tables 4 and 5, the top two categories are combined for high involvement, the bottom two for low involvement.

TABLE 1. LENGTH OF TIME SERVED AND CONFORMITY TO STAFF ROLE EXPECTATIONS

Length of Time Served	Percent High Conformity	Percent Medium Conformity	Percent Low Conformity	Total	n
Less than 6 months	47	44	09	100	77
6 months–2 years	32	54	14	100	99
Over 2 years	16	61	24	100	38
Total					214

χ^2 (4df) = 12.00 p < .01
γ = −.35

TABLE 2. LENGTH OF TIME SERVED AND CONFORMITY TO STAFF ROLE EXPECTATIONS, FOR OFFENDERS DIFFERING IN PRIOR PENAL COMMITMENTS

	Percent High Conformity			
Length of Time Served	No Prior Adult Commitment	n	Prior Adult Commitment	n
Less than 6 months	49	51	40	25
6 months–2 years	31	64	33	33
Over 2 years	19	26	06	12
Total		141		70

χ^2 (2df) = 7.56 p < .025 χ^2 (2df) = 2.50 p > .10
γ = −.40 γ = −.38

port to the proposition that both the speed and degree of prisonization are a function of informal inmate involvement. During the first time period there is no significant relation between involvement and conformity to staff opinion. However, the percentage of high conformists drops rapidly for inmates who are highly involved. For those who have little contact with other inmates as assessed by our items, the process of prisonization appears to operate, but the major impact is delayed until after two years have been served, and even then does not oper-

ate to the same degree as for highly involved inmates.

While our data do not enable us to specify clearly the time relationship between involvement and conformity, it is instructive to examine the relationship as though the reverse time sequence were in operation—as though the sequence were from conformity to involvement. As Table 6 shows, the proportion of high conformists who are also involved in intimate interaction with other inmates decreases through time, while there is an increase in social contacts among the nonconformists.

These results of course raise the question of the interplay between social involvement on the one hand, attitudes and values on the other. Rather than thinking of one of these variables as an effect of the other, a more appropriate model of their interaction in the prison community might stress the structural incompatibility of being both highly involved with inmates and an attitudinal conformist to staff expectations. The dominant normative order among inmates (at least in terms of power and visibility if not numbers) is strongly opposed to that of the staff. The inmate who values friendship among his

TABLE 3. PERCENTAGE HIGH CONFORMITY FOR FIRST-TERMERS OVER THE FIRST 12 MONTHS OF INCARCERATION

Length of Time Served	Percent High Conformity	n
Less than 3 weeks	56	18
3 to 6 weeks	48	21
6 weeks to 6 months	42	12
6 months to 1 year	28	25
Total		76

χ^2 (1df) = 2.05 p < .10
γ = −.37

TABLE 4. LENGTH OF TIME SERVED AND CONFORMITY TO STAFF ROLE EXPECTATIONS, FOR INMATES DIFFERING IN EXTENSIVENESS OF PRIMARY GROUP CONTACTS

	Percent High Conformity			
Length of Time Served	High Group Contacts*	n	Low Group Contacts*	n
Less than 6 months	45	31	48	46
6 months–2 years	20	44	42	55
Over 2 years	06	18	30	20
Total		93		121

$$\chi^2 (2df) = 8.37 \; p < .01 \qquad \chi^2 (2df) = 1.82 \; p > .25$$
$$\gamma = -.62 \qquad\qquad\qquad \gamma = -.20$$

* See footnote 10 for item wording.

TABLE 5. LENGTH OF TIME SERVED AND CONFORMITY TO STAFF ROLE EXPECTATIONS, FOR INMATES DIFFERING IN INTENSITY OF INMATE CONTACTS

	Percent High Conformity			
Length of Time Served	High Group Intensity*	n	Low Group Intensity*	n
Less than 6 months	42	40	51	35
6 months–2 years	21	61	49	39
Over 2 years	00	16	27	22
Total		117		96

$$\chi^2 (2df) = 9.75 \; p < .005 \qquad \chi^2 (2df) = 3.58 \; p < .10$$
$$\gamma = -.63 \qquad\qquad\qquad \gamma = -.27$$

* See footnote 10 for item wording.

TABLE 6. LENGTH OF TIME SERVED AND EXTENSIVENESS OF PRIMARY GROUP CONTACTS, FOR INMATES DIFFERING IN CONFORMITY TO STAFF EXPECTATIONS

	Percent High Extensiveness			
Length of Time Served	High Conformists	n	Low Conformists	n
Less than 6 months	39	36	41	41
6 months–2 years	28	32	52	67
Over 2 years	14	7	55	31
Total		75		139

$$\chi^2 (1df) = 1.33 \; p > .10 \qquad \chi^2 (1df) = 1.17 \; p > .10$$
$$\gamma = -.31 \qquad\qquad\qquad \gamma = .17$$

peers and also desires to conform to the staff's norms faces a vivid and real role conflict. The conflict is not apparent or perhaps is not felt so intensely during the earliest stages of confinement, but with increasing length of time in the prison the strain becomes more acute; inmates move to resolve the strain either by giving up or being excluded from primary ties, or by a shift in attitudes. In either case the result leads to a polarization of non-involved conformists and involved nonconformists. One group of inmates becomes progressively prisonized, the other progressively isolated. And as the marginal frequencies of Tables 4 and 6 suggest, the dominant tendency is to move in the direction of nonconformity rather than isolation.[11]

---

[11] The strain may be similar to that noted in small group research, between the expressive and instrumental roles. Persons who initially play both the best-ideas and best-liked roles tend to drop the former role for the latter as interaction continues. Talcott Parsons, Robert F. Bales and Edward A. Shils, *Working Papers in the Theory of Action* (Glencoe: The Free Press, 1953), pp. 150–61.

This interpretation of changes over time in the prison community awaits panel longitudinal data for its validation.

A problem posed by the above data, as well as Clemmer's earlier analysis concerns the absence of social bonds among the conforming inmates. Neither in our data nor in the language system of the prison is there evidence of a category characterized both by conformity to the staff *and* by strong social bonds with other inmates. What is it about the structure of the correctional community that makes conformity possible, apparently, only at the cost of isolation? The question is too complex to receive detailed treatment here, involving as it does at least in part the question of the origin of the negative inmate culture in prisons. Once established, however, the culture exerts pressure on both the inmates and the staff which operates largely to suppress the formation of solidary ties among the conformists. Evidence from other parts of this study suggests that inmates perceive the opinions of others to be more opposed to the staff than they actually are.[12] The resulting pattern of pluralistic ignorance operates to restrain even the initial seeking out of like-minded individuals. The same pressures lead to the frequent warnings from staff members to stay out of involvements with other inmates, and "do your own time." Thus the conforming inmate may be restrained from establishing supportive ties with others by both the official and the inmate systems. If the withdrawal pattern characteristic of those who conform to the staff is not offset by strong ties to persons outside the institution, the effects of social isolation may be quite severe. For these inmates, the modern institution may accomplish by social and psychological pressure what the Pennsylvania system accomplished by its physical design, and perhaps with some of the same consequences.[13]

---

[12] "Role Conflict in Correctional Communities," in Donald R. Cressey, editor, *The Prison: Studies in Institutional Organization and Change* (New York: Holt, Rinehart, and Winston, 1961).

[13] The suggestion that prisonization and social isolation are alternative forms of response to the prison, each posing different problems of adjustment upon release, does not preclude the possibility that inmates may adopt both forms of response at different stages in their incarceration. Again, panel studies are required to trace the interactions between these forms of response. For some suggestions of possible linkages between the two patterns, see Lloyd E. Ohlin, *Sociology and the Field of Corrections* (New York: Russell Sage Foundation, 1956), pp. 37–40.

RESULTS: INSTITUTIONAL CAREER PHASE AND CONFORMITY TO STAFF EXPECTATIONS

In the following analysis inmates are classified into three categories: 1) those who have served less than six months in the correctional community and are thus in an *early phase* of their commitment; 2) those who have less than six months remaining to serve—the *late phase* inmates; and 3) those who have served more than six months and have more than six months left to serve—the *middle phase* inmates. This procedure enables us to examine changes in response that may occur as inmates are preparing for return to the broader community.

The relationship between phase of institutional career and conformity of staff expectations is presented in Table 7. Two trends are apparent. First there is a steady increase in the proportion of low conformity responses. Second, there is a U-shaped distribution of high conformity responses. The trends suggest that two processes may be in operation. One process is that of prisonization. A progressive opposition to staff norms is observed when inmates are classified either by length of time served or by institutional career phase.

TABLE 7. PHASE OF INSTITUTIONAL CAREER AND CONFORMITY TO STAFF ROLE EXPECTATIONS

Institutional Career Phase	Percent High	Percent Medium	Percent Low	Total	n
Early phase	47	44	09	100	77
Middle phase	21	65	14	100	94
Late phase	43	33	25	100	40
Total					211

$$\chi^2 (4df) = 20.48 \quad p < .001$$
$$\gamma = -.21$$

The second process appears to be one of differential attachment to the values of the broader society. The U-shaped distribution of high-conformity responses suggests that inmates who recently have been in the broader community and inmates who are soon to return to that community are more frequently oriented in terms of conventional values. Inmates conform least to conventional standards during the middle phase of their institutional career. These inmates appear to shed the prison culture before they leave it, such that there are almost as many conforming inmates at time of release as at time of entrance into the system.[14]

Empirical verification of these two processes will require panel [longitudinal] studies. If future research supports the findings reported here, other important questions would be raised. What types of inmates follow the pattern of prisonization vs. the pattern of reattachment to the extra-institutional world? Where are these types located within the prison social structure? What events or conditions lead to one process rather than the other? Can institutional authorities exert control over the processes by policy decisions?

The resocialization effect is apparent among inmates who have established close friendships in the institution, as well as among those who have not. Table 8 shows that inmates who stay out of close friendship ties exhibit as great an attachment to law-abiding standards during the late phase as during the early phase. The process of resocialization is evident among highly involved inmates, but not to the same degree.[15] And as the marginal distributions indicate, the rate of group involvement is highest during the

middle phase. When the rate of involvement is examined separately for high and low conformists, the high conformists show a decline at each stage and the low conformists a sharp rise during the middle phase with a decline as time for release approaches.

Further evidence regarding the process of resocialization appears when recidivists are compared with first offenders. As presented in Table 9, the pattern for recidivists is similar to that for first termers. Both groups show the decline in conformity during the middle phase with a rise in conformity in the late phase. The recidivists begin at a lower point and end at a lower point, but the adaptive response pattern is still evident.

The findings concerning career phase for first termers and recidivists suggest some revision of our thinking regarding the impact of time. Instead of viewing successive institutional careers as the development of an increasingly negative pattern, the results would suggest that a cyclical pattern of adjustment may hold for a sizable number of inmates—a cycle which has its lowest point during the middle of a period of institutional confinement, and may have its high point at some period on parole. If observations could be made on parolees it is possible that we could locate other points in the cycle. The results suggest a complex process of socialization and resocialization as offenders move into and out of the correctional community. The model is that of a cycle with a negative trend rather than a monotonically increasing commitment to a criminal value system.[16]

DISCUSSION

The prisonization theory is strongly supported when inmates are classified according to the length of time they have served. When they are classified into phases of their institutional career, however, the prisonization theory is inadequate as a description of changes over time. While it accounts for the increase in extreme nonconformity, it fails to account for the U-shaped dis-

---

[14] Another potential bias required analysis at this point. Inmates receiving the longest sentences are more likely to be included in the middle phase, while inmates receiving short sentences are over-represented in the late phase. The differences between middle and late phase inmates could thus be due to selective factors.

The best available check on the existence of such a bias is to consider the responses of middle and late phase inmates separately in terms of total expected time to be served. If the result is due to selection, the differences between middle and late phases should disappear.

This procedure yielded the following results: For low total time inmates, the percentage high conformity was 28 percent in the middle phase, 44 percent in the late phase, for low conformity from 11 percent to 25 percent. For high total time inmates, the percent high conformity moved from 21 percent in the middle phase to 38 percent in the late phase; for low conformity from 15 percent to 25 percent. Thus the relationships hold when total length of sentence is controlled. Use of other cutting points for total time served produced roughly similar results, though suggesting that resocialization operates more strongly for inmates with short sentences, much less strongly for inmates with long sentences.

[15] One may question the use of gamma as a measure of association for U-shaped distributions such as those indicated in Table 8, for (provided the marginals are balanced) the measure will give a value of zero for a perfectly U-shaped distribution, although obviously there is "a relationship." One might think of the measure in the present case as reflecting the "net effect" of imprisonment, in which case the measure appropriately gives a value of zero if changes between the early and middle phase are offset by changes between the middle and late phase. Table 8 also demonstrates the dependence of gamma on the marginal distribution. If our sample contained equal numbers of inmates in the early, middle and last phases, the gamma for the relationship among the "high contacts" group would drop from −.38 to −.18, and for the "low contacts" group from −.07 to zero.

[16] A pattern similar to that found here has been observed in a state penitentiary. See Peter Garabedian, *Western Penitentiary: A Study in Social Organization*, unpublished Ph.D. Dissertation (University of Washington, 1959).

TABLE 8. PHASE OF INSTITUTIONAL CAREER AND CONFORMITY TO STAFF ROLE EXPECTATIONS, FOR INMATES DIFFERING IN EXTENSIVENESS OF PRIMARY GROUP CONTACTS

Institutional Career Phase	Percent High Conformity			
	High Group Contacts	n	Low Group Contacts	n
Early phase	45	31	48	46
Middle phase	12	50	30	47
Late phase	33	12	48	27
		—		—
Total		93		120

$$\chi^2 \text{ (2df)} = 11.38 \text{ p} < .01 \qquad \chi^2 \text{ (2df)} = 4.06 \text{ p} > .10$$
$$\gamma = -.38 \qquad\qquad\qquad \gamma = -.07$$

tribution of high conformity responses. Recent attempts to develop a theory accounting for the content of the inmate culture provide some understanding of the possible bases for these two types of change.

The Inmate Culture

Two explanations have been offered to account for the content of the inmate culture, one focussing on the process of "negative selection," the other on problem-solving processes. The *negative selection* approach begins with the obvious fact that the single trait held in common by all inmates is participation in criminal activity. Their criminal acts indicate in varying degrees an opposition to conventional norms. It follows that the inmate culture should give expression to the values of those who are most committed to a criminal value system—the long termers, those who have followed systematic criminal careers, etc. And if the culture is viewed as an outgrowth of the criminogenic character of inmates, it is reasonable to expect a reinforcement process

operating throughout the duration of confinement. This is consistent with the image of correctional institutions as "crime schools" and with a theory that accounts for changes in response to the prison largely in terms of prisonization.

The alternative view stresses the problem-solving nature of subcultures, and interprets the content of the inmate culture as a response to the adjustment problems posed by imprisonment, with all its accompanying frustrations and deprivations. In his analysis of social types in a state penitentiary, Schrag noted the way in which these types are focussed around the problems of loyalty relations, of "doing time," of sexual outlet, etc.—problems which are not a direct carry-over from the outside world.[17] In a more recent functional analysis of the inmate social system, Sykes and Messinger note five major deprivations or attacks on the inmate's self-conception,

---

[17] Clarence C. Schrag, "Some Foundations for a Theory of Correction," in Donald R. Cressey, ed., *The Prison* (New York: Holt, Rinehart and Winston, 1961). See also Gresham M. Sykes, *The Society of Captives* (Princeton: Princeton University Press, 1958), pp. 84–108.

TABLE 9. PHASE OF INSTITUTIONAL CAREER AND CONFORMITY TO STAFF ROLE EXPECTATIONS, FOR OFFENDERS DIFFERING IN PRIOR PENAL COMMITMENTS

Institutional Career Phase	Percent High Conformity			
	No Prior Adult Commitment	n	Prior Adult Commitment	n
Early phase	49	51	40	25
Middle phase	21	63	22	32
Late phase	44	27	33	12
		—		—
Total		141		69

$$\chi^2 \text{ (2df)} = 11.1 \text{ p} < .01 \qquad \chi^2 \text{ (2df)} = 1.44 \text{ p} > .30$$
$$\gamma = -.19 \qquad\qquad\qquad \gamma = -.19$$

including the rejected status of being an inmate, the material and sexual deprivations of imprisonment, the constant social control exercised by the custodians, and the presence of other offenders. They conclude:[18]

"In short, imprisonment 'punishes' the offender in a variety of ways extending far beyond the simple fact of incarceration. However just or necessary such punishments may be, their importance for our present analysis lies in the fact that they form a set of harsh social conditions to which the population of prisoners must respond or *adapt itself*. The inmate feels that the deprivations and frustrations of prison life, with all their implications for the destruction of his self-esteem, somehow must be alleviated. It is, we suggest, as an answer to this need that the functional significance of the inmate code or system of values exhibited so frequently by men in prison can best be understood."

Elsewhere they note:[19]

"The maxims of the inmate code do not simply reflect the individual values of imprisoned criminals; rather, they represent a system of group norms that are directly related to mitigating the pains of imprisonment under a custodial regime having nearly total power."

If this interpretation is valid we might expect that the culture would exert its major impact on inmates during the *middle* of their stay, at the point in time when they are farthest removed from the outside world. We might also expect that as time for release approaches, the problems deriving from imprisonment recede relative to prospective adjustment problems on parole. Such a shift in reference should give rise to a resocialization process beginning prior to release. And if the culture has this problem-solving character, then recidivists as well as first termers should exhibit the U-shaped pattern of response.[20]

These observations merely indicate that the two trends suggested by the data are consistent with two different interpretations of the inmate culture. On both theoretical and empirical grounds, the adaptive pattern would seem to deserve more attention than it has received in discussions of socialization in the prison. But whether either or both of these types of response are dominant patterns of adjustment in the prison cannot be assessed with the cross-sectional design used in the present study. A panel study in which inmates were interviewed in the early, middle, and late phases of incarceration, and scored as conformist $(+)$ or deviant $(-)$ in their orientation to the staff and the outside world, would yield eight possible response patterns describing the inmate's movement through his institutional career. In addition to the prisonization and adaptation patterns $(+ - -$ and $+ - +)$ there are patterns of stable conformity and stable deviance $(+ + +$ and $- - -)$, a delayed prisonization pattern $(+ + -)$, patterns of rehabilitation or delayed rehabilitation $(- + +$ and $- - +)$, and a counter-adaptive pattern $(- + -)$ in which the inmate appears to move toward a conventional orientation during the middle of his stay only to return to the deviant response as he approaches parole. Anecdotal evidence and informal observation suggest that all of these patterns might be found, though the prisonization and adaptation patterns may be the most frequent of those in which change occurs. One suggestion emerging from our analysis of the adaptive pattern is that while changes from early to middle phase may reflect events within the institution, changes near release are largely a response to the external world. As correctional programs develop their emphases on liberal visiting, family counseling and pre-release programs they may be able to strengthen tendencies toward a positive change in attitude during the late phases of imprisonment. In turn, current sociological accounts of the inmate culture and adjustment processes may have to be revised to deal more systematically with these external influences.

Conditions affecting type of response. When

---

[18] Gresham M. Sykes and Sheldon L. Messinger, "The Inmate Social System," p. 15.

[19] *Ibid.*, p. 19.

[20] A third possible interpretation is that the U-shaped distribution would disappear if one could control adequately for a "social desirability" response set which may be more likely during the early and late stages of confinement. The conditions of administration of the research were designed, of course, to reduce this possibility, but further controls are necessary before this interpretation can be ruled out. The increase in extreme nonconformity during the late stage shows that the effect is not a general one. Also, one would expect that if the effect is operating, it would be sustained at least until inmates had received their sentences, (sometime be-

tween the third and sixth month of incarceration). But the evidence from Table 3 suggests that the decline in conformity operates before this major administrative decision is made.

Clemmer wrote *The Prison Community* it was perhaps reasonable to note under "conditions affecting degree of prisonization" only the personal characteristics of offenders. Prisons were pretty much alike, classification between institutions was weak, and the processes Clemmer noted could be assumed to be relatively constant across a range of institutions. Current correctional systems increasingly depart from this image, and it is likely that both type of clientele and institutional program exert an effect on socialization processes. For example, the fate of those who enter prison with an initially conformist orientation probably depends in large part on the balance between initial conformists and deviants: as the proportion of initial deviants increases, there is greater pressure on the conformists to move away from the pattern of stable conformity. This relationship in turn probably depends on the average age of offenders in the institution. Thus adult maximum security prisons tend to get a very large proportion of inmates who are deviant at time of entrance, but the advanced age of initial conformists may mean that they are less susceptible to influence from the inmate culture. Juvenile institutions are likely to receive a larger number of offenders whose frames of reference are not solidified, and who may thus be more susceptible to peer-group influence. A less "negative" inmate culture may still produce the prisonization response. These features of the inmate population probably interact with staff programs (including the attempts in some institutions to neutralize the inmate culture) to create further modifications in the socialization process in different institutions. The growing differentiation of correctional institutions reinforces the need for comparative analyses and serves as a reminder of the limits of generalization from studies of the type reported in this paper.

Prison and Parole Adjustment

The suggestion that the inmate's response to the prison is adaptive—that he becomes deprisonized as well as prisonized—raises the question of the impact of incarceration on parole conduct. Failure on parole is frequently viewed as the result of internalization of a criminal value system while in prison. But evidence of a cyclical type of adjustment suggests that the process is more complex than is implied in the prisonization scheme. The value system learned in prison may serve as a set of rationalizations activated only when the parolee faces what he defines as barriers to success on parole. Even though the inmate sheds the culture of the prison it will have provided him with justifications for criminal behavior that may be invoked in the event of post-release adjustment difficulties. The prisonization effect may still be operating, though not in the simple and direct fashion implied by the "crime school" image. Its effect is probably modified in important ways by different types of parole settings.

There is a danger, however, of pressing the concept of prisonization too far as an explanation of the prison's impact on parole behavior. Another feature of imprisonment would appear to have an extremely potent influence. This is the impact on the offender's self-conception rather than upon his attitudes toward the outside world. Almost all accounts of correctional processes note what Ohlin has referred to as the "self-defining character of the experiences to which the offender is exposed by correctional agencies."[21] In many instances, these effects appear to be highly related to the prisonization process. The offender learns to reject society and in doing so comes to accept a conception of himself as a criminal, with an elaborate set of supporting justifications. But much of the impact of imprisonment appears to lie along another dimension of self-image—the tendency for the offender to internalize the social rejection implicit in his status and suffer the pains of a lowered self-esteem and self rejection. In the work of McCorkle and Korn and more recently in Sykes and Messinger, these potential attacks on the offender's self-image are taken as a crucial condition giving rise to the inmate value system. Self esteem is restored by participation in a system that enables the offender to "reject his rejectors, rather than himself."[22] But if the

---

[21] Ohlin, *Sociology and the Field of Corrections*, p. 33.
[22] Lloyd W. McCorkle and Richard Korn, "Resocialization Within Walls," *The Annals of the Academy of Political and Social Science* 293 (May, 1954), pp. 88–98.

inmate culture has the problem solving function stressed in these accounts, and if many men show an adaptive response, it follows that the salience of the culture is reduced as men prepare to leave it. This reduction is probably "functional" in the sense that many of the problems of imprisonment do in fact decrease as the inmate nears release. This would seem to be true of most of the threats to self noted by Sykes and Messinger, including the extensive social control of the custodians, the constant presence of other inmates, and the material and sexual deprivations. However, the sense of rejection and degradation implicit in the offender's status does not necessarily decline with release, for the ex-con label still applies. The inmate who sheds the negative outlook required by the inmate system may inherit in its place the rejecting feelings the culture served largely to deny. In this sense the function of the inmate culture may be to *delay* the facing of problems imposed by a degraded social status, rather than to solve them.

This interpretation may help account for the profound states of anxiety and lack of confidence in themselves which even seemingly "tough" inmates frequently display prior to release.[23] As the inmate turns his attention from the inside to the free community, as he makes contacts with employers and relatives, the definition of his status provided by the inmate code loses much of its significance. But it is precisely at this point when the meaning of being an inmate, *as it is viewed by the outside world,* is most likely to have its impact. Some inmates find an atmosphere of acceptance and encouragement. Many others may find that certain jobs are not open to them, that there is some question as to how welcome they are in the community, that they are generally defined as "risks" and not accorded full status. They may return to association with other ex-offenders not so much to continue a criminal career as to find a more supportive social setting, though further crimes may well grow out of such contacts.

If this interpretation is correct, many of the psychological pains of imprisonment are revealed most clearly at time of release rather than entry. It suggests a basis for a cyclical fluctuation of attitudes as the offender sheds the culture of the prison, experiences social rejection, finds support among other former inmates, returns to crime and to prison, reincorporates prison values, and so on. If true, it points to another possible reason for the organization of therapeutic efforts around the time of release, as well as to the limitations of such efforts unless they can bring about a change in the response to the offender on the part of those in his parole environment. And it suggests that sociological research should be as concerned with the process of re-entry into the community as it has been historically with the problem of assimilation in prison.[24]

One final problem may be noted. Prisons along with other types of "total institutions" are usually assumed to have deep and long-lasting effects on the values of their members. The assumption is natural, deriving as it does largely from the potential effect of 24 hour living establishments that allow only psychological means of escape. The view is supported by a tendency to study the processes of *induction* into such institutions, where the initial effects stand out very clearly.[25] But in most such institutions, membership is temporary. Inmates leave as well as enter. If the institutions tend to develop subcultures specific to the problems imposed by their rather unique character, their members may be insulated from lasting socialization effects. In the case of prisons, this insulation provides a less negative picture of the effects of the institution than emerges from analysis of the inmate culture. In therapeutically oriented total institutions, the positive effects may be suppressed. We

---

[23] Robert Lindner, *Stone Walls and Men* (New York: Odyssey Press, 1946), p. 422.

[24] Prison officials have long been aware of the potential changes in offenders as they near release, and in some institutions special programs are devoted to "pre-release" training or therapy. Useful information on changes in adjustment associated with release is being developed by Daniel Glaser in his panel study of inmates in the federal prison system.

[25] It appears that studies of mental hospitals as well as prisons have emphasized the induction process. For a perceptive account of induction phenomena in mental hospitals, see Erving Goffman, "The Moral Career of the Mental Patient," *Psychiatry* 22 (May, 1959), pp. 123–42. For a suggestion that the effects of these processes in mental hospitals and other types of total institutions may well disappear with release, see Goffman, "On the Characteristics of Total Institutions," *Proceedings of the Symposium on Preventive and Social Psychiatry* (Walter Reed Army Institute of Research, Washington, D.C., April 1957), pp. 35–36.

might expect this suppression of lasting effects to occur particularly in institutions where membership is involuntary. Another relevant condition

may be a known and relatively brief duration of confinement.[26] Both of these conditions are present in reformatories.

---

[26] Some of the effects of involuntary membership have been outlined by Festinger, "An Analysis of Compliant Behavior," in Sherif and Wilson, editors, *Group Relations at the Crossroads* (New York: Harper and Brothers, 1953). See also John W. Thibaut and Harold H. Kelly, *The Social Psychology of Groups* (New York: John Wiley, 1959), pp. 168–90. The concept of voluntary membership itself deserves further clarification. Membership in colleges and professional schools is usually regarded as voluntary since the member chooses to apply. Since membership in such institutions is frequently the only means of achieving other desired ends, (such as the legal right to teach, practice medicine, etc.) elements of involuntary membership are present. Membership may be something to be endured rather than enjoyed. Such settings may produce less overall change in values than is usually supposed. Thus Becker and Geer found a U-shaped attitud-

inal shift in medical students similar in form to our findings, for the reformatory. The idealism of entering students was corroded during the middle of their stay, under the pressure to get the training and grades necessary for graduation, though it emerged again as they neared "release." See "The Fate of Idealism in Medical School," *American Sociological Review* 23 (February, 1958), pp. 50–56. Newcomb's finding of a steadily increasing commitment to the institution's values at Bennington College may be attributed in part to the relatively earlier age at entrance, the spirit of newness, and the high prestige of the institution and its staff. As such it may not be typical of the pattern of value change to be found in many colleges or universities lacking these qualities. Theodore Newcomb, *Personality and Social Change* (New York: Dryden Press, 1943).

C. CONSEQUENCES

In "The Corruption of Authority and Rehabilitation," Sykes reveals some important consequences that may stem from the antagonistic prison subculture. Guards are charged with maintaining strict internal order, which means rigid inmate adherence to prison rules. Since the prison subculture restrains inmates from cooperating with prison officials, greater surveillance by the guards is necessary. However, guards cannot be everywhere—the costs of surveillance are too great. Consequently, they may relax some rules in exchange for the inmates' voluntary compliance with others. The guards' authority may be undermined as a result. Other corruptive influences are the prisoners' assumption of certain of the guards' duties, and the friendships that develop between guards and prisoners. Sykes suggests that while these processes may relax the totalitarian atmosphere of prison life, they have negative effects on prisoner rehabilitation.

THE CORRUPTION OF AUTHORITY AND REHABILITATION
GRESHAM M. SYKES

I

Few problems in modern criminology are more perplexing than the role of imprisonment in reforming the adult criminal. Many writers argue that our prisons are a dismal failure as far as rehabilitation is concerned; they point to the numerous studies indicating that more than 50 percent of imprisoned offenders commit new crimes after being released. Other observers claim that it is a basic fallacy of the sentimental approach to penology to assume that all inmates can be reformed, particularly since it is the hardened criminal who is apt to be sent to prison; we are urged to call the prison a success and emphasize the smaller proportion of salvaged offenders.[1]

If the problem were simply a matter of attaching a label of "success" or "failure" to the penal system of the United States, it could be left to the field of polemics. In fact, however, much more serious questions are involved. If an inmate does not commit a crime after being released, has he reformed because of imprisonment or in spite of it? If an inmate does commit a crime after being released, has imprisonment exercised a harmful influence or no influence at all? Is it possible for imprisonment to reform only to have its achievements negated or undone by forces operating in the community? If imprisonment is failing to reform, are there any possibilities for future improvements? If improvements are possible, can they be made within the existing structure of penal institutions or are radical innovations required? To what extent are improvements in the prison's ability to reform in conflict with the objectives of custody and internal discipline?

We have no precise answers to these questions at the present time and much of the confusion is due to the uncertain meaning of the word rehabilitation itself; the term has been used to refer to everything from "instilling good work habits" to "realizing the individual's capacities." This vagueness of aim has been matched by arguments over means, but there appears to be a growing area of agreement: imprisonment's effectiveness in reformation depends on a profound change in the criminal's personality structure, and this change is not to be won by exhortation; rather, conformity with the norms of society is to be secured by making the individual responsive to the reaction of others, in the sense that the social approval or disapproval of law-abiding groups becomes effective in channelling the individual's motives, drives, needs, or impulses.

Attitudes which "neutralize" social controls and make the individual unresponsive to the demands of society are partially familiar under the label of rationalization—the individual justifies his action by unconsciously distorting reality and the ego-image is protected from hurt or destruction under the attacks of self-blame. Recent work by Redl and others, however, has disclosed the intricate system of conscious ego-defenses which the deviant constructs to ward off the reactions of the social groups to which he belongs.[2] *They're picking on me; I couldn't help myself; I didn't do it for myself; they asked for it; it's a deal; it's all a matter of luck:* these become the slogans which the individual uses to deflect the blame and praise of others.[3]

A major portion of the prison's task in reforming the adult criminal consists of modifying these attitudes which neutralize social sanctions. Such modifications, if they are to be achieved at all, are to be achieved through the daily process of social interaction within the institutional setting.

Reprinted with permission of the author and publisher from *Social Forces* 34 (December, 1956), pp. 257–62. The data for this paper have been gathered in connection with a study of the determinants and consequences of social adjustment in prison. The institution being studied is an eastern state maximum security prison with an inmate population of approximately 1,100. Portions of the article appear in *Crime and Society,* copyright © 1956 by Random House, Inc.

[1] See George B. Vold, "Does the Prison Reform?" *The Annals of the American Academy of Political and Social Science* 293 (May, 1954), pp. 42–50.

[2] F. Redl and D. Wineman, *Children Who Hate* (Glencoe: The Free Press, 1951).

[3] Such attitudes appear to be very similar to Sutherland's "definitions favorable to the violation of law." As far as a theory of criminal behavior is concerned, they are subject to variation along two critical dimensions: (1) the extent to which they reflect reality; and (2) the extent to which they are cultural constructs rather than idiosyncratic beliefs.

It is clear that the prison guard must play a vital role in this process. The guard stands as the surrogate of society and it is he who must bring the massive power of the state to bear against the individual in concrete and detailed terms. Unfortunately, the portrayal of the correctional officer's strategic role has been distorted. The common stereotype of social interaction within the maximum security prison presents a brutal and sadistic guard exercising a maximum of social control over a criminal locked by himself in a cell. In fact, however, this picture seems to have little correspondence with reality. The prison community is best seen as resting in uneasy equilibrium between two theoretical poles. At one extreme all inmates would be constantly secured in solitary confinement; at the other, all inmates would roam freely within the limits set by the wall and its armed guards. Actually neither of these theoretical conditions could long endure, and the prison seeks a *modus vivendi* at an intermediate point.[4] The prisoner has limited freedom of movement (a freedom which the inmate population attempts to enlarge, legitimately if possible, by guile and conniving if necessary), and this sets the stage for a wide range of social interaction with officials and other inmates. The inmate leaves his cell to work, eat, engage in recreation, undergo examination by the prison doctor, attend the prison school, etc. And it is in this required compromise of partial freedom that we can begin to see emerge the realities of life in prison. Guards and prisoners become involved in a complex pattern of social relationships in which the authority of the guard is subject to a number of corrupting influences; it is only by understanding the nature and extent of this corruption that we can understand the effectiveness or ineffectiveness of imprisonment in rehabilitating the adult criminal.

II

The prison community has been well described as a social group made up of "custodial and professional employees, habitual petty thieves, one-time offenders, gangsters, professional racketeers, psychotics, pre-psychotics, neurotics, and psychopaths, all living under extreme conditions of physical and psychological compression."[5] The prison officials represent a custodial force charged with the primary function of preventing escapes and maintaining internal order. Standing in opposition to the official system of control there exists an inmate social system—a more or less organized criminal group.[6]

The proliferation of prison regulations and the officials' emphasis on internal discipline is often attributed to institutional inertia of the bureaucratic mind. This viewpoint overlooks the potential danger which may lie in the most innocent appearing action when large groups of criminals are confined for long periods of time under conditions of deprivation. Gambling, stealing, note-writing, quarrelling, or loitering may appear as trivial offenses to the casual observer. The difficulty is that such offenses can be symptomatic of, or prepare the ground for, far more serious situations. The unpaid gambling debt can lead to a knifing; stealing food, clothing, or objects to decorate a cell can provide a route of exchange which can be used for the transmission of weapons, drugs, or the materials necessary for an escape attempt; the illegal communication can establish a rendezvous for a homosexual relationship which may in turn lead to a vicious fight; a minor argument can easily flare into a dangerous battle under conditions of enforced, prolonged intimacy and this may touch off an uncontrollable riot; and loitering or "being out of place" may provide the momentary escape from supervision needed to perform a variety of illegal acts.

But the crisis is usually potential, not actual. Many infractions of the rules are in fact minor, not indicative of serious offenses, and only some of the inmates, not all, present major problems

[4] Public opinion, programs of rehabilitation, the use of prison labor, and the demands of institutional house keeping all serve as forces moving the prison community from the extreme of complete confinement. Elementary requirements of security prohibit the opposite solution.

[5] L. W. McCorkle and R. Korn, "Resocialization Within Walls," *The Annals of the American Academy of Political and Social Science* 293 (May, 1954), pp. 88–98.

[6] Cf. D. Clemmer, *The Prison Community* (Boston: Christopher, 1940); N. Hayner and E. Ash, "The Prison Community as a Social Group," *American Sociological Review* 4 (June, 1939), pp. 362–69; F. E. Haynes, "The Sociological Study of the Prison Community," *Journal of Criminal Law and Criminology* 39 (November-December, 1948), pp. 432–40; S. K. Weinberg, "Aspects of the Prison's Social Structure," *American Journal of Sociology* 47 (March, 1942), pp. 717–25; C. Schrag, "Leadership among Prison Inmates," *American Sociological Review* 19 (February, 1954), pp. 37–42.

of discipline and security. The guard in the cell-block may rigidly enforce all rules on the grounds that a trivial violation of prison regulations *may* be the first symptom of a serious breach in the institution's defenses; or—and this is probably the more frequent case—he may be lulled into forgetting the possible dangers of his position. Like many social roles organized around the theme of potential crisis, the guard's position demands a fine edge of readiness which is difficult to maintain. The correctional officer is called on to make decisions in the daily flux of human affairs in which he must weigh the consequences of treating a possibly serious offense as actually minor against the consequences of treating a possibly minor offense as actually serious; and in such decisions (although this implies, perhaps, too great a degree of conscious rationality) he is under great pressure to take into account the reaction of the men he controls as well as the institution's requirements of security.

III

The guard in charge of a cellblock is required to perform a number of routine tasks during his tour of duty which have as their major aim the prison's function of custody and internal order. Counting inmates, periodically reporting to the center of communications, signing passes, checking mass movements of inmates, inspecting bars, windows, gratings, and other possible escape routes, searching cells for contraband material—these make up the minutiae of the eight-hour shift. In addition, the cellblock officer is supposed to be constantly alert for violations of prison rules which fall outside of his sphere of routine supervision and control.

In the exercise of authority, the deep and pervasive schism which is supposed to separate the captors and captives is actually bridged at innumerable points in the maximum security prison. Guards frequently fail to report infractions of the regulations; guards transmit forbidden information to inmates, neglect elementary security requirements, and join inmates in outspoken criticisms of higher officials. This "corruption" of the guard's authority is apparently seldom to

be attributed to bribery—bribery is usually unnecessary, for far more subtle influences are at work which tend to destroy the authority of the cellblock guard.

Corruption through Friendship

The correctional officer is in close and intimate association with his prisoners throughout the course of the working day. He can remain aloof only with difficulty for he possesses few of those devices which normally serve to separate rulers and the ruled. He cannot withdraw physically in symbolic affirmation of social distance; he has no intermediaries to bear the brunt of resentment springing from orders which are disliked; he cannot fall back on the dignity adhering to his office—he is a "hack" or "screw" in the eyes of those he controls and an unwelcome display of officiousness evokes that great destroyer of respect, the ribald humor of the dispossessed.

There are many pressures in American culture to "be nice," to "be a good Joe," and the guard in the maximum security prison is not immune.[7] The guard is constantly exposed to a sort of moral blackmail in which the first signs of condemnation or estrangement are immediately countered by the inmates with the threat of ridicule or hostility. In this complex interplay, the guard does not always start from a position of determined opposition to "being friendly." The cellblock officer holds an intermediate post in a bureaucratic structure between top prison officials—his captains, lieutenants, and sergeants—and the prisoners in his charge. Like many "unlucky" Pierres always in the middle, the guard is caught in a conflict of loyalties. He resents many of the actions of his superiors—the reprimands, the lack of ready appreciation, the incomprehensible order—and in the inmates he finds willing sympathizers: they too claim to suffer from the unreasonable caprice of power.

Furthermore, the guard in many cases is marked by a basic ambivalence towards the criminals under his supervision. Although condemned by society through its instrument the law, many criminals are a "success" in terms of

---

[7] For an incisive analysis of this theme in more general terms, see D. Riesman, *The Lonely Crowd* (New Haven, Conn.: Yale University Press, 1950).

a mundane system of values which places a high degree of prestige on notoriety and wealth even though won by devious means. The poorly paid guard may be gratified to associate with a famous racketeer. This ambivalence in the correctional officer's attitudes toward his captives cuts deeper than a discrepancy between the inmate's position in the power structure of the prison and his possible status in a *sub rosa* stratification system. There may also be a discrepancy between the judgments of society and the guard's work-a-day values as far as the "criminality" of the inmate is concerned. The bookie, the man convicted of deserting his wife, the inmate who stridently proclaims his innocence and is believed—the guard often holds that these men are not seriously to be viewed as criminals, as desperate prisoners to be rigidly suppressed.

Corruption through Reciprocity

To a large extent the guard is dependent on inmates for the satisfactory performance of his duties and like many figures of authority, the guard is evaluated in terms of the conduct of the men he controls—a troublesome, noisy, dirty cell-block reflects on the guard's ability to "handle prisoners," and this forms an important component of the merit rating which is used as the basis for pay raises and promotions. A guard cannot rely on the direct application of force to achieve compliance, for he is one man against hundreds; and if he continually calls for additional help he becomes a major problem for the shorthanded prison administration. A guard cannot easily rely on threats of punishment, for he is dealing with men who are already being punished near the limits permitted by society, and if the guard insists on constantly using the last few negative sanctions available to the institution—the withdrawal of recreation facilities and other privileges, solitary confinement, or loss of good time—he again becomes burdensome to the prison administration which realizes that its apparent dominance rests on some degree of uncoerced cooperation. The guard, then, is under pressure to achieve a smoothly running cellblock not with the stick but with the carrot, but here again his stock of rewards is limited. One of the best "offers" he can make is ignoring minor offenses or making sure that he never places himself in a position to discover infractions of the rules.

Aside from winning routine and superficial compliance, the guard has another favor to be secured from inmates which makes him willing to forego strict enforcement of prison regulations. Many prisons have experienced a riot in which the tables are momentarily turned and the captives hold sway over their *quondam* captors. The guard knows that he may some day be a hostage and that his life may turn on the settling of old accounts. A fund of good will becomes a valuable form of insurance.[8]

Corruption through Default

Finally, much of the guard's authority tends to be destroyed by the innocuous encroachment of inmates on the guard's duties. Making out reports, checking cells at the periodic count, locking and unlocking doors—in short, all the minor chores which the guard is called on to perform during the course of the day—may gradually be transferred to the hands of the inmates whom the guard has come to trust. The cellblock "runner," formally assigned the tasks of delivering mail, housekeeping duties, and similar jobs, is of particular importance in this respect. Inmates in this position function in a manner analogous to that of the company clerk in the armed forces, and at times they may wield great power and influence in the life of the cellblock. For reasons of indifference, laziness, or naivete, the guard may find much of his authority whittled away; nonfeasance, rather than malfeasance, has corrupted the theoretical guard-inmate relationship.

Authority, like a woman's virtue, once lost is hard to regain. The measures to break up an established pattern of abdication need to be much more severe than those required to stop the first steps in the corruption of authority. In the first place, a guard assigned to a cellblock in which a large portion of control has been transferred in the past from the correctional officer

---

[8] This fear for personal safety in an uprising is rarely noticed by the guards themselves, perhaps because it represents an explicit capitulation to the inmate social system. Conversations with the wives of guards are, however, much more revealing.

to the inmates is faced with the weight of precedent. It requires a good deal of moral courage on his part to face the gibes and aggression of inmates who fiercely defend the legitimacy of the status quo established by custom. In the second place, if the guard himself has allowed his authority to be subverted, he may find his attempts to rectify his error checked by a threat from the inmates to send a "snitch-kite"—an anonymous note—to the guard's superior officers explaining his past derelictions in detail. This simple form of blackmail may on occasion be sufficient to maintain the existing balance of power.

IV

The corruption of authority in the maximum security prison provides an illuminating example of the limits of totalitarian power.[9] To view the inmate social system of an American prison as an organized expression of rebellion against totalitarianism is undoubtedly misleading in a number of ways. We must take into account the matrix of the democratic community in which the prison is embedded, the lack of a well-developed political ideology which serves as a focus of resistance, the lack of cohesiveness in the inmate population itself, the prison administrators' adherence to democratic beliefs and practices, etc. Nonetheless, the maximum security prison is confronted with many of the problems of a system of total, or almost total, power; and foremost among these problems is the transmutation of orders and standard operating procedures in the process of their execution, particularly at the point where authority flows across the line separating the rulers from the ruled.

We do not know the extent of the corruption or destruction of the guard's authority and for rather obvious reasons such information would be difficult to obtain.[10] There is enough evidence, however, to suggest that it is a chronic problem of prison administration.[11] The pressures which tend to shift power from the hands of the guard to the hands of the inmates are often realized in fact and this raises a critical question: What are the implications of such a shift for the rehabilitation of the adult criminal? If we are correct in assuming that reformation depends on modifying those attitudes which neutralize the sanctions of society and its surrogates, it would appear that the corruption of the guard's authority makes the criminal still more unresponsive to legitimate social controls by encouraging the criminal in patterns of conniving, deception, and counterattacks against the normative order.

Insofar as the prison inmates manage to destroy the guard's role as an impersonal enforcer of the rules, the path is opened for a host of beliefs and attitudes which negate the approval or disapproval of legitimate society. When guards and inmates are enmeshed in a pattern of quasi-friendship and reciprocity, punishments by prison officials easily come to be interpreted as personal, vindictive attacks and thus lose their moral force. Similarly, rewards tend to be redefined as a "pay-off," an expedient product of a "deal," rather than social approval for conforming behavior.[12] The guard, the dominant symbol of law-abiding society in the daily life of the prison inmate, becomes a figure to be manipulated, coerced, and hoodwinked. It seems likely,

---

[10] It should be noted here that the accumulation of data for this study has been made possible only because of the extraordinary cooperation of the prison officials in the institution being investigated. Not only has this made possible a marked frankness on the part of the guards and other prison employees—it has also made possible the interviewing of inmates under conditions which have led to a high degree of rapport.

[11] See C. McKendrick, "Custody and Discipline," in P. W. Tappan, ed., *Contemporary Correction* (New York: McGraw-Hill Book Co., 1951), pp. 157–71.

[12] The line here is a fine one, but legitimate rewards appear to be distinguishable from the "pay-off" on the following basis: if the individual views rewards as a necessary condition for the performance of a prescribed act, we are approaching the idea of the "deal"; if the individual views rewards as lagniappe, as a fortunate concomitant of duty, we are approaching legitimate positive sanctions. The important point is that when normative conformity is based on the principle of a favor for a favor, the individual is not subject to the critical social control of an internalized moral imperative. Cf. K. Davis, *Human Society* (New York: The Macmillan Co., 1949), chap. 3.

---

[9] David Riesman has noted that "resistance movements" are not simply heroic acts of individual defiance but also turn on the social organization of those who are subject to extremes of social control. Cf. D. Riesman, "Some Observations on the Limits of Totalitarian Power," *Antioch Review* 12 (1952), pp. 155–68. For a further discussion see K. W. Deutsch, "Cracks in the Monolith: Possibilities and Patterns of Disintegration in Totalitarian Systems," in C. F. Friedrich, ed., *Totalitarianism* (Cambridge, Mass.: Harvard University Press, 1954).

therefore, that a major barrier to the rehabilitation of the adult criminal in a maximum security prison is to be attributed not only to the "unnaturalness" of his social environment and the lack of scientifically tested therapeutic devices but also to the corruption of the guard's authority in maintaining custody and discipline. Since these functions have long been held to be opposed to the aim of reformation, it would appear that a profound reevaluation of the importance of these functions for the rehabilitation of the adult criminal is needed.

CHAPTER SIX

DEVIANT SEX ROLES:
MALE AND FEMALE HOMOSEXUALITY

The distinction between normal and deviant sexual behavior is not as apparent as it might appear. Not only does sexually approved conduct vary among societies,[1] it varies according to education, social class, race, religion, and region within the United States.[2] For example, the frequency of as well as the attitude toward such sexual activities as masturbation and petting are different in different social classes. Furthermore, since many sex norms are unwritten and institutionalized informally, conclusions as to what is or is not deviant sexual behavior are not always easy to make. The case of homosexuality is less problematical, at least in the United States, since this is a clearcut deviation from generally approved sexual conduct. In some instances it results in court conviction and imprisonment. Selections in this chapter explore some of the possible causes, social relations, and consequences associated with homosexuality.

The term homosexuality applies to females as well as males, although considerably more has been written on homosexuality among males than among females. Also, according to the available evidence, homosexuality is more frequent among males. According to Kinsey and his associates, 37 percent of the white male population in the United States has at least one homosexual experience during adolescence or later, in comparison to a figure of half that, 19 percent, for females.[3]

Given the high figure among males, one might be inclined to question the extent to which homosexuality is really a form of deviant behavior; 37 percent is high enough to raise the question of whether homosexuality really deviates from the statistically normal. And the 19 percent

---

[1] Clellan S. Ford and Frank A. Beach, *Patterns of Sexual Behavior* (New York: Harper and Row, Publishers, 1951).

[2] Alfred C. Kinsey, Wardell B. Pomeroy, and Clyde E. Martin, *Sexual Behavior in the Human Male* (Philadelphia: W. B. Saunders Co., 1948); Alfred C. Kinsey, Wardell B. Pomeroy, Clyde E. Martin, and Paul H. Gebhard, *Sexual Behavior in the Human Female* (Philadelphia: W. B. Saunders Co., 1953).

[3] Kinsey, Pomeroy, and Martin, *Sexual Behavior in the Human Male*, p. 650, and Kinsey, Pomeroy, Martin, and Gebhard, *Sexual Behavior in the Human Female*, pp. 452–54.

of females represent about one in five. These figures can be misleading. While they indicate that a large proportion of the population does engage in homosexual practices, Kinsey's data also reveal that these practices are exceptional for most of them. Only about 4 percent of Kinsey's male sample were exclusively homosexual throughout their lives.[4] Moreover, studies show that homosexuality is definitely outside of the normative expectations of most Americans. For example, in a study where individuals were asked to list acts and persons that they considered deviant, homosexuality was mentioned more often than any other act.[5] A Harris Poll in 1969 reports that 63 percent of a national sample believed homosexuals harmful to American life.[6] A number of other studies also reveal the normative rejection of homosexuality.[7]

A. ANTECEDENTS AND DETERMINANTS

There are two prominent views of the determinants of homosexuality. One focusses on the societal determinants of the homosexual role, the other on the factors that lead individuals to adopt the role. Both views are dealt with in the two selections in this section, one of which concerns male homosexuality, the other female homosexuality.

In the United States and most Western societies, male homosexuality is seen as a "condition" which characterizes certain persons. Male homosexuals are viewed as exclusively homosexual, having feminine attributes and behaving in ways which set them off from males who are not homosexuals. A certain set of behaviors and attributes are associated with homosexuality, and individuals who engage in homosexuality are assumed to express those behaviors and to possess those attributes. That is, a role is defined and the people who fill this role are assumed to fit the characteristics described in that definition. It is generally assumed that such a role is universal and not limited to a particular society. However, in "The Societal Context of the Homosexual Role," Mary McIntosh points out that societies not only vary in whether they define a homosexual role, but in societies where such a role is defined, the definition varies. McIntosh suggests that the basic determinants of the homosexual role in Western societies are found in the cultural conception of homosexuality—the perception of homosexual behavior as incompatible with heterosexual behavior —with a corresponding societal reaction to homosexuality and the existence of institutions which reinforce these perceptions and reactions. Although McIntosh emphasizes that the role (as defined by society) may not cor-

[4] Kinsey, Pomeroy, and Martin, *Sexual Behavior in the Human Male*, p. 651.

[5] J. L. Simmons, "Public Stereotypes of Deviants," *Social Problems* 13 (Fall, 1965), pp. 223–32.

[6] *Time*, October 31, 1969.

[7] See Martin S. Weinberg and Colin J. Williams, *Male Homosexuals: Their Problems and Adaptations* (New York: Oxford University Press, 1974), pp. 17–21.

respond precisely with reality—all homosexuals in the United States are not effeminate or exclusively homosexual—the existence of this role does influence the behavior of homosexuals and the way homosexual and homosexually related activities are arranged and organized.

The most frequently heard explanation of the determinants of the individual male's tendency to adopt the homosexual role focusses on the individual's relations with his parents during childhood. Hypotheses revolve around the notion of "mother-fixation" or "mother domination": supposedly, homosexuals are those people, overprotected and indulged by their mothers, who view their mothers as stronger and more competent than their fathers and who, therefore, take their mothers as role models. Other theories argue that this mother-son relation must be combined with a rejecting, hostile father before generating homosexual trends, while still others contend that an unsatisfactory father-son relation itself may be a sufficient cause. Although several studies have been made of parent-child relations and homosexuality, most are limited in that they are based on what may be an unrepresentative sample of homosexuals (e.g., psychiatric patients) and/or they do not include a control group of heterosexuals with whom homosexuals may be compared.[8] Moreover, results from such research are not consistent enough to permit definitive conclusions.

Female homosexuals are less apt to be viewed in terms of their relationships with parents; more often female homosexuals are viewed in terms of the current social conditions that encourage sexual relations with other females. For example, conditions that deprive females of satisfying sexual relations with males—imprisonment, prostitution, stripping—may provide structural conditions that are causally related to female homosexual behavior. This is the basic thesis of McCaghy and Skipper in "Lesbian Behavior as an Adaptation to the Occupation of Stripping," which examines the factors associated with the stripper role that encourage female homosexuality among strippers. Strippers tend to be isolated from emotional relationships with others, their relationships with males tend to be unsatisfactory, and they have opportunities to engage in a wide range of sexual behavior. Thus, the analysis shows how one role can provide the determining conditions for another role.

---

[8] For a study which largely overcomes both of these problems, see Eve Bene, "On the Genesis of Male Homosexuality: An Attempt at Clarifying the Role of the Parents," *British Journal of Psychiatry* 111 (September, 1965), pp. 803–13.

SOCIETAL CONTEXT AND THE HOMOSEXUAL ROLE

MARY McINTOSH

Recent advances in the sociology of deviant behavior have not yet affected the study of homosexuality, which is still commonly seen as a condition characterizing certain persons in the way that birthplace or deformity might characterize them. The limitations of this view can best be understood if we examine some of its implications. In the first place, if homosexuality is a condition, then people either have it or do not have it. Many scientists and ordinary people assume that there are two kinds of people in the world: homosexuals and heterosexuals. Some of them recognize that homosexual feelings and behavior are not confined to the persons they would like to call "homosexuals" and that some of these persons do not actually engage in homosexual behavior. This should pose a crucial problem; but they evade the crux by retaining their assumption and puzzling over the question of how to tell whether someone is "really" homosexual or not. Lay people too will discuss whether a certain person is "queer" in much the same way as they might question whether a certain pain indicated cancer. And in much the same way they will often turn to scientists or to medical men for a surer diagnosis. The scientists, for their part, feel it incumbent on them to seek criteria for diagnosis.

Thus one psychiatrist, discussing the definition of homosexuality, has written:

> I do not diagnose patients as homosexual unless they have engaged in overt homosexual behavior. Those who also engage in heterosexual activity are diagnosed as bisexual. An isolated experience may not warrant the diagnosis, but repetitive (sic) homosexual behavior in adulthood, whether sporadic or continuous, designates a homosexual.[1]

Along with many other writers, he introduces the notion of a third type of person, the "bisexual," to handle the fact that behavior patterns cannot be conveniently dichotomized into heterosexual and homosexual. But this does not solve the conceptual problem, since bisexuality too is seen as a condition (unless as a passing response to unusual situations such as confinement in a one-sex prison). In any case there is no extended discussion of bisexuality; the topic is usually given a brief mention in order to clear the ground for the consideration of "true homosexuality."

To cover the cases where the symptoms of behavior or of felt attractions do not match the diagnosis, other writers have referred to an adolescent homosexual phase or have used such terms as "latent homosexual" or "pseudo homosexual." Indeed one of the earliest studies of the subject, by Krafft-Ebing, was concerned with making a distinction between the "invert" who is congenitally homosexual and others who, although they behave in the same way, are not true inverts.[2]

A second result of the conceptualization of homosexuality as a condition is that the major research task has been seen as the study of its etiology. There has been much debate as to whether the condition is innate or acquired. The first step in such research has commonly been to find a sample of "homosexuals" in the same way that a medical researcher might find a sample of diabetics if he wanted to study that disease. Yet, after a long history of such studies, the results are sadly inconclusive and the answer is still as much a matter of opinion as it was when Havelock Ellis published *Sexual Inversion*[3] seventy years ago. The failure of research to answer the question has not been due to lack of scientific rigor or to any inadequacy of the available evidence; it results rather from the fact that the wrong question has been asked. One might as well try to trace the etiology of "committee-chairmanship" or "Seventh-Day Adventism" as of "homosexuality."

Reprinted with permission of the author and the Society for the Study of Social Problems, from "The Homosexual Role," *Social Problems* 16 (Fall, 1968), pp. 182–92.
[1] Irving Bieber, "Clinical Aspects of Male Homosexuality," in Judd Marmor, editor, *Sexual Inversion* (New York: Basic Books, 1965), p. 248; this but one example among many.

---

[2] R. von Krafft-Ebing, *Psychopathia Sexualis*, 1889.
[3] Later published in H. Ellis, *Studies in the Psychology of Sex*, Vol. 2 (New York: Random House, 1936).

The vantage point of comparative sociology enables us to see that the conception of homosexuality as a condition is, in itself, a possible object of study. This conception and the behavior it supports operate as a form of social control in a society in which homosexuality is condemned. Furthermore, the uncritical acceptance of the conception by social scientists can be traced to their concern with homosexuality as a social problem. They have tended to accept the popular definition of what the problem is and they have been implicated in the process of social control.

The practice of the social labeling of persons as deviant operates in two ways as a mechanism of social control.[4] In the first place it helps to provide a clear-cut, publicized, and recognizable threshold between permissible and impermissible behavior. This means that people cannot so easily drift into deviant behavior. Their first moves in a deviant direction immediately raise the question of a total move into a deviant role with all the sanctions that this is likely to elicit. Secondly, the labeling serves to segregate the deviants from others, and this means that their deviant practices and their self-justifications for these practices are contained within a relatively narrow group. The creation of a specialized, despised, and punished role of homosexual keeps the bulk of society pure in rather the same way that the similar treatment of some kinds of criminals helps keep the rest of society law-abiding.

However, the disadvantage of this practice as a technique of social control is that there may be a tendency for people to become fixed in their deviance once they have become labeled. This, too, is a process that has become well-recognized in discussions of other forms of deviant behavior such as juvenile delinquency and drug taking and, indeed, of other kinds of social labeling such as streaming in schools and racial distinctions. One might expect social categorizations of this sort to be to some extent self-fulfilling prophecies: if the culture defines people as falling into distinct types—black and white, criminal and non-criminal, homosexual and normal

—then these types will tend to become polarized, highly differentiated from each other. Later in this paper I shall discuss whether this is so in the case of homosexuals and "normals" in the United States today.

It is interesting to notice that homosexuals themselves welcome and support the notion that homosexuality is a condition. For just as the rigid categorization deters people from drifting into deviancy, so it appears to foreclose on the possibility of drifting back into normality and thus removes the element of anxious choice. It appears to justify the deviant behavior of the homosexual as being appropriate for him as a member of the homosexual category. The deviancy can thus be seen as legitimate for him and he can continue in it without rejecting the norms of the society.[5]

The way in which people become labeled as homosexual can now be seen as an important social process connected with mechanisms of social control. It is important, therefore, that sociologists should examine this process objectively and not lend themselves to participation in it, particularly since, as we have seen, psychologists and psychiatrists on the whole have not retained their objectivity but become involved as diagnostic agents in the process of social labeling.[6]

It is proposed that the homosexual should be seen as playing a social role rather than as having a condition. The role of "homosexual," however, does not simply describe a sexual behavior pattern. If it did, the idea of a role would be no more useful than that of a condition. For the purpose of introducing the term "role" is to enable us to handle the fact that behavior in this sphere does not match popular beliefs: that sexual behavior patterns cannot be dichotomized in the way that the social roles of homosexual and heterosexual can.

It may seem rather odd to distinguish in this way between role and behavior, but if we accept a definition of role in terms of expectations (which may, or may not be fulfilled), then the distinction is both legitimate and useful. In modern societies where a separate homosexual role

---

[4] This is a grossly simplified account. Edwin Lemert provides a far more subtle and detailed analysis in "Sociopathic Individuation," *Social Pathology* (New York: McGraw-Hill, 1951), ch. 4.

[5] For discussion of situations in which deviants can lay claim to legitimacy, see Talcott Parsons, *The Social System* (New York: Free Press, 1951), pp. 292–93.

[6] The position taken here is similar to that of Erving Goffman in his discussion of becoming a mental patient; *Asylums* (Garden City, N.Y.: Doubleday-Anchor, 1961), pp. 128–46.

is recognized, the expectation, on behalf of those who play the role and of others, is that a homosexual will be exclusively or very predominantly homosexual in his feelings and behavior. In addition, there are other expectations that frequently exist, especially on the part of nonhomosexuals, but affecting the self-conception of anyone who sees himself as homosexual. These are: the expectation that he will be effeminate in manner, personality, or preferred sexual activity; the expectation that sexuality will play a part of some kind in all his relations with other men; and the expectation that he will be attracted to boys and very young men and probably willing to seduce them. The existence of a social expectation, of course, commonly helps to produce its own fulfillment. But the question of how far it is fulfilled is a matter for empirical investigation rather than *a priori* pronouncement. Some of the empirical evidence about the chief expectation—that homosexuality precludes heterosexuality—in relation to the homosexual role in America is examined in the final section of this paper.[7]

In order to clarify the nature of the role and demonstrate that it exists only in certain societies, we shall present the cross-cultural and historical evidence available. This raises awkward problems of method because the material has hitherto usually been collected and analyzed in terms of culturally specific modern Western conceptions.

THE HOMOSEXUAL ROLES IN VARIOUS SOCIETIES

To study homosexuality in the past or in other societies we usually have to rely on secondary evidence rather than on direct observation. The reliability and the validity of such evidence is open to question because what the original observers reported may have been distorted by their disapproval of homosexuality and by their definition of it, which may be different from the one we wish to adopt.

For example, Marc Daniel tries to refute accusations of homosexuality against Pope Julian II by producing four arguments: the Pope had many enemies who might wish to blacken his name; he and his supposed lover, Alidosi, both had mistresses; neither of them was at all effeminate; and the Pope had other men friends about whom no similar accusations were made.[8] In other words Daniel is trying to fit an early sixteenth century Pope to the modern conception of the homosexual as effeminate, exclusively homosexual, and sexual in relation to all men. The fact that he does not fit is, of course, no evidence, as Daniel would have it, that his relationship with Alidosi was not a sexual one.

Anthropologists too can fall into this trap. Marvin Opler, summarizing anthropological evidence on the subject, says,

> Actually, no society, save perhaps Ancient Greece, pre-Meiji Japan, certain top echelons in Nazi Germany, and the scattered examples of such special status groups as the berdaches, Nata slaves, and one category of Chuckchee shamans, has lent sanction in any real sense to homosexuality.[9]

Yet he goes on to discuss societies in which there are reports of sanctioned adolescent and other occasional "experimentation." Of the Cubeo of the Northwest Amazon, for instance, he says, "*true* homosexuality among the Cubeo is rare if not absent," giving as evidence the fact that no males with persistent homosexual patterns are reported.[10]

Allowing for such weaknesses, the Human Relations Area Files are the best single source of comparative information. Their evidence on homosexuality has been summarized by Ford and Beach,[11] who identify two broad types of accepted patterns: the institutionalized homosexual role and the liaison between men or boys who are otherwise heterosexual.

The recognition of a distinct role of *berdache* or transvestite is, they say, "the commonest form of institutionalized homosexuality." This form shows a marked similarity to that in our own

---

[7] For evidence that many self-confessed homosexuals in England are not effeminate and many are not interested in boys, see Michael Schofield, *Sociological Aspects of Homosexuality* (London: Longmans, 1965).

[8] Marc Daniel, "Essai de methodologie pour l'étude des aspects homosexuels de l'histoire," *Arcadie* 133 (January, 1965), pp. 31–37.

[9] Marvin Opler, "Anthropological and Cross-Cultural Aspects of Homosexuality," in Marmor, editor, *Sexual Inversion*, p. 174.

[10] *Ibid.*, p. 117.

[11] C. S. Ford and F. A. Beach, *Patterns of Sexual Behavior* (New York: Harper, 1951), ch. 7.

society, though in some ways it is even more extreme. The Mohave Indians of California and Arizona, for example,[12] recognized both an *alyhā*, a male transvestite who took the role of the woman in sexual intercourse, and a *hwamē*, a female homosexual who took the role of the male. People were believed to be born as *alyhā* or *hwamē*, hints of their future proclivities occurring in their mothers' dreams during pregnancy. If a young boy began to behave like a girl and take an interest in women's things instead of men's, there was an initiation ceremony in which he would become an *alyhā*. After that he would dress and act like a woman, would be referred to as "she" and could take "husbands."

But the Mohave pattern differs from ours in that although the *alyhā* was considered regrettable and amusing, he was not condemned and was given public recognition. The attitude was that "he was an *alyhā*, he could not help it." But the "husband" of an *alyhā* was an ordinary man who happened to have chosen an *alyhā*, perhaps because they were good housekeepers or because they were believed to be "lucky in love," and he would be the butt of endless teasing and joking.

This radical distinction between the feminine passive homosexual and his masculine active partner is one which is not made very much in our own society,[13] but which is very important in the Middle East. There, however, neither is thought of as being a "born" homosexual, although the passive partner, who demeans himself by his feminine submission, is despised and ridiculed, while the active one is not. In most of the ancient Middle East, including among the Jews until the return from the Babylonian exile, there were male temple prostitutes.[14] Thus even cultures that recognize a separate homosexual role may not define it in the same way as our culture does.

Many other societies accept or approve of homosexual liaisons as part of a variegated sexual pattern. Usually these are confined to a particular stage in the individual's life. Among the Aranda of Central Australia, for instance, there are long-standing relationships of several years' duration, between unmarried men and young boys, starting at the age of ten to twelve.[15] This is rather similar to the well-known situation in classical Greece, but there, of course, the older man could have a wife as well. Sometimes, however, as among the Siwans of North Africa,[16] all men and boys can and are expected to engage in homosexual activities, apparently at every stage of life. In all of these societies there may be much homosexual behavior, but there are no "homosexuals."

THE DEVELOPMENT OF THE HOMOSEXUAL ROLE IN ENGLAND

The problem of method is even more acute in dealing with historical material than with anthropological, for history is usually concerned with "great events" rather than with recurrent patterns. There are some records of attempts to curb sodomy among minor churchmen during the medieval period,[17] which seem to indicate that it was common. At least they suggest that laymen feared on behalf of their sons that it was common. The term "catamite" meaning "boy kept for immoral purposes," was first used in 1593, again suggesting that this practice was common then. But most of the historical references to homosexuality relate either to great men or to great scandals. However, over the last seventy years or so various scholars have tried to trace the history of sex,[18] and it is possible to glean a good deal from what they have found and also from what they have failed to establish.

Their studies of English history before the sev-

---

[12] George Devereux, "Institutionalized Homosexuality of the Mohave Indians," *Human Biology* 9 (1937), pp. 498–527; reprinted in Hendrik M. Ruitenbeek, editor, *The Problem of Homosexuality in Modern Society* (New York: Dutton, 1963).

[13] The lack of cultural distinction is reflected in behavior; Gordon Westwood found that only a small proportion of his sample of British homosexuals engaged in anal intercourse and many of these had been both active and passive and did not have clear preference. See *A Minority* (London: Longmans, 1960), pp. 127–34.

[14] Gordan Rattray Taylor, "Historical and Mythological Aspects of Homosexuality," in Marmor, *Sexual Inversion;* Fernando Henrique, *Prostitution and Society,* Vol. 1 (London: MacGibbon and Kee, 1962), pp. 341–43.

[15] Ford and Beach, *Patterns of Sexual Behavior,* p. 132.
[16] *Ibid.,* pp. 131–32.
[17] Geoffrey May, *Social Control of Sex Expression* (London: Allen and Unwin, 1930), pp. 65 and 101.
[18] Especially Havelock Ellis, *Sexual Inversion,* (London: Wilson and Macmillan, 1897); Iwan Bloch (E. Dühren, pseud.), *Sexual Life in England Past and Present,* English translation, (London: Francis Aldor, 1938); German edition, Charlottenberg, Berlin, 1901–03; Gordon Rattray Taylor, *Sex in History* (London: Thames and Hudson, 1953); Noel I. Garde, *Jonathan to Gide: The Homosexual in History* (New York: Vantage, 1964).

enteenth century consist usually of inconclusive speculation as to whether certain men, such as Edward II, Christopher Marlowe, William Shakespeare, were or were not homosexual. Yet the disputes are inconclusive not because of lack of evidence but because none of these men fits the modern stereotype of the homosexual.

It is not until the end of the seventeenth century that other kinds of information become available and it is possible to move from speculations about individuals to descriptions of homosexual life. At this period references to homosexuals as a type and to a rudimentary homosexual subculture, mainly in London, begin to appear. But the earliest descriptions of homosexuals do not coincide exactly with the modern conception. There is much more stress on effeminacy and in particular in transvestism, to such an extent that there seems to be no distinction at first between transvestism and homosexuality.[19] The terms emerging at this period to describe homosexuals—Molly, Nancy-boy, Madge-cull—emphasize effeminacy. In contrast the modern terms—like fag, queer, gay, bent—do not have this implication.[20]

By the end of the seventeenth century, homosexual transvestites were a distinct enough group to be able to form their own clubs in London.[21] Edward Ward's *History of the London Clubs*, published in 1709, describes one called "The Mollies' Club" which met "in a certain tavern in the City" for "parties and regular gatherings." The members "adopt[ed] all the small vanities natural to the feminine sex to such an extent that they try to speak, walk, chatter, shriek and scold as women do, aping them as well in other respects." The other respects apparently included the enactment of marriages and childbirth. The club was discovered and broken up by agents of the Reform Society.[22] There were a number of

similar scandals during the course of the eighteenth century as various homosexual coteries were exposed.

A writer in 1729 describes the widespread homosexual life of the period:

> They also have their Walks and Appointments, to meet and pick up one another, and their particular Houses of Resort to go to, because they dare not trust themselves in an open Tavern. About twenty of these sort of Houses have been discovered, besides the Nocturnal Assemblies of great numbers of the like vile Persons, what they call the *Markets,* which are the Royal Exchange, Lincoln's Inn, Bog Houses, the south side of St. James's Park, the Piazzas in Covent Garden, St. Clement's Churchyard, etc.
>
> It would be a pretty scene to behold them in their clubs and cabals, how they assume the air and affect the name of Madam or Miss, Betty or Molly, with a chuck under the chin, and "Oh, you bold pullet, I'll break your eggs," and then frisk and walk away.[23]

The notion of exclusive homosexuality became well-established during this period. When "two Englishmen, Leith and Drew, were accused of paederasty.... The evidence given by the plaintiffs was, as was generally the case in these trials, very imperfect. On the other hand the defendants denied the accusation, and produced witnesses to prove their predeliction for women. They were in consequence acquitted."[24] This could only have been an effective argument in a society that perceived homosexual behavior as incompatible with heterosexual tastes.

During the nineteenth century there are further reports of raided clubs and homosexual brothels. However, by this time the element of transvestism had diminished in importance. Even the male prostitutes are described as being of masculine build and there is more stress upon sexual license and less upon dressing up and play-acting.

The Homosexual Role and Homosexual Behavior

Thus, a distinct, separate, specialized role of "homosexual" emerged in England at the end of the seventeenth century and the conception of

---

[19] Dr. Evelyn Hooker has suggested that in a period when homosexual grouping and a homosexual subculture have not yet become institutionalized, homosexuals are likely to behave in a more distinctive and conspicuous manner because other means of making contact are not available. This is confirmed by the fact that lesbians are more conspicuous than male homosexuals in our society, but does not seem to fit the 17th century, where the groups are already described as "clubs."

[20] However, "fairy" and "pansy," the commonest slang terms used by non-homosexuals, have the same meaning of effeminate as the earlier terms.

[21] Bloch, *Sexual Life in England*, p. 328, gives several examples, but attributes their emergence to the fact that "the number of homosexuals increased."

[22] Quoted in *ibid.*, pp. 328–29.

[23] Anon., *Hell upon Earth: or the Town in an Uproar* (London, 1729), quoted by G. R. Taylor in Marmor, editor, *Sexual Inversion*, p. 142.

[24] Bloch, *Sexual Life in England*, p. 334.

homosexuality as a condition which characterizes certain individuals and not others is now firmly established in our society. The term role is, of course, a form of shorthand. It refers not only to a cultural conception or set of ideas but also to a complex of institutional arrangements which depend upon and reinforce these ideas. These arrangements include all the forms of heterosexual activity, courtship, and marriage as well as the labeling processes—gossip, ridicule, psychiatric diagnosis, criminal conviction—and the groups and networks of the homosexual subculture. For simplicity we shall simply say that a specialized role exists.

How does the existence of this social role affect actual behavior? And, in particular, does the behavior of individuals conform to the cultural conception in the sense that most people are either exclusively heterosexual or exclusively homosexual? It is difficult to answer these questions on the basis of available evidence because so many researchers have worked with the preconception that homosexuality is a condition, so that in order to study the behavior they have first found a group of people who could be identified as "homosexuals." Homosexual behavior should be studied independently of social roles, if the connection between the two is to be revealed.

This may not sound like a particularly novel program to those who are familiar with Kinsey's contribution to the field.[25] He, after all, set out to study "sexual behavior"; he rejected the assumptions of scientists and laymen:

> that there are persons who are "heterosexual" and persons who are "homosexual," that these two types represent antitheses in the sexual world and that there is only an insignificant class of "bisexuals" who occupy an intermediate position between the other groups... that every individual is innately—inherently—either heterosexual or homosexual... (and) that from the time of birth one is fated to be one thing or the other....[26]

But, although some of Kinsey's ideas are often referred to, particularly in polemical writings, surprisingly little use has been made of his actual data.

Most of Kinsey's chapter on the "Homosexual Outlet"[27] centers on his "heterosexual-homosexual rating scale." His subjects were rated on this scale according to the proportion of their "psychologic reactions and overt experience" that was homosexual in any given period of their lives. It is interesting, and unfortunate for our purposes, that this is one of the few places in the book where Kinsey abandons his behavioristic approach to some extent. However, "psychologic reactions" may well be expected to be affected by the existence of a social role in the same way as overt behavior. Another problem with using Kinsey's material is that although he gives very full information about sexual behavior, the other characteristics of the people he interviewed are only given in a very bald form.[28] But Kinsey's study is undoubtedly the fullest description there is of sexual behavior in any society and as such it is the safest basis for generalizations to other Western societies.

The ideal way to trace the effects on behavior of the existence of a homosexual role would be to compare societies in which the role exists with societies in which it does not. But as there are no adequate descriptions of homosexual behavior in societies where there is no homosexual role, we shall have to substitute comparisons within American society.

(1) Polarization

If the existence of a social role were reflected in people's behavior, we should expect to find that relatively few people would engage in bisexual behavior. The problem about investigating this empirically is to know what is meant by "relatively few." The categories of Kinsey's rating scale are, of course, completely arbitrary. He has five bisexual categories, but he might just as well have had more or less, in which case the number

---

[25] Alfred C. Kinsey et al., *Sexual Behavior in the Human Male* (Philadelphia and London: Saunders, 1953).

[26] Kinsey et al., *Sexual Behavior in the Human Male*, pp. 636–37.

[27] *Ibid.*, ch. 21, pp. 610–66.

[28] The more general drawbacks of Kinsey's data, particularly the problem of the representativeness of his sample, have been thoroughly canvassed in a number of places; see especially William G. Cochran et al., *Statistical Problems of the Kinsey Report on Sexual Behavior in the Human Male*, Washington: American Statistical Society, 1954.

falling into each would have been smaller or larger. The fact that the distribution of his scale is U-shaped, then, is in itself meaningless. (See Table 1).

It is impossible to get direct evidence of a polarization between the homosexual and the heterosexual pattern, though we may note the suggestive evidence to the contrary that at every age far more men have bisexual than exclusively homosexual patterns. However, by making comparisons between one age group and another and between men and women, it should be possible to see some of the effects of the role.

(2) Age Comparison

As they grow older, more and more men take up exclusively heterosexual patterns, as Table 1, Column 2 shows. The table also shows that *each* of the bisexual and homosexual categories, columns 3–8, contains fewer men as time goes by after the age of 20. The greatest losses are from the fifth bisexual category, column 7, with responses that are "almost entirely homosexual." It is a fairly small group to begin with, but by the age of 45 it has almost entirely disappeared. On the other hand the first bisexual category, column 3, with only "incidental homosexual histories" has its numbers not even halved by the age of 45. Yet at all ages the first bisexual category represents a much smaller proportion of those who are almost entirely heterosexual (columns 2 and 3) than the fifth category represents of those who are almost entirely homosexual (columns 7 and 8). In everyday language, it seems that proportionately more "homosexuals"

dabble in heterosexual activity than "heterosexuals" dabble in homosexual activity and such dabbling is particularly common in the younger age groups of 20 to 30. This indicates that the existence of the despised role operates at all ages to inhibit people from engaging in occasional homosexual behavior, but does not have the effect of making the behavior of many "homosexuals" exclusively homosexual.

On the other hand, the overall reduction in the amount of homosexual behavior with age can be attributed in part to the fact that more and more men become married. While the active incidence of homosexual behavior is high and increases with age among single men, among married men it is low and decreases only slightly with age. Unfortunately the Kinsey figures do not enable us to compare the incidence of homosexuality among single men who later marry and those who do not.

(3) Comparison of Men and Women

The notion of a separate homosexual role is much less well-developed for women than it is for men and so too are the attendant techniques of social control and the deviant subculture and organization. So a comparison with women's sexual behavior should tell us something about the effects of the social role on men's behavior.

Fewer women than men engage in homosexual behavior. By the time they are 45, 26 percent of women have had *some* homosexual experience, whereas about 50 percent of men have. But this is probably a cause rather than an effect of the difference in the extent to which the ho-

TABLE 1. HETEROSEXUAL-HOMOSEXUAL RATING: ACTIVE INCIDENCE BY AGE

| | Percent of Each Age Group of Male Population Having Each Rating | | | | | | | | |
Age	(1) X	(2) 0	(3) 1	(4) 2	(5) 3	(6) 4	(7) 5	(8) 6	(9) 1–6
15	23.6	48.4	3.6	6.0	4.7	3.7	2.6	7.4	28.0
20	3.3	69.3	4.4	7.4	4.4	2.9	3.4	4.9	27.4
25	1.0	79.2	3.9	5.1	3.2	2.4	2.3	2.9	19.8
30	0.5	83.1	4.0	3.4	2.1	3.0	1.3	2.6	16.4
35	0.4	86.7	2.4	3.4	1.9	1.7	0.9	2.6	12.9
40	1.3	86.8	3.0	3.6	2.0	0.7	0.3	2.3	11.9
45	2.7	88.8	2.3	2.0	1.3	0.9	0.2	1.8	8.5

Note: Based on Kinsey (1948) p. 652, Table 148. X = unresponsive to either sex; 0 = entirely heterosexual; 1 = largely heterosexual, but with incidental homosexual history; 2 = largely heterosexual but with a distinct homosexual history; 3 = equally heterosexual and homosexual; 4 = largely homosexual but with distinct heterosexual history; 5 = largely homosexual but with incidental heterosexual history; 6 = entirely homosexual.

mosexual role is crystallized, for women engage in less nonmarital sexual activity of any kind than men. For instance, by the time they marry 50 percent of women have had some pre-marital heterosexual experience to orgasm, whereas as many as 90 percent of men have.

The most revealing contrast is between the male and female distributions on the Kinsey rating scale, shown in Table 2. The distributions for women follow a smooth J-shaped pattern, while those for men are uneven with an increase in numbers at the exclusively homosexual end. The distributions for women are the shape that one would expect on the assumption that homosexual and heterosexual acts are randomly distributed in a ratio of 1 to 18.[29] The men are relatively more concentrated in the exclusively homosexual category. This appears to confirm the hypothesis that the existence of the role is reflected in behavior.

Finally, it is interesting to notice that although at the age of 20 far more men than women have homosexual and bisexual patterns (27 percent as against 11 percent), by the age of 35 the figures are both the same (13 percent). Women seem to broaden their sexual experience as they get older whereas more men become narrower and more specialized.

None of this, however, should obscure the fact that, in terms of behavior, the polarization between the heterosexual man and the homosexual man is far from complete in our society.

Some polarization does seem to have occurred, but many men manage to follow patterns of sexual behavior that are between the two, in spite of our cultural preconceptions and institutional arrangements.

CONCLUSION

This paper has dealt with only one small aspect of the sociology of homosexuality. It is, nevertheless, a fundamental one. For it is not until he sees homosexuals as a social category, rather than a medical or psychiatric one, that the sociologist can begin to ask the right questions about the specific content of the homosexual role and about the organization and functions of homosexual groups.[30] All that has been done here is to indicate that the role does not exist in many societies, that it only emerged in England toward the end of the seventeenth century, and that, although the existence of the role in modern America appears to have some effect on the distribution of homosexual behavior, such behavior is far from being monopolized by persons who play the role of homosexual.

---

[29] This cannot be taken in a rigorously statistical sense, since the categories are arbitrary and do not refer to numbers, or even proportions, of actual sexual acts.

[30] But an interesting beginning has been made by Evelyn Hooker in "The Homosexual Community," *Proceedings XIVth International Congress of Applied Psychological Personality Research*, Vol. 2, Copenhagen, Munksgaard, 1962; and "Male Homosexuals and the Worlds," Marmor, editor, *Sexual Inversions*, pp. 83–107; there is much valuable descriptive material in Donald Webster Cory, *The Homosexual in America* (New York: Greenberg, 1951); and in Gordon Westwood, *Minority: A Report on the Life of the Male Homosexual in Great Britain* (London: Longmans, 1960, as well as elsewhere).

TABLE 2. COMPARISON OF MALE AND FEMALE HETEROSEXUAL-HOMOSEXUAL RATINGS: ACTIVE INCIDENCE AT SELECTED AGES

	Age	Percent of Each Age Group Having Each Rating								
		(1) X	(2) 0	(3) 1	(4) 2	(5) 3	(6) 4	(7) 5	(8) 6	(9) 1–6
Male	20	3.3	69.3	4.4	7.4	4.4	2.9	3.4	4.9	27.4
Female		15	74	5	2	1	1	1	1	11
Male	35	0.4	86.7	2.4	3.4	1.9	1.7	0.9	2.6	12.9
Female		7	80	7	2	1	1	1	1	13

Note: Based on Kinsey (1948) p. 652, Table 148 and Kinsey (1953) p. 499, Table 142. For explanation of the ratings, see Table 1.

LESBIAN BEHAVIOR AS AN ADAPTATION TO THE OCCUPATION OF STRIPPING

CHARLES H. McCAGHY AND JAMES K. SKIPPER, JR.

In recent publications Simon and Gagnon[1] contend that too frequently students of deviant behavior are prepossessed with the significance of the behavior itself and with the "exotic" trappings which accompany it. One finds exhaustive accounts of the demographic characteristics of deviants, the variety of forms their behavior may take, and the characteristics of any subculture or "community," including its argot, which emerge as a direct consequence of a deviant status. Furthermore, Simon and Gagnon chide researchers for being locked into futile searches for ways in which inappropriate or inadequate socialization serves to explain their subjects' behavior.

Simon and Gagnon argue that these research emphases upon descriptions of deviant behavior patterns and their etiology provide an unbalanced and misleading approach to an understanding of deviants. Deviants do or, at least, attempt to accommodate themselves to the "conventional" world, and they play many roles which conform to society's expectations. Yet, for the most part, deviants' learning and playing of nondeviant or conventional roles are either ignored by researchers or interpreted strictly as being influenced by a dominant deviant role. The focus of most research obscures the fact that with few exceptions a deviant role occupies a minor portion of the individuals' behavior spectrums. What is not recognized is the influence which commitments and roles of a nondeviant nature have upon deviant commitments and roles. To illustrate their contention, Simon and Gagnon discuss how homosexual behavior

patterns are linked with the identical concerns and determinants which influence heterosexuals: aging problems, identity problems, making a living, management of sexual activity, etc. The authors argue convincingly for damping concern over ultimate causes of homosexuality and for concentrating on factors and contingencies shaping the homosexual role. In their words: "Patterns of adult homosexuality are consequent upon the social structures and values that surround the homosexual after he becomes, or conceives himself as, homosexual rather than upon original and ultimate causes."[2]

Since past research on homosexuals has been dominated by an emphasis upon the sexual feature of their behavior and its consequences, it is fitting that Simon and Gagnon draw attention to linking deviant with nondeviant behaviors or roles. However, since in their scheme the choice of sexual object is taken as given, a complementary perspective is still needed to gain an understanding of the process by which individuals engage in homosexual behavior. We suggest a structural approach. Because sexual behavior, deviant or not, emerges out of the context of social situations, it would seem that the structure of certain situations might contribute to becoming involved in homosexual behavior and to the formation of a homosexual self-concept. We are not suggesting such structures as "ultimate" causes; rather, we are saying that different social structures may provide conditions, learning patterns, and justifications differentially favorable to the occurrence of homosexual contacts and self-concepts. This is not strictly a matter of etiology, then, but an epidemiological concern over differential incidences of deviance, regardless of how episodic or pervasive homosexual behavior may be for an individual case.

A pertinent, albeit extreme, example here is the incidence of homosexual behavior occurring

Reprinted with permission of author and the Society for the Study of Social Problems, *Social Problems* 17 (Fall, 1969), pp. 262–72. Footnotes have been added.

This paper is a revised and expanded version of one presented before joint meetings of The Midwest and The Ohio Valley Sociological Societies in Indianapolis May 1–3, 1969. We would like to express our appreciation to David Gray for his assistance during the data collection stage of this research.

[1] John H. Gagnon and William Simon, "Sexual Deviance in Contemporary America," *The Annals of the American Academy of Political and Social Science* 376 (March, 1968), pp. 106–22, and "The Social Meaning of Prison Homosexuality," *Federal Probation* 32 (March, 1968), pp. 23–30.

[2] William Simon and John H. Gagnon, "Homosexuality: The Formulation of a Sociological Perspective," *Journal of Health and Social Behavior* 8 (September, 1967), p. 179.

among incarcerated populations. A large proportion of prisoners can be identified as "jail house turnouts": those whose homosexual behavior is limited to within an institutional setting.[3] Evidence indicates that contingencies and opportunities inherent in the prison setting are related to the onset and possible continuation of homosexual behavior. There is no question that for some prisoners homosexual behavior emerges as an adaptation to the prison structure which not only curtails avenues of heterosexual release, but deprives inmates of meaningful affective relationships they would otherwise have.[4]

We have little reliable information concerning the incidence of homosexuality among various populations outside the setting of total institutions.[5] Most researchers agree that homosexuals will be found across the entire socioeconomic spectrum.[6] There is, however, continual speculation that relatively high proportions of male homosexuals are contained in certain occupational groups such as dancers, hairdressers, etc. Assuming this speculation to be correct it is still unclear which is prior: occupational choice or commitment to homosexual behavior. The sociological literature is replete with examples of how occupation influences other aspects of social life; there is no apparent reason why choice of sexual objects should necessarily vary independently. This is not to say that occupations are as extreme as total institutions in their control

over life situations regarding sexual behavior. We do suggest that *some* occupations, like the prison setting, may play a crucial role in providing pressures, rationales, and opportunities leading to involvement in, if not eventual commitment to, homosexual behavior.

In the course of conducting a study of the occupational culture of stripping, we found that homosexual behavior was an important aspect of the culture which apparently stemmed less from any predisposition of the participants than from contingencies of the occupation.

NATURE OF THE RESEARCH

The principal research site was a midwestern burlesque theater which employed a different group of four touring strippers each week. With the permission and support of the theater manager, two male researchers were allowed access to the backstage dressing room area during and after afternoon performances. The researchers were introduced to each new touring group by the female stage manager, a person whom the girls trusted. After the stage manager presented them as "professors from the university who are doing an anthology on burlesque," the researchers explained that they were interested in how persons became strippers and what these persons thought about stripping as an occupation. After this, the researchers bided their time with small talk, card playing, and general questions to the girls about their occupation.[7] The purposes of this tactic were to make the girls more comfortable and to allow the researchers to survey the field for respondents.

The primary data were gathered through in-depth interviews with 35 strippers.[8] Although

[3] Gresham M. Sykes, *The Society of Captives: A Study of a Maximum Security Prison* (New York: Atheneum, 1965), pp. 72, 95–99; and David A. Ward and Gene G. Kassebaum, *Women's Prison: Sex and Social Structure* (Chicago: Aldine, 1965), pp. 76, 96 [see also pp. 247–54 of this volume].

[4] Gagnon and Simon, "The Social Meaning of Prison Homosexuality"; and Rose Giallombardo, *Society of Women: A Study of a Woman's Prison* (New York: John Wiley, 1966), pp. 133–57.

[5] Estimates of the proportion of males having homosexual contacts during imprisonment range between 30 and 45 percent, depending on the institution, characteristics of the population, and length of sentences (Gagnon and Simon, "The Social Meaning of Prison Homosexuality," p. 25). In one women's institution researchers estimated that 50 percent of the inmates had at least one sexual contact during their imprisonment (Ward and Kassebaum, *Women's Prison*, p. 92).

[6] Alfred C. Kinsey, Wardell B. Pomeroy, and Clyde E. Martin, *Sexual Behavior in the Human Male* (Philadelphia: Saunders, 1948), pp. 639–55; Alfred C. Kinsey, Wardell B. Pomeroy, Clyde E. Martin, and Paul H. Gebhard, *Sexual Behavior in the Human Female* (Philadelphia: Saunders, 1953), pp. 459–60, 500; John Gerassi, *The Boys of Boise: Furor, Vice, and Folly in an American City* (New York: MacMillan); and Maurice Leznoff and William A. Westley, "The Homosexual Community," *Social Problems* 3 (April, 1956), pp. 257–63 (see pp. 269–74 of this volume).

[7] Data concerning stripteasers and the occupation of stripping may be found in a paper by James K. Skipper, Jr., and Charles H. McCaghy, "Stripteasers and the Anatomy of a Deviant Occupation." (Paper read at the American Sociological Association meetings in San Francisco, September, 1969).

[8] The social characteristics of the interviewed sample of strippers are as follows: All were white and ranged in age from 19 to 45, with 60 percent between the ages of 20 and 30. On the Hollingshead (1957) two-factor index of social position, ten came from families in classes I and II, nine from class III, and 12 from classes IV and V. (Family background data were not obtained in four cases.) Their range of education was from seven to 16 years: 22 had graduated from high school, eight of whom had at least one year of college.

there was no systematic method of selecting respondents from each touring group, an attempt was made to obtain a range of ages, years in the occupation, and salary levels. There were only four cases of outright refusals to be interviewed, one coming after the girl had consulted with a boyfriend. In six cases no convenient time for the interview could be arranged because the potential subjects were "busy." It was impossible in these instances to determine whether the excuses really constituted refusals. In general, the researchers found the girls eager to cooperate and far more of them wanted to be interviewed than could be accommodated.

The interviews, lasting an average of an hour and a half, were conducted in bars, restaurants, and, on occasion, backstage. Although difficult at times, the interviewing took place in a manner in which it was not overheard by others. In all but one case, two researchers were present. Interviews were also conducted with others, both male and female, whose work brought them in contact with strippers: the theater manager, stage manager, union agent, and sales persons selling goods to strippers backstage. The interviews were semi-structured and designed to elicit information on background, the process of entering the occupation, and aspects of the occupational culture.

INCIDENCE OF HOMOSEXUALITY

Ideally, in order to posit a relationship between the occupation and homosexual contacts it would be necessary to establish that the incidence of such behavior is relatively higher among strippers than in other female occupations. However, statistics comparing rates of homosexuality among specific female occupational groups are simply not available. Ward and Kassebaum[9] did find as part of female prison lore that lesbianism is prominent among models and strippers. In our research the restricted sample and relatively brief contact with the subjects did not allow us to ascertain directly the extent of homosexual behavior among strippers. We were, however, able to gauge the salience of such behavior in the occupation by asking the subjects to estimate what proportion of strippers had homosexual contacts. Estimates ranged from 15 to 100 percent of the girls currently being at least bisexual in their contacts; most responses fell within the 50 to 75 percent range. We also have evidence, mostly self-admissions, that nine of the thirty-five respondents (26 percent) themselves engaged in homosexual behavior while in the occupation, although in no case did we request such information or have prior evidence of the respondents' involvement. We did make some attempt to include subjects in the sample whom we suspected were maintaining relatively stable homosexual relationships. But these deliberate efforts were futile. In two cases strippers known to be traveling with unemployed and unrelated female companions refused to be interviewed, saying they were "too busy."

Despite our inability to fix an exact proportion of strippers who had engaged in homosexuality, it is clear from the subjects' estimates and their ensuing discussions that such behavior is an important facet of the occupation. The estimates of 50 to 75 percent are well above Kinsey's finding that 19 percent of his total female sample had physical sexual contact with other females by age 40.[10] This difference is further heightened when we consider that a large majority of our sample (69 percent) were or had been married; Kinsey found that only three percent of married and nine percent of previously married females had homosexual contacts by age 40.[11]

CONDITIONS CONTRIBUTING TO HOMOSEXUALITY

More relevant to the hypothesis of this paper, however, are the conditions of the occupation which our subjects claimed were related to the incidence of homosexual behavior, whatever its magnitude. It was evident from their discussions that a great part, if not most, of such behavior could be attributed to occupational conditions. Specifically, conditions supportive of homosexual

[9] Ward and Kassebaum, *Women's Prison*, pp. 75, 148–49.

[10] Kinsey, Pomeroy, Martin, and Gebhard, *Sexual Behavior in the Human Female*, pp. 452–53.

[11] *Ibid.*, pp. 453–54.

behavior in the stripping occupation can be classified as follows: (1) isolation from affective social relationships; (2) unsatisfactory relationships with males; and (3) an opportunity structure allowing a wide range of sexual behavior.

Isolation from affective social relationships. Evidence from our research indicates that in general strippers have difficulty maintaining permanent affective social relationships, judging by their catalogues of marital difficulties and lack of persons whom they say they can trust. Aside from such basic inabilities, it is apparent that the demands of the occupation as a touring stripper make it exceedingly difficult for the girls to establish or maintain immediate affective relationships, even on a temporary basis. The best way to demonstrate this is to describe their working hours. Generally, strippers on tour spend only one week in each city and work all seven days from Friday through Thursday evening. They must be in the next city by late Friday morning for rehearsal. Their working day usually begins with a show about 1 P.M. and ends around 11 P.M., except on Saturday when there may be a midnight show. Although the girls' own acts may last only about 20 minutes in each of four daily shows, they also perform as foils in the comedians' skits. As a consequence, the girls usually are restricted to the theater every day from 1 to 11 P.M. except for a two and a half hour dinner break. After the last show most either go to a nearby nightclub or to their hotel rooms to watch television. Many girls spend over 40 weeks a year on tour.

Such working conditions effectively curtail the range of social relationships these girls might otherwise have. It should not be surprising that a nearly universal complaint among strippers is the loneliness they encounter while on tour. One girl claimed: "When you are lonely enough you will try anything." By itself this loneliness is not necessarily conducive to homosexual activities since, aside from other girls in the troupe, there is isolation from females as well as from males. But strippers find that contacts with males are not only limited but often highly unsatisfactory in content, and homosexuality can become an increasingly attractive alternative.

Unsatisfactory relationships with males. As stated above, women prisoners claim that lesbianism is very frequent among strippers. Data

from our research tends to confirm this rumor. There is also some evidence that homosexual behavior is relatively frequent among prostitutes.[12] It is a curious paradox that two occupations dedicated to the sexual titillation of males would contain large numbers of persons who frequently obtain their own gratification from females. Tempting as it may be to turn to some exotic psychoanalytic explanations concerning latent homosexuality, the reasons may not be so covert. Ward and Kassebaum[13] and others[14] note that among prostitutes homosexual behavior may result less from inclination or predisposition than from continual experiences which engender hostility toward males in general.

A recurring theme in our interviews was strippers' disillusionment with the male of the species. This disillusionment often begins on stage when the neophyte first witnesses audience reactions which prove shocking even to girls who take off their clothes in public. Due to lighting conditions the stripper is unable to see beyond the second row of seats, but from these front rows she is often gratuitously treated to performances rivaling her own act: exhibitionism and masturbation. There is no question that strippers are very conscious of this phenomenon for they characterize a large proportion of their audience as "degenerates." This term, incidentally, occurred so often in the course of our interviews it could be considered part of the stripper argot. Strippers know that "respectable" people attend their performances, but they are usually out in the dark where they cannot be seen. Furthermore, a sizable proportion of these "respectables" are perceived by strippers to be "couples," hence most of the unattached male audience is suspect.

There is no indication that strippers on tour have more off-stage contact with their audience than does any other type of performer. But the precedent set by the males in rows one and two persists for strippers even in their off-stage contacts with men. They find that their stage identifications as sex objects are all too frequently taken at face value. Initially, strippers may find this identification flattering but many eventually become irritated by it. As one subject put it:

---

[12] Ward and Kassebaum, *Women's Prison*, 126–32.
[13] *Ibid.*
[14] Harry Benjamin and R. E. L. Masters, *Prostitution and Morality* (New York: Julian Press, 1964), pp. 245–46n.

If a guy took me out to dinner and showed me a good time, I'd sleep with him. But most of them just call up and say "Let's fuck."

When checking into hotels while on tour, most girls register under their real rather than their stage name. Several girls pointed out to us that the purpose of this practice was to eliminate being phoned by their admirers. Furthermore, many of the girls avoid identifying themselves in public as strippers, preferring to call themselves dancers, entertainers, and the like. This enables them not only to steer clear of a pariah label but to minimize unwelcome sexual reactions which they feel the name "stripper" engenders.

When strippers do form relatively prolonged liaisons with males during the course of their stripping career, chances are good that they will result in another embittering experience. In some cases the man will insist that the girl abandon the occupation, something she may not be inclined to do; hence a breakup occurs. But more frequently the girls find themselves entangled with males who are interested only in a financial or sexual advantage. One of our male informants closely connected with the stripping profession claimed, "You know the kind of jerks these girls tie up with? They're pimps, leeches, or weirdos." This, of course, is an oversimplification; yet the strippers themselves confirm that they seem to be involved with more than their share of rough, unemployed males who are more than happy to enjoy their paycheck.

Strippers probably are not without fault themselves in their difficulties with heterosexual relationships; in our sample of 35 we found that of the 24 who had ever been married, 20 had experienced at least one divorce. It is evident, however, that their problems are compounded by the exploitive males who gravitate toward them. Under these circumstances contacts with lesbians are often seen as respites from importunate males. One subject claimed that although she did not care to engage in homosexual activities she would frequently go to a lesbian bar where she could "have a good time and not be bothered." Another said that lesbians are the only ones who "treat you like a person." As one reasoned:

Strippers go gay because they have little chance to meet nice guys. They come in contact with a lot of degenerate types. If they do meet a nice guy chances are he will ask them to stop stripping. If he doesn't he's likely to be a pimp. So the girls got to turn to a woman who understands them and their job. It is very easy for them to listen to the arguments of lesbians who will tell them basically that men are no good and women can give them better companionship.

Our argument should in no way be interpreted to mean that most strippers are anti-male or have completely severed all contacts with males. From our research it appears that the "career" homosexual is the exception among strippers. At best, the majority can be described as bisexual. The point is that experiences gained in the course of their occupation promote the homosexual aspect by generating caution and skepticism where relationships with males are concerned. Limited contacts with males plus the wariness which accompanies these contacts can be instrumental in severely curtailing the sexual activity of strippers outside of prostitution. Thus an opportunity for a warm, intimate relationship unaccompanied by masculine hazards becomes increasingly attractive. According to one of our subjects, when faced by the lesbian ploy, "Men are no good; I can do things for you they can't," many strippers find themselves persuaded, at least temporarily.

Opportunity structure allowing a wide range of sexual behavior. The final occupational condition contributing to the incidence of homosexual behavior among strippers involves the existence of both opportunities and tacit support for such behavior. As male researchers we found it difficult to fathom the opportunities available for female homosexual activities. Our respondents pointed out, however, that there is no want in this regard. Strippers on tour have easy access to information on the location of gay bars in any city they play; furthermore, the reception strippers receive in these bars is especially hospitable. More immediate opportunities are available, obviously, with the presence of homosexuals in the touring group itself. The group which, of necessity, spends most of the day together provides the novice stripper with at least an opportunity for sexual experimentation without the risks inherent in becoming involved with complete strangers.

There is some indication also that some strippers experienced in homosexual behavior are not particularly quiescent when obtaining partners. One subject informed us that she avoids touring with certain groups simply because homosexual contacts within the group are an expected mode of behavior and noncompliance is punished by ostracism. She claimed that being on tour was boring enough without having the other girls refusing to talk or associate with her. In this same vein, several of our subjects stated that certain older and established women in the occupation actively recruit partners with promises of career rewards. We were at first skeptical of such "casting couch" tactics among strippers, but the same stories and names recurred so often from such diverse sources that the possibility cannot be ignored.

We do not wish to overdramatize the pressures placed on the girls by others to engage in lesbian practices. No doubt such pressures do occur, but sporadically. More important is the fact that opportunities for homosexual contacts occur in an atmosphere of permissiveness toward sexual behavior which characterizes the workday philosophy of strippers. The strippers' principal salable product is sex; the music, dancing, and costumes are only accessories. The real product becomes, over time, effectively devoid of any exclusiveness and is treated with the same detachment as grocers eventually view their radishes. For some strippers sexual contacts are regarded not only with detachment but with a sense of indifference:

> I usually don't get kicks out of other women, not really, but there are times. Sometimes you come home and you are just too tired to work at it. Then it's nice to have a woman around. You can lay down on the floor, relax, watch T.V. and let her do it.

Add to this a sense of cynicism regarding sexual mores. Sexual behavior is generally not characterized by strippers as right or wrong by any universal standard but in terms of its presumed incidence in the general society; many of our respondents firmly expressed their view that lesbianism and prostitution are easily as common among women outside the occupation as among strippers. One respondent reasoned:

> Strippers are no different in morality than housewives, secretaries, waitresses, or anybody else. There is a certain amount of laxity of behavior which would occur in anybody, but with the occupational hazard of being lonely and moving from town to town, well, that's the reason.

The end effect of such attitudes is that no stigma is attached to either homosexual behavior or prostitution[15] among strippers as long as the participants are discreet, do not bother others, and do not allow their activities to interfere with the stability of the touring group. It appears, then, that strippers work in a situation where opportunities for homosexuality are not only available but where social pressures restricting sexual choice to males are minimal or nonexistent.

SUMMARY

Previous research indicates that most homosexual careers, male or female, begun outside the total institutional setting involve enlistment rather than a system of recruitment through peer group or subcultural pressures.[16] As sociologists, however, we must not lose sight of the importance of situational conditions as explanatory variables for understanding rates of deviant behavior. We have attempted to demonstrate how sexual behavior may be an adaptation to social factors immediately impinging upon the actors; specifically, we have argued that the stripping occupation may be analogous to the prison setting in that its structural characteristics contribute to the incidence of homosexual behavior.

---

[15] One perceptive respondent even questioned the rationality of the legal definition of prostitution: there is a very hazy line between what people call prostitution and just going to bed with a man. What is the difference between taking $50 for it, or receiving flowers, going out to dinner, and then the theater, and then getting laid? One has preliminaries, otherwise there is no difference. There is a payment both ways.

[16] Gagnon and Simon, "Sexual Deviance in Contemporary America," pp. 116, 118.

B. SOCIAL RELATIONS AND PROCESS

The first selection on social relations and process is to some extent an extension of McCaghy and Skipper's analysis. In the selection, "Female Homosexual Roles," David A. Ward and Gene G. Kassebaum investigate female homosexuality in prisons. Although they also view female homosexuality as an adaptation to the situation, the description of the various role relationships and ideology that characterize prison homosexuality illustrates types of social relations in this form of deviant behavior.

Homosexuality, like all bisexual behavior, involves a social relationship between two persons. Often the participants are two homosexuals, and the exchange of sexual favors is the basis for their relationship. (Relationships sometimes go beyond just sexual exchange, of course, and involve deeper personal commitments; in some instances homosexual "marriages" take place.) Sometimes, however, the relationship will involve a non-homosexual partner. In the second selection in this section, "The Social Integration of Queers and Peers," Albert J. Reiss, Jr., shows that one partner may be a young male prostitute, or "peer." In this case, the basis of the relationship is a sexual-economic exchange.

Reiss describes various facets of peer-queer relations, including places where peers and queers meet, processes of peer recruitment, and the norms by which the relationship is controlled. Norms sharply delimit the peer-queer relation to sexual-economic transaction, allowing peers to interpret the relationship in purely economic terms. In this way the peer is able to protect his sex identity. Peer norms allow peers to participate in sexual activity with homosexuals while placing limits on how far such participation may go.

FEMALE HOMOSEXUAL ROLES AND RELATIONSHIPS
DAVID A. WARD AND GENE G. KASSEBAUM

Estimates of the prevalence of homosexuality in the prison vary widely. Official records identify 19 percent of the population as homosexual. In the survey of staff members, more than half of the respondents estimated between 30 and 70 percent of the inmates "have sexual affairs while in prison." Estimates were higher on the inmate questionnaire, with 69 percent of the respondents estimating that between 30 and 70 percent of the girls were having homosexual affairs and an additional 7 percent estimating as high as 90 percent or more. These data, with comparative estimates made by prisoners in a medium security prison for men located in the same state, can be seen in Table 1.[1]

Excerpted with permission of authors and the Society for the Study of Social Problems, from "Homosexuality: A Mode of Adaptation in a Prison for Women," *Social Problems* 12 (Fall, 1964), pp. 166–75. Table and footnotes have been renumbered.

[1] In addition to our own data estimating the incidence of homosexuality among male prisoners, Donald Clemmer's study of an institution for adult male felons indicated that

TABLE 1. ESTIMATES OF PREVALENCE OF INSTITUTIONAL HOMOSEXUALITY (PERCENT)

Replies of women's prison staff and female and male inmates to the statement: "A rough estimate of the number of women (men) who have sexual affairs at one time or another with women (men) while in prison would be:"

Estimate of Homosexuality	Women's Prison Staff	Female Inmates	Male Inmates
5 percent or less	12	12	29
15 percent	31	12	25
30 percent	29	25	25
50 percent	14	22	12
70 percent	9	22	6
90 percent or more	5	7	3
(N)	100(58)	100(263)	100(744)

Note: 6 staff members, 30 female inmates, and 127 male inmates refused or were unable to make an estimate.

In the interviews with female inmates, guesses of the extent of homosexuality were never less than 50 percent, with most estimating 60 to 75 percent. Individual conversations with staff members yielded similar estimates. Overall, it can be conservatively estimated that at least 50 percent of the inmates are sexually involved at least once during their prison terms. By sexually involved we mean kissing and fondling of the breasts, manual and oral stimulation of the clitoris and simulation of intercourse. Our definition of homosexuality does not include mere emotional arousal, or kissing, hand holding and embracing, when these activities are not followed by overt sexual behavior and are not seen as being sexual in intent by the participants.[2]

Reliable estimates of the extent of homosexual involvement of women in other institutional settings—the military, mental hospital, schools—are nonexistent. However, in the outside community, data from the Kinsey Report indicate that, of their national sample, 13 percent experienced orgasm in homosexual relations, an additional 6 percent had had homosexual experience, and another 9 percent had experienced "psychological arousal" for a total of 28 percent of the population.[3] Comparatively, the incidence of overt homosexual behavior in this prison is high.

HOMOSEXUAL ROLES

In the prison setting the total number of women involved sexually with other inmates is less interesting sociologically than the sharp distinction between those referred to by the inmates as "true" homosexuals and those identified as "jailhouse turnouts."

The *jailhouse turnout* or *J.T.O.*, in contrast to the true homosexual, has her introduction to homosexuality in jail or prison. All inmates interviewed and 80 percent of the staff who filled out the questionnaire asserted that 90 percent or more of the homosexually involved women had their first affair in jail or prison. In addition, 84 percent of the inmates and 85 percent of the staff agreed on the questionnaires that most of the homosexually involved women return to heterosexual relationships when they leave prison.

The *true homosexual* is, as defined by the in-

"16 percent of the sampling admitted to homosexual activity during their present incarceration. Of these 38 men, only two were partners with each other in the abnormal acts, so it is suggested that since homosexuality cannot occur singly, that the actual percentage of men engaging in this practice is 32 percent." Donald Clemmer, "Some Aspects of Sexual Behavior in the Prison Community," *Proceedings of the Eighty-Eighth Annual Congress of Correction of The American Correctional Association* (Detroit, Michigan, 1958), p. 383.

[2] These figures may be compared with other data that have been gathered on homosexuality among girls in youth institutions. A study by Selling, published in 1931, estimated that 2 percent of the population of a girl's institution were involved in an overt homosexual existence and another 40 percent engaged in behavior which involved embracing, kissing and fondling of another inmate. Lowell S. Selling, "The Pseudo Family," *The American Journal of Sociology* 37 (September, 1931), pp. 247–53. A more recent study by Halleck and Hersko indicates that 69 percent of the girls in a training school were homosexually involved. The majority of these cases did not, however, involve breast fondling, or direct genital contact. Seymour L. Halleck and Marvin Hersko, "Homosexual Behavior in a Correctional Institution for Adolescent Girls," *American Journal of Orthopsychiatry* XXXII (October, 1962), pp. 911–17.

[3] Alfred C. Kinsey, Wardell B. Pomeroy, Clyde E. Martin and Paul H. Gebhard, *Sexual Behavior in the Human Female* (Philadelphia, Pa.: W. B. Saunders, 1953), pp. 452–54.

mates, a woman who was homosexual before she arrived at the institution and will be after she leaves. Incidentally, a few of the true homosexuals remain faithful to lovers on the outside and do not become involved with other inmates. Such persons would not, therefore, be included in our estimate of institutional homosexuality.

Those true homosexuals who are active in prison come to the relationship with a perspective based on experience. They believe the impact of a homosexual affair is never forgotten, and they feel that they enter such relationships more for the positive features they perceive than in reaction to the negative features of confinement. It is also likely that the labels of "criminal" and "prisoner" are less traumatic for people who already have a self-conception of being stigmatized by most of the general community. As a result of homosexual affairs many of these women appear to have made adjustments in their self-conceptions which make adjustment to the pains of imprisonment less difficult. Our data indicate that among those few inmates who can be classified as prison politicians and merchants, there is a large number of true homosexuals. Like the experienced male con, they are more concerned with alleviating the material deprivations of confinement, getting a good prison job and living quarters, and doing time without attracting attention. In the following remarks a young woman who is a true homosexual playing the masculine or *butch* role, speaks with disdain of the blatant and opportunistic behavior of the jailhouse turnouts:

They want companionship, they just want to play a little game with you, you know, and they LOVE you, oh, everybody loves you, God, they're in love with you. They've seen you once, but they're in love with you. They turn out right away because they need somebody to care, someone to look up to. They're afraid, and somehow a butch is sort of a protective symbol—"She'll take care of me so nobody will hurt me." They need somebody to talk to, they're lonesome. And they've been taken away from everything they love, and they sort of project all of this love into the butch. ... But mostly, it's just a big game with them. They're lonesome, there's nothing else to do, and I'm the closest thing they can get to a man.... These other ones [butch turnouts] I can't see at all—the ones that come in here with long hair and all of a sudden they're big rompstomping butches.... I can respect a person that's been

that way all their life and knows what's happening, but these kids that just cut their hair and think they're really hitting on something, and then they can't wait to get out on the streets to get with a dude again—they make me sick. While they're in here you'd swear to God they'd been gay their whole life. There's nothing but women in this world for them—while they're in here. They have their hair short one week and then, God, they're just too lovely the next—I mean it. One week they're my brother and the next week they're hitting on me. They swagger and drop their belt and all of a sudden they're big stuff. When really they're not. They don't feel any of this inside, they don't go through any of the emotions that a butch [true homosexual] goes through, they're not involved in this and they're gonna forget it as soon as they're out of the institution.

Whether homosexuality is learned prior to imprisonment or is restricted to the prison experience, another distinction involves the roles played by homosexuals in their affairs. These roles are represented by a combination of appearance, behavior, and personality characteristics, and are found among both true homosexuals and jailhouse turnouts. The most obvious is the *butch, stud broad,* or *drag butch,*[4] the aggressive, active sexual partner. Her hair is close-cropped or worn in pixie or "D.A." style; she wears no makeup; her legs are unshaven; she usually wears pedal pushers or, if a dress, the belt is worn low on the hips. Masculine gait, manner of smoking and other gestures are adopted. A variation of this is the woman who dresses femininely, but acts aggressively and plays the dominant role in her homosexual relationship. The transition to the role of butch is a dramatic manifestation of inversion of sexual role, representing such a change that a disproportionately small number of women in prison actually make it. Our personal observation is that many of the jailhouse turnouts who are butches are singularly unattractive, according to some of the criteria used to judge feminine attractiveness in our society. Many of these women are overweight or underweight, have skin disorders or appear

---

[4] Neither staff nor inmates use the term lesbian. Staff members use the term homosexual because it is consistent with departmental directives, rule books and references to male prisoners. Inmates use more colloquial terms such as playing, being together, making it, and turning out. The term lesbian apparently suggests what staff and inmates agree is usually not the case—a long-term definite commitment to homosexuality.

unusually wiry or muscular.[5] Some of the severely unattractive women and the women possessing aggressive personality traits and inclined toward masculine habits and demeanor express themselves in the butch role when these predisposing factors are combined with the experience of imprisonment. In prison they have found that by emphasizing dissimilarity to the female role and appearance, they can attract attention from some members of their own sex. Here they can take the initiative in both social and sexual interaction and these women find in prison a functional role they did not find outside.[6] The role of the butch in the prison community seems to be an effort to solve a variety of problems and conflicts of which adjustment to imprisonment is one.

The complementary role of the butch is the *femme,* who maintains a feminine appearance and ideally plays a more submissive, passive role. Of the two, the butch appears to have a greater commitment to homosexuality. The butch changes the love object and her behavior, thereby substituting a role. The femme changes only the love object. It is less difficult to describe and to understand the role of the femme because she often does in the homosexual affair what she did in heterosexual relationships. She continues to play the role often expected of women—to be relatively more submissive and passive in sexual relations, to be dependent, and to provide housekeeping services. The role of the femme provides relief from the need to fend for oneself in a strange and threatening environment. This role provides for the establishment of supportive relationships similar to those which characterized relationships with fathers, husbands or lovers. The femme does not have to make the radical

transition to a new role that the butch has made. She often comes to view herself as bisexual and she expects to resume heterosexual relations upon release—both of which militate against homosexual self-definition.

While the butch can display her role in terms of dress, mannerisms and appearance, the femme emphasizes her role largely in behavior. She walks with her arms around the butch, embraces and kisses her in public, and allows the butch to speak in her behalf.[7] Recently the staff has attempted to reduce these public demonstrations of affection by making inmates liable for disciplinary action. Couples flaunting their relationship are often housed in separate cottages in an effort to prevent them from seeing one another. The staff has also required 48 butches to change their hair style to a less masculine coiffure and more effort has been devoted to preventing personal (bodily) contact on the institution grounds. While there has been less visible evidence of homosexuality, these efforts, to date, have not reduced the number of homosexual involvements.

THE DYNAMICS OF PRISON LOVE AFFAIRS

For many girls the pressure to *turn out* begins when they enter the receiving unit. Two types of women in particular are the object of concerted attention by the general population. The arrival of a *butch broad* causes a stir on the campus as the femmes vie for her affection. The rush is intense, and the femme makes it clear that she is available:

It's just like the outside. I flirted, I got things for her, I did her clothes, I woke her in the morning, we went to dances—the same things you do for a man on the outside. Girls are approached in the same way a man approaches a woman. He . . . she . . . looks at her and the way she looks back gives him the clue as to further action. He . . . she . . . looks at you like she wants you, a look of desire.

---

[5] There is, however, no evidence of any unusual physiological or anatomical features which characterize these masculine-appearing women. Physicians at the prison reported that they had observed no constitutional differences in terms of distribution and abundance of body hair, size of the clitoris, muscle distribution or any other factor.

[6] For a description of the butch role among female homosexuals living in the free world, see Jane McKinnon, "I Am a Homosexual Woman," in A. M. Krich, editor, *The Homosexuals* (New York: The Citadel Press, 1954), pp. 119–22. The butch role played by call girls is described by Harold Greenwald in *The Call Girl* (New York: Ballantine Books, 1958), pp. 119–22. See also Frank S. Caprio, *Female Homosexuality* (New York: Grove Press, Inc., 1954), pp. 16–18. While the author has a more general point to make, an excellent discussion of the "masculine protest" can be found in Simone De Beauvoir, *The Second Sex* (New York: Bantam Books, 1961), pp. 379–99.

---

[7] For descriptions of the butch role in a girl's school, see Halleck and Hersko, "Homosexual Behavior in a Correctional Institution for Adolescent Girls," p. 912, and for the femme role see the description of the soft mama by Romolo Toigo, "Illegitimate and Legitimate Cultures in a Training School for Girls," *Proceedings of the Rip Van Winkle Clinic* 13, No. 3 (Summer, 1962), pp. 9–11.

The rushing process includes plying the butch with love notes, candy, coffee, cigarettes and other articles, referred to as *commissary*.

This adaptation by femmes of the usual tactics employed by males in heterosexual affairs was explained by our respondents as a matter of supply and demand because there are fewer butches than femmes in the population. (Our interviews and analysis of inmate file data indicate that about one-third of the jailhouse turn-out population are butch, with a somewhat higher proportion of butches among the true homosexuals.) In addition, broken love affairs sustain a supply of femmes who express great interest in the relatively small number of new butches. A twenty-year-old true homosexual butch described her reception at the institution:

When I came into the institution I didn't go after anybody. I had a bad experience on the street that was part of what got me here, and I didn't want anything to do with any more women. So I was very bitter. But I got here and all of a sudden I was getting all these kites [notes] and I had all these girls come to me—I never went to them. They're real aggressive with a new butch, everybody wants to snatch her up before somebody else gets her. And so I looked around at some of the people I was getting messages from—I checked them out and there wasn't too much there that I wanted. But I played the field for about six weeks, and like I said, I'd get a message from a girl to please come over and see her and she'd give me cigarettes and, you know, give me everything I needed. So I'd walk her out to the field, or to the canteen, and then I dated a few girls, I took some of them to the show, but I never saw anybody that I wanted.

In other instances butches approach new arrivals, exert special attention on young, homosexually uninitiated and attractive girls, win them over and then exploit them for contraband, commissary items, and other services.

Once the butch has secured the affection of the femme, she may then exact tribute in the form of goods and services in exchange for her assurance that she will not play around with anyone else (as one woman paraphrased the song: "I love you for commissary reasons"). In each of these cases the butch role has the advantage of material gain in addition to sexual recompense. However, many of the homosexual pairs do not involve exploitation of one lover by the other and are not dissimilar to love af-

fairs between males and females on the outside. Exploitation, when it does occur in these relationships, comes when one of the parties is tiring of the other. There was only one report that butch broads had stables (more than one femme of her own). This case, it is our impression, involved a transitional stage at which time a butch was getting over her affair with one femme and beginning another. There were no indications of homosexual families or clans.[8] Finally, in contrast to prisons for men, no inmate reported, nor was there any evidence of, any inmate using force to exact sexual favors from another.

The behavior of one partner often appears to be exploitative of the other in the actual sexual relationship. Interviews conducted with both homosexual and non-homosexual inmates indicated that in about one-third of the homosexual relationships at the institution the butch refuses to let the femme touch her or reciprocate sexually. Some butches remain completely clothed during sexual activity. This seems in part to facilitate maintaining the illusion of masculinity which would be exposed by the removal of her clothing. The role of the femme, in these cases, is one of complete passivity in which the butch *gives work* (also referred to as *giving some head*), i.e., engages in cunnilingus, manual manipulation of the clitoris, and breast fondling. While the butch gives work, the denial of sexual gratification for herself is called *giving up the work*. Such self-denial militates against becoming obligated to the femme and from developing emotional ties that would be painful to disturb or break. Participation in a relationship where only the butch gives work is

---

[8] The building of family constellations has been reported in studies of youth institutions for females by Sheriff in Michela Robbins, "The Inside Story of a Girl's Reformatory," *Colliers* 132 (October 30, 1953), p. 76; Sidney Kosofsky and Albert Ellis, "Illegal Communication Among Institutionalized Female Delinquents," *The Journal of Social Psychology* 48 (August 1958), pp. 155–60; see also Charles A. Ford, "Homosexual Practices of Institutionalized Females," *The Journal of Abnormal and Social Psychology* 23 (January–March, 1929), p. 446; by Selling, "The Pseudo Family," pp. 248–53 and by Toigo, "Illegitimate and Legitimate Cultures," pp. 3–29. It is not surprising to find young girls who are still oriented toward the consangual family establishing substitute daddies, brothers and cousins. The separation from parents, siblings and other relatives seems to be less a source of real stress for older women. Most of them have established their own families and the pain of separation comes from being away from conjugal rather than the consangual family.

functional for some femmes as well. They can receive sexual satisfaction and at the same time avoid viewing themselves as homosexual. For a number of women, homosexual self-definition only follows active participation in sexual activity.[9]

The following statement from a tape-recorded interview describes the practice of giving up the work as seen by a femme jailhouse turnout:

> Giving up the work means who's gonna do who. I mean, which one of you is going to commit the sexual act on the other one. Usually the one that's the aggressor and doing the lovemaking is the one that's giving up the work. [Note the butch is *giving* work at the same time she is giving *up* reciprocal sexual interaction.] The other one isn't giving up anything, she's receiving. It usually refers to the stud broad and usually the stud broad will be very modest and strict about who knows if she's been receiving any work or not.
>
> I think it's that butches realize a woman is satisfied by a man, as a rule, this is the natural role, and that they want to satisfy you as much as a man would, if not more. They want to get this certain edge over you, this certain control over you. But being aware in the back of their minds that they're a woman too, they know that it's just as possible for you to get control over them, and I think that they fight this because in their minds their main goal is to satisfy and control you, and keep you.

The butch partner of the respondent quoted above reported her reason for wishing to have a relationship where only she gave work:

> In myself—the only desire I have is to make love and not have love made to me. I don't feel the need for it or the desire for it. The desire for it can be aroused and has been—I'm not saying that a girl hasn't made love to me—but it's very few and far between that I want somebody to make love to me. I want to do the work, and that's the way I get my pleasure, by making love to her, a woman. When I make love to a woman I like the power of being able to satisfy her. It gives me

a good feeling to know that she responds to me and that I can satisfy her desires. And this is where I get my enjoyment.

Q. When you talk about satisfaction for yourself, is this satisfaction in terms of orgasm, or is satisfaction in other terms?

> It's a satisfaction more or less mentally, and not really—it's a physical satisfaction but merely because I know I've done a good job, or I hope I have, and I'm satisfied with knowing that I've pleased her and I'm just relaxed through the whole act. Otherwise, no, I don't reach a climax. I have, but it's very seldom that I do. I don't lose myself that much, and I don't like to lose that much control. I like to keep my mind as clear as I can so I'm aware of exactly what I'm doing, and I'm aware of my timing, and I'm aware of the girl —if she's responsive at a certain time then I know that's what she likes, and then if she's not responding then I can do something else. Where, if I was just lost in passion I don't recognize any of these things, and I don't feel that I would satisfy her as fully as if I didn't lose myself all that much and kept concentrating on her, watching her— that's what I do. And when the act is over I'm tired and that tiredness brings on a satisfaction in itself. And it gives me a form of release, the tension sort of release, after I've made love to somebody. But I don't reach a climax—not generally.

In practice, however, giving up the work seems to characterize the early stage of a homosexual relationship. Presuming that there is some mutual attraction to begin with, it seems to be difficult to have such intimate contact without, over time, developing more intense affectional ties. It often happens that the butch comes to ask for sexual reciprocity and that the femme is then ready to reciprocate. Hence, this behavior can, in some cases, be an effective means of total seduction in which the femme who is resistant or feeling guilty is brought along slowly. Stresses accompanying attempted transitions from giving up the work to reciprocal sexuality result in the failure of some sexual affairs that are carried on satisfactorily until the femme finally refuses to reciprocate. Such refusal is interpreted by the butch as lack of affection and low degree of commitment to the homosexual role.

There is an apparent parallel between a prostitute receiving the attentions of a customer and the femme receiving a butch who gives up the work, but there is a major difference im-

---

[9] The attitude of the femme here is similar to that of the young male delinquents who permit male adults to perform fellatio on them but who do not think of themselves as homosexuals. The boys define themselves and each other not on the basis of the homosexual behavior per se, but on the basis of nonparticipation in the role which is perceived as the homosexual role, that of the fellator. Albert J. Reiss, Jr., "The Social Integration of Queers and Peers," *Social Problems* 9 (Fall, 1961), pp. 118–19. [See pp. 254–67 of this volume.]

plicit in the rationale for the latter. The male customer, while an active sex partner and to some degree the aggressor, is not viewed as being in danger of becoming emotionally involved with the prostitute. The action of the active and aggressive butch is specifically directed toward preventing herself from becoming more deeply attached to her partner. For many women who have assumed the butch role because they were unsuccessful in heterosexual affectional relationships, there is still the danger of being rejected again. For the butch then, the initial period during which the femme remains passive serves the important function of screening out femmes who are "chippying" (promiscuous). As one respondent said, "You check them out, to see if she's gonna stay." In addition, the period of giving up the work serves to more deeply involve the femme, as she may experience satisfaction with the relationship. Thus, after this trial period, the butch may ask for reciprocity if the femme has not indicated that she wants to play a more active sexual role. It is beyond this point that some femmes refuse to go, and this usually terminates the affair. Enough women stop here to confirm the fears of butches so that they must continue the same testing process.

The term jailhouse turnout indicates, and inmates confirm, that most prison love affairs are temporary and situational.[10] The insecurity and anxiety which is promoted by the movement of the population out of the institution results in the use of certain defense mechanisms to protect oneself from being hurt too badly. This is especially the case for butches who have made a more definite and dramatic commitment to homosexuality. They cannot count on holding the affection of the femme, not only because of

separation by staff or parole, but also because femme jailhouse turnouts do not have a long-term commitment to the *gay life*. This is apparent in the high percentage of women whom the inmates believe will return to heterosexual affairs once they leave prison. The prison homosexuals who are expected to revert to heterosexuality are the femmes and not the butches.

In summary, the process of turning out seems to represent socialization of the new inmates into practices which provide support, guidance and emotional satisfactions during a period when these are lacking. This mechanism for coping with the stress of imprisonment is presented to the new inmate at a time when she is likely to be most responsive and when she is least aware of alternative courses of action. Turning out often involves a series of steps through which both partners initially seek to insulate themselves from strong involvement. Reciprocity of sexual behavior if often delayed until confidence in the stability of the union is felt. This is particularly true for those butches who have made more definite commitments to homosexuality. However, instability is not unknown for other butches who change from homosexual involvements to heterosexual involvements and back again as they are paroled, violate parole and are returned to prison. (This role alteration prompted one inmate to remark, "There's something hypocritical about a pregnant butch.")

Inmates believe that most homosexual involvement occurs early in imprisonment, that most affairs are situational, with heterosexual relationships to be resumed upon release, and that many are "once-only" affairs.[11] The folklore of the female prison community provides

[10] In the male homosexual community, Hooker reports that there is a constant searching for sexual partners, and that long-enduring relationships are rare, with change not stability the rule. Evelyn Hooker, "A Preliminary Analysis of Group Behavior of Homosexuals," *The Journal of Psychology* 42 (October, 1956), pp. 223–24. Halleck and Hersko report that homosexual relationships among the girls in the youth institution they studied were usually short-lived and characterized by jealousy and unfaithfulness. Halleck and Hersko, "Homosexual Behavior in a Correctional Institution for Adolescent Girls," p. 913. The shifting of homosexual roles among girls in the youth institution is also reported by Toigo, "Illegitimate and Legitimate Cultures," p. 16. The ability to play both roles—active and passive—is reported by Helene Deutsch, "On Female Homosexuality," in Robert Fliess, editor, *The Psychoanalytic Reader* (New York: International Universities Press, 1948), p. 243.

[11] In view of these characteristics of institutional homosexuality, Ford questions whether such involvements represent true sexual inversion. See Ford, "Homosexual Practices of Institutionalized Females," p. 448. Deviant behavior in prison may be temporary because ties to significant others in the free world are not voluntarily severed. Their absence is forced and they remain significant others. Thus while escape into institutional deviance can be rationalized on the basis of "they aren't around" or "they won't know," long-term commitment is unlikely because it is to these others and not to those in prison that long-run loyalty is given. Loyalty to a homosexual partner in prison is fortuitous. For a discussion of deviant careers and of the important implications of membership in an organized deviant group see Howard S. Becker, *Outsiders* (New York: The Free Press of Glencoe), pp. 25–39.

rationalizations for homosexuality by emphasizing that women involved in prison affairs are not homosexual but bisexual, by referring to those who do not play as "prudes," by emphasizing the alleviation of loneliness that such involvements can bring, by alleging greater satisfactions than can be found in heterosexual affairs and by repeating stories about the women who return to men upon release. While the intrinsic satisfactions are described it is made clear that one may return to heterosexual relationships without any damaging effects....

THE SOCIAL INTEGRATION OF QUEERS AND PEERS
ALBERT J. REISS, JR.

Sex delinquency is a major form of behavior deviating from the normative prescriptions of American society. A large number of behaviors are classified as sex delinquency—premarital heterosexual intercourse, pederasty, and fellation, for example.

Investigation of sex behavior among males largely focusses on the psychological structure and dynamic qualities of adult persons who are described as "sexual types" or on estimating the incidence, prevalence, or experience rates of sex acts for various social groups in a population. There is little systematic research on the social organization of sexual activity in a complex social system unless one includes descriptive studies of the social organization of female prostitution.

An attempt is made in this paper to describe the sexual relation between "delinquent peers" and "adult queers" and to account for its social organization. This transaction is one form of homosexual prostitution between a young male and an adult male fellator. The transaction is limited to fellation and is one in which the boy develops no self-conception as a homosexual person or sexual deviator, although he perceives adult male clients as sexual deviators, "queers" or "gay boys."

There has been little research on social aspects of male homosexual prostitution; hence the exploratory nature of the investigation reported here and the tentative character of the findings. Although there are descriptions of "marriage" and of the "rigid caste system of prison homosexuality"[1] which contribute to our understanding of its social organization in the single sex society of deviators, little is known about how homosexual activity is organized in the nuclear communities of America.

A few recent studies discuss some organizational features of male prostitution.[2] Ross distinguishes three types of male homosexual prostitutes on the basis of the locus of their hustling activity:[3] (1) the *bar-hustler* who usually visits bars on a steady basis in search of queer clients; (2) the *street-hustler,* usually a teen-aged boy who turns "tricks" with older men; and (3) the *call-boy* who does not solicit in public. The street-hustler has the lowest prestige among hustlers, partly because his is the more hazardous and less profitable form of activity. One might expect their prestige status in the organized "gay world" to be low since they apparently are marginal to its organization. Street-hustlers, therefore, often become bar-hustlers when they are able to pass in bars as of legal age.

Reprinted with permission of author and publisher from *Social Problems* 9 (Fall, 1961), pp. 102–20. Editorial adaptations. Footnotes have been renumbered. The word "queer" is of the "straight" and not the "gay" world. In the "gay" world it has all the qualities of a negative stereotype but these are not intended in this paper. The paper arose out of the perspective of boys in the "straight" world.

I am particularly indebted to Howard S. Becker, Evelyn Hooker, Everett Hughes, John Kitsuse, Ned Polsky, H. Laurence Ross and Clark Vincent for their helpful suggestions and encouragement in publishing this article.

---

[1] Arthur V. Huffman, "Sex Deviation in a Prison Community," *The Journal of Social Therapy* 6 (Third Quarter, 1960), pp. 170–81; Joseph E. Fishman, *Sex in Prison* (New York: The Commonwealth Fund, 1930); Donald Clemmer, *The Prison Community* (Boston: The Christopher Publishing House, 1940), pp. 260–73.

[2] William Marlin Butts, "Boy Prostitutes of the Metropolis," *Journal of Clinical Psychopathology* 8 (1946–1947), pp. 673–81; H. Laurence Ross, "The 'Hustler' in Chicago," *The Journal of Student Research* 1 (September, 1959), pp. 13–19; Jens Jersild, *Boy Prostitution* (Copenhagen: C. E. Gad, 1956). (Translation of *Den Mandlige Prostitution* by Oscar Bojesen.)

[3] H. Laurence Ross, "The 'Hustler' in Chicago," p. 15.

The boys interviewed for this study could usually be classified as street-hustlers, given the principal locus of their activity. Yet, the street-hustlers Ross describes are oriented toward careers as bar-hustlers, whereas none of the boys I studied entered hustling as a career. For the latter, hustling is a transitory activity, both in time and space.

There apparently are crucial differences among hustlers, however, in respect to the definition of the hustler role and the self-concept common to occupants in the role. The hustlers Ross studied are distinguished by the fact that they define themselves as both prostitute and homosexual. The boys I studied *do not define themselves either as hustlers or as homosexual.* Most of these boys see themselves as "getting a queer" only as a substitute activity or as part of a versatile pattern of delinquent activity.[4] The absence of a shared definition of one another as hustlers together with shared definitions of when one "gets a queer" serve to insulate these boys from self-definitions either as street-hustlers or as homosexual.

The boys interviewed in this study regard hustling as an acceptable substitute for other delinquent earnings or activity. Although the sexual transaction itself may occur in a two-person *or a* larger group setting, the prescribed norms governing this transaction are usually learned from peers in the delinquent gang. Furthermore, in many cases, induction into the queer-peer transaction occurs through participation in the delinquent group. They learn the prescribed form of behavior with adult fellators and are inducted into it as a business transaction by means of membership in a group which carries this knowledge in a common tradition and controls its practices. In particular, it will be shown that the peer group controls the amount of activity and the conditions under which it is permitted. Finally, it is postulated that this is a shared organizational system between peer hustlers and adult fellators.

There apparently exist the other possible types of males who engage in homosexual sex acts based on the elements of self-definition as homosexual and hustler. John Rechy in several vignettes describes a third type who conceive of themselves as hustlers but do not define themselves as homosexual.[5]

> The world of queens and male-hustlers and what they trive on, the queens being technically men but no one thinks of them that way—always "she"—their "husbands" being the masculine vagrants—"fruithustlers"—fleetingly sharing the queens' pads—never considering they're involved with another man (the queen), and as long as the hustler goes only with queens—and with fruits only for scoring (which is making or taking sex money, getting a meal, making a pad) *he is himself not considered queer.* (Italics mine)[6]

The importance of being defined as nonhomosexual while acknowledging one's role as a hustler is brought forth in this passage:

> Like the rest of us on that street—who played the male role with other men—Pete was touchy about one subject—his masculinity. In Bickford's one afternoon, a good looking masculine young man walked in, looking at us, walks out again hurriedly. 'That cat's queer,' Pete says, glaring at him. 'I used to see him and I thought he was hustling, and one day he tried to put the make on me in the flix. It bugged me, him thinking I'd make it with him for free. I told him to f . . . off, go find another queer like him.' He was moodily silent for a long while and then he said almost belligerently: 'No matter how many queers a guy goes with, if he goes for money, that don't make him queer. You're still straight. It's when you start going for free, with other young guys, that you start growing wings.'[7]

The literature on male homosexuality, particularly that written by clinicians, is abundant with reference to the fourth possible type—those who define themselves as homosexual but not as hustlers.

THE DATA

Information on the sexual transaction and its social organization was gathered mostly by interviews, partly by social observation of their meeting places. Though there are limitations to in-

---

[4] The distinction made here is not intended to suggest that other types of hustlers do not also define themselves in other deviant roles. Hustlers may occupy a variety of deviant roles which are classified as delinquent or criminal; they may be "hooked," blackmailers, thieves, etc.

[5] I am indebted to Ned Polsky for bringing Rechy's stories to my attention.

[6] John Rechy, "The Fabulous Wedding of Miss Destiny," *Big Table 1.* No. 3 (1959), p. 15.

[7] John Rechy, "A Quarter Ahead," *Evergreen Review* 5, No. 19 (July-August, 1961), p. 18.

ferring social organization from interview data (particularly when the organization arises through behavior that is negatively sanctioned in the larger society), they provide a convenient basis for exploration.

Sex histories were gathered from 18.6 percent of the 1008 boys between the ages of 12 and 17 who were interviewed in the Nashville, Tennessee, SMA for an investigation of adolescent conforming and deviating behavior. These represent all of the interviews of one of the interviewers during a two-month period, together with interviews with all Nashville boys incarcerated at the Tennessee State Training School for Boys.

The largest number of interviews was taken with lower-class delinquent boys. There is a reason for this: when it was apparent that delinquents from the lowest social class generally had some contact with adult male fellators, an attempt was made to learn more about how this contact was structured and controlled. Sex histories, therefore, were obtained from all of the white Nashville boys who were resident in the Tennessee State Training School for Boys during the month of June, 1958.

HOW PEERS AND QUEERS MEET

Meetings between adult male fellators and delinquent boys are easily made, because both know how and where to meet within the community space. Those within the common culture know that contact can be established within a relatively short period of time, if it is wished. The fact that meetings between peers and queers can be made easily is mute evidence of the organized understandings which prevail between the two populations.

There are a large number of places where the boys meet their clients, the fellators. Many of these points are known to all boys regardless of where they reside in the metropolitan area. This is particularly true of the central city locations where the largest number of contact points is found within a small territorial area. Each community area of the city and certain fringe areas, inhabited by substantial numbers of lower-class persons, also have their meeting places, generally known only to the boys residing in the area.

Queers and peers typically establish contact in public or quasi-public places. Major points of contact include street corners, public parks, men's toilets in public or quasi-public places such as those in transportation depots, parks or hotels, and "second" and "third-run" movie houses (open around the clock and permitting sitting through shows). Bars are seldom points of contact, perhaps largely because they are plied by older male hustlers who lie outside the peer culture and groups, and because bar proprietors will not risk the presence of under-age boys.

There are a number of prescribed modes for establishing contact in these situations. They permit the boys and fellators to communicate intent to one another privately despite the public character of the situation. The major form of establishing contact is the "cruise," with the fellator passing "queer-corners" or locations until his effort is recognized by one of the boys. A boy can then signal—usually by nodding his head, a hand gesticulation signifying OK, following, or responding to commonly understood introductions such as "You got the time?"—that he is prepared to undertake the transaction. Entrepreneur and client then move to a place where the sexual activity is consummated, usually a place affording privacy, protection and hasty exit. "Dolly," a three-time loser at the State Training School, describes one of these prescribed forms for making contact:

> Well, like at the bus station, you go to the bathroom and stand there pretendin' like . . . and they're standin' there pretendin' like . . . and then they motions their heads and walks out and you follow them, and you go some place. Either they's got a car, or you go to one of them hotels near the depot or some place like that . . . most any place.

Frequently contact between boys and fellators is established when the boy is hitchhiking. This is particularly true for boys' first contacts of this nature. Since lower-class boys are more likely than middle-class ones to hitch rides within a city, particularly at night when such contacts are most frequently made, they perhaps are most often solicited in this manner.

The experienced boy who knows a "lot of queers," may phone known fellators directly from a public phone, and some fellators try to establish continued contact with boys by giving them their phone numbers. However, the boys seldom use this means of contact for reasons inherent in their orientation toward the transaction, as we shall see below.

We shall now examine how the transaction is facilitated by these types of situations and the prescribed modes of contact and communication. One of the characteristics of all these contact situations is that they provide a *rationale* for the presence of *both* peers and queers in the *same* situation or place. This rationale is necessary for both parties, for were there high visibility to the presence of either and no ready explanation for it, contact and communication would be far more difficult. Public and quasi-public facilities provide situations which account for the presence of most persons since there is relatively little social control over the establishment of contacts. There is, of course, some risk to the boys and the fellators in making contact in these situations since they are generally known to the police. The Morals Squad may have "stakeouts," but this is one of the calculated risks and the communication network carries information about their tactics.

A most important element in furnishing a rationale is that these meeting places must account for the presence of delinquent boys of essentially lower-class dress and appearance who make contact with fellators of almost any class level. This is true despite the fact that the social settings which fellators ordinarily choose to establish contact generally vary according to the class level of the fellators. Fellators of high social class generally make contact by "cruising" past street-corners, in parks, or the men's rooms in "better" hotels, while those from the lower class are likely to select the public bath or transportation depot. There apparently is some general equation of the class position of boys and fellators in the peer-queer transaction. The large majority of fellators in the delinquent peer-queer transaction probably are from the lower class ("apes"). But it is difficult to be certain about the class position of the fellator clients since no study was made of this population.

The absence of data from the fellator population poses difficulties in interpreting the contact relationship. Many fellators involved with delinquent boys do not appear to participate in any

overt or covert homosexual groups, such as the organized homosexual community of the "gay world."[8] The "gay world" is the most visible form of organized homosexuality since it is an organized community, but it probably encompasses only a small proportion of all homosexual contact. Even among those in the organized homosexual community, evidence suggests that the homosexual members seek sexual gratification outside their group with persons who are essentially anonymous to them. Excluding homosexual married couples, Leznoff and Westley maintain that there is "... a prohibition against sexual relationships within the group. ..."[9] Ross indicates that young male prostitutes are chosen, among other reasons, for the fact that they protect the identity of the client.[10] Both of these factors tend to coerce many male fellators to choose an anonymous contact situation.

It is clear that these contact situations not only provide a rationale for the presence of the parties to the transaction but a guarantee of anonymity. The guarantee does not necessarily restrict social visibility as both the boys and the fellators may recognize cues (including, but not necessarily, those of gesture and dress) which lead to mutual role identification.[11] But anonymity is guaranteed in at least two senses: anonymity of presence is assured in the situation and their personal identity in the community is protected unless disclosed by choice.

There presumably are a variety of reasons for the requirement of anonymity. For many, a homosexual relationship must remain a secret since their other relationships in the community—families, business relationships, etc.—must be protected. Leznoff and Westley refer to these men as the "secret" as contrasted with the "overt" homosexuals,[12] and in the organized "gay world," they are known as "closet fags."

---

[8] See, for example, Maurice Leznoff and William A. Westley, "The Homosexual Community," *Social Problems* 4 (April, 1956), pp. 257–63. [In this volume, pp. 269–74.]

[9] *Ibid.*, p. 258.

[10] H. Laurence Ross, "The 'Hustler' in Chicago," p. 15.

[11] The cues which lead to the queer-peer transaction can be subtle ones. The literature on adult male homosexuality makes it clear that adult males who participate in homosexual behavior are not generally socially visible to the public by manner and dress. Cf., Jess Stearn, *The Sixth Man* (Garden City, N.J.: Doubleday and Co., 1961). Chapters 1 and 3.

[12] Leznoff and Westley "The Homosexual Community." pp. 260–61.

For some, there is also a necessity for protecting identity to avoid blackmail.[13] Although none of the peer hustlers reported resorting to blackmail, the adult male fellator may nonetheless hold such an expectation, particularly if he is older or of high social class. Lower-class ones, by contrast, are more likely to face the threat of violence from adolescent boys since they more often frequent situations where they are likely to contact "rough trade."[14] The kind of situation in which the delinquent peer-queer contact is made and the sexual relationship consummated tends to minimize the possibility of violence.

Not all male fellators protect their anonymity; some will let a boy have their phone number and a few "keep a boy." Still, most fellators want to meet boys where they are least likely to be victimized, although boys sometimes roll queers by selecting a meeting place where by prearrangement, their friends can meet them and help roll the queer, steal his car, or commit other acts of violence. Boys generally know that fellators are vulnerable in that they "can't" report their victimization. Parenthetically, it might be mentioned that these boys are not usually aware of their own institutional invulnerability to arrest. An adolescent boy is peculiarly invulnerable to arrest even when found with a fellator since the mores define the boy as exploited.[15]

Situations of personal contact between adolescent boys and adult male fellators also provide important ways to *communicate intent* or to carry out the transaction *without* making the contact particularly visible to others. The wall writings in many of these places are not without their primitive communication value, e.g., "show it hard," and places such as a public restroom provide a modus operandi. The entrepreneur and his customer in fact can meet with little more than an exchange of non-verbal gestures,

transact their business with a minimum of verbal communication and part without a knowledge of one another's identity. In most cases, boys report "almost nothing" was said. The sexual transaction may occur with the only formal transaction being payment to the boy.

INDUCTION INTO THE PEER-QUEER TRANSACTION

The peer-queer culture operates through a delinquent peer society. Every boy interviewed in this study who voluntarily established contacts with fellators was also delinquent in many other respects. The evidence shows that contact with fellators is an institutionalized aspect of the organization of lower-class delinquency-oriented groups. This is not to say that boys outside these groups never experience relationships with adult male fellators: some do, but they are not participants in groups which sanction the activity according to the prescribed group standards described below. Nor is it to say that all delinquent groups positively sanction the peer-queer transaction since its distribution is unknown.

How, then, do lower-class delinquent boys get to meet fellators? Most boys from the lowest socioeconomic level in large cities are prepared for this through membership in a delinquent group which has a knowledge of how to make contact with fellators and relate to them. This is part of their common culture. Often, too, the peer group socializes the boy in his first experiences or continuing ones with fellators. The behavior is apparently learned within the framework of differential association.

The peer group actually serves as a school of induction for some of its members. The uninitiated boy goes with one or more members of his peer group for indoctrination and his first experience. Doy L., a lower-class boy at a lower-class school and a two-time loser at the State Training School, explains how he got started:

I went along with these older boys down to the bus station, and they took me along and showed me how it was done . . . they'd go in, get a queer, get blowed and get paid . . . if it didn't work right, they'd knock him in the head and get their money . . . they showed me how to do it, so I went in too.

---

[13] Ross notes that, failing in the con-man role, some hustlers resort to extortion and blackmail since they provide higher income. See Ross, "The 'Hustler' in Chicago," p. 16. Sutherland discusses extortion and blackmail of homosexuals as part of the practice of professional thieves. The "muzzle" or "mouse" is part of the role of the professional thief. See Edwin Sutherland, *The Professional Thief* (Chicago: University of Chicago Press, 1937), pp. 78–81. See also the chapter on "Blackmail" in Jess Stearn, *The Sixth Man,* Chapter 16.

[14] Jess Stearn, *The Sixth Man,* p. 47.

[15] Albert J. Reiss, Jr., "Sex Offenses: The Marginal Status of the Adolescent," *Law and Contemporary Problems* 25 (Spring, 1960), pp. 322–24 and 326–27.

In any case, boys are socialized in the subcultural definitions of peer-queer relations by members of their group and many apply this knowledge when an opportunity arises. Within the group, boys hear reports of experiences which supply the cultural definitions: how contacts are made, how you get money if the queer resists, how much one should expect to get, what kind of behavior is acceptable from the queer, which is to be rejected and how. Boys know all this *before* they have any contact with a fellator. In the case of street gangs, the fellators often pass the neighborhood corner; hence, even the preadolescent boy learns about the activity as the older boys get picked up. As the boy enters adolescence and a gang of his own which takes over the corner, he is psychologically and socially prepared for his first experience, which generally occurs when the first opportunity presents itself. Lester H. illustrates this; his first experience came when he went to one of the common points of convergence of boys and fellators— The Empress Theatre—to see a movie. Lester relates:

> I was down in the Empress Theatre and this gay came over and felt me up and asked me if I'd go out ... I said I would if he'd give me the money as I'd heard they did, and I was gettin' low on it ... so he took me down by the river and blowed me.

In a substantial number of cases, a brother introduces the boy to his first experience, much as he introduces him to other first experiences. Jimmie M. illustrates this pattern. Jimmie describes how he was led into his first heterosexual experience:

> When I was almost 14, my younger brother said he'd screwed this woman and he told me about it, so I went down there and she let me screw her too.

His induction into the peer-queer transaction also occurred through his younger brother:

> Well, my younger brother came home and told me this gay'd blowed him and he told me where he lived ... And, I was scared to do it, but I figured I'd want to see what it was like since the other guys talked about it and my brother'd done it. So I went down there and he blowed me.

The impression should not be gained that most lower-class boys who are solicited by fellators accept the solicitation. A majority of all solicitations are probably refused when the initial contact is made unless several other conditions prevail. The first is that the boy must be a member of a group which permits this form of transaction, indoctrinates the boy with its codes and sanctions his participation in it. Almost all lower-class boys reported they were solicited by a queer at least once. A majority refused the solicitation. Refusal is apparently easy since boys report that queers are seldom insistent. There apparently is a mutual willingness to forego the transaction in such cases, perhaps because the queer cannot afford the risk of exposure, but perhaps also because the probability of his establishing contact on his next try is sufficiently high so that he can "afford" to accept the refusal. Looked at another way, there must be a set of mutual gains and expectations for the solicitation to be accepted and the transaction to proceed. Boys who refuse to be solicited are not vulnerable for another reason: they usually are members of groups which negatively sanction the activity. Such groups generally "bug" boys who go out with fellators and use other techniques of isolation to discourage the transaction. There also are gangs which look upon queers as "fair game" for their aggressive activity. They beat them, roll, and otherwise put upon them. A third condition that must prevail is that the boy who accepts or seeks solicitation from fellators must view the offer as instrumental gain, particularly monetary gain (discussed below).

There are boys, however, particularly those who are quite young, who report a solicitation from a man which they were unable to refuse but which they subsequently rejected as neither gratifying nor instrumentally acceptable. It is these boys who can be said to be "exploited" by adult fellators in the sense that they are either forced into the act against their will, or are at least without any awareness of how to cope with the situation. One such instance is found in the following report:

> This guy picked me up down at Fourth and Union and said he was going over to East Nashville, so I got in ... but he drove me out on Dickerson Pike. (What'd he do?) ... Well, he

blowed me and it made me feel real bad inside
... but I know how to deal with queers now ...
ain't one of 'em gonna do that to me again ... I
hate queers. ... They're crazy.

There is an important admission in the statement, "but I know how to deal with 'em now."
The lower-class boy as he grows older learns
how to deal with sexual advances from fellators.
Boys exchange experiences on how they deal
with them and it becomes quite difficult to "exploit" a lower-class boy who is socialized in a
peer group. It is perhaps largely the very young
boy, such as the one in the case above, or those
isolated from peer groups, who are most vulnerable to solicitation without previous preparation
for it.

Lower-class boys, as we have seen, have the
highest probability of being in situations where
they will be solicited by fellators. But, *the lower-
class boy who is a member of a career-oriented
gang which positively sanctions instrumental relationships with adult male fellators and which
initiates members into these practices, and a boy
who at the same time perceives himself as "needing" the income which the transaction provides,
is most likely to establish personal contact with
adult male fellators on a continuing basis.*

It is suggested that the peer-queer transaction
is behavior learned through differential association in delinquent gangs. This cannot be demonstrated without resort to a more specific test of
the hypothesis. But, as Sutherland has pointed
out, "Criminal behavior is partially a function of
opportunities to commit special classes of
crimes. ... It is axiomatic that persons who commit a specific crime have the opportunity to
commit that crime. ... While opportunity may
be partially a function of association with criminal patterns and of the specialized techniques
thus acquired, it is not entirely determined in
this manner, and consequently differential association is not a sufficient cause of criminal behavior."[16] Middle-class boys are perhaps excluded from the peer-queer transaction as much
through lack of opportunity to commit this special class of crime in their community of exposure as through any criterion of differential

association. The structure of the middle-class
area is incompatible with the situational requirements for the peer-queer transaction.

NORMS GOVERNING THE TRANSACTION

Does the peer society have any norms about personal relations with fellators? Or, does it simply
induct a boy into a relationship by teaching him
how to effect the transaction? The answer is that
there appear to be several clear-cut norms about
the relations between peers and queers, even
though there is some deviation from them.

The first major norm is that *a boy must
undertake the relationship with a queer solely as
a way of making money; sexual gratification
cannot be actively sought as a goal in the relationship.* This norm does not preclude a boy
from sexual gratification by the act; he simply
must not seek this as a goal. Put another way, a
boy cannot admit that he failed to get money
from the transaction unless he used violence
toward the fellator and he cannot admit that he
sought it as a means of sexual gratification.

The importance of making money in motivating a boy to the peer-queer transaction is succinctly stated by Dewey H.:

This guy in the Rex Theatre came over and sat
down next to me when I was 11 or 12, and he
started to fool with me. I got over and sat down
another place and he came over and asked me,
didn't I want to and he'd pay me five bucks. I
figured it was *easy money* so I went with him ...
I didn't do it before that. That wasn't too long
after I'd moved to South Nashville. I was a pretty
good boy before that ... not real good, but I
never ran with a crowd that got into trouble before that. But, I met a lot of 'em there. (Why do
you run with queers?) It's *easy money* ... like I
could go out and break into a place when I'm
broke and get money that way ... but that's
harder and *you take a bigger risk* ... with a
queer it's *easy money.*

Dewey's comments reveal two important motivating factors in getting money from queers,
both suggested by the expression, "easy money."
First, the money is easy in that it can be made
quickly. Some boys reported that when they
needed money for a date or a night out, they
obtained it within an hour through the sexual
transaction with a queer. All a boy has to do is

---

[16] Albert Cohen, Alfred Lindesmith and Karl Schuessler,
editors, *The Sutherland Papers* (Bloomington, Indiana: The
University of Indiana Press, 1956), p. 31.

go to a place where he will be contacted, wait around, get picked up, carried to a place where the sexual transaction occurs, and in a relatively short period of time he obtains the money for his service.

It is easy money in another and more important sense for many of these boys. Boys who undertake the peer-queer transaction are generally members of career-oriented delinquent groups. Rejecting the limited opportunities for making money by legitimate means or finding them inaccessible, their opportunities to make money by illegitimate means may also be limited or the risk may be great. Theft is an available means, but it is more difficult and involves greater risk than the peer-queer transaction. Delinquent boys are not unaware of the risks they take. Under most circumstances, delinquents may calculate an act of stealing as "worth the risk." There are occasions, however, when the risk is calculated as too great. These occasions occur when the "heat" is on the boy or when he can least afford to run the risk of being picked up by the police, as is the case following a pick-up by the police, being put on probation or parole, or being warned that incarceration will follow the next violation. At such times, boys particularly calculate whether they can afford to take the risk. Gerald L., describing a continuing relationship with a fellator who gave him his phone number, reflects Dewey's attitude toward minimizing risk in the peer-queer transaction: "So twic'd after that when I was gettin' real low and couldn't risk stealin' and gettin' caught, I called him and he took me out and blowed me." Here is profit with no investment of capital and a minimum of risk in social, if not in psychological, terms.

The element of risk coupled with the wish for "easy money" enters into our understanding of the peer-queer relationship in another way. From a sociological point of view, the peer-queer sexual transaction occurs between two major types of deviators—"delinquents" and "queers." Both types of deviators risk negative sanctions for their deviant acts. The more often one has been arrested or incarcerated, the more punitive the sanctions from the larger social system for both types of deviators. At some point, therefore, both calculate risks and seek to minimize them, at least in the very short run. Each

then becomes a means for the other to minimize risk.

When the delinquent boy is confronted with a situation in which he wants money and risks little in getting it, how is he to get it without working? Illegitimate activities frequently provide the "best" opportunity for easy money. These activities often are restricted in kind and number for adolescents and the risk of negative sanctions is high. Under such circumstances, the service offered a queer is a chance to make easy money with a minimum of risk.

Opportunities for sexual gratification are limited for the adult male fellator, particularly if he wishes to minimize the risk of detection in locating patrons, to avoid personal involvement and to get his gratification when he wishes it. The choice of a lower-class male, precisely because of his class position, somewhat reduces the risk. If the lower-class male also is a delinquent, the risk is minimized to an even greater degree.

This is not to say that the parties take equal risks in the situation. Of the two, the fellator perhaps is less able to minimize his risk since he still risks violence from his patron, but much less so if a set of expectations arise which control the use of violence as well. The boy is most able to minimize his risk since he is likely to be defined as "exploited" in the situation if caught.

Under special circumstances, boys may substitute other gratifications for the goal of money, provided that these gratifications do not include sexual gratification as a major goal. These special circumstances are the case where an entire gang will "make a night (or time) of it" with one or more adult male fellators. Under these circumstances, everyone is excepted from the subcultural expectations about making money from the fellator because everyone participates and there is no reason for everyone (or anyone) to make money. For the group to substitute being given a "good time" by a "queer" for the prescribed financial transaction is, of course, the exception which proves the rule.

Several examples of group exemption from the prescribed norm of a financial gain were discovered. Danny S., leader of the Black Aces, tells of his gang's group experiences with queers: "There's this one gay who takes us to the Colonial Motel out on Dickerson Pike . . . usually it's a bunch of us boys and we all get drunk and get blowed by this queer . . . we don't get any money then . . . it's more a drinking party." The Black Aces are a fighting gang and place great stress on physical prowess, particularly boxing. All of its members have done time more than once at the State Training School. During one of these periods, the school employed a boxing instructor whom the boys identified as "a queer," but the boys had great respect for him since he taught them how to box and was a game fighter. Danny refers to him in accepting terms: "He's a real good guy. He's fought with us once or twice and we drink with him when we run into him. . . . He's taken us up to Miter Dam a coupla times; he's got a cabin up there on the creek and he blows us. . . . But mostly we just drink and have a real good time." These examples illustrate the instrumental orientation of the gang members. If the expense of the gang members getting drunk and having a good time is borne by a "queer," each member is released from the obligation to receive cash. The relationship in this case represents an exchange of services rather than that of money for a service.

The second major norm operating in the relationship is that *the sexual transaction must be limited to mouth-genital fellation. No other sexual acts are generally tolerated.*[17] The adult male fellator must deport himself in such a way as to reinforce the instrumental aspects of the role relationship and to insure affective neutrality.[18] For the adult male fellator to violate the boy's expectation of "getting blowed," as the boys refer to the act, is to risk violence and loss of service. Whether or not the boys actually use violent means as often as they say they do when expectations are violated, there is no way of knowing with precision. Nevertheless, whenever boys reported they used violent means, they al-

ways reported some violation of the subcultural expectations. Likewise, they never reported a violation of the subcultural expectations which was not followed by the use of violent means, unless it was clearly held up as an exception. Bobby A. expresses the boys' point of view on the use of violent means in the following exchange: "How much did you usually get?" "Around five dollars; if they didn't give that much, I'd beat their head in." "Did they ever want you to do anything besides blow you?" "Yeh, sometimes . . . like they want me to blow them, but I'd tell them to go to hell and maybe beat them up."

Boys are very averse to being thought of in a queer role or engaging in acts of fellation. The act of fellation is defined as a "queer" act. Most boys were asked whether they would engage in such behavior. All but those who had the status of "punks" denied they had engaged in behavior associated with the queer role. Asking a boy whether he is a fellator meets with strong denial and often with open hostility. This could be interpreted as defensive behavior against latent homosexuality. Whether or not this is the case, strong denial could be expected because the question goes counter to the subcultural definitions of the peer role in the transaction.

A few boys on occasion apparently permit the fellator to perform other sexual acts. These boys, it is guessed, are quite infrequent in a delinquent peer population. Were their acts known to the members of the group, they would soon be defined as outside the delinquent peer society. Despite the limitation of the peer-queer sexual transaction to mouth-genital fellation, there are other sexual transactions which the peer group permits members to perform under special circumstances. They are, for example, permitted to perform the *male* roles in "crimes against nature," such as in pederasty ("cornholing" to the boys), bestiality (sometimes referred to as buggery) and carnal copulation with a man involving no orifice (referred to as "slicklegging" among the boys) provided that the partner is roughly of the same age and not a member of the group and provided also that the boys are confined to the single-sex society of incarcerated delinquent boys. Under no circumstances, however, is the female role in carnal copulation acceptable in any form. It is taboo. Boys who

---

[17] It is not altogether clear why mouth-genital fellation is the only sexual act which is tolerated in the peer-queer transaction. The act seems to conform to the more "masculine" aspects of the role than do most, but not all possible alternatives. Ross has suggested to me that it also involves less bodily contact and therefore may be less threatening to the peers' self-definitions. One possible explanation therefore for the exclusiveness of the relationship to this act is that it is the most masculine alternative involving the least threat to peers' self-definition as nonhustler and nonhomosexual.

[18] Talcott Parsons in *The Social System* (Glencoe: The Free Press, 1951), Chapter III, discusses this kind of role as "the segregation of specific instrumental performances, both from expressive orientations other than the specifically appropriate rewards and from other components of the instrumental complex." (P. 87.)

accept the female role in sexual transactions occupy the lowest status position among delinquents. They are "punks."

The third major norm operating on the relationship is that *both peers and queers, as participants, should remain affectively neutral during the transaction.* Boys within the peer society define the ideal form of the role with the fellator as one in which the boy is the entrepreneur and the queer is viewed as purchasing a service. The service is a business deal where a sexual transaction is purchased for an agreed upon amount of money. In the typical case, the boy is neither expected to enjoy or be repulsed by the sexual transaction; mouth-genital fellation is accepted as a service offered in exchange for a fee. It should be kept in mind that self-gratification is permitted in the sexual act. Only the motivation to sexual gratification in the transaction is tabooed. But self-gratification must occur without displaying either positive or negative affect toward the queer. In the prescribed form of the role relationship, the boy sells a service for profit and the queer is to accept it without show of emotion.

The case of Thurman L., one of three brothers who are usually in trouble with the law, illustrates some aspects of the expected pattern of affective neutrality. Thurman has had a continuing relationship with a queer, a type of relationship in which it would be anticipated that affective neutrality would be difficult to maintain. This relationship continued, in fact, with a 21-year-old "gay" until the man was "sent to the pen." When queried about his relationship with this man and why he went with him, Thurman replied:

> Don't know . . . money and stuff like that I guess. (What do you mean? . . . stuff like that?) Oh, clothes. . . . (He ever bought you any clothes?) Sure, by this one gay. . . . (You mind being blowed?) No. (You like it?) Don't care one way or the other. I don't like it, and I don't not like it. (You like this one gay?) Nope, can't say that I liked anythin' about him. (How come you do it then?) Well, the money for one thing. . . . I need that. (You enjoy it some?) Can't say I do or don't.

More typical than Thurman's expression of affective neutrality is the boy who accepts it as "OK," or "It's all right; I don't mind it." Most frequent of all is some variant of the statement:

"It's OK, but I like the money best of all." The definition of affective neutrality fundamentally requires only that there be no positive emotional commitment to the queer *as a person.* The relationship must be essentially an impersonal one, even though the pure form of the business relationship may seldom be attained. Thus, it is possible for a boy to admit self-gratification without admitting any emotional commitment to the homosexual partner.

Although the peer group prescribes affective neutrality toward the queer in the peer-queer transaction, queers must be regarded as low-prestige persons, held in low esteem, and the queer role is taboo. The queer is most commonly regarded as "crazy, I guess." Some boys take a more rationalistic view, "They're just like that, I guess," or "They're just born that way." While there are circumstances under which one is permitted to like a particular fellator, as in the case of all prejudices attached to devalued status, the person who is liked must be the exception which states the rule. Though in many cases both the boy and the fellator are of very low class origins, and in many cases both are altogether repulsive in appearance, cleanliness and dress by middle-class standards, these are not the standards of comparison used by the boys. The deviation of the queers from the boy's norms of masculine behavior places the fellator in the lowest possible status, even "beneath contempt." If the fellator violates the expected affective relationship in the transaction, he may be treated not only with violence but with contempt as well. The seller of the service ultimately reserves the right to set the conditions of his patrons.

Some boys find it difficult to be emotionally neutral toward the queer role and its occupants; they are either personally offended or affronted by the behavior of queers. JDC is an instance of a boy who is personally offended by their behavior; yet he is unable to use violence even when expectations governing the transaction are violated. He does not rely very much on the peer-queer relationship as a source of income. JDC expresses his view: "I don't really go for that like some guys; I just do it when I go along with the crowd. . . . You know. . . . That, and when I do it for money. . . . And I go along. . . . But . . . I hate queers. They embarrass me." "How?" "Well, like you'll be in the lobby at the theatre, and they'll come up and pat your ass or your prick right in front of everybody. I just can't go for that—not me." Most of the boys wouldn't either, but they would have resorted to violent means in this situation.

Two principal types of boys maintain a continuing relationship with a known queer. A few boys develop such relationships to insure a steady income. While this is permitted within peer society for a short period of time, boys who undertake it for extended periods of time do so with some risk, since in the words of the boys, "queers can be got too easy." The boy who is affectively involved with a queer or his role is downgraded in status to a position, "Ain't no better'n a queer." There are also a few boys affectively committed to a continuing relationship with an adult male homosexual. Such boys usually form a strong dependency relationship with him and are kept much as the cabin boys of old. This type of boy is clearly outside the peer society of delinquents and is isolated from participation in gang activity. The sociometric pattern for such boys is one of choice into more than one gang, none of which is reciprocated.

Street-hustlers are also downgraded within the peer society, generally having reputations as "punk kids." The street-hustler pretty much "goes it alone." Only a few street-hustlers were interviewed for this study. None of them was a member of an organized delinquent group. The sociometric pattern for each, together with his history of delinquent activity, placed them in the classification of nonconforming isolates.

A fourth major norm operating on the peer-queer relationship serves as a primary factor in stabilizing the system. This norm holds that *violence must not be used so long as the relationship conforms to the shared set of expectations between queers and peers.* So long as the fellator conforms to the norms governing the transaction in the peer-queer society, he runs little risk of violence from the boys.

The main reason, perhaps, for this norm is that uncontrolled violence is potentially disruptive of any organized system. All organized social systems must control violence. If the fellator clients were repeatedly the objects of violence, the system as it has been described could not exist. Most boys who share the common expectations of the peer-queer relationship do not use

violent means unless the expectations are violated. To use violence, of course, is to become affectively involved and therefore another prescription of the relationship is violated.

It is not known whether adult male fellators who are the clients of delinquent entrepreneurs share the boys' definition of the norm regarding the use of violence. They may, therefore, violate expectations of the peer society through ignorance of the system rather than from any attempt to go beyond the set of shared expectations.

There are several ways the fellator can violate the expectations of boys. The first concerns money: refusal to pay or paying too little may bring violence from most boys. Fellators may also violate peer expectations by attempting to go beyond the mouth-genital sexual act. If such an attempt is made, he is usually made an object of aggression as in the following excerpt from Dolly's sex history:

(You like it?) It's OK. I don't mind it. It feels OK. (They ever try anything else on you?) They usually just blow that's all. (Any ever try anything else on you?) Oh sure, but we really fix 'em. I just hit 'em on the head or roll 'em . . . throw 'em out of the car. . . . Once a gay tried that and we rolled him and threw him out of the car. Then we took the car and stripped it (laughs with glee).

Another way the fellator violates a boy's expectations is to introduce considerable affect into the relationship. It appears that affect is least acceptable in two forms, both of which could be seen as "attacks on his masculinity." In one form, the queer violates the affective neutrality requirement by treating the adolescent boy as if he were a girl or in a girl's role during the sexual transaction, as for example, by speaking to him in affectionate terms such as "sweetie." There are many reasons why the feminine sex role is unacceptable to these lower-class boys, including the fact that such boys place considerable emphasis on being "tough" and masculine. Walter Miller, for example, observes that:

The almost compulsive lower class concern with "masculinity" derives from a type of compulsive reaction-formation. A concern over homosexuality runs like a persistent thread through lower-class culture—manifested by the institutionalized practice of "baiting queers," often accompanied by violent physical attacks, an expressed contempt for "softness" or frills, and the use of the local term for "homosexual" as a general pejorative epithet (e.g., higher-class individuals or upwardly mobile peers are frequently characterized as "fags" or "queers").[19]

Miller sees violence as part of a reaction-formation against the matriarchal lower-class household where the father often is absent. For this reason, he suggests, many lower-class boys find it difficult to identify with a male role, and the "collective" reaction-formation is a cultural emphasis on masculinity. Violence toward queers is seen as a consequence of this conflict. Data from our interviews suggests that among career-oriented delinquents, violation of the affective neutrality requirement in the peer-queer relationship is at least as important in precipitating violence toward "queers." There are, of course, gangs which were not studied in this investigation which "queer-bait" for the express purpose of "rolling the queer."

The other form in which the fellator may violate the affective neutrality requirement is to approach the boy and make suggestive advances to him when he is with his age-mates, either with girls or with his peer group when he is not located for "business." In either case, the sexual advances suggest that the boy is not engaged in a business relationship within the normative expectations of the system, but that he has sexual motivation as well. The delinquent boy is expected to control the relationship with his customers. He is the entrepreneur "looking" for easy money or at the very least he must appear as being merely receptive to business; this means that he is receptive only in certain situations and under certain circumstances. He is not in business when he is with girls and he is not a businessman when he is cast in a female role. To be cast in a female role before peers is highly unacceptable, as the following account suggests:

This gay comes up to me in the lobby of the Empress when we was standin' around and starts feelin' me up and callin' me Sweetie and like that ... and, I just couldn't take none of that there ... what was he makin' out like I was a queer or somethin' ... so I jumps him right then and there and we like to of knocked his teeth out.

---

[19] Walter Miller, "Lower-Class Culture as a Generating Milieu of Gang Delinquency," *The Journal of Social Issues* 14, No. 3 (1958), p. 9.

The sexual advance is even less acceptable when a girl is involved:

I was walkin' down the street with my steady girl when this gay drives by that I'd been with once before and he whistles at me and calls, "Hi Sweetie." ... And, was I mad ... so I went down to where the boys was and we laid for him and beat on him 'til he like to a never come to ... ain't gonna take nothin' like that off'n a queer.

In both of these instances, not only is the boys' masculinity under attack, but the affective neutrality requirement of the business transaction is violated. The queer's behavior is particularly unacceptable, however, because it occurs in a peer setting where the crucial condition is the maintenance of the boy's status within the group. A lower-class boy cannot afford to be cast in less than a highly masculine role before lower-class girls nor risk definition as a queer before peers. His role within his peer group is under threat even if he suffers *no* anxiety about masculinity. Not only the boy himself but his peers perceive such behavior as violating role expectations and join him in violent acts toward the fellator to protect the group's integrity and status.

If violence generally occurs only when one of the major peer norms has been violated, it would also seem to follow that *violence is a means of enforcing the peer entrepreneurial norms of the system.* Violence or the threat of violence is thus used to keep adult male fellators in line with the boys' expectations in his customer role. It represents social control, a punishment meted out to the fellator who violates the cultural expectation. Only so long as the fellator seeks gratification from lower-class boys in a casual pick-up or continuing relationship where he pays money for a "blow-job," is he reasonably free from acts of violence.

There is another, and perhaps more important reason for the use of violence when the peer defined norms of the peer-queer relationship are violated. The formally prescribed roles for peers and queers are basically the roles involved in all institutionalized forms of prostitution, the prostitute and the client. But in most forms of prostitution, whether male or female, the hustlers perceive of themselves in hustler roles, and furthermore the male hustlers also develop a conception of themselves as homosexual whereas *the peer hustler in the peer-queer relationship develops no conception of himself either as prostitute or as homosexual.*

The fellator risks violence, therefore, if he threatens the boy's self-conception by suggesting that the boy may be homosexual and treats him as if he were.

Violence seems to function, then, in two basic ways for the peers. On the one hand, it integrates their norms and expectations by controlling and combatting behavior which violates them. On the other hand, it protects the boy's self-identity as nonhomosexual and reinforces his self-conception as "masculine."

The other norms of the peer society governing the peer-queer transaction also function to prevent boys in the peer-queer society from defining themselves as homosexual. The prescriptions that the goal is money, that sexual gratification is not to be sought as an end in the relationship, that affective neutrality be maintained toward the fellator and that only mouth-genital fellation is permitted, all tend to insulate the boy from a homosexual self-definition. So long as he conforms to these expectations, *his "significant others" will not define him as homosexual;* and this is perhaps the most crucial factor in his own self-definition. The peers define one as homosexual not on the basis of homosexual *behavior* as such, but on the basis of participation in the homosexual *role,* the "queer" role. The reaction of the larger society, in defining the *behavior* as homosexual, is unimportant in their own self-definition. What is important to them is the reactions of their peers to violation of peer group norms which define roles in the peer-queer transaction.

TERMINATING THE ROLE BEHAVIOR

Under what circumstances does a boy give up earning money in the peer-queer transaction? Is it altogether an individual matter, or are there group bases for abandoning the practice? We have little information on these questions since interviews were conducted largely with boys who were still participants in the peer-queer culture. But a few interviews, either with boys who had terminated the relationship or spoke of those who had, provide information on how such role behavior is terminated.

Among lower-class adolescent boys, the new roles one assumes with increasing age are important in terminating participation in the peer-queer relationship. Thus older boys are more likely to have given up the transaction as a source of income. Several boys gave as their reason, "I got a job and don't need that kind of money now." An older boy, who recently married, said that he had quit when he was married. Another responded to the question, "When do you think you'll quit?" with, "When I quit school, I reckon. . . . I don't know a better way to make money afore then." A few boys simply said that they didn't care to make money that way any more, or that since they got a steady girl, they had quit.

The reasons older boys have for giving up the peer-queer transaction as a means of making money are perhaps different for the career-oriented than for the peer-oriented delinquent boy. As career-oriented delinquents get older, the more serious crimes direct their activity and the group is more actively involved in activities which confer status. The boy has a "rep" to maintain. The peer-hustler role clearly contributes nothing to developing or maintaining a reputation, and the longer one gets money this way, the more one may risk it. The older career-oriented delinquent boy perhaps gives up peer-hustling activity, then, just as he often gives up petty theft and malicious destruction of property. These are activities for younger boys.

As peer-oriented delinquents get older, they enter adult groups where a job becomes one of the acceptable ways of behaving. Many of them may also move out of the "tight little island" of the peer group which inducted them into the activity. If one gets enough money from a job, there is no socially acceptable reason for getting money in the peer-queer transaction. One risks loss of status if one solicits at this age, for this is the age to move from one steady girl to another and perhaps even settle on one and get married, as often one "has to."

Regardless of the reasons for moving out, it seems clear that most boys do move out of their roles as peer hustlers and do not go on to other hustling careers. The main reason perhaps that most boys do not move on in hustling careers is that they never conceived of themselves in a hustling role or as participants in a career where there was a status gradation among hustlers. Hustling, to the peer hustler, is simply another one of the activities which characterizes a rather versatile pattern of deviating acts. It is easier, too, to move out when one has never defined oneself as homosexual. It is in this sense, perhaps, that we have reason to conclude that these boys are not involved in the activity primarily for its homosexual basis. Peer hustlers are primarily oriented toward either delinquent, and later criminal, careers, or toward conventional conformity in lower-class society. They become neither hustlers nor queers.

SUMMARY

This paper explores a special form of male prostitution in American society, a homosexual relationship between adult male fellators and delin-

quents. It is seen as a financial transaction between boys and fellators which is governed by delinquent peer norms. These norms integrate the two types of deviators into an institutionalized form of prostitution and protect the boys from self-definitions either as prostitutes or as homosexuals.

The conclusions offered in this paper must be regarded as tentative, because of limitations inherent in the data. Study of the fellator population might substantially change the conclusions. Cross-cultural studies also are necessary. Discussion of these findings with criminologists in Denmark and Sweden and exploratory investigations in several larger American cities, however, suggest that the description and explanation offered in this paper will hold for other American cities and for some other social systems.

C. CONSEQUENCES

Homosexuality is more than just a form of sexual behavior. It is also a deviant subculture. Burgess has remarked:

> Every large city has its homosexual world with its rendevous, parties, and celebrities. This world has its own language, incomprehensible to outsiders. It has its own literature, group ways, and code of conduct. It is a world where members find moral support, sympathy, and fellowship. The group lore identifies, not always too accurately, certain famous men, past and present, as homosexuals, thus providing a justification of their aberrant way of life.[1]

The subculture is primarily a consequence of two factors. One is the social ostracism and legal punishment to which known homosexuals are subjected; as a result, homosexuals frequently attempt to conceal their identity. The second is that homosexuals are normally dependent upon other homosexuals for sexual gratification. The homosexual subcommunity solves both of these problems. It gives homosexuals access to sexual partners and at the same time it protects them from the surveillance of the community. As Leznoff and Westley contend in "The Homosexual Community," homosexual groups exist so that the individual homosexual may evade societal social controls. Also, since the homosexual community is the only context in which a homosexual is "normal," it gives him a sense of social support and acceptance. The burdens of concealment are

---

[1] Ernest W. Burgess, "The Sociologic Theory of Psychosexual Behavior," in P. H. Hoch and J. Zubin, eds., *Psychosexual Development in Health and Disease* (New York: Grove and Stratton, 1949), p. 234.

thereby mitigated. Leznoff and Westley also reveal that all homosexuals are not equally threatened by public exposure, however. This may lead to two types of groups within the homosexual world—secret groups and overt groups.

Once developed, homosexual communities of course help to perpetuate homosexuality. The free interaction between homosexuals reinforces homosexual trends as well as homosexual self-conceptions. As Burgess states:

> [The homosexual's] full development as a homosexual comes only when he identifies himself as a homosexual. This typically coincides with his entrance into the homosexual world.[2]

In the final selection in this chapter, "Coming Out in the Gay World," Barry M. Dank describes in detail this function of homosexual communities. The function is viewed from the perspective of homosexuals who are in the process of moving from the primary stage of deviant behavior to the secondary stage. In the former stage, we recall, an individual engages in deviant behavior without viewing himself as a deviant while in the second stage he does view himself as such. "Coming out" is the process by which a "primary homosexual" becomes a "secondary homosexual." We have already noted that the societal reaction to homosexual behavior has as a consequence the development of homosexual subcultures and subcommunities. Dank's analysis allows us to view this consequence from another perspective; in his analysis, homosexual communities provide the settings in which individuals become socialized into homosexual behavior. Accordingly, his analysis allows us to see that homosexual behavior is much more than a psychiatric or medical "condition"; it is social behavior. The process of becoming a "secondary" homosexual is closely related to the existence of homosexual communities which are themselves consequences of homosexuality.

---

[2] *Ibid.*

THE HOMOSEXUAL COMMUNITY

MAURICE LEZNOFF AND WILLIAM A. WESTLEY

The significance of homosexuality in our society has been minimized and obscured by the force of social taboo. Yet there is evidence that homosexuals are distributed throughout all geographical areas and socioeconomic strata.[1] Furthermore, the subjection of homosexuals to legal punishments and social condemnation has produced a complex structure of concealed social relations which merits sociological investigation. The psychological isolation of the homosexual from society, his dependence upon other deviants for the satisfaction of sexual needs and self-expression, the crystallization of social roles and behavior patterns within the deviant group, the reciprocal obligations and demands within the homosexual community, and their significance for the larger society in which they occur, are but a few of the areas of theoretical interest to the sociologist.

In this paper we shall confine our discussion to the social organization of one homosexual community and its constituent social groups: their function, etiology, and interrelationships.

The report is based upon an intensive study of 60 homosexuals in a large Canadian city. The data consist of four-hour interviews with 40 homosexuals and briefer interviews with 20 others.[2] In addition, the data include information based on the observation of many homosexual parties and gatherings in bars and restaurants, and a series of 30 letters written by one homosexual to another.

FUNCTIONS OF HOMOSEXUAL GROUPS

The primary function of the homosexual group is psychological in that it provides a social context within which the homosexual can find acceptance as a homosexual and collective support for his deviant tendencies. Most homosexuals fear detection and are often insecure and anxious because of this. The following statement illustrates this:

> The thought that you are "gay" is always with you and you know it's there even when other people don't. You also think to yourself that certain of your mannerisms and your ways of expression are liable to give you away. That means that there is always a certain amount of strain. I don't say that it's a relief to get away from normal people, but there isn't the liberty that you feel in a gay crowd. When I associate with normal people I prefer very small groups of them. I don't like large groups and I think I try to avoid them when I can. You know, the only time when I really forget I'm gay is when I'm in a gay crowd.

To relieve this anxiety the deviant seeks collective support and social acceptance. Since the homosexual group provides the only social context in which homosexuality is normal, deviant practices moral, and homosexual responses rewarded, the homosexual develops a deep emotional involvement with his group, tending toward a ready acceptance of its norms and dictates, and subjection to its behavior patterns. The regularity with which he seeks the company of his group is a clear expression of this dependency.

A prohibition against sexual relationships within the group, in a manner suggestive of the incest taboo, indicates the extent to which the group culture is oriented to this function. The quotation which follows is indicative of this taboo:

Reprinted with permission of authors and publisher from *Social Problems* 3 (April, 1956), pp. 257–63.

[1] Kinsey reports that 37 percent of the total male population have at least some overt homosexual experience to the point of orgasm between adolescence and old age; 30 percent of all males have at least incidental homosexual experience or reactions over at least a three-year period between the ages of 16 and 55; 25 percent of the male population have more than incidental homosexual experience or reactions for at least three years between the ages of 16 and 55; 18 percent of the males have at least as much of the homosexual as the heterosexual in their histories for at least three years between the ages of 16 and 55; 4 percent of the white males are exclusively homosexual throughout their lives, after the onset of adolescence. Homosexual practices are reported among all occupational groups with the percentage for professionals approximately 50 percent lower than those of other groups. Further confirmation of the distribution of homosexuals among all social strata was obtained from police files and the testimony of homosexuals.

[2] Access to this homosexual community was obtained through a client at a social welfare agency. The authors are indebted to the Canadian Social Science Research Council and to the McGill University Research Fund for grants in support of this study.

As far as I know, people who hang around with each other don't have affairs. The people who are friends don't sleep with each other. I can't tell you why that is, but they just don't. Unless you are married[3] you have sex with strangers mostly. I think if you have sex with a friend it will destroy the friendship. I think that in the inner mind we all respect high moral standards, and none of us want to feel low in the eyes of anybody else. It's always easier to get along with your gay friends if there has been no sex. Mind you, you might have sex with somebody you just met and then he might become your friend. But you won't have sex with him any more as soon as he joins the same gang you hang around with.

Within these groups the narration of sexual experiences and gossip about the sexual exploits of others is a major form of recreation. The narration of sexual experiences functions to allocate prestige among the members because of the high evaluation placed upon physical attraction and sexual prowess. Yet it creates hostility and sexual rivalry. The intense involvement of homosexuals in the results of this sexual competition is illustrated in the following statement which was overheard in a restaurant:

Who wouldn't blow up. That bitch is trying to get her[4] clutches into Richard. She can't leave anybody alone. I wouldn't be surprised if she ended up with a knife in her back. I don't mean to say I'm threatening her. But she's not going to get away with that stuff forever... playing kneesies under the table all night long. I had to get her away from Richard. That lousy bitch. From now on she better keep away from me.

An additional function is the provision of a social situation in which the members can dramatize their adherence to homosexual values. Thus, the gossip about sex, the adoption and exaggeration of feminine behavior, and the affectation of speech, represent a way of affirming that homosexuality is frankly accepted and has the collective support of the group. The extreme but not uncommon instance of this is the homosexual institution of the "drag" in which the members of the group dress and make themselves up as women. A good description of a drag is contained in the following letter:

_____
[3] A stable social and sexual relationship between two homosexuals is frequently referred to as "marriage."
[4] The substitution of the female for the male pronoun is a common practice within homosexual groups.

Well, doll, last night was one to remember. Raymond of B. [city] gave me a letter of introduction to one of the local belles. He phoned yesterday and we arranged to go out in the evening. Met at my room and proceeded to the Frederick Hotel where I was introduced to my new acquaintances. It was decided to hold a party afterwards, Chez Norman, my new acquaintance. He told me they were supposed to be discontinued but we were going ahead in my honor. And in drag. One queen about 45–50 who is a window dresser brought some materials of fine nylon net, 2 yards wide and changing color across the width from yellow to flaming orange. There must have been about 25 yds. Well, he made his entrance wearing nothing but his shorts and this stuff wound around him and proceeded to do an exotic dance. Included in the costume was a blond wig from one of the store mannequins and artificial tropical fruits. It was something to see. It was very ludicrous to begin with and much more so when you realize that he is by no means graceful and has so much hair on him that I am smooth by comparison. Throughout the evening he kept on making variations of the costume —each becoming briefer until he was down to nothing. Really!

Another one, very slim, put on a pair of falsies, a turban hat to hide short hair, and a dress with a wide flair skirt. Other than hair on the chest which showed, the effect of femininity was so convincing (even his heels) that I promptly lost interest. Actually produced a beautiful effect— the kind of woman I would like if I could. Beautiful dancer, and performed all evening. Later borrowed some of the nylon net of the old queen and did a dance with flowing material and wearing nothing, but nothing else.

There were only three of us not in drag, including yrs. truly. But when it came time to leave (not alone, I might add) I couldn't resist flinging about my coat a fox fur which happened to be lying around. Really, my dear, it was quite an affair.

These functions reflect the common needs and problems which homosexuals face in hostile society.

Etiology: The Evasion of Social Controls

In our society, homosexuality is defined both legally and socially as a criminal and depraved practice and the homosexual is threatened by powerful legal and social sanctions such as imprisonment, physical violence [William A. Westley, "Violence and the Police," chapter three], social and occupational ostracism, and ridicule. Therefore, all homosexuals face the problem of evading social controls. They do this in two predominant ways.

Some pass for heterosexuals on the job and in most of their social relationships. They mix regularly with heterosexuals for business, entertainment, and other social activities. They avoid situations and persons publicly recognized as homosexual for they fear that discovery will threaten their career and expose them to sanctions. This is illustrated in the following statement of a lawyer:

> I know a few people who don't care. They are really pitiful. They are either people who are in very insignificant positions or they are in good positions but are independent. I know of one who is in the retail business. He doesn't care. A lot of artists don't care. For that reason I have never cultivated the friendship of artists. I just don't get along with anybody who doesn't care. That's why I really can't give you information about those who don't. It's just that I can't afford to get to know them very well, and I try to avoid them. Sometimes personal friends become this way. Then there is a mutual rejection of the friendship. From my point of view I am just no longer interested when they adopt that kind of attitude. From their point of view it means completely living outside of society and they are no longer interested in people who they consider hypocrites.

Others openly admit and practice homosexuality. They usually work in occupations where the homosexual is tolerated, withdraw from uncompromising heterosexual groups, and confine most of their social life to homosexual circles. The attitude is expressed in the following statement by a hairdresser:

> Rosenstein can go to hell as far as I care. She works you to the bone if she can get away with it. She told me I run around the place like a regular pansy. So I told her I am a pansy and if she doesn't like it she can get somebody else to do her dirty work for her. I knew she wouldn't fire me. All the ladies ask for me and I don't have to pretend to nobody.

While the problem of evasion is common to all homosexuals, the mechanisms of evasion present various alternatives. Most homosexuals find themselves compelled to conform outwardly to societal demands. They are conscious of their social position within society and seek such satisfactions as occupational mobility and prestige. They endeavor to retain intimate associations within the heterosexual community, and fear recognition as a status threat. Such homosexuals rely upon secrecy and the concealment of their deviant practices. They will therefore be referred to as "secret" homosexuals. A minority retreats from the demands of society and renounces societal goals. Such individuals will be referred to as "overt" homosexuals.

The mode of adaptation is largely dependent upon the extent to which identification as a homosexual is a status threat. While economic status cannot be equated with social status, the individual's position within the work world represents the most significant single factor in the prestige scale. Therefore, the extent to which homosexuality is tolerated in various occupations determines to a great extent the mode of evasion chosen by the homosexual. Thus, there are many occupations, of which the professions are an obvious example, where homosexuals are not tolerated. In other areas, the particular occupation may have traditionally accepted homosexual linkages in the popular image or be of such low rank as to permit homosexuals to function on the job. The artist, the interior decorator, and the hairdresser exemplify the former type; such positions as counter man or bellhop, the latter. Thus we find a rough relationship between form of evasion and occupation. The overt homosexual tends to fit into an occupation of low-status rank; the secret homosexual into an occupation with a relatively high-status rank. The relationship is shown in Table 1.

Distinctions Between the Secret and Overt Groups

The chief distinctions between homosexual groups correspond to the differences in the general modes of evading social controls which homosexuals have developed. Thus, secret and overt homosexuals form distinctive groups.

The distinctions between these groups are maintained by the secret homosexuals who fear identification and refuse to associate with overt homosexuals. This statement by a secret homosexual is illustrative:

If someone who is gay wanted to be spiteful they could say something in the wrong quarter. Nobody who cared about himself would say anything. The trouble is that some don't care. I make it a rule to avoid anybody who is perfectly open about himself. It's easy not to become friendly with those people but it's hard to avoid them entirely. You certainly don't want to snub them because that might make them antagonistic. You just don't call them or see them at social gatherings. But you do meet them at bars and that's where you can be introduced to them. If they remember you and continue to say hello to you on the street, you have to acknowledge them or they might feel that you are trying to snub them.

TABLE 1. OCCUPATION OF 40 SECRET AND OVERT HOMOSEXUALS*

Occupation	Secret†	Overt	Total
Professional and managerial	13	0	13
Clerical and sales	9	4	13
Craftsmen	2	1	3
Operatives	1	1	2
Service	0	6	6
Artists	0	3	3
Totals	25	15	40

* Except for artists the categories and ranking are those established by the National Opinion Research Center. [National Opinion Research Center, *Opinion News* IX (September, 1947), pp. 3–13.] Artists have been listed as a separate category because they often represent a group which is apart from the status structure of the community.

† The secret homosexuals gave the following reasons for concealment: (1) desire to avoid social ridicule—22 cases; (2) fear of dismissal from the job, or where self-employed, inability to get clients—20 cases; (3) a desire to protect others such as family or friends—18 cases.

As a result of this social distance a certain amount of reciprocal hostility has developed between the members of secret and overt groups. This hostility helps maintain the social distance and distinctions between these groups. This is demonstrated in the following statements by an overt and a secret homosexual respectively:

I know some of them because sometimes they stoop down and have an affair with somebody from our gang. They even come to a party over at Robert's once in a while but they never hang around for very long and then you don't see them again. They go over to the Red Room sometimes but we don't have much to say to each other and the same thing happens when we go over to the Burning Flame.[5] We just might

say hello. But sometimes they will cruise us and try to take someone home to bed. I think you could say we mix sexually but not socially.

There are some people who I don't like and I wish these people didn't know about me. Then there are the people I don't know too well: people who are obvious or what I uncharitably call the riff-raff. I have always attempted to avoid them and I avoid them now. It is inevitable that you bump into a lot of people you would rather not know. Homosexuals are very democratic people. To achieve their own ends they overlook a lot they wouldn't overlook in other fields. People are bound to each other like a link of a chain. You try to avoid being a link in this chain by carefully choosing.

This poses serious problems for the homosexual who is socially mobile. He is forced to change his primary group affiliations within the homosexual community.

The following statement by the manager of an appliance shop shows how the homosexual tends to change his orientation from "overt" to "secret" as he becomes upwardly mobile.

My promotions have made me more conscious of the gang I hang around with. You see, for the first time in my life I have a job that I would really like to keep and where I can have a pretty secure future. I realize that if word were to get around that I am gay I would probably lose my job. I don't see why that should be, because I know that I'm the same person gay or not. But still that's the way it works. I don't want to hang around with Robert[6] any more or any of the people who are like Robert. I don't mind seeing them once in a while at somebody's house, but I won't be seen with them on the street any more.

Both types of groups were identified and observed in the course of this research. Each group consisted of fourteen members. The descriptions which follow are based on the study of these groups.

Secret Groups

The secret homosexuals form groups which consist of a loose amalgamation of small cliques. Interaction within the cliques is frequent, with members meeting at each other's homes and in

[5] The Burning Flame refers to a bar which tended to draw its clientele from secret homosexuals; the Red Room was the acknowledged gathering place of overt homosexuals.

[6] Robert is the leader of an overt group of which the respondent was a member at the time he was contacted.

bars and restaurants. The clique structure is a product of the diverse interests and occupations and of the desire to limit homosexual contacts which characterize secret homosexuals. The clique unites its several members in common specialized interests apart from the larger group.

The following chart shows the clique structure and occupational composition of a secret homosexual group.

TABLE 2. THE CLIQUE STRUCTURE AND OCCUPATIONAL COMPOSITION OF A SECRET HOMOSEXUAL GROUP

Clique A	Clique B
Lawyer	Clerk-bookkeeper
Personnel manager	Auditing clerk
University student	Assistant office manager
Economist	University student
	Secretary

Clique C	Clique D
Stenographer	Accountant
Store manager	Interior decorator
Manager of statistical dept.	

A secret homosexual group is generally characterized by: (1) informal standards of admission; (2) discretion in the manner in which homosexuality is practiced; (3) an attempt at concealment; (4) partial rather than complete involvement in the homosexual world.

Overt Groups

Overt homosexuals gather in cohesive social groups which become the dominant focus of their lives. These groups are openly homosexual in character. The members make little effort to conceal their deviation, spend almost all their free time with the group, and tend to regard their other activities as peripheral.

These groups generally draw their members from persons of low socioeconomic status who have jobs where concealment is not a prerequisite. Table 3 presents the occupation composition of the overt group identified in this study.

The members of the group met daily either at a bar, a restaurant, or at the house of the acknowledged leader or "queen."[7] They spent their

TABLE 3. OCCUPATIONAL COMPOSITION OF AN OVERT HOMOSEXUAL GROUP

Occupation	Frequency
Manager of appliance shop*	1
School teacher	1
Hospital attendant	1
Hairdresser	4
Sales clerk	2
Foundry worker	1
Baker	1
Salesman	1
Waiter	1
Cashier	1
Total	14

* This individual had just been promoted and was beginning to leave the group. Both he and the school teacher retained for a time their affiliation with an overt group while at the same time concealing their homosexuality at work.

time in endless gossip about the sexual affairs of the members or other homosexuals known to them. Often they would go to bars and restaurants in the attempt to make a "pick-up," or spend the evening "cruising" individually or in groups of two's and three's.

The queen seems to characterize only "overt" groups. Functionally, the role of the queen is very important in the life of these groups. He provides a place where the group may gather and where its individual members may have their "affairs." He helps finance members in distress, functions as an intermediary in making sexual contacts, partially controls the entrance of new members, and warns the members of hoodlums who would prey upon them. Generally the queen is an older homosexual who has had wide experience in the homosexual world.

The following statement about the queen by a member of the overt group provides insight into the functioning of the queen and tells something of the way in which the individuals relate to him.

A queen really means the leader of the group. You see how that is in a small town where there are not many people who are gay and willing to admit it. She knows who's who and what's what. She will know every gay person in town and will arrange things just the way Roberta does.[8] The queen is always somebody pretty old and pretty much out of the game as far as getting anything

[7] Our data with respect to the prevalence of this role are incomplete. However, homosexuals regularly refer to the queens of other cities, suggesting that the practice is widespread.

[8] The adoption of feminine names is a widespread practice among all homosexuals interviewed.

for herself is concerned. But she doesn't have anything else to do, so she spends all her time on this. I don't know of any queen as commercial as Roberta. But that's because Roberta is so goddam crude. I know the queen in Hillsburg and she was a perfect lady if I ever saw one. She knows everything. She used to make quite a bit but it was always in the form of getting invitations for dinner or as a present. You feel grateful to somebody who does something for you and you pay off. It's like a debt.

Overt groups are characterized by: (1) no particular standards of admission; (2) unselfconscious and unrestrained practice of homosexuality; (3) little or no concealment; (4) high degree of social isolation with little involvement in heterosexual activities; (5) little concern with identification as a status threat or the sanctions of heterosexual society.

The Homosexual Community

The diverse secret and overt homosexuals are linked together either through bonds of sex or of friendship. Within the primary group, the emphasis upon friendship rather than sex serves to eliminate excessive sexual competition and preserves group unity. However, this creates a sexual interdependency upon those outside the group with important social consequences.

In the first place, it forces the secret homosexual out into the open in an attempt to solicit sexual partners. He thus frequents the known homosexual meeting places within the city such as specific bars, hotel lobbies, street corners, and lavatories. These activities make him an increasingly familiar figure within the homosexual world.

Secondly, this solicitation leads to the interaction of secret and overt homosexuals on a sexual as opposed to a social basis. While these contacts occur in a spirit of anonymity, an approach to the other often requires an exchange of confidences.

Thirdly, this sexual interdependency increases the anxiety of secret homosexuals since it forces them to contact the overt ones whom they fear as a threat to their security.

Thus, it is the casual and promiscuous sexual contacts between the members of different categories of evasion (i.e., the secret and the overt) which weld the city's homosexuals into a community.

Conclusion

The homosexual community thus consists of a large number of distinctive groups within which friendships bind the members together in a strong and relatively enduring bond and between which the members are linked by tenuous but repeated sexual contacts. The result is that homosexuals within the city tend to know or know of each other, to recognize a number of common interests and common moral norms, and to interact on the basis of antagonistic cooperation. This community is in turn linked with other homosexual communities in Canada and the United States, chiefly through the geographical mobility of its members.[9]

---

[9] The queen of the overt group studied maintained an address book containing the names of approximately 3,000 homosexuals scattered across North America.

COMING OUT IN THE GAY WORLD
BARRY M. DANK

There is almost no sociological literature on "becoming" homosexual. There is a vast literature on the etiology of homosexuality—that is,

the family background of homosexuals[1]—but little is known concerning how the actor learns

---

Reprinted with permission of the author and by special permission of The William Alanson White Psychiatric Foundations, Inc., from *Psychiatry* 34 (1971), pp. 180–97. Footnotes have been renumbered.

---

[1] See E. Bergler, *Neurotic Counterfeit-Sex* (New York: Grune and Stratton, 1951); Irving Bieber et al., *Homosexuality, A Psychoanalytic Study of Male Homosexuals* (New York: Vintage Books, 1965); Sigmund Freud, *Three Contributions to the Theory of Sex* (New York: Dutton,

that he is a homosexual, how he decides that he is a homosexual. In terms of identity and behavior, this paper is concerned with the transition to a homosexual identity, not in the learning of homosexual behavior per se, or the antecedent or situational conditions that may permit an actor to engage in a homosexual act. One may engage in a homosexual act and think of oneself as being homosexual, heterosexual, or bisexual. One may engage in a heterosexual act and think of oneself as being heterosexual, homosexual, or bisexual, or one may engage in no sexual acts and still have a sexual identity of heterosexual, homosexual, or bisexual. This study is directed toward determining what conditions permit a person to say, "I am a homosexual."[2]

RESEARCH METHOD

This report is part of a study that has been ongoing for over two years in a large metropolitan area in the United States. The analysis is based on data obtained from lengthy interviews with 55 self-admitted homosexuals, on observations of and conversations with hundreds of homosexuals, and on the results of a one-page questionnaire distributed to 300 self-admitted homosexuals attending a meeting of a homophile organization. The statistical data are based on the 182 questionnaires that were returned.

The 4 to 5-hour interviews with the 55 self-

admitted homosexuals were generally conducted in the subject's home, and in the context of a "participant-observation" study in which the researcher as researcher became integrated into friendship networks of homosexuals. The researcher was introduced to this group by a homosexual student who presented him correctly as being a heterosexual who was interested in doing a study of homosexuals as they exist in the "outside world." He was able to gain the trust of the most prestigious person in the group, which enabled him, on the whole, to gain the trust of the rest of the group. The guidelines employed in the study were based on those outlined by Polsky for participant-observation studies.

There is no way of determining whether the sample groups studied here, or any similar sample, would be representative of the homosexual population. Thus it remains problematic whether the findings of this study can be applied to the homosexual population in general or to other samples of homosexuals.[3] Since age is a critical variable in this study, the questionnaire sample was used in the hope that the replies to a questionnaire would represent a fairly wide age range. The age distribution of the questionnaire sample is shown in Table 1.

COMING OUT

The term "coming out" is frequently used by homosexuals to refer to the identity change to homosexual. Hooker states: "Very often, the debut, referred to by homosexuals as the coming out, of a person who believes himself to be homosexual but who has struggled against it will occur when he identifies himself publicly for the first time as a homosexual in the presence of other homosexuals by his appearance in a bar."[4] Gagnon and Simon refer to coming out as that

1962); Paul Gebhard et al., *Sex Offenders, Analysis of Types* (New York: Hoeber-Harper, 1965); Evelyn Hooker, "Parental Relations and Male Homosexuality in Patient and Non-Patient Samples," *Journal of Consulting and Clinical Psychology* 33 (1969), pp. 140–42; A. M. Krich, ed., *The Homosexuals* (New York: Citadel Press, 1965); Lionel Ovesey, *Homosexuality and Pseudohomosexuality* (New York: Science House, 1969); Hendrick Ruitenbeck, ed., *The Problem of Homosexuality in Modern Society* (New York: Dutton, 1963); Michael Schofield, *Sociological Aspects of Homosexuality* (New York: Little, Brown, 1965); Donald J. West, "Parental Figures in the Genesis of Male Homosexuality," *International Journal of Social Psychiatry* 5 (1969), 85–97; and Gordon Westwood, *A Minority: A Report on the Life of the Male Homosexual in Great Britain* (London: Longmans Green, 1960).
[2] It should also be pointed out that from the subjective viewpoint of the actor, it becomes problematic exactly at which point a "homosexual" act should be viewed as such. A male actor may have a sexual contact with another male but fantasize during the sexual act either that the other male is a female or that he himself is a female; in either case he may view the act as being heterosexual. Or a male actor may have a sexual contact with a female, but fantasize the female as being a male or himself as being a female; in such a case he might view the act as being homosexual. Robert Stoller, *Sex and Gender* (New York: Science House, 1968).

[3] In addition, it should be pointed out that the sample employed may be skewed in an unknown direction since the questionnaire response rate was approximately 60 percent. In the interview sample, the researcher received excellent cooperation from both those who viewed themselves as being psychologically well-adjusted and those who did not; those more reluctant to participate tended to occupy high socioeconomic positions.
[4] Evelyn Hooker, "Male Homosexuals and Their 'Worlds,'" in Judd Marmor, ed., *Sexual Inversion: The Multiple Roots of Homosexuality* (New York: Basic Books, 1965), p. 99.

"... point in time when there is self-recognition by the individual of his identity as a homosexual and the first major exploration of the homosexual community."[5]

In this study it was found that the meaning that the informant attached to this expression was usually directly related to his own experiences concerning how he met other gay[6] people and how and when he decided he was homosexual. For purposes of this study the term "coming out" will mean identifying oneself as being homosexual.[7] This self-identification as being homosexual may or may not occur in a social context in which other gay people are present. One of the tasks of this paper is to identify the social contexts in which the self-definition of homosexual occurs.

THE SOCIAL CONTEXTS OF COMING OUT

The child who is eventually to become homosexual in no sense goes through a period of anticipatory socialization;[8] if he does go through such a period, it is in reference to heterosexuality, not homosexuality. It is sometimes said that the homosexual minority is just like any other minority group;[9] but in the sense of early childhood socialization it is not, for the parents of a Negro can communicate to their child that he is a Negro and what it is like to be a Negro, but the parents of a person who is to become homosexual do not prepare their child to be homosexual—they are not homosexual themselves,

and they do not communicate to him what it is like to be a homosexual.[10]

The person who has sexual feelings or desires toward persons of the same sex has no vocabulary to explain to himself what these feelings mean. Subjects who had homosexual feelings during childhood were asked how they would have honestly responded to the question, "Are you a homosexual?" at the time just prior to their graduation from high school. Some typical responses follow:

> SUBJECT 1: I had guilt feelings about this being attracted to men. Because I couldn't understand why all the other boys were dating, and I didn't have any real desire to date.
> INTERVIEWER: Were you thinking of yourself as homosexual?
> SUBJECT 1: I think I did but I didn't know how to put it into words. I didn't know it existed. I guess I was like everybody else and thought I was the only one in the world. . . . I probably would have said I didn't know. I don't think I really knew what one was. I would have probably asked you to explain what one was.

> SUBJECT 2: I would have said, "No. I don't know what you are talking about." If you had said "queer," I would have thought something about it; this was the slang term that was used, although I didn't know what the term meant.

> SUBJECT 3: I don't think I would have known then. I know now. Then I wasn't even thinking about the word. I wasn't reading up on it.

Respondents were asked the age at which they first became aware of any desire or sexual feeling toward persons of the same sex; subsequently they were asked when they decided they were homosexual. Results are presented in Table 1. On the average, there was a six-year interval

---

[5] John H. Gagnon and William Simon, "Homosexuality: the Formulation of a Sociological Perspective," in Mark Lefton et al., eds., *Approaches to Deviance* (New York: Appleton-Century-Crofts, 1968), p. 356.

[6] In homosexual argot, "gay" means homosexual and "straight" means heterosexual. These terms are acceptable to homosexuals whether used by gay or straight persons.

[7] Sometimes homosexuals use the expression "to bring out" or "bringing out." The meaning attached to these expressions varies; they are sometimes used interchangeably with "coming out." However, as used by my informants, they usually refer to the first complete homosexual act which the subject found enjoyable. The statement, "He brought me out," usually means, "He taught me to enjoy real homosexual acts."

[8] Robert K. Merton, *Social Theory and Social Structure*, rev. ed. (New York: Free Press of Glencoe, 1957).

[9] Donald W. Cory, *The Homosexual in America* (New York: Greenberg, 1951), and Westwood, *A Minority*.

[10] Some homosexuals are parents. In the homosexual social networks that I am involved in, there are many persons who once played the role of husband and father—generally before they decided they were homosexual. In addition, there are homosexual couples who are raising children they adopted or children from a former heterosexual marriage; however, such couples tend to be lesbian. In some cases one parent has decided that he or she is homosexual, but both parents have remained together as husband and wife. "Front" marriages also occur, in which a male homosexual marries a female homosexual and they adopt children or have children of their own; such marriages are generally for purposes of social convenience. What the effects are, if any, of being raised by at least one homosexual parent have not been determined. In this sample, there were no cases in which a subject had a homosexual mother or father.

TABLE 1. AGE CHARACTERISTICS OF SAMPLE

Age	Age Distribution		Age of First Sexual Desire Toward Same Sex		Age at Which Decision Was Made That Respondent Was a Homosexual	
	N	(%)	N	(%)	N	(%)
0–4	0	(0)	1	(0.5)	0	(0)
5–9	0	(0)	28	(15)	1	(0.5)
10–14	0	(0)	83	(46)	27	(15)
15–19	13	(7)	54	(29)	79	(44)
20–24	36	(20)	14	(8)	52	(29)
25–29	39	(22)	1	(0.5)	11	(6)
30–34	28	(16)	1	(0.5)	4	(2)
35–39	21	(12)	0	(0)	3	(2)
40–44	18	(10)	0	(0)	1	(0.5)
45–49	6	(3)	0	(0)	0	(0)
50–59	11	(6)	0	(0)	0	(0)
60–69	8	(4)	0	(0)	1	(0.5)
Total	180	(100)	182	(99.5)	179	(99.5)
	$\bar{X} = 32.5, S = 11.3$		$\bar{X} = 13.5, S = 4.3$		$\bar{X} = 19.3, S = 6.4$	

between time of first sexual feeling toward persons of the same sex and the decision that one was a homosexual. The distribution of the differing time intervals between a person's awareness of homosexual feelings and the decision that he is homosexual is presented in Table 2. As Table 2 indicates, there is considerable variation in this factor.[11]

The fact that an actor continues to have homosexual feelings and to engage in homosexual behavior does not mean that he views himself as being homosexual. In order for a person to view himself as homosexual he must be placed in a new social context, in which knowledge of homosexuals and homosexuality can be found; in such a context he learns a new vocabulary of motives, a vocabulary that will allow him to identify himself as being a homosexual. This can occur in any number of social contexts—through

meeting self-admitted homosexuals, by meeting knowledgeable straight persons, or by reading about homosexuals and homosexuality. Knowledge of homosexuals and homosexuality can be found in numerous types of physical settings: a bar, a park, a private home, a psychiatrist's office, a mental hospital, and so on (see Table 3). It is in contexts where such knowledge tends to be concentrated that the actor will be most likely to come out. It is therefore to be expected that an actor is likely to come out in a context in

TABLE 2. TIME INTERVAL BETWEEN FIRST HOMOSEXUAL DESIRE AND THE DECISION THAT ONE IS A HOMOSEXUAL

Time Interval (years)	Distribution	
	N	%
0	29	(16)
1–4	66	(37)
5–9	49	(27)
10–14	21	(12)
15–19	7	(4)
20–29	5	(3)
30–39	1	(0.5)
40–49	0	(0)
50–59	1	(0.5)
Total	179	(100)
	$\bar{X} = 5.7, S = 6.4$	

[11] First sexual desire toward persons of the same sex was chosen instead of first sexual contact with persons of the same sex since it is quite possible for one to have homosexual desires, fight against those desires, and have no homosexual contacts of any type for an extensive period of time. The mean age of first homosexual contact of any type was 13, which was not significantly different at the .01 level from age of first homosexual desire. In reference to which came first, homosexual act or homosexual desire, 31 percent (56) had desire before the act; 49 percent (87) had act before desire; 20 percent (36) had first homosexual desire and first homosexual act at approximately the same time.

which other gay people are present; they are usually a ready and willing source of knowledge concerning homosexuals and homosexuality. In the questionnaire sample, 50 percent came out while associating with gay people.

It is also to be expected that a likely place for an actor to come out would be in one-sex situations or institutions. Sexually segregated environments provide convenient locales for knowledge of homosexuality and homosexual behavior. Examples of these one-sex environments are mental institutions, YMCAs, prisons, the military, men's rooms, gay bars, and school dormitories. The first six case histories below illustrate the influence of such milieux.

TABLE 3. SOCIAL CONTEXTS IN WHICH RESPONDENTS CAME OUT

Social Contexts	N*	(%)
Frequenting gay bars	35	(19)
Frequenting gay parties and other gatherings	46	(26)
Frequenting parks	43	(24)
Frequenting men's rooms	37	(21)
Having a love affair with a homosexual man	54	(30)
Having a love affair with a heterosexual man	21	(12)
In the military	34	(19)
Living in a YMCA	2	(1)
Living in all-male quarters at a boarding school or college	12	(7)
In prison	2	(1)
Patient in a mental hospital	3	(2)
Seeing a psychiatrist or professional counselor	11	(6)
Read for the first time about homosexuals and/or homosexuality	27	(15)
Just fired from a job because of homosexual behavior	2	(1)
Just arrested on a charge involving homosexuality	7	(4)
Was not having any homosexual relations	36	(20)

* Total N of social contexts is greater than 180 (number of respondents) because there was overlap in contexts.

The first example of an actor coming out in the context of interacting with gay persons concerns a subject who came out in a mental hospital. The subject was committed to a mental hospital at age 20; his commitment did not in-

volve homosexuality and the hospital authorities had no knowledge that the subject had a history of homosexual behavior. Prior to commitment he had a history of heterosexual and homosexual behavior, thought of himself as bisexual, had had no contact with self-admitted homosexuals, was engaged to marry, and was indulging in heavy petting with his fiancée. In the following interview excerpt the subject reports on his first reaction to meeting gay persons in the hospital:

SUBJECT: I didn't know there were so many gay people, and I wasn't use to the actions of gay people or anything, and it was quite shocking walking down the halls, going up to the ward, and the whistles and flirting and everything else that went on with the new fish, as they called it.

And there was this one kid who was a patient escort and he asked me if I was interested in going to church, and I said yes ... and he started escorting me to church and then he pulled a little sneaky to see whether I'd be shocked at him being gay. There was this queen[12] on the ward, and him and her, he was looking out the hall to see when I'd walk by the door and they kissed when I walked by the door and this was to check my reaction. And I didn't say a word. So he then escorted me to the show, and we were sitting there and about half-way through the movie he reaches over and started holding my hand, and when he saw I didn't jerk away, which I was kind of upset and wondering exactly what he had in mind, and then when we got back to the ward, he wrote me a long love letter and gave it to me; before we knew it we were going together, and went together for about six months.

[After 3 weeks] he had gotten me to the point where I'd gotten around the hospital, where I picked up things from the other queens and learned how to really swish and carry on and got to be one of the most popular queens in the whole place. [About that same time] I'd gotten to consider myself—I didn't consider myself a queen. I just considered myself a gay boy; we sat down, a bunch of us got together and made out the rules about what was what as far as the joint was concerned, drew definitions of every little thing ... if someone was completely feminine, wanted to take the female role all the time, then they were a "queen," if they were feminine but butchy, then they were a "nellie-butch," and I was considered a "gay boy" because I could take any role, I was versatile.

INTERVIEWER: Before this bull session were you considering yourself gay?

[12] In gay argot, the meaning of the term "queen" is variable. Depending on the context, it can mean any homosexual or a homosexual on the female side.

SUBJECT: Yes, I had definitely gotten to be by this time; after three months my folks came down to see me and I told them the whole thing point blank.

INTERVIEWER: What would you say was the most important effect the hospital had on you?

SUBJECT: It let me find out it wasn't so terrible. . . . I met a lot of gay people that I liked and I figured it can't be all wrong. If so and so's a good Joe, and he's still gay, he can't be all that bad. . . . I figured it couldn't be all wrong, and that's one of the things I learned. I learned to accept myself for what I am—homosexual.

This subject spent a year and a half in the mental hospital. After release he did not engage in heterosexual relations, and has been actively involved in the gay subculture for the past four years.

The above example clearly demonstrates how a one-sex environment can facilitate the development of a homosexual identity. Although some one-sex environments are created for homosexuals, such as gay bars, any one-sex environment can serve as a meeting and recruiting place for homosexuals, whether or not the environment was created with that purpose in mind.

The YMCA is a one-sex environment that inadvertently functions as a meeting place for homosexuals in most large urban areas in the United States.[13] The following subject came out while living and working at a YMCA. He was 24 when he first visited a Y, never had had a homosexual experience, and had just been separated from his wife.

I became separated from my wife. I then decided to go to Eastern City. I had read of the Walter Jenkins case and the name of the YMCA happened to come up, but when I got to the city it was the only place I knew of to stay. I had just $15.00 in my pocket to stay at the Y, and I don't think I ever had the experience before of taking a group shower. So I went into the shower room, that was the first time I remember looking at a man's body and finding it sexually enticing.[14] So I started wondering to myself—that guy is good-looking. I walked back to my room and left the door open and the guy came in, and I happened to fall in love with that guy.

After this first experience, the subject became homosexually active while living and working at the Y and became part of the gay subculture that existed within the Y.

I found that the kids who were working for me, some of them I had been to bed with and some of them I hadn't, had some horrible problems and trying to decide the right and wrong of homosexuality . . . and they would feel blunt enough or that I had the experience enough to counsel them along the lines of homosexuality or anything else. . . . Part of this helped me realize that one of the greatest things that you can do is to accept what you are and if you want to change it, you can go ahead and do it. . . .

This subject spent six months living in this Y; by the end of three months he had accepted himself as being homosexual and has been exclusively homosexual for the last two years.

The prison is another one-sex environment in which homosexual behavior is concentrated. Although there have been studies of situational homosexuality in prison[15] and of how homosexual activities are structured in prison, there have been no studies that have looked at the possible change of the sexual identity of the prisoner. In the following case the subject was sentenced to prison on a charge of sodomy at the age of 32, and spent five years in prison. He had been homosexually active for 22 years, and before his arrest he had been engaging predominantly in homosexual behavior, but he had not defined himself as being a homosexual. He had had only peripheral contacts with the gay subculture before his arrest, largely because he was married and held a high socioeconomic position.

INTERVIEWER: In prison did you meet homosexuals?

SUBJECT: Yes.

INTERVIEWER: I'm not talking about people who are just homosexual while in prison.

---

[13] YMCAs have not been studied in their relation to homosexual society. It appears that YMCAs function as meeting places for homosexuals and for those desiring homosexual relations but defining themselves as straight. This is not a regional phenomenon but is, according to my informants, true for almost all YMCAs in large metropolitan areas. YMCAs are often listed in gay tourist guides.

[14] This subject later admitted that he had previously been attracted to other males.

[15] Rose Giallombardo, *Society of Women, An Analysis of Types* (New York: Hoeber-Harper, 1965); Gresham M. Sykes, *Society of Captives* (Princeton: Princeton University Press, 1958); Charles R. Tittle, "Inmate Organization: Sex Differentiation and the Influence of Criminal Subcultures," *American Sociological Review* 34 (1969), pp. 492–05; and David A. Ward and Gene G. Kassebaum, *Women's Prisons: Sex and Social Structure* (Chicago: Aldine, 1965). [See also pp. 247–54 of this volume.]

SUBJECT: People who are homosexual, period. I became educated about the gay world, how you can meet people and not lay yourself open to censure, and how to keep from going to prison again. And still go on being homosexual. While in prison I definitely accepted myself as being homosexual. . . . I had frequent meetings with psychiatrists, various social workers. We were all pretty much in tacit agreement that the best thing to do would be to learn to live with yourself. Up until then, I rationalized and disillusioned myself about a lot of things. As I look back on it, I was probably homosexual from ten years on.

After his release from prison, this subject became involved in the gay subculture and has been exclusively homosexual for the last eight years.

The military is a one-sex environment that is a most conducive setting for homosexual behavior. In the military, a large number of young men live in close contact with one another and are deprived of heterosexual contacts for varying periods of time; it is not surprising that a homosexual subculture would arise. Given the young age of the military population, it should also be expected that a certain proportion of men would be entering military service with homosexual desires and/or a history of homosexual behavior, but without a clearly formulated homosexual identity. Approximately 19 percent of the sample came out while in military service. The following subject had a history of homosexual desires and behavior previous to joining the Navy, but came out while in military service.

INTERVIEWER: How did you happen to have homosexual relations while in the Navy?
SUBJECT: We were out at sea and I had heard that one of the dental technicians was a homosexual, and he had made advances toward me, and I felt like masturbation really wouldn't solve the problem so I visited him one night. He started talking about sex and everything. I told him I had never kissed a boy before. And he asked me what would you do if a guy kissed you, and I said you mean like this and I began kissing him. Naturally he took over then. . . . There were other people on the ship that were homosexual and they talked about me. A yeoman aboard ship liked me quite a bit, was attracted to me; so he started making advances toward me, and I found him attractive, so we got together, and in a short period of time, we became lovers. He started to take me to the gay bars and explain what homosexuality was all about. He took me to gay bars when we were in port.

INTERVIEWER: Did you start to meet other gay people aboard ship?
SUBJECT: The first real contact with gay people was aboard ship. . . .
INTERVIEWER: Was it while you were in the Navy that you decided you were a homosexual?
SUBJECT: Yes. Once I was introduced to gay life, I made the decision that I was a homosexual.

Public restrooms, another part of society which is sexually segregated, are known in the gay world as T-rooms, and some T-rooms become known as meeting places for gay persons and others who are looking for homosexual contacts.[16] Sex in T-rooms tends to be anonymous, but since some nonsexual social interaction also occurs in this locale, some homosexuals do come out in T-rooms. In the sample studied here 21 percent came out while frequenting T-rooms for sexual purposes. The following subject came out in the context of going to T-rooms when he was 15. Previously he had been homosexually active, but had not thought of himself as being a homosexual.

I really didn't know what a homosexual was. In the back of my mind, my definition of a homosexual or queer was someone who wore girls' clothes and women's shoes, 'cause my brothers said this was so, and I knew I wasn't.

At the age of 15 this subject had a sexual relationship with a gay man.

And he took me out and introduced me to the gay world. I opened the door and I went out and it was a beautiful day and I accepted this whole world, and I've never had any guilt feelings or hang-ups or regrets. . . . I was young and fairly attractive and I had men chasing me all the time. . . . He didn't take me to bars. We went to restrooms, that was my outlet. He started taking me to all the places they refer to in the gay world as T-rooms, and I met other people and I went back there myself and so on.

After meeting other gay persons by going to T-rooms, this subject quickly discovered other segments of the gay world and has been exclusively homosexual for the last nine years.

Gay bars are probably the most widespread

---

[16] Laud Humphreys, *Tearoom Trade* (Chicago: Aldine, 1970).

and well-known gay institutions.[17] For many persons who become homosexual, gay bars are the first contact with organized gay society and therefore a likely place to come out. In this sample 19 percent came out while going to gay bars. Since gay bars apparently are widespread throughout the nation, this could be viewed as a surprisingly low percentage. However, it should be remembered that generally the legal age limit for entering bars is 21. If the age limit is enforced, this would reduce the percentage of persons coming out in gay bars. T-rooms and gay private parties and other gatherings perform the same function as gay bars, but are not hampered by any age limit. Thus, it is not really surprising that the percentages of persons who came out in several other ways are higher than the percentage coming out in gay bars.

The following subject came out in the context of going to gay bars. He had been predominantly homosexual for a number of years and was 23 at the time he came out.

> SUBJECT: I knew that there were homosexuals, queers and what not; I had read some books, and I was resigned to the fact that I was a foul, dirty person, but I wasn't actually calling myself a homosexual yet. . . . I went to this guy's house and there was nothing going on, and I asked him, 'Where is some action?" and he said, "There is a bar down the way." And the time I really caught myself coming out is the time I walked into this bar and saw a whole crowd of groovy, groovy guys. And I said to myself, there was the realization, that not all gay men are dirty old men or idiots, silly queens, but there are some just normal looking and acting people, as far as I could see. I saw gay society and I said, "Wow, I'm home."
> INTERVIEWER: This was the first time that you walked into this gay bar that you felt this way?
> SUBJECT: That's right. It was that night in the bar. I think it saved my sanity. I'm sure it saved my sanity.

This subject has been exclusively homosexually active for the last 13 years.

Even after an introduction to gay bars, labeling oneself as homosexual does not always occur as rapidly as it did in the previous example.

Some persons can still, for varying periods of time, differentiate themselves from the people they are meeting in gay bars. The following subject came out when he was 22; he had been predominantly homosexual before coming out. He interacted with gay people in gay bars for several months before he decided he was a homosexual. He attempted to differentiate himself from the other homosexuals by saying to himself, "I am not really homosexual since I am not as feminine as they are."

> Finally after hanging around there for so long, some guy came up to me and tried to take me for some money, and I knew it, and he said, "You know, you're very nellie."[18] And I said I wasn't, and he said, "Yes, you are, and you might as well face facts and that's the way it is, and you're never going to change." And I said, "If that's the case, then that's the way it's going to be." So I finally capitulated.

This subject has been predominantly homosexually active for the last 21 years.

It should be made clear that such a change in sexual identity need not be accompanied by any change in sexual behavior or any participation in homosexual behavior. It is theoretically possible for someone to view himself as being homosexual but not engage in homosexual relations just as it is possible for someone to view himself as heterosexual but not engage in heterosexual relations. Approximately 20 percent of this sample came out while having no homosexual relations. The following subject is one of this group; he came out during his late twenties even though he had had his last homosexual experience at age 20.

> I picked up a copy of this underground newspaper one day just for the fun of it . . . and I saw an ad in there for this theatre, and after thinking about it I got up enough nerve to go over there. . . . I knew that they had pictures of boys and I had always liked boys, and I looked at the neighborhood and then I came home without going in. . . . I went back to the neighborhood again and this time I slunk, and I do mean slunk through the door . . . and I was shocked to see what I saw on the screen, but I found it interesting and stimulating and so I went back several more times.

---

[17] Nancy Achilles, "The Development of the Homosexual Bar as an Institution," in John H. Gagnon and William Simon, eds., *Sexual Deviance* (New York: Harper and Row, 1967), and Hooker, "Male Homosexuals and Their 'Worlds'."

---

[18] In gay argot, "nellie" means feminine or feminine-appearing. The word is not usually used in a complimentary manner.

Eventually this subject bought a copy of a gay publication, and subsequently he went to the publication's office.

> I visited with the fellows in the office and I had time on my hands and I volunteered to help and they were glad to have me. And I have been a member of the staff ever since and it was that way that I got my education of what gay life is like.... For the last ten years, I had been struggling against it. Back then if I knew what homosexuality was, if I had been exposed to the community ... and seen the better parts, I probably would have admitted it then.

This subject has been very active socially but not sexually in the gay subculture for the last year.

In contrast to the previous examples, there are cases in which the subject has no direct contact with any gay persons, but yet comes out in that context. Fifteen percent (27) of the sample came out upon first reading about homosexuals or homosexuality in a book, pamphlet, etc.; 10 of these (about 6 percent of the sample) were not associating with gay people at the time they came out. The following subject came out in this context. He was 14 at the time, had just ended a homosexual relationship with a person who considered himself to be straight, and had had no contact with gay society.

> I had always heard like kids do about homosexuals and things, but that never really entered my mind, but when I read this article, when I was in the 8th grade, and it had everything in it about them sexually, not how they looked and acted and where they go. It was about me and that was what I was thinking. I just happen one day to see a picture of a guy and thought he was kind of cute, so I'll read the article about him. But before that I didn't realize what was happening. I didn't even realize I wasn't right as far as heterosexuals were concerned. I didn't realize that what I was thinking wasn't kosher.... If people don't like it I'll keep my mouth shut. The article said people wouldn't like it, so I decided to keep my mouth shut. That's the way I was, so I accepted it.

This subject has been active sexually and socially in the gay subculture for the last five years.

Another context in which a subject can come out is that of having a homosexual relationship with a person who defines himself as being heterosexual; 12 percent (21) of the sample came

out in such a context. Of these, 12 (about 7 percent of the sample) had never met any self-admitted homosexuals and had never read any material on homosexuality. The following case involves a subject who came out in such a context. At the age of 21 he was having an intense love affair with a serviceman who defined himself as straight. The subject also became involved in a triangular relationship with the serviceman's female lover.

> This got very serious. I told him I loved him.... He wanted me for a sex release; I didn't admit it then, but now I see, through much heartbreak. He liked me as a person.... At the same time he was dating a married woman; he was dating her and having sex with her.... She couldn't admit to having a relationship with him 'cause she was married, but he told me and I was extremely jealous of her. [We worked together] and privately she was a very good friend of mine. So I started feeling hatred toward her because she was coming between he and I, competition. I was strong competition, 'cause I frankly dominated it, and she sensed this; so one day she said, "I bet he'd be very good in bed." So I said, "You know he is." She said, "What did you say?" and I said, "Oh, I guess he would be." And I wanted to tell her; so I finally acted like I just broke down and I told her everything in order to make her not like him. So she got on his tail and told him to stop seeing me or she wouldn't have anything to do with him.... I taped all their phone conversations and told her if she wouldn't leave him alone, I'd play them for her husband. She got furious, so she said if I tried to blackmail her she would go to the police with the whole thing ... it all backfired on me and I really didn't want to hurt her, but my love for him was so strong; I'd hurt anybody to keep him, so I erased the tape. And later I bawled and bawled and cried about it to her because I was very sensitive at this time and I told her I was sorry, didn't want to hurt her, but I loved him so much.... After I fell in love with him I knew I was homosexual. I talked to my brother about it and he said I wasn't really in love. He said you're just doing it cause you want to; it's not right, boys don't fall in love with boys. He wasn't nasty about it.... I really loved him; he was my first love; I even dream about him once in a while to this very day.... It was during this time that I came out, and I was extremely feminine, not masculine in any way. I wore male clothing, but dressed in a feminine way, in the way I carried myself, the way I spoke.... I realized that I was homosexual because I loved him. I was afraid of gay people; heard they did all kinds of weird things from straight people talking about them.

Before this relationship, the subject had engaged in both homosexual and heterosexual petting. Shortly after the relationship terminated the subject became involved in the gay subculture and has been almost exclusively homosexual since that time.

COGNITIVE CHANGE

What is common to all the cases discussed is that the subject placed himself in a new cognitive category,[19] the category of homosexual. In some cases, such placement can occur as soon as the person learns of the existence of the category; an example of this is the boy who placed himself in that category after reading about homosexuals in a magazine. However, probably most persons who eventually identify themselves as homosexuals require a change in the meaning of the cognitive category *homosexual* before they can place themselves in the category.

The meaning of the category must be changed because the subject has learned the negative stereotype of the homosexual held by most heterosexuals, and he knows that he is no queer, pervert, dirty old man, and so on.[20] He differentiates himself from the homosexual image that straight society has presented to him. Direct or indirect contact with the gay subculture provides the subject with information about homosexuals that will challenge the "straight" image of the homosexual. The subject will quite often see himself in other homosexuals, homosexuals he finds to be socially acceptable. He now knows who and what he is because the meaning of the cognitive category has changed to include himself. As one subject said: "Wow, I'm home"; at times that is literally the case since the homosexual now feels that he knows where he really belongs.

A person's identification of himself as being homosexual is often accompanied by a sense of relief, of freedom from tension. In the words of one subject:

I had this feeling of relief; there was no more tension. I had this feeling of relief. I guess the fact that I had accepted myself as being homosexual had taken a lot of tensions off me.

Coming out, in essence, often signifies to the subject the end of a search for his identity.

IDENTIFICATION AND SELF-ACCEPTANCE

Identifying oneself as being homosexual and accepting oneself as being homosexual usually come together, but this is not necessarily the case. It can be hypothesized that those who identify themselves as being homosexual, but not in the context of interacting with other homosexuals, are more likely to have guilt feelings than those who identify themselves as being homosexual in the context of interacting with other homosexuals. Interaction with other homosexuals facilitates the learning of a vocabulary that will not simply explain but will also justify the homosexual behavior.

Identifying oneself as homosexual is almost uniformly accompanied by the development of certain techniques of neutralization.[21] In this self-identification, it would be incorrect to state that the homosexual accepts himself as being deviant, in the evaluative sense of the term. The subject may know he is deviant from the societal standpoint but often does not accept this as part of his self-definition. Lemert has defined secondary deviation as the situation in which "a person begins to employ his deviant behavior or a role based upon it as a means of defense, attack or adjustment to the overt and covert problems created by the consequent societal reaction to him."[22] Once the subject identifies himself as being homosexual, he does develop means, often in the process of the change in self-definition, of adjusting to the societal reaction to the behavior. The means employed usually involve the denial, to himself and to others, that he is really deviant. Becker explained the situation when he stated:

[19] C. J. McCall and J. L. Simmons, *Identities and Interactions* (New York: Free Press of Glencoe, 1966).
[20] J. L. Simmons, "Public Stereotypes of Deviants," *Social Problems* 13 (1965), pp. 223–32.
[21] Gresham M. Sykes and David Matza, "Techniques of Neutralization: A Theory of Delinquency," *American Sociological Review* 22 (1957), pp. 664–70.
[22] Edwin Lemert, *Social Pathology* (New York: McGraw-Hill, 1951).

But the person thus labeled an outsider may have a different view of the matter. He may not accept the rule by which he is being judged and may not regard those who judge him as either competent or legitimately entitled to do so.[23]

The societal reaction to homosexuality appears to be expressed more in a mental health rhetoric[24] than in a rhetoric of sin and evil or crime and criminal behavior. In order to determine how the subjects adjusted to this societal reaction to homosexuality, they were asked to react to the idea that homosexuals are sick or mentally ill. With very few exceptions, this notion was rejected.

SUBJECT 1: I believe this idea to be very much true, if added that you are talking from society's standpoint and society has to ask itself why are these people sick or mentally ill.... In other words, you can't make flat statements that homosexuals are sick or mentally ill. I do not consider myself to be sick or mentally imbalanced.

SUBJECT 2: That's a result of ignorance; people say that quickly, pass quick judgments. They are not knowledgeable, fully knowledgeable about the situation.

SUBJECT 3: I don't feel they are. I feel it's normal. What's normal for one person is not always normal for another. I don't think it's a mental illness or mental disturbance.

SUBJECT 4: Being a homosexual does not label a person as sick or mentally ill. In every other capacity I am as normal or more normal than straight people. Just because I happen to like strawberry ice cream and they like vanilla, doesn't make them right or me right.

It is the learning of various ideas from other homosexuals that allows the subject to in effect say, "I am homosexual, but not deviant," or, "I am homosexual, but not mentally ill." The cognitive category of *homosexual* now becomes socially acceptable, and the subject can place himself in that category and yet preserve a sense of his self-esteem or self-worth.

It should be emphasized that coming out often involves an entire transformation in the meaning of the concept of homosexual for the subject. In each of these cases the subject had been entirely unaware of the existence of gay bars or an organized gay society, of economically successful homosexuals, of homosexually "married" homosexuals, and so on. In the words of one subject:

I had always thought of them as dirty old men that preyed on 10, 11, 12-year-old kids, and I found out that they weren't all that way; there are some that are, but they are a minority. It was a relief for me 'cause I found out that I wasn't so different from many other people. I had considered consulting professional help prior to that 'cause at the time I thought I was mentally ill. Now I accept it as a way of life, and I don't consider it a mental illness. It's an unfortunate situation.... I consider myself an outcast from general society, but not mentally ill.

PUBLIC LABELING

It should be made clear that the self-identification as a homosexual does not generally take place in the context of a negative public labeling, as some labeling theorists imply that it does.[25] No cases were found in the interview sample in which the subject had come out in the context of being arrested on a charge involving homosexuality or being fired from a job because of homosexual behavior. In the questionnaire sample, 4 percent (7) had just been arrested and 1 percent (2) had just been fired from a job. A total of 8 respondents or 4.5 percent of the sample came out in the context of public exposure.

It can be hypothesized that the public labeling of an actor who has not yet identified himself as being homosexual will reinforce in his mind the idea that he is not homosexual. This is hypothesized because it is to be expected that at the time of the public labeling the actor will be presented with information that will present homosexuals and homosexuality in a highly negative manner. For example, the following subject was arrested for homosexual activities at the age of 11. Both before and after the arrest he did

---

[23] Howard S. Becker, *Outsiders: Studies in the Sociology of Deviance* (New York: Free Press of Glencoe, 1963), pp. 1-2.

[24] Bieber et al., *Homosexuality;* Samuel B. Hadden, "A Way Out for Homosexuals," *Harper's Magazine,* March, 1967, pp. 107-20; Ovesey, *Homosexuality and Pseudohomosexuality;* Charles W. Socarides, "Homosexuality and Medicine," *Journal of American Medical Association* 212 (1970), pp. 1199-1202; and Thomas Szasz, *The Manufacture of Madness* (New York: Harper and Row, 1970).

[25] Harold Garfinkle, "Conditions of Successful Degradation Ceremonies," *American Journal of Sociology* 61 (1956), pp. 420-24; Lemert, *Social Pathology;* and Thomas Scheff, *Being Mentally Ill* (Chicago: Aldine, 1966).

not consider himself to be a homosexual. His reaction to the arrest was:

> SUBJECT: The officer talked to me and told me I should see a psychiatrist. It kind of confused me. I really didn't understand any of it.
> INTERVIEWER: And were you thinking of yourself at that time as a homosexual?
> SUBJECT: I probably would have said I wasn't. 'Cause of the way the officer who interrogated me acted. It was something you never admit to. He acted as if I were the scum of the earth. He was very rude and impolite.

If the actor has not yet identified himself as being homosexual, it can probably be assumed that to a significant degree he already accepts the negative societal stereotype; the new information accompanying the public labeling will conform to the societal stereotype, and the actor consequently will not modify his decision not to place himself in the homosexual category. This is not to say that public labeling by significant others and/or official agents of social control does not play a significant role in the life of the homosexual; all that is hypothesized is that public labeling does not facilitate and may in fact function to inhibit the decision to label oneself as being homosexual.

THE CLOSET QUEEN

There are some persons who may continue to have homosexual desires and may possibly engage in homosexual relations for many years, but yet do not have a homosexual identity. Self-admitted homosexuals refer to such persons as "closet queens."[26] Such persons may go for many years without any contact with or knowledge of self-admitted homosexuals. The subject previously cited who came out in prison was a closet queen for 20 years.

An interval of 10 or more years between first awareness of sexual attraction toward males and the decision that one is a homosexual, would probably classify one as having been a closet

queen. As Table 2 shows, the questionnaire sample included 35 respondents (20 percent of the sample) who at one time were closet queens.

It is the closet queen who has most internalized the negative societal stereotype of the homosexual. It is to be expected that such persons would suffer from a feeling of psychological tension, for they are in a state of cognitive dissonance[27]—that is, feelings and sometimes behavior are not consistent with self-definition.

The following subject was a closet queen for over 50 years. He had his first homosexual experience at the age of 12, has had homosexual desires since that time, and has been exclusively homosexual for 53 years. At the time the subject was interviewed, he expressed amazement that he had just come out during the last few months. Over the years, his involvement with the gay subculture was peripheral; at the age of 29 for about one year he had some involvement with overt homosexuals, but otherwise he had had only slight contact with them until recently. During that earlier involvement:

> I was not comfortable with them. I was repressed and timid and they thought I was being high-hat, so I was rejected. It never worked out; I was never taken in. I felt uncomfortable in their presence and I made them feel uncomfortable. I couldn't fit in there, I never wanted to, never sought to; I was scared of them. I was scared of the brazen bitches who would put me down.

During the years as a closet queen he was plagued with feelings of guilt; for varying periods of time he was a patient in over 20 mental hospitals. His social life was essentially nil; he had neither gay friends nor straight friends. His various stays in mental hospitals relieved continuing feelings of loneliness. At the age of 65 he attended a church whose congregation was primarily homosexual. It was in the context of interacting with the gay persons who were associated with this church that after 53 years this subject came out.

> SUBJECT: I had never seen so many queens in one place; I was scared somebody would put me down, somebody would misunderstand why I was there. I had this vague, indescribable fear. But all

---

[26] In gay argot, the meaning of the term "closet queen" varies, but usually it is applied to one who does not admit to being homosexual. However, the term is sometimes used to refer to a self-admitted homosexual who does not like to associate with other homosexuals, or who may be trying to pass as being straight most of the 24 hours of the day.

[27] Leon Festinger, *Theory of Cognitive Dissonance* (New York: Harper and Row, 1957).

this was washed away when I saw all were there for the one purpose of fellowship and community in the true sense of the term.... I kept going and then I got to be comfortable in the coffee hour.... Then out in the lobby a young fellow opened his heart to me, telling me all his troubles and so forth, and I listened patiently, and I thought I made a couple of comforting remarks. Then I went out to the car, and when I got in the car I put my hand out to shake hands and he kissed my hand.... It's hard for you to understand the emotional impact of something like this —that I belong, they love me, I love them.

Until the last few weeks, in all my life I had never been in a gay bar for more than a few minutes, I was acutely uncomfortable. But now I can actually go into it; this is the most utterly ludicrous transformation in the last few weeks. ... There's no logic whatsoever. I'm alive at 65.

It's a tremendous emotional breakthrough. I feel comfortable and relieved of tensions and self-consciousness. My effectiveness in other fields has been enhanced 100 percent. I have thrown off so many of the prejudices and revulsions that were below the surface.... I'm out of the closet. In every way, they know, where I work, in this uptight place where I work; I've told them where I live; I've written back east. What more can I do?

INTERVIEWER: Do you think you are now more self-accepting of yourself?

SUBJECT: Brother! I hope you're not kidding. That's the whole bit. How ironical it would come at 65. The only thing that I wouldn't do now is to go to the baths. I told the kids the other day; it's the only breakthrough I cannot bring myself to.

One can only speculate why after all these years this subject came out. The reason may have been that he had had a very religious upbringing and could not conceive of homosexuals in a religiously acceptable manner. The church he attended for the first time at age 65 presented homosexuals as being religiously acceptable, and presented to the subject highly religious homosexuals.[28] Contact with this church may have

helped change the meaning of the category homosexual so that he could now include himself.[29]

In a sense the closet queen represents society's ideal homosexual, for the closet queen accepts the societal stereotype of the homosexual and feels guilt because he does the same sort of things that homosexuals do, yet believes he is really different from homosexuals in some significant way. This inability of the closet queen to see himself in other homosexuals prevents him from placing himself in the cognitive category of *homosexual,* and he will not come out until some new information is given to him about homosexuals which permits him to say, "There are homosexuals like myself" or "I am very much like them."

There may be significant differences between ex-closet queens and those closet queens who never come out. Of course, I had contact only with ex-closet queens, and they uniformly reported that their own psychological adjustment has been much better since coming out. Their only regret was that they had not come out sooner. Possibly the closet queen who remains a closet queen reaches some sort of psychological adjustment that ex-closet queens were unable to reach.

THE ROLE OF KNOWLEDGE

The change of self-identity to *homosexual* is intimately related to the access of knowledge and information concerning homosexuals and homosexuality. Hoffman has observed:

Society deals with homosexuality as if it did not exist. Although the situation is changing, this subject was not even discussed and was not even the object of scientific investigation until a few decades ago. We just didn't speak about these things; they were literally unspeakable and so loathsome

---

[28] It may be that among closet queens, or those who have been closet queens for many years, one would find a disproportionately high number of very religious persons; the traditional negative religious reaction would probably prevent highly religious persons from easily placing themselves in the homosexual category. It would therefore be expected that clergymen who have homosexual feelings would tend to be closet queens for many years. Not only do clergymen have a more difficult time in resolving problems of guilt, but also interaction with other homosexuals could lead to their losing their jobs. In this sample, there were 10 respondents who were ministers or who were studying for the ministry at the time they came out. Their mean age for coming out was 22, and the mean time interval between first homosexual desire and the homosexual self-identification was 10.4 years. I hope to publish a report in the near future on the social life of homosexual ministers.

[29] There have been some recent actions that challenge the traditional religious reaction against homosexuality and homosexuals. Particularly, see: John Dart, "Church for Homosexuals," *Los Angeles Times,* Dec. 8, 1969, Part 2, pp. 1–3; Edward B. Fiske, "Homosexuals in Los Angeles ... Establish Their Own Church," *New York Times,* Feb. 15, 1970, Sec. 1, p. 58; "The Homosexual Church," *Newsweek,* Oct. 12, 1970, p. 107. Some churches have openly accepted homosexuals; I am currently preparing an article on such a church.

that nothing could be said in polite society about them. . . .[30]

The traditional silence on this topic has most probably prevented many persons with homosexual feelings from identifying themselves as being homosexual. Lofland has noted that the role of knowledge in creating a deviant identity is an important one. If significant others or the actor himself does not know of the deviant category, his experience cannot be interpreted in terms of that category; or if his experience appears to be completely alien from that category he will not interpret his experience in terms of that category. If the societal stereotype of homosexuals is one of dirty old men, perverts, Communists, and so on, it should not be surprising that the young person with homosexual feelings would have difficulty in interpreting his experience in terms of the homosexual category.

The greater tolerance of society for the freer circulation of information concerning homosexuality and homosexuals has definite implications in reference to coming out. The fact that there is greater overt circulation of homophile magazines and homophile newspapers, that there are advertisements for gay movies in newspapers, and that there are books, articles, and movies about gay life, permits the cognitive category of homosexuals to be known to a larger proportion of the population and, most importantly, permits more information to be circulated that challenges the negative societal stereotype of the homosexual.

Since there has been a freer circulation of information on homosexuality during the past few years, it can be hypothesized that the development of a homosexual identity is now occurring at an increasingly earlier age. Indeed, older gay informants have stated that the younger homosexuals are coming out at a much earlier age. In order to test this hypothesis, the sample was dichotomized into a 30-and-above age group and a below-30 age group. It can be seen in Table 4 that the below-30 mean age for developing a homosexual identity was significantly lower (at the .01 level) than the above-30 mean age; the

drop in mean age was from approximately 21 to 17.[31]

TABLE 4. RELATIONSHIP OF RESPONDENT AGE TO AGE AT HOMOSEXUAL SELF-IDENTIFICATION

| Age at Homosexual Self-Identification | Age of Respondents | | | |
| | 30 and above | | Below 30 | |
	N	(%)	N	(%)
5–9	0	(0)	1	(1)
10–14	8	(9)	19	(22)
15–19	35	(38)	44	(50)
20–24	29	(32)	23	(21)
25–29	10	(11)	1	(1)
30–39	7	(8)	0	(0)
40–49	1	(1)	0	(0)
50–59	0	(0)	0	(0)
60–69	1	(1)	0	(0)
Total	91	(100)	88	(100)
Mean	21.4*		17.2*	
Standard Deviation	7.7		3.8	

* Means significantly different at .01 level.

Indications are that the present trend toward greater circulation of information that is not highly negative about homosexuals and homosexuality will continue. The fact that a mass-circulation magazine such as *Time* gave its front cover to an article entitled "The Homosexual in America" (Oct. 31, 1969) and that this article was not highly negative represents a significant breakthrough. The cognitive category of homosexual is now being presented in a not unfavorable manner to hundreds of thousands of people who previously could not have been exposed to such information through conventional channels. This is not to say that more information about homosexuals and homosexuality will lead to a significantly greater prevalence of persons engaging in homosexuality. What is being asserted is that a higher proportion of those with homosexual desires and behavior will develop a homosexual identity, and that the development of that identity will continue to occur at an increasingly younger age.

---

[30] Martin Hoffman, *The Gay World, Male Homosexuality and the Social Creation of Evil* (New York: Basic Books, 1968), p. 195.

[31] It can be argued that this was not a meaningful test because of sample bias, since the sample could not include subjects of the younger generation who had still not come out. However, the age of 30 was chosen as the dividing point because only 9 respondents (5 percent) had come out after the age of 30. Any remaining bias in the sample from this source should presumably be insignificant.

CONCLUSION

This study has suggested that the development of a homosexual identity is dependent on the meanings that the actor attaches to the concepts of homosexual and homosexuality, and that these meanings are directly related to the meanings that are available in his immediate environment; and the meanings that are available in his immediate environment are related to the meanings that are allowed to circulate in the wider society. The commitment to a homosexual identity cannot occur in an environment where the cognitive category of homosexual does not exist. Hoffman in essence came to the same conclusion when he hypothesized that the failure to develop a homosexual identity is due to a combination of two factors:

> the failure of society to make people aware of homosexuality as an existent way of life (and of the existence of the gay world), and the strong repressive forces that prevent people from knowing what their real sexual feelings are. One might consider this a psychological conspiracy of silence, which society insists upon because of its belief that it thereby safeguards existent sexual norms.[32]

In an environment where the cognitive category of homosexual does not exist or is presented in a highly negative manner, a person who is sexually attracted to persons of the same sex will probably be viewed and will probably view himself as sick, mentally ill, or queer.

It can be asserted that one of the main functions of the viewpoint that homosexuality is mental illness is to inhibit the development of a homosexual identity. The *homosexuality-as-mental-illness* viewpoint is now in increasing competition with the *homosexuality-as-way-of-life* viewpoint. If the homosexuality-as-way-of-life viewpoint is increasingly disseminated, one would anticipate that the problems associated with accepting a homosexual identity will significantly decrease, there will be a higher proportion of homosexually oriented people with a homosexual identity, and this identity will develop at an earlier age.[33]

If the homosexuality-as-way-of-life philosophy does become increasingly accepted, the nature of the homosexual community itself may undergo a radical transformation. To have a community one must have members who will acknowledge to themselves and to others that they are members of that community. The increasing circulation of the homosexuality-as-way-of-life viewpoint may in fact be a self-fulfilling prophecy. It may lead to, and possibly is leading to, the creation of a gay community in which one's sex life is becoming increasingly less fragmented from the rest of one's social life.

---

[32] Hoffman, *The Gay World*, p. 138.

[33] Weinberg has recently reported that younger homosexuals have on the whole a worse psychological adjustment than older homosexuals. As the age for the development of a homosexual identity drops, the psychological adjustment of younger homosexuals may significantly improve.

CHAPTER SEVEN

ALCOHOLISM

National surveys consistently report that approximately two-thirds of the adult American population drink some form of alcoholic beverage.[1] Most of this group are occasional drinkers or moderate and social drinkers who, although they drink with some regularity, do not drink to excess. In all, about $14,500,000 was spent on alcohol in 1967, which figure represents about 3 percent of all personal expenditures.[2] Considering the frequency with which it occurs and the amount of money spent on it, drinking itself is not deviant in American society over all. However, drinkers who continuously drink to the point of creating adverse economic, social and psychological consequences for themselves and others are considered deviant; such drinkers are defined as alcoholics.[3] Estimates of the number of alcoholics among American adults vary between 4 and 10 percent, depending on the method of estimation used.[4] Thus, even deviant (that is, alcoholic) drinking is not particularly rare in the United States. Problems associated with alcoholism are not limited to the United States, of course, but plague most societies in the world today.[5]

Most persons are probably aware of the problems associated with excessive drinking, and governments of many societies have attempted to suppress drinking altogether as in this country earlier in this century. Such efforts are usually short-lived and unsuccessful as was exemplified by the continued drinking of U.S. citizens during the period of Prohibition and the

[1] See the following: John W. Riley, Jr., and Charles F. Mardin, "The Social Pattern of Alcoholic Drinking," *Quarterly Journal of Studies on Alcohol* 8 (September 1947), pp. 265–73; Harold A. Mulford, "Drinking and Deviant Drinking in the U.S.A., 1963," *Quarterly Journal of Studies on Alcohol* 25 (December, 1964), pp. 634–50; and D. Cahalan, I. M. Crisin and H. M. Crossley, *American Drinking Practices: A National Study of Drinking Behavior and Attitudes* (New Brunswick, New Jersey: Rutgers Center of Alcohol Studies, 1969).

[2] U.S. Bureau of the Census, *Statistical Abstract of the United States, 1969* (Washington, D.C.: U.S. Government Printing Office, 1969), p. 314.

[3] This is the most frequently accepted definition of alcoholism. See Mark Keller, "The Definition of Alcoholism and the Estimation of Its Prevalence," in David J. Pittman and Charles R. Snyder, eds., *Society, Culture, and Drinking Patterns* (New York: John Wiley, 1962), p. 313.

[4] *Ibid.*, pp. 318–29. See also Robert Straus, "Alcoholics and Alcoholism," in Robert K. Merton and Robert A. Nisbet, eds., *Contemporary Social Problems*, 3rd ed. (New York: Harcourt Brace Jovanovich, 1971), p. 256.

[5] Mark Keller and Mary McCormick, *A Dictionary of Words about Alcohol* (New Brunswick, New Jersey: Rutgers Center of Alcohol Studies, 1968), p. xv.

subsequent official actions which repealed the Act. Although most persons would like to eliminate excessive drinking and the problems that are associated with it, they do not want to eliminate the forms of drinking that must precede before excessive drinking.

A. ANTECEDENTS AND DETERMINANTS

In identifying causal factors of alcohol use, causes of drinking behavior among nonalcoholics must be distinguished from causes of drinking among alcoholics. This is because alcohol use itself is an etiological factor of alcoholism. Through a prolonged period of heavy drinking, drinkers may become dependent upon alcohol and develop a "need" for it. The exact nature of this "need" is not clearly understood. It has been described as "a state of stress, discontent, or inner tension, the origin of which may be physiological, psychological, or social, or a blending of all three."[6] What seems clear, however, is that among alcoholics, "alcohol is used to relieve these discomforts."[7] Subsequent dependence on alcohol to relieve such discomforts develops after a prolonged period of drinking. Consequently, drinking itself is one of the determinants of the dependence on alcohol.

The two selections on causes of drinking are concerned with different types of drinking. The first, "Norm Qualities and Deviant Drinking Behavior," by Larsen and Abu-Laban, is concerned with the relationship between group norms about drinking and the level of drinking. Some sociologists argue that the level of drinking is higher in groups which prohibit all forms of drinking (proscriptive norms) than in groups which prescribe drinking at least on certain occasions, such as during religious ceremonies and during meals (prescriptive norms).[8] The general explanation offered is that groups which proscribe drinking do not provide rules which guide and control drinking behavior; consequently when drinking occurs, it tends to take an extreme form. Larsen and Abu-Laban, however, find little support for this theory. In addition to prescriptive and proscriptive norms, they distinguish nonscriptive norms, which neither prohibit nor encourage drinking. Heaviest drinking is associated with nonscriptive norms, in their view, while abstinence is most apt to occur among groups which proscribe drinking. At the same time, prescriptive norms do appear to place restraints on drinking (since they are associated with less drinking than are nonscriptive norms) by defining the circumstances under which drinking should occur, thus limiting alcohol consumption. The absence of norms—

---

[6] Straus, "Alcoholics and Alcoholism," p. 247–48.
[7] *Ibid.,* p. 248.
[8] See Ephraim H. Mizruchi and Robert Perruci, "Norm Qualities and Differential Effects of Deviant Behavior: An Exploratory Analysis," *American Sociological Review* 27 (June, 1962), pp. 391–99. See also Jerome H. Skolnick, "Religious Affiliation and Drinking Behavior," *Quarterly Journal of Studies on Alcohol* 19 (September, 1958), pp. 452–70.

whether prescriptive or proscriptive—regulating drinking appears to result in the heaviest drinking. The heavy drinkers in Larsen and Abu-Laban's study are not necessarily alcoholic drinkers; we do not know which of the heavy drinkers drink to the point of dependence on alcohol and the creation of adverse consequences for themselves and others. Still as noted above, heavy drinking over a period of time is a necessary antecedent to alcoholism.

But other factors are involved; all persons who drink to "excess" do not become dependent upon alcohol. (In fact, some nonalcoholics consume more alcohol than some alcoholics but can resist drinking when the occasion demands it.) Nor do all groups and societies with high consumption rates have high alcoholic rates. Heavy drinking is a necessary condition for alcoholism but in itself is insufficient to explain it.

Some explanations of alcoholism emphasize personality factors. Compulsive drinking is said to be an expression of unconscious psychopathological tendencies, such as neurosis, homosexuality, sexual fears, and unresolved Oedipus problems. Also, the belief that alcoholics have certain personality traits that differentiate them from the nonalcoholics is not uncommon among psychiatrists, psychologists, and the public. Actually, however, there is little evidence for any of the personality theories.[9]

In "Cultural Differences in Rates of Alcoholism," Robert Freed Bales argues that although compulsive drinking may be an expression of a psychological state ("inner tension"), this state is *socially* induced. More significantly, he believes this leads to alcoholism only under certain social conditions. He hypothesizes that the level of compulsive drinking is likely to be high in societies that generate high levels of inner tension (such as anxiety, repressed sex, and aggression) only if these societies do not instill anti-alcohol attitudes and offer few alternatives for relieving anxiety. Inner tension as a cause of alcoholism varies with social and cultural conditions. The rate of alcoholism for any particular group, therefore, can be determined only when the combined influence of these factors is known. In some groups, such as the Irish, all these factors may encourage compulsive drinking; however, in other groups, such as the Jews, one of the factors may be absent, in which case the rate will be lower. Thus, while Larsen and Abu-Laban show that drinking behavior is associated with group attitudes (social norms), Bales argues that additional factors are necessary in the etiology of *alcoholic* drinking.

---

[9] See Edwin H. Sutherland, H. G. Schroeder and G. L. Tordella, "Personality Traits and the Alcoholic," *Quarterly Journal of Studies on Alcohol* 11 (September, 1950), pp. 547–61; Leonard Symes, "Personality Characteristics and the Alcoholic: A Critique of Current Studies," *Quarterly Journal of Studies on Alcohol* 17 (June, 1957), pp. 288–302; and John D. Armstrong, "The Search for the Alcoholic Personality," *Annals of the American Academy of Political and Social Science* 315 (January, 1958), pp. 40–47.

NORM QUALITIES AND DEVIANT DRINKING BEHAVIOR

DONALD E. LARSEN AND BAHA ABU-LABAN

The relationship between norm qualities and drinking behavior has become a subject of growing theoretical interest among sociologists.[1] Discussions of this relationship explicitly identify two types of norms. These are the proscriptive norms, which negatively sanction drinking of alcoholic beverages, and the prescriptive norms which sanction drinking positively. The focus of recent discussions has been the association between these two types of norms and deviant drinking behavior.[2] Deviation from the proscriptive norms is defined by any degree of drinking, whereas deviation from the prescriptive norms is defined only by heavy drinking.

Two related generalizations regarding norm qualities and drinking behavior are discernible in the literature. First, members of groups for which the consumption of alcoholic beverages is proscribed tend to become heavy drinkers if they begin to drink. Conversely, excessive drinking tends to be curbed in groups which provide their members with prescriptions about drinking.[3] Second, there is a relatively high degree of deviant drinking behavior associated with proscriptive norms.[4]

These generalizations are based on the findings of the Yale-sponsored College Drinking Survey conducted from 1949 to 1951. The findings of two subsequent surveys of drinking behavior do not fully support the Yale survey. Specifically, the Yale survey showed that among Mormon and ascetic Protestant students who drink, there is a higher rate of extreme drinking behavior than among Jewish and Italian Catholic students.[5] In contrast, a nation-wide survey of drinkers in the United States showed that Methodists and Baptists, who proscribe drinking, have the same low rates of heavy drinking as the Jews.[6] Another study of adult drinkers in Cedar Rapids, Iowa, revealed that Methodists have the lowest rate of heavy drinking of all the denominations studied, but Baptists have the highest rate.[7]

A second notable fact about the available evidence is the wide and unexplained variability in the degree of deviation in groups with the same type of norms. For example, among religious groups which proscribe drinking, such as Mormons, Methodists, and Baptists, the proportions of deviants (i.e., drinkers) vary from a low of 48 to a high of 82 percent. Similarly, the proportions of deviants (in this case, heavy drinkers) among Catholics and Jews, who positively sanction drinking, range from 7 to 28 percent.[8]

The purpose of this paper is to report the findings of a study which examined the relationship between norm qualities and deviant drinking behavior within a broader analytical framework than that used in previous studies. The unique

Adapted with permission of the authors and The Society for the Study of Social Problems, from "Norm Qualities and Deviant Drinking Behavior," *Social Problems* 15 (Spring, 1968), pp. 442–50.

[1] Ephraim H. Mizruchi and Robert Perrucci, "Norm Qualities and Differential Effects of Deviant Behavior: An Exploratory Analysis," *American Sociological Review* 27 (June, 1962), pp. 391–99. This paper later appeared in a revised and extended form under the title "Norm Qualities and Deviant Behavior" in Ephraim H. Mizruchi, editor, *The Substance of Sociology* (New York: Appleton-Century-Crofts, 1967), pp. 259–70. Subsequent references are to the original article.

[2] See, for example, Robert Straus and Selden D. Bacon, *Drinking in College* (New Haven: Yale U., 1954); Charles R. Snyder, *Alcohol and the Jews* (Glencoe, Ill.: Free Press, 1958); Jerome H. Skolnick, "Religious Affiliation and Drinking Behavior," *Quarterly Journal of Studies on Alcohol* 19 (September, 1958), pp. 452–70; Albert D. Ullman, "Sociocultural Backgrounds of Alcoholism," *The Annals* 315 (January, 1958), pp. 48–54; and Mizruchi and Perrucci, "Norm Qualities and Differential Effects."

[3] See, for example, Mizruchi and Perucci, "Norm Qualities and Differential Effects."

[4] See, for example, Skolnick, "Religious Affiliation and Drinking Behavior," fn. 16, p. 460.

[5] Straus and Bacon, *Drinking in College*, pp. 141–45; Skolnick, "Religious Affiliation and Drinking Behavior," *passim;* and Snyder, *Alcohol and the Jews*, pp. 189–192.

[6] Harold A. Mulford, "Drinking and Deviant Drinking, U.S.A., 1963," *Quarterly Journal of Studies on Alcohol* 25 (December, 1964), pp. 634–50.

[7] National Center for Health Statistics, *Identifying Problem Drinkers in a Household Health Survey* (Washington, D.C.: U.S. Department of Health, Education, and Welfare, 1966), pp. 22–23.

[8] Straus and Bacon, *Drinking in College*, pp. 51 and 111; Skolnick, "Religious Affiliation and Drinking Behavior," fn. 16, p. 460; Harold A. Mulford and Donald A. Miller, "Drinking in Iowa. I. Sociocultural Distribution of Drinkers," *Quarterly Journal of Studies on Alcohol* 20 (December, 1959), pp. 704–26; Harold A. Mulford and Donald A. Miller, "Drinking in Iowa. II. The Extent of Drinking and Selected Sociocultural Categories," *Quarterly Journal of Studies on Alcohol* 21 (March, 1960) pp. 26–39; Mulford, "Drinking and Deviant Drinking"; and National Center for Health Statistics, *Identifying Problem Drinkers.*

features of this framework are (1) the recognition of a third type of norm, in addition to proscriptive and prescriptive norms, and (2) the consideration of the norms of five different groups rather than only one's religio-ethnic group. An important outcome of this study is that its findings suggest a possible explanation for the conflicting and variable evidence that has been reported in the literature.

RESEARCH PROCEDURES

The Community and the Sample. This study was conducted in Edmonton, Alberta, in the summer of 1966. With a population of 374,406 in 1966, Edmonton is the largest city in the province and is the seat of the provincial government.[9]

Self-administered questionnaires were distributed to the first six households in each of 36 residential blocks which were randomly selected from a city map. Two questionnaires were left in each household in which there were at least two adults, and only one questionnaire was left in a household consisting of a single adult. Respondents were given stamped and addressed envelopes in which to return their questionnaire.

A total of 440 questionnaires were distributed. One hundred and ninety-two questionnaires (or 44 percent of the total distributed) were returned, of which 180 were usable. The returns included slightly more female than male respondents (or 56 and 44 percent respectively). The modal age group of the entire sample was 35–49 years, and the most commonly represented ethnic group was British (54 percent), followed by German (19 percent), and Ukrainian (11 percent).[10] The religious affiliation most frequently reported (25 percent) was the United Church (consisting of Methodists, Congregationalists, and Presbyterians), followed by Roman Catholic (16 percent), Anglican (14 percent), and Baptist (11 percent).[11] A large majority of the respondents (84 percent) were married. Both husband and wife returned their questionnaires in 56 cases.

Quality of Norms. In addition to acknowledging the prescriptive and proscriptive norms, this study recognizes a third type of norm which we call *nonscriptive.* As applied to drinking, this norm refers to those situations where a group neither prohibits drinking nor provides a person with adequate guidelines, if any, for the consumption of alcoholic beverages. Nonscriptive norms incorporate an element of permissiveness, an element of incompleteness of directives for how to act, and an element of generality (rather than specificity) of standards. It is important to note that these descriptive qualities are relative rather than absolute. The term "nonscriptive norms" should not be equated with "permissive norms," although the two norms have in common the notion of individual determination of limits. Further, nonscriptive norms can exist in periods of normative transformation as well as in culturally stable conditions.

Nonscriptive and proscriptive norms are similar in that both types provide little guidance, if any, for those who drink; but they are different in that proscriptive norms disallow drinking while nonscriptive norms do not disallow it. Moreover, nonscriptive and prescriptive norms are similar in that they permit drinking; but they are different in that nonscriptive norms provide limited guidance regarding drinking whereas prescriptive norms provide an elaborate set of guidelines for drinking.

Source of Norms. The norms of five different groups were investigated. These groups included a respondent's parents, the religious group in which he was raised, his immediate family (if married), his close friends, and his co-workers. To obtain information about a group's norms,

---

[9] Edmonton is also the fastest growing city in Canada, having increased in population by nearly 100,000—or 33 percent—since 1961. No claim is made that Edmonton is a "typical" Canadian city, nor can we say that it is a unique city in any significant respect which may affect the results of our research.

[10] The representativeness of our sample may be examined with reference to the ethnic composition of the entire city. In 1951, 46.3 percent of the city population were of British origin; 12.2 percent were of German origin; and 11.6 percent were of Ukrainian origin. (See *1961 Census of Canada, Population and Housing Characteristics by Census Tracts, Edmonton,* Bulletin CT-21, [Ottawa: Dominion Bureau of Statistics, 1963]). These proportions are highly similar to those found in the sample. We have no evidence, however, that those who did not return questionnaires came from the "same population" as the actual respondents.

[11] These proportions may also be compared with those of the entire city. In 1961, 31 percent of the city population were affiliated with the United Church; 22.9 percent were affiliated with the Roman Catholic Church; 12.2 percent were affiliated with the Anglican Church; and 3.4 percent of the city population were affiliated with the Baptist Church. (*Ibid.*) Except for an overrepresentation of Baptists in our sample, the results show considerable similarity in the proportions of religious groups in the sample and in the city.

respondents were given the following instructions:

> People may have different rules concerning drinking of alcoholic beverages. For example, some tend to emphasize that one should not drink. Others tend to emphasize definite guidelines concerning acceptable drinking behavior (such as when, where, how much, and with whom to drink). A third group tends not to emphasize any rules or guidelines.
>
> For each of the five groups listed below, please place a check next to the category which, in your judgment, comes closest to what has been made known to you, either directly or indirectly, by that group.

The three categories, representing proscriptive, prescriptive, and nonscriptive norms respectively, are: (1) Made known to me that one should not drink; (2) Made known to me definite guidelines concerning acceptable drinking behavior; and (3) Made known to me either few guidelines concerning drinking, or none at all.

This method of measuring norm qualities differs from the technique used in previous studies in two significant ways. First, whereas previous investigations focused only on the norms of a person's religio-ethnic group, this study distinguishes among several sources of drinking norms. This approach assumes that an individual can acquire rules about drinking from a number of groups, and not just from the religio-ethnic group to which he is related. Second, norm qualities are determined on the basis of an individual's *perception* of a group's drinking norms, rather than on what is commonly believed to be the position of a particular group with respect to drinking. The significance of the perceptual data derives from the fact that, at least among certain religious groups, norms are neither transmitted uniformly nor perceived identically by parishioners.

Degree of Drinking. Operationally, this variable was defined by a "Quantity-Frequency Index" similar to the one developed by Straus and Bacon.[12] Each respondent was asked to indicate how much beer, liquor, and/or wine he ordinarily consumed in one sitting, and how often he had one or more drinks on the average during the past twelve months. On the basis of this evidence, persons were classified as either abstainers, or light, moderate, or heavy drinkers.[13]

Deviant Drinking. As indicated at the outset, deviation from proscriptive norms refers to any degree of drinking, whereas deviation from prescriptive norms refers only to heavy drinking. The line of demarcation between conformity and deviation in relation to nonscriptive norms is drawn at the point of heavy drinking (as in the case of prescriptive norms). This decision is based on the assumption that nonscriptive norms are likely to incorporate such general injunctions as "don't drink too much" and "stay out of trouble."

FINDINGS

Table 1 indicates the extent to which five different groups are perceived to emphasize proscriptive, prescriptive, and nonscriptive norms in regard to the consumption of alcoholic beverages.

---

[12] Straus and Bacon, *Drinking in College,* pp. 101–05.

[13] Light Drinker: drinks once a month or less and consumes one to three bottles or glasses of beer, liquor, or wine.

Moderate Drinker: drinks every two or three weeks or once a week and consumes one to three bottles or glasses of beer, liquor, or wine.

Heavy Drinker: drinks at least once a month or more often and consumes four or more bottles or glasses of beer, liquor, or wine; or drinks twice a week or more often and consumes three or more bottles or glasses of beer, liquor, or wine.

TABLE 1. PERCENTAGE OF RESPONDENTS RECEIVING EITHER PROSCRIPTIVE, PRESCRIPTIVE, OR NONSCRIPTIVE NORMS FROM FIVE GROUPS

Type of Norm Received	Source of Norms				
	Parents	Family	Friends	Co-workers	Church
Proscriptive	26%	16%	10%	6%	35%
Prescriptive	45	48	45	42	39
Nonscriptive	29	36	46	52	26
Total%	100	100	100	100	100
(N)	(174)	(154)	(166)	(146)	(168)

In general, the three types of norms are emphasized to a substantial degree. However, there is variability in the degree to which each type of norm is attributed to one or the other of the reference groups investigated. For example, about one-half of the respondents believe that co-workers' and friends' norms regarding the use of beverage alcohol are nonscriptive. In comparison, only one-fourth to one-third of the respondents attribute the same quality to norms transmitted by church, parents, and immediate family. Also, whereas about three out of ten persons perceive church and parents' norms as proscriptive, only about one out of ten perceive co-workers' and friends' norms as prohibitive.

The data which bear upon the relationship between proscriptive, prescriptive, and nonscriptive norms and deviant drinking behavior, with source of norms held constant, are presented in Table 2. One of the important findings from this table is that the proportion of deviants from proscriptive norms (i.e., drinkers) varies according to the source of the norms. The highest degree of deviation occurs in relation to church norms, within which approximately seven out of ten persons, whose religious group is perceived to prohibit drinking, deviate from its norms; that is, they do drink. The proportion of deviants declines steadily as the norms of parents, co-workers, immediate family, and friends (in that order) are examined. The lowest degree of deviation occurs in relation to peer group norms—only three out of ten persons who attribute the norm of abstinence to the peer group deviate from this norm.

The findings which relate type and source of norms to degree of heavy drinking are also presented in Table 2. It is evident that within each

TABLE 2. TYPE OF NORM RECEIVED FROM FIVE GROUPS AND DRINKING BEHAVIOR

Drinking Behavior	Proscriptive Norms by Source									
	Parents		Family		Friends		Co-workers		Church	
Abstainer	40%		60%		69%		57%		29%	
Drinker	60		40		31		43		71	
Light		54%		75%		75%		67%		44%
Moderate		23		12		—		—		27
Heavy		23		12		25		33		29
Total %	100		100		100		100		100	
(N)	(37)		(20)		(13)		(7)		(48)	

	Prescriptive Norms by Source									
	Parents		Family		Friends		Co-workers		Church	
Abstainer	4%		8%		7%		3%		5%	
Drinker	96		92		93		97		95	
Light		39%		49%		41%		39%		41%
Moderate		33		28		29		32		36
Heavy		28		23		30		29		23
Total %	100		100		100		100		100	
(N)	(78)		(71)		(71)		(58)		(64)	

	Nonscriptive Norms by Source									
	Parents		Family		Friends		Co-workers		Church	
Abstainer	12%		7%		10%		16%		11%	
Drinker	88		93		90		84		89	
Light		37%		31%		29%		39%		44%
Moderate		28		31		38		30		23
Heavy		35		38		33		31		33
Total %	100		100		100		100		100	
(N)	(49)		(55)		(72)		(73)		(44)	

of the three normative orientations there is variation in the proportion of heavy drinkers associated with the different reference groups. For example, among those exposed to proscriptive norms, the proportions range from 12 to 33 percent; among those exposed to prescriptive norms, they range from 23 to 30 percent; and among those exposed to nonscriptive norms, the proportions of heavy drinkers range from 31 to 38 percent.

The same table shows that the proportion of heavy drinkers in relation to religious groups which proscribe drinking is higher than in relation to religious groups which prescribe drinking.[14] This has also been observed in previous studies.[15] It is noteworthy, however, that for three other groups—namely, parents, immediate family, and friends—just the opposite relationship obtains: the proportion of heavy drinkers is higher among those with prescriptive than with proscriptive norms.

Finally, the data in Table 2 indicate that the degree of heavy drinking associated with nonscriptive norms is higher than that associated with either prescriptive or proscriptive norms. This generalization holds for each of the five groups investigated.

Since the norms which a person receives from any one of the five groups investigated are only a part of his total normative environment, it would be important to examine the relationship between types of norms and heavy drinking with the norms of all five groups considered simultaneously. For this purpose, a respondent's normative environment was classified as predominantly proscriptive, prescriptive, or nonscriptive if at least three of the five groups were perceived to have the same type of norm.[16]

The results of this analysis, which are presented in Table 3, tend to support our earlier

conclusion. Again, it is evident that heavy drinking is highest among those generally exposed to nonscriptive norms, slightly lower in relation to prescriptive norms, and lowest with respect to proscriptive norms. It is interesting to note that when a person's total normative environment is considered, about four out of ten persons deviate from the norm of abstinence. In contrast, when only the proscriptive norms of the church are examined, about seven out of ten persons deviate from these norms. (See Tables 2 and 3.)

The relationship between predominant type of norm and degree of drinking remains essentially the same when the effects of five background characteristics—sex, occupation, education, age, and church attendance—are alternately controlled.[17] Table 4 shows only the proportion of heavy drinkers among those who drink. Although the small N's limit the generality of the findings, the table reveals that those who come from a predominantly proscriptive environment tend to have the lowest degree of heavy drinking. Furthermore, in seven out of eleven comparisons, the proportion of heavy drinkers is considerably higher among those who come from a predominantly nonscriptive compared to a prescriptive normative background. This relationship is reversed only with regard to persons with more than a high school education. The remainder of the comparisons reveal a very slight difference in the proportion of heavy drinkers from these two normative environments.

DISCUSSION AND CONCLUSIONS

The findings uphold our assumption that nonscriptive norms constitute a significant segment of the system of norms regarding the consumption of alcoholic beverages, and should therefore be considered along with proscriptive and prescriptive norms. Furthermore, the utility of taking into account the norms of groups other than an individual's religious group is supported by the data. Although some studies have assumed that the norms of an individual's religious group have a predominant influence on his drinking

---

[14] Although the same relationship holds in regard to co-workers, this finding is unreliable because it is based on the responses of only three persons who report that their co-workers proscribe drinking.

[15] Direct comparisons between the findings of this study and previous research may not be entirely appropriate, since our evidence is based on the respondents' perceptions of their church's norms while earlier studies rated a church's norms on the basis of what is commonly believed to be its position regarding the consumption of alcoholic beverages.

[16] Omitted from the analysis are those cases in which the norms which a person attributes to different groups are so dissimilar that no more than two groups have the same type of norms.

[17] Because of the relatively small number of respondents, it is not possible to control simultaneously these background variables.

TABLE 3. PREDOMINANT TYPE OF NORM AND DEGREE OF DRINKING

Drinking Behavior	Predominant Type of Norm		
	Proscriptive	Prescriptive	Nonscriptive
Abstainer	59%	4%	10%
Drinker	41	96	90
Light	71%	46%	34%
Moderate	15	25	30
Heavy	15	29	36
Total %	100	100	100
(N)	(17)	(66)	(59)

TABLE 4. PERCENTAGE OF HEAVY DRINKERS BY PREDOMINANT TYPE OF NORM AND SELECTED BACKGROUND FACTORS

Control Variable	Predominant Norms of Heavy Drinkers		
	Proscriptive	Prescriptive	Nonscriptive
I. Sex:			
Male	33% (1)	41% (11)	48% (14)
Female	—	19 (7)	21 (5)
II. Occupation:			
White-collar	—	18 (6)	32 (10)
Blue-collar	33 (1)	41 (11)	50 (9)
III. Education:			
Grade 9 or less	—	30 (3)	44 (4)
Grades 10–12	50 (1)	26 (10)	40 (10)
Beyond grade 12	—	36 (5)	26 (5)
IV. Age:			
34 years or less	—	33 (11)	32 (10)
35 years or more	25 (1)	23 (7)	41 (9)
V. Church attendance:			
Very or fairly regularly	25 (1)	26 (5)	22 (4)
Occasionally or rarely	—	32 (13)	39 (15)

behavior,[18] the findings of this study show that people receive, and apparently are strongly influenced by, norms of groups other than the church. In many cases the norms of these groups conflict or compete with the norms of the church. Thus, many people do not live in a monolithic normative environment concerning what is appropriate drinking behavior. The significance of this fact for understanding drinking behavior has not yet been adequately recognized.

As indicated at the beginning of this paper, one of the major questions that has been raised in the literature concerns the relationship between the qualities of drinking norms and extreme drinking behavior. Our most significant finding in relation to this question is that among persons who drink, those who have received few, if any, guidelines (nonscriptions) regarding appropriate drinking behavior are more likely to become heavy drinkers than those who are given specific directives—either positive (prescriptions) or negative (proscriptions). In other words, heavy drinking is associated with a *relative* lack of norms regarding the consumption of alcoholic beverages in an environment which does not prohibit drinking.

This finding may appear to support Mizruchi and Perrucci's proposition that "pathological drinking behavior is associated with a relative

---

[18] See, for example, Skolnick, "Religious Affiliation and Drinking Behavior."

absence of directives for the act of drinking alcoholic beverages itself."[19] However, it is important to note the difference in the social context to which their generalization and ours applies. Their hypothesis was intended to refer to drinkers from an abstinence background; our finding refers to drinkers from a nonscriptive environment. Further, Mizruchi and Perrucci based their proposition on Yale's College Drinking Survey which found higher rates of "pathological drinking behavior" (e.g., intoxication) among students whose religion proscribes drinking compared to those whose religion provides explicit directives for drinking.

As stated earlier, not all studies support the proposition of extreme reactions to drinking among those whose religion proscribes drinking. The present investigation shows that, when the church is taken as a frame of reference, a higher degree of heavy drinking is associated with proscriptive than with prescriptive norms. But when the norms of three other groups are considered, the relationship is reversed: heavy drinking is related more to prescriptive than to proscriptive norms. In short, the data do not confirm Mizruchi and Perrucci's hypothesis that "predominantly proscriptive norms are more likely than predominantly prescriptive norms to lead to extreme degrees of pathological reactions when deviation occurs."[20]

This study has also shown that, in general, there is a higher level of deviance associated with proscriptive norms than with prescriptive norms, but that within each normative framework the proportion of deviants changes with the source of the norms. Although these findings may indicate that prescriptive norms are more effective than proscriptive norms in controlling deviation, they also suggest several factors other than the quality of the norms which influence the level of conformity to the norms.

One relevant factor suggested by the data is the *importance* of a group to an individual. That is, whether or not a person abides by the norms of a group will depend on the degree to which the group has meaning or relevance for him. This can be inferred, for example, from the finding that persons whose church proscribes drinking are more likely to be abstainers *if they attend church regularly.* Persons for whom the church is relatively unimportant, as indicated by low or no church attendance, tend to ignore the norm of abstinence.

The level of conformity to a group's drinking norm is also likely to be influenced by the extent to which its members are exposed to competing or conflicting definitions of appropriate drinking behavior. Thus, it is difficult for an individual to conform to his church's demand for abstinence if his friends urge or expect him to drink. On the other hand, if the norms of other reference groups are consistent with those of the church, it would be socially and emotionally easier for him to live up to the church's norms.

These results provide a possible explanation for (1) the conflicting evidence in the literature regarding the relation of heavy drinking to proscriptive religious norms, and (2) the variation in the proportion of deviants from both proscriptive and prescriptive norms. Our data suggest that persons who deviate from the proscriptive norms of the church do not inevitably become heavy drinkers because their drinking behavior may be guided by the positive norms of other groups, such as family or friends. Thus, the conflicting data of earlier studies may be related to the fact that the populations which were studied differed in the degree to which individuals discern specific guidelines for drinking from groups other than the church. To control for variation in exposure to various sources of norms, future studies should employ a measure of norms which simultaneously considers the norms of several relevant reference groups.

We have also suggested that conformity to the drinking norms of a group is influenced by the relative importance of that group to an individual and by the degree to which the group's norms are consistent with the norms of other reference groups. Failure to control for variation in these two factors may also be related to the problematic evidence which research has thus far produced.

---

[19] Mizruchi and Perrucci, "Norm Qualities and Differential Effects," p. 395. The above statement assumes that "pathological" and "heavy" drinking are comparable.

[20] *Ibid.,* p. 398.

CULTURAL DIFFERENCES IN RATES OF ALCOHOLISM

ROBERT FREED BALES

In analyzing cultural differences in "rates of alcoholism" it is necessary at the outset to avoid confusion between the degree to which alcohol is used in a given culture and the degree to which it creates problems in that culture. The first aspect is approached through "rates of consumption"; the second through rates of arrest for drunkenness, commitment to mental hospitals for alcoholic disorders, and death from alcoholism, which are sometimes broadly grouped together and referred to as "rates of alcoholism."

High rates of consumption do not necessarily mean high rates of alcoholism. Among most aboriginal peoples of the world before their contact with Europeans, drinking tended to take place on set social occasions, and it is probably accurate to say that on these special occasions they usually drank to a degree that would be considered excessive in our culture. It would not be accurate to assume, however, that these societies therefore had high rates of alcoholism. It is true that drinking on these occasions tended to create or at least to sharpen certain social problems. It tended to stir up aggression and sexuality in certain aspects, and to interfere with the performance of specialized functions such as the defense of the group. At the same time, however, it seems to have helped in the solution of certain crucial problems, such as the attainment of convincing religious experience, the promotion of solidarity, and the periodic catharsis of certain internal tensions, such as anxiety, suppressed aggression and sexuality. In most of these societies the immediate temporary problems which drinking created were endured for the sake of the more pressing and lasting problems which it helped to solve.

In other words, a high rate of consumption of alcohol for a particular society does not necessarily mean that individuals in that society will be more maladjusted than they would be without alcohol. It does not mean that there will necessarily be a high proportion of members who persistently get into trouble with authorities, develop various alcoholic disorders, or finally die from the effects of excessive drinking. "Rates of alcoholism" refer primarily to the frequency of these social and physical complications. Whether or not these complications occur depends upon factors other than gross consumption of alcoholic beverages by the whole group, although a certain minimum consumption on the part of individuals directly involved is of course presumed.

Whether rates of arrest for drunkenness, commitment to mental hospitals for alcoholic disorders, and death from alcoholism will be high in a given society seems to depend in large degree upon whether or not a large proportion of individuals become compulsive drinkers. Where drinking is not compulsive it can be confined to specific social occasions and its undesirable consequences can be dealt with by taking special precautions as among aboriginal peoples. Where a great many persons become compulsive drinkers, however, society loses its control over those persons and they tend to become progressively more deviant and disordered. In extreme cases resembling addiction, individuals continue to drink compulsively regardless of the harm to themselves and their families, regardless of repeated arrests and punishments. Some of them develop alcoholic psychoses and some eventually die from the effects of their excesses. Where these things happen frequently, it is fairly certain that rates of inebriety or compulsive drinking are high even though these rates cannot at present be measured directly. In the general discussion to follow it will not always be necessary to specify just what rate or combination of rates is used as the index. Ideally, the reference is to rates of compulsive drinking.

The formation of compulsive drinking is taken as the strategic point in this discussion of cultural differences not only because other rates more or less follow from it but also because it is during the formation of the compulsive habit

Reprinted with permission of author and publisher from the *Quarterly Journal of Studies on Alcohol* 6 (1949), pp. 480–99. Copyright 1949 by the Journal of Studies on Alcohol, Inc., New Brunswick, New Jersey. Footnotes have been renumbered.

that the influences of the society and its culture come to a critical focus in the individual person and work their effect. The effective motivation of the individual at any given time may be considered as the outcome of two sets of influences: the needs or urges which he carries within himself, and the opportunities which he finds in his situation. No matter how the individual acts as a result of these two sets of influences, his action is recorded in his personality and becomes a part of his habit system. Because of this the ways of behaving suggested or required by the culture become a part of the habit system of the individual, and thus a part of the motivation he brings to new situations. Thus, in the case of the individual with a compulsive desire to drink, it may be assumed that this motivation is in part a result of his past action, and that this past action in turn was influenced by the means of satisfaction offered by the society in which he lived. Although the desire to drink has finally become compulsive, and neither society nor the individual himself is able to control it, the desire might not have become compulsive if the society and culture had been different. In another culture the individual might not have had such severe needs for adjustment, or might have been offered something other than drinking as a means of satisfying these needs.

This account might be simplified by saying that there are three general ways in which culture and social organization can influence rates of alcoholism. The first is *the degree to which the culture operates to bring about acute needs for adjustment, or inner tensions, in its members.* There are many of these; culturally induced anxiety, guilt, conflict, suppressed aggression, and sexual tensions of various sorts may be taken as examples. The second way is *the sort of attitudes toward drinking which the culture produces in its members.* Four different types of attitudes will be suggested later. The crucial factor seems to be whether a given attitude toward drinking positively suggests drinking to the individual as a means of relieving his inner tensions, or whether such a thought arouses a strong counteranxiety. The third general way is *the degree to which the culture provides suitable substitute means of satisfaction.* In other words, there is reason to believe that if the inner ten-

sions are sufficiently acute certain individuals will become compulsively habituated in spite of opposed social attitudes unless substitute ways of satisfaction are provided.

These three factors may be used as the outline for the rest of this discussion. Under each heading one or more cultural groups will be discussed whose particular rates seem to reflect the factor in question. It is taken for granted that the three factors work together, and that any given rate depends upon their particular combination. If this is not mentioned explicitly in each case the omission is only a means of simplifying and saving time. It should also be noted that biological or physiological differences may play a part in some of these differences in rates; but if they do, what they may be or how they may operate is still unknown. Various theories to this effect have been offered in the past but they are hardly accepted by biologists and physiologists now. The three factors mentioned seem to make sense, both theoretically and practically. However, scientists are still very much in the process of interpreting cultural differences in rates, and in some ways the rates offer more problems than answers.

There is fairly good evidence that inebriety tends to be pronounced where the inner tensions or needs for adjustment of many individuals are high, other things being equal. In a careful statistical study of all the primitive societies for which data were available, Horton[1] found that societies with inadequate techniques or resources for maintaining their physical existence also tended to have "strong degrees of insobriety." This does not necessarily mean that the members become compulsive drinkers, but that on the occasions when they drink they do so to the point of unconsciousness and their bouts of drunkenness are likely to last for days. Their drinking, in other words, shows a semicompulsive character when once started, although it starts only on socially sanctioned occasions. The direct factor seems to be the anxiety induced by the basic insecurities of their lives, such as the constant danger of drought, insect plagues,

---

[1] D. Horton, "The Functions of Alcohol in Primitive Societies: A Cross-cultural Study," *Quarterly Journal of Studies on Alcohol* 4 (1943), pp. 199–220.

floods, crop failures or other threats to the food supply. Those societies which were being broken up by contact with other more powerful groups invariably had high degrees of insobriety. In most of the societies with high subsistence anxiety there was also a great deal of pent-up aggression which emerged in the periods of drunkenness, sometimes in very extreme form.

Repressed aggression seems to be a very common maladjustment. It can be created by the way the social organization is set up, as well as by other sorts of deprivation or frustration. The data gathered by Hallowell[2] on the Northeastern Woodlands Indians relating to the time of their contact with the whites indicate a high degree of inhibition of aggressive impulses. They were forced by their culture to be restrained, stoic, amiable and mild under all provocations, and had to suppress all open criticism of one another. It is assumed that they had a great deal of pent-up aggression, because they had a highly developed system of witchcraft directed against one another. When they were introduced to alcohol the consequences were disastrous. In their bouts of drunkenness they strangled and beat themselves—a form of aggression directed against the self. They broke up everything in their wigwams and quarreled for hours together. Brothers cut the throats of sisters, husbands attacked their wives, mothers threw their children into the fire or into the river, fathers choked their children and children attacked their parents. Many others of the Indian tribes of the Eastern United States showed similar reactions. Their culture was broken up by the whites. They were crowded off their lands, beaten and cheated in their economic dealings, kidnaped and sent into slavery, and exposed to the ravages of strange diseases. In short, they were subject to the strongest sort of subsistence anxiety. This laid a part of the groundwork for the devastation alcohol worked among them. There was another factor, however, tied up with the fact that they had not known alcohol previously, which will be discussed shortly.

To illustrate more definitely the way in which the social organization can induce inner tensions in its members, the Irish peasantry may be taken as an example.[3] The Irish have been noted for their inebriety during the past several centuries. In statistics of admissions for alcoholic disorders to various hospitals in this country the Irish have consistently had rates two to three times as high as any other ethnic group. In 1840 an Irish priest[4] wrote:

> In truth, not only were our countrymen remarkable for the intemperate use of intoxicating liquors, but intemperance had already entered into, and formed a part of the national character. An Irishman and a drunkard had become synonymous terms. Whenever he was to be introduced in character, either in the theatre or on the pages of the novelist, he should be represented habited in rags, bleeding at the nose, and waving a shillelah. Whiskey was everywhere regarded as our idol.

The English at this time wished to keep the Irish an agricultural people, so that the Irish would raise the sort of farm produce needed in England. As a part of this program they hampered the development of adequate means of transportation in order to prevent industrialization in Ireland. They had control of the land, with a complicated system of absentee landlords, and squeezed every last penny they could out of the Irish farmers. The farmers, for the most part, lived on the bare edge of existence. They raised so few different kinds of food that the potato blight resulted in severe periodic famines. Many people died during these famines because food could not be transported to them in time.

The small farms were crowded to capacity. There was no room on them for more than one extended family. The grandparents, who had retired, lived in the West Room of the cottage. The farmer and his wife with their children made up the rest of the family. They all had to work hard for their existence, the girls helping their mother around the cottage and farmyard, the boys help-

---

[2] A. I. Hallowell (Unpublished ms., cit. Horton).

[3] The material on Irish social structure has been drawn chiefly from the following: C. M. Arensberg, *The Irish Countryman* (New York: The Macmillan Co., 1937); C. M. Arensberg, and S. T. Kimball, *Family and Community in Ireland* (Cambridge, Mass.: Harvard Univ. Press, 1940); M. J. F. McCarthy, *Irish Land and Irish Liberty* (London: Robert Scott, 1911).

[4] J. Birmingham, *A Memoir of the Very Rev. Theobald Mathew* (Dublin: Milliken & Son, 1840).

ing their father in the fields. There was a strict separation of the sexes which they managed to maintain in spite of the fact that the whole family usually slept in the same room. The training of the children was apparently a very contradictory affair. The elders teased the little boys unmercifully—"codding" it was called—and sometimes prodded them into "scuffing" with one another. It was not unusual for a child to receive extravagant love and affection at one moment, and the next moment to be cuffed about or even beaten in a fit of anger. There was also a marked tendency to attempt to control children through an exaggerated fear of the "bogey man," "spooks," and "fairies." Conflict between family members was likely to be frequent and severe. Many children must have grown up in an atmosphere of fear and insecurity, both in the family and outside.

Because the farms were so small they could not be divided. The boys could not marry until the "old fellow" was ready to give up the farm and retire. Then only one of the boys would get the farm. The other brothers and sisters would have to leave. Some of the brothers went into the priesthood. Others were apprenticed to tradesmen in town, or emigrated. One or two of the girls received a dowry and married. The others became nuns, were apprenticed, or emigrated. Very often the "old fellow" was not willing to give up the farm until his physical powers were spent, and this caused a great deal of resentment. So long as his sons stayed on the farm they had to work for him as "boys" and were treated as boys, even though they might be 45 or 50 years old. By the same token they had to stay away from girls. There were very severe sanctions on premarital sexual activity which were enforced both by the church and the peasantry. Thus there were many physically mature men, ready for a life of their own, who were kept under the father's thumb as "boys," dependent upon him even for their spending money, and deprived of sexual contacts.

Even social contacts between the two sexes were at a minimum. It was apparently not considered a good idea to encourage love affairs when the land would not support more families. When the "boys" were not working as laborers for their father, they were expected to spend their time with the other boys. Small male groups of every age met at various farmhouses or taverns to pass the time. Drinking and aggressive "horseplay" were major activities. The "teetotaler," as a matter of fact, was regarded as a suspicious character, since this implied he was not likely to be with the other boys and might be wandering around with the idea of molesting innocent girls. In short, the culture was such as to create and maintain an immense amount of suppressed aggression and sexuality. Both of these suppressed tensions found their outlet in drinking.

It is not entirely clear just what happened to this family system in urban America, but it seems to have broken down in various ways and created still other conflicts.[5] The males came in at the bottom of our occupational ladder, and no longer had the ownership of a farm as the mainstay of their self-respect and prestige. The tenement was not a place where aged parents could easily be kept after their working days were over. It was not easy to provide the money for their support out of small day-wages. There was uncertainty and inner conflict as to whether one was obligated to keep them at all. There was usually nothing a father could pass on to his son, or if he died and left a little property there was likely to be conflict over how it should be divided, since equal inheritance was not the rule in Ireland as it is here. The father in many cases seems to have dropped into a role of impotence and insignificance, and the mother became the dominant member of the family. She tended to bind her sons to her in the way which was usual and natural in Ireland. In this country, however, a strong attachment between a son and his mother made it very difficult, and in some cases impossible, for the son to make a successful transition to independent adult status. In a survey of some 80 cases of alcoholic patients of Irish descent I found this mother-son dependence and conflict in some 60 percent. Whether this is a higher percentage than would be found in other ethnic groups it is impossible to say at present, but the mother-son dependence pattern was certainly a prominent factor causing maladjustment in these Irish cases.

---

[5] These interpretations are based on a study by the present author of some 80 detailed hospital case records of Irish alcoholic patients.

Bunzel[6] has made a study of a community in Guatemala, called Chichicastenango, which has many similarities to the Irish peasant organization. The father owns the land and there is an unequal system of land tenure. Blind obedience to the father is demanded. He is the representative of the ancestors, and they are supposed to support him in his claims. All aggression must be inhibited. Similarly, sexual chastity before marriage and absolute fidelity after marriage are demanded. There is a great deal of sorcery which is widely feared. No act can be hidden from the supernatural ancestors and there is a great deal of anxiety about sin. Although drinking begins ceremonially in this society, it soon becomes disorganized. There are "colossal sprees in which men stay drunk for days on end." During these sprees a great deal of aggression and sexuality is expressed. The woman follows her husband around, and when his violence is exhausted she picks him up and takes him home.

Although severe inner tensions or needs for adjustment are nearly always found as a background for compulsive drinking, this factor always works in conjunction with the particular attitudes toward drinking which are structured in the culture. Where these attitudes arouse strong counteranxiety there may be little compulsive drinking in spite of severe maladjustments. Other outlets will be sought. On the other hand, where the attitudes are such as to permit or positively suggest drinking as a means of satisfying minor tensions, the effects of the drinking itself may generate acute maladjustments which result in its perpetuation. It is possible to distinguish four different types of attitudes which are represented in various cultural groups and which seem to have different effects on the rates of alcoholism.

The first is an attitude which calls for *complete abstinence.* For one reason or another, usually religious in nature, the use of alcohol as a beverage is not permitted for any purpose. The second might be called a *ritual attitude* toward drinking. This is also religious in nature, but it requires that alcoholic beverages, sometimes a particular one, should be used in the performance of religious ceremonies. Typically the beverage is regarded as sacred, it is consecrated to that end, and the partaking of it is a ritual act of communion with the sacred. This is a characteristic attitude toward drinking among many aboriginal peoples. The third can be called a *convivial attitude* toward drinking. Drinking is a "social" rather than a religious ritual, performed both because it symbolizes social unity or solidarity and because it actually loosens up emotions which make for social ease and good will. This is what is often called "social drinking." The fourth type seems best described as a *utilitarian attitude* toward drinking. This includes medicinal drinking and other types calculated to further self-interest or exclusively personal satisfaction. It is often "solitary" drinking, but not necessarily so. It is possible to drink for utilitarian purposes in a group and with group approval. The distinction is that the purpose is personal and self-interested rather than social and expressive.

One of the outstanding instances of the adoption of the attitude of *complete abstinence,* total prohibition on a large scale, is that of the Moslems.[7] The taboo rests on a religious basis, the command given by Mohammed. According to one of the translators of the Koran, during the fourth year of the Hegira, or flight from Mecca, Mohammed and his men were engaged in expeditions against neighboring tribes. In the midst of this some of his leaders quarreled while gambling and drinking, and upset the plans of warfare. Mohammed then forbade the use of wine and games of chance forever. He supported his decree by a fable of two angels who were sent to Babylon to teach men righteousness. They disobeyed God's commandment not to drink, got into trouble with a woman, and were severely punished by God, who then forbade the use of wine to His servants forever after. It is evident here how the usual dangers to social order, excess aggression and sexuality, played a part in the prohibition. Another factor, perhaps operative in the beginning and certainly afterward in maintaining the taboo, was the danger that intoxication would profane the performance of religious duties. These duties were very strict and

---

[6] R. Bunzel, "The Role of Alcoholism in Two Central American Cultures," *Psychiatry* 3 (1940), pp. 361–87.

[7] S. Morewood, *A Philosophical and Statistical History of the Inventions and Customs of Ancient and Modern Nations in the Manufacture and Use of Inebriating Liquors* (Dublin: W. Curry, Jun. & Co., and W. Carson, 1838).

exact. A man might soil himself while intoxicated and say a prayer while in an unclean condition.

There do not seem to be any statistical data which might be used as an index to the actual extent of drinking among the Moslems but there is a great deal of evidence to show that the taboo has been very unevenly observed in the course of history, and in some cases flagrantly violated. All sorts of expedients and rationalizations have been employed to evade the spirit of the law if not the letter of it. One of these was to mislabel the contents of wine containers. Some Moslems assumed that all other alcoholic beverages except wine were permitted. Some protested that the law referred only to excessive drinking. Smuggling and private use have been common. All in all, the Moslem can hardly be regarded as a model of successful total prohibition. One of the chief defects of total prohibition seems to be the extreme difficulty of getting a genuine acceptance of the attitude. The breaking of this taboo becomes an ideal way of expressing dissent and aggression, especially where the original solidarity of the group is weak and aggression is strong. Thus total prohibition sometimes overshoots the mark and encourages the very thing it is designed to prevent. This situation is frequently found among individual alcoholics whose parents were firm teetotalers and absolutely forbade their son to drink.

A similar situation arose among many of our East Coast Indian tribes when they were first introduced to alcohol. They made repeated attempts to enforce total prohibition when they saw the effects of the alcoholic beverages brought by the traders and colonists. They produced some famous temperance reformers, but they were unable to stem the tide.[8] The old men were usually the most concerned, but the young men could not be controlled. The Hopi and Zuni Indians in western New Mexico form an interesting exception.[9] Although information about them is somewhat confused and contradictory, it appears that in their aboriginal state they used alcoholic beverages in a ritual manner, and often

ended up with some rioting and sexual expression. When liquor was brought in by the Spaniards it was used for a period and then rejected entirely. It is not known just how this came about. It may be that the objectionable effects were accentuated by the new insecurity and stronger beverages. These people now put great emphasis on a quiet, calm, orderly existence. Everybody is expected to cooperate peacefully with his neighbors, and nobody tries to be outstanding. Insanity is greatly feared, and they seem to have identified drunkenness with insanity. Their life is highly and meticulously ritualized. It may be that their ritualism adequately took care of their insecurities and fears. It may be surmised, however, that if they had not previously used alcoholic beverages in a ritual manner, thus accepting its prohibition for all other purposes, they could not have been able to make total prohibition effective. The fact that they drank ritually before contact with the whites is one factor which distinctly sets them off from the East Coast Indians who had no alcoholic beverages before and hence had not been able to build up any stable attitudes toward drinking, ritually or otherwise. An attitude capable of restraining strong impulses in all the members of a group cannot be created by fiat or even by rational decision of all the members. It has to be a natural part of the emotional training of the child, repeated and actively practiced throughout the life cycle, in order to be firmly built into the personality.

It would be hard to find a better test of the hypothesis of the significance of the *ritual attitude* than the case of the orthodox Jews. They are not total abstainers, as some people suppose. They drink regularly, mostly in a ritual manner, although to some extent in a social way. Yet they are very seldom apprehended for drunkenness, and their rate of admission with alcoholic psychoses to mental hospitals is remarkably low. In almost any table showing rates of this sort for different ethnic groups in this country the Jews are at the bottom, just as the Irish are at the top. There have been many attempts to explain this. Immanuel Kant,[10] who was one of the first to

[8] "Aborigines of North America," in *Standard Encyclopedia of the Alcohol Problem*, vol. 1.
[9] Horton, "The Functions of Alcohol in Primitive Societies."

[10] Immanuel Kant, *Anthropologie in Pragmatischer Hinsicht* (Koenigsberg: Nivolovius, 1793), cf. E. M. Jellinek, "Immanuel Kant on Drinking," *Quarterly Journal of Studies on Alcohol* 1 (1941), pp. 777–78.

offer an explanation, believed that since the Jews' civic position was weak they had to be very rigidly self-controlled and cautious. They had to avoid the scandal and perhaps persecution which might result from drunkenness. Fishberg[11] emphasizes that the Jews have had to live under persecution, and says that the Jew knows it does not pay to be drunk. Myerson[12] emphasized the Jewish tradition itself and the hatred the Jews have developed for the drunkard, along with the factors of danger. These hypotheses are not necessarily contradictory—they simply emphasize different aspects of a ramified pattern. Yet it may be seriously questioned whether any of these factors could have remained truly effective without the ritual use of alcohol. In my opinion it is the ritual activity, repeated and participated in from childhood up, which positively stamps into the personality the sentiments or emotions to back up the rational realization of the dangers. Our East Coast Indians certainly saw the dangers rationally, and repeatedly decided to avoid alcohol, but had no success. They simply did not have the time nor the ritual technique for building into the personality the necessary emotional support for their rational decision. Hence the rational decision could not hold up in a crisis.

If it should be supposed that the Jews simply do not have acute needs for adjustment, or inner tensions, strong evidence may be advanced to the contrary. Besides all of the reasons for maladjustment to be expected from their position and historic role, it can be shown that with one or two minor exceptions they are quite as frequently represented in the major mental disorders as other groups. It is the impression of most psychiatrists that the Jews have higher rates of neuroses, that is the milder disturbances, than most other ethnic groups. If it should be imagined that the Jews have some kind of mysterious immunity to compulsive habits in general, no supporting evidence can be found. Jews are known to have high rates of drug addiction, at least in certain areas. In a study made in this country of all draftees rejected in World War I for psychiatric reasons, the Jews were found to have a higher rate of drug addiction than any other ethnic group.[13] This emphasizes the fact that their immunity to alcoholism can hardly be explained in terms of either a general immunity to addiction or a lack of acute inner tensions.

The essential ideas and sentiments which may come to be embodied in the attitude toward drinking as a result of ritual drinking, and which seem to operate as a counterinfluence to the formation of the habit of excessive drinking, may be clearly seen in the Jewish culture. In the Jewish family at least one male child is greatly desired, so that he may say prayers for his parents after their death. The continuity of the family is through the male line. Eight days after the birth of the male child a ceremony is held for his circumcision. There should be at least 10 adult males present to make up the "minyan," or legal and ritually sufficient quorum, to represent the community and carry on worship in the synagogue. The circumcision is performed because of God's commandment, and signifies the entry of the son into the covenant between Jehovah and the Jewish people. The people say, "Even as he has entered into the Covenant, so may he enter into the Law, the nuptial canopy, and into good deeds." A benediction is then offered over a cup of wine, with the following words: "Blessed art Thou, O Lord our God, king of the universe, creator of the fruit of the vine." The drinking of the cup of wine is a visible symbol and seal of the completed act of union.

In the Jewish culture wine stands for a whole complex of sacred things. Wine is variously alluded to as "the word of God" and "the commandment of the Lord." Similarly, the Torah (the sacred body of the Law), Jerusalem (the sacred place), Israel (the sacred community), and "the Messiah" (the righteous) are all compared to wine. The wine must be ritually pure, untouched by an idolater, and any vessel in which it is put must be "kosher," or ritually clean. Drinking, like eating, has a sacrificial character and is vested with an element of holiness. The dietary laws are symbolic of the separateness of

[11] M. Fishberg, *The Jews; a Study of Race and Environment* (New York: Scribners, 1911).
[12] A. Myerson, "Alcoholism and Induction into Military Service," *Quarterly Journal of Studies on Alcohol* 3 (1942), pp. 204–20. "Social Psychology of Alcoholism," *Diseases of the Nervous System* 1 (1940), pp. 42–50.

[13] P. Bailey, "A Contribution to the Mental Pathology of Races in the United States," *Archives of Neurological Psychiatry* 7 (1922), pp. 183–201.

the Jewish people. They constitute a discipline of all appetites to the end of attaining the all-inclusive state of holiness which is so much desired in the Jewish religion. Undisciplined appetites are a defilement of the self.

The first religious education of the child is directed to the teaching of the proper benedictions for bread, fruit, milk and other foods. He is told very early, "Thou shalt not eat any abominable thing." He also learns to observe the prohibition against touching that which is "holy unto the Lord." The "fruit of the vine" in the form of grapes falls in this class of sacred things. They must not be eaten before the fifth year of the life of the vine. In the first three years they are "uncircumcised," and in the fourth year they are "holy, to praise the Lord withal." Jewish parents impress their children with a great awe and reverence for things sacred and divine. Both grapes and wine are referred to as the "fruit of the vine," as in the customary benediction over wine.

There are four rituals each Sabbath in which the drinking of wine is the central act of communion. The first is on Friday evening and is called "Kiddush," that is, the ritual which "sanctifies" the holy day. After a thanksgiving prayer by the master of the house, a cup of wine is blessed. The master first partakes, and the cup is then passed from member to member, in the order of their precedence, down to and including the domestics if they are also Jewish. The males wear their hats, as in the synagogue, for this is a religious as well as a familistic ceremony. Then one of the two special Sabbath loaves is broken and each person is given a portion. After the meal, grace is recited and another cup of wine is blessed and passed around as before. This is called the "cup of benediction." A similar ritual, ironically called "Great Kiddush," because of its lesser importance, precedes the benediction over bread before breakfast on the morning of the Sabbath and other festival days. The ritual called the "Habdalah," on the Sabbath evening, marks the separation of the holy day from the rest of the week. The father chants a prayer of separation, the winecup is poured to overflowing to symbolize the overflowing of blessing which is hoped for, is blessed in the regular way, and partaken of first by the master of the house and then by the other males. The females do not partake on this occasion. The wine is again

blessed and this time the father drinks alone. He moistens his eyes with the wine, saying, "The commandment of the Lord is pure, enlightening the eyes." The remaining wine is finally poured upon a plate and the burning candle is extinguished by dipping it into the wine. It is interesting and important to note that the order in which the family members partake of the wine, first the father, then the lesser males, then the females, and then the domestics, emphasizes their relative status and also their relative closeness to the sacred. The same order in reverse is observed in the Habdalah, where first the females abstain and then the lesser males, so that finally only the father drinks. The various members are separated from the sacred in the order of the lesser first, and finally the most important.

The drinking of wine, or the specific abstention from drinking, figures in the various feasts and fasts of the yearly cycle. In general, where food is forbidden as a sign of mourning or as a sign of guilt and expiation, that is, where the ritual state is one of estrangement from the sacred, wine is forbidden. This is true of the "Black Fast" and of "Yom Kippur"—the Day of Atonement. After the season of estrangement, comes the season of reunion and restored favor with God in the Festival of the Booths. This reunion and restored favor is indicated by the taking of food and wine. On Purim, a more secular holiday, the Talmud says that the Jew should drink until he can no longer distinguish between "cursed be Haman" (the ancient persecutor of the Jews) and "blessed be Mordecai" (their ancient savior). Sometimes the old men pretend to become drunk to amuse the youngsters. Actually, however, this appears to be another one of those ironic inversions, like "Great Kiddush," and only emphasizes the extreme foolishness and danger of drunkenness by linking it with the memory of old persecutions. At the celebration of the Passover there are four ritual partakings of wine, each with a blessing. After this no more wine may be tasted that night. A cup of wine, which one of the boys tastes, is left for Elijah, who may come during the night. Finally, in the Rejoicing of the Law, a festival celebrating the time when the Law was given, wine is partaken of in the usual ritual manner.

At the time of marriage, the social union par excellence, the bridal couple and their nearest relatives partake of a consecrated cup of wine, and the glass is broken, apparently with the connotation of the finality and exclusiveness of the union. At the time of death, the final separation, the deep mourning is indicated by abstention from all food and wine. In all of these rituals, in which the child participates from the time he is able to understand, the partaking of the consecrated wine indicates a union with the sacred and the solidarity of the Jewish people in their covenant with God, while abstention from the wine indicates a temporary estrangement from Divine favor, a state of guilt, and the sad dispersion of the Jewish people.

In the Jewish culture the wine is sacred and drinking is an act of communion. The act is repeated again and again and the attitudes toward drinking are all bound up with attitudes toward the sacred in the mind and emotions of the individual. In my opinion this is the central reason why drunkenness is regarded as so "indecent"— so unthinkable—for a Jew. Rational precaution also probably plays a part, but the ritual use is the main mechanism which builds in the necessary emotional support for the attitudes. Drunkenness is a profanity, an abomination, a perversion of the sacred use of wine. Hence the idea of drinking "to become drunk" for some individualistic or selfish reason arouses a counteranxiety so strong that very few Jews ever become compulsive drinkers.

We have other evidence that the counteranxiety connected with drinking can act as a factor to prevent drunkenness. Among the Balinese[14] alcoholic beverages are distilled and used ceremonially by the people, but they very seldom become intoxicated. The anxiety here, however, seems not to have been created through specific ceremonial use but because it is so extremely important to these people to maintain their exact spatial and geographic orientation. If a Balinese is put into a car and taken suddenly by a winding way to a place where he loses his directions he becomes extremely anxious and actually sick. Eastward, inland toward their sacred mountain, and upward toward its summit are sacred directions. Westward, outward to the sea, and downward are profane. Each member is very careful to keep other members of higher status than himself to the eastward, inland, or on a higher seat. Drunkenness is likely to make one lose his directions and become confused in these relations. In the weaving and confusion of drunkenness one is likely to trespass on the sacred, put sacred things in profane places, or wander off into the dangerous jungle which they fear greatly. Hence the anxiety connected with drunkenness is so strong and immediate that Balinese avoid it almost entirely. This is true in spite of the fact that they have extremely strong suppressed emotions, as is known from other facts about their culture.

Convivial drinking is a mixed type, tending toward the ritual in its symbolism of solidarity, and toward the utilitarian in the "good feeling" expected. Wherever it is found highly developed it seems to be in danger of breaking down toward purely utilitarian drinking. This breakdown is to be found in marked form in the Irish culture. A drinking party is in order at all of the principal occasions in the life cycle, in the meeting of friends, in business dealings, political affairs, pilgrimages, and every other occasion when people come together. One writer[15] in the last century says, "Hallow-E'en, St. Patrick's Day, Easter, and all extra-ordinary days are made apologies for a drinking bout; a week's excess is taken at Christmas." He continues:

> Baptisms are generally debauches; launching a ship; making men pay their footing [on board a crowded ship where the men had to stand on the deck], births, wakes, funerals, marriages, churns in the country, are all jovial and vehement occasions of universal revelry. Pledging, toasting, and offering spirits in courtesy is much in vogue; and if a visitor do not taste at any time a day, he gives offence, as in Scotland. Washerwomen, wet nurses, coach drivers, carmen, porters, and others are all treated by their employers with whiskey. There are no dry bargains; and in provision stores and other places, allowances of whiskey are bound to the workmen in their articles of service. An Irishman is in the last stage when he begins to drink alone; which is the case also with the Scotsman; and numbers treat for the mere purpose of obtaining pleasant company.

---

[14] G. Bateson and M. Mead, *Balinese Character* (New York: New York Academy of Sciences, 1942).

---

[15] Testimony of John Dunlop. In "Evidence on Drunkenness Presented to the House of Commons," J. S. Buckingham, Esq. in the Chair (London: S. Bagster, Jun., Printer [ca. 1834]).

It is important to note that although drinking is a part of gatherings for occasions such as marriages, which have a ritual or ceremonial core, the people never drink as a part of the ritual itself. In the Mass the priest partakes of the wine but not the laity. On the sort of occasions where there is a ritual core, drinking is a purely secular, convivial celebration, before or after. Whisky is always liberally provided. No "good fellow" would be niggardly in providing whisky for a celebration. It is thought to be only "decent" to treat a friend. One shows that he regards the other as "a good fellow" by drinking with him. When relatives, or "friends" as they are called in Ireland, or acquaintances of the same social standing meet in a public house, it is a matter of strict obligation for one to "stand" for all the others. He must order drinks all around and pay for them himself. Each man is then obligated to "stand" in his turn, and so on until all have bought at least one drink around. If there are more than three or four in the party, they are necessarily fairly well intoxicated by the time each has done his duty. It is an unforgivable insult to refuse to take a drink with a man without a long involved explanation and a profuse apology.

The breakdown into a *utilitarian attitude* can be observed in the use of drinking in economic transactions. At the fairs, where the livestock is sold, there is usually a long, heated argument about the price. When an agreement is finally reached, the bargain is sealed with one or more drinks. Sometimes the seller takes his customer to the public house before the agreement is reached and treats him a few times to "soften him up." In making the bargain for a marriage it is necessary to reach extensive economic agreements in the evaluation of the farm and livestock, since this determines the amount of the dowry the young lady's father will give. In one of these matchmakings the bargainers treat back and forth until all are well fuddled. One writer[16] says, "To one who has lived for some time in England, the mixture of tippling and business seems like some incredible dream. Little bits of business get in, as if by stealth, between the drinks during the day!" The farmer typically comes home from a day at the fair in a very intoxicated condition indeed. His wife does not usually complain. In fact, if she is a very good wife, she may treat her husband the next morning with "a hair of the dog that bit him." Drunken men are usually treated with care and affection in Ireland. To the mother the drunken man is "the poor boy." Laborers seeing an intoxicated man coming home from the fair are prone to regard him with envy, rather than pity, since he is in a much better state than they.

Drinking to get over a hang-over, "a hair of the dog that bit you," is a pure example of individualistic, utilitarian drinking. Here the alcohol is regarded as a medicine. According to Morewood,[17] an Irish historian, whisky, or aqua vitae, as it was called, "was first used in Ireland only as a medicine, considered a panacea for all disorders, and the physicians recommended it to patients indiscriminately for preserving health, dissipating humours, strengthening the heart, curing colic, dropsy, palsy, quartan fever, stone, and even prolonging existence itself beyound the common limits." Aqua vitae was sold only in apothecaries' shops until sometime in the sixteenth or seventeenth century, and it has retained its medicinal virtues in the mind of the people to this day. It was the universal folk remedy, to "keep the cold out of the stomach," to produce a feeling of warmth after exposure, to restore consciousness in case of fainting, to cure the stomach-ache, to cure insomnia, to reduce fatigue, to whet the appetite, to feel stronger, and to get rid of hang-overs. In the cholera plagues of 1831 and 1849, which struck a mortal fear into the hearts of the people, brandy was firmly believed to be a preventive. People even sold their beds in their anxiety to get it. The country doctors prescribed it widely and used it themselves. In fact legends grew up about some of these old topers to the effect that the Divine inspiration to cure did not possess them unless they were more or less "under the influence." In many cases a glass of whisky was all the poor peasant had to offer the doctor by way of payment. Whisky was given to children as a reward for good behavior. Drinking was the recommended cure-all for young men in low spirits,

---

[16] McCarthy, *Irish Land and Irish Liberty.*

[17] Morewood, *Philosophical and Statistical History of Inebriating Liquors.*

for whatever reason, just as prayer was recommended to women and old people.

There is little reason to doubt that the utilitarian attitude toward drinking, if commonly held, is the one of the four types which is most likely to lead to widespread compulsive drinking. There is no counter-anxiety attached to the process of drinking in this case, and there is every suggestion for the individual to adopt drinking as the means of dealing with his particular maladjustment. The prevalence of this attitude in the culture of the Irish, along with widespread inner tensions, seems adequately to explain their high rate of alcoholism.

There are certain occupational groups with high rates that seem to trace mainly to an occupationally induced utilitarian attitude toward drinking. It is well known, for example, that rates are particularly high among individuals connected with the manufacture and sale of alcoholic beverages, such as brewery employees, public-house, hotel and innkeepers, barmen, waiters and traveling salesmen. Certain manual laborers, who do heavy exhausting work, such as longshoremen, drink to reduce their fatigue or to escape chronic unpleasant conditions of work. They are likely to have high rates. Sullivan[18] in a statistical study of England made in 1905, drew a distinction between "convivial drinking," much as it is defined here, and "industrial drinking," which is one type of utilitarian drinking. He found that the highest rates of alcoholic disorders were associated with "industrial drinking, and not with convivial drunkenness." It is a well-known fact that a very high percentage of prostitutes become inebriates. The use of alcohol, both for themselves and as an attraction to their customers, is an indispensable part of their trade.

Finally, there is the third cultural factor which seems to have a bearing on rates of alcoholism— the degree to which the culture provides suitable substitutes for the inner tensions and needs for adjustment which it creates. One of the most common substitutes is the use of other narcotic drugs. The high rate of drug addiction among the Jews has been mentioned. Many Moslems,

it is said, are users of hashish, and seem to be habituated to very strong tea and coffee. Among the Brahmins, who have a severe prohibition against alcoholic beverages, opium is used to a considerable degree, and this pattern seems to have spread to some of the peoples in the East Indies. The Japanese, who are supposed to have a low rate of alcoholism, are frequently users of opium.

Among the Balinese, who avoid drunkenness because of their anxiety about orientation, there is a peculiar trancelike state which seems to act as an outlet for their tensions. Their childhood training is one of constant stimulation to emotional response, followed by frustration. The mother fondles the child, but as soon as he notices and begins to respond emotionally, she "cuts him dead." Under this treatment the children finally withdraw into themselves and refuse to respond. But in their ceremonial dances, which symbolically recall the childhood situation, they go into trances and express extreme self-aggression with mingled emotions of "agony and ecstasy." Thus the trances seem to provide a way of restoring the balance, and to give the emotional purging which, in another culture, alcohol might provide. The complicated ritualism of the Hopi and Zuni Indians, who were successful in total prohibition, may provide a somewhat similar substitute for reducing anxiety.

It is impossible to name all the sorts of things which might possibly serve as substitute means of adjustment, since this would depend upon the maladjustments which are acute in particular cultures, and these are very numerous and complicated. The three general factors discussed, the acute inner tensions or needs for adjustment, the attitudes toward drinking, and the provision of substitutes, seem to be fairly adequate in an over-all logical way, and give some insight into a few of the outstanding cultural differences in rates of alcoholism. There are many rates, however, which are not yet understood. It is still not possible to formulate precisely all the different types of maladjustment or tension which can be involved in compulsive drinking, to say nothing of our inability to measure just how acute they are in specific cultural settings. As to the types of attitude toward drinking, very little is known concerning just how they come about, what makes them endure or break down, or just how

---

[18] W. C. Sullivan, "Industrial Alcoholism," *Economic Review*, London 15 (1905), pp. 150–63.

widespread particular attitudes are in particular places and cultures. These problems still require an immense amount of careful theoretical and research work.

It can safely be said, however, that all three factors are important. They all work together, and the rates are complicated end-results. With regard to the problem of reducing the rates of alcoholism in a particular place, there is no doubt that it must be attacked from all three angles. Anything which can be done to relieve the acute tensions of people, or steer them away from utilitarian attitudes toward drinking, or provide them with suitable and effective substitutes for the rewards which drinking brings them, may have a preventive effect in the long run. It seems clear, however, that no very conspicuous success can be expected unless all three factors can be modified together, and modified considerably for the whole group.

B. SOCIAL RELATIONS AND PROCESS

In many instances the alcoholic's drinking leads to serious interpersonal discord with his family, especially his wife. In "Wives of Alcoholics," Thelma Whalen argues, however, that there may be another dimension to the husband-wife relationship. Whalen thinks that females may marry alcoholics or pre-alcoholics because they need to suffer pain, to dominate, to punish, to depreciate, and so forth. When anyone marries, according to Whalen (and others), they may select, albeit unconsciously, individuals who satisfy deep-seated personality needs. A female who needs to suffer, to dominate, etc., may select an alcoholic for a husband. Consequently, she may derive significant unconscious pleasure from her husband's drinking.

Whalen's analysis, of course, applies only to alcoholics who are married. Evidence indicates, however, that many alcoholics are single, divorced, widowed, or separated. This is particularly true of alcoholics who, because of their drinking, are unable to continue their normal occupational and social roles, who therefore drop in status and sometimes end up on "skid row." Not only are the alcoholic's relations with relatives and friends severed by this process, but some investigators report that such persons are deficient in social relations in general. Although skid roaders may interact with each other, social relations are reported to be weak, fleeting, and easily broken. Skid row alcoholics, then, are said to be "undersocialized." However, James F. Rooney's study of skid row in three California cities, reported in "Group Processes Among Skid Row Winos," suggests that this conception is not wholly valid. Rooney finds that winos may establish quite meaningful social relations through their contacts in "bottle groups." "Bottle groups" consist of winos who pool their funds to purchase a bottle. Although the group dissolves once the bottle is empty, a wino may join several bottle groups in the course of a day. According to Rooney, these groups provide winos with the rewards of belonging, prestige, and security. They are like other groups in that norms serve to structure and regulate group relations. As an example, skid roaders are expected to reciprocate when they have been "treated" and are negatively sanctioned (labelled "chiselers") if they don't. Social relations and processes in bottle groups are thus similar to those in all groups. The difference is in content and group objectives.

WIVES OF ALCOHOLICS

THELMA WHALEN

The alcoholic marriage is a marriage, and as such is not exempt from all the things that are true of other marriages even though it is often discussed as though it were. Men and women marry in an effort to meet their own needs. The needs for which the husband and wife seek satisfaction are complex and varied and represent different degrees of maturity in different individuals. When people verbalize these needs, they usually describe them in such terms as the need to love and be loved; to care for and be cared for; to have a home, children and companionship. There are other needs, unconscious and unexpressed, which may motivate a man or a woman to marry. These may include the wish to depreciate, to control, to hurt, to seek pain or to suffer. These needs, both conscious and unconscious, occur in a variety of combinations. But each individual has a dominating characteristic which is the nucleus of his personality. It is this dominating characteristic which governs his selection of a marriage partner. In some way the person he selects must appear to him to be the person who can meet his particular needs. This is not to imply that people go about getting married in a thoughtful, reasoned way. They obviously do not. It is their feelings toward another person that guide them, and many of these feelings they do not understand or interpret accurately because they are unconscious feelings.

When the needs to be met by the marriage relationship are predominantly positive and mature, the resulting marriage is essentially a "good" or happy one which results in personally satisfying and socially useful living for the whole family. When the needs to be met by the marriage relationship are predominantly negative and unhealthy, the marriage may become a vehicle for unhappiness and destructive social living for everyone in the family.

The woman who marries an alcoholic or a man who subsequently becomes an alcoholic is usually viewed by the community as a helpless victim of circumstance. She sees herself and other people see her as someone who, through no fault of her own and in spite of consistent effort on her part, is defeated over and over again by her husband's irresponsible behavior. This is certainly not true. It merely appears to be true. The wife of an alcoholic is not simply the object of mistreatment in a situation which she had no part in creating. Her personality was just as responsible for the making of this marriage as her husband's was; and in the sordid sequence of marital misery which follows, she is not an innocent bystander. She is an active participant in the creation of the problems which ensue.

With this background of psychological insight, let us look at some of the women who come to a family service agency for counseling in relation to the problems of being married to an alcoholic.

THE SUFFERER

The first of these women I shall call Suffering Susan because it is clear that her need to punish herself is the dominating characteristic which forms the nucleus of her personality. That was why she chose a marriage partner who was obviously so troublesome that her need to be miserable would always be gratified. Her husband's alcoholism usually insures hardship, which she bears with composure and equanimity. He usually earns and supports poorly. He may be abusive; he is sure to be irresponsible. When she starts to have labor pains he is never around to help her get to the hospital. And when the baby is born he cannot be found anywhere. He found the strain too great to bear, became gloriously "lit," and is now sleeping it off—heaven knows where. The suspicions of infidelity, characteristic of many alcoholics, cause him to be hostile and insulting when drunk, and moody when sober. Even the mildest of men are able to inflict severe pain upon their families by simply staying away and letting their wives worry about their safety and their lost wages.

Susan, however, is a model of deportment.

Reprinted with permission of author and publisher, from *Quarterly Journal of Studies on Alcohol* 14 (October, 1953), pp. 632–41. Copyright 1953 by Journal of Studies on Alcohol, Inc., New Brunswick, N. J.

She is a good housekeeper and feels great responsibility for homemaking. She sees this as her proper womanly function and may be so exclusively devoted to practical aspects of planning and management that she is not aware that the home is a cheerless place for husband and children. She is likely to be drab and colorless in appearance and manner. She has few contacts outside the home because of her limited self-regard and self-assertiveness. She is unable to reach out for what are usually called "the good things of life." She is invariably apologetic in the way she relates to the counselor, sometimes expressing concern about "taking so much of your time." She presents a picture of uncomplaining endurance in dealing with intolerable situations. Susan does not see problems accurately but presents them in a roundabout, devious manner. She interprets them in terms of unfortunate situations or conditions, quite beyond her control, and for which no one is really to blame. It is from this manner of presenting her situation and from the fact that the problems are of long standing that we sense this woman's need for discomfort and suffering. She feels that there is "goodness" in this meek, self-effacing attitude and manner. To her, the pronoun "I" is spelled a-y-e.

With her children, Susan enforces a conventional level of behavior with particular emphasis on neatness, orderliness and repression of hostile feelings. This becomes especially difficult when the alcoholic father is being troublesome, hostile or abusive. The shy, patient child may have trouble in his schoolwork; the more spirited one may become rebellious and belligerent and come to the attention of the court. The parental attitudes are particularly confusing to children in these families. Daughters are prone to develop the pain-seeking patterns laid down by their mother. The boys, with such a faulty pattern in their father, are likely to assume a dependent relationship with their mother, for a child needs someone to cling to.

To the skilled counselor it is clear that alcoholism is merely a red herring here which tends to obscure the essence of this marital relationship. As a matter of fact, Susan does not always choose an alcoholic for a husband. Her need to be miserable is sometimes served just as effectively by marrying a sadistic, belittling man who is a strict teetotaler and a deacon in the church; or a man who is handicapped physically or intellectually or both; or one who is ineffectual in some other way. It can also happen that Susan marries a psychopath. But it is always someone who is certain to provide much less in love, security and support than she properly should expect. . . .

THE CONTROLLER

In a different category are the alcoholics who wake up some fine morning and find themselves married to Controlling Catherine. Catherine is quite a girl. She knew all about his drinking but knew things would be different once he had her to look out for him. And she looks out for him. She dominates each and every aspect of their life together. She does this because there is no doubt in her mind that, of the two of them, she is more capable of making decisions than her husband. Generally speaking, this is quite true too. The unique character of this relationship lies in the fact that, in spite of the affection, sympathy and compassion implied in the act of marrying someone because he needed her, this union serves as a vehicle for expressing Catherine's distrustful, resentful attitudes toward men in general. She could not possibly have wanted to marry a more adequate man. It would have been too threatening to her. In her view of life, men have all the advantages anyway. Why risk marrying one over whom you do not have some advantage? Consequently her husband's ineptitude is not only acceptable but even gratifying— up to a point. Controlling Catherine always marries a man whom she feels to be inadequate or inferior in some way. He is not always an alcoholic, though he frequently is. Sometimes he is a cripple, or a person with less education or a poorer social background than her own. Or he may be a person of a different racial or national background, in which case Catherine can look down on him because he is "different" and therefore, to her, inferior. We meet Catherine quite as often in the so-called mixed marriages as we do in the alcoholic marriage.

When Catherine's husband is an alcoholic he tends to become more and more incapacitated as the marriage continues. Economic insecurity usually is present as a result of irregular work. Catherine usually decides to take a job herself, and having done so, she controls the family purse strings with an iron hand and uses this as a further means of monitoring her husband. Unlike Susan, Catherine is highly critical and resentful of her husband's behavior. There is no doubt whatever in her mind who is at fault for the family problems. Has not her husband told her in one of his fits of repentance that he is not good enough for her? She tends to be coldly angry in presenting her complaints and problems, and there is a quality of hardness and unforgivingness in her manner of expressing criticisms. She wants her husband to change and to act differently; to stop drinking and to support her more adequately, so that she may have a happy marriage. Before she comes to us, she has usually sought an ally in a clergyman or a lawyer. She does not look to herself or to her own behavior and attitudes for a possible explanation of her situation. . . .

THE WAVERER

Next there is Wavering Winnifred. We see her more often than either Susan or Catherine. Winnifred appears to be the balance wheel of the family. It is she who gathers up the pieces and holds the family together when her husband is on a spree. She manages the money. She knows how to plan. She has worked outside the home at various times ever since the beginning of her marriage, and her earnings have helped to meet the payments to the building and loan company and the doctor. Sometimes she loses patience with her husband and takes him to court; but the judge, if he takes her seriously, speedily discovers that she didn't mean it because she relents almost at once and begs him to dismiss the case. She may separate from her husband for a few weeks or months, but she always comes back when he pleads with her and makes promises. She does not easily admit love for her husband. Her friends and relatives have told her that she is a fool to stay with him, and she fears that the counselor may have the same opinion. Her "official" position is, therefore, that her husband's behavior has killed her love for him. When she has learned to trust the counselor,

however, she will express verbally her continuing affection for her husband. If he leaves home, she expresses great anxiety about his comfort and safety. Suppose he should get run over when he is not quite himself? Winnifred seldom expresses this affection in ways that would really help this man to work out his problem. She shares her husband's blindness about the depth of his difficulties, and she resists, almost as much as he does, any suggestion from the counselor that these difficulties, if untreated, will continue to recur. When he is drinking, she is furious and despairing; when he is sober, she recovers her good spirits, tries to forget the past, and expresses a childlike hope that this time he will keep his promises and there will never again be any trouble.

Winnifred appears quite capable when conditions are favorable. She is a good housekeeper, an affectionate mother, and keeps her family well organized. She is likeable, good-natured and pleasant. She has a pseudocapacity for relationships—"pseudo" in that it gives the outward appearance of genuine motherly interest in both husband and children. Actually, out of her own great need to be loved, appreciated and given to, Winnifred searches out the weak and helpless to form relationships with. She can be giving only to those who seem to need her. She always chooses a husband who, to her, is weak, who she thinks "needs her" and would therefore be unlikely to leave her. As long as she can be sure that a man cannot get along without her, she can feel secure in a relationship with him. The fact that he is also often an alcoholic appears to strike her as a surprising but somewhat irrelevant factor. Basically, Winnifred is fearful and insecure. She is unable to reach out for relationships with adequate, self-sufficient individuals because, since they have no need of her, she doubts her ability to hold their interest. Alcoholism increases her husband's need of her, and that is why Winnifred can be tolerant of it for a long time. It sometimes looks as if she expects him to drink, although she may fuss and nag about it. When it continues for a long time, or is markedly excessive, however, her tolerance wears thin. She becomes disturbed and disorganized as the situation gets too far out of control —when her husband stays away from home too long drinking, or when he has lost one job and is slow about finding another and the creditors get nasty. She sometimes leaves him under stress of this kind, but her own need for love, appreciation and emotional response is so great that she is quite unable to resist his urgent plea for her to return, to make a fresh start. Wavering Winnifred can always believe what she wants to believe. She doesn't always marry an alcoholic, however. Sometimes she chooses a man who is a steady, faithful worker and quite responsible about holding a job but so dependent and passive in nature that he never gets a promotion and would be the last man in the world to request a raise. Such a marriage usually works out satisfactorily in most respects except for the fact that there are always financial worries and economic deprivation.

Winnifred's children also have felt the effects of her need to be needed. Outwardly they are likely to be well-behaved, well-cared for children who achieve satisfactorily in school. The boys may have a rough time of it because of their close tie to their mother and their lack of a strong, successful father to pattern after. In her insecurity and hunger for relationship, however, Winnifred has shut her children off from normal participation in activities outside the home. She has kept them tied closely to herself.

THE PUNISHER

Last, but not least, there is Punitive Polly, whose relationship to her husband resembles that of a boa constrictor to a rabbit. Such a relationship is often mutually satisfactory; some rabbits seem to like being swallowed. But quite often the rabbit rebels and goes out and gets drunk. Punitive Polly is often, though not always, a career woman. Sometimes she is a clubwoman. She either earns more money than her husband, or it is her influence and maneuvering which gets and holds his job for him or is responsible for the orders or accounts or contracts given him. Polly's relationships with people in general, and with men in particular, are characterized by rivalrous, aggressive and envious attitudes. This makes for great loneliness, although she is so busy being successful that she is seldom aware of it. Polly despises housework and the care of children and usually succeeds in avoiding them.

Since her goal in life is to achieve outstandingly in business or industry, or perhaps politics, where her chief competitors are men, she naturally feels that men are her chief enemies in the world of people. Obviously she could risk marriage only with a man whom she felt to be vulnerable in some way, as a man. In describing her husband, Polly will refer to him as being "boyish" or "sweet." That is when he is sober, of course. In point of fact, he is quite often several years her junior. But regardless of whether or not he is younger than she, Polly's husband always seems to her to be limited in some way in his essential masculinity. If he did not, she would never have married him. It is not surprising that this appealing vulnerability often takes the form of alcoholism.

Polly does not require a great deal of her husband—at least she thinks not. She is quite willing to earn most of the living, to carry most of the responsibility, to pay the rent and buy the television set. All she requires in return is that the rabbit remain swallowed. She wants him to behave like the becoming household accessory she intended him to be and not embarrass her by going out and getting drunk and waking up in the wrong beds. She will not insist on his taking care of her adequately, as Catherine does, or require him to make himself over for her. She is willing for him to have almost anything he wants —except his manhood. When he does not meet these modest requirements Polly can be very punitive, indeed. Since drinking is often the only way he can find to assert himself, Polly is never free from underlying angry feelings and her behavior toward her husband is likely to be quite harsh and unforgiving. One such husband commented, "My wife is stronger than I am—she's got me down." In this marriage Polly finds an outlet for her aggressive impulses in a partnership with a man who is partially dependent on her and who is constantly maneuvering himself into situations that seem to justify her punishing him. Polly's husband finds in his wife a partial outlet for his submissive and passive impulses: someone to scold him when he is bad, to think and plan for him when he is puzzled, to extricate him from his scrapes and, most important of all, to worry about him. The relationship is in many ways similar to that of a mother—a scolding but indulgent mother—and her very small boy.

Under favorable circumstances, if there is adequate income and good enough social standing to avert scandal, these marriages last for years. The children are the ones who suffer the most emotional damage. Polly is too preoccupied to really know her children. She finds no pleasure in giving them the physical care through which mothers build relationships with their children when they are small, and therefore usually turns this responsibility over to someone else. She finds older children and adolescents particularly bothersome, and when they develop emotional problems, as Polly's children frequently do, she gladly turns these over to someone else too. Thus, in counseling we meet Polly as the parent of a teenager with whom we are working no less often than as the wife of an alcoholic. The general public is prone to say, "Of course those children are poorly adjusted. What else can you expect? Their father is an alcoholic!" It is necessary to point out that the children's problems can only partly be explained in this way. It is true that they suffer from the lack of a strong, masculine figure as a father. They cannot easily respect him and this deprives them of an anchor which every child needs. But it is also true that Polly has never given them the warm, close, loving relationship, the personal

mothering, that is equally important to a child's normal development. They have been doubly deprived.

SUMMARY

In summary then, the family of the alcoholic continues to be a concern of the family counseling agency today not because we attempt to treat alcoholism per se but because the alcoholic is often one factor among others in a family constellation which is productive of emotional problems. It is our observation that certain kinds of women are attracted to the alcoholic man and marry him hoping to find in him an answer to deep unconscious needs of their own. These women will inevitably choose a husband who has certain psychological characteristics, although he does not always express them through alcoholism. Our work with these wives consists of helping them to understand their own motivations and to find less destructive ways of meeting their own needs.

It will not be thought that the four personality types sketched here constitute a complete gallery. They represent the ones we meet most often. No doubt there are other well-known types.

GROUP PROCESSES AMONG SKID ROW WINOS
A Reevaluation of the Undersocialization Hypothesis

JAMES F. ROONEY

Men composing the Skid Row population of the United States are nearly completely lacking in family ties, and many maintain few or irregular employment relationships by means of which individuals may be brought into contact with others. In a study of 444 men on the Bowery in

New York City, Straus and McCarthy[1] found that half had never married, over one-third had been divorced or separated from their wives, and 12 percent were widowers. None had regular contact with any other class of relative. Although the men in this social group interact among themselves, their mutual associations are meager. Their personal relationships do not connote responsibility for the future and very easily

Reproduced by permission of the author and publisher from the *Quarterly Journal of Studies on Alcohol* 22 (June, 1961) pp. 444–60. Footnotes have been renumbered. The author wishes to express gratitude to Thomas E. Shipley, Jr., and to Leonard Blumberg, of Temple University, for insights into the concept of socialization as used in this paper, as well as to Jane Phillips, Betty Segal and Francis H. Hoffman for suggestions in preparing the manuscript.

[1] R. Straus and R. G. McCarthy, "Nonaddictive Pathological Drinking Patterns of Homeless Men," *Quarterly Journal of Studies on Alcohol* 12 (1951), pp. 601–11.

can be broken or merely disintegrate without meaningful effect on the individuals.

A variety of psychological adjustments appears to be used to adapt to the dearth of meaningful interpersonal relationships. That alcohol is not the only means of adjustment is shown by the fact that perhaps only one-third of the Chicago Skid Row population are excessive drinkers,[2] other inhabitants being both steady and seasonal workers, aged and disabled men seeking low-cost living quarters, and beggars and thieves.[3]

Chronic excessive use of alcohol, however, is one of the chief means used by Skid Row men to adjust to the loneliness of this way of life and has been interpreted as a means of escape from the feelings of inadequacy which underlie it.[4] Straus[5] describes this mode of living as both cause and effect of undersocialization:

> Deficiently socialized persons are usually deprived of the opportunity of sharing experiences with others, of belonging to social groups and participating in social activities. They are deprived, also, of certain important personal satisfactions, such as affection, prestige, the feeling of security, the rewarding aspects of identifying with others, and the like. The satisfactions of these personal needs usually come through association with other people. Because they have not learned the ways of society, undersocialized persons are insecure, and acts of "sharing" become difficult, distasteful and even dangerous to them. They therefore choose a way of life which avoids associations of "sharing."

For Pittman and Gordon,[6] undersocialization

means that an individual's life history is marked by a lack of participation in primary groups such as the family, play groups, and peer groups, these being the sine qua non of personality formation. An individual who has limited opportunities to develop intimate personal relationships in the primary groups is handicapped in sharing experiences with others; his interpersonal relationships are inept.

Pittman and Gordon support the hypothesis that chronic excessive drinkers are undersocialized by presenting a wealth of facts gained from intensive background interviews with 187 prisoners arrested for habitual drunkenness in Rochester, N.Y. The orientation of families of the prisoners frequently was marked by disruption (death, divorce or separation occurring in 39 percent of the cases), low regular church attendance (41 percent), and almost complete lack of participation in voluntary church societies and community activities (2 percent). As a group they not only appeared to lack experience in all types of sharing situations on the formal level of social organization but also appeared not to have had the opportunity to learn to form a satisfying emotional bond with family members.

Pittman and Gordon further hypothesize that lack of socialization into the primary-group roles encountered in childhood results in an inadequate basis for participation in the important secondary-task roles occurring in education, occupation, and marriage.[7] Inadequate preparation and lack of self-confidence frequently result in an "adaptive flight" syndrome by which the individual separates himself from family and employment and seeks dependency upon drinking.[8] Entry into the Skid Row population frequently accompanies the pattern of flight. Complementarily the tavern group is described as a refuge in which the undersocialized person is welcome. "The demands which the other members of the drinking group place upon him are limited, and he is able to handle these with his small competence in interpersonal relationships."[9]

Straus and McCarthy point out that the majority of Skid Row imbibers are capable of controlling their drinking within quite strict limits. Thus they are not properly alcohol addicts but rather are nonaddictive symptomatic excessive drinkers who seek a sense of removal and relief,

---

[2] "The Homeless Man on Skid Row," (Chicago: National Opinion Research Center, 1958, Report No. 65-1, D. J. Bogue, study director), Table 6–1.

[3] *Ibid.,* chap. 4.

[4] Straus and McCarthy, "Drinking Patterns of Homeless Men," p. 610.

[5] R. Straus, "Alcohol and the Homeless Man," *Quarterly Journal of Studies on Alcoholism* 7 (1946), pp. 360–404.

[6] D. J. Pittman and C. W. Gordon, *Revolving Door: A Study of the Chronic Police Case Inebriate* (New Haven: Publications Division, Yale Center of Alcohol Studies; and Glencoe, Ill.: Free Press, 1958).

[7] *Ibid.,* p. 109.

[8] *Ibid.,* p. 129.

[9] *Ibid.,* p. 69.

but not complete escape, through alcohol.[10] Jellinek[11] has defined such behavior patterns as constituting a form of nonaddictive alcoholism. He states that the basic problem for such individuals is not irrevocably bound up with their relationship to alcohol but rather to the underlying personality problems or harsh environmental conditions from which they seek relief.

There are many different types of drinking groups on Skid Row. Peterson and Maxwell[12] state that entry into Skid Row is a process of progressive enculturation into the drinking patterns, and that two major groups are distinguished by the inhabitants: "drunks" and "winos," these being points on a continuum of progressive excessive drinking. Jackson and Connor[13] divide the Skid Row excessive drinkers into two general classes: "lushes," who can afford to drink in taverns and consider themselves the prestige group; and the more deteriorated class who consume the cheapest wine or nonbeverage alcohol as frequently as possible, called "winos" or "rubby-dubs." Although their particular jargon is not used in all Skid Rows of the United States, the division does correspond with Peterson and Maxwell's "drunks" and "winos." The present investigator's field work corroborates this general dichotomy, which is recognized by Skid Row inhabitants themselves. The drinking pattern of "drunks" is characterized by occasional sprees of extended drinking followed by longer periods of control during which the individual may or may not consume liquor. This drinking pattern permits an individual to engage in seasonal employment. A wino may be defined as one whose need can no longer be met by occasional sprees, but who has reached the point of needing alcohol nearly every day, with a resulting pattern that limits him to day-labor participation in the economy. The wino no longer looks upon himself as primarily a worker and thus can no longer consider himself a temporary resident of Skid Row. He has given up real hope of steady employment and has come to accept Skid Row as "home."

Bain[14] likewise described two major types of Skid Row drinking groups in Chicago: tavern-centered groups and street-drinking groups. Tavern groups are composed of more regularly employed and hence fairly affluent persons who form relatively stable associational ties based upon continued attendance at the same establishment. Bain found that the norms of groups in different taverns may be ranked by the differential affluence required for membership and by the degree to which "panhandling" is prohibited within the barroom. Individuals continually lacking sufficient funds to participate in the more costly tavern drinking are forced to purchase liquor in bulk and to drink on the street, if they are to obtain liquor at all. Bain reports that these street drinking groups are of short duration and do not develop the stability or structure of the barroom groups.

The present study is concerned particularly with the meaning of drinking among this outcast group of street drinkers—the Skid Row winos.

Jackson and Connor[15] and Peterson and Maxwell[16] in particular have reported that Skid Row drinkers consume liquor in small groups. Their studies, however, were done at a distance. Their informants were inmates of a municipal jail or correctional institution, resulting in a stilted view of the bottle-group social structure and conveying none of the quality of the interactional patterns comprising the group structure.

METHOD

Material for this study was gathered during the investigator's visits to the Skid Row areas of Pacific Coast cities, particularly those of Stockton, Sacramento and Fresno, Calif. He lived on each Skid Row for 1 to 2 weeks at a time as a participant observer and identified himself to the inhabitants of the area as a currently unem-

[10] Straus and McCarthy, "Drinking Patterns of Homeless Men," p. 609.

[11] E. M. Jellinek, "Phases of Alcohol Addiction," *Quarterly Journal of Studies on Alcohol* 13 (1952), pp. 673–84.

[12] W. J. Peterson and M. A. Maxwell, "The Skid Row 'Wino,'" *Social Problems* 5 (1958), pp. 308–16.

[13] J. K. Jackson and R. Connor, "The Skid Row Alcoholic," *Quarterly Journal of Studies on Alcohol* 14 (1953), pp. 468–86.

[14] H. G. Bain, "A Sociological Analysis of the Chicago Skid-Row Lifeway," unpublished Master's Thesis (Chicago: University of Chicago, 1950).

[15] Jackson and Connor, "Skid Row Alcoholic."

[16] Peterson and Maxwell, "Skid Row 'Wino.'"

ployed traveling worker or "fruit tramp." Days were passed by participating in the normal routines of Skid Row life: sleeping in the "flop-houses," listening to sermons and eating free meals in the gospel missions, and standing around the streets and talking and drinking with the men during the daytimes. The investigator participated in the drinking rituals and was able to form a better conception of their structure through observing the patterns occurring repeatedly, day after day.

The following sections will describe the social structure of the Skid Row "bottle gang" and will interpret the social relations according to their functions in satisfying external (instrumental) and internal (affective) goals of the group members. The concept of undersocialization will be analyzed as it applies to the most enculturated of Skid Row drinkers.

SOCIAL RELATIONS ON SKID ROW

Men on Skid Row clearly do not participate in social relations in a manner which characterizes the other classes in American society. Close examination reveals, however, that even the most enculturated groups of Skid Row drinkers manifest consistent efforts to structure situations so as to involve interpersonal contact and emotional reinforcement. The investigator in his field of work has found that winos do participate in cooperative activities and form social groups in which they experience the rewards of belonging, prestige, and a feeling of security. Yet they strive to accomplish these ends in ways distinctively different from those of other classes of society.

These unattached men attempt to satisfy their need for interpersonal contacts by structuring social relations around an activity which meets one of their major physical needs—purchasing and drinking wine.

GROUP PROCESSES

The quality of the interactional pattern of winos perhaps may be best interpreted according to a dichotomy of group processes proposed by

Hubert S. Coffey:[17] socio-group processes and psyche-group processes. The socio-group process is that by which the members consciously seek out external goals and direct their activities toward the selected goals. Psyche-group processes are those by which group members find satisfaction of their own emotional needs for interpersonal contact but are not concerned with the attainment of an external goal.

Coffey points out that few human groups fulfill either socio- or psyche-group functions exclusively. Most socio-groups have a latent function of partially meeting the members' psychic needs through the interaction which occurs in conducting the contractual relations. Conversely, most groups in which the members interact primarily for personal satisfaction accomplish this objective through participation in goal-focussed activities. Hence, nearly every group combines both psyche-group and socio-group processes, and focuses on the business involved in achievement while simultaneously meeting the members' needs for interpersonal contact.

The Skid Row winos integrate these two aspects of group process in procuring their most imminently felt need: alcohol. Individuals band together, pool resources and purchase their wine communally. The purchasing of wine by a group of men fulfills two functions simultaneously: (1) it permits individuals with very limited financial resources to purchase the maximum amount of alcohol per monetary unit; (2) the interpersonal association resulting from this transaction permits satisfaction of emotional needs for personal contact. The former is a socio-group function; the latter is a psyche-group function. In the following section the economic aspect or socio-group functions of communal purchasing of wine will be examined.

FORMATION OF THE BOTTLE GROUP

Socio-Group Functions

Men who can afford to drink hard liquor in taverns, or who prefer beer, can meet social needs

---

[17] H. S. Coffey, "Socio and Psyche Group Processes: Integrative Concepts," *Journal of Social Issues* 3 (1952), pp. 65–74.

by associating with other tavern habitués. The men in the wino group cannot afford to purchase hard liquor nor can they satisfy their need for alcohol with beer. They are thus forced to drink fortified wine, the beverage which provides the most alcohol per penny. Purchasing wine by the bottle is much cheaper than wine over the bar. This places poverty-stricken winos in an economic dilemma, for they can purchase little wine with the small sums they beg or earn by odd jobs. Their poverty could prevent them from experiencing both the satisfactions derived from liquor and those of interpersonal contact. The winos, however, have capitalized on their deficits and have developed an alternate institution capable of satisfying both economic and social needs simultaneously. This institution is the wino bottle group.

The wino bottle group or "bottle gang" is similar to a corporate group in that a number of individuals pool their capital for a common goal. The management of the capital is handled by a leader who acts as general chairman. Each member is a stockholder and maintains rights to consumption of the communally purchased bottle of wine.

A bottle group is developed through the efforts of an initiator with some capital who recruits other members willing and able to contribute to the purchase of a bottle. The initiator must have a "substantial" sum to start with—at least 10 cents. However, two or three regular associates may pool nickels and pennies to the amount of one-third or one-half the price of a bottle and then go out to look for other investors.

The initiator and the other members proceed along the sidewalk asking passers-by whether they are interested in "going in on a bottle." The solicitor has the obligation to inform the prospective partner of the amount of money collected and the number of men with whom he will have to share the wine, for example: "Three of us have 28 cents in on a bottle. Do you want to get in on it?" As the statement is made the leader holds the announced cash out in his hand so that the prospect may know the offer is genuine and that he is not being exploited to purchase wine for a group of destitute "promoters." Thus the prospective stockholder can appraise the value of the corporation before investing.

If the solicited person has sufficient money and is willing to participate, he gives his contribution to the leader. The handing over of money toward the purchase of a "jug" of wine establishes a contractual relation by which a contributor becomes a member of the group. The contract forms a corporation in which the members hold certain rights to the consumption of the proposed bottle of wine, and the leader has the obligation to purchase and share the wine with the members. The size of the group is governed by the price of a bottle and is usually between three and five men. The corporation continues in existence until the emptying of the bottle dissolves the contract.

Although the actual drinking group as such does not have temporal continuity, there are both temporary and quite regular associates in these bottle groups. Men living permanently in one Skid Row area may become regular associates by the fact of engaging in the common activity of group drinking. Because each individual frequently seeks drinking companions, these men often join forces and may thereby develop specialized patterns of interpersonal responses. Frequent participation may promote recognition of a special relationship between a group of men who then can come to regard themselves as a clique distinct from others.

Two factors prevent the development of a strong feeling of group solidarity: First, the boundaries of the clique are seldom defined. Almost any individual is substitutable for another. The only reason the clique has continuity is that the same men are there day after day in the same habitat. Second, the members appear not to make close personal ties but, instead, tend to interact in an instrumental pattern, not making great adjustments to individual personality differences.

Temporary associates are men who have never met previously or who meet only infrequently and hence have not developed any sense of group identity. The membership of the bottle group at any one time, however, is determined strictly by those available men who are willing and able to "go in on a bottle." This most frequently will include those who associate regularly by reason of their spatial proximity, but actually includes also any available men who have funds to contribute. The so-called "permanent" bottle gangs, then, are composed of a core of regular associates with one or two strangers recruited expediently. The "temporary" groups are composed of men who most likely never met before but are brought together for an occasion of wine drinking and social interaction.

The bottle gang is not an on-going association with temporal continuity. As stated above, the emptying of the bottle dissolves the contract. At this time some members may leave. Those wishing to "go in on another bottle" then assess their finances and go out again to recruit the necessary additional individuals to finance another bottle. Although there may be carry-over of personnel, each group is started anew with each new bottle.

Psyche-Group Functions

The formation of a bottle gang and the consequent contractual relations, as described, are socio-group functions of wine-drinking activity. The psyche-group functions or structured interpersonal contacts which fulfill emotional needs will now be examined, beginning with the leader's role.

The Leader-Host. The role of initiator or leader requires the performance of exactly prescribed duties. It calls for the exertion of more effort in soliciting additional members for the purchase of the bottle, as well as for serving as treasurer. In addition, the leader actually plays the psyche-function role of host to the men in the group. When sufficient money has been acquired, the leader enters a liquor store or tavern and makes the purchase, selecting the variety of wine to be consumed. In California, tokay is by far the most popular variety on Skid Row, with muscatel, port and sherry following in order. Rarely does anyone make a suggestion as to which variety of wine should be selected. This is the prerogative of the leader. The purchase completed, the buyer places the bottle in an inner pocket of his coat and rejoins the group, which then moves to a place convenient for drinking.

It is best to consume the wine in a somewhat secluded spot in the Skid Row neighborhood rather than on the main street. A degree of seclusion is desirable for three major reasons: (1)

The members can chat more easily and freely. (2) The possibility of annoyance by potential "moochers" is diminished. (3) It insures avoidance of the police who frequently arrest persons drinking on the street or in other public places.

The leader walks at the front of the group carrying the bottle. Upon arriving in a doorway or alley, the men form a circle. After looking around to see that no police are in sight, the leader takes the bottle from his inner pocket and nicks the celluloid protective band with his fingernail before removing it by grasping the raised edge of the band with his teeth. He then takes off the cap and offers the bottle to the first man on his left. Almost without exception the bottle is passed to the left because the leader generally uses his right hand to unscrew the cap. This necessitates holding the bottle in the left hand, which facilitates passing it to the left or in a clockwise direction. Each man takes two swallows in his turn as the bottle is passed to him. If an individual takes more than the allotted number of gulps, one of the members is certain to protest and to grab the bottle from his mouth. Not until the bottle has toured the entire group does the leader take his drink. Upon completing the circle, the cap is replaced on the bottle and it is returned to the leader's pocket for a few minutes until any member calls for another round. The leader, in his role of host, has the major obligation of leading the conversation, which consists of ego-building mechanisms and recapitulations of past experiences, with frequent disparagement of the local police force as grossly unjust, and condemnation of the gospel missions as "rackets."

The leader-host feels he has prestige because the others are dependent upon him for providing the initial capital and especially the impetus to organize the group. By assuming such important socio-group functions the leader gains the right to play the psyche-group role of host, which consists of selecting the type of wine and regulating the consumption and conduct of his guests.

The Members. For the other members of the group, too, participation in the contractual relations provides a structure for the operation of psyche-group functions, activities for the structuring of affective relations which meet the psychic needs of the members.

The initial contractual relation forms a small primary group in which all members are aware of their statuses and of the exclusion of all others. While the wine is being consumed the men converse in a convivial mood and the group members tend to accept the stories and claims of each individual quite uncritically. During drinking the men exchange ego-boosting rationalizations, reaffirm their status as "good men," offer boastful stories of their accomplishments, and retell past experiences, especially experiences in common.

A portion of the inveterate wine drinkers prefer to regard themselves still as members of the working class but temporarily out of the labor market. Although some may not have had stable employment for as long as 10 years, a few still cling tenaciously to their identification as working men. An individual can continue to maintain this rationalizing facade by talking only of his past work experience and not considering any future employment plans. By interacting with another individual who has performed the same kinds of work, or better yet, who has worked at the same places, a wino can engage in esoteric small talk about the specific details of the job. By this means a man is able to bolster his identification with his reference group and to keep alive for a while longer his illusion of being a participant in his former occupation. The fully enculturated wino, however, has relinquished all identification with his former working class status and has come to accept Skid Row as "home."

The group drinking experience is the only situation in the Skid Row social system in which a man receives personal recognition and affectional response. The men may not know each other's names, perhaps never having met before. This does not dim or alter the nature of their feelings toward each other; for by contributing money toward the group goal a man automatically becomes an insider and is afforded full acceptance.

Equal Consumption Without Equal Contribution. Another manifestation of the psyche-group functions of the bottle gang is the fact that although not all individuals contribute equally to the purchase of a bottle, all are full and equal members and consume the beverage in equal proportions. As the bottle is passed around the group, each man takes his two swallows in turn and passes the bottle on to the next man. The fact of contribution makes one a member; the amount of contribution is not a relevant factor. This may be due to mutual interdependence for obtaining the wine.

The purchasing of the bottle is a group action which results in satisfaction of individual needs. No one individual has sufficient funds to purchase a bottle; hence, all members are mutually interdependent for the attainment of their individual goals. The wine becomes a group goal because its procurement is possible only through the group effort. Since no individual in the group had sufficient funds to buy a bottle for himself, the man with 25 cents had as much need for the man with 5 cents as the poorer man did for the more affluent one. All therefore share equally in the wine purchased through the combined efforts of the members. Furthermore, the desire for personal association is an independent additional motive in forming the group.

The banding together to purchase liquor is a contractual relationship, the structure of which permits the functioning of interpersonal contacts for the satisfaction of psychic needs. It is at this point that the desire for psyche-group relations alters the operation of the socio-group contractual relations. This is a nonpecuniary motive for forming the contractual relationship, and appears to influence the members to overlook all but the grossest monetary differences.

Economically the differential contributions may balance out through time, if the individuals are permanent residents in one Skid Row. The man who one day contributes a larger amount to a "jug" may have only a few pennies on the following day, but he will be fully welcome in a group because of his past associations. The men do not calculate the balance of monetary relationships over a period of time but rather accept a former drinking "buddy" because he is considered a "good guy."

In a survey of the drinking habits of men on the Bowery in New York City, Straus and McCarthy[18] found that 90 percent usually or always had drinking companions. This is not surprising, since the bottle group is the only

---

18 Straus and McCarthy, "Drinking Patterns of Homeless Men."

structured emotional contact a wino experiences —it is the only psyche-group experience by which his social needs can be satisfied. Thus it is evident that relations are sought for their own sake and not merely as an appendage of the necessary contractual relations by which the wine is purchased.

Treating and "Chiseling." Another institution operating within this context is the "treat," in which one individual who has earned a substantial sum or who has just received a subsistence check purchases a bottle and shares it with one or two of his friends. "The treat is the Skid Row version of conspicuous consumption."[19] The treater experiences a sense of prestige in being able to buy liquor for his less fortunate friends; it permits him temporarily to feel superior to his dependent associates. The treater has the right to tell the others his troubles and they in turn have the obligation to listen and to agree.

But the sharing of the wine incurs an obligation to reciprocate when one comes into money. At this point difficulties and animosities may arise. One who continually fails to return the treat, if suspected of being able to do so, soon finds himself excluded from wino society and is no longer invited to share drinks.

The obligation of eventual reciprocation can lead to trouble for an individual who wishes to maintain a large number of "treating" relationships but has insufficient income for treating. Financially the most advantageous manner of repayment is to invite former benefactors to share in a corporate bottle and thus to repay with wine for which the reciprocator has borne only part of the cost. That is, a man becomes a legitimate stockholder in a bottle gang by contributing his share toward the purchase of wine, and after the bottle has been purchased, if he meets former benefactors on the street, he invites them to have a drink out of "his" bottle.

By this method a man may repay debts to former hosts largely at the expense of other stockholders. This maneuver gains the shrewd operator future invitations to share drinks, since he has "returned the compliment" to his benefactors. But this frequently leads to arguments,

resentments, and eventual banishment of the offender. Such a person is called a "chiseler." Chiselers attempt to persuade the other members to invite the outsiders because they are "old buddies" and "such nice guys" that it would be a severe breach of etiquette not to offer them a drink. This low-cost technique of providing for a future liquor supply is most frequently tolerated by the group members because many of them do not care to appear rude. There may be protest by some. The outcome is determined by the relative strengths of the appeal of the inviting man balanced against the strengths of the protests. Usually the most vociferous win.

Although there is some resentment by the group members when outsiders are invited, this is compensated to some degree by a sense of superiority because of the dependency relationship of the outsider. The resentment is a natural result of a breach of the contractual or socio-group relations. The compensating feeling of superiority is a psyche-function which alters the operation of the initial contractual relations. Nevertheless, some resentment remains against both the outsider and, especially, the chiseler. An individual who continually treats his own friends at the expense of group members is likely to find himself excluded from wino society.

EXPEDIENCY VERSUS PERSONALITY

In wino society, personnel for interaction and emotional rapport must be recruited most of the time on the basis of expediency. The psyche-group functions are structured around the socio-group functions. And the socio-group functions consist of the contractual relations by which money is collected for the purchase of wine. Ability to participate in the bottle gang is influenced at any particular time by the individual's financial resources. Hence the social relationships of each individual are determined solely by his pecuniary condition.

Selection on the basis of expediency does not allow focus on the value of a particular personality and thus prohibits the formation of a close personal bond. Rather, the choice of an individual for interaction, of necessity, must be with one who can meet the necessary financial re-

---

[19] Bain, "Chicago Skid-Row Lifeway," p. 137.

quirements by which the bottle—the focal point of the social relations—is purchased.

The overt form of interaction is the affirmation of one's status as a "good man" and the expression of ego-boosting rationalizations. To this end, one only needs others who will cooperate in these sets of behavior patterns. Because the majority of winos in the Skid Row population can participate in this social institution, a great number of individuals can be easily substituted for any man. Thus there is no need to make a strong investment of libido in any individual.

The selection of associates on the basis of expediency is shown quite clearly in the acceptance of Negroes into white drinking groups. Negroes comprise 10 to 15 percent of the Skid Row population of the California cities studied. Negroes were excluded by the management from the majority of "flophouses" and low-priced hotels. This exclusion was sanctioned by the white residents of the area who professed that Negroes were "dirty" and "low," and that the majority were untrustworthy in that they would pilfer from other hotel residents and even "cut up" those who attempted to stop them.

In soliciting membership for a bottle group, however, Negroes as well as whites on the streets of the Skid Row area were asked to participate. No willing Negro was refused membership if he had the cash. Negro members appeared to be accorded the same degree of acceptance in the psyche-group relationships as were the white members. Interaction, thus, does not appear to involve mutual adjustment of personalities by which individuals invest part of themselves, through the mutual exchange of libidinal bonds, to form affective ties. Rather, there is selection of personalities according to ability and willingness to participate in a preestablished pattern of behavior. Selection on such a basis does not call for investment of self. The prevalence of this phenomenon inhibits the formation of strong personal ties among Skid Row winos.

DISCUSSION

The social relations of Skid Row residents differ most markedly from those of other residents of American communities in the relative lack of family ties. Because Skid Row residents have few contacts with kinsmen they are more dependent upon peer associates for social satisfactions. For the wino, participation in the bottle gang is one of the most rewarding emotional experiences. This limited social participation is not due to original enculturation into a different set of norms. Quite the contrary, all the members of this unattached population have been downwardly mobile from former higher prestige statuses which tended to demand more responsibility.

Even the most enculturated of Skid Row men actively seek and participate in psyche-groups in which an individual receives the satisfactions of acceptance, prestige and security, and which bolster his self-conception. The hypothesis of under-socialization as advanced by Straus[20] and by Pittman and Gordon[21] appears to be applicable inasmuch as there is inability to participate in a repertoire of varied social relations requiring a broader range of interpersonal skills. But the present observations indicate that these men are quite adept at certain interpersonal functions, however limited in scope.

The Straus and the Pittman and Gordon formulations of undersocialization of Skid Row men are partially inapplicable in that they consider undersocialization as a whole unit of personality. This conceptualization regards individuals as varying along a unidimensional scale of socialization. A person is socialized continuously throughout life by participation in meaningful roles. The "better developed" or "adequately" socialized personalities are those which have been conditioned to participate in a wide variety of roles demanding various types of interpersonal skills involved in a broad range of life experiences. By this consideration, the "less adequately" socialized are those personalities whose conditioning has been limited to acquiring facility in a smaller number of roles.

Socialization is a process by which a person develops facility and confidence, and learns to experience satisfactions from interacting with others. According to this view socialization is a multidimensional process through which a person may develop different skills at varying rates and intensities. Hence, any given individual may

---

[20] Straus, "Alcohol and the Homeless Man."
[21] Pittman and Gordon, *Revolving Door*.

be below average, or "undersocialized," in the development of facility in some skills and above average in others—the development of each trait being partially independent.

Given this multidimensional view of socialization, any individual may be considered socialized to the extent that, and in the activities in which, he has learned to participate with others in meaningful contexts.

In addition to differential development of interpersonal skills, the loss of former skills also influences interpersonal participation. Undoubtedly individuals of the lower class who lack facility in key social roles are more prone to enter Skid Row. Upon entry into that social system, an individual is subject to situations quite different from those he formerly experienced. Participation in an all-male society requires fewer and different skills than does participation in the family-oriented social systems of the other societal strata. Not only are no new skills acquired by participation in the Skid Row social system, but in addition former skills are lost by disuse or perhaps owing to anxiety associated with the use of a skill.

That men can lose acquired skills is shown by the fact that the majority of Skid Row men, including the winos, once held responsible employment for which they no longer have the skills or the stability to qualify. This loss of ability to perform accustomed roles is actually a process of "desocialization."

These findings corroborate those of Pittman and Gordon who state that Skid Row excessive drinkers seek social situations in which demands are minimal and do not require much competence in interpersonal relationships. But the fact that even the most enculturated of Skid Row winos actively seek participation in social relations indicates a considerable degree of interpersonal skill. The present evidence fails to indicate whether the socialization of these men in childhood and youth was initially faulty or limited, and if so, in what areas; nor does it indicate to what extent these men have lost former social skills through disuse and emotional blocks.

SUMMARY

Undersocialization has been considered the major psychological trait characterizing the Skid Row population. The unattached men have been described as inept in social relationships and therefore avoiding interpersonal contacts. An investigation of Skid Rows in three California cities, utilizing the participant observation method, revealed that the group with lowest prestige on Skid Row—the winos—takes deliberate steps to structure social relationships around the activity of wine drinking. The social relationships were analyzed in terms of socio-group and psyche-group processes. Through the socio-group processes the men form a contractual relationship for the purchase and consumption of a bottle of wine. This contractual relationship serves as a structure for meeting the winos' emotional needs for interpersonal contacts. The contract forms a small intimate group in which individuals seek acceptance and personal affirmation. That such a bottle gang is formed more for the sake of personal interaction than for economic necessity is indicated by the case of individuals with sufficient money to purchase their own wine who prefer to participate in a series of groups successively throughout the day.

This evidence indicates that, although Skid Row men generally are limited in the range of social relationships, even the winos are not completely inept in interpersonal relationships. The partial inapplicability of the Straus and the Pittman and Gordon formulations suggesting a complete lack of interpersonal skills is thought to arise from consideration of undersocialization as a whole unit of personality.

The present evidence suggests that this unidimensional view should be replaced by a multidimensional view of the process of socialization which regards persons as developing skills at varying rates and intensities—the development of each trait being partially independent. In addition to differential experience in acquiring behavior traits, interaction skills may also be lost through disuse, a process of desocialization.

C. CONSEQUENCES

Repeated heavy drinking can lead to a number of physical symptoms, such as delirium tremens, cirrhosis of the liver, and convulsions. It may also lead to a number of behavioral and social problems as well. While some of these problems are unique to alcoholic drinking (for example, arrests for public drunkenness), many are not, as King *et al.* show in "Alcoholic Abuse: A Crucial Factor in the Social Problems of Negro Men." Unemployment and marital instability as well as several forms of deviant behavior besides problems unique to alcoholic drinking are also more frequent among those who are heavy drinkers than among those who are not. The effect of alcoholic drinking in the generation of these problems is to eliminate many of the advantages of certain background factors (for example, higher education and coming from an intact home). But in addition, alcoholic drinking is seen as a factor which perpetuates a cycle of broken homes, deviance, and problems of employment among urban blacks. For example, heavy drinkers are more apt to come from broken homes and to have unstable family relations as adults. (In the last chapter of this book we will examine another form of deviance that is a consequence of alcoholism, though one that is less frequent among blacks than among whites.[1])

The consequences of alcoholism are not always limited to the alcoholic himself, as King *et al.* show in reference to their findings for marital disruptions. Others have noted, also, that the alcoholic's drinking has serious consequences for the drinker's family; for example, public drunkenness, sexual deviation, and unemployment may lead to his rejection by family, friends, and associates. The alcoholic's behavior is particularly disruptive and embarrassing to his family, whose economic welfare and community status he may threaten.[2] Even short of actual family rejection, alcoholic drinking may generate severe interpersonal ruptures within the family. Such discord, in turn, may have serious psychological and physical consequences for family members. Paul W. Haberman shows, in "Childhood Symptoms in Children of Alcoholics and Comparison Group Parents," that childhood problems that are frequently assumed to have a psychiatric origin (such as stuttering and bed wetting) are apt to occur in children with alcoholic parents. This suggests that the interpersonal problems created by alcoholic drinking are manifest in pathological symptoms of the alcoholics' children.

---

[1] See pp. 475–79 below.
[2] See Joan K. Jackson, "The Adjustment of the Family to Alcoholism," *Journal of Marriage and Family Living* 18 (November, 1956), pp. 361–69.

ALCOHOL ABUSE: A CRUCIAL FACTOR IN THE SOCIAL PROBLEMS OF NEGRO MEN

LUCY JANE KING, GEORGE E. MURPHY, LEE N. ROBINS, AND HARRIET DARVISH

Recent events have tragically emphasized the major points of Moynihan's well-known review of sociological data entitled *The Negro Family: The Case for National Action.* In 1965 he wrote:

> The emergence and increasing visibility of a Negro middle class may beguile the nation into supposing that the circumstances of the remainder of the Negro community are equally prosperous, whereas just the opposite is true.... Nearly a quarter of Negro women living in cities who have ever married are divorced, separated, or living apart from their husbands.... Nearly one-quarter of Negro births are now illegitimate.... Unemployment among Negroes outside the South has persisted at catastrophic levels since the first statistics were gathered in 1930....[1]

> What then is [the] problem? We feel the answer is clear enough. Three centuries of injustice have brought about deep-seated structural distortions in the life of the Negro American. At this point, the present tangle of pathology is capable of perpetuating itself without assistance from the white world. The cycle can be broken only if these distortions are set right.[2]

A study of young, urban Negro men in St. Louis[3] has pointed out a crucial variable in this cycle that should be of particular concern to psychiatry as it contributes to community programs. That crucial variable is alcohol abuse. Heavy drinking was found to be twice as common in urban Negro men as in a sample of urban white men of similarly lower socioeconomic class origins.[4] Drinking began early among young Negro boys: 84 percent had begun drinking before age 19. Early drinking was associated with becoming a heavy drinker. Heavy drinking and problems related to drinking were predicted by the usual predictors of deviant behavior: i.e., school problems, dropouts, delinquency, and deviant parental roles. Unfortunately, both the family instability and the childhood behavior predictive of drinking problems are much more common in the urban Negro ghetto than in the white community. Consequently, the adult penalties are much more prevalent. In this paper we have examined the adult social penalties brought about by the addition of alcohol abuse to the already unstable ghetto family pattern.

Method

The sample was obtained from public school records. The criteria for eligibility were being male, born in St. Louis between 1930 and 1934, attending a Negro St. Louis public elementary school for six years or more, having an IQ score of at least 85 while in elementary school, and guardian's name and occupation appearing on the school record. From this population of 930 individuals, 235 names were selected in such a way as to provide approximately equal numbers in each of eight categories created by taking all permutations of three dichotomized variables: (1) father's presence or absence in the home during the subject's childhood through the completion of elementary school; (2) guardian's occupation at the lowest level versus a higher level; and (3) no school problems versus truancy and/or academic problems in elementary school.

Presence of the father in the childhood home was determined originally from school records showing a male guardian with the same last name as the subject. Interviews revealed that this had resulted in an overestimation of the number of fathers present. Thus, 60 percent of

---

Reprinted with permission of the authors and the American Psychiatric Association, from *American Journal of Psychiatry* 125 (June, 1969), pp. 1682–90.

[1] Daniel P. Moynihan, *The Negro Family: The Case for National Action.* Washington, D.C.: Department of Labor, Office of Policy Planning and Research, 1965), chapter 2, 3.
[2] *Ibid.,* introduction to Chapter 5.
[3] L. N. Robins and G. E. Murphy, "Drug Use in a Normal Population of Young Negro Men," *American Journal of Public Health* 57 (1967), pp. 1580–96; and L. N. Robins, G. E. Murphy, and M. B. Breckenridge, "Drinking Behavior in Young Urban Negro Men," *Quarterly Journal of Studies on Alcohol* 29 (1968), pp. 657–84.
[4] *Ibid.*

the boys grew up in homes where the father was absent at some time during elementary school. The guardian's occupation at the lowest level included those occupations scoring 10 or below on Duncan's SEI scale (domestic servants, unskilled laborers, unemployed), and the higher level included all with a score of 11 or greater on the 96-point scale.[5] School problems included academic difficulties, defined as being held back two or more quarters or being placed in an ungraded room, and truancy, defined as being absent more than 20 percent of school days in five or more quarters.[6]

In 1965 and 1966 systematic structured interviews were obtained with 223 (95 percent) of the men so selected. In addition, records indicating problems with alcohol among these men were sought in St. Louis police files, prison, probation, and parole records; armed forces, Veterans Administration, and public welfare records; and in the records of the five hospitals and three outpatient clinics which serve the medical needs of the vast majority of Negroes in St. Louis.

For purposes of the present paper, the sample of 223 men has been divided into three groups on the basis of their answers to specific questions in the interview about drinking habits:[7] (1) recent problems with alcohol (medical and/or social problems related to alcohol abuse since age 25); (2) heavy drinker without recent alcohol problems; and (3) never heavy drinker (has never drunk heavily at any age). To be counted as having recent problems with alcohol, a man had to report any one of the following: delirium tremens, liver disease, convulsions, or hospitalization due to drinking; or any two of the following: shakes (tremulousness relieved by drinking), benders (drinking 48 hours or more without sobering up), arrests, wife or child beating, job loss, and lateness or absence at work due to drinking since age 25.[8] A heavy drinker was a

man who reported drinking seven or more drinks[9] weekly and either seven or more drinks per occasion or at least four drinks daily.[10] This behavior may or may not have been current, but it had not produced criterion problems since age 25.

This paper will explore the extent to which these three groups differ with respect to such adult social variables as family problems, unemployment problems, and contact with law enforcement agencies as determined both by interview and from official records. Data comparisons are by the chi-square method, with continuity correction (Yates correction) when applicable. A p value of .05 is the maximum accepted for statistical significance.

Results

A history of heavy drinking was found in 62 percent of the men interviewed. Division of the sample as described produced the following groups: (1) recent problems related to alcohol, 37 subjects; (2) heavy drinkers without recent problems, 101 subjects; (3) never heavy drinkers at any time, 85 subjects. The most commonly reported problems in group I were shakes, benders, and arrests (Table 1). Men with problems averaged 2.9 problems each. As can be noted in the table the more serious medical complications occurred recently in 14 men, or 38 percent of all the men who had recent problems, and in six percent of the total sample.

Because the definition of recent alcohol problems includes some social consequences (arrests, wife or child beating, job loss), it is by definition true that recent problems due to alcohol will be associated with adult social problems. However, every effort was made to separate criteria from findings. It is particularly important to note that the arrests considered in defining group I include only those directly related to intoxication (drunk driving, public drunkenness, peace disturbance, affray, common assault) while arrests to be discussed later are exclusive of these. This paper will show that alcohol abuse leads to

[5] A. J. Reiss, Jr., *Occupations and Social Status* (New York: The Free Press of Glencoe, 1961).

[6] The research design is described in greater detail in Robins and Murphy, "Drug Use of Young Negro Men."

[7] Robins, Murphy, and Breckenridge, "Drinking Behavior in Young Urban Negro Men."

[8] Recent problems with alcohol is defined somewhat differently here than in a previous paper (*ibid.*), where the criterion was any one problem after age 30 reported by interview or in records.

[9] A drink was the equivalent of 1½ ounces of whiskey or a 12-ounce bottle of beer.

[10] Included are four men who averaged less than seven drinks per week but regularly drank very large amounts *when* they drank.

TABLE 1. CONCURRENCE OF ALCOHOL PROBLEMS SINCE AGE 25 AMONG RECENT PROBLEM DRINKERS (N = 37)

Symptom	Number Suffering from Symptom	2	3	Concurrence with Other Symptoms 4	5	6	7	8	9	10	Average Number of Other Nine Symptoms Suffered Concurrently
1. Delirium tremens	5	1	0	1	5	4	3	1	1	1	3.4
2. Liver disease	5		0	1	3	4	3	1	2	1	3.2
3. Convulsions	3			1	2	0	2	1	0	0	2.0
4. Hospitalization	5				4	2	2	3	0	0	2.8
Any of the above	14				10	8	8	4	2	1	
5. Shakes	28					17	16	7	6	2	2.2
6. Benders	23						11	5	6	2	2.2
7. Arrests	20							6	3	1	2.4
8. Wife/child beating	9								1	0	2.8
9. Job Loss	6									1	3.3
10. Late or absent at work	3										2.7

Note: Criterion for inclusion in group I was reporting any one of symptoms 1 through 4 or any two of symptoms 5 through 10. A total of 14 men qualified by having one of symptoms 1 through 4, and 31 men qualified by having at least two of symptoms 5 through 10. Since some subjects qualified in both ways, the total number in group I was 37.

social problems *other* than those used as criteria for alcohol problems and that heavy drinking, in the *absence* of problems attributed to alcohol, also is associated with a high level of adult social difficulties.

Thirty percent of the men studied were currently either divorced or permanently separated from their wives. This is more than twice the census rate of 13.7 percent for urban Negro men in this age bracket.[11] The high rate we found is due at least in part to our restricting ourselves to an urban-born population.

When our subjects had had recent alcohol problems, the percent divorced or separated was 57, more than four times the census rate (table 2). Among men without drinking problems, the rate was 18 percent, close to the rate for the

[11] U.S. Bureau of the Census, "Marital and Family Characteristics of the Metropolitan Population," *Population Characteristics* series P-20, no. 165 (May 9, 1967).

urban population of Negro men aged 30–34. This rate is, of course, still considerably higher than the comparable rate for white men (3.7 percent). Heavy drinkers without recent alcohol problems were currently separated or divorced in 30 percent of cases.

As a measure of social deviance, having lived in common-law arrangement with a woman—i.e., a marital arrangement without legal sanction—reflects transiency and limited commitment. Such arrangements were common in this population sample, having been entered into by nearly one-third (32.3 percent) of the men at some time. The relationship of this behavior to alcohol problems is as striking as that for broken marriages (Table 2). Three-fifths of group I (those with recent alcohol problems) had lived in common-law arrangements, as compared to less than one-fifth of group III (those who had never been heavy drinkers). Group II (heavy drinkers without recent problems) occupies a

TABLE 2. FAMILY PROBLEMS IN RELATION TO DRINKING HISTORY

Item	I Recent Problems* (N = 37)	II Heavy Drinkers* (N = 101)	III Never Heavy* (N = 85)	Probability
	(in Percent)			
Currently divorced or separated**	57	30	18	<.001
Ever lived "common-law"	61	36	17	<.001
Any illegitimate children	44	36	20	<.02

* See text for definitions.
** "Currently" means at the time of interview, when the subjects were in their early 30s. Separation is without expectation of reconciliation.

middle position. The differences are highly significant statistically (p < .001).

Having sired one or more illegitimate children was admitted to by 30 percent of the men interviewed. The proportion of men in group I with illegitimate children was more than twice as great as that in group III (Table 2), with group II again between them. The differences are significant (p < .02). The three groups had almost identical mean numbers of *legitimate* children, but group I had the highest mean number of total children (2.81), group II was second (2.44), and group III had fewest, with 2.18 children per man. The difference is accounted for by illegitimate children. One-third of all the children sired by men in group I were illegitimate, as compared to one-fourth of the children of group II men, and one-eighth of those of group III. This difference is also highly significant statistically (p < .001).

Underemployment has been shown to be much higher among Negro men than among whites. Moynihan[12] has quoted Bureau of Labor Statistics data giving the unemployment rate for nonwhite males aged 14 or over as 10.6 percent. It is believed that Negro unemployment in St. Louis is higher than elsewhere. For example, the unemployment rate for nonwhite males was 12.7 percent of the work force in St. Louis in November, 1966.[13]

In the present sample of Negro men in their

early to mid-30s, 11 percent were unemployed, an additional six percent did not have full-time employment at the time of the interview, and 30.5 percent reported having been without full-time employment for a total of at least one year in the past five.

Underemployment was found to be very substantially related to alcohol abuse. Over one-third of those with recent problems with alcohol were not fully employed at the time of the interview (Table 3), as compared to 18 percent of heavy drinkers without recent alcohol problems and only six percent of those who were never heavy drinkers (p < .001). Further, nearly two-thirds of those with recent problems had lacked full-time employment for as much as one year in the last five, compared to 25 and 22 percent in the other two groups respectively (p < .001).

Median income of those who had earned anything during the year prior to interview was $5,547. This low figure reflects not only the fact of less than full-time employment for many men but also the relatively lower level of jobs held by those with drinking problems. Only those who were never heavy drinkers had an average salary ($6,526) similar to that given by Moynihan.[14] He quotes $6,800 as the approximate average salary of employed Negro males (his table 17). Men with recent drinking problems had a median income of only $3,714.

It is well known that Negro men are subject to arrest more frequently than are white men. It is nevertheless surprising to realize that two-fifths

[12] Moynihan, *The Negro Family.*
[13] Department of Labor, *Sub-employment in the Slums of St. Louis* (Washington: U.S. Government Printing Office, November, 1966).

[14] Moynihan, *The Negro Family.*

TABLE 3. EMPLOYMENT PROBLEMS IN RELATION TO DRINKING HISTORY

Item	I Recent Problems (N = 37)	II Heavy Drinkers (N = 101)	III Never Heavy (N = 85)	Probability
	(in Percent)			
Not employed full time currently*	38	18	6	<0.01
Underemployed one or more years in past five years	65	25	22	<.001
Median income in past year**	$3,714	$5,522	$6,526	I vs. II, <.001
				I vs. III, <.001
				II vs. III, <.02

* "Currently" and "past five years" were determined in reference to the time of interview, 1965 or 1966, at which time subjects were in their early 30s. Figures for "not employed full time" exclude one man who was a full-time student when interviewed.
** Assessment of median income for the year prior to interview excludes those with no income during that year and those for whom this information is unavailable (ten in group I, seven in group II, and ten in group III).

(43.1 percent) of the men in this sample have a history of police arrests since 1959, excluding traffic arrests and "suspicion" arrests. Arrests for drunkenness, however, make up a large part of the total arrest picture in the U.S. Indeed, arrests for drunkenness have been reported to constitute one-half of all nontraffic arrests.[15] It was important, therefore, to learn whether alcohol abuse was associated with arrests for causes *other* than drunkenness. When we omitted all arrests that could conceivably be called drunk arrests (public drunkenness, drunk driving, peace disturbance, affray, common assault), we still found that 34 percent of the population had an arrest record since 1959. When alcohol problems were present, the rate was almost double this (61 percent); among men who had never been heavy drinkers it was reduced almost to half (19 percent) (Table 4).

Arrests were catalogued as *crimes against property, crimes against persons,* and *crimes of conduct* (Table 4). Nearly half (47 percent) of group I (recent problems with alcohol), as compared to one-third (34 percent) of group II (heavy drinkers without recent alcohol problems) and one-seventh (14 percent) of group III (never heavy drinkers) had been arrested for *crimes against property.* The charges included burglary, robbery, larceny, forgery, counterfeiting, auto theft, embezzlement, fraud, destruction of property, and buying, possessing, or receiving stolen property. The difference in frequency of

---

[15] M. Zax, E. A. Gardner, and W. T. Hart, "Public Intoxication in Rochester: A Survey of Individuals Charged During 1961," *Quarterly Journal of Studies on Alcohol* 25 (1964), pp. 669–78.

such arrests between the groups is highly significant (p < .001).

Arrests for *crimes against persons* (murder, aggravated assault, forcible rape) were more common in group I than in the remainder, but differences just fail to achieve statistical significance. *Crimes of conduct* for which any subjects had been arrested include commercial vice (e.g., prostitution, contributing to the delinquency of a minor), postal law violations, nonsupport, neglect, vagrancy, loitering, gambling, statutory rape, homosexual practices, possession of weapons or concealed weapons, and possession or sale of narcotics. Exclusive of drunk arrests, nearly half (47 percent) of group I, compared to one-quarter (26 percent) of group II and one-fifth (18 percent) of group III had records of such arrests (p < .01).

About half of the men arrested for a crime in any category between 1959 and 1964 had been convicted at least once during that time. The proportion of those convicted to those ever arrested was similar in all three groups. However, of those ever arrested, the men in group I had a higher mean number of arrests than those in the other groups.

To summarize thus far, those with recent alcohol problems were much more likely than those without to have marital and family difficulties, employment and income problems, and nondrunk arrests. Heavy drinkers without recent alcohol problems were less likely than those with recent problems to have these difficulties. Those who had never been heavy drinkers were least likely to have these adult problems. It is clear therefore that increasing degrees of alcohol abuse

TABLE 4. CONTACTS WITH POLICE, 1959–64, IN RELATION TO DRINKING HISTORY

Item	I Recent Problems (N = 37)	II Heavy Drinkers (N = 95)	III Never Heavy (N = 84)	Probability
	(in Percent)			
Arrests other than for drunkenness,*				
1959–1964	61	40	19	<.001
Property offense	47	34	14	<.001
Person offense	19	10	6	<.06
Conduct offense other than				
drunkenness	47	26	18	<.01

* Excluded are arrests that might have been due to drunkenness, such as peace disturbance, drunk driving, public drunkenness, fighting or affray, as well as all traffic arrests and arrests for "suspicion" not further described. Excludes one man in group I, six in group II, and one in group III who were in the armed forces for the entire five years and therefore not subject to civilian arrest.

are increasingly associated with various measures of social deviance.

However, it is still possible that alcohol abuse is yet another measure of deviance and yet another reflection of some broader underlying factor. In order to examine the contribution made by alcohol abuse itself, it would be desirable to hold constant other contributors to deviant behavior. Absence of father from the home has been shown to predict heavy drinking in this sample.[16] Elementary school problems and failure to graduate from high school predicted both heavy drinking *and* alcohol problems. Dropping out of high school frequently follows elementary school problems, but dropping out may be the more important predictor of adult status inasmuch as a high school diploma is required for the more secure and better paying jobs. Education is known to be positively correlated with stable marriage[17] and freedom from arrest.[18]

To be sure that our findings are not simply evidence that the dropout *both* becomes alcoholic and fails to make a good social adjustment in other ways, we needed to see what effect alcohol abuse has on the social adjustment of the high school graduate. To be certain that any effect found would not be due to our other variable associated with heavy drinking—the broken home—we looked at the effect of alcohol upon men reared in intact homes who graduated from high school. There are only 65 such men in the sample.[19] Because the total number of men with an apparently good start is small, it was necessary to combine current problem drinkers (group I) and heavy drinkers without current problems (group II) in order to have groups of a reasonable size.

It is at once striking to find that only 37 percent (24 men) of those 65 men with the favorable background ever became heavy drinkers, while 72 percent (114 men) of the less favored 158 men did drink heavily (Figures 1 and 2). Stated another way, of the 138 men who have ever been heavy drinkers, only 17 percent (24 men) have the favorable background of their father present and high school graduation, while 48 percent (41 men) of the 85 who never drank heavily were so favored.

Comparing heavy drinkers with others with respect to each measure of adult adjustment previously discussed (Figures 1 and 2), the heavy drinkers prove to be more deviant, both among men from advantaged backgrounds and among those with less advantage. It is also noteworthy that becoming a heavy drinker appears to wipe out most of the social advantage of coming from an intact home and graduating from high school. Among men who never drank heavily, the advantages of an intact childhood home and a high school diploma have a marked impact for each measure except divorce and separation. But among men with a history of heavy drinking, those from an advantaged background are hardly distinguishable from the less favored in terms of family life and have a much narrower advantage in employment and arrest records. For instance, among men who have not been heavy drinkers, the rate of major unemployment in the last five years is three times as high among the disadvantaged as among the advantaged, but among heavy drinkers the rate among the disadvantaged is only one and one-third times that among the advantaged.

Heavy drinking is, therefore, *not* simply one more adult expression of deviant behavior beginning in childhood. It is predictive of a variety of social, economic, and legal troubles, independent of the background variables of the father's presence in childhood and graduation from high school.

Discussion

Moynihan[20] has stated that "a national effort towards the problems of Negro Americans must be directed towards the question of family structure. The object should be to strengthen the

---

[16] Robins, Murphy, and Breckenridge, "Drinking Behavior in Young Urban Negro Men."

[17] P. Glick, *American Families* (New York: John Wiley, 1957), pp. 155–56.

[18] N. Christie, *Unge Norske Lovovertredere* (Oslo-Bergen, Norway: Universitetsvorlaget, 1960, 11-page English summary), and G. E. Gardner and N. Godlman, "Childhood and Adolescent Adjustment of Naval Successes and Failures," *American Journal of Orthopsychiatry* 15 (1945), pp. 584–96.

[19] This small number is in part due to the balanced design of the study, in which half of the men were chosen for having records of school problems and half for records indicating father's absence. Also, fewer fathers than expected were found to have been present when we combined interview and record information.

---

[20] Moynihan, *The Negro Family.*

FIGURE 1. RELATIONSHIP OF HEAVY DRINKING TO FAMILY LIFE

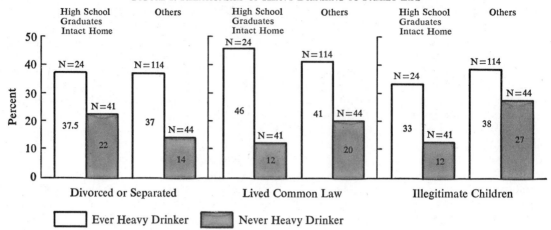

High school graduates whose fathers had been present throughout elementary school ("intact home") and who themselves drank heavily (N = 24) are compared with similarly advantaged men who never drank heavily (N = 41). These two groups, in turn, are compared with all others ("others"): i.e., men who had not graduated and/or whose fathers had been absent and who themselves drank heavily (N = 114) and similarly disadvantaged men who never drank heavily (N = 44).

Numbers in the center of each bar represent the percent of those in each group who were divorced or separated, had lived in "common law" relationships, or had had illegitimate children (figure 1) and who were not currently employed, had been out of full-time employment for more than one year in the past five, or who had had arrests other than those related to drunkenness (figure 2). (In the arrests 1959–64 category, N's are not as large as in the other categories because men in the armed services throughout the period were excluded.)

FIGURE 2. RELATIONSHIP OF HEAVY DRINKING TO EMPLOYMENT AND ARRESTS

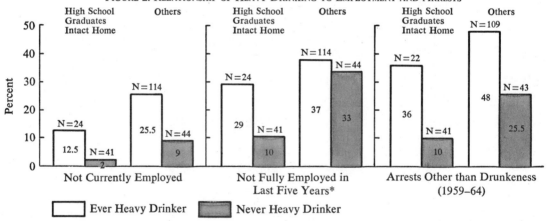

High school graduates whose fathers had been present throughout elementary school ("intact home") and who themselves drank heavily (N = 24) are compared with similarly advantaged men who never drank heavily (N = 41). These two groups, in turn, are compared with all others ("others"): i.e., men who had not graduated and/or whose fathers had been absent and who themselves drank heavily (N = 114) and similarly disadvantaged men who never drank heavily (N = 44).

Numbers in the center of each bar represent the percent of those in each group who were divorced or separated, had lived in "common law" relationships, or had had illegitimate children (figure 1) and who were not currently employed, had been out of full-time employment for more than one year in the past five, or who had had arrests other than those related to drunkenness (figure 2). (In the arrests 1959–64 category, N's are not as large as in the other categories because men in the armed services throughout the period were excluded.)

* Underemployed one or more years in past five years.

Negro family so as to enable it to raise and support its members as do other families." In order to plan and carry out such a strengthening, it is necessary to identify and attempt to deal with those forces that tend to weaken the family structure. Continuing discrimination against Negroes in all areas of living is clearly a major factor.

The special impact of restricted employment opportunities for the Negro male is reflected in his apparent dispensability as head of the household. "Nearly a quarter of Negro women living in cities who have ever married are divorced, separated, or are living apart from their husbands," according to Moynihan.[21] In the present study, 29.6 percent of the men were either divorced or permanently separated. Of those *ever* married, over one-third were currently divorced or separated.

Apart from broken marriages, fatherless families are produced by illegitimate births. Moynihan[22] reports that 23.6 percent of Negro children born in 1963 were illegitimate, as compared to 3.07 percent of white children. In the present study, 22.3 percent of the children sired by the men interviewed were illegitimate, a figure almost identical with the national data.

Both the frequency of broken marriages and that of illegitimate children are strikingly related to a history of heavy drinking. The poorest marital histories occur in men whose drinking caused recent medical, social, legal, and/or employment problems. Men who never drank heavily have considerably more stable marriages. The difference is not accounted for by the man's having come from a broken home himself or by his failure to achieve at least a high school education, although the father's presence and high school graduation ameliorate slightly the likelihood of having illegitimate children. (Or it may be that siring an illegitimate child sometimes interferes with graduating from high school.)

Moynihan reports that "in 1963, a prosperous year, 29.2 percent of all Negro men in the labor force were unemployed at some time during the year. Almost half of these men were out of work fifteen weeks or more."[23] In the present study 16.6 percent of the men were either unemployed or employed less than full time when interviewed. Further, 30.5 percent of them had been underemployed (out of work or with less than full-time employment) for one year or longer in the previous five years. We are not aware of comparable national figures, and Moynihan cites a general lack of inquiry. The implications of this degree of nonproductiveness for the national economy are staggering. Again, although coming from an intact home and achieving high school graduation ameliorates the magnitude of the problem, a history of heavy drinking is strikingly related to both aspects of underemployment (Figure 2).

Studies have shown that coming from a broken home predisposes to delinquency.[24] Logically it should therefore also predict adult arrests. Controlling for the father's presence does reduce the arrest rate in the present sample, but the factor of heavy drinking remains a significant variable.

The reader is reminded that the findings presented here refer to a population sample of Negro men born and educated in a large city and who fall within the normal IQ range. It is not possible at this point to say how far the conclusions may be generalized to rural or Southern-born Negro men or to those of lower IQ. The close comparability of our data to more general data from public sources suggests that they may be more representative than not.

The findings appear to support Moynihan's[25] hypothesis of a vicious cycle of broken home, delinquency, reproductive irresponsibility, underemployment, and broken home. Alcohol abuse emerges as a crucial intervening variable. The Negro boy who comes from a broken home is least likely to complete even a high school education.[26] His drinking will begin early and he is likely to drink heavily.[27] If he does drink heavily he is more likely than others to live in a common-law arrangement, to leave his wife if he marries, and to sire illegitimate children. He is likely to have trouble with the law. He will fail to support many of his children,[28] and those he supports will share in a poverty-level subsistence. Those who do not live with him—the majority[29] —will be less likely to complete high school and more likely to drink heavily. Thus the cycle is renewed.

It is urgent that social planning concerned

[21] *Ibid.*
[22] *Ibid.*, p. 8.
[23] *Ibid.*, p. 21.

[24] L. N. Robins, *Deviant Children Grown Up: A Sociological and Psychiatric Study of Sociopathic Personality* (Baltimore: Williams and Wilkens, 1966).
[25] Moynihan, *The Negro Family.*
[26] I. J. King, G. E. Murphy, L. N. Robins, and H. Darvish (unpublished data).
[27] Robins, Murphy, and Breckenridge, "Drinking Behavior in Young Urban Negro Men."
[28] King, Murphy, Robins, and Darvish (unpublished data).
[29] *Ibid.*

with the urban problems of crime, poverty, and disrupted family structure take into account the damaging role that alcohol abuse plays in canceling out the gains to be expected from improved economic and educational opportunity.

Summary

Two hundred twenty-three Negro men in their early 30s, born and raised in a metropolis, were selected without knowledge of their drinking habits and were interviewed with respect to social functioning, alcohol use, and evidences of serious alcohol abuse (e.g., delirium tremens, liver disease, convulsions, "benders," "shakes"). A history of heavy drinking was found in 62 percent and of recent serious difficulties secondary to alcohol use in 17 percent.

Increasing degrees of alcohol use were increasingly associated with various measures of social deviance. Those with recent serious alcohol problems, those who drank heavily but had no alcohol problems, and those who had never drunk heavily comprised three groups statistically significantly different from one another in terms of marital and family difficulties, employment and income problems, and arrests.

Absence of a father in the childhood home and failure to graduate from high school predicted heavy drinking and alcohol problems. However, even those who came from homes where the father was present and who themselves completed high school—if they became heavy drinkers—had the same high frequency of marital and family difficulties, employment and income problems, and nondrunk arrests as did those without these early advantages. Conversely, among those whose fathers had been absent and who had not completed high school, the absence of a history of heavy drinking was associated with significantly fewer family and employment problems and arrests.

This study demonstrates for the first time the significance of alcohol abuse in the urban Negro ghetto cycle of broken home, delinquency, reproductive irresponsibility, and underemployment. Alcohol abuse emerges as a crucial intervening variable which must be taken into account in any attempts to deal with the crisis in our cities and to free the American Negro from this vicious circle.

CHILDHOOD SYMPTOMS IN CHILDREN OF ALCOHOLICS AND COMPARISON GROUP PARENTS

PAUL W. HABERMAN

There has been general agreement that parental alcoholism has a harmful effect on children. However, there have been very few published works on this subject, and only one has been found which discusses the characteristics and symptomatology of the children of alcoholics in a specific manner.[1] Children of alcoholics, children of parents with stomach ulcers or other chronic stomach trouble, and children of parents with neither pathology are examined in this paper for differences in the extent and type of symptoms. Interview responses of mothers in the three groups were analyzed with the expectation of confirming and elaborating upon previously reported and conjectured symptomatology for children of alcoholics. In addition, Social Service Exchange clearance was obtained as an independent source of identifying problem children in the alcoholic and comparison groups.

METHODOLOGY

In one section of the current project, a comparative study of family interaction and role performance, mothers were asked some questions

---

Reprinted with permission of the author and the National Council on Family Relations, from *Journal of Marriage and the Family* 2 (May, 1966), pp. 152–54.
[1] Ingvar Nylander, "Children of Alcoholic Fathers," *Acta Paediatricia* 49, supplement 121 (March 1960), Uppsala, Sweden.

about their children including the eight childhood symptoms listed in Table 1. These women had been initially interviewed in a large-scale representative community study, the Master Sample Survey, conducted by the Columbia University School of Public Health and Administrative Medicine in the Washington Heights Health District of New York City in 1960 and 1961. This was a cooperative project, with the participation of the National Council on Alcoholism and several other health agencies, which has been previously described.[2]

Members of Master Sample Survey families who were identified as presumed alcoholics, their spouses, and separated women who indicated that their former spouses had been problem drinkers were reinterviewed as part of the current study. In the present research, as in the

_____

[2] Margaret B. Bailey, Paul W. Haberman, and Harold Alksne, "The Epidemiology of Alcoholism in an Urban Residential Area," *Quarterly Journal of Studies on Alcohol* 26 No. 1 (March, 1965), pp. 19–40.

earlier study, alcoholism was defined in terms of problems in the areas of health, work, or interpersonal relationships because of too much drinking.

After respondents in the alcoholic group were reinterviewed, controls with stomach ulcers or other chronic stomach trouble, and controls with neither pathology, hereafter called the general comparison group, were matched with alcoholic group respondents and reinterviewed on a case-for-case basis. General comparison persons were matched with the alcoholics on the following background characteristics: sex, age group, marital and family status, educational group, and ethnicity.

As a possible "sick" comparison group, persons for whom stomach ulcers or other chronic stomach trouble were reported in the Master Sample Survey most closely resembled the alcoholics in reported frequency, sex, and age distribution. Since there were too few such cases for more precise demographic control, only married persons with stomach trouble, matched with

TABLE 1. SYMPTOM DATA FOR CHILDREN OF ALCOHOLIC AND
COMPARISON GROUP PARENTS

Symptom Data	Group: Family N: Children N:	All Families		Currently Married Families		
		Alcoholic 41 89	General comparison 41 92	Alcoholic 24 53	General comparison 24 58	Stomach trouble 24 55
Families with one or more children with at least one symptom		63.4%	51.2%	62.5%	45.8%	45.8%
Eight specific symptoms:						
Stuttering or stammering		19.5%	14.6%	16.7%	12.5%	8.3%
Unreasonable fears		19.5	12.2	20.8	16.7	12.5
Frequent temper tantrums		39.0	22.0	37.5	20.8	29.2
Constant fighting with other children		19.5	9.8	20.8	4.2	0.0
Often in trouble in neighborhood		9.8	7.3	4.2	4.2	0.0
Staying by self and rarely playing with other children		14.6	12.2	12.5	12.5	4.2
Bed wetting after age 6		17.1	14.6	16.7	8.3	16.7
Frequent trouble in school because of bad conduct or truancy		19.5	9.8	20.8	4.2	4.2
Families with child known to correctional agency, child guidance clinic, or attendance bureau		17.1%	2.4%	16.7%	4.2%	0.0%
Children with one or more symptoms		35.9%	24.7%	38.2%	22.6%	20.6%
Average number of symptoms per child		0.8	0.5	0.8	0.4	0.3

alcoholics on sex and age group, and their spouses were reinterviewed.

The resultant sample available for this investigation consists of two groups of 41 currently or previously married alcoholic and general comparison group mothers and three groups of 24 currently married women in the alcoholic, general comparison, and stomach trouble groups.[3] The median ages for these five groups of women ranged from 38 to 43 years, with the median years of education completed nine or ten in all cases.

The four major ethnic groups in the Washington Heights Health District were Negroes, Puerto Ricans, Jewish, and Irish. About one-quarter of the alcoholic groups and one-sixth of the comparison groups were Negro. Slightly more than one-half of the stomach trouble group, one-quarter of the general comparison groups, and one-sixth of the alcoholic groups were Jewish. The Irish and Puerto Ricans had approximately equal representation among the sample groups except for fewer Puerto Rican women in the stomach trouble group.

FINDINGS

As shown in Table 1, childhood symptoms were more often reported for children in alcoholic families. As corroborating evidence of disturbance, these children were more likely to be known to correctional or school authorities than those in the general comparison or stomach trouble groups. Although all eight symptoms

occurred more frequently among the children of alcoholics, temper tantrums, fighting with peers, and trouble in school were the ones with the most difference in occurrence between alcoholic and comparison groups. The over-all symptomatology and specific symptom patterns shown in this study seem to confirm the earlier findings by Nylander,[4] using 229 children of alcoholics and 163 controls. The Social Service Exchange clearance data support specifically the occurrence of trouble in school among the alcoholic and comparison groups.

The results suggest that parental alcoholism frequently involves harmful interpersonal behavior which is reflected in their children's symptoms. On the other hand, parents with chronic stomach trouble more often may have internalized manifestations of disorder which are not as damaging to their children. However, the rather small sample size must be considered in any interpretation of these findings. Likewise, although demographic factors were partially controlled, symptom differences to some extent may have reflected sociocultural variations among the comparison groups. In particular, there were more Negro alcoholic families and more Jewish children with parents in the stomach trouble group.

In conclusion, the children with alcoholic parents had more implicative symptoms than those in the comparison groups, although children in the stomach trouble group did not differ substantially from their general comparison counterparts. In addition, children of alcoholics were more frequently identified as having been in trouble by Social Service Exchange clearance. Thus, some aspects of the detrimental effects of parental alcoholism upon their children have been demonstrated in these findings.

---

[3] The husband was the alcoholic in 18 of the 24 currently married cases, the wife in two such cases, and both spouses were alcoholics in four cases. None of the 17 separated women with alcoholic husbands had drinking problems themselves. Of the 24 currently married stomach trouble cases, the husband was the sick person in 21 such cases, the wife in 1 case, and both spouses in 2 cases.

---

[4] Nylander, "Children of Alcoholic Fathers."

CHAPTER EIGHT

DRUG USE AND ADDICTION

To many persons, drug use in the United States has reached crisis proportions. Federal, state, and local governments have strengthened law enforcement agencies in order to slow the "drug traffic," and numerous facilities where drug addicts can get treatment have been established.[1]

In 1960, the Federal Bureau of Narcotic and Dangerous Drugs listed 45,391 known drug addicts; the number increased to 57,199 in 1965[2] and 68,088 by 1969.[3] The figures refer to addicts known to the police and so may underestimate the actual numbers. For example, the official register of addicts in New York City obtains names from a wider variety of sources than does the federal agency, with less reliance on law-enforcement agencies and comparatively greater reliance on social and medical agencies. And for 1969 this register showed that there were 52,104 addicts in New York City, substantially more than the 32,240 that the federal agency reported for the entire state of New York (though admittedly almost all New York addicts are in New York City). Assuming that the rate is under-reported in similar proportion in other areas of the country, based on the figures reported by the federal bureau, there were about 109,000 addicts in the United States as of 1969.[4] Some believe that even this figure is low since it is also based on official statistics.[5] Estimates based on other calculations yield higher figures.

Only half of the persons whose deaths were attributed directly or indirectly to heroin in New York City in 1969 were found listed in the

---

[1] See Raymond Glasscote, James N. Sussex, Jerome H. Jaffe, John Ball and Leon Brill, *The Treatment of Drug Abuse: Programs, Problems, Prospects* (Washington: American Psychiatric Association, 1974), pp. 23–26, 44–46.

[2] Robert W. Winslow, *Crime in a Free Society: Selections from the President's Commission on Law Enforcement and Administration of Justice* (Belmont, California: Dickenson Publishing Company, 1968), p. 221.

[3] Louise G. Richards and Eleanor E. Carroll, "Illicit Drug Use and Addiction in the United States," *Public Health Reports,* 85 (December, 1970), p. 1036.

[4] *Ibid.,* p. 1037.

[5] Some question whether official statistics underestimate actual numbers very much. Glosscote et al. state: "If one assumes . . . that most addicts, because of the many illegal transactions in which they are regularly involved to maintain their supply of drugs, will come to official attention within any one five-year period, then the additional number (beyond the official record) will not be great." *The Treatment of Drug Abuse,* p. 16.

city's narcotics register that year.[6] On this basis one might assume that the official register contains only half of all addicts in New York, which in 1969 would indicate a total of 104,208 addicts. Again assuming that 50 percent of all addicts are in New York, there would have been over 200,000 addicts in the United States as a whole. And federal estimates of the number of addicts in 1971 were as high as 300,000.[7]

But regardless of the exact figures, official statistics, known deaths from drug overdose, arrest and court records, and surveys of public schools and colleges indicate that drug use (not just addiction) increased greatly during the years after 1960.[8] For example, the number of deaths from drug abuse in New York City increased threefold from 1961 to 1969, from 311 to 950.[9] Along with the overall increase in drug use there has been an increase in the variety of drugs that are used. Prior to the years 1960 to 1965, the "drug problem" was largely confined to users of heroin and opiate derivatives. Recently, however, the use of LSD, marijuana, and even barbituates, tranquillizers, and amphetamines are viewed as reaching crisis proportions.

The problem is no doubt serious for society, and in individual cases the consequences are often tragic. Nevertheless, perceptions of and beliefs about drugs are frequently erroneous and distorted. There is a tendency for the public to believe that drug addiction is much higher than it is. To illustrate, public estimates of heroin addiction among Army enlisted men who served in Vietnam in 1970 to 1971 ran as high as 200,000. Scientific surveys indicated, however, that the number was closer to 4,000.[10] In addition, assuming that there are 300,000 addicts in the U.S. today, there are still fewer than would be expected if the percentage of the population addicted were as high as in 1918. Based on a survey of physicians who were asked to report the number of addicts under their care in that year, it is estimated that there were 238,000 addicts,[11] or about one for every four hundred persons. If this were the rate today, we would have almost 500,000 addicts. And other evidence suggests that drug use was more frequent prior to the passage of federal legislation that restricted drug use, beginning with the Harrison Act in 1914.[12] From this perspective, then, it does not appear that the rate of drug addiction is higher today than in the past.

What is clear is that changes have occurred in the patterns of drug use. First, the legal regulation of drug use made drug users dependent on

[6] Richards and Carroll, "Illicit Drug Use and Addiction," p. 1037.

[7] Glasscote et al., *The Treatment of Drug Abuse*, p. 16.

[8] See David Malikin, Sheldon D. Bacon, John D. Case, Ken Jackson, and Edmund W. Gordon, *Social Disability: Alcoholism, Drug Addiction, Crime and Social Disadvantage* (New York: New York University Press, 1973), pp. 101–08.

[9] Milton Helpern and Yong-Myun Rho, "Deaths from Narcotism in New York City: Incidence, Circumstances, and Postmortem Findings," *New York State Journal of Medicine* (Sept. 15, 1966), p. 2394; and Richards and Carroll, "Illicit Drug Use and Addiction," p. 1040.

[10] *Time* (May 7, 1973).

[11] C. E. Terry and M. Pellens, "The Extent of Chronic Opiate Use in the United States Prior to 1921," in John C. Ball and C. D. Chambers, eds., *The Epidemiology of Opiate Addiction in the United States* (Springfield, Illinois: Charles C. Thomas, 1971).

[12] *Ibid.*, Glasscote et al., *The Treatment of Drug Abuse*, pp. 15–16.

criminals for their supply of drugs. Laws restricting drugs actually brought a criminal element into existence—criminal structures emerged to meet a demand that could not be met through legal structures. This does not mean, however, that a substantial proportion of crime is associated with drug use. A *realistic* estimate of the proportion of crimes committed by addicts who need money to satisfy their habits cannot be made on the basis of existing evidence.

Another emerging pattern is the change in the social characteristics of drug users. Prior to the 1914 to 1918 period of federal legislation, drug users were predominantly older (40 years and above) middle and upper-class females. After this period, users increasingly were young males from minority groups (predominantly blacks) who lived in urban slums. In recent years, use has spread to middle-class public schools and to college campuses.[13] Thus, "What started as a middle-class phenomenon and then became for a time mainly a problem of the slums now appears to be extending to the middle-class...."[14] The socially defined drug crisis of post-1960 may not be a reaction to the increased drug usage so much as a reaction to the spread of drug usage into the middle and upper classes.

A. ANTECEDENTS AND DETERMINANTS

The question of what causes illegal drug use and subsequent addiction is clouded by controversy. A number of causal theories have been presented emphasizing environmental, social, cultural, familial, physiological, and psychological factors.[15] No single theory is universally accepted, and no one theory appears to receive greater acceptance than any other. There are several areas of agreement, however.

For example, it is believed that the reason for or cause of initial drug use is frequently different from the cause of addictive use. The determinants of initial use are diverse; a first time user may wish to vent anger (indirectly) at society, need help in weathering a personal crisis, desire to gain group acceptance, or need any number of things. However, the motive for the *maintenance* of the habit is to obtain the specific effects produced by the drug, such as euphoria ("highs" and "kicks") or, in the

---

[13] Glasscote et al., *The Treatment of Drug Abuse*, pp. 17–18. For studies of different patterns in drug use see John C. Ball, "Two Patterns of Narcotic Addiction in the United States," *Journal of Criminal Law, Criminology and Police Science* 56 (June, 1965), pp. 203–11; John C. Ball and William M. Bates, "Migration and Residential Mobility of Narcotic Drug Addicts," *Social Problems* 14 (Summer, 1966), pp. 56–69; and William M. Bates, "Narcotics, Negroes and the South," *Social Forces* 45 (September, 1966), pp. 61–67.
[14] Glasscote et al., *The Treatment of Drug Abuse*, p. 18.
[15] See *ibid.*, pp. 19–21, and Malikin et al., *Social Disability*, pp. 108–13.

case of opiate addiction, to reduce "withdrawal symptoms" that occur when the last dosage has worn off.[16]

But regardless of motivation, initial use tends to occur through association with one or more addicts;[17] drugs are usually first consumed at the invitation of an addict friend or acquaintance. In other instances, initial use is related to the ready legal access to narcotics, as through physicians and possibly other members of the "white coat" professions (pharmacists, dentists and nurses). According to some estimates, as many as 1 percent of U.S. physicians are drug addicts. Hence, initial use is causally associated with opportunity and availability. This alone is not a sufficient explanation in most instances, however, because many persons who have the opportunity to use drugs do not do so.[18] Why some individuals accept and some refuse an opportunity is not known, although a number of studies have been conducted in an effort to identify personality characteristics of users.[19]

Finally, there seems to be a growing consensus that, regardless of motivation and opportunity, the effects of drugs on users are variable. This opinion rejects what has been called the "chemicalistic fallacy" or the view that a "specific drug has a specific effect or set of effects on everyone who uses it."[20] Instead, the nature of the effect will vary with the social setting. "It is not the chemical composition of the drug that determines the most important features of drug effects and drug-related behavior, but the social and cultural setting surrounding use."[21] Exactly what the individual experiences when he ingests a drug depends on the *meaning* he *assigns* to the effect, and this in turn depends on social definitions available to him in his social setting. This is not to say that drugs have no universal biochemical effects or that the effects are totally dependent on social definition; that would be a "sociologistic fallacy." Nevertheless, the process of *"assigning meanings* to internal states, to behavior, to drug 'effects,' " varies with the social setting, and this may indeed be the most important aspect of drug use.[22] Certainly from a sociological standpoint, a central question about the etiology of drug use concerns the origin of assigned

---

[16] In the case of maintenance motives for opiate addiction, schools of thought are split. Lindesmith argues that compulsive heroin use—addiction—begins when the user has learned that withdrawal symptoms disappear shortly after the drug is injected. See Alfred R. Lindesmith, *Opiate Addiction* (Bloomington, Ind.: Principia Press, 1947). On the other hand, others argue that withdrawal symptoms are not as painful as many believe, that the continued use of heroin stems from the thrill, "kick," or euphoric feeling that one gets from the drug. The alleviation of withdrawal symptoms only enhances the drug's euphoric action. See David P. Ausuble, *Drug Addiction: Physiological, Psychological, and Sociological Aspects* (New York: Random House, 1958). The best and most recent evidence supports the latter position. See William E. McAuliffe and Robert A. Gordon, "A Test of Lindesmith's Theory of Addiction: The Frequency of Euphoria among Long-Term Addicts," *American Journal of Sociology* 79 (January, 1974), pp. 794–840.

[17] For an early study showing this, see Bingham Dai, *Opium Addiction in Chicago* (Shanghai, China: The Commercial Press, 1937).

[18] See Isador Chen et al., *The Road to H: Narcotics and Public Policy* (New York: Basic Books, 1964), p. 153.

[19] Malikin et al., *Social Disability*, pp. 108–13.

[20] Erich Goode, *The Drug Phenomenon: Social Aspects of Drug Taking* (Indianapolis: Bobbs-Merrill Company, 1973), p. 38.

[21] *Ibid.*, p. 39.

[22] *Ibid.* (Author's emphasis.)

meanings, which is always influenced by societal and group conceptions about the effects of drugs.

Accordingly, the selections on antecedents and determinants deal with this issue. In "History, Culture and Subjective Experience: An Exploration of the Social Bases of Drug-Induced Experiences," Howard S. Becker argues that the effect of the drug—the way the drug is experienced—varies according to how long the particular drug has been used in society. When drugs have been used in society for a considerable period of time, experience with the effects of the drug accumulates, and a culture and social organization surrounding the use of that drug develop. This provides the user with a set of definitions in which his subjective experience can be interpreted and which provide a set of controls for subsequent behavior. It is in the early stages of drug use in a society that "psychotic" episodes are most apt to occur; this is because a culture—a set of expectations—about the effects of the drug and how to handle them have not yet developed. (In this respect, note that the findings of Larsen and Abu-Laban for alcohol use are consistent with Becker's theory.) Becker notes, however, that his theory may be most descriptive of drugs that have highly variable physical effects on an individual, such as marijuana and LSD.

In the next selection, Harold Finestone argues that the subjective experience among male Negro adolescents is rooted in the "cat" role characteristic of many Negro adolescents. This role includes "playing it cool," being an "operator," having a "hustle," and, above all, cultivating a "kick." The ultimate "kick" is drug use. "Kicks" are especially important because they are strongly tabooed by "squares," and "cats" view themselves as the antithesis of "squares." Finestone views drug use, then, as a manifestation of a social type or role. This role provides a social context that shapes the subjective effects of the drug and allows a basis for assigning meaning to the drug experience. Note, too, that Finestone views the "cat" role, in turn, as a collective response to the blocked status frustrations that originate in social denials and racial discriminations.

HISTORY, CULTURE AND SUBJECTIVE EXPERIENCE
An Exploration of the Social Bases of Drug-Induced Experiences

HOWARD S. BECKER

In 1938, Albert Hoffman discovered the peculiar effects of lysergic acid dieythlamide (LSD-25) on the mind. He synthesized the drug in 1943 and, following the end of World War II, it came into use in psychiatry, both as a method of simulating psychosis for clinical study and as a means of therapy.[1] In the early 1960's, Timothy Leary, Richard Alpert and others began using it with normal subjects as a means of "consciousness expansion." Their work received a great deal of publicity, particularly after a dispute with Harvard authorities over its potential danger. Simultaneously, LSD-25 became available on the underground market and, although no one has accurate figures, the number of people who have used or continue to use it is clearly very large.

The publicity continues and a great controversy now surrounds LSD use. At one extreme, Leary considers its use so beneficial that he has founded a new religion in which it is the major sacrament. At the other extreme, psychiatrists, police and journalists allege that LSD is extremely dangerous, that it produces psychosis, and that persons under its influence are likely to commit actions dangerous to themselves and others that they would not otherwise have committed. Opponents of the drug have persuaded the Congress and some state legislatures to classify it as a narcotic or dangerous drug and to attach penal sanctions to its sale, possession, or use.

In spite of the great interest in the drug, I think it is fair to say that the evidence of its danger is by no means decisive.[2] If the drug does prove to be the cause of a bona fide psychosis, it will be the only case in which anyone can state with authority that they have found *the* unique cause of any such phenomenon; a similar statement applies to causes of crime and suicide. Whatever the ultimate findings of pharmacologists and others now studying the drug, sociologists are unlikely to accept such an asocial and unicausal explanation of any form of complex social behavior. But if we refuse to accept the explanations of others we are obligated to provide one of our own. In what follows, I consider the reports of LSD-induced psychoses and try to relate them to what is known of the social psychology and sociology of drug use. By this means I hope to add both to our understanding of the current controversy over LSD and to our general knowledge of the social character of drug use.

In particular, I will make use of a comparison between LSD use and marihuana use, suggested by the early history of marihuana in this country. That history contains the same reports of "psychotic episodes" now current with respect to LSD. But reports of such episodes disappeared at the same time as the number of marihuana users increased greatly. This suggests the utility of considering the historical dimension of drug use.

I must add a cautionary disclaimer. I have not

Reprinted with permission of the author and the American Sociological Association, from the *Journal of Health and Social Behavior* 7 (June, 1967), pp. 163–76.

[1] See "D-Lysergic Acid Diethylamide-LSD," *Sandoz Excerpta* 1 (1955), pp. 1–2, quoted in Sanford M. Unger, "Mescaline, LSD, Psilocybin and Personality Change," in David Solomon, editor, *LSD: The Consciousness-Expanding Drug* (New York: Berkley Publishing, 1966), p. 206.

[2] On this point, to which I return later, the major references are: Sydney Cohen, "Lysergic Acid Diethylamide: Side Effects and Complications," *Journal of Nervous and Mental Diseases* 130 (January, 1960), pp. 30–40; Sydney Cohen and Keith S. Ditman, "Prolonged Adverse Reactions to Lysergic Acid Diethylamide," *Archives of General Psychiatry* 8 (1963), pp. 475–80; Sydney Cohen and Keith S. Ditman, "Complications Associated with Lysergic Acid Diethylamide (LSD–25)," *Journal of the American Medical Association* 181 (July 14, 1962), pp. 161–62; William A. Frosch, Edwin S. Robbins and Marvin Stern, "Untoward Reactions to Lysergic Acid Diethylamide (LSD) Resulting in Hospitalization," *New England Journal of Medicine* 273 (December 2, 1965), pp. 1235–39; A. Hoffer, "D-Lysergic Acid Diethylamide (LSD): A Review of its Present Status," *Clinical Pharmacology and Therapeutics* 6 (March, 1965), pp. 183–255; S. H. Rosenthal, "Persistent Hallucinosis Following Repeated Administration of Hallucinogenic Drugs," *American Journal of Psychiatry* 121 (1964), pp. 238–44; and J. Thomas Ungerleider, Duke D. Fisher and Marielle Fuller, "The Dangers of LSD: Analysis of Seven Month's Experience in a University Hospital's Psychiatric Service," *Journal of the American Medical Association* 197 (August 8, 1966), pp. 389–92.

examined thoroughly the literature on LSD, which increases at an alarming rate.[3] What I have to say about it is necessarily speculative with respect to its effects; what I have to say about the conditions under which it is used is also speculative, but is based in part on interviews with a few users. I present no documented conclusions, but do hope that the perspective outlined may help orient research toward generalizations that will fit into the corpus of sociological and social psychological theory on related matters.

THE SUBJECTIVE EFFECTS OF DRUGS

The physiological effects of drugs can be ascertained by standard techniques of physiological and pharmacological research. Scientists measure and have explanations for the actions of many drugs on such observable indices as the heart and respiratory rates, the level of various chemicals in the blood, and the secretion of enzymes and hormones. In contrast, the subjective changes produced by a drug can be ascertained only by asking the subject, in one way or another, how he feels. (To be sure, one can measure the drug's effect on certain measures of psychological functioning—the ability to perform some standardized task, such as placing pegs in a board or remembering nonsense syllables—but this does not tell us what the drug experience is like.)[4]

We take medically prescribed drugs because we believe they will cure or control a disease from which we are suffering; the subjective effects they produce are either ignored or defined as noxious side effects. But some people take some drugs precisely because they want to experience these subjective effects; they take them, to put it colloquially, because they want to get "high." These recreationally used drugs have be-

come the focus of sociological research because the goal of an artificially induced change in consciousness seems to many immoral, and those who so believe have been able to transform their belief into law. Drug users thus come to sociological attention as lawbreakers, and the problems typically investigated have to do with explaining their lawbreaking.

Nevertheless, some sociologists, anthropologists, and social psychologists have investigated the problem of drug-induced subjective experience in its own right. Taking their findings together, the following conclusions seem justified.[5] First, many drugs, including those used to produce changes in subjective experience, have a great variety of effects and the user may single out many of them, one of them, or none of them as definite experiences he is undergoing. He may be totally unaware of some of the drug's effects, even when they are physiologically gross, although in general the grosser the effects the harder they are to ignore. When he does perceive the effects, he may not attribute them to drug use but dismiss them as due to some other cause, such as fatigue or a cold. Marihuana users, for example, may not even be aware of the drug's effects when they first use it, even though it is obvious to others that they are experiencing them.[6]

Second, and in consequence, the effects of the same drug may be experienced quite differently by different people or by the same people at different times. Even if physiologically observable effects are substantially the same in all members of the species, individuals can vary

---

[3] Hoffer's recent review of this literature, for which he disclaims completeness cites 411 references (Hoffer, "D-Lysergic Acid Diethylamide").

[4] See, for instance: New York City Mayor's Committee on Marihuana, *The Marihuana Problem in the City of New York* (Lancaster, Penn.: Jacques Cattell Press, 1944), pp. 69–77; and C. Knight Aldrich, "The Effect of a Synthetic Marihuana-Like Compound on Musical Talent as Measured by the Seashore Test," *Public Health Reports* 59 (1944), pp. 431–33.

[5] I rely largely on the following reports: Howard S. Becker, *Outsiders* (New York: The Free Press, 1963), pp. 41–58 (marihuana); Alfred R. Lindesmith, *Opiate Addiction* (Bloomington, Ind.: Principia Press, 1947) (opiates); Richard Blum and associates, *Utopiates* (New York: Atherton Press, 1964) (LSD); Ralph Metzner, George Litwin, and Gunther M. Weil, "The Relation of Expectation and Mood to Psilocybin Reactions: A Questionnaire Study," *Psychedelic Review* No. 5 (1965), pp. 3–39 (Psilocybin); David F. Aberle, *The Peyote Religion Among the Navaho* (Chicago: Aldine Publishing Co., 1966), pp. 5–11 (Peyote); Stanley Schacter and Jerome E. Singer, "Cognitive, Social and Physiological Determinants of Emotional State," *Psychological Review* 69 (September, 1962), pp. 379–99 (Adrenalin); and Vincent Newlis and Helen H. Newlis, "The Description and Analysis of Mood," *Annals of the New York Academy of Science* 65 (1956), pp. 345–55 (benzedrine, seconal and dramamine). Schacter and Singer propose a similar approach to mine to the study of drug experiences, stressing the importance of the label the person attaches to the experience he is having.

[6] Becker, *Outsiders*.

widely in those to which they choose to pay attention. Thus, Aberle remarks on the quite different experiences Indians and experimental subjects have with peyote[7] and Blum reports a wide variety of experiences with LSD, depending on the circumstances under which it was taken.[8]

Third, since recreational users take drugs in order to achieve some subjective state not ordinarily available to them, it follows that they will expect and be most likely to experience those effects which produce a deviation from conventional perceptions and interpretations of internal and external experience. Thus, distortions in perception of time and space and shifts in judgments of the importance and meaning of ordinary events constitute the most common reported effects.

Fourth, any of a great variety of effects may be singled out by the user as desirable or pleasurable, as the effects for which he has taken the drug. Even effects which seem to the uninitiated to be uncomfortable, unpleasant or frightening —perceptual distortions or visual and auditory hallucinations—can be defined by users as a goal to be sought.[9]

Fifth, how a person experiences the effects of a drug depends greatly on the way others define those effects for him.[10] The total effect of a drug is likely to be a melange of differing physical and psychological sensations. If others whom the user believes to be knowledgeable single out certain effects as characteristics and dismiss others, he is likely to notice those they single out as characteristic of his own experience. If they define certain effects as transitory, he is likely to believe that those effects will go away. All this supposes, of course, that the definition offered the user can be validated in his own experience,

that something contained in the drug-induced melange of sensations corresponds to it.

Such a conception of the character of the drug experience has its roots, obviously, in Mead's theory of the self and the relation of objects to the self.[11] In that theory, objects (including the self) have meaning for the person only as he imputes that meaning to them in the course of his interaction with them. The meaning is not given in the object, but is lodged there as the person acquires a conception of the kind of action that can be taken with, toward, by, and for it. Meanings arise in the course of social interaction, deriving their character from the consensus participants develop about the object in question. The findings of research on the character of drug-induced experience are therefore predictable from Mead's theory.

DRUG PSYCHOSES

The scientific literature and, even more, the popular press frequently state that recreational drug use produces a psychosis. The nature of "psychosis" is seldom defined, as though it were intuitively clear. Writers usually seem to mean a mental disturbance of some unspecified kind, involving auditory and visual hallucinations, an inability to control one's stream of thought, and a tendency to engage in socially inappropriate behavior, either because one has lost the sense that it is inappropriate or because one cannot stop oneself. In addition, and perhaps most important, psychosis is thought to be a state that will last long beyond the specific event that provoked it. However it occurred, it is thought to mark a more-or-less permanent change in the psyche and this, after all, is why we usually think of it as such a bad thing. Overindulgence in alcohol produces many of the symptoms cited but this frightens no one because we understand that they will soon go away.

Verified reports of drug-induced psychoses are

---

[7] Aberle, *Peyote Religion Among the Navaho,* and Anthony F. C. Wallace, "Cultural Determinants of Response to Hallucinatory Experience," *Archives of General Psychiatry* 1 (July, 1959), pp. 58–69 (especially Table 2 on p. 62). Wallace argues that "both the subjective feeling, tone and the specific content of the hallucination are heavily influenced by . . . the cultural milieu in which the hallucination, and particularly the voluntary hallucination, take place." (P. 62.)

[8] Blum et al., *Utopiates,* p. 42.

[9] See the case cited in Becker, *Outsiders,* pp. 55–56.

[10] The studies cited in footnote 5, *supra,* generally make this point.

[11] See George Herbert Mead, *Mind, Self and Society* (Chicago: University of Chicago Press, 1934); and Herbert Blumer, "Sociological Implications of the Thought of George Herbert Mead," *American Journal of Sociology* 71 (March, 1966), pp. 535–44.

scarcer than one might think.[12] Nevertheless, let us assume that these reports have not been fabricated, but represent an interpretation by the reporter of something that really happened. In the light of the findings just cited, what kind of event can we imagine to have occurred that might have been interpreted as a "psychotic episode"? (I use the word "imagine" advisedly, for the available case reports usually do not furnish sufficient material to allow us to do more than imagine what might have happened.)

The most likely sequence of events is this. The inexperienced user has certain unusual subjective experiences, which he may or may not attribute to having taken the drug. He may find his perception of space distorted, so that he has difficulty climbing a flight of stairs. He may find his train of thought so confused that he is unable to carry on a normal conversation and hears himself making totally inappropriate remarks. He may see or hear things in a way that he suspects is quite different from the way others see and hear them.

Whether or not he attributes what is happening to the drug, the experiences are likely to be upsetting. One of the ways we know that we are normal human beings is that our perceptual world, on the evidence available to us, seems to be pretty much the same as other people's. We see and hear the same things, make the same kind of sense out of them and, where perceptions differ, can explain the difference by a difference in situation or perspective.[13] We may take for granted that the inexperienced drug user, though he wanted to get "high," did not expect an experience so radical as to call into question that common sense set of assumptions.

In any society whose culture contains notions of sanity and insanity, the person who finds his subjective state altered in the way described may think he has become insane. We learn at a young age that a person who "acts funny," "sees things," "hears things," or has other bizarre and unusual experiences may have become "crazy," "nuts," "loony" or a host of other synonyms.[14] When a drug user identifies some of these untoward events occurring in his own experience, he may decide that he merits one of those titles —that he has lost his grip on reality, his control of himself, and has in fact "gone crazy." The interpretation implies the corollary that the change is irreversible or, at least, that things are not going to be changed back very easily. The drug experience, perhaps originally intended as a momentary entertainment, now looms as a momentous event which will disrupt one's life, possibly permanently. Faced with this conclusion, the person develops a full-blown anxiety attack, but it is an anxiety caused by his reaction to the drug experience rather than a direct consequence of drug use itself. (In this connection, it is interesting that, in the published reports of LSD psychoses, acute anxiety attacks appear as the largest category of untoward reactions.)[15]

It is perhaps easier to grasp what this must feel like if we imagine that, having taken several social drinks at a party, we were suddenly to see varicolored snakes peering out at us from behind the furniture. We would instantly recognize this as a sign of delirium tremens, and would no doubt become severely anxious at the prospect of having developed such a serious mental illness. Some such panic is likely to grip the recreational user of drugs who interprets his experience as a sign of insanity.

Though I have put the argument with respect

[12] See the studies cited in footnotes 2, *supra,* and the following reports of marihuana psychoses: Walter Bromberg, "Marihuana: A Psychiatric Study," *Journal of the American Medical Association* 113 (July 1, 1939), pp. 4–12; Howard C. Curtis, "Psychosis Following the Use of Marihuana with Report of Cases," *Journal of the Kansas Medical Society* 40 (1939), pp. 515–17; and Marjorie Nesbitt, "Psychosis Due to Exogenous Poisons," *Illinois Medical Journal* 77 (1940), pp. 278–81.

[13] See Alfred Schutz, *Collected Papers,* vols. I and II (The Hague: Martinus Nijhoff, 1962 and 1964); and Harold Garfinkel, "A Conception of and Experiments with 'Trust' as a Condition of Stable Concerted Actions," in O. J. Harvey, editor, *Motivation and Social Interaction* (New York: Ronald Press Co., 1963), pp. 187–238.

[14] See Thomas J. Scheff, *Being Mentally Ill: A Sociological Theory* (Chicago: Aldine Publishing Co., 1966).

[15] See Frosch et al., "Untoward Reactions to Lysergic Acid Diethylamide," Cohen and Ditman, "Prolonged Adverse Reactions to LSD," and Ungerleider et al., "The Dangers of LSD." It is not always easy to make a judgment, due to the scanty presentation of the material, and some of the reactions I count as anxiety are placed in these sources under different headings. Bromberg, "Marihuana," makes a good case that practically all adverse reactions to marihuana can be traced to this kind of anxiety, and I think it likely that the same reasoning could be applied to the LSD reports, so that such reactions as "hallucination," "depression" and "confused" (to use Ungerleider's categories) are probably reactions to anxiety.

to the inexperienced user, long-time users of recreational drugs sometimes have similar experiences. They may experiment with a higher dosage than they are used to and experience effects unlike anything they have known before. This can easily occur when using drugs purchased in the illicit market, where quality may vary greatly, so that the user inadvertently gets more than he can handle.

The scientific literature does not report any verified cases of people acting on their distorted perceptions so as to harm themselves and others, but such cases have been reported in the press. Press reports of drug-related events are very unreliable, but it may be that users have, for instance, stepped out of a second story window, deluded by the drug into thinking it only a few feet to the ground.[16] If such cases have occurred, they too may be interpreted as examples of psychosis, but a different mechanism than the one just discussed would be involved. The person, presumably, would have failed to make the necessary correction for the drug-induced distortion, a correction, however, that experienced users assert can be made. Thus, a novice marihuana user will find it difficult to drive while "high," but experienced users have no difficulty. Similarly, novices find it difficult to manage their relations with people who are not also under the influence of drugs, but experienced users can control their thinking and actions so as to behave appropriately.[17] Although it is commonly assumed that a person under the influence of LSD must avoid ordinary social situations for 12 or more hours, I have been told[18] of at least one user who takes the drug and then goes to work; she explained that once you learn "how to handle it" (i.e., make the necessary corrections for distortions caused by the drug) there is no problem.

In short, the most likely interpretation we can make of the drug-induced psychoses reported is that they are either severe anxiety reactions to an event interpreted and experienced as insanity, or failures by the user to correct, in carrying out some ordinary action, for the perceptual distortions caused by the drug. If the interpretation is correct, then untoward mental effects produced by drugs depend in some part on its physiological action, but to a much larger degree find their origin in the definitions and conceptions the user applies to that action. These can vary with the individual's personal makeup, a possibility psychiatrists are most alive to, or with the groups he participates in, the trail I shall pursue here.

THE INFLUENCE OF DRUG-USING CULTURES

While there are no reliable figures, it is obvious that a very large number of people use recreational drugs, primarily marihuana and LSD. From the previous analysis one might suppose that, therefore, a great many people would have disquieting symptoms and, given the ubiquity in our society of the concept of insanity, that many would decide they had gone crazy and thus have a drug-induced anxiety attack. But very few such reactions occur. Although there must be more than are reported in the professional literature, it is unlikely that drugs have this effect in any large number of cases. If they did there would necessarily be many more verified accounts than are presently available. Since the psychotic reaction stems from a definition of the drug-induced experience, the explanation of this paradox must lie in the availability of competing definitions of the subjective states produced by drugs.

Competing definitions come to the user from other users who, to his knowledge, have had sufficient experience with the drug to speak with authority. He knows that the drug does not produce permanent disabling damage in all cases, for he can see that these other users do not suffer from it. The question, of course, remains whether it may not produce damage in some cases and whether his is one of them, no matter how rare.

---

[16] Although LSD is often said to provoke suicide, there is very little evidence of this. Cohen, "Lysergic Acid Diethylamide," after surveying 44 investigators who had used LSD with over 5,000 patients, says that the few cases reported all occurred among extremely disturbed patients who might have done it anyway; Hoffer, "D-Lysergic Acid Diethylamide," remarks that the number is so low that it might be argued that LSD actually lowers the rate among mental patients. Ungerleider reports that 10 of 70 cases were suicidal or suicide attempts, but gives no further data.

[17] See Becker, *Outsiders*, pp. 66–72.

[18] By David Oppenheim.

When someone experiences disturbing effects, other users typically assure him that the change in his subjective experience is neither rare nor dangerous. They have seen similar reactions before, and may even have experienced them themselves with no lasting harm. In any event, they have some folk knowledge about how to handle the problem.

They may, for instance, know of an antidote for the frightening effects; thus, marihuana users, confronted with someone who has gotten "too high," encourage him to eat, an apparently effective countermeasure.[19] They talk reassuringly about their own experiences, "normalizing" the frightening symptom by treating it, matter-of-factly, as temporary. They maintain surveillance over the affected person, preventing any physically or socially dangerous activity. They may, for instance, keep him from driving or from making a public display that will bring him to the attention of the police or others who would disapprove of his drug use. They show him how to allow for the perceptual distortion the drug causes and teach him how to manage interaction with nonusers.

They redefine the experience he is having as desirable rather than frightening, as the end for which the drug is taken.[20] What they tell him carries conviction, because he can see that it is not some idiosyncratic belief but is instead culturally shared. It is what "everyone" who uses the drug knows. In all these ways, experienced users prevent the episode from having lasting effects and reassure the novice that whatever he feels will come to a timely and harmless end.

The anxious novice thus has an alternative to defining his experience as "going crazy." He may redefine the event immediately or, having been watched over by others throughout the anxiety attack, decide that it was not so bad after all and not fear its recurrence. He "learns" that

his original definition was "incorrect" and that the alternative offered by other users more nearly describes what he has experienced.

Available knowledge does not tell us how often this mechanism comes into play or how effective it is in preventing untoward psychological reactions; no research has been addressed to this point. In the case of marihuana, at least, the paucity of reported cases of permanent damage coupled with the undoubted increase in use suggests that it may be an effective mechanism.

For such a mechanism to operate, a number of conditions must be met. First, the drug must not produce, quite apart from the user's interpretations, permanent damage to the mind. No amount of social redefinition can undo the damage done by toxic alcohols, or the effects of a lethal dose of an opiate or barbiturate. This analysis, therefore, does not apply to drugs known to have such effects.

Second, users of the drug must share a set of understandings—a culture—which includes, in addition to material on how to obtain and ingest the drug, definitions of the typical effects, the typical course of the experience, the permanence of the effects, and a description of methods for dealing with someone who suffers an anxiety attack because of drug use or attempts to act on the basis of distorted perceptions. Users should have available to them, largely through face-to-face participation with other users but possibly in such other ways as reading as well, the definitions contained in that culture, which they can apply in place of the common-sense definitions available to the inexperienced man in the street.

Third, the drug should ordinarily be used in group settings, where other users can present the definitions of the drug-using culture to the person whose inner experience is so unusual as to provoke use of the common-sense category of insanity. Drugs for which technology and custom promote group use should produce a lower incidence of "psychotic episodes."

The last two conditions suggest, as is the case, that marihuana, surrounded by an elaborate culture and ordinarily used in group settings, should produce few "psychotic" episodes.[21] At the same

---

[19] Cf. the New York City Mayor's Committee on Marihuana, p. 13: "The smoker determines for himself the point of being 'high,' and is over-conscious of preventing himself from becoming 'too high.' This fear of being 'too high' must be associated with some form of anxiety which causes the smoker, should he accidentally reach that point, immediately to institute measures so that he can 'come down.' It has been found that the use of beverages such as beer, or a sweet soda pop, is an effective measure. A cold shower will also have the effect of bringing the person 'down.'"

[20] *Ibid.*, and Becker, *Outsiders.*

[21] I discuss the evidence on this point below.

time, they suggest the prediction that drugs which have not spawned a culture and are ordinarily used in private, such as barbiturates, will produce more such episodes. I suggest possible research along these lines below.

NON-USER INTERPRETATIONS

A user suffering from drug-induced anxiety may also come into contact with non-users who will offer him definitions, depending on their own perspectives and experiences, that may validate the diagnosis of "going crazy" and thus prolong the episode, possibly producing relatively permanent disability. These non-users include family members and police, but most important among them are psychiatrists and psychiatrically oriented physicians. (Remember that when we speak of reported cases of psychosis, the report is ordinarily made by a physician, though police may also use the term in reporting a case to the press.)

Medical knowledge about the recreational use of drugs is spotty. Little research has been done, and its results are not at the fingertips of physicians who do not specialize in the area. (In the case of LSD, of course, there has been a good deal of research, but its conclusions are not clear and, in any case, have not yet been spread throughout the profession.) Psychiatrists are not anxious to treat drug users, so few of them have accumulated any clinical experience with the phenomenon. Nevertheless, a user who develops severe and uncontrollable anxiety will probably be brought, if he is brought anywhere, to a physician for treatment. Most probably, he will be brought to a psychiatric hospital, if one is available; if not, to a hospital emergency room, where a psychiatric resident will be called once the connection with drugs is established, or to a private psychiatrist.[22]

Physicians, confronted with a case of drug-induced anxiety and lacking specific knowledge of its character or proper treatment, rely on a kind of generalized diagnosis. They reason that people probably do not use drugs unless they are suffering from a severe underlying personality disturbance; that use of the drug may allow repressed conflicts to come into the open where they will prove unmanageable; that the drug in this way provokes a true psychosis; and, therefore, that the patient confronting them is psychotic. Furthermore, even though the effects of the drug wear off, the psychosis may not, for the repressed psychological problems it has brought to the surface may not recede as it is metabolized and excreted from the body.

Given such a diagnosis, the physician knows what to do. He hospitalizes the patient for observation and prepares, where possible, for long-term therapy designed to repair the damage done to the psychic defenses or to deal with the conflict unmasked by the drug. Both hospitalization and therapy are likely to reinforce the definition of the drug experience as insanity, for in both the patient will be required to "understand" that he is mentally ill as a precondition for return to the world.[23]

The physician then, does *not* treat the anxiety attack as a localized phenomenon, to be treated in a symptomatic way, but as an outbreak of a serious disease heretofore hidden. He may thus prolong the serious effects beyond the time they might have lasted had the user instead come into contact with other users. This analysis, of course, is frankly speculative; what is required is study of the way physicians treat cases of the kind described and, especially, comparative study of the effects of treatment of drug-induced anxiety attacks by physicians and by drug users.

Another category of non-users deserves mention. Literary men and journalists publicize definitions of drug experiences, either of their own invention or those borrowed from users, psychiatrists or police. (Some members of this category use drugs themselves, so it may be a little confusing to classify them as non-users; in any case, the definitions are provided outside the

---

[22] It may be that a disproportionate number of cases will be brought to certain facilities. Ungerleider et al., "The Dangers of LSD," say (p. 392): "A larger number of admissions, both relative and real, than in other facilities in the Los Angeles area suggests the prevalence of a rumor that 'UCLA takes care of acid heads,' as several of our patients have told us."

[23] See Thomas Szasz, *The Myth of Mental Illness* (New York: Paul B. Hoeber, 1961).

ordinary channels of communication in the drug-using world.) The definitions of literary men—novelists, essayists and poets—grow out of a long professional tradition, beginning with De Quincey's *Confessions,* and are likely to be colored by that tradition. Literary descriptions dwell on the fantasy component of the experience, on its cosmic and ineffable character, and on the threat of madness.[24] Such widely available definitions furnish some of the substance out of which a user may develop his own definition, in the absence of definitions from the drug-using culture.

Journalists use any of a number of approaches conventional in their craft; what they write is greatly influenced by their own professional needs. They must write about "news," about events which have occurred recently and require reporting and interpretation. Furthermore, they need "sources," persons to whom authoritative statements can be attributed. Both needs dispose them to reproduce the line taken by law enforcement officials and physicians, for news is often made by the passage of a law or by a public statement in the wake of an alarming event, such as a bizarre murder or suicide. So journalistic reports frequently dwell on the theme of madness or suicide, a tendency intensified by the newsman's desire to tell a dramatic story.[25] Some journalists, of course, will take the other side in the argument, but even then, because they argue against the theme of madness, the emphasis on that theme is maintained. Public discussion of drug use thus tends to strengthen those stereotypes that would lead users who suffer disturbing effects to interpret their experience as "going crazy."

AN HISTORICAL DIMENSION

A number of variables, then, affect the character of drug-induced experiences. It remains to show that the experiences themselves are likely to vary according to when they occur in the history of use of a given drug in a society. In particular, it seems likely that the experience of acute anxiety caused by drug use will so vary.

Consider the following sequence of possible events, which may be regarded as a natural history of the assimilation of an intoxicating drug by a society. Someone in the society discovers, rediscovers or invents a drug which has the properties described earlier. The ability of the drug to alter subjective experience in desirable ways becomes known to increasing numbers of people, and the drug itself simultaneously becomes available, along with the information needed to make its use effective. Use increases, but users do not have a sufficient amount of experience with the drug to form a stable conception of it as an object. They do not know what it can do to the mind, have no firm idea of the variety of effects it can produce, and are not sure how permanent or dangerous the effects are. They do not know if the effects can be controlled or how. No drug-using culture exists, and there is thus no authoritative alternative with which to counter the possible definition, when and if it comes to mind, of the drug experience as madness. "Psychotic episodes" occur frequently.

But individuals accumulate experience with the drug and communicate their experiences to one another. Consensus develops about the drug's subjective effects, their duration, proper dosages, predictable dangers and how they may be avoided; all these points become matters of common knowledge, validated by their acceptance in a world of users. A culture exists. When a user experiences bewildering or frightening effects, he has available to him an authoritative alternative to the lay notion that he has gone mad. Every time he uses cultural conceptions to interpret drug experiences and control his response to them, he strengthens his belief that the culture is indeed a reliable source of knowledge. "Psychotic episodes" occur less frequently in proportion to the growth of the culture to cover the range of possible effects and its spread to a greater proportion of users. Novice users, to whom the effects are most unfamiliar and who therefore might be expected to suffer most from

[24] For a classic in the genre, see Fitzhugh Ludlow, *The Hasheesh Eater* (New York: Harper and Brothers, 1857). A more modern example is Alan Harrington, "A Visit to Inner Space," in Solomon, ed., *LSD,* pp. 72–102.

[25] Examples are J. Kobler, "Don't Fool Around with LSD," *Saturday Evening Post* 236 (November 2, 1963), pp. 30–32, and Noah Gordon, "The Hallucinogenic Drug Cult," The *Reporter* 29 (August 15, 1963), pp. 35–43.

drug-induced anxiety, learn the culture from older users in casual conversation and in more serious teaching sessions and are thus protected from the dangers of "panicking" or "flipping out."

The incidence of "psychoses," then, is a function of the stage of development of a drug-using culture. Individual experience varies with historical stages and the kinds of cultural and social organization associated with them.

Is this model a useful guide to reality? The only drug for which there is sufficient evidence to attempt an evaluation is marihuana; even there the evidence is equivocal, but it is consistent with the model. On this interpretation, the early history of marihuana use in the United States should be marked by reports of marihuana-induced psychoses. In the absence of a fully formed drug-using culture, some users would experience disquieting symptoms and have no alternative to the idea that they were losing their minds. They would turn up at psychiatric facilities in acute states of anxiety and doctors, eliciting a history of marihuana use, would interpret the episode as a psychotic breakdown. When, however, the culture reached full flower and spread throughout the user population, the number of psychoses should have dropped even though (as a variety of evidence suggests) the number of users increased greatly. Using the definitions made available by the culture, users who had unexpectedly severe symptoms could interpret them in such a way as to reduce or control anxiety and would thus no longer come to the attention of those likely to report them as cases of psychosis.

Marihuana first came into use in the United States in the 1920s and early '30s, and all reports of psychosis associated with its use date from approximately that period.[26] A search of both *Psychological Abstracts* and the *Cumulative Index Medicus* (and its predecessors, the *Current List of Medical Literature* and the *Quarterly Index Medicus*) revealed no cases after 1940. The disappearance of reports of psychosis thus fits the model. It is, of course, a shaky index, for it depends as much on the reporting habits of

physicians as on the true incidence of cases, but it is the only thing available.

The psychoses described also fit the model, insofar as there is any clear indication of a drug-induced effect. (The murder, suicide and death in an automobile accident reported by Curtis, for instance, are equivocal in this respect; in no case is any connection with marihuana use demonstrated other than that the people involved used it.)[27] The best evidence comes from the 31 cases reported by Bromberg. Where the detail given allows judgment, it appears that all but one stemmed from the person's inability to deal with either the perceptual distortion caused by the drug or with the panic at the thought of losing one's mind it created.[28] Bromberg's own interpretation supports this:

> In occasional instances, and these are the cases which are apt to come to medical attention, the anxiety with regard to death, insanity, bodily deformity and bodily dissolution is startling. The patient is tense, nervous, frightened; a state of panic may develop. Often suicide or assaultive acts are the result [of the panic]. The anxiety state is so common ... that it can be considered a part of the intoxication syndrome.[29]

> The inner relationship between cannabis [marihuana] and the onset of a functional psychotic state is not always clear. The inner reaction to somatic sensation seems vital. Such reactions consisted of panic states which disappeared as soon as the stimulus (effects of the drug) faded.[30]

Even though Bromberg distinguishes between pure panic reactions and those in which some underlying mental disturbance was present (the "functional psychotic state" he refers to), he finds, as our model leads us to expect, that the episode is provoked by the user's interpretation of the drug effects in terms other than those contained in the drug-using culture.

The evidence cited is extremely scanty. We do not know the role of elements of the drug-using culture in any of these cases or whether the decrease in incidence is a true one. But we are not likely to do any better and, in the absence of conflicting evidence, it seems justified to take the

---

[26] Bromberg, "Marihuana," Curtis, "Psychosis Following the Use of Marihuana," and Nesbitt, "Psychosis Due to Exogenous Poisons."

[27] Curtis, "Psychosis Following the Use of Marihuana."
[28] See Table 1 in Bromberg, "Marihuana," pp. 6–7.
[29] *Ibid.*, p. 5.
[30] *Ibid.*, pp. 7–8.

model as an accurate representation of the history of marihuana use in the United States.

The final question, then, is whether the model can be used to interpret current reports of LSD-induced psychosis. Are these episodes the consequence of an early stage in the development of an LSD-using culture? Will the number of episodes decrease while the number of users rises, as the model leads us to predict?

LSD

We cannot predict the history of LSD by direct analogy to the history of marihuana, for a number of important conditions may vary. We must first ask whether the drug has, apart from the definitions users impose on their experience, any demonstrated causal relation to psychosis. There is a great deal of controversy on this point, and any reading of the evidence must be tentative. My own opinion is that LSD has essentially the same characteristics as those described in the first part of this paper; its effects may be more powerful than those of other drugs that have been studied, but they too are subject to differing interpretations by users,[31] so that the mechanisms I have described can come into play.

The cases reported in the literature are, like those reported for marihuana, mostly panic reactions to the drug experience, occasioned by the user's interpretation that he has lost his mind, or further disturbance among people already quite disturbed.[32] There are no cases of permanent derangement directly traceable to the drug, with one puzzling exception (puzzling to those who report it as well as to me). In a few cases the visual and auditory distortions produced by the drug recur weeks or months after it was last ingested; this sometimes produces severe upset among those who experience it. Observers are at a loss to explain the phenomenon, except for Rosenthal, who proposes that the drug may have a specific effect on the nerve pathways involved in vision; but this theory, should it prove correct, is a long way from dealing with questions of possible psychosis.[3]

The whole question is confused by the extraordinary assertions about the effects of LSD made by both proponents and opponents of its use. Both sides agree that it has a very strong effect on the mind, disagreeing only as to whether this powerful effect is benign or malignant. Leary, for example, argues that we must "go out of our minds in order to use our heads,"[34] and that this can be accomplished by using LSD. Opponents[35] agree that it can drive you out of your mind, but do not share Leary's view that this is a desirable goal. In any case, we need not accept the premise simply because both parties to the controversy do.

Let us assume then, in the absence of more definitive evidence, that the drug does not in itself produce lasting derangement, that such psychotic episodes as are now reported are largely a result of panic at the possible meaning of the experience, that users who "freak out" do so because they fear they have permanently damaged their minds. Is there an LSD-using culture? In what stage of development is it? Are the reported episodes of psychosis congruent with what our model would predict, given that stage of development?

Here again my discussion must be speculative, for no serious study of this culture is yet available.[36] It appears likely, however, that such a culture is in an early stage of development. Several conceptions of the drug and its possible effects exist, but no stable consensus has arisen. Radio, television, and the popular press present a variety of interpretations, many of them contradictory. There is widespread disagreement, even among users, about possible dangers. Some certainly believe that use (or injudicious use) can lead to severe mental difficulty.

At the same time, my preliminary inquiries and observations hinted at the development (or at least the beginnings) of a culture similar to that surrounding marihuana use. Users with some experience discuss their symptoms and translate from one idiosyncratic description into another, developing a common conception of

[31] Blum et al., *Utopiates*, p. 42.
[32] See footnote 2, *supra*.
[33] Rosenthal, "Persistent Hallucinosis Following Repeated Administration of Hallucinogenic Drugs."

[34] Timothy Leary, "Introduction" to Solomon, ed., *LSD*, p. 13.
[35] Frosch et al., "Untoward Reactions to LSD"; and Ungerleider et al., "The Dangers of LSD."
[36] The book by Blum et al., *Utopiates*, attempts this, but leaves many important questions untouched.

effects as they talk. The notion that a "bad trip" can be brought to a speedy conclusion by taking thorazine by mouth (or, when immediate action is required, intravenously) has spread. Users are also beginning to develop a set of safeguards against committing irrational acts while under the drug's influence. Many feel, for instance, that one should take one's "trip" in the company of experienced users who are not under the drug's influence at the time; they will be able to see you through bad times and restrain you when necessary. A conception of the appropriate dose is rapidly becoming common knowledge. Users understand that they may have to "sit up with" people who have panicked as a result of the drug's effects, and they talk of techniques that have proved useful in this enterprise.[37] All this suggests that a common conception of the drug is developing which will eventually see it defined as pleasurable and desirable, with possible untoward effects that can however be controlled.

Insofar as this emergent culture spreads so that most or all users share the belief that LSD does not cause insanity, and the other understandings just listed, the incidence of "psychoses" should drop markedly or disappear. Just as with marihuana, the interpretation of the experience as one likely to produce madness will disappear and, having other definitions available to use in coping with the experience, users will treat the experience as self-limiting and not as a cause for panic.

The technology of LSD use, however, has features which will work in the opposite direction. In the first place, it is very easily taken; one need learn no special technique (as one must with marihuana) to produce the characteristic effects, for a sugar cube can be swallowed without instruction. This means that anyone who gets hold of the drug can take it in a setting where there are no experienced users around to redefine frightening effects and "normalize" them. He may also have acquired the drug without acquiring any of the presently developing

cultural understandings so that, when frightening effects occur, he is left with nothing but current lay conceptions as plausible definitions. In this connection, it is important that a large amount of the published material by journalists and literary men places heavy emphasis on the dangers of psychosis.[38] It is also important that various medical facilities have become alerted to the possibility of patients (particularly college students and teenagers) coming in with LSD-induced psychoses. All these factors will tend to increase the incidence of "psychotic episodes," perhaps sufficiently to offset the dampening effect of the developing culture.

A second feature of LSD which works in the opposite direction is that it can be administered to someone without his knowledge, since it is colorless, tasteless and odorless. (This possibility is recognized in recent state legislation which specifies *knowing* use as a crime; no such distinction has been found necessary in laws about marihuana, heroin, peyote or similar drugs.) It is reported, for instance, that LSD has been put in a party punchbowl, so that large numbers of people have suffered substantial changes in their subjective experience without even knowing they had been given a drug that might account for the change. Under such circumstances, the tendency to interpret the experience as a sudden attack of insanity might be very strong.[39] If LSD continues to be available on the underground market without much difficulty, such events are likely to continue to occur. (A few apocalyptic types speak of introducing LSD into a city water supply—not at all impossible, since a small amount will affect enormous quantities of water—and thus "turning a whole city on." This might provoke a vast number of "psychoses," should it ever happen.)

In addition to these technological features,

---

[37] Ungerleider et al., deny the efficacy of these techniques (pp. 391–392): "How do we know that persons taking LSD in a relaxed friendly environment with an experienced guide or 'sitter' will have serious side effects? We have no statistical data to answer this, but our impression (from our weekly group sessions) is that bad experiences were common with or without sitters and with or without 'the right environment.' This does not minimize the importance of suggestion in the LSD experience."

[38] For journalistic accounts, see Kobler, "Don't Fool Around with LSD," Gordon, "The Hallucinogenic Drug Cult," R. Coughlan, "Chemical Mind-Changers," *Life* 54 (March 15, 1963); and H. Asher, "They Split My Personality," *Saturday Review* 46 (June 1, 1963), pp. 39–43. See also two recent novels in which LSD plays a major role: B. H. Friedman, *Yarborough* (New York: Knopf, 1964); and Alan Harrington, *The Secret Swinger* (New York: World Publishing Co., 1966).

[39] Cf. Cohn and Ditman, "Complications Associated with Lysergic Acid Diethylamide," p. 161: "Accidental ingestion of the drug by individuals who are unaware of its nature has already occurred. This represents a maximally stressful event because the perceptual and ideational distortions then occur without the saving knowledge that they were drug induced and temporary."

many of the new users of LSD, unlike the users of most illicit recreational drugs, will be people who, in addition to never having used any drug to alter their subjective experience before, will have had little or nothing to do with others who have used drugs in that way. LSD, after all, was introduced into the United States under very reputable auspices and has had testimonials from many reputable and conventional persons. In addition, there has been a great deal of favorable publicity to accompany the less favorable—the possibility that the drug can do good as well as harm has been spread in a fashion that never occurred with marihuana. Finally, LSD has appeared at a time when the mores governing illicit drug use among young people seem to be changing radically, so that youth no longer reject drugs out of hand. Those who try LSD may thus not even have had the preliminary instruction in being "high" that most novice marihuana users have before first using it. They will, consequently, be even less prepared for the experience they have. (This suggests the prediction that marihuana users who experiment with LSD will show fewer untoward reactions than those who have had no such experience.)[40]

These features of the drug make it difficult to predict the number of mental upsets likely to be "caused" by LSD. If use grows, the number of people exposed to the possibility will grow. As an LSD-using culture develops, the proportion of those exposed who interpret their experience as one of insanity will decrease. But people may use the drug without being indoctrinated with the new cultural definitions, either because of the ease with which the drug can be taken or because it has been given to them without their knowledge, in which case the number of episodes will rise. The actual figure will be a vector made up of these several components.

A NOTE ON THE OPIATES

The opiate drugs present an interesting paradox. In the drugs we have been considering, the development of a drug-using culture causes a decrease in rates of morbidity associated with drug use, for greater knowledge of the true character of the drug's effects lessens the likelihood that users will respond to those effects with uncontrolled anxiety. In the case of opiates, however, the greater one's knowledge of the drug's effects, the more likely it is that one will suffer its worst effect, addiction. As Lindesmith has shown,[41] one can only be addicted when he experiences physiological withdrawal symptoms, recognizes them as due to a need for drugs, and relieves them by taking another dose. The crucial step of recognition is most likely to occur when the user participates in a culture in which the signs of withdrawal are interpreted for what they are. When a person is ignorant of the nature of withdrawal sickness, and has some other cause to which he can attribute his discomfort (such as a medical problem), he may misinterpret the symptoms and thus escape addiction, as some of Lindesmith's cases demonstrate.[42]

This example makes clear how important the actual physiology of the drug response is in the model I have developed. The culture contains interpretations of the drug experience, but these must be congruent with the drug's actual effects. Where the effects are varied and ambiguous, as with marihuana and LSD, a great variety of interpretations is possible. Where the effects are clear and unmistakable, as with opiates, the culture is limited in the possible interpretations it can provide. Where the cultural interpretation is so constrained, and the effect to be interpreted leads, in its most likely interpretation, to morbidity, the spread of a drug-using culture will increase morbidity rates.

CONCLUSION

The preceding analysis, to repeat, is supported at only a few points by available research; most of what has been said is speculative. The theory, however, gains credibility in several ways. Many of its features follow directly from a Meadian social psychology and the general plausibility of that scheme lends it weight. Furthermore, it is consistent with much of what social scientists have discovered about the nature of drug-induced experiences. In addition, the theory makes

---

[40] Negative evidence is found in Ungerleider et al., "The Dangers of LSD." Twenty-five of their 70 cases had previously used marihuana.

[41] Lindesmith, *Opiate Addiction.*
[42] *Ibid.,* cases 3, 5 and 6 (pp. 68–69, 71, 72).

sense of some commonly reported and otherwise inexplicable phenomena, such as variations in the number of "psychotic" episodes attributable to recreational drug use. Finally, and much the least important, it is in accord with my haphazard and informal observations of LSD use.

The theory also has the virtue of suggesting a number of specific lines of research. With respect to the emerging "social problem" of LSD use, it marks out the following areas for investigation: the relation between social settings of use, the definitions of the drug's effects available to the user, and the subjective experiences produced by the drug; the mechanisms by which an LSD-using culture arises and spreads; the difference in experiences of participants and non-participants in that culture; the influence of each of the several factors described on the number of harmful effects attributable to the drug; and the typical response of physicians to LSD-induced anxiety states and the effect of that response as compared to the response made by experienced drug-culture participants.

The theory indicates useful lines of research with respect to other common drugs as well. Large numbers of people take tranquilizers, barbiturates and amphetamines. Some frankly take them for "kicks" and are participants in drug-using cultures built around those drugs, while others are respectable middle-class citizens who probably do not participate in any "hip" user culture. Do these "square" users have some shared cultural understandings of their own with respect to use of these drugs? What are the differential effects of the drugs—both on subjective experience and on rates of morbidity associated with drug use—among the two classes of users? How do physicians handle the pathological effects of these drugs, with which they are relatively familiar, as compared to their handling of drugs which are only available illicitly?

The theory may have implications for the study of drugs not ordinarily used recreationally as well. Some drugs used in ordinary medical practice (such as the adrenocortical steroids) are said to carry a risk of provoking psychosis. It may be that this danger arises when the drug produces changes in subjective experience which the user does not anticipate, does not connect with the drug, and thus interprets as signs of insanity. Should the physician confirm this by diagnosing a "drug psychosis," a vicious circle of increasing validation of the diagnosis may ensue. The theory suggests that the physician using such drugs might do well to inquire carefully into the feelings that produce such anxiety reactions, interpret them to the patient as common, transient and essentially harmless side effects, and see whether such action would not control the phenomenon. Drugs that have been incriminated in this fashion would make good subjects for research designed to explore some of the premises of the argument made here.

The sociologist may find most interesting the postulated connection between historical stages in the development of a culture and the nature of individual subjective experience. Similar linkages might be discovered in the study of political and religious movements. For example, at what stages in the development of such movements are individuals likely to experience euphoric and ecstatic feelings? How are these related to shifts in the culture and organization of social relations within the movement? The three-way link between history, culture and social organization, and the person's subjective state may point the way to a better understanding than we now have of the social bases of individual experience.

CATS, KICKS, AND COLOR
HAROLD FINESTONE

Growing recognition that the most recent manifestation of the use of opiates in this country has been predominantly a young peoples' problem has resulted in some speculation as to the nature of this generation of drug users. Is it possible to form an accurate conception as to what "manner of man" is represented by the current species of young drug addict? Intensive interviews between 1951 and 1953 with over fifty male black users of heroin in their late teens and early twenties selected from several of the areas of highest incidence of drug use in Chicago served to elicit from them the expression of many common attitudes, values, schemes of behavior, and general social orientation. Moreover, since there was every reason to believe that such similarities had preceded their introduction to heroin, it appeared that it was by virtue of such shared features that they had been unusually receptive to the spread of opiate use. Methodologically, their common patterns of behavior suggested the heuristic value of the construction of a social type. The task of this paper is to depict this social type, and to present a hypothetical formulation to account for the form it has taken.

No special justification appears to be necessary for concentrating in this paper on the social type of the young colored drug user. One of the distinctive properties of the distribution of drug use as a social problem, at least in Chicago, is its high degree of both spatial and racial concentration. In fact, it is a problem which in this city can be pinpointed with great accuracy as having its incidence preponderantly among the young male colored persons in a comparatively few local community areas. The following delineation of the generic characteristics of young colored drug users constitutes in many respects an ideal type. No single drug addict exemplified all of the traits to be depicted but all of them revealed several of them to a marked degree.

The young drug user was a creature of contrasts. Playing the role of the fugitive and pariah as he was inevitably forced to do, he turned up for interviews in a uniformly ragged and dirty condition. And yet he talked with an air of superiority derived from his identification with an elite group, the society of "cats." He came in wearing a nonfunctional tie clip attached to his sport shirt and an expensive hat as the only indications that he was concerned with his appearance and yet displayed in his conversation a highly developed sense of taste in men's clothing and a high valuation upon dressing well. He came from what were externally the drabbest, most overcrowded, and physically deteriorated sections of the city and yet discussed his pattern of living as though it were a consciously cultivated work of art.

Despite the location of his social world in the "asphalt jungle" of the "Blackbelt" he strictly eschewed the use of force and violence as a technique for achieving his ends or for the settling of problematic situations. He achieved his goals by indirection, relying, rather, on persuasion and on a repertoire of manipulative techniques. To deal with a variety of challenging situations, such as those arising out of his contacts with the police, with his past or potential victims, and with jilted "chicks," etc., he used his wits and his conversational ability. To be able to confront such contingencies with adequacy and without resort to violence was to be "cool." His idea was to get what he wanted through persuasion and ingratiation; to use the other fellow by deliberately outwitting him. Indeed, he regarded himself as immeasurably superior to the "gorilla," a person who resorted to force.

The image of himself as "operator" was projected onto the whole world about him and led to a complete skepticism as to other persons' motives. He could relate to people by outsmarting them, or through open-handed and often ruinous

Reprinted from *Social Problems* 5 (Summer, 1957), pp. 3–13. Footnotes have been renumbered. This investigation was supported by research grant 3M 9030 from the National Institute of Mental Health, Public Health Service, and was carried on under the direction of Clifford R. Shaw and Solomon Kobrin. The writer acknowledges the generous assistance received in the clarification of the problems dealt with in this paper through discussions with Clifford R. Shaw, Henry D. McKay, and Solomon Kobrin, supervising sociologists at the Illinois Institute for Juvenile Research and the Chicago Area Project.

generosity, but his world seemed to preclude any relationship which was not part of a "scheme" or did not lend itself to an "angle." The most difficult puzzle for him to solve was the "square," the honest man. On the one hand the "square" was the hard-working plodder who lived by routine and who took honesty and the other virtues at their face value. As such he constituted the prize victim for the cat. On the other hand the cat harbored the sneaking suspicion that some squares were smarter than he, because they could enjoy all the forbidden pleasures which were his stock in trade and maintain a reputation for respectability in the bargain.

The cat had a large, colorful, and discriminating vocabulary which dealt with all phases of his experience with drugs. In addition, he never seemed to content himself with the conventional word for even the most commonplace objects. Thus he used "pad" for house, "pecks" for food, "flicks" for movies, "stick hall" for pool hall, "dig the scene" for observe, "box" for record player, "bread" for money, etc. In each instance the word he used was more concrete or earthier than the conventional word and such as to reveal an attitude of subtle ridicule towards the dignity and conventionality inherent in the common usage.

His soft convincing manner of speaking, the shocking earthiness and fancifulness of his vocabulary, together with the formidable gifts of charm and ingratiation which he deployed, all contributed to the dominant impression which the young drug user made as a person. Such traits would seem to have fitted naturally into a role which some cats had already played or aspired to play, that of the pimp. To be supported in idleness and luxury through the labors of one or more attractive "chicks" who shoplifted or engaged in prostitution or both and dutifully handed over the proceeds was one of his favorite fantasies. In contrast with the milieu of the white underworld, the pimp was not an object of opprobrium but of prestige.

The theme of the exploitation of the woman goes close to the heart of the cat's orientation to life, that is, his attitude towards work. Part of the cat's sense of superiority stems from his aristocratic disdain for work and for the subordination of self to superiors and to the repetitive daily routine entailed by work, which he

regards as intolerable. The "square" is a person who toils for regular wages and who takes orders from his superiors without complaint.

In contrast with the "square," the cat gets by without working. Instead he keeps himself in "bread" by a set of ingenious variations on "begging, borrowing, or stealing." Each cat has his "hustle,"[1] and a "hustle" is any nonviolent means of "making some bread" which does not require work. One of the legendary heroes of the cat is the man who is such a skillful con-man that he can sell "State Street" to his victim. Concretely, the cat is a petty thief, pickpocket, or pool shark, or is engaged in a variety of other illegal activities of the "conning" variety. A very few cats are actually living off the proceeds of their women "on the hustle."

The main purpose of life for the cat is to experience the "kick." Just as every cat takes pride in his "hustle," so every cat cultivates his "kick." A "kick" is any act tabooed by "squares" that heightens and intensifies the present moment of experience and differentiates it as much as possible from the humdrum routine of daily life. Sex in any of its conventional expressions is not a "kick" since this would not serve to distinguish the cat from the "square," but orgies of sex behavior and a dabbling in the various perversions and byways of sex pass muster as "kicks." Some "cats" are on an alcohol "kick," others on a marihuana "kick," and others on a heroin "kick." There is some interchangeability among these various "kicks" but the tendency is to select your "kick" and stay with it. Many of these young drug users, however, had progressed from the alcohol to the marihuana to the heroin "kick." Each "kick" has its own lore of appreciation and connoisseurship into which only its devotees are initiated.

In addition to his "kick" the cat sets great store on the enjoyment of music and on proper dress. To enjoy one's "kick" without a background of popular music is inconceivable. The cat's world of music has a distinctive galaxy of stars, and the brightest luminaries in his firmament are performers such as "Yardbird" (the late Charlie Parker) and disc jockeys such as Al Benson. Almost every cat is a frustrated musi-

---

[1] Harold Finestone, "Narcotics and Criminality," *Law and Contemporary Problems* 22 (Winter, 1957), pp. 60–85.

cian who hopes some day to get his "horn" out of pawn, take lessons, and earn fame and fortune in the field of "progressive music."

The cat places a great deal of emphasis upon clothing and exercises his sartorial talents upon a skeletal base of suit, sport shirt, and hat. The suit itself must be conservative in color. Gaiety is introduced through the selection of the sport shirt and the various accessories, all so chosen and harmonized as to reveal an exquisite sense of taste. When the cat was not talking about getting his clothes out of pawn, he talked about getting them out of the cleaners. With nonchalant pride one drug user insisted that the most expensive sport shirts and hats in the city of Chicago were sold in a certain haberdashery on the South Side. The ideal cat would always appear in public impeccably dressed and be able to sport a complete change of outfit several times a day.

The cat seeks through a harmonious combination of charm, ingratiating speech, dress, music, the proper dedication to his "kick," and unrestrained generosity to make of his day to day life itself a gracious work of art. Everything is to be pleasant and everything he does and values is to contribute to a cultivated aesthetic approach to living. The "cool cat" exemplifies all of these elements in proper balance. He demonstrates his ability to "play it cool" in his unruffled manner of dealing with outsiders such as the police, and in the self-assurance with which he confronts emergencies in the society of "cats." Moreover, the "cat" feels himself to be any man's equal. He is convinced that he can go anywhere and mingle easily with anyone. For example, he rejects the type of music designated "the blues" because for him it symbolizes attitudes of submission and resignation which are repugnant and alien to his customary frame of mind.

It can be seen now why heroin use should make such a powerful appeal to the cat. It was the ultimate "kick." No substance was more profoundly tabooed by conventional middle-class society. Regular heroin use provides a sense of maximal social differentiation from the "square." The cat was at last engaged, he felt, in an activity completely beyond the comprehension of the "square." No other "kick" offered such an instantaneous intensification of the immediate moment of experience and set it apart from every-

day experience in such spectacular fashion. Any words used by the cat to apply to the "kick," the experience of "being high," he applied to heroin in the superlative. It was the "greatest kick of them all."

In the formulation now to be presented the cat as a social type is viewed as a manifestation of a process of social change in which a new type of self-conception has been emerging among the adolescents of the lower socioeconomic levels of the black population in large urban centers. It is a self-conception rooted in the types of accommodation to a subordinate status achieved historically by the black race in this country, a self-conception which has become increasingly articulated as it responded to and selected various themes from the many available to it in the milieu of the modern metropolis. Blumer's classification of social movements into general, specific, or expressive appears to provide a useful framework for the analysis of the social type of the cat.[2]

In terms of these categories the cat as a social type is the personal counterpart of an expressive social movement. The context for such a movement must include the broader community, which, by its policies of social segregation and discrimination, has withheld from individuals of the black population the opportunity to achieve or to identify with status positions in the larger society. The social type of the cat is an expression of one possible type of adaptation to such blocking and frustration, in which a segment of the population turns in upon itself and attempts to develop within itself criteria for the achievement of social status and the rudiments of a satisfactory social life. Within his own isolated social world the cat attempts to give form and purpose to dispositions derived from but denied an outlet within the dominant social order.

What are these dispositions and in what sense may they be said to be derived from the dominant social order? Among the various interrelated facets of the life of the cat two themes are central, those of the "hustle" and the "kick." It is to be noted that they are in direct antithesis to two of the central values of the dominant cul-

[2] Herbert Blumer, "Social Movements," in Robert E. Park, ed., *An Outline of the Principles of Sociology* (New York: Barnes & Noble, 1939), pp. 255–78.

ture, the "hustle" versus the paramount importance of the occupation for the male in our society, and the "kick" versus the importance of regulating conduct in terms of its future consequences. Thus, there appears to be a relationship of conflict between the central themes of the social type of the cat and those of the dominant social order. As a form of expressive behavior, however, the social type of the cat represents an indirect rather than a direct attack against central conventional values.

It is interesting to speculate on the reasons why a type such as the cat should emerge rather than a social movement with the objective of changing the social order. The forces coercing the selective process among colored male adolescents in the direction of expressive social movements are probably to be traced to the long tradition of accommodation to a subordinate status on the part of the Negro as well as to the social climate since the Second World War, which does not seem to have been favorable to the formation of specific social movements.

The themes of the "hustle" and "kick" in the social orientation of the cat are facts which appear to be overdetermined. For example, to grasp the meaning of the "hustle" to the cat one must understand it as a rejection of the obligation of the adult male to work. When asked for the reasons underlying his rejection of work the cat did not refer to the uncongenial and relatively unskilled and low paid jobs which, in large part, were the sole types of employment available to him. He emphasized rather that the routine of a job and the demand that he should apply himself continuously to his work task were the features that made work intolerable for him. The self-constraint required by work was construed as an unwarranted damper upon his love of spontaneity. The other undesirable element from his point of view was the authoritarian setting of most types of work with which he was familiar.

There are undoubtedly many reasons for the cat's rejection of work but the reasons he actually verbalized are particularly significant when interpreted as devices for sustaining his self-conception. The cat's feeling of superiority would be openly challenged were he to confront certain of the social realities of his situation, such as the discrimination exercised against black persons looking for work and the fact that only the lowest status jobs are available to him. He avoided any mention of these factors which would have forced him to confront his true position in society and thus posed a threat to his carefully cherished sense of superiority.

In emphasizing as he does the importance of the "kick" the cat is attacking the value our society places upon planning for the future and the responsibility of the individual for such planning. Planning always requires some subordination and disciplining of present behavior in the interest of future rewards. The individual plans to go to college, plans for his career, plans for his family and children, etc. Such an orientation on the part of the individual is merely the personal and subjective counterpart of a stable social order and of stable social institutions, which not only permit but sanction an orderly progression of expectations with reference to others and to one's self. Where such stable institutions are absent or in the inchoate stages of development, there is little social sanction for such planning in the experience of the individual. Whatever studies are available strongly suggest that such are the conditions which tend to prevail in the lower socioeconomic levels of the Negro urban community.[3] Stable family and community organization is lacking in those areas of the city where drug use is concentrated. A social milieu which does not encourage the subordination and disciplining of present conduct in the interests of future rewards tends by default to enhance the present. The "kick" appears to be a logical culmination of this emphasis.

Accepting the emergence of the self-conception of the cat as evidence of a developing expressive social movement, we may phrase the central theoretical problem as follows: What are the distinctive and generic features of the cat's social orientation? Taking a cue from the work of Huizinga as developed in *Homo Ludens*,[4] we propose that the generic characteristics of the social type of the cat are those of play. In what

[3] St. Clair Drake and Horace R. Cayton, "Lower Class: Sex and Family," *Black Metropolis* (New York: Harcourt, Brace & Co., 1945), pp. 564–99.

[4] Johan Huizinga, *Homo Ludens, A Study of the Play Element in Culture* (Boston: Beacon Press, 1955).

follows, Huizinga's conception of play as a distinctive type of human activity will be presented and then applied as a tool of analysis for rendering intelligible the various facets of the social orientation of the cat. It is believed that the concept of play indicates accurately the type of expressive social movement which receives its embodiment in the cat.

According to Huizinga the concept of play is a primary element of human experience and as such is not susceptible to exact definition.

"The *fun* of playing resists all analysis, all logical interpretation. . . . Nevertheless it is precisely this fun-element that characterizes the essence of play."[5]

The common image of the young black drug addict pictures him as a pitiful figure, a trapped unfortunate. There is a certain amount of truth in this image but it does not correspond to the conception which the young colored addict has of himself or to the impression that he tries to communicate to others. If it were entirely true it would be difficult to square with the fact that substantial numbers of young black persons continue to become drug users. The cat experiences and manifests a certain zest in his mode of life which is far from self-pity. This fun element seemed to come particularly to the fore as the cat recounted his search for "kicks," the adventure of his life on the streets, and the intensity of his contest against the whole world to maintain his supply of drugs. Early in the cycle of heroin use itself there was invariably a "honeymoon" stage when the cat abandoned himself most completely to the experience of the drug. For some cats this "honeymoon" stage, in terms of their ecstatic preoccupation with the drug, was perpetual. For others it passed, but the exigencies of an insatiable habit never seemed to destroy completely the cat's sense of excitement in his way of life.

While Huizinga declines to define play, he does enumerate three characteristics which he considers to be proper to play. Each one of them when applied to the cat serves to indicate a generic feature of his social orientation.

(1) "First and foremost . . . all play is a voluntary activity."[6] "Here we have the first main characteristic of play: that it is free, is in fact freedom."[7]

The concept of an expressive social movement assumes a social situation where existing social arrangements are frustrating and are no longer accepted as legitimate and yet where collective activity directed towards the modification of these limitations is not possible. The cat is "free" in the sense that he is a preeminent candidate for new forms of social organization and novel social practices. He is attempting to escape from certain features of the historical traditions of the Negro which he regards as humiliating. As an adolescent or young adult he is not fully assimilated into such social institutions as the family, school, church, or industry which may be available to him. Moreover, the social institutions which the Negroes brought with them when they migrated to the city have not as yet achieved stability or an adequate functioning relationship to the urban environment. As a Negro, and particularly as a Negro of low socioeconomic status, he is excluded from many socializing experiences which adolescents in more advantaged sectors of the society take for granted. He lives in communities where the capacity of the population for effective collective action is extremely limited, and consequently there are few effective controls on his conduct besides those exercised by his peer group itself.

He is fascinated by the varied "scenes" which the big city spreads out before him. Granted this setting, the cat adopts an adventurous attitude to life and is free to give his allegiance to new forms of activity.

(2) . . . A second characteristic is closely connected with this (that is, the first characteristic of freedom), namely, that play is not "ordinary" or "real" life. It is rather a stepping out of "real" life into a temporary sphere of activity with a disposition all of its own. Every child knows perfectly well that he is "only pretending," or that it was "only for fun." . . . This "only pretending" quality of play betrays a consciousness of the inferiority of play compared with "seriousness," a

---

[5] *Ibid.,* p. 3.

[6] *Ibid.,* p. 7.
[7] *Ibid.,* p. 8.

feeling that seems to be something as primary as play itself. Nevertheless . . . the consciousness of play being "only a pretend" does not by any means prevent it from proceeding with the utmost seriousness, with an absorption, a devotion that passes into rapture and, temporarily at least, completely abolishes that troublesome "only" feeling.[8]

It is implicit in the notion of an expressive social movement that, since direct collective action to modify the sources of dissatisfaction and restlessness is not possible, all such movements should appear under one guise, as forms of "escape." Persons viewing the problem of addiction from the perspective of the established social structure have been prone to make this interpretation. It is a gross oversimplification, however, as considered from the perspective of the young drug addict himself. The emergence of the self-conception of the cat is an attempt to deal with the problems of status and identity in a situation where participation in the life of the broader community is denied, but where the black adolescent is becoming increasingly sensitive to the values, the goals, and the notions of success which obtain in the dominant social order.

> The caste pressures thus make it exceedingly difficult for an American Negro to preserve a true perspective of himself and his own group in relation to the larger white society. The increasing abstract knowledge of the world outside—of its opportunities, its rewards, its different norms of competition and cooperation—which results from the proceeding acculturation at the same time as there is increasing group isolation, only increases the tensions.[9]

Such conditions of group isolation would appear to be fairly uniform throughout the Negro group. Although this isolation may be experienced differently at different social levels of the Negro community, certain features of the adaptations arrived at in response to this problem will tend to reveal similarities. Since the struggle for status takes place on a stage where there is acute sensitivity to the values and status criteria of the dominant white group, but where access to the means through which such values may be

achieved is prohibited, the status struggle turning in on itself will assume a variety of distorted forms. Exclusion from the "serious" concerns of the broader community will result in such adaptations manifesting a strong element of "play."

Frazier in *Black Bourgeoisie* discusses the social adaptation of the Negro middle class as "The World of Make-Believe."

> The emphasis upon "social" life or "society" is one of the main props of the world of make-believe into which the black bourgeoisie has sought an escape from its inferiority and frustrations in American society. This world of make-believe, to be sure, is a reflection of the values of American society, but it lacks the economic basis that would give it roots in the world of reality.[10]

In the Negro lower classes the effects of frustrations deriving from subordination to the whites may not be experienced as personally or as directly as it is by the Negro middle class, but the massive effects of residential segregation and the lack of stable social institutions and community organization are such as to reinforce strong feelings of group isolation even at the lowest levels of the society.

It is here suggested that the function performed by the emergence of the social type of the cat among Negro lower-class adolescents is analogous to that performed by "The World of Make-Believe" in the Negro middle class. The development of a social type such as that of the cat is only possible in a situation where there is isolation from the broader community but great sensitivity to its goals, where the peer group pressures are extremely powerful, where institutional structures are weak, where models of success in the illegitimate world have strong appeals, where specific social movements are not possible, and where novel forms of behavior have great prestige. To give significance to his experience, the young male addict has developed the conception of a heroic figure, the "ideal cat," a person who is completely adequate to all situations, who controls his "kick" rather than letting it control him, who has a lucrative "hustle," who has no illusions as to what makes the world

---

[8] *Ibid.*, p. 8.
[9] Gunnar Myrdal, *An American Dilemma* (New York: Harper & Brothers, 1944), p. 760.

[10] E. Franklin Frazier, *Black Bourgeoisie* (Glencoe, Illinois: Free Press, 1957), p. 237.

"tick," who is any man's equal, who basks in the admiration of his brother cats and associated "chicks," who hob-nobs with "celebs" of the musical world, and who in time himself may become a celebrity.

The cat throws himself into his way of life with a great deal of intensity but he cannot escape completely from the perspective, the judgments, and the sanctions of the dominant social order. He has to make place in his scheme of life for police, lockups, jails, and penitentiaries, to say nothing of the agonies of withdrawal distress. He is forced eventually to confront the fact that his role as a cat with its associated attitudes is largely a pose, a form of fantasy with little basis in fact. With the realization that he is addicted he comes only too well to know that he is a "junky," and he is fully aware of the conventional attitudes towards addicts as well as of the counter-rationalizations provided by his peer group. It is possible that the cat's vacillation with regard to seeking a cure for his addiction is due to a conflict of perspectives, whether to view his habit from the cat's or the dominant social order's point of view.

> (3) Play is distinct from "ordinary" life both as to locality and duration. This is the third main characteristic of play: its secludedness, its limitedness. It is "played out" within certain limits of time and place. It contains its own course and meaning.[11]

It is this limited, esoteric character of heroin use which gives to the cat the feeling of belonging to an elite. It is the restricted extent of the distribution of drug use, the scheming and intrigue associated with underground "connections" through which drugs are obtained, the secret lore of the appreciation of the drug's effects, which give the cat the exhilaration of participating in a conspiracy. Contrary to popular conception most drug users were not anxious to proselyte new users. Of course, spreading the habit would have the function of increasing the possible sources of supply. But an equally strong disposition was to keep the knowledge of drug use secret, to impress and dazzle the audience with one's knowledge of being "in the know."

When proselyting did occur, as in jails or lockups, it was proselyting on the part of a devotee who condescended to share with the uninitiated a highly prized practice and set of attitudes.

As he elaborates his analysis of play, Huizinga brings to the fore additional aspects of the concept which also have their apt counterpart in the way of life of the cat. For instance, as was discussed earlier, the cat's appreciation of "progressive music" is an essential part of his social orientation. About this topic Huizinga remarks, "Music, as we have hinted before, is the highest and purest expression of the *facultas ludendi*."[12] The cat's attitude toward music has a sacred, almost mystical quality. "Progressive music" opens doors to a type of highly valued experience which for him can be had in no other way. It is more important to him than eating and is second only to the "kick." He may have to give up his hope of dressing according to his standards but he never gives up music.

Huizinga also observes, "Many and close are the links that connect play with beauty."[13] He refers to the "profoundly aesthetic quality of play."[14] The aesthetic emphasis which seems so central to the style of living of the cat is a subtle elusive accent permeating his whole outlook but coming to clearest expression in a constellation of interests, the "kick," clothing, and music. And it certainly reaches a level of awareness in their language. Language is utilized by the cat with a conscious relish, with many variations and individual turns of phrase indicating the value placed upon creative expression in this medium.

It is to be noted that much of the description of the cat's attributes did not deal exclusively with elements unique to him. Many of the features mentioned are prevalent among adolescents in all reaches of the status scale. Dress, music, language, and the search for pleasure are all familiar themes of the adolescent world. For instance, in his description of the adolescent "youth culture" Talcott Parsons would appear to be presenting the generic traits of a "play-form" with particular reference to its expression in the middle class.

---

[11] Huizinga, *Homo Ludens*, p. 9.

[12] *Ibid.*, p. 7.
[13] *Ibid.*, p. 7.
[14] *Ibid.*, p. 2.

It is at the point of emergence into adolescence that there first begins to develop a set of patterns and behavior phenomena which involve a highly complex combination of age grading and sex role elements. These may be referred to together as the phenomena of the "youth culture"....

Perhaps the best single point of reference for characterizing the youth culture lies in its contrast with the dominant pattern of the adult male role. By contrast with the emphasis on responsibility in this role, the orientation of the youth culture is more or less specifically irresponsible. One of its dominant roles is "having a good time"....It is very definitely a rounded humanistic pattern rather than one of competence in the performance of specified functions.[15]

Such significant similarities between this description and the themes of the social type of the cat only tend to reinforce the notion that the recent spread of heroin use was a problem of adolescence. The cat is an adolescent sharing many of the interests of his age-mates everywhere but confronted by a special set of problems of color, tradition, and identity.

The social orientation of the cat, with its emphasis on nonviolence, was quite in contrast to the orientation of the smaller group of young white drug users who were interviewed in the course of this study. The latter's type of adjustment placed a heavy stress upon violence. Their crimes tended to represent direct attacks against persons and property. The general disposition they manifested was one of "nerve" and brashness rather than one of "playing it cool." They did not cultivate the amenities of language, music, or dress to nearly the same extent as the cat. Their social orientation was expressed as a direct rather than an indirect attack on the dominant values of our society. This indicates that the "youth culture" despite its generic features may vary significantly in different social settings.

In his paper, "Some Jewish Types of Personality," Louis Wirth made the following suggestive comments about the relationship between the social type and its setting.

A detailed analysis of the crucial personality types in any given area or cultural group shows that they depend upon a set of habits and attitudes in the group for their existence and are the direct expressions of the values of the group. As the life of the group changes there appears a host of new social types, mainly outgrowths and transformations of previous patterns which have become fixed through experience.[16]

What are some of the sources of the various elements going to make up the social type of the cat which may be sought in his traditions? The following suggestions are offered as little more than speculation at the present time. The emphasis upon nonviolence on the part of the cat, upon manipulative techniques rather than overt attack, is a stress upon the indirect rather than the direct way towards one's goal. May not the cat in this emphasis be betraying his debt to the "Uncle Tom" type of adjustment, despite his wish to dissociate himself from earlier patterns of accommodation to the dominant white society? May not the "kick" itself be a cultural lineal descendant of the ecstatic moment of religious possession so dear to revivalist and storefront religion? Similarly, may not the emphasis upon the exploitation of the woman have its origin in the traditionally greater economic stability of the black woman?

W. I. Thomas in one of his references to the problems raised by the city environment stated, "Evidently the chief problem is the young American person."[17] In discussing the type of inquiry that would be desirable in this area he states that it should

lead to a more critical discrimination between that type of disorganization in the youth which is a real but frustrated tendency to organize on a higher plane, or one more correspondent with the moving environment, and that type of disorganization which is simply the abandonment of standards. It is also along this line ... that we shall gain light on the relation of fantastic phantasying to realistic phantasying....[18]

Posed in this way the problem becomes one of evaluating the social type of the cat in relation to the processes of social change. This social

---

[15] *Ibid.*, p. 9.

[16] Louis Wirth, "Some Jewish Types of Personality," in Ernest W. Burgess, ed., *The Urban Community* (Chicago: University of Chicago Press, 1926), p. 112.

[17] William I. Thomas, "The Problem of Personality in the Urban Environment," in Ernest W. Burgess, ed., *The Urban Community* (Chicago: University of Chicago Press, 1926), p. 46.

[18] *Ibid.*, p. 47.

type is difficult to judge according to the criterion suggested by Thomas. Since many of the cat's interests are merely an extreme form of the adolescent "youth culture," in part the problem becomes one of determining how functional the period of adolescence is as preparation for subsequent adult status. However, the central phases of the social orientation of the cat, the "hustle" and the "kick," do represent a kind of disorganization which indicates the abandonment of conventional standards. The young addicted cat is "going nowhere." With advancing age he cannot shed his addiction the way he can many of the other trappings of adolescence. He faces only the bleak prospect, as time goes on, of increasing demoralization. Although the plight of the young colored addict is intimately tied to the conditions and fate of his racial group, his social orientation seems to represent a dead-end type of adjustment. Just as Handlin in *The Uprooted* suggests that the first generation of immigrant peoples to our society tends to be a sacrificed generation,[19] it may be that the unique problems of Negro migrants to our metropolitan areas will lead to a few or several sacrificed generations in the course of the tortuous process of urbanization.

The discussion of the social type of the cat leads inevitably to the issue of social control. Any attempt to intervene or modify the social processes producing the "cat" as a social type must have the objective of reducing his group isolation. For instance, because of such isolation and because of the cat's sensitivity to the gestures of his peers, the most significant role models of a given generation of cats tend to be the cats of the preceding age group. Where, in a period of rapid change, the schemes of behavior of the role models no longer correspond to the possibilities in the actual situation, it is possible for attitudes to be transmitted to a younger generation which evidence a kind of "cultural lag." Thus the condition of the labor market in Chicago is such as to suggest the existence of plentiful employment opportunities for the Negro in a variety of fields. But because such openings are not mediated to him through role models it is possible that the cat is unable to take advantage of these opportunities or of the facilities available for training for such positions.

The social type of the cat is a product of social change. The type of social orientation which it has elaborated indicates an all too acute awareness of the values of the broader social order. In an open class society where upward mobility is positively sanctioned, an awareness and sensitivity to the dominant values is the first stage in their eventual assimilation. Insofar as the social type of the cat represents a reaction to a feeling of exclusion from access to the means towards the goals of our society, all measures such as improved educational opportunities which put these means within his grasp will hasten the extinction of this social type. Just as the "hoodlum" and "gangster" types tend to disappear as the various more recently arrived white ethnic groups tend to move up in the status scale of the community,[20] so it can confidently be expected that the cat as a social type will tend to disappear as such opportunities become more prevalent among the black population.

---

[19] Oscar Handlin, *The Uprooted* (New York: Grosset and Dunlap, 1951), p. 243.

[20] Daniel Bell, "Crime as an American Way of Life," *Antioch Review* 13 (June, 1953), pp. 131–54.

B. SOCIAL RELATIONS AND PROCESS

Becker's analysis of the drug situation emphasizes historical conditions for a drug subculture and the causal role of that subculture in the subjective experience of drug effects. Drug subcommunities, which facilitate the transmission of this culture, have two other functions as well. First, a drug subcommunity brings together individuals who have a mutual dependence on drugs and interest in the continuation of drug traffic. As a group, users can facilitate the flow of drugs and hence maintain their own individual access to drugs. Second, certain activities of the drug community shield drug traffickers and users from the surveillance of police and legitimate society. In these two respects, drug subcommunities resemble homosexual subcommunities (see pp. 267–68 above). In a very real sense, drug subcommunities exist because they are illegal.

In "The Social Structure of a Heroin Copping Community," Hughes et al. describe the roles and social relationships within one such community. The authors describe a system of roles that is more complex than the relationship between just a dealer or "pusher" and a user. Indeed, most individuals involved in the network are users as well as sellers, so that the distinction between buyer and seller is not very appropriate within the system. The authors also describe the social, psychological, and demographic differences that distinguish individuals in the various roles and raise questions as to whether the subcommunity (rather than the individual addict) should not be the object of treatment and prevention programs.

THE SOCIAL STRUCTURE OF A HEROIN COPPING COMMUNITY

PATRICK H. HUGHES, GAIL A. CRAWFORD,
NOEL W. BARKER, SUZANNE SCHUMANN,
AND JEROME H. JAFFE

We have been studying heroin addicts in their natural setting in an effort to understand the factors contributing to the spread and maintenance of addiction. In previous studies[1] we reported that (1) the majority of active street addicts in our urban area appeared to be organized for purposes of heroin distribution into neighborhood "copping communities"; (2) members of an epidemiologic field team located at these drug distribution sites, called "copping areas," were able to obtain demographic and other epidemiologic data on the majority of cop-

ping community members; and (3) the field team was able to remove special samples from the copping community through experimental treatment projects.

During our visits to copping areas in various ethnic neighborhoods, we were impressed by the structural similarities of these drug distribution networks and their high degree of social and geographical stability. The characteristic features of local distribution systems can be accounted for by two unique aspects of heroin addiction. The first is the addict's need for a continuous drug supply to prevent onset of withdrawal symptoms. When he is sick and has money, he needs a place where he can go for symptom relief. Second, because these locations are frequently under police surveillance, the addict cannot walk up to a dealer, pass him money, and walk away. Therefore, copping communities tend to develop a rather complex organization to

Reprinted with permission of the author and the American Psychiatric Association, from *American Journal of Psychiatry* 128 (November, 1971), pp. 551–57.

[1] P. H. Hughes, G. A. Crawford, and N. W. Barker, "Developing an Epidemiologic Field Team for Drug Dependence," *Archives of General Psychiatry* 24 (1971), pp. 389–94; and P. H. Hughes, and J. H. Jaffe, "The Heroin Copping Area: A Location for Epidemiologic Study and Intervention Activity," *Archives of General Psychiatry* 24 (1971), pp. 394–401.

protect their membership from constant police pressure. In this way they resemble delinquent gangs and other criminal organizations.

In this paper we will describe the role structure elaborated by the membership of a copping community that we studied for a period of one year. Data are presented showing the distribution of the membership in the various roles and the social and treatability characteristics of the occupants of these roles. The implications of these findings for prevention and control programs are also discussed.

Method

Ex-addict field workers maintained on methadone were assigned to four major copping areas on Chicago's South Side where they were known and trusted. We chose one particular copping area for intensive study because of the unusual competence of the field worker. By administering a card in the field, he obtained demographic and drug use data on the majority of addicts frequenting this copping area. A weekly log was kept on the current addiction status of all copping community members for a 12-month period. A "member" was defined as a heroin distributor or consumer who frequented the copping area for at least four weeks of the study period. The field worker's recordings were verified by members of the professional staff through visits to the copping area and through personal interviews.

Fifty-two members who were active during the months of April, May, and June 1969 were offered a 50 percent chance of immediate treatment if they participated in a home-visit study. The random assignment of participants to immediate treatment or to the waiting list (with a four-month delay) was made upon completion of the interviews. Thirty-four (65 percent) cooperated with the project. A comparison of the effects of immediate treatment versus placement on the waiting list will be reported elsewhere.

Each subject was rated on the Addict Psychosocial Functioning Scale.[2] This instrument evaluates addicts on eight subscales that assess severity of addiction and psychological and occupational functioning. Ratings were arrived at by the consensus of a psychiatrist and two psychologists, one of whom conducted a clinical interview during the home visit. To provide a basis for the ratings, the clinician who conducted the interview prepared a psychiatric history of each subject on the basis of questionnaire responses, interview material, and the field worker's report of how the addict's peers in the copping community viewed his social functioning.

Results

During the year of observation, 125 heroin addicts and two nonusers were judged by the field staff to be members of this copping community. The field team determined that the majority could be assigned to one of the following primary roles: big dealer, street dealer, part-time dealer, bag follower, tout, hustler, and worker.

Big dealers are defined as local wholesalers who supply street dealers or part-time dealers, though they may sell directly to a few trusted customers. Street dealers sell heroin directly to consumers. Part-time dealers supplement their income by hustling or working, and move in and out of the dealer role for varying lengths of time. Touts carry out liaisons between dealers and consumers, sometimes steering customers to a particular dealer. They may also buy drugs for addicts who have no established connection with dealers. Bag followers attach themselves to dealers to support their habits. The three in our study were attractive women who earned their drugs by enhancing a dealer's prestige or by carrying heroin on their persons since the police are reluctant to search women on the street. Hustlers engage in various illegal activities other than drug distribution to support their habits; most commonly they are shoplifters. Workers maintain at least a part-time legitimate job, although most hustle as well.

This division of labor follows the functional requirements of drug distribution originally described by Preble and Casey.[3] However our classification does not include roles in the distribution hierarchy above the neighborhood level. It

[2] S. Schumann, P. H. Hughes, and E. Caffrey, "Addict Psychosocial Functioning Scale."

[3] E. Preble, and J. J. Casey, "Taking Care of Business—the Heroin User's Life on the Street," *International Journal of the Addictions* 4 (1969), pp. 1–24.

also differs slightly from Preble's classification because we wanted to assign each person to one primary role. "Part-time dealer" is the only label that we developed to meet this classificatory need. All the other roles and definitions are based on the current use of these terms by the heroin addicts in our community. Although some members occupied several distribution roles during the period of study, weekly recordings for a four-month period suggested a great deal of role stability over time.

The distribution of this copping community's membership according to functional roles is portrayed in Figure 1. One notes that a high proportion, 34 percent, are primarily engaged in drug distribution. Only two members of this copping community are nonaddicted dealers, i.e., are motivated purely by economic gain. The figure also shows the distribution of women and police informers within the various roles.

Although 127 men and women were considered to be active members of this copping community at some time during the 12 months, on the average only 56 percent were reported to visit the area during any given week. New members entered after relapsing into addiction or moving from other copping areas when higher quality heroin became available. Others stopped visiting because they were in jail or in treatment, etc. For example, during the last week of August 1969, there was a total of 77 active members: seven big dealers, three street dealers, 11 part-time dealers, one bag follower, five touts, 31 hustlers, and 19 workers.

Demographic and Drug Use Characteristics

Occupants of the various roles are compared by age and drug use characteristics in Table 1. Men's roles in the distribution structure were not related to age or formal education. Women were most frequently hustlers and bag followers.

Age at first use of heroin did not differentiate the roles, although touts had been heroin users longer than others. This finding lends some support to the belief among addicts that chronic heroin use and repeated arrests cause some to

FIGURE 1. THE COMPOSITION OF A HEROIN COPPING COMMUNITY

	Number	Percent
● Questionnaire and/or home visit	34	27
◒ Survey card or intake questionnaire	71	56
○ Field Observation Only	22	17
♀ Female	23	18
★ Police Informer	11	9
□ Nonaddict	2	2

BIG DEALERS (6%)

STREET DEALERS (6%)

PART-TIME STREET DEALERS (15%)

BAG FOLLOWERS (2%)

TOUTS (4%)

(34%)

(66%)

Hustlers (38%)

Workers (28%)

TABLE 1. COMPARISON OF AGE AND DRUG USE AMONG THE DISTRIBUTION ROLES

Role	Age		Years of Heroin Use		Weekly Cost of Habit	
	Number	Mean	Number	Mean	Number	Mean
Big dealers	4	33.3	4	14.2	1	$1,000
Street dealers	6	37.3	6	17.0	—	—
Part-time dealers	16	37.1	16	18.2	5	205
Bag followers	3	23.0	3	2.7	2	150
Touts	5	42.6	5	22.6	1	100
Hustlers	40	36.2	41	15.4	7	268
Workers	30	39.1	30	18.9	10	111
Total	104	37.1	105	16.8	26	208

lose their "nerve," i.e., they avoid dealing and hustling because of the higher risk of arrest. Instead they "hang out" in the copping area in low-status roles, hoping to receive small amounts of drugs for their touting services. Bag followers had shorter addiction histories than others, which would be expected since the role requires that they be young and attractive.

Individuals in higher-level distribution roles reported more frequent heroin use and more expensive habits. However, the cost of their drugs might be considered an auxiliary expense of maintaining the distribution system and not a personal expenditure. This framework for analyzing the economics of addiction, then, shows that it is erroneous to equate the huge habits of dealers with direct economic loss to the innocent public. Furthermore workers, who reported less frequent use and less expensive habits, paid for their drugs largely through their own legitimate income. The true economic loss to the public would more appropriately be based upon the cost of the average daily habit of hustlers, who bring into this illicit marketing system real dollars or goods obtained from illegal activities. It must be emphasized that the net dollar loss to the public occurs only once, no matter how many times money may change hands after it enters this system.

Standard of Living

The popular stereotype of the drug dealer pictures him as living in luxury, with the street addict reduced to sleeping in abandoned buildings. To bring some clarification to this question, the subjects of our home visit study were ranked on several measures of standard of living: (1) relative condition of their housing, (2) general con-

dition of the neighborhood, and (3) monthly nondrug expenses such as rent, food, and clothing. Housing and neighborhood rankings were made on a standardized seven-point scale. A score of one signified unusual comfort and luxury; a score of four, average accommodations; and a score of seven, extremely substandard conditions. A score of eight was assigned to addicts who were "carrying the stick" (had no fixed place of residence).

Although the two big dealers did live better than other members of the sample, their housing and neighborhood ratings were only average (4.0). One big dealer lived in a lower-middle-class neighborhood in a neat but modestly furnished apartment. His working wife paid for food and rent and occasionally contributed to his legal fees on court cases. The other big dealer lived in hotel rooms, which he frequently changed because he kept drugs there. Some may be surprised by the relatively low standard of living of these big dealers, but it must be remembered that these men were defined as big dealers in this one copping community. Had we studied distribution roles above the neighborhood level or in other copping areas, we might have found the higher standards of living commonly associated with those whom narcotics officers consider to be big dealers.

The three bag followers ranked just below big dealers on housing (4.7) and neighborhood condition (4.7). The eleven workers followed, with ratings of 4.9 and 5.4 on housing and neighborhood condition, respectively. The six part-time dealers ranked next with a housing rating of 5.7 and a neighborhood rating of 5.5. The one street dealer we visited received a rating of 6.0 on both housing and neighborhood. Hustling addicts ranked lowest on housing (6.9) and neighborhood condition (7.1), with five of the ten visited "carrying the stick."

Many of us assume that the addict pays rent, board, and family expenses just as we do (perhaps $200 to $400 per month) and that these living costs are borne by the public through theft and other illegal activities. This stereotype did not hold for the sample studied. Although three members of the intensive study sample were totally self-supporting, six "carried the stick" and the remaining 25 lived with others. When an addict lived with others this almost always meant that his family or girl friend paid the room and board, with the addict spending his entire income on drugs.

Psychosocial Functioning

Subjects who participated in the home visit study were assigned scores of zero to 100 on the following eight subscales: economic autonomy, severity of addiction, degree of subjective discomfort, fitness for employment, degree of mental health, quality of interpersonal relationships, degree of criminality, and social attractiveness. A score of zero on any subscale indicated severe malfunctioning; a score of 100 indicated perfect functioning in an area.

Compared with the rest of the sample, the two big dealers ranked high on economic autonomy, stability of interpersonal relations, and social attractiveness. They showed relatively little subjective discomfort and the lowest degree of mental disturbance. These findings are consistent with the requirements of the dealer role. Higher-level dealers must possess a certain degree of reliability and responsibility in order to maintain a stable distribution system in spite of constant threats from law enforcement agents and internal manipulation by addict members. This role also requires enough self-discipline to keep a cash reserve on hand and to use only a portion of one's heroin supply for one's own habit. Big dealers' high ratings on criminality and low ratings on employment fitness suggest that they would require extensive rehabilitation. Although the one street dealer in our sample exhibited a relatively high degree of mental disturbance, his other subscale scores, particularly employment fitness and criminality, were similar to those of big dealers.

The six part-time dealers in our sample tended to be addicts who had difficulty meeting the requirements of the dealer role. They were frequently unable to "discipline" their habits or maintain a cash reserve in case they were "burned" (i.e., sold poor-quality drugs). Some part-time dealers held jobs and dealt only enough drugs to support their own habits. They tended to score high on subjective discomfort, stability of interpersonal relationships, and social attractiveness. They tended to score low on economic autonomy.

Although the three bag followers did not have long addiction histories, they showed relatively high economic dependence and subjective discomfort. They were rated low on employment fitness, mental health, and stability of interpersonal relationships.

The ten hustlers tended to score low on all subscales except subjective discomfort. Although there was considerable variation among members, the group as a whole scored low since the most severely disturbed persons appeared to be in this category. The relatively high degree of mental disturbance among hustlers suggests that this is a catchall category with minimal role requirements. A severely disturbed individual who would have trouble meeting the requirements of a dealer role or the demands of steady employment could still hustle, even though unsuccessfully.

As a group, the nine workers were rated highest on employment fitness and lowest on criminality. They were also rated relatively high on mental health and social attractiveness, suggesting that they might be good treatment prospects.

Although the Addict Psychosocial Functioning Scale is still in its early stages of development, the findings presented here suggest that occupants of particular functional roles share certain characteristics that may be related to their choice of these roles as well as their ability to maintain them.

Treatability Characteristics

In an attempt to assess the treatability characteristics of the different roles, we compared the proportions entering treatment and the proportions remaining in treatment six months after their date of admission. Although the majority of our subjects were assigned to methadone maintenance, some were assigned to such other modalities as a therapeutic community or in-patient withdrawal. Our findings on treatment success must therefore be viewed with caution.

Of the 125 addicted members of this copping community, 50 (40 percent) entered treatment, and 30 (60 percent of those entering) remained in treatment six months later (see Table 2). As

TABLE 2. TREATABILITY ACCORDING TO DISTRIBUTION ROLES

Role	Number	Admitted to Treatment		In Treatment After Six Months	
		Number	Percent	Number	Percent
Big dealers	7	3	43	1	33
Street dealers	7	1	14	0	—
Part-time dealers	19	9	47	6	67
Bag followers	3	3	100	1	33
Touts	5	1	20	0	—
Hustlers	48	17	35	9	53
Workers	36	16	44	13	81
Total	125	50	40	30	60

Note: Includes all members of the copping community known to have entered treatment during the 21 months from January 1969 to September 1970.

a group, workers were found to be the most favorable treatment prospects, i.e., 16 of the 36 entered treatment and 13 remained after six months. The relative success of workers can be partially explained by their having already over-come one of the major hurdles to rehabilitation —obtaining legitimate employment. Not so readily explained is the finding that part-time dealers were most likely to enter treatment, with nine of the 19 entering and six remaining after six months.

The finding that big dealers, street dealers, bag followers, and touts can be involved in treatment but tend to do poorly is consistent with our clinical experience. For example, we have ob-served a number of dealers who, after entering treatment, continued to sell drugs rather than seek legitimate employment. By continuing their illegal activities and by periodically returning to heroin use, they came under increasing pressure from clinical staff and they eventually withdrew from the program.

Discussion

We found that the drug distribution community under study had elaborated a more highly differ-entiated system of roles than is usually con-sidered, i.e., dealer and user. By studying drug use, personality, and treatability characteristics of the occupants of different roles, we were able to bring some empirical definition to this social system. Since drug distribution roles were not the basis for selection of the intensive study group, the sample sizes for most roles were too small to permit meaningful statistical compari-sons. It must also be noted that the copping area studied was only one of perhaps 20 known to exist in the Chicago metropolitan area. The find-ings, then, should be viewed only as suggestive. Despite these limitations, the data suggest that the membership and dynamics of local heroin distribution systems can be studied and perhaps altered by treatment programs.

Further field studies of the addict as a mem-ber of a definable distribution system should help to eliminate many of the myths surround-ing the so-called addict subculture. For example, dealers in this neighborhood were not "pushing" heroin. The addicts, in fact, were in a seller's market, i.e., they had to seek out the dealers. It may be that in such neighborhoods, where ad-diction is of long standing, police surveillance and penetration prompt dealers to minimize the risk of arrest by selling only to trustworthy cus-tomers. One might expect an addict community that experiences less pressure from agencies of law enforcement to exhibit less structural differ-entiation, with dealers being more directly ac-cessible to consumers. In such a setting one might see the "pushing" phenomenon and a buyer's market. It is interesting to note that Moore[4] arrived at similar conclusions from purely theoretical considerations.

The distribution of police informers within this addict community is consistent with effective local police penetration. For example, there is a concentration of informers in the tout role, which is perhaps the key communication posi-tion in the system. Although this aspect of our study is in an early stage, the ability to investi-gate police penetration into these systems may yield important clues to control. For example, the high degree of police penetration seen here may be partially responsible for the low inci-

[4] M. Moore, "Economics of Heroin Distribution," *Policy Concerning Drug Abuse in New York State*, Vol. 3 (New York: Hudson Institute, 1970).

dence of new cases of addiction observed in this neighborhood.[5]

Despite the strategic location of informers, the system operates in a way that makes it difficult for local law enforcement officials to arrest higher-level dealers. For example, during the period of our study we noted that one big dealer in this copping area acquired four different felony charges for the sale and possession of heroin. Shortly thereafter he became suspected of being a police informer, lost his connections with the "main people" for drugs, and was forced to support his habit by hustling.

Although all heroin addicts share the same physical withdrawal symptoms, our findings indicate that addicts do not share the same psychological disturbance. By looking at the variations in psychopathology among addicts in their natural setting, our approach differs from that of studies carried out with the biased samples available in treatment or correctional settings. The approach used here permitted us to examine how differences in psychopathology might relate to the functional requirements of various distribution roles. It also incorporates standards used by addicts themselves to judge one another in terms of social functioning. Although some professionals may consider all addicts to be sick, many members of the addict community are viewed by their peers as success models. Another result of our attempt to relate psychopathology to the social structure of this community was the location of the most disturbed members in the role with the lowest performance requirements.

The findings on treatability, if confirmed by future studies, may suggest improved treatment typologies and certain modifications in clinical practice. Our impression that major distribution

roles were associated with lower motivation for treatment and higher dropout rates suggests that voluntary community programs might consider special approaches for involving and holding these groups. For example, one might obtain better results with big dealers through immediate hospitalization, thereby removing them from the temptation to continue dealing purely for profit. Alternatively, the demand for immediate behavioral change among big dealers might be postponed until they have worked through their initial difficulties in accepting the lower prestige of the patient role.

We are currently replicating our approach in different ethnic neighborhoods in order to assess local variations in role structure, distribution of the membership, and social and treatability characteristics of role occupants. Our search for an effective, medically oriented control strategy requires that we explore the usefulness of different operational models. For example, should local heroin distribution networks be defined as disease maintenance systems that might be eradicated through the use of public health field teams that would involve the majority of active addicts in voluntary treatment and employ short-term quarantine for the small percentage who refuse treatment? Would it be useful to define these networks as illegal heroin maintenance systems that might be readily converted to neighborhood methadone maintenance clinics? Or does their criminal role structure require that they be defined as deviant social systems best controlled by local law enforcement pressure?

In the absence of short-term quarantine laws, our intervention approach is limited to voluntary outreach projects. Nevertheless, we hope this intervention can be varied enough to permit experimental manipulation of the size, structure, and other characteristics of these drug distribution networks, perhaps leading to their complete removal from some neighborhoods.

------

[5] Hughes, Crawford and Barker, "Developing an Epidemiologic Field Team for Drug Dependence."

C. CONSEQUENCES

In the first selection of this section on the basis of data obtained from the Federal Bureau of Narcotics (now the Federal Bureau of Narcotics and Dangerous Drugs), Charles Winick provides one answer to the often asked question, "What happens to most drug addicts?" In an earlier study Winick reported that most addicts "mature out" of addiction, that is, they quit: by the age of 47 years, 87 percent of former addicts become inactive. In the current selection, he explores the relationship between length of drug career and age of initial addiction. He finds that the younger one is when addicted, the longer the addiction is apt to last. It is possible that higher death rates for older age groups contribute to this pattern. It is not likely, however, that this is the sole factor. In any case, it is clear that most addiction careers end by the time the addict is in his middle forties and are definitely related to the age at which the individual entered the career.

In the final selection, "The Cycle of Abstinence and Relapse Among Heroin Addicts," Marsh Ray indicates that the termination of drug use, whether from "maturing out" or otherwise, is not an easy or simple process and that more is involved than having to suffer through withdrawal symptoms. Relapse and abstention may be associated with the character of an addict's social relations, that is, they may be related to the response of others. Abstention occurs, according to Ray, because the addict has a "socially disjunctive experience" that causes him to reject his drug addict identity. Most cures are not permanent, however, and Ray argues that this is due primarily to the way significant others interact with and define the addict after the "cure" has taken place. Certain secondary characteristics are associated with an addict, and society continues to attribute such characteristics to him after abstention. A former addict is treated as though he were still an addict, and because of this a relapse may occur.

THE LIFE CYCLE OF THE NARCOTIC ADDICT AND OF ADDICTION

CHARLES WINICK

One goal of a scientific investigation of any subject is to determine the underlying regularities that permit us to make generalizations about the subject. Generalizations that are confirmed may enable us not only to explain but to predict, and prediction is the hallmark of a mature science. A number of investigators have made contributions towards our understanding of the regularities that may underlie the phenomenon of nar-

cotic addiction. For example, the statement by Himmelsbach and his associates of the near-schematic pattern of withdrawal behavior suggests that a deep-rooted mechanism has manifested itself in withdrawal.[1] The formulation by Wikler of a theory of narcotic use as a gratification of certain primary needs is another example of a broad-gauge generalization that seems to

Reprinted with permission of the author and publisher, from *Bulletin on Narcotics*, January-March, 1964, pp. 1–11.

[1] C. K. Himmelsbach, "The Morphine Abstinence Syndrome: Its Nature and Treatment," *Annals of Internal Medicine* 15 (1941), pp. 829–35.

explain previously heterogeneous phenomena and that has predictive value.[2] A number of other generalizations about addiction have also enabled us to observe mechanisms or response patterns that appear to have predictive value.

Age is one of the very few continuous variables that it is possible for us to examine in the study of narcotic addiction. Interest in the phenomena of the length of addiction and age of the addict when he ceases to use narcotic drugs led to the analysis of data on former narcotic users obtained through the vary generous and helpful co-operation of the Honorable H. J. Anslinger and the Honorable Henry L. Giordano, the former and incumbent Commissioner of Narcotics, respectively. The Federal Bureau of Narcotics made a tabulation of the age and number of years of addiction of those persons who had not used narcotics for five years, as of 31 December 1960.[3] Of these 7,234 former drug users, there was a concentration of persons in their thirties. The average age at which they became inactive was 35.1 and their average length of addiction was 8.6 years. By the age of 47, 87.3 percent of the total number of former narcotic users had become inactive.

These figures clearly suggest that there are fewer and fewer drug addicts who cease drug use in the later years of life and, contrariwise, that there is a considerable concentration of persons ceasing drug use in the years of prime adulthood. This phenomenon was identified as maturing out of narcotic addiction. It was speculated that, as the stresses of adolescence became less insistent and the drug user felt less threatened by the need to respond to such stresses, he tended to stop taking narcotics. The data, interpreted in the light of the maturing-out concept, suggested that addiction might be a self limiting process for perhaps two-thirds of addicts.

The maturing-out phenomenon has received independent confirmation from other sources. A recent personal interview follow-up study in New York of 1,359 addicts released from the U.S. Public Health Service Hospital at Lexington found that patients over 30 had a significantly higher abstinence rate than younger patients.[4] Five years after release from the hospital, 61 percent of the group over 30 was abstinent. This is approximately the proportion of this age group which had become inactive in the author's earlier study.[5]

Another kind of confirmation comes from psychopaths. The dropout curve for psychopaths is almost identical with that of the addicts who had ceased taking drugs after five years. Students of psychopathy have noted that psychopaths seem to "disappear" by their early thirties. There is reason to believe that they "disappear" because they have matured out of their psychopathy. Diethelm has summarized the experience of many psychiatrists with psychopaths: "During adult life, with the subsiding of instinctual desires ... many psychopathic difficulties may disappear.... In a survey of patients ... it was possible to single out some patients of an age over 45 years whose lives represented that of a psychopath until about 30. These patients might be considered recovered psychopaths."[6]

The same phenomenon has been noted with juvenile delinquents, a large proportion of whom seem to begin functioning within the "legitimate" society and "going straight" when they reach the age of about 30. Our most distinguished students of delinquency, the Gluecks, have observed a sharp drop in recidivism when offenders are about 30. They have also noted that even "repeaters" may shift from aggressive behavior to "nuisance" offenses after reaching their thirties. They have consistently found, in several different follow-up studies of delinquents, that there is a significant drop in the incidence of recidivism among young adult offenders.[7] The drop occurs in the late twenties and early and mid-thirties.

[2] A. Wikler, "A Psychodynamic Study of a Patient During Experimental Self Regulated Re-Addiction to Morphine," *Psychiatric Quarterly* 26 (1952), pp. 270–93.

[3] C. Winick, "Maturing Out of Narcotic Addiction," *Bulletin on Narcotics* 14 (1962), pp. 1–7.

[4] H. J. Duvall, B. Z. Locke, and L. Brill, "Follow-up Study of Narcotic Drug Addicts Five Years after Hospitalization," *Public Health Reports* 78 (1963), pp. 185–93.

[5] Winick, "Maturing Out of Narcotic Addiction."

[6] O. Diethelm, "Basic Considerations of the Concept of the Psychopathic Personality," in Edward Podolsky, ed., *Encyclopedia of Aberrations* (New York: Philosophical Library, 1953), pp. 452–56.

[7] Grateful acknowledgement is made of some very suggestive and helpful comments about research data on juvenile delinquency that were made by Dr. Sheldon Glueck, Roscoe Pound Professor of Law at Harvard University. With his wife Eleanor T. Glueck, his pioneering applications of the scientific method to the study of delinquency have helped enormously to clarify this difficult area.

Dr. Richard C. Cabot, in the preface to an early publication of the Gluecks, speculates that "Perhaps this type of crime is a symptom of a self-limited disease of personality, which ordinarily runs its course during the years from sixteen to thirty-five or forty...."[8] Concluding a fifteen-year follow-up of 510 young adult offenders who had been convicted and served their sentences, the Gluecks reported "a rising trend toward improvement in all aspects of the activities of our men accompanying the passage of time (ageing) or maturation. This proceeds to approximately the age of 36...."[9] In the same study, they note that "a basic problem of this research was to determine which of the 63 factors studied were chiefly responsible for the reduction in criminality.... Such analysis revealed that only within the factor of *ageing* was a significant explanation to be found for the increasing trend away from criminal conduct...."

A similar fifteen-year follow-up study on an entirely different sample of 1,000 juvenile delinquents came to essentially similar conclusions.[10] Their thinking on maturation as a contributor to de-recidivism has been confirmed by several different studies.[11] It is therefore within the realm of possibility that the same underlying forces that contribute to the settling down of delinquents or to their change from aggressive criminalism to petty offenses of the nuisance type underlie both the phenomenon of de-recidivism and the analogous phenomenon of de-addiction. It is possible that de-addiction is simply one facet of de-recidivism. If this larger process of de-recidivism did not occur, our already large adult criminal population would be many times larger than it already is.

A similar phenomenon has been observed in delinquents who are incarcerated. Prison officials have noticed prisoners who commit infractions against the prison rules are usually under the age of 30. Even in the closed community of a prison, there appears to be a self selection of prisoners who flaunt established procedures and engage in behavior that is frowned upon. The great majority of those who behave in this way are at roughly the same age as the addicts who stop taking drugs. That younger inmates in prison commit more infractions than older inmates is not unexpected; the younger people commit more infractions outside as well as inside a prison, and probably as a reflection of the same process of maturation. The infractions committed by young prisoners usually involve the expression of aggression—fighting, assaulting a guard, or overt stealing. It is difficulty with the expression of aggression that may turn some young persons to narcotics, and some violent "bopping" street gangs have turned to narcotics when they stopped "bopping." The experience of prison officials is thus in line with what we know about what some young people do with feelings of aggression. Such young people may turn to narcotics, for so long as they experience difficulties in handling their aggression.

Parole officers working closely with addict parolees of all ages have observed that parolees in their thirties increasingly say "I'm too old for that stuff. I've had it. Who needs it?" Such parolees may not like to stop taking drugs, but they dislike the consequences of return to drug use even more. What is curious is that the parolees' feeling that they have "had it" seems to become intensified by the time they reach their thirties. Many parolees in their thirties who are former addicts reject narcotics, even though they have improved their knowledge of techniques of evasion, like using a very fine needle, applying cocoa butter to facilitate the healing of needle scars, and using different drugs on different days in order to avoid dependence on any one drug. The parolees who turn their backs on narcotics by their thirties tend to be those whose prison experiences are most radically different from their non-prison situations.[12]

In all of these situations, persons who since adolescence have been violating the law or behaving in an antisocial manner, somewhere between their late twenties and mid-thirties, increasingly seem to be able to modify their

[8] S. Glueck and E. T. Glueck, *500 Criminal Careers* (New York: Alfred A. Knopf, 1930), p. xii.
[9] S. Glueck and E. T. Glueck, *Later Criminal Careers* (New York: Commonwealth Fund, 1937), pp. 122, 199–200.
[10] S. Glueck and E. T. Glueck, *Juvenile Delinquents Grown Up* (New York: Commonwealth Fund, 1940), pp. 90–91, 268–70.
[11] S. Glueck and E. T. Glueck, *After-conduct of Discharged Offenders* (London: Macmillan, 1946).

[12] Dr. Kurt Konietzko of the Philadelphia Parole Narcotics Project has helped greatly to clarify the psychology of the addict parolee.

TABLE 1. AGE AT CESSATION OF ADDICTION AND LENGTH OF ADDICTION

Age at Drop Out	Length of Addiction in Years																									
	5	6	7	8	9	10	11	12	13	14	15	16	17	18	19	20	21	22	23	24	25	26	27	28	29	30
18	1																									
19	5																									
20	3	3		1																						
21	12	6	4		1																					
22	23	17	4	2	1																					
23	53	37	18	3	3	3	1																			
24	86	43	26	17	1	4	1																			
25	102	63	39	21	15	3	2		2																	
26	131	81	62	29	27	18	9	3	4	1																
27	134	96	58	38	30	25	21	7	3																	
28	175	84	56	39	39	38	21	9	4	4																
29	146	72	57	44	42	31	13	18	19	1	4															
30	161	96	66	54	42	32	24	19	13	4	3															
31	161	66	46	47	18	36	23	16	10	8	3		1	1												
32	144	69	53	43	34	42	23	23	12	7	10			1	1											
33	127	57	56	28	24	41	26	18	14	4	9	4	1	3				1								
34	129	40	38	28	32	24	11	10	8	7	7	6	3		2	1					1					
35	89	39	35	29	21	25	9	14	8	5	3	4	3	4	2	2	1									
36	81	43	22	16	20	27	13	12	7	4	5	3	1	1		1	1	2	1							
37	80	28	29	12	23	20	12	5	2	3	3	3	3	3	1	3	1									
38	51	17	15	6	11	10	10	10	9	1	5	1		1	3	1		1	1		1					
39	34	23	12	10	14	13	5	3	7	2	7				3					2						
40	46	21	13	10	4	7	5	6	3		7		1	1	1					1						
41	35	20	9	7	3	9	3	3	6	1	8		3	1	2	3	1	1		1	1					
42	35	13	13	7	5	5	9	2	5	1	2	1			2	2	2	1		1	1					1
43	25	17	8	7	7	5	2	1	1	1	9		3		1	5	1	1	1	1	3		1			
44	27	13	3	6	3	3	2	1	5		4				1	2	1		2	1		2	1			
45	25	11	9	5	3	5	2	2	3	2	3			4	1	1	2		1		3				1	
46	27	5	3	6	4	1	2		1	1	4	1		1	2	9				1	4	1			1	2
47	20	5	5	1		1	5	1	2	1	7		2	1		4		1	1		3	1		1		
48	22	6	2	3		5	1	3	3		1		1		1	3	2	1	1	6						
49	14	3	5	4	2	4	2	2	2		4		2			5		1			4	1		2		
50	23	2	1	3	1	1	1		1	2	8	1			2	1		1			3	1			1	2

behavior patterns and to adapt to the larger society. This process is not automatic, and it does not happen to all the members of these groups, but it does happen to a significant proportion. To say that these persons have matured out of their earlier pattern of antisocial behavior is to suggest the end product of a combination of forces: insight, possible regression to neurosis or perhaps psychosis, the effect of years of jail or harassment by authorities, difficulties in obtaining narcotics, the passage of time, reaching a point of satiation or saturation, and the decreasing pressure that the community applied on the drug user to make decisions.

The young man who turns to antisocial behavior during his teens is likely to be responding to the many decisions—job, family, home—that he is called upon to make in our society during this period of his life. Basic human motivational systems are called into play in the late teens with a force that adds urgency to the decisions they require. The decision to use narcotics or to engage in other antisocial activity provides opportunities for gratifications that bypass the ordinary personal and social procedures for coping. In some cases, it may be a protection against a near-psychotic response. Drug use may represent a response to a physiological change. It may reflect a predisposing need which in turn reflects certain childhood experiences, and espe-

TABLE 1. (continued)

	Length of Addiction in Years																											
	31	32	33	34	35	36	37	38	39	40	41	42	43	44	45	46	47	48	49	50	51	52	53	54	55	56	Total	
18																											1	18
19																											5	19
20																											7	20
21																											23	21
22																											47	22
23																											118	23
24																											178	24
25																											247	25
26																											365	26
27																											412	27
28																											469	28
29																											447	29
30																											514	30
31																											436	31
32																											462	32
33																											413	33
34																											347	34
35																											293	35
36																											260	36
37																											231	37
38																											154	38
39																											135	39
40																											126	40
41	1																										118	41
42																											108	42
43		1																									101	43
44	1																										78	44
45																											83	45
46																											76	46
47		1	1																								64	47
48				1	1																						63	48
49																											57	49
50	1			1	1																						58	50

cially certain kinds of parent-child relations. It may be a safeguard against feelings of inadequacy, or a means of lowering the organism's drive state. It may involve the counterphobic mechanism of repetitive exposure to narcotics' dangerous effect.[13]

The young person's separation from school during this period, whether by graduation or dropout, removes whatever blunting effect the school has had in absorbing the motives and drives that may manifest themselves in narcotics use. In our society, the place of a puberty rite is taken by the complex of decisions and actions that are the age-graded expectations that we have toward the adolescent moving into young adulthood. The implied threat posed by this complex may be faced by commencing narcotics use.

The commencement of narcotics use is likely to be reciprocally and complementarily related to the factor(s) that led to the maturing out of the use of drugs. For example, the young person who began using drugs as one way of coping with physiological changes seems to tend to mature out of narcotics use when these physiological changes lose their salience.

---

[13] T. Szasz, "The Role of the Counterphobic Mechanism is Addiction," *Journal of the American Psychoanalytic Association* 6 (1958), pp. 309–25.

TABLE 1. (continued)

Age at Drop Out	Length of Addiction in Years																									
	5	6	7	8	9	10	11	12	13	14	15	16	17	18	19	20	21	22	23	24	25	26	27	28	29	30
51	14	3	5	1	1	1	3	4	3		2	3				1	1	1	1		5		1	1		4
52	11	3	4	4		2	2	1		1	3	1	2			1	1		1		2	3	1	1	2	2
53	27	4	1	3	1	3	1	2	2		5		1	2	1	4	1	1	1		4		2			2
54	12	1	5	1		2	1		2	1	3					4				1	10			1		1
55	13	4	1	3	2	5	2	3		1	1	3				2	1		1		4		1	2		3
56	10		4		1	1	1	1	1		2	1				2					6			2		1
57	12	2	4	2	1	2		1		1	1	1				1		2			3				1	1
58	26	3	3	3	1	1		2	1		1			1		3	1				1	1				
59	16		3	2		1		2	3		1	1				1			1		2					2
60	20	2	1	1		2				1	7					3					7	1			1	1
61	10	1		1		1					3		1					2		2						1
62	16	1	2				1				1			1							1				1	2
63	13	1	1		1	1							1		2			1		1	1					1
64	8	3									1			1	1	1		1		1						1
65	10		1			1	1						1								3					2
66	13		3		2																				1	1
67	8	3	1																						1	2
68	6	1	1								1					1		1								1
69																						1				
70																										
71														1												
72																2										
73																					1					
74																										
75																									1	
76	1																									
Total	2,473	1,128	807	547	438	463	270	204	166	65	148	29	34	27	24	76	18	16	19	7	82	13	8	12	11	35

The data available in the earlier study did not make it possible to establish whether an addict's cessation of drug use is a function of either the age at which he begins using drugs or the life cycle of the disease of addiction itself, or some combination of both. It appeared important to attempt to clarify the relationship between the age at which drug use begins and the number of years that a person uses drugs. The data for such a study were made available through the very generous cooperation of Commissioners H. J. Anslinger and Henry L. Giordano of the Federal Bureau of Narcotics.[14] The Bureau prepared a cross-tabulation of the number of years of addiction of each age group in the population of 7,234 former drug users that had become inactive as of 1960. These records of the Federal Bureau of Narcotics are the only national figures on narcotic addiction. Great care has been taken to eliminate duplications from these records and to keep them up to date. Table 1 gives the age at cessation of drug use of the sample, in terms of the number of persons in each age category cross-tabulated against the length of their addiction. These are persons reported as drug users during 1955 and not subsequently reported as of the end of 1960. The criterion of five years of freedom from symptoms is the traditional medical criterion for recovery from a chronic disease.

There is obviously a tremendous range in these data, from an eighteen-year-old with five years of drug use to a man of seventy-one with

[14] Grateful acknowledgement is made of the extensive and helpful cooperation of Commissioners Anslinger and Giordano in providing this tabulation and in making these data available completely unconditionally. All students of narcotics addiction are indebted to the Federal Bureau of Narcotics for its continuing efforts to keep its records as complete and reliable as possible. The author alone is, of course, responsible for the interpretations suggested for the Bureau data.

TABLE 1. (continued)

	31	32	33	34	35	36	37	38	39	40	41	42	43	44	45	46	47	48	49	50	51	52	53	54	55	56	Total	
51	1		2																								58	51
52		1		2					1																		52	52
53	2			2							1																73	53
54	2	1		1	1		1																				54	54
55	1		1		2	2																					58	55
56					5			1							1												40	56
57					1				1																		37	57
58					3		1			2																	54	58
59	1				3								1														39	59
60					1						1				1												51	60
61	1				2				1	2					1	1											32	61
62	1		1			1			1	1		1															32	62
63					1		1					1			2												29	63
64								1	3		1																23	64
65					2						1	1			2		1										26	65
66												2			1												23	66
67					1										1												19	67
68					3			1									1										16	68
69															1									1			3	69
70					1		1			1					1					1			1				6	70
71															1						1				1	1	5	71
72															1						1						3	72
73																											1	73
74			1																								1	74
75							1																				2	75
76																											1	76
	12	3	7	3	32	1	6	2	4	11	4	7	1		11	1	2				1		1	1	2	1	7,234	

fifty-six years of drug use. The majority of the dropouts, however, clearly are clustered in the years of mid-adulthood and have an addiction history of less than a decade. It is possible to take these data and, by subtraction, to compute the number of persons beginning drug use at each age.[15] This is shown in Table 2.

In the original report on maturing out, it had been speculated that there is a heavy concentration of commencement of drug use in the years of late adolescence and early adulthood, probably as one way of coping with the problems and decisions of these stressful years. Such a speculation appears to be confirmed by these data. Although the number of teenagers commencing drug use is most disturbing, even as-

suming a considerable period of time before these young users come to the attention of the authorities, the proportion of new teenage users to the total number of new users seems less than is sometimes assumed to be the case.

We are interested not only in how many persons commence drug use at each age, but also in how long they continue to use drugs. The median would probably be the best measure of central tendency for these data, but the limited number of cases in the very young and especially in the older age groups makes the median relatively impractical for this computation. The mean number of years of duration of addiction, at each age of onset, was therefore computed, and is shown in Table 3.

The mean number of years that the persons in this sample used drugs suggests that the younger a person starts on narcotics, the longer is his period of drug use likely to last. The qualitative

---

[15] The statistical analysis of these data was directed by Professor David W. Miller of Columbia University. Professor Miller's imaginative and thoughtful analysis uncovered relationships that were not at all apparent.

TABLE 2. NUMBER OF PERSONS BEGINNING
DRUG USE AT VARIOUS AGES

Age	Number of Persons	Age	Number of Persons
7	1	37	76
10	1	38	81
11	3	39	57
12	10	40	58
13	16	41	52
14	46	42	40
15	59	43	43
16	167	44	33
17	253	45	50
18	320	46	33
19	405	47	30
20	449	48	33
21	499	49	25
22	462	50	22
23	505	51	19
24	438	52	22
25	416	53	30
26	430	54	20
27	347	55	24
28	293	56	14
29	268	57	17
30	214	58	17
31	151	59	11
32	153	60	11
33	122	61	17
34	103	62	9
35	126	63	6
36	90	71	1

TABLE 3. MEAN NUMBER OF YEARS OF DURATION OF
ADDICTION AT EACH AGE OF ONSET

Age	Average Duration	Age	Average Duration
7	27	37	7.7
10	31	38	9.8
11	36.3	39	7.9
12	19.9	40	9.2
13	16.1	41	8.0
14	13.8	42	6.7
15	13.7	43	8.9
16	10.9	44	7.5
17	10.4	45	8.3
18	10.2	46	9.2
19	8.7	47	7.5
20	8.7	48	6.4
21	8.9	49	6.5
22	8.2	50	6.2
23	8.2	51	6.3
24	8.3	52	7.6
25	7.7	53	5.7
26	8.2	54	5.6
27	7.6	55	5.4
28	7.8	56	5.9
29	8.1	57	5.1
30	7.9	58	5.3
31	8.1	59	5.6
32	8.0	60	5.2
33	8.4	61	5.3
34	8.8	62	5.1
35	9.3	63	5.0
36	8.8	71	5.0

observations that can be made on each age group and each age decade doubtless have some value in making predictions about the life cycle of addiction. It was felt that the relationships between age at onset and length of addiction could be seen more clearly by smoothing the curve of these data, by dropping these cases that had been addicted for sixteen years or more. Table 4 gives the percentage of addicts at each age of onset who had used narcotics for sixteen or more years.

It will be noted that the proportion of those using narcotics for over fifteen years is relatively high in those starting on narcotics in their early teens and mid-thirties. From age 34 to 43, the proportions are very erratic. For ages over 48, there are practically no cases of more than fifteen years of use, probably because of the decreased life span possible. There are 525 cases of narcotics use for more than fifteen years, or

7.26 percent of the total. When we subtract those cases from the mean number of years of drug use at each age of onset, the mean number of years of drug use appears to follow a clear-cut pattern, as can be seen in Table 5.

If we look at the mean number of years of addiction at the ages of onset up to 30, we see that a correlation (r) of -0.95 obtains between age at onset and length of addiction. This extraordinarily high correlation documents how, in this age group, the length of addiction declines progressively and consistently as the age at onset increases. We do not know whether this relationship is the result of a decrease in need, an increase in resistance, external factors, or a combination of these and other factors.

The correlation (r) between length of addiction and age at onset between ages 38 and 60 is -0.80, which is also extremely high. The reason for the correlation being lower in the old-

TABLE 4. PROPORTION OF FORMER DRUG USERS AT EACH AGE LEVEL WHO HAVE BEEN ADDICTED FOR MORE THAN FIFTEEN YEARS

Age	Proportion (*Percent*)	Age	Proportion (*Percent*)
14	19.6	32	7.8
15	25.4	33	9.0
16	8.4	34	13.6
17	9.5	35	14.3
18	9.4	36	11.1
19	5.7	37	5.3
20	5.4	38	14.8
21	7.2	39	5.3
22	4.8	40	15.5
23	5.9	41	5.8
24	6.4	42	2.5
25	3.6	43	13.9
26	7.2	44	3.0
27	5.8	45	4.0
28	5.1	46	6.1
29	9.0	47	3.3
30	8.0	48	6.1
31	7.2		

TABLE 5. AVERAGE LENGTH OF ADDICTION FOR THOSE ADDICTED FIFTEEN YEARS OR LESS, IN YEARS

Age	Length of Addiction	Age	Length of Addiction
14	9.9	38	7.4
15	9.9	39	6.9
16	9.3	40	7.0
17	9.0	41	7.1
18	8.3	42	6.4
19	7.8	43	7.1
20	7.7	44	7.1
21	7.4	45	7.8
22	7.3	46	8.2
23	7.1	47	7.1
24	6.9	48	5.4
25	7.0	49	6.5
26	6.9	50	6.2
27	6.6	51	6.3
28	6.6	52	5.6
29	6.5	53	5.7
30	6.4	54	5.6
31	6.8	55	5.4
32	6.6	56	5.7
33	6.5	57	5.1
34	6.9	58	5.3
35	7.1	59	5.6
36	7.1	60	5.2
37	6.6		

er than in the younger age group is probably a function of the diminishing life expectancy and much smaller number of cases in each cell in the older group. The ages 31 to 37 present a less clear picture. It is possible to present these relationships graphically, in Figure 1. The length of addiction is the dependent variable, and is plotted against age at onset.

Figure 1 makes it clear that there are essentially three different groups in this population of former drug users: the group starting drug use at ages up to 30, the group starting from 38 to 60, and an intermediate group starting between 30 and 38.

We can establish a regression equation for each of the two major age groups. The equation for the 19 to 30 group is $y = 10.09 - 0.126x$, with y the average length of addiction and x the age at onset. This equation enables us to predict the length of drug use of the average person starting drug use at any age in this range. The results of this equation provide the best estimate on how long a person starting at any given age will use narcotics. It will be noticed that the younger a person in this age range begins drug use, the longer he is likely to continue using drugs. A person, however, who has held off using drugs until a later age will use them for a shorter

period. If we now look at the older age group from 38 to 60, the regression equation $y = 11.58 - .0.107x$ enables us to predict how long a person commencing drug use within this age group will continue to use narcotics. These two age groups are distinct and separate, but roughly the same equation helps to clarify the duration of their drug use. The two regression lines drawn on Figure 1 are almost exactly parallel and have essentially the same slope, suggesting the operation of some profound underlying principle.

The reason for considering the 32 to 36 group separately is that it appears to offer data that seem to depart from either of the two regression formulae. Inspection of the length of addiction at each of the years in this group suggests that some unusual factors are operating. The regression line that was developed for this age group is shown in Figure 1. Perhaps the simplest way of interpreting these data is to assume that each age group from 32 to 36 contains different proportions of the two age groups that appear to be present at each step in the series. We can

FIGURE 1. MEAN LENGTH OF ADDICTION AT EACH AGE OF ONSET

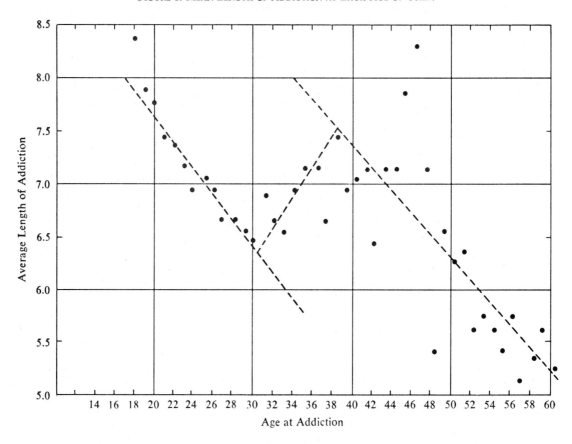

assume, if there are two distinct groups in this population of former addicts, that the intermediate group is a mixture of the trend lines of the two groups. The components of the mixture are shown in Table 6. The first column gives the

TABLE 6. PROPORTIONS OF TWO AGE GROUPS IN FORMER DRUG USERS COMMENCING DRUG USE BETWEEN 32 AND 38

Age	Actual Mean Length of Addiction	Mean Length of Addiction if Younger Group	Mean Length of Addiction if Older Group	Proportion of Younger Group at This Age (*Percent*)
32	6.6	6.1	8.15	76
34	6.9	5.85	7.95	50
36	7.18	5.60	7.70	25

age and the second column gives the mean length of the addiction period. The third column gives the mean length of addiction at each age

if the younger group's regression equation ($y = 10.09 - 0.126x$) were to be applied to the addicts commencing drug at each age. The fourth column gives the mean length of addiction at each age if the older group's regression equation ($y = 11.58 - 0.107x$) were to be applied to the addicts commencing drug use at each age.

It will be noticed that there is an extraordinary symmetry in the progression. The 32-year-old group has 76 percent of the under-30 proportions, the 34-year-old group has 50 percent and the 36-year-old group has 25 percent of the younger group. Although the group from 32 to 36 did not seem to cease drug use with the predictable regularity of the other ages, it appears to be similar to them if we assume a symmetrically varying proportion of each of the two established age groups at each step in the continuum. The relative importance of the two age groups changes as the addict between 32 and 36 grows older, which is not surprising. As his age increases, the salience and importance of the older group increases, and vice versa. Even the intermediate group thus appears to be understandable in the light of the existence of the two separate but analogous age groups in this population of addicts who ceased taking drugs.

The length of a narcotic user's addiction will be between one-eighth and one-ninth of a year less for each year that the onset of his addiction is delayed. This relationship, and its implications of maturing out, appear to apply to almost two-thirds of addicts. This straight-line regression relationship does not apply, of course, to the relatively small number of addicts who continue narcotics use for over fifteen years. Why is there such a precise consistent decline in the average length of addiction, as the age at onset increases? These average lengths might have remained constant, or might have increased. The decrease in the number of years, and its remarkable consistency, suggest the possibility of a pervasive relationship that involves some causal force that counters the development of the addiction.

Why does the curve representing the older group, even though this group is smaller in number, so closely parallel that of the younger group? There is no reason why it should. It may be that both groups are responding to the same kind of life pressures, but that accessibility of narcotics and contact with peers may lead the younger group to start drug use earlier. The older users may have been able to cope with their symptoms without using drugs up to a certain point in their lives. An addiction that begins at age 19 is likely to serve different purposes for the addict than an addiction that begins at age 38. The 19-year-old is likely to be responding to the decisions that he is asked to make. The older man's decision to use narcotics, on the other hand, may be a response to the realization that decisions such as those about jobs, family and home will be less and less possible. The realization that decisions of significance to the life situation are decreasingly likely may lead some persons in their late thirties and early forties to begin to use narcotic drugs on whatever level such a decision may be made.

It is a reasonable assumption that the persons who begin drug use at different ages do so for different reasons, because the urgency of the drives that may have led to the beginning of drug use varies with a person's place on the life cycle. Another way of saying this is that the co-efficient which expresses a person's predilection for addiction is a function of age. This coefficient takes a track through time. The earlier addiction starts, the longer it lasts. This suggests that a person who has yielded relatively early in life to addiction has less resistance than someone who starts later. The user who begins with drugs relatively later in life has withstood yielding to drug use for a long enough period of time to manifest the kind of resilience that shows itself in a shorter period of drug use. Resistiveness to drug use in the earlier age groups is all the more impressive a sign of the ability to defer gratifications because drugs are more available to young people, who are more likely to be in contact with drug-using peers. Their turning away from the anchorage provided by narcotics is a clue to their possession of resources for coping with their life space.

It is important to remember that the addicts in this sample began their drug use at different times, although the majority probably began as contributors to the localized "epidemics" which began in 1946. The year or decade or era in which a person begins narcotics use may be a major contributor to his having done so, because it contributes to the kind of socialization process that occurs. Such dimensions doubtless contribute to the age at which narcotics use begins. The addicts commencing drug use in the 1930s, for example, were perhaps ten years older on the average than those beginning drug use in the 1950s.

Strong evidence for the operation of some kind of inherent mechanism in the life cycle of addiction is provided by the extraordinary similarity between the two regression lines, and their having essentially the same slope. It is almost as if a constant is added to the regression line for the younger group to make the regression line for the older group.

While we recognize that opiates may serve varying functions for their users, and that it is difficult to generalize about a phenomenon as complex as narcotics addiction, it should not be surprising that there is a certain larger regularity in the pattern of commencement and cessation of drug use. A number of authorities have suggested that opiate addiction meets certain underlying needs and follows a unique cycle of its own, almost independent of the personalities of its users. It would seem possible that one parameter like length of addiction adequately explains much drug addiction. This one parameter may be the end product of an interaction or combination of biological forces, personality, propinquity to drugs, environmental pressures, subcultures, social conditions, differential socialization within a delinquent subculture, the alertness of enforcement agencies, comparative life expectancy and morbidity, and similar factors.

The data that are the basis for this study are not perfect, although they represent the best information available. The five-year criterion of nonuse of drugs, an addict becoming a medical addict, or death may contribute to possible imperfections in the data. The criterion of five years of drug inactivity before assuming that a person may be deemed not to be a user is, of course, relatively conservative. Since these former users had no official record of narcotics use after 1955, many doubtless ceased drug use long before 1960. The actual age at which these former users cease drug use may thus be less than the age at which they are officially credited with doing so. An appreciable number of addicts disappear from the active list by acquiring some pathology which requires narcotic medication, so that they are classified as medically addicted persons. Some may die from "hot shots," overdoses, or conditions related to addiction. Others may cease drug use as a result of their regression to another or deeper level of symptomatology.

Another possible imperfection in our data is that cessation of drug use is, for statistical purposes, treated as a phenomenon. One possible implication of such an approach is that addicts are assumed to stop using drugs as of a specific date. The likelihood is, of course, that many addicts refrain from drug use for a brief period of time, return to drug use, refrain for a longer period of time, return to drugs, refrain for yet a longer period of time, and so forth. It may be a relatively long-term process, which proceeds by an accretion of insight and experience. There are some addicts who vow not to use narcotics on a birthday or anniversary or other occasion that has special symbolic meaning for them, and can sustain such a decision. They would seem, however, to be in a minority. It is therefore often difficult to determine precisely when a given narcotics user ceased using drugs.

We have previously noted that approximately two-thirds of addicts seem to mature out, and that this study is based on a sample of all of the addicts who had ceased using drugs as of one year. Even in this sample, however, there is a small group that has been using narcotics for over fifteen years that seems to be different from the others. The average addict who matures out, we may speculate, seems to have contact with narcotics for a range of time the upper limit of which is fifteen years. This suggests that people who use narcotic drugs for a very long time differ from those who use them for an intermediate period, and that the latter differ from short-term users. We refer to each of these three groups as "addicts," although the likelihood is that there ought to be different designations for each group, and for the different degrees of craving for and dependence on narcotics that exist.

THE CYCLE OF ABSTINENCE AND RELAPSE AMONG HEROIN ADDICTS

MARSH B. RAY

Those who study persons addicted to opium and its derivatives are confronted by the following paradox: a cure from physiological dependence on opiates may be secured within a relatively short period, and carefully controlled studies indicate that use of these drugs does not cause psychosis, organic intellectual deterioration, or any permanent impairment of intellectual function.[1] But, despite these facts, addicts display a high rate of recidivism. On the other hand, while the rate of recidivism is high, addicts continually and repeatedly seek cure. It is difficult to obtain definitive data concerning the number of cures the addict takes, but various studies of institutional admissions indicate that it is relatively high,[2] and there are many attempts at home cure that go unrecorded.

This paper reports on a study[3] of abstinence and relapse in which attention is focussed on the way the addict or abstainer orders and makes meaningful the objects of his experience, including himself as an object,[4] during the critical periods of cure and of relapse and the related sense of identity or of social isolation the addict feels as he interacts with significant others. It is especially concerned with describing and analyzing the characteristic ways the addict or abstainer defines the social situations he encounters during these periods and responds to the status dilemmas he experiences in them.

SECONDARY STATUS CHARACTERISTICS OF ADDICTS

The social world of addiction contains a loose system of organizational and cultural elements, including a special language or argot, certain artifacts, a commodity market and pricing system, a system of stratification, and ethical codes. The addict's commitment to these values gives him a status and an identity.[5] In addition to these direct links to the world of addiction, becoming an addict means that one assumes a number of secondary status characteristics in accordance with the definitions the society has of this activity.[6] Some of these are set forth in federal and local laws and statutes, others are defined by the stereotypic thinking of members of the larger society about the causes and consequences of drug use.

The addict's incarceration in correctional institutions has specific meanings which he finds reflected in the attitudes adopted toward him by members of non-addict society and by his fellow addicts. Additionally, as his habit grows and the demands for drugs get beyond any legitimate means of supply, his own activities in satisfying

Reprinted as abridged with permission of author and publisher from *Social Problems* 9 (Fall, 1961), pp. 132–40. The author wishes to thank Howard S. Becker for his interest, encouragement, and valuable suggestions as he worked out the ideas for this paper. In addition, thanks are also due G. Lewis Penner, Executive Director of the Juvenile Protective Association of Chicago who made office space available for some of the interviews.

[1] See as examples: C. Knight Aldrich, "The Relationship of the Concept Formation Test to Drug Addiction and Intelligence," *Journal of Nervous and Mental Diseases* 100 (July, 1944), pp. 30–34; Margaret E. Hall, "Mental and Physical Efficiency of Women Drug Addicts," *Journal of Abnormal and Social Psychology* 33 (July, 1938), pp. 332–45; A. Z. Pfeffer and Dorothy Cleck, "Chronic Psychoses and Addiction to Morphine," *Archives of Neurology and Psychiatry* 56 (December, 1946), pp. 665–72.

[2] Michael J. Pescor, *A Statistical Analysis of the Clinical Records of Hospitalized Drug Addicts,* Supplement No. 143 to the Public Health Reports, United States Public Health Service (Washington: Government Printing Office, 1943), p. 24; Victor H. Vogel, "Treatment of the Narcotic Addict by the U. S. Public Health Service," *Federal Probation* 12 (June, 1948), pp. 45–50.

[3] The basic data consisted of case histories collected in repeated depth interviews with 17 addicts and abstainers over a two-year period. During this time several of the active addicts became abstainers and vice versa. Additional material was gathered while the author worked for a year as a social worker in a rehabilitation program for addicts.

[4] "Object" is employed here in the sense intended by George Herbert Mead in his development of the concept in *Mind, Self and Society* (Chicago: University of Chicago Press, 1934), Part III, pp. 135–226. Two earlier studies have applied this kind of thinking in studying the behavior of addicts; see: L. Guy Brown, "The Sociological Implications of Drug Addiction," *Journal of Educational Sociology* 4 (February, 1931), pp. 358–69, and Alfred R. Lindesmith, *Opiate Addiction* (Bloomington, Ind.: Principia Press, 1947).

[5] Marsh B. Ray, "Cure and Relapse Among Heroin Addicts" (unpublished M.A. thesis, Department of Sociology, University of Chicago, 1958).

[6] For a general discussion of the important role that auxiliary status characteristics play in social situations, see Everett C. Hughes, "Dilemmas and Contradictions in Status," *American Journal of Sociology* 50 (March, 1945), pp. 253–59.

his increased craving give him direct experiential evidence of the criminal aspects of self. These meanings of self as a criminal become internalized as he begins to apply criminal argot to his activities and institutional experiences. Thus shoplifting becomes "boosting," the correctional settings become "joints," and the guards in such institutions become "screws."

The popular notion that the addict is somehow psychologically inadequate is supported by many authorities in the field. In addition, support and definition are supplied by the very nature of the institution in which drug addicts are usually treated and have a large part of their experience since even the names of these institutions fix this definition of addiction. For example, one of the out-patient clinics for the treatment of addicts in Chicago was located at Illinois Neuropsychiatric Institute, and the connotations of Bellevue Hospital in New York City, another treatment center for addicts, are socially well established. Then, too, the composition of the staff in treatment centers contributes substantially to the image of the addict as mentally ill, for the personnel are primarily psychiatrists, psychologists, and psychiatric social workers. How such a definition of self was brought forcefully home to one addict is illustrated in the following quotation:

> When I got down to the hospital, I was interviewed by different doctors and one of them told me, "You now have one mark against you as crazy for having been down here." I hadn't known it was a crazy house. You know regular people [non-addicts] think this too.

Finally, as the addict's habit grows and almost all of his thoughts and efforts are directed toward supplying himself with drugs, he becomes careless about his personal appearance and cleanliness. Consequently non-addicts think of him as a "bum" and, because he persists in his use of drugs, conclude that he lacks "will power," is perhaps "degenerate," and is likely to contaminate others.

The addict is aware that he is judged in terms of these various secondary social definitions, and while he may attempt to reject them, it is difficult if not impossible to do so when much of his interpersonal and institutional experience serves to ratify these definitions. They assume importance because they are the medium of exchange in social transactions with the addict and non-addict world in which the addict identifies himself as an object and judges himself in relation to addict and non-addict values. Such experiences are socially disjunctive and become the basis for motivated acts.

THE INCEPTION OF CURE

An episode of cure begins in the private thoughts of the addict rather than in his overt behavior. These deliberations develop as a result of experience in specific situations of interaction with important others that cause the addict to experience social stress, to develop some feeling of alienation from or dissatisfaction with his present identity, and to call it into question and examine it in all of its implications and ramifications. In these situations the addict engages in private self-debate in which he juxtaposes the values and social relationships which have become immediate and concrete through his addiction and those that are sometimes only half remembered or only imperfectly perceived.

> I think that my mother knew that I was addicted because she had heard rumors around the neighborhood. Around that time [when he first began to think about cure] she had been telling me that I looked like a "bum," and that my hair was down the back of my neck and that I was dirty. I had known this too but had shoved it down in the back of my mind somewhere. She used to tell me that to look like this wasn't at all like me. I always wanted to look presentable and her saying this really hurt. At that time I was going to [college] and I wanted to look my best. I always looked at myself as the clever one—the "mystery man"—outwitting the "dolts." I always thought that no one knew, that when I was in my room they thought I was studying my books when actually I wasn't studying at all.

> After mother said those things I did a lot of thinking. I often used to sit around my room and think about it and even look at myself in the mirror and I could see that it was true. What is it called . . .? When you take yourself out of a situation and look at yourself . . .? "Self-appraisal" . . . I guess that's it. Well I did this about my appearance and about the deterioration of my character. I didn't like it because I didn't want anything to be master over me because this was contrary to my character. I used to sit and look

at that infinitesimal bit of powder. I felt it changed my personality somehow.

I used to try staying in but I would get sick. But because I had money I couldn't maintain it [withstand the demands of the withdrawal sickness] and when the pain got unbearable, at least to me it was unbearable, I would go out again. I wanted to be independent of it. I knew then that if I continued I would have to resort to stealing to maintain my habit and this I couldn't tolerate because it was contrary to my character. The others were robbing and stealing but I couldn't be a part of that. I first talked with my uncle about it because my mother was alive then and I thought she would crack up and maybe not understand the problem. I didn't want to be reprimanded, I knew I'd done wrong. I had been through a lot and felt I wanted to be rid of the thing. He was very understanding about it and didn't criticize me. He just talked with me about going to the hospital and said he thought this would be the best way to do it.

In the above example, the meanings of the complex of secondary status characteristics of the addict identity when used as self-referents in bringing this identity into question are shown in dramatic fashion.

But the social psychological prerequisites to the inception of an episode of abstinence need not precede physical withdrawal of the drug. It is frequently the case that, following the enforced withdrawal that begins a period of confinement in a correctional institution or hospital, the addict engages in self-debate in which the self in all of its ramifications emerges as an object and is brought under scrutiny. Such institutional situations constrain the addict's perspectives about himself and have a dual character. On the one hand, they serve to ratify a secondary status characteristic, while on the other, as addicts interact with older inmates of jails and hospitals they provide daily concrete models of what life may be like in later years as a consequence of continued use of drugs.

On occasion, however, the addict group itself, rather than non-addict society, provides the socially disjunctive experience that motivates the addict to abstain, although the non-addict world and its values are still the reference point. An addict who had been addicted for several years and had had several involuntary cures in correctional institutions describes such an experience as follows:

When I first started using we were all buddies, but later we started "burning" each other. One guy would say, "Well, I'll go 'cop' " [buy drugs]. Then he'd take the "bread" [money] and he'd never come back. I kicked one time because of that. I didn't have no more money and I got disgusted. First I started to swear him up and down but then my inner conscience got started and I said maybe he got "busted" [arrested]. Then I said, "Aw, to hell with him and to hell with all junkies—they're all the same." So I went home and I tried to read a couple of comic books to keep my mind off it. I was very sick but after a couple of days I kicked.

While the above situation may not be typical, it illustrates the same process to be observed in the other example—a disruption of the social ordering of experience that has become familiar, a calling into question of the addict identity, and the rejection of this identity and the values associated with it. The more typical situations that evoke such conduct would appear to involve a non-addict or some concrete aspect of the non-addict world as the catalytic agent.

THE ADDICT SELF IN TRANSITION

The addict who has successfully completed withdrawal is no longer faced with the need to take drugs in order to avert the disaster of withdrawal sickness, and now enters a period which might best be characterized as a "running struggle" with his problems of social identity. He could not have taken such a drastic step had he not developed some series of expectations concerning the nature of his future relationships with social others. His anticipations concerning these situations may or may not be realistic; what matters is that he has them and that the imagery he holds regarding himself and his potentialities is a strong motivating force in his continued abstinence. Above all, he appears to desire ratification by significant others of his newly developing identity, and in his interactions during an episode of abstinence he expects to secure it.

In the early phases of an episode of cure, the abstainer manifests considerable ambivalence about where he stands in addict and non-addict groups, and in discussions of addiction and addicts, he may indicate his ambivalence through his alternate use of the pronouns "we" and "they" and thus his alternate membership in addict and non-addict society. He may also indicate his ambivalence through other nuances of language and choice of words. Later, during a successful episode of abstinence, the ex-addict indicates his non-membership in the addict group through categorizations that place addicts clearly in the third person, and he places his own addiction and matters pertaining to it in the past tense. For example, he is likely to preface a remark with the phrase "When I was an addict. . . ." But of equal or greater importance is the fact that the ex-addict who is successful in remaining abstinent relates to new groups of people, participates in their experience, and to some extent begins to evaluate the conduct of his former associates (and perhaps his own when he was an addict) in terms of the values of the new group.

I see the guys around now quite often and sometimes we talk for a while but I don't feel that I am anything like them anymore and I always leave before they "make up" [take drugs]. I tell them, "You know what you are doing but if you keep on you'll just go to jail like I did." I don't feel that they are wrong to be using but just that I'm luckier than they are because I have goals. It's funny, I used to call them "squares" for not using and now they call me "square" for not using. They think that they are "hip" and they are always talking about the old days. That makes me realize how far I've come. But it makes me want to keep away from them, too, because they always use the same old vocabulary —talking about "squares" and being "hip."

Thus, while some abstainers do not deny the right of others to use drugs if they choose, they clearly indicate that addiction is no longer a personally meaningful area of social experience for them. In the above illustration the abstainer is using this experience as something of a "sounding board" for his newly developed identity. Of particular note is the considerable loss of meaning in the old symbols through which he previously ordered his experience and his concern with one of the inevitable consequences of drug use. This is a common experience for those who have maintained abstinence for any length of time.

During the later stages of the formation of an abstainer identity, the ex-addict begins to perceive a difference in his relations with significant others, particularly with members of his family. Undoubtedly their attitudes, in turn, undergo modification and change as a result of his apparent continued abstinence, and they arrive at this judgment by observing his cleanliness and attention to personal neatness, his steady employment, and his resubscription to other values of non-addict society. The ex-addict is very much aware of these attitudinal differences and uses them further to bolster his conception of himself as an abstainer.

Lots of times I don't even feel like I ever took dope. I feel released not to be dependent on it. I think how nice it is to be natural without having to rely on dope to make me feel good. See, when I was a "junkie" I lost a lot of respect. My father wouldn't talk to me and I was filthy. I have to build up that respect again. I do a lot of things with my family now and my father talks to me again. It's like at parties that my relatives give, now they are always running up to me and giving me a drink and showing me a lot of attention. Before they wouldn't even talk to me. See, I used to feel lonely because my life was dependent on stuff and I felt different from regular people. See, "junkies" and regular people are two different things. I used to feel that I was out of place with my relatives when I was on junk. I didn't want to walk with them on the street and do things with them. Now I do things with them all the time like go to the show and joke with them and I go to church with my uncle. I just kept saying to myself that "junkies" are not my people. My relatives don't say things behind my back now and I am gaining their respect slow but sure.

In this illustration there may be observed a budding sense of social insight characteristic of abstainers in this period of their development. Another characteristic feature is the recognition that subscription to non-addict values must be grounded in action—in playing the role of non-addict in participation with non-addicts and thus sharing in their values and perspectives.

THE PROCESS OF RELAPSE

The tendency toward relapse develops out of the meanings of the abstainer's experience in social situations when he develops an image of himself as socially different from non-addicts, and relapse occurs when he redefines himself as an addict. When his social expectations and the expectations of others with whom he interacts are not met, social stress develops and he is required to reexamine the meaningfulness of his experience in non-addict society and in so doing question his identity as an abstainer. This type of experience promotes a mental realignment with addict values and standards and may be observed in the abstainer's thoughts about himself in covert social situations, in his direct interpersonal relations with active addicts, and in his experience with representatives of non-addict society. It is in these various settings that his developing sense of self as an abstainer is put to the test.

Experiences with Other Addicts that Promote Relapse

Readdiction most frequently occurs during the period immediately following the physical withdrawal of the drug—the period described earlier as a time of "running struggle" with identity problems for the ex-addict. It is at this point, when the old values and old meanings he experienced as an addict are still immediate and the new ordering of his experience without narcotics is not well established, that the ex-addict seems most vulnerable to relapse. Sometimes the experiences that provoke the questioning of identity that precedes relapse occur within the confines of the very institution where the addict has gone to seek cure. The social expectations of other addicts in the hospital are of vital importance in creating an atmosphere in which identification with the values of non-addict society is difficult to maintain.

[The last time we talked you said that you would like to tell me about your experiences in the hospital. What were they like?]

Well, during the first time I was at the hospital most of the fellows seemed to hate [to give] the "square" impression, not hate it exactly but refuse to admit [to] it. My own feelings were that everyone should have been a little different in expressing themselves that I would like to accept the extreme opposite. But I felt that I would have disagreements about this with the fellow inmates. They thought I was a very queer or peculiar person that constantly showed disagreement about the problem as they saw it. I never did reach an understanding with them about the problem.

But addicts do not always relapse on first contact with members of the old group. In fact, there is nothing to indicate that addicts relapse only as a result of association. Instead, contacts may go on for some time during which the ex-addict carries on much private self-debate, feeling at one point that he is socially closer to addicts and at another that his real interest lies in future new identities on which he has decided. Typically he may also call to mind the reason he undertook cure in the first place and question the rationality of relapsing. An interesting example of the dilemma and ambivalence experienced under these circumstances and the partial acceding to social pressures from the addict group by applying the definitions of that group to one's own conduct are the experiences of another addict.

[He had entered the hospital "with the key" and after completing withdrawal he stayed at the hospital for three weeks before voluntarily signing out, although the required period of treatment for a medical discharge at the time was four and one-half months.]

This one kid who was a friend of mine came to me one night and said, "Let's get out of here." So I went and checked out too. Then I got to thinking, "I don't want to go home yet—I'm still sick —and what did I come down here for anyway." So I went up and got my papers back from the officer and tore them up. Then I found this kid and told him that I was staying and he said, "Oh we knew you weren't going to do it—we knew you'd chicken out." Then I went back and put my papers through again. I felt they were trying to "put me down."

When we got out I could have had a shot right away because one of these guys when we got to town said he knew a croaker who would fix us up, but I didn't go with them. I didn't care what they thought because I got to figuring that I had went this far and I might as well stay off.

When I got home I stayed off for two months but my mother was hollering at me all the time and there was this one family in the neighborhood that was always "chopping me up." I wanted to tell this woman off because she talked all right to my face but behind my back she said things like she was afraid I would turn her son on because I was hanging around with him. She would tell these things to my mother. I never turned anybody on! She didn't know that but I wanted to tell her. Finally I just got disgusted because nobody wanted to believe me and I went back on.

The experiences of this addict provide an interesting denial of the notion that addicts relapse because of association *per se* and support the thesis that relapse is a function of the kind of object ex-addicts make of themselves in the situations they face.

Relations with Non-addicts as a Prelude to Relapse

While the ex-addict's interaction with addict groups is often a source of experiences which cause him to question the value to him of an abstainer identity, experiences with non-addict groups also play a vital role. In most instances the addict has established a status for himself in the eyes of non-addicts who may be acquainted with his case—members of his family, social workers, law enforcement officers, physicians and so forth. Through gestures, vocal and otherwise, these non-addicts make indications to the ex-addict concerning his membership and right to participation in their group, for example, the right to be believed when he attempts to indicate to the non-addict world that he believes in and subscribes to its values. In his contacts with non-addicts, the former addict is particularly sensitive to their cues.

During the early phases of an episode of abstinence the abstainer enters various situations with quite definite expectations concerning how he should be defined and treated. He indicates his desire for ratification of his new status in many ways, and finds it socially difficult when he sees in the conduct of others toward him a reference to his old identity as an addict. He is not unaware of these doubts about his identity.

> My relatives were always saying things to me like "Have you really quit using that drug now?" and things like that. And I knew that they were doing a lot of talking behind my back because when I came around they would stop talking but I overheard them. It used to burn my ass.

On the other hand, the non-addicts with whom he has experience during this period have their own expectations concerning the abstainer's probable conduct. Based in part on the stereotypic thinking of non-addict society concerning addiction, in part on unfortunate previous experiences, they may exhibit some skepticism concerning the "cure" and express doubt about the abstainer's prognosis.[7]

THE SOCIAL PSYCHOLOGICAL MEANING OF RELAPSE

On an immediate concrete level, relapse requires that the individual reorient himself to the market conditions surrounding the sale of illicit drugs. He must reestablish his sources of supply and, if he has been abstinent for very long, he may have to learn about new fads and fashions in drug use. He may learn, for example, that Dolophine is more readily available than heroin at the moment of his return to drug use, that it requires less in the way of preparation, that it calls for such and such amount to safely secure a certain effect, what the effects will be, and so on.

But the ex-addict's reentrance into the social world of addiction has much deeper meanings. It places demands and restraints upon his interactions and the meaningfulness of his experience. It requires a recommitment to the norms of addiction and limits the degree to which he may relate to non-addict groups in terms of the latter's values and standards. It demands participation in the old ways of organizing conduct and experience and, as a consequence, the readoption of the secondary status characteristics of addiction. He again shows a lack of concern about his personal appearance and grooming. Illicit activities are again engaged in to get money for drugs, and as a result the possibility of more firmly establishing the criminal aspect of his identity becomes a reality.

The social consequence of these experiences and activities is the reestablishment of the sense of social isolation from the non-addict group and a recaptured sense of the meaningfulness of experience in the social world of addiction. It is through these familiar meanings and the reapplication of the symbolic meanings of the addict

---

[7] Family members may have been subjected to thefts by the addict, or other kinds of trickery, and they tend to be on their guard lest the experience be repeated. Interestingly, the matter of thefts of either money or small household objects (a radio or a clock) is often used by family members as an index as to whether "he's back on that stuff again" or not. His physical appearance is another gauge.

world to his own conduct that identity and status as an addict are reaffirmed. The ex-addict who relapses is thus likely to comment, "I feel like one of the guys again," or as Street has put it, "It was like coming home."[8]

While repeated relapse on the addict's part may more firmly convince him that "once a junkie, always a junkie" is no myth but instead a valid comment on his way of life, every relapse has within it the genesis of another attempt at cure. From his however brief or lengthy excursions into the world of non-addiction, the relapsed addict carries back with him an image of himself as one who has done the impossible—one who has actually experienced a period when it was unnecessary to take drugs to avoid the dreaded withdrawal sickness. But these are not his only recollections. He recalls, too, his identification of himself as an abstainer, no matter how tentatively or imperfectly this may have been accomplished. He thinks over his experiences in situations while he occupied the status of abstainer and speculates about the possible other outcomes of these situations had he acted differently.

[Originally from Chicago, he experienced the only voluntary period of abstinence in a long career of addiction while living with his wife in Kansas City, Missouri. After an argument with his wife, during which she reminded him of his previous addiction and its consequences for her, he left her and returned to Chicago, where he immediately relapsed. After three weeks he was using about $12 worth of morphine daily.] He reports on his thoughts at the time as follows:

Now and then I'm given to rational thinking or reasoning and somehow I had a premonition that should I remain in Chicago much longer, shoplifting and doing the various criminal acts I did to get money for drugs, plus the criminal act of just using the drug, I would soon be in jail or perhaps something worse, for in truth one's life is at stake each day when he uses drugs. I reflected on the life I had known in Kansas City with Rose in contrast to the one I had returned to. I didn't know what Rose thought had become of me. I thought that more than likely she was angry and thoroughly disgusted and glad that I was

gone. However, I wanted to return but first thought it best to call and see what her feelings were.

[At his wife's urging he returned to Kansas City and undertook a "cold turkey" cure in their home. He remained abstinent for a considerable period but subsequently relapsed again when he returned to Chicago.]

Reflections of the above kind provide the relapsed addict with a rich body of material for self-recrimination and he again evaluates his own conduct in terms of what he believes are the larger society's attitudes toward addicts and addiction. It is then that he may again speculate about his own potential for meaningful experiences and relationships in a non-addict world and thus set into motion a new attempt at cure.

SUMMARY

Addiction to narcotic drugs in our society commits the participant in this activity to a status and identity that has complex secondary characteristics. These develop through shared roles and common interpersonal and institutional experience, and as a consequence addicts develop perspectives about themselves and about non-addict values. They evaluate social situations, and in turn are evaluated by the other participants in these situations, in these terms, often with the result that the value of the addict's identity relative to the social world of addiction is brought into question. When this happens the identification of oneself as an addict, committed to the values and statuses of the addict group, is contrasted with new or remembered identities and relationships, resulting in a commitment to cure with its implications of intense physical suffering. In the period following physical withdrawal from heroin, the addict attempts to enact a new social reality which coincides with his desired self-image as an abstainer, and he seeks ratification of his new identity from others in the situations he faces.

But the abstainer's social expectations during a period when he is off drugs are frequently not gratified. Here again, socially disjunctive experiences bring about a questioning of the value of an abstainer identity and promote reflections in

---

[8] Leroy Street (pseudonym) and D. Loth, *I Was a Drug Addict*, Pyramid Books (New York: Random House, 1953), p. 71.

which addict and non-addict identities and relationships are compared. The abstainer's realignment of his values with those of the world of addiction results in the redefinition of self as an addict and has as a consequence the actions necessary to relapse. But it should be noted that the seeds of a new attempt at abstinence are sown, once addiction has been reestablished, in the self-recriminations engaged in upon remembrance of a successful period of abstinence.

CHAPTER NINE

MENTAL ILLNESS AND HOSPITALIZATION

Sometimes a person's actions are so bizarre and deviate so far from normal social intercourse that they create serious difficulties for others. When it is difficult for others to understand such behavior, they are apt to label the person as "crazy" or "insane." Mental illness is thus inferred from behavior. In this sense, lay opinion is similar to psychiatric diagnosis, which is also inferred from behavior.

Persons who are believed to be mentally ill are treated as deviants. In the past they have been accused of being witches, madmen, lunatics, and demons; they have been confined in jails, locked in dungeons, stowed away in "lunatic asylums," and executed. Although treated less harshly today, they are still placed in institutions and isolated from "normal" society, and their treatment in hospitals frequently falls short of standards recommended by the psychiatric profession.[1] Moreover, such persons may be stigmatized.[2]

Serious debate exists, however, as to whether persons who are labelled by society as mentally ill and who are in mental hospitals are really mentally ill or whether these persons are any sicker than those outside the hospital. Research by Scheff and others (see pp. 412–22 below) suggests that the societal reaction or labelling process rather than the psychiatric condition is the crucial factor in hospitalization. Yet in several critiques and evaluations of this research, Gove contends that most mental hospital patients are indeed mentally sick and in need of hospitalization.[3] In response, Scheff claims that Gove's "evaluations" contain serious errors and distortions. In addition, Scheff's review of relevant studies gives

---

[1] See Ivan Belknap, "The Mental Patient in the Hospital Ward System," pp. 422–32 below.

[2] See for example, Derek L. Phillips, "Rejection: A Possible Consequence of Seeking Help for Mental Disorder," *American Sociological Review* 28 (December, 1963), pp. 963–72. Gove and Fain attribute considerably less significance to the stigmatization process for former mental patients. See Walter Gove and Terry Fain, "The Stigma of Mental Hospitalization: An Attempt to Evaluate Its Consequences," *Archives of General Psychiatry* 28 (April, 1973), pp. 404–500.

[3] Gove's position is probably the most extreme of sociologists in this respect. See for example, Walter Gove, "Societal Reaction as an Explanation of Mental Illness: An Evaluation," *Amercian Sociological Review* 35 (October, 1970), pp. 873–84, and "Who Is Hospitalized? A Critical Review of Some Sociological Studies of Mental Illness," *Journal of Health and Social Behavior* 10 (December, 1970), pp. 294–303.

a great deal of support to the view that at least many, if not most, mental patients are in hospitals largely because they have been labelled as mentally ill and not primarily because they are mentally ill.[4]

The controversy is difficult to resolve because of problems associated with the criteria for determining who is mentally ill. These criteria are often so general and vague that almost anyone could be designated mentally ill. As Slovenko observes, almost anyone would be covered by one of the diagnostic categories in the American Psychiatric Association manual of mental disorders.[5] Legal definitions, in contrast to medical (that is, psychiatric) definitions, are no better since as a rule they are "appallingly vague, circular and tied to no observable referents."[6] This raises serious research problems. If the definition for mental illness is without clear, unambiguous behavioral criteria, it is difficult to know which and how many persons are mentally ill. Indeed, studies show wide variation in this regard. In 1966 there were about 600,000 adults in mental hospitals.[7] According to the United States census for 1970, there were about 116,000,000 persons 20 years of age and over.[8] On the basis of this information, slightly more than .5 percent of the adult population are in mental institutions. The actual rate of mental illness may be higher than this, since all persons who are mentally ill are not in institutions. (But there are also questions as to whether all persons in mental institutions are psychiatrically disturbed.[9]) Surveys of the population give varied estimates of the proportion reported to be mentally ill.[10] Some report a figure of 6 to 7 percent[11] whereas others report figures much higher than this. One well-known study of the Manhattan population reports that 23.4 percent of the population are psychiatrically impaired and that 81.5 percent have some form of psychiatric symptom.[12] A study of Nova Scotia reports that over 65 percent of the population exhibit symptoms of mental illness.[13] While these findings have not gone unchallenged,[14] the figures, taken together,

---

[4] A number of studies by sociologists and psychiatrists have shown this to be the case. For a review of the evidence, see Thomas J. Scheff, "The Labelling Theory of Mental Illness," *American Sociological Review* 39 (June, 1974), pp. 444–52.

[5] Ralph Slovenko, "Civil Commitment in Perspective," *Emory Journal of Public Law* 20 (1971), p. 14.

[6] Nolan E. Penn, Ronald Sindberg, and Allyn Robert, "The Dilemma of Involuntary Commitment: Suggestions for a Measurable Alternative," *Mental Hygiene* 53 (January, 1969), pp. 4–13.

[7] John A. Clauson, "Mental Disorders," in Robert K. Merton and Robert A. Nisbet, eds., *Contemporary Social Problems*, 2nd ed. (New York: Harcourt, Brace and World, 1966), p. 26.

[8] U. S. Bureau of the Census, 1970, *General Population Characteristics*, Final Report PC(1)-B1 United States Summary (Washington: U.S. Government Printing Office, 1972), p. 1–263.

[9] See for example, Scheff's paper below; pp. 412–22.

[10] See Bruce P. Dohrenwend, "Social Status and Psychological Disorder: An Issue of Substance and an Issue of Method," *American Sociological Review* 39 (June, 1974), pp. 444–52.

[11] See William F. Roth and Frank Luton, "The Mental Health Program in Tennessee: I. Description of the Original Study Program, II: Statistical Report of a Psychiatric Survey in a Rural County," *American Journal of Psychiatry* 99 (1943), pp. 662–75; and Paul Lemkau, Christopher Tietze, and Marcia Cooper, "Mental Hygiene Problems in an Urban District," *Mental Hygiene* 25 (1941), pp. 624–46.

[12] Leo Srole et al., *Mental Health in the Metropolis: the Midtown Manhattan Study* (New York: McGraw-Hill Book Company, 1962), p. 138.

[13] Dorothea Leighton et al., *The Character of Disorder* (New York: Basic Books, 1963).

[14] See Jerome G. Manis, Milton J. Brawer, Chester L. Hunt, and Leonard C. Kercher, "Validating a Mental Health Scale," *American Sociological Review* 28 (1963), pp. 108–16, and Frank E. Hartung, "Manhattan Madness: The Social Movement of Mental Illness," *Sociological Quarterly* 4 (1963), pp. 261–72. See also, Dohrenwend, "Social Status and Psychological Disorder."

reveal one demonstrable fact: estimates of the rate of mental illness in the population depend to a large degree on the instruments used in making the estimates; different instruments were used in each of the studies cited.

According to my definition of deviant behavior in Chapter One, it is far from clear that all (or most) forms of attributed mental illness should be considered as deviant behavior. This is certainly true if the majority, and especially if upwards of 80 percent, of a community exhibit psychiatric symptoms. In the eyes of some writers, we are a sick or insane society, a society in which the majority of us are sick and where those who are not sick are the deviants.[15] Consequently, behavior designated by mental health professionals as manifesting mental illness, except for the most severe forms of bizarre behavior (the existence of which has been *objectively* confirmed, that is, observed by different observers using clear and unambiguous procedures), may not be deviant behavior at all, at least from the perspective of the behavior patterns that are typical in society.

This, however, does not hold for persons who are institutionalized in mental hospitals. Regardless of their mental status, mental hospital patients are clearly deviant. Such persons are a minority in society,[16] and by virtue of being in the hospital, they deviate from the norms expected of most persons in society. Moreover, in contrast to the vague criteria for defining mental illness, the criteria as to who is and is not in a mental hospital are unambiguous. Also, one might argue that hospitalization is a far more significant phenomenon, to both the individual and the sociologist, than is mental illness. It is the hospitalized patient, rather than the outside person, whom professionals label as mentally ill and who is victimized, incarcerated, stigmatized, and unable to perform (by virtue of his institutionalization) his or her normal role in society. Hospitalization may be far more significant to both the individual and the functioning of society than mental illness itself, however that is defined. Consequently, selections in this chapter deal with the causes, processes, and consequences of mental hospitalization rather than with mental illness per se. Emphasis is on the sociological rather than the psychiatric factors that are associated with these three aspects of mental hospitalization.

A. ANTECEDENTS AND DETERMINANTS

Probably, the social factor that has shown the most consistent relationship to deviant behavior is social class. Many theories of deviant behavior are based on this relationship, and a wide range of empirical studies has

---

[15] The thesis or implication is found in the works of a number of psychoanalytic and psychiatric oriented social critics. For one example, see Eric Fromm, *The Sane Society* (New York: Holt, Rinehart and Co., 1955).

[16] Still it is estimated that one in twelve U. S. citizens will spend at least some time in a mental hospital during his lifetime. See Clausen, "Mental Disorders," p. 60.

reported the existence of the relationship. The same is true for studies of mental illness and mental hospitalization: studies consistently show that the rate of hospitalization is inversely related to social class. In the first selection, "Two Patterns in the Relationship Between Social Class and Mental Hospitalization," the editor investigates this relationship somewhat more precisely than other studies have done. He finds that there is indeed an inverse relationship between social class and hospitalization but that the relationship is curvilinear. While rates decrease continuously as one moves upward across class strata, there is a sudden, very large decrease from the lowest strata to the second-lowest. Therefore, there are two patterns in the relationship, and alternative causal interpretations that emphasize the role of social class must account for both patterns. A question that is not answered in this paper is whether the relationship occurs between social class and mental illness or only between social class and hospitalization.

In the second selection, "Individual Resources, Societal Reactions, and Hospital Commitment," the relationship between social class and *type* of hospitalization is investigated. A distinction is made between voluntary and involuntary hospitalization. The author argues that the distinction corresponds to differences in societal reaction—involuntary admission represents a more severe reaction than does voluntary admission. This is true because the former is accompanied by the trauma of a court trial and because the individual is identified with the stigma of being legally "insane" and is institutionalized against his will (hence, the term involuntary) by virtue of a court order. He must stay in the hospital until the hospital authorities are ready to release him (the length of stay is much longer for the involuntary patient; see pp. 449–52 below). Findings show that coercive institutionalization is most apt to occur among individuals whose social and economic resources are most limited, thus the more disadvantaged persons are apt to receive the more disadvantaged form of hospitalization. And in this sense, the level of one's social and economic resources is causally related to the type of hospital commitment.

TWO PATTERNS IN THE RELATIONSHIP BETWEEN SOCIAL CLASS AND MENTAL HOSPITALIZATION

WILLIAM A. RUSHING

Although most research on social class and mental hospitalization indicates that the two are negatively related,[1] questions about this relationship continue to be raised. For example, on the basis of studies using a five-class breakdown, which show that class V has a disproportionately high rate with little difference between the rates for the other four,[2] some have concluded that social class and mental illness are not *inversely* related.[3] This raises the question: is the relationship continuous or discrete, i.e., do rates of mental illness consistently increase from the highest class to the lowest, or are rates relatively uniform for all classes except for the lowest class, which has an appreciatively higher rate? A related issue is whether differences in socioeconomic status *within* class levels are related to mental hospitalization.

THE PROBLEM

The first issue may be illustrated with findings from two studies based on data for England and Wales. For classes I through V, Goldberg and Morrison[4] find the ratio of observed to expected schizophrenics to be 1.00, .48, .88, .95, and 2.31[5] respectively, while Morris[6] reports rates

per 100,000 males as 51, 57, 92, 103, and 229. The first distribution shows a high concentration of cases in class V; except for class II, the differences between the other classes are quite small and no general relationship among them can be discerned. Results suggest a discrete relationship more than a continuous relationship. In the second distribution the largest break is also between class IV and V, but rates consistently increase as class status decreases; this finding indicates a continuous relationship, with an unusually sharp increase at the lowest level.

A major difference in these two studies is sample size. The first is based on 353 first admissions aged 24–35 for 1956, the second on approximately 13,150 first admissions between 20 and 64 for 1949 through 1953.[7] If class placement of only nine cases in the first study is changed—six cases from class I to class II and 3 from class III to class IV—results would be .50, .61, .86, 1.00, and 2.31, which is almost identical to the findings in the second study. While these precise errors in class placement may not actually exist, the example does illustrate how even a few changes and errors can distort results when sample size is small. This suggests, therefore, that different results may be an artifact of sample size.

Studies of *incidence*[8] suggest that results *are* affected by sample size. Dunham's findings for psychotics are based on one-year samples of 40 and 42 patients from two subcommunities of

Reprinted with permission of the American Sociological Association, from *American Sociological Review* 34 (August, 1969), pp. 533–41, as abridged.

[1] Robert J. Kleiner and Seymour Parker, "Goal-Striving, Social Status and Mental Disorder: A Research Review," *American Sociological Review* 28 (April, 1963), pp. 189–203; Elliott G. Mishler and Norman A. Scotch, "Sociocultural Factors in the Epidemiology of Mental Disorders," *International Journal of Psychiatry* 1 (April, 1965), pp. 258–305; and Melvin L. Kohn, "Social Class and Schizophrenia: A Critical Review," *Journal of Psychiatric Research* 6 (Supplement 1, 1968), pp. 155–73.

[2] August B. Hollingshead and Frederick C. Redlich, *Social Class and Mental Illness* (New York: John Wiley, 1958).

[3] S. M. Miller and Elliott, "Social Class, Mental Illness, and American Psychiatry: An Expository Review," *Millbank Memorial Fund Quarterly* 37 (April, 1959), pp. 174–99, and H. Warren Dunham, *Community and Schizophrenia* (Detroit: Wayne State University Press, 1965), p. 178.

[4] E. M. Goldberg and S. L. Morrison, "Schizophrenia and Social Class," *British Journal of Psychiatry* 109 (1963), pp. 785–802.

[5] These rates are the author's computations based on data presented by Goldberg and Morrison.

[6] J. N. Morris, "Health and Social Class" (address given to the British Sociological Association, January 24, 1959), *Lancet* 1 (February 7, 1959), pp. 303–5.

[7] The second figure is an estimate based on the rates given by Morris, and the 1950 population in each of the five social classes used in the British Census. Source of population data is General Registrar's Office, *Census of 1951. England and Wales. Occupational Titles* (London: Her Majesty's Stationery Office, 1958), Table 17, p. 148.

[8] Studies of prevalence are not included in this review. Prominent among these are studies by Benjamin Pasamanick, Dean W. Roberts, Paul W. Lemkau, and Dean B. Krueger, "A Survey of Mental Disease in an Urban Population: Prevalence by Race and Income," in Benjamin Pasamanick, ed., *Epidemiology of Mental Disorder* (Washington, D.C.: American Association for the Advancement of Science, 1959); Leo Srole, Thomas S. Langner, Stanley T. Michael, in K. Opler, and Thomas A. C. Rennie, *Mental Health in the Metropolis* (New York: McGraw-Hill, 1962); and Dorothea C. Leighton, John S. Harding, David B. Macklin, Allister M. MacMillan, and Alexander H. Leighton, *The Character of Danger: Psychiatric Symptoms in Selected Communities* (New York: Basic Books, 1963).

Detroit, and Hollingshead and Redlich's[9] findings covering a six-month period for New Haven are based on approximately 100 cases;[10] both studies report a discrete relationship. However, Clausen and Kohn[11] fail to find a relationship of any kind for 59 schizophrenics covering a twelve-year period for Hagerstown, Maryland.[12] On the other hand, studies with much larger samples reveal a relationship more consistent with the findings of Morris. These studies include 12,186 Chicago males, twelve-year period;[13] 10,633 New York State males, three-year period;[14] 6,683 Ohio males, four and one half year-period;[15] 3,943 New York males, six-year period;[16] 1,192 Ohio males, one-year period;[17] and 279 males from the Buffalo, New York area, three-year period.[18] These studies suggest a continuous relationship, but with the greatest increase at the lowest class level.[19] Thus, both a continuous and a discrete pattern are indicated.

A related problem concerns variation *within* social classes. All studies have been concerned with the difference *between* class strata. However, the possibility of a continuous trend suggests that socioeconomic differences within class strata may be related to differences in hospitalization.

The objective of this paper is to show, somewhat more clearly than previous studies, the form of the relationship between social class and hospitalized mental illness. Data are based on 4,650 male patients, ages 21–64, who had been admitted to and discharged from state hospitals in Washington between 1954 and 1965. The relatively large number of cases covering an extended time interval makes generalizations about class status and mental illness statistically more reliable than those of most other studies. In addition, since the relationship between socioeconomic differences and mental hospitalization *within* strata is investigated, the analysis will be more refined than in other studies.

DATA AND PROCEDURE

Data

Occupational data for all male first admissions, ages 21–64, between December 31, 1954 and April 31, 1965 were derived from patient records in the three state hospitals in Washington. Since data are limited to hospitalized patients, no conclusions can be made about "true" incidence; strictly speaking, reference is to mental hospitalization rather than mental illness. Data are also limited in that private hospital patients are excluded, as are patients in one Veteran Administration (VA) hospital.[20] Nevertheless, for the period of study, the three state hospitals had more than 87 percent of all psychiatric hospital beds in the state, received 76 percent of all admissions, and, on the basis of patient census figures, they had about 87 percent of all hospital patients at a given time.[21] Also, it is probable that the occupational distribution of VA patients

[9] Hollingshead and Redlich, *Social Class and Mental Illness*.

[10] Total number of psychotics included in Hollingshead and Redlich's study is not given; "100" is an estimate based on the rate and the total population which they present.

[11] John A. Clausen and Melvin L. Kohn, "Relation of Schizophrenia to the Social Structure of a Small City," in Benjamin Pasamanick, ed., *Epidemiology of Mental Disorder*.

[12] Clausen and Kohn, "Relation of Schizophrenia to the Small City," suggest that the correlation between socioeconomic status and mental illness (schizophrenia) may be higher in large cities than in medium-sized cities. Their explanation is in terms of differences in the social-psychological significance of social status in communities of different size as well as migration differentials. The hypothesis advanced in this paper is not inconsistent with findings indicating a difference by community size, but *sample* size, rather than the social-psychological and social system dynamices of community size, is postulated as a crucial factor.

[13] Robert E. Clark, "Psychosis, Income, and Occupational Prestige," *American Journal of Sociology* 54 (March, 1949), pp. 433–40.

[14] Dorothy Swaine Thomas and Ben Z. Locke, "Marital Status, Education, and Occupational Differentials in Mental Disease," *Millbank Memorial Fund Quarterly* 41 (1963), pp. 145–60.

[15] *Ibid.*, p. 148.

[16] Robert H. Hardt and Sherwin J. Feinhandler, "Social Class and Mental Hospitalization Prognosis," *American Sociological Review* 24 (December, 1959), pp. 815–21.

[17] Robert M. Frumkin, "Occupation and Mental Disorders," in Arnold M. Rose, ed., *Mental Health and Mental Disorder: A Sociological Approach* (New York: W. W. Norton and Company, 1955), pp. 135–60.

[18] Rema Lapouse, Mary A. Monk, and Melton Terris, "The Drift Hypothesis in Socio-Economic Differentials in Schizophrenia," *American Journal of Public Health* 46 (August, 1956), pp. 978–86.

[19] This is not to say that sample size is the only factor, since Jaco finds for Texas that rates are highest for the high status professional group. E. Gartley Jaco, *The Social Epidemiology of Mental Disorders* (New York: Russell Sage Foundation, 1960).

[20] Excluded also are patients admitted to psychiatric wards in general hospitals in the state. It is not possible to estimate the number involved. In addition, data are limited to patients who were both admitted and discharged during a 10-year period.

[21] These estimates are based on figures presented in the "Guide" issues of the *Journal of the American Hospital Association* for the years 1954–1965.

is not unlike that of male patients in state hospitals. If this is granted, only about 10 percent of all admissions have an occupational distribution that could be significantly different from that of the admissions to state hospitals. This is a maximum figure because an unknown number of private hospital admissions are also admitted to state hospitals. Admissions to private hospitals have an average stay of only 44 days in comparison to 159 and 157 for the state and VA hospitals respectively;[22] this suggests that a high proportion of the more severe cases of hospitalized illness are represented. Inasmuch as the Detroit study shows that practically all patients of private practitioners also spent time as inpatients,[23] most severe cases of all treated persons may be represented. Also, the Louisville study finds virtually identical class distributions for state hospital schizophrenics and schizophrenics referred to a treatment center by private physicians, welfare, and other social agencies.[24] Finally, studies show that the inclusion of private hospital patients[25] does not eliminate a negative relationship between social class and treated mental illness. Thus, the class bias in the sample of state hospital patients is probably not extreme, if it exists at all.[26]

Procedure

Patients' occupations were taken from their records and, where possible, classified in one of the detailed census occupational categories (e.g., accountant, barber, carpenter, stevedore, etc.). In all there are approximately 500 such occupations in the census categories. Duncan has developed a socioeconomic index score for each of the

occupations in accordance with transformed NORC values.[27] Socioeconomic scores assigned to patients in this study are based on the values as derived by Duncan.

In most instances the appropriate occupational category of patients was clear, as a great deal of rather detailed and specific occupational information was entered in patients' records beginning in January, 1958. Patients were classified in the job held during most of their work life. (Patients with more than one job, or a history of many jobs, were classified in the major job held at the time of commitment provided they had held the major job for at least three years. Unemployed patients were classified in their last job if it had been held for three years.) This procedure probably reduces the influence of "drift." Recent occupational changes might be due to "drift," and hence lead to high rates for low status occupations. Consequently, our procedure may impose a somewhat more stringent test on the hypothesis of a negative relationship than would be the case if patients were classified in their current occupation. In all, 4,048 cases (approximately 87 percent) could be classified in one of the detail categories.

Reliability. Partial checks revealed that percentages of agreement between three coders in classifying patients were 81, 84, and 88. Occupational information on most patients was sufficiently adequate, therefore, to permit their classification. [This problem has been discussed by Gross[28] and Olson.[29]] One reason is that patients could often be placed in one of the residual categories ("other" and "not elsewhere classified" categories) when information was not adequate to place them in a more specific category. As will be seen below, however, a large percentage could be classified in specific categories.

Coders were also able to classify patients *consistently.* Agreement between coders on the exact category varied only from 78 to 87 percent and

---

[22] These figures are based on the average number of patients per bed for the different types of hospitals.

[23] Dunham, *Community and Schizophrenia,* p. 262.

[24] Benjamin Pasamanick, Frank R. Scarpitti, and Simon Dinitz, *Schizophrenia in the Community: An Experimental Study in the Prevention of Hospitalization* (New York: Appleton-Century-Crofts, 1967).

[25] Hollingshead and Redlich, *Social Class and Mental Illness,* and Dunham, *Community and Schizophrenia.*

[26] Patients were not classified by diagnosis. Evidence that psychiatric diagnoses are not very reliable is well known and need not be cited here. The author's impressions based on observations of diagnostic conferences in psychiatric settings in several states are consistent with the published evidence. Also, staff members from two of the hospitals advised that many of the diagnoses in patient records are not very meaningful. For these reasons no effort was made to obtain diagnostic information.

---

[27] Otis Dudley Duncan, "A Socio-Economic Index for All Occupations," and "Properties and Characteristics of the Socio-Economic Index," in Albert J. Reiss, Jr., *Occupation and Social Status* (New York: The Free Press of Glencoe, 1961).

[28] Edward Gross, "The Occupational Variable as a Research Category," *American Sociological Review* 24 (October, 1959), pp. 640–49.

[29] Philip Olson, "On Occupational Classification," *American Sociological Review* 25 (April, 1960), pp. 267–69.

between one coder at different points in time by only 82 percent and 88 percent. Most disagreements involved no more than a few points in socioeconomic score. Although systematic analysis was not made of differences by major categories, it was clear that titles in the professional, craftsmen, and service categories presented fewer coding difficulties than titles in other categories. These occupational titles are generally more specific; the jobs often entail a period of training; and a number of them require license and/or union membership, all of which facilitate the determination of occupational identity.[30]

Coders had difficulty making certain distinctions called for by the detailed classification; therefore, combined categories were necessary. The distinction between 21 pairs of salaried and self-employed managers was particularly difficult to make. In these cases, rates were based on the total for the pair (e.g., "construction managers" include both salaried and self-employed), and socioeconomic scores were averaged. All such combinations were made *after* the coding process; had they been made prior to coding, coder agreement would have undoubtedly been greater.

FINDINGS

Socioeconomic scores for Duncan's values range from a low of 20 for unskilled workers in tobacco manufacturing to a high of 93 for dentists and osteopaths. Scores were grouped into five categories as follows: 45 and below; 46–55; 56–65; 66–75; and 76 and above. Hospitalization rates per 100,000 employed males of 14 years and over were computed based on census figures for 1960. Inspection revealed an extremely sharp increase in hospitalization rates for occupations with socioeconomic scores of 45 and below (see Table 1). However, a continuous relationship is

TABLE 1. AVERAGE ANNUAL HOSPITALIZATION RATE BY SOCIOECONOMIC SCORE

Socioeconomic Strata	Hospitalization Rate	Rate of Increase*
76 and above	21	
66–75	39	1.86
56–65	49	1.26
46–55	64	1.31
45 and below	270	4.22

Source: *U. S. Census of Population: 1960. Detailed Characteristics. Washington,* Final Report PC(1)-49D. (Washington, D. C.: U. S. Government Printing Office, 1962), Table 123.

Note: Hospitalization Rate is the number of patients per 100,000 employed males 14 years and over.

* Between adjacent categories.

also indicated, with rates consistently increasing as socioeconomic status decreases. This is especially clear from Figure 1. The average socioeconomic scores are computed for patients in each of the five strata (for example, the average for patients with scores of 45 and below is 43.18), and the hospitalization rate is plotted against this score. As Figure 1 shows, there is a very steep decline from the lowest stratum to the next lowest, at which point there is a gradual but continuous decline to the highest stratum. Hence, a *general* social class effect is indicated as well as one that is specific to the lowest class.

Specific Occupations Above the Lowest Stratum

To ascertain more precisely the nature of the relationship, analysis was conducted based on categories with only one specific occupation. Since the major question is whether a relationship exists above the lowest stratum in the class structure, all occupations 45 and below in socioeconomic score were eliminated. A number of categories above this level were also eliminated; only those with one specific occupation were retained. Therefore, all residual categories (e.g., "other" and "not elsewhere classified") were eliminated[31] as were several managerial categories (e.g., "ship officers, pilots, pursers, engineers"). Industry categories among operatives

---

[30] McTavish has shown that greater validity may be achieved by using the *Alphabetic Index of Occupations and Industries* as an intermediate step. He finds, however, that the correlation between classification based on "direct" coding and the intermediate step is quite high (r = .91), and that correlations between occupational status coded by each of the two procedures and other variables are virtually identical. (Donald G. McTavish, "A Method for More Reliably Coding Detailed Occupations into Duncan's Socio-Economic Categories," *American Sociological Review* 29 [June, 1964], pp. 402–6.) For these reasons, as well as the limited resources available for the study, the intermediate step was not used.

[31] Two exceptions were made. "Teachers (not elsewhere classified—n.e.c.)" are combined with "elementary teachers" and "secondary teachers." However, "teachers (n.e.c.)" represent less than 10 percent of the total in the teacher category. "Foremen (n.e.c.)" were retained, although distinctions were not made in foremen by industry.

FIGURE 1. PLOT OF HOSPITALIZATION RATE ON AVERAGE OCCUPATIONAL SOCIOECONOMIC INDEX FOR FIVE OCCUPATIONAL-SOCIAL CLASS STRATA

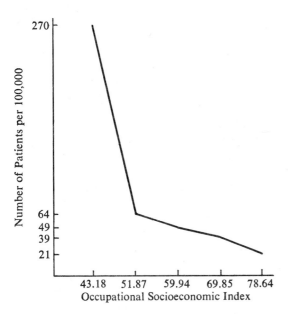

is small, all categories with fewer than 500 members were excluded.[33]

Sample Characteristics. The elimination of categories left 130 occupations with 1,683 patients representing 65 percent of Washington employed males, 14 years and over, in eight major census categories. Representativeness varies with occupational status, however; as noted, the occupations with socioeconomic scores below 45 are eliminated, and occupations eliminated on the grounds of occupational heterogeneity or age distribution are concentrated in the lower socioeconomic levels. The proportions of the population from the major categories represented are given in Table 2.

TABLE 2. NUMBER OF OCCUPATIONS AND PERCENTAGE OF POPULATION REPRESENTED, BY MAJOR OCCUPATIONAL CATEGORY

Occupational Category	Number of Detailed Occupations Represented	Percentage of Population
Professional	30	80
Managerial[1]	23	84
Clerical	8	31
Sales	6	84
Craftsmen	34	83
Operatives	15	43
Service	11	82
Laborers	3	17
Total	130	66

Source: *U. S. Census of Population: 1960.*
[1] Includes farmers and farm managers.

and laborers were omitted. The sales categories of manufacturing, wholesale, and retail salesmen are borderline cases; strictly speaking, these are industrial rather than occupational distinctions. At the same time, however, sales skills are generally adaptable to different settings and products, especially in retail sales. Consequently, these three categories were retained.

In addition, all occupational categories in which the proportion of incumbents below 20 years was unusually high were eliminated. In several instances the elimination was based on information given in the nationwide census, because the age distribution was not given for that occupation in the state census. Seven such categories were eliminated.[32]

Categories with small populations were also eliminated. Since only a few patients may produce a very high rate when the population base

Results. A scattergram of all 130 occupations was made; except for two extreme deviant cases,[34] there were no major departures from linearity. When the two deviant cases are eliminated, the product-moment correlation and correlation ratio (η) are —.42 and .48. Control for age has no apparent influence. Age distribution by occupations for Washington is given in 61 of the 128 cases, and to cancel out the effects of

---

[32] Categories eliminated are as follows: messenger and office boys (median age =15.6); newsboys (median age = 19.7); attendants, recreation and amusement (median age = 19.7); apprentices (median age = 22.9); auto service and parking attendants (median age = 23.8); private household workers (median age = 19.8); garage laborers and car washers and greasers (median age = 26.6); and wholesale and retail laborers (median age = 18.1).

[33] One exception was made. "Shoemakers and repairers," with a population of 484, was retained in the analysis. Since this category had a rather large number of patients (9), we assume that its high rate is statistically reliable. The elimination of this category had only a slight effect on the results.

[34] The two deviant cases are "credit men" (socioeconomic score of 79 and hospitalization rate of 1,372) and "sailors and deck hands" (socioeconomic score of 55 and hospitalization rate of 3,589).

age, rates standardized for age were computed;[35] $r = -.47$ and $\eta = .49$. The significance of occupational prestige above the lowest stratum is clearly indicated.

Results thus reveal two patterns in the relationship between social class and mental hospitalization. (1) There is a discrete pattern, with the increase from the next lowest to the lowest level being much greater than between any other two levels. (2) For occupations above the lowest level, the relationship is continuous and basically linear. This pattern suggests that socioeconomic differences *within* class levels are inversely related to mental hospitalization.

Relationship Within Strata

As expected, considerable variation in mental illness within class levels is present. That there are factors other than socioeconomic is clear from the following examples:

Occupation	Socio-economic Score	Average Annual Hospitalization Rate
Artists and art teachers	76	73
Real estate agents	76	18
Bakers	60	100
Upholsterers	60	64
Fishermen and oystermen	49	139
Gardeners	50	31

Nevertheless, socioeconomic score and hospitalization rate are inversely related within occupational classes.

Occupations are grouped according to major census category, and correlations (r's) and regression coefficients (b's) are computed separately for each category (see Table 3). The b's are expressed in terms of average annual increase for the period of study; hence, the b of 2.32 for professional occupations means that, on

TABLE 3. PRODUCT-MOMENT AND REGRESSION CO-EFFICIENTS BETWEEN OCCUPATIONAL SOCIOECONOMIC SCORE AND HOSPITALIZATION RATE, BY MAJOR OCCUPATIONAL CATEGORY

Occupational Category	r	b
Professional	−.44	−2.32
Managerial[1]	−.58	−1.66
Clerical and sales	−.23	−1.01
Craftsmen	−.41	−3.25
Operatives	−.18	−0.71
Service and laborers	−.34	−2.39

[1] Farmers and farm managers included.

the average, the difference between two occupations, each with 1,000 incumbents but different by 10 points on the socioeconomic scale, is 2.32 admissions per year. Because of the small number of cases, clerical and sales and service and laborer occupations are combined.

All relationships are negative and four of six r's are above −.33, and b's range from −0.71 to −3.25. The regression coefficients show no particular class pattern while the two highest correlations are for professional and managerial categories. Therefore, the slope of the regression line[36] is about the same at all class levels, and deviations around the regression line appear to be somewhat less at high class levels. Hence, the hypothesis of an inverse *relationship* between occupational status and mental illness (as reflected by r's) is at least as good and the actual *effect* of socioeconomic status (as reflected by b's) is just as strong at higher class levels as at lower class levels.

Clerical-sales and operatives have the lowest r's and b's; however, for sales alone (N = 6), r = −.50. Also, in 1960 only 31 percent of all employed male clerical employees above 13 years were in the eight clerical occupations, and for operatives the figure is only 43 percent (see Table 2). Coefficients are highest for groups with over 80 percent of their populations represented; hence, the weak findings for clerical and operatives may result because occupations in

[35] The technique used to standardize by age is the same as that used by the Department of Health, Education and Welfare in computing mortality rates. See Lillian Guralnick, "Mortality by Industry and Cause of Death among Men 20 to 64 Years of Age: United States, 1950," *Vital Statistics–Special Reports* 53 (September, 1963), pp. 344–45. The measure is the ratio of tabulated cases in an occupation to the number to be expected in that occupation if the hospital rate for each of seven age categories (21–24, 25–29, . . . 60–64) had been the same as for the total sample.

[36] The use of regression analysis here implies that socioeconomic position leads to hospitalization rather than the reverse. The direction of causality in this relation is far from clear, however, and could be the other way, as implied by "drift" and social selection hypotheses. This is discussed in the final section.

these categories are less representative of their respective populations than are the others.

In any case, results show that mental hospitalization is not only inversely related across socioeconomic strata, but that it is inversely related to socioeconomic differences within socioeconomic strata as well. This is further indicated by the similarity between the correlation ratios and product-moment coefficients for the three largest groups (η and r for professionals, managers, and craftsmen are .49 and —.44; .67 and —.58; and .55 and —.41 respectively). Still there are relatively few occupations in each of these groups, and since the correlation ratio is extremely sensitive to a small number of cases in the columns, the finding of linearity should be accepted cautiously. Nevertheless, results are consistent with each other and with those for the total sample. Findings consistently show that occupational status is inversely related to mental hospitalization at all class levels above the lowest, and that differences in occupational status are just as important at higher-status levels as at lower levels.

As for the lowest level, results presented in Table 1 suggest that other factors (e.g., "lower-class subculture") may combine with occupational status and thus help account for the unusually high rate at this level. Regression and correlation coefficients for this level cannot be compared with other levels since there are only three occupations below 45 in socioeconomic status with at least 500 incumbents.

DISCUSSION

The correlation between incidence of mental illness and social class has been given a variety of interpretations. These include etiological hypotheses, as well as social reaction and differential tolerance[37] and social selection (intergeneration downward mobility) and "drift" (intragenerational downward mobility).[38] Any explanation of our results, however, must be consistent with

the fact that there are two patterns in the relationship. Most explanations tend to emphasize a discrete relationship, and thus explain only why the lower-class rate is so high. This is true of etiological explanations which emphasize economic and social insecurity[39] and blocked aspirations and disparagement,[40] which presumably characterize the lower class. The same applies, of course, to other arguments which postulate a lower-class subculture or a high degree of social disorganization at the lower end of the class structure. At best, these only explain the high rate in the lower class. They do not explain the continuous character of the relationship.

A discrete relationship is also implied and sometimes explicit in social selection hypotheses. For example, Dunham argues that the mentally ill, and persons prone to illness, "experience difficulty in being fitted into the (class) hierarchy, except for the lowest rank position," so that it is "natural to expect that in our type of society many persons destined for schizophrenia would be placed in the lowest ranking position. . . ."[41] On the other hand, one could postulate the "drift" process of a constant tendency for occupations to receive the "rejects," failures, and "misfits" from occupations immediately above each in status, and that the large number in the lowest ranks results because there are no lower positions for persons to "drift" into. Arguing against this hypothesis is the evidence that only a very small percentage of mental patients are downwardly mobile during the ten years prior to their hospitalization.[42]

As for societal reaction hypotheses, it is probable that societal reactions cause more lower-status persons to be hospitalized than higher-status persons. Lower-class persons are more apt to have contact with official agencies (jails, welfare organizations, etc.) through which the hospitalization process is often initiated; also, once in contact with such agencies, a lower-class person may be more apt to be hospitalized than a person of higher status. In addition, with decreases in status, tolerance for aberrant behavior

[37] J. M. Wanklin, D. F. Fleming, C. W. Buck, and G. E. Hobbs, "Factors Influencing the Rate of First Admission to Mental Hospital," *Journal of Nervous and Mental Disease* 121 (February, 1955), pp. 103–16.

[38] R. Jay Turner and Morton O. Wagenfeld, "Occupational Mobility and Schizophrenia: An Assessment of the Social Causation and Social Selection Hypotheses," *American Sociological Review* 32 (February, 1967), pp. 104–13.

[39] Lapouse, *et al.*, "The Drift Hypothesis."

[40] Srole et al., *Mental Health in the Metropolis*, pp. 194–200, esp. 200.

[41] Dunham, *Community and Schizophrenia*, p. 191.

[42] Turner and Wagenfeld, "Occupational Mobility and Schizophrenia," p. 110.

may be lower and the need to hospitalize may be greater; a family's *economic* ability to tolerate nonproductive persons decreases with socioeconomic status. These factors may be valid as explanations for differences between classes, and especially the high rate at the lowest-class level, but it is doubtful if they are valid for the findings within strata at higher status levels.

In general, most interpretations fail to explain the continuous and linear character of the relationship above the lowest-class level. A plausible explanation for this relationship would seem to be one which incorporates the concept of relative deprivation. Regardless of the level in the class structure, and therefore the degree of *absolute* deprivation, persons who have fewer life chances than others—that is, who are characterized by *objective* relative deprivation—have higher hospitalization rates. However, the extent to which perceived objective deprivation leads to *subjective* relative deprivation cannot be answered with the data at hand. Even if such data were available, the question of why subjective relative deprivation should lead to mental illness, or at least hospitalization, would have to be investigated. It may be, however, as others have argued, that social frustrations and deprivations generate tendencies toward mental illness and other forms of deviance.[43] In any case, given this postulate,

the linear results are consistent with the interpretation. However, since the most variance explained for any class is only 43 percent (for managers), and as low as 3 percent for operatives, a theory based on relative deprivation, as related to differentials in occupational status, explains only a small proportion of variation in hospitalization. It is clear that other factors besides socioeconomic status are involved, especially at the lowest level. Such factors may be social selection, "drift," and social and subcultural conditions characteristic of lower-class life, or a combination of these and possibly other processes. Nevertheless, the existence of two patterns in the relationship between social class and mental illness (or hospitalization) is hard to deny.

Finally, there is the question of whether the same patterns are manifest by other correlates of social class, particularly other forms of deviance. If they are, theories of deviance may need to be qualified or extended to account for the general as well as specific social class effects. At the same time, such findings would indicate a socioeconomic theory of deviance is, in general, plausible. Whether the influence is due to social selection, relative deprivation, differential societal reaction, anomie, class subcultures, or some combination of these and other variables, are matters that need to be investigated.

---

[43] See Jacob Tuckman and Robert H. Kleiner, "Discrepancy Between Aspiration and Achievement as a Predictor of Schizophrenia," *Behavioral Science* 7 (October, 1962), pp.

143–47; and Robert K. Merton, *Social Theory and Social Structures* (Glencoe: The Free Press, 1957), pp. 131–60.

INDIVIDUAL RESOURCES, SOCIETAL REACTION, AND HOSPITAL COMMITMENT

WILLIAM A. RUSHING

A number of sociologists contend that deviant behavior is less a function of a person's overt acts than an interpretation and definition of those acts by others.[1] Advocates of this perspective, which is variously referred to as the societal reaction, labeling, and interactionist approach to deviant behavior, have devoted particular attention to mental illness.[2] Several investigators report results which they contend are consistent with the perspective.[3] On the other hand, others question the validity of this approach,[4] and particularly the interpretations of research findings that have been taken as support for it.[5] They

argue instead for a behavior pathology perspective, contending that most persons who are labeled as mentally ill and hospitalized are indeed mentally ill.

Probably both perspectives are valid. Behavior pathology and societal reactions are probably involved to some degree in most cases of mental hospitalization, although their relative importance may vary from case to case. One only needs to observe admission conferences in state hospitals to appreciate that at least some admissions are truly mentally disturbed, even by the narrowest of definitions. On the other hand, since a large proportion of admissions to state mental hospitals are committed by the courts, societal reactions are clearly involved in a substantial number of cases. If members of society had not reacted as they did, many court commitments would never have occurred, and in consequence, persons would be less apt to have been labeled as "crazy" and considered incompetent by public record.

Operationally, it is probably impossible to determine precisely the proportion of hospitalization rates contributed by behavior pathology and by societal reactions.[6] More accessible to investigation is the study of contingencies in the societal reaction, which is the concern of this paper. Types of admissions to state mental hospitals (voluntary and involuntary) provide the basis for the analysis.

Involuntary admissions (court commitments) reflect explicit societal reactions; they are clear-cut manifestations of the societal tendency to isolate and exclude.[7] While some court-committed patients may have consented to court proceedings and to subsequent hospitalization, many others are committed against their will. Of course, some voluntary commitments are infor-

Reprinted with permission of the University of Chicago Press, from *The American Journal of Sociology* 77 (November, 1971), pp. 511–26.

[1] E. Lemert, *Social Pathology* (New York: McGraw-Hill, 1951); H. Becker, *Outsiders* (New York: Free Press, 1963); K. Erikson, *Wayward Puritans* (New York: John Wiley, 1966); J. Kitsuse, "Societal Reaction to Deviant Behavior: Problems of Theory and Method," *Social Problems* 9 (Winter, 1962), pp. 247–56; T. Scheff, *Being Mentally Ill: A Sociological Theory* (Chicago: Aldine, 1966); and E. Schur, "Reactions to Deviance: A Critical Assessment," *American Journal of Sociology* 75 (November, 1969), pp. 309–22.

[2] See especially E. Goffman, *Asylums: Essays on the Social Situation of Mental Patients and Other Inmates* (Garden City, N.J.: Doubleday, 1961); T. Szasz, *The Myth of Mental Illness* (New York: Harper and Row, 1961); and Scheff, *Being Mentally Ill.*

[3] Scheff, *Being Mentally Ill;* D. Miller and M. Schwartz, "County Lunacy Commission Hearings: Some Observations of Commitments to a State Mental Hospital," *Social Problems* 14 (Summer, 1966), pp. 26–35; C. Haney and R. Michielutte, "Selective Factors Operating in the Adjudication of Incompetency," *Journal of Health and Social Behavior* 9 (September, 1968), pp. 233–52; D. Wenger and C. Fletcher, "The Effects of Legal Counsel on Admission to a State Mental Hospital: A Confrontation of Professions," *Journal of Health and Social Behavior* 19 (March, 1960), pp. 66–72; W. Wilde, "Decision-Making in a Psychiatric Screening Agency," *Journal of Health and Social Behavior* 9 (September, 1969), pp. 215–21; C. Haney and K. Miller, "Definitional Factors in Mental Incompetency," *Sociology and Social Research* 54 (July, 1970), pp. 520–32; A. Linsky, "Who Shall Be Excluded: The Influence of Personal Attributes in Community Reaction to the Mentally Ill," *Social Psychiatry* 5 (July, 1970), pp. 166–71.

[4] W. Gove, "Societal Reaction as an Explanation of Mental Illness: An Evaluation," *American Sociological Review* 35 (October, 1970), pp. 873–84 and H. Dunham, "Comment on Gove's Evaluation of Societal Reaction Theory as an Explanation for Mental Illness," *American Sociological Review* 36 (April, 1971), pp. 313–14.

[5] Gove, "Societal Reaction as an Explanation of Mental Illness," and W. Gove, "Who Is Hospitalized?—A Critical Review of Some of Sociological Studies of Mental Illness," *Journal of Health and Social Behavior* 11 (December, 1970), pp. 873–84.

[6] Even if this were known, there would be the further problem of knowing to what extent the relationship for behavior pathology is due to social causation and how much to self-selection factors (e.g., "drift").

[7] Linsky, "Who Shall Be Excluded."

mally pressured into "volunteering" for treatment. Nevertheless, pressure is probably greater for involuntary patients; they are less apt to have a "positive orientation" toward their hospitalization (e.g., they are more likely to say they did not want to come to the hospital and to feel that they were coerced into coming).[8] Moreover, the force manifest in the societal reaction is greater for the involuntary patient. The courts, after all, are institutionalized representatives of society; decisions are made by them on behalf of society and thus symbolize society's rejection of the individual. Although both voluntary and involuntary rates may be due both to illness behavior and to societal reactions, reactions are present to a much greater degree in court commitments and certainly the quality of the reaction is different. Consequently, the ratio of involuntary to voluntary admissions, taken as a reflection of the extent of formal societal force, rejection, and degradation in hospitalization, was examined for patients entering the three state hospitals in Washington between 1956 and 1965. The relationships between this ratio and socioeconomic-occupational and marital status of patients are examined; it is hypothesized that these two status variables are important contingencies in the societal reaction.[9]

Despite their central concern with contingencies, social reaction theorists have not usually presented systematic propositions concerning those contingencies. For example, although Becker recognizes that the reaction does not necessarily reflect the commission of deviant acts, his analysis is directed to constructing definitions and typologies in terms of acts and reactions[10] rather than to accounting for variation in reactions.[11] Scheff, however, does suggest that

the societal reaction depends on several factors, one of which is the social power of the individual.[12] Since power is a function of resources, individuals with limited social and economic resources because of their low social status have limited power and are more apt to be involuntarily confined than individuals whose resources and power are less limited. We shall refer to this as the "status resource hypothesis" of mental hospitalization.

Social and economic resources are assumed to be inversely related to an individual's socioeconomic status, a relationship that need not be discussed. As for marital status, resources are assumed to be highest for the married and lowest for the single, with disrupted-estranged (divorced, separated, and widowed) in between. Married persons have the support of a spouse (and possibly children), as well as relationships with other persons that result from having a spouse and children. Since the social networks of single persons are usually not as extensive or as interconnected[13] as those of married persons, the single person has fewer social supports in time of need, as when altercations occur that result in the initiation of court proceedings against him. While the disrupted-estranged may be without the support of a spouse and children, remnants of such supports may be available, even if these relationships are not as extensive or as viable as for the married.

Pacific Sociological Review 9 (Spring, 1966), pp. 9–14. For a more positive evaluation of the general perspective, see Shur, "Reactions to Deviance." For a negative evaluation with specific reference to mental illness, see Gove, "Societal Reaction as an Explanation of Mental Illness." Scheff argues, however, that Gove seriously distorts the positions of others. T. J. Scheff, "The Labelling Theory of Mental Illness," *American Sociological Review* 39 (June, 1974), pp. 444–52.

[12] Scheff, *Being Mentally Ill*, p. 96.

[13] An interconnected network is one in which A has a relationship with B, B with C, and C with A, as opposed to one in which A has a relationship with B, B with C, but where C has no relationship with A. An interconnected network is "closed" rather than "open"; see E. Bott, *Family and Social Networks* (London, Tavistock, 1957). It is probable that closed networks are more apt to occur in connection with family relationships. This is true not only within the family but beyond it—as when a spouse has a relationship with an outside member—because a relationship with the other spouse and the outsider usually accompanies or is consequential to such a relationship. Hammer has shown that persons with networks of interconnected social relations are less apt to be hospitalized as rapidly as those whose networks are not interconnected. M. Hammer, "Influence of Small Social Networks as Factors in Mental Hospital Admission," *Human Organization* 22 (Winter, 1964), pp. 254–51.

---

[8] L. Linn, "Social Characteristics and Patient Expectations Toward Mental Hospitalization," *Archives of General Psychiatry* 20 (April, 1969), p. 462.

[9] In addition, the relationship between the ratio and degree of community integration and visibility will also be investigated, but to a more limited extent. This hypothesis will be introduced below in connection with the analysis of specific occupational categories. Linsky, "Who Shall Be Excluded," examines several relationships that are similar to some of those we examine.

[10] Becker, *Outsiders*, p. 20.

[11] Criticism that this approach fails to explain variation in deviant acts applies also to its failure to explain variation in the reactions. Gibbs' criticism that the approach represents a "conception" of deviant behavior (or even a theory only poorly systematized) is generally well taken. See J. Gibbs, "Conceptions of Deviant Behavior: The Old and the New,"

RATIONALE FOR THE HYPOTHESIS

The status resource hypothesis[14] of societal reactions is a specific case of a more general hypothesis, independent of the societal reaction perspective on deviant behavior—namely, that social advantages and disadvantages are cumulative.[15] Socioeconomic status and life chances are interrelated, so that people who are disadvantaged in one area tend to be disadvantaged in others. The disadvantages of involuntary hospitalization[16] include the following: social stigma of a court record, loss of civil liberties, trauma of court proceedings,[17] longer period of hospitalization,[18] and denial of freedom. Voluntary patients are also denied freedom, but they are more likely to accept their hospitalization.[19] Moreover, if a voluntary patient requests release after a pre-scribed period, the hospital staff must comply, whereas the wishes of the involuntary patient can be ignored.[20] In the words of Mr. Justice Brennan, "No matter how sweetly disguised or delicate the language, involuntary confinement [in a mental hospital] is a loss of freedom."[21]

Since low socioeconomic status and nonmarried status confront most American males with tangible economic and social disadvantages, relationships between the involuntary/voluntary confinement ratio and socioeconomic and marital status can be expected. Considering the disadvantages of involuntary admissions, then, we see that it is advantageous to have a network of social relations, even if we assume that members of that network may persuade and pressure one into voluntary admission. More specific reasons for expecting the involuntary/voluntary ratio to be associated with socioeconomic and marital status derive from the initiation process of court commitments along with the court procedures themselves.

The Initiation Process

In a large percentage of court commitments, police and social agencies are involved from the beginning.[22] It is precisely those people with limited social and economic resources who are most apt to have contact with representatives of law enforcement and social agencies. Also, once in contact with such agencies, a prospective candidate for a state mental hospital whose resources are limited is more likely to be brought to court because of the restraints surrounding the initiation process.[23] Important legal responsibility rests with those who sign the petition that

[14] We could just as well call this an individual "power hypothesis," since it is the translation of status resources into power that is the crucial phenomenon in the hypothesis. The term status resource is preferred for two reasons. First, social power is usually conceptualized in the sociological literature along quite different lines from that employed here; consequently, a focus on status resources rather than social power may lead to less terminological confusion and debate. Second, our measures of occupational and marital status are more directly measures of status resources than of social power; only as indirect indicators may they be considered as measures of power.

[15] S. Lipset and R. Bendix, *Social Mobility and Industrial Society* (Berkeley: University of California Press, 1959), and W. Rushing, *Class, Culture and Alienation: A Study of Farmers and Farm Workers* (Lexington, Mass.: D. C. Heath, 1972), Chapter 3.

[16] H. Weihofen, "Hospitalizing the Mentally Ill," *Michigan Law Review* 50 (1952), pp. 837–42.

[17] We should note, however, that no systematic studies have been conducted of the effect of court proceedings on the defendant's mental status. Some suggest, however, that involuntary patients may be sicker than voluntary patients; see N. Barr, "Voluntary Imprisonment: Its Usefulness in the Rehabilitation of Criminal Offenders," *American Journal of Psychiatry* 124 (March, 1967), pp. 170–78. If this is true, it may be a *consequence* of differences in the way patients are admitted. Although this makes sense from sociological and social-psychological perspectives, some psychiatrists seem unready to accept it. According to one report, most psychiatrists seem to think the type of admission has little effect on the patient and the patient's subsequent progress—that these are matters of the severity and nature of the illness rather than the way the patient is admitted. See A. Klots et al., *Mental Illness and Due Process* (Ithaca: Cornell University Press, 1962), p. 57. At the same time, we are told that psychiatrists think voluntary admissions are best from a therapeutic standpoint—they tend 'to promote an attitude favorable to effective treatment" (Klots et al., *Mental Illness and Due Process*, p. 59).

[18] R. Morgan and L. Cook, "Relationships of Methods of Admission to Length of Stay in State Hospitals," *Public Health Reports* 78 (July, 1963), pp. 619–29. In the present study, 61 percent of the voluntary patients were released within two months, whereas only 19 percent of the involuntary patients were.

[19] Linn, "Social Characteristics and Patient Expectations Toward Mental Hospitalization," p. 462.

[20] A clinician in one of the hospitals volunteered the comment that the staff preferred involuntary patients to voluntary patients because they could be retained for as long as the staff considered necessary.

[21] Klots et al., *Mental Illness and Due Process*, p. 145.

[22] See R. Rock, with M. Jacobson and R. Janopaul, *Hospitalization and Discharge of the Mentally Ill* (Chicago: University of Chicago Press, 1968).

[23] In a study of the decision of mental health screening centers for potential court cases, Wilde ("Decision Making in a Psychiatric Screening Agency") reports that the center's decision to send the case to court for hearing is not significantly associated with the behavioral characteristics of the potential patient, but is significantly associated with characteristics of the petitioner and the identity of the interviewer. Unfortunately, however, Wilde does not report the status characteristics of the potential patient.

initiates the hospitalization process. The petitioner is subject to both criminal and civil charges if his act is judged to have been malicious and careless.[24] While such court actions are rare, a study of hospitalization proceedings in five states concludes that their possibility deters private physicians, police officers, and representatives of social agencies from initiating court commitment proceedings.[25] But such restraints are apt to be weaker against individuals who, because of their limited resources, are less able to initiate a defense.

On the basis of his study of restraints on social agency participation in court and hospitalization proceedings in seven states, Wade[26] concludes that when agencies deal "with persons whose social supports are more stable and available," they are less apt to initiate court proceedings. One agency supervisor reports that the general rule in his agency is against involvement, "but that there is less hesitancy if no relatives or others can be found."[27] Wade reports that those agencies most willing to participate, such as Traveler's Aid, deal with persons who "are usually absent, at least temporarily, from their accustomed social supports, families, and friends."[28] Even here, however, effort is usually made to refer the individual to family or others, and hospitalization proceedings are initiated only after such efforts have failed. In one such agency, for example, the informant relates that "if no family or friends can be found, Traveler's Aid takes the responsibility of seeing that the individual is cared for either through hospitalization or outpatient treatment."[29] Thus it appears that it is not the presence of illness symptoms or even the need for hospitalization that prompts social agency initiation of the hospitalization process (although these may be present), but the absence of a social relation network to which the individual may be referred.[30]

In addition to the important legal risks, the stigma for the patient and his family may be an important deterrent to the family bringing court action against one of its members; it apparently restrains physicians as well, thus other procedures may be sought to minimize such risk.[31] Implied here is that an effort is made to persuade the individual to volunteer for admission; if this fails, hospitalization proposals may be dropped. It is probable that the stigma of a court appearance and the restraints generated by stigma are positively related to socioeconomic status.

Court Proceedings

Evidence suggests that court proceedings are perfunctory and based on the presumption that the defendant is mentally ill.[32] Probably, however, the presumption is more apt to be rejected if the defendant has sufficient counterpower—that is, economic and social resources—to challenge it. Indeed, some evidence suggests that when patients do show serious legal resistance, the state may drop the case[33] or the court may rule for the defendant.[34] Moreover, Scheff[35] con-

---

[24] The Washington Code states that the petitioner must have acted "in good faith" (*Revised Code, Washington, Annotated,* 71.02.100).

[25] Rock et al., *Hospitalization and Discharge of the Mentally Ill,* esp. p. 121. For a discussion of restraints on police in *emergency* admissions, see E. Bittner, "Police Discretion in Emergency Apprehension of Mentally Ill Persons," *Social Problems* 10 (Winter, 1967), pp. 278–92.

[26] A. Wade, "Social Agency Participation in Hospitalization for Mental Illness," *Social Service Review* 26 (January, 1967), pp. 27–43.

[27] *Ibid.,* p. 29.

[28] *Ibid.,* p. 38.

[29] *Ibid.*

[30] Another factor cited by Wade to be related to social agency willingness to participate in court proceedings is the status of the agency in the community; "the lower the status of the agency, the more likely it is to participate—even though reluctantly—in the hospitalization of the mentally ill" (*ibid.*). Although Wade does not provide systematic data on this point, it is probable that the lower the status of the agency, the lower the status of persons it serves.

[31] Rock et al., *Hospitalization and Discharge of the Mentally Ill,* p. 135.

[32] L. Kutner, "The Illusion of Due Process in Commitment Proceedings," *Northwestern University Law Review* 57 (September, 1962), pp. 383–99; Scheff, *Being Mentally Ill* [and pp. 412–22 below]; and Rock et al., *Hospitalization and Discharge of the Mentally Ill.* Unlike some other states, Washington requires only one person to petition the court, and the petition need not be signed by a medical practitioner before court proceedings can be initiated. At the hearing, however, the court must hear the testimony of at least two physicians who have been appointed by the court. The defendant (or others acting in his behalf) can provide his own medical witnesses, of course. (*Revised Code, Washington, Annotated,* 71.01.020.170).

[33] Rock et al., *Hospitalization and Discharge of the Mentally Ill,* p. 193.

[34] Miller and Schwartz, "County Lunacy Commission Hearings," p. 30; Wenger and Fletcher, "Effects of Legal Counsel on Admissions." A case cited by Miller and Schwartz of an obviously affluent female who, through legal counsel of her own choosing, was able to gain a favorable verdict ("County Hearings," p. 30), illustrates my point about the significance of socioeconomic status in involuntary hospitalization.

[35] See p. 421 below.

tends that one reason for the presumption of illness is the political pressure the court is under to hospitalize those persons brought before it. Counterpressure (implied as well as overt) is apt to be greater if the defendant's occupational status is high and there is a network of social relations that can exert pressure.

Miller and Schwartz[36] note that persons who have a spouse are more apt to resist commitment, and that, among the resisters, individuals with spouses are more likely to be released. Socioeconomic status may have an effect on subtle behavioral styles as well as the more obvious economic and social resources. Miller and Schwartz conclude: "Those persons who are able to approach the judge in a controlled manner, use proper eye contact, sentence structure, posture, etc., and who presented their stories without excessive emotional response or blandness and with proper demeanor, were able to obtain the decision they wanted (regardless of) 'psychiatric symptomatology.'"[37]

But even when the presumption of illness is not challenged, there is the further question of whether the court's disposition depends on the individual's power and resources.[38] Rock et al. state: "In case after case that we observed, the consensus [of the court participants] was that commitment to a state hospital was necessary *only* because it was *the* available resource and not because it was the best disposition of the case" (first emphasis supplied).[39] In many instances, a mental hospital is the only alternative because the individual's social and economic supports are so limited. In one case, for example:

The public defender added that the real problem was that the patient was alone and had no relatives or friends in the state, or anywhere in the country for that matter. He had tried to find someone who would agree to take care of her but

was unsuccessful. He believed that if he had found someone who would do this he could have persuaded the court not to hospitalize her but to commit her to the care of the custody of that person. The District Attorney indicated that he would have agreed to such a disposition.[40]

The point here is not whether most persons who are committed are actually ill; Scheff,[41] Miller and Schwartz,[42] and Wengler and Fletcher[43] raise serious questions about that. On the other hand, Rock et al.[44] contend that, in most cases they observed, illness was "not contestable," although they do question whether hospitalization is necessary in most cases.[45] Their conclusion indicates that the defendant's social rather than mental status is the determining factor. The "need" for hospitalization, and the decision to deny a person his freedom, are partially contingent on whether the defendant has a family or others to which the court can refer him.[46] Thus, the actual decision by the court to commit a person may reflect the same limited resources that were significant factors in his being brought to court in the first place.[47]

DATA AND MEASURES

Data are based on all twenty-one- to sixty-four-year-old male involuntary (court-committed)

---

[36] Miller and Schwartz, "County Lunacy Commission Hearings," p. 29.

[37] *Ibid.*, p. 34.

[38] This is not to say, of course, that nonmedical factors besides social and economic resources are involved in court commitments. Haney and Michielutte ("Selective Factors Operating in the Adjudication of Lunacy") report, for example, that the decision is also contingent on residence (urban-rural), availability of hospital beds, age of the defendant, type of petition (from family or nonfamily), and the involvement of psychiatrists in the proceedings.

[39] *Ibid.*, p. 173.

[40] *Ibid.*, p. 171.

[41] See pp. 412–22 below.

[42] *Ibid.*

[43] *Ibid.*

[44] *Ibid.*, p. 124.

[45] *Ibid.*, pp. 193–94.

[46] The finding that defendants are less apt to be committed by the court when a family member is included among petitioners than when this is not the case (Haney and Michielutte, "Selective Factors Operating in the Adjudication of Lunacy," p. 239) may stem from the fact that defendants who do not have family members among the petitioners are less likely to come from intact families than defendants whose petitioners include at least one family member. Miller and Schwartz ("County Lunacy Commission Hearings") also cite instances in which the defendant is released although the spouse is the petitioner.

[47] The relations of the individual's economic and social resources to the process involved in court initiation and court proceedings is complex and involves several dimensions. Four may be distinguished: (1) the tendency of others to initiate proceedings, (2) the individual's power to resist and abort the proceedings once they are initiated, (3) the tendency of the court to rule in the defendant's favor regardless of the defendant's resistance, and (4) the defendant's power to resist court action to commit him. We postulate that each of these is associated with the individual's social and economic resources. However, we do not postulate that the relationship is stronger for one dimension than the others, although this may be the case.

and voluntary admissions who had been admitted to and discharged from any of the three state mental hospitals in Washington between 1956 and 1965. Analysis is limited to first admissions only; there were 2,262 involuntary and 1,496 voluntary first admissions.

Based on an examination of each patient's record, he was classified in one of the detailed census occupational categories. As in the previous paper, patients were classified into one of five socioeconomic strata in accordance with Duncan's socioeconomic scores for all census occupations (see pp. 397–98). The ratio of involuntary admissions to voluntary admissions is then derived for each stratum. Rates per 100,000 for the 10-year period are also derived using 1960 as the population base.

In addition, patients were classified in three marital categories—married, disrupted-estranged, and single; information was available on almost all cases (2,214 and 1,490 involuntary and voluntary admissions, respectively). Ratios are reported, as well as rates, per 100,000 on a 10-year basis.

FINDINGS

Socioeconomic Status

The findings reveal that the involuntary/voluntary ratio increases as socioeconomic status decreases (Table 1). Differences between adjacent

TABLE 1. RATIO OF INVOLUNTARY TO VOLUNTARY FIRST ADMISSIONS BY SOCIOECONOMIC STATUS

Socioeconomic Strata	Involuntary Admissions	Voluntary Admissions	Ratio
I	99 (88)*	97 (86)	1.02
II	295 (156)	313 (166)	0.94
III	361 (241)	274 (189)	1.32
IV	314 (308)	216 (212)	1.45
V	814 (1,328)	365 (593)	2.23

* Figure in parenthesis is rate per 100,000. Source of figures for population base: U.S. Bureau of the Census 1962, table 121.

strata vary, however. There is little difference between strata I and II or between strata III and IV, although ratios for both strata III and IV are higher than for strata I and II. The most striking

difference, however, is between strata IV and V. While results are generally consistent with the status resource hypothesis, coercive hospitalization is especially probable at the lowest level of the class structure (i.e., at the poverty level).

Occupational Status

The same pattern occurs for major occupational categories (Table 2); ratios are higher for manual than for nonmanual workers, and the largest differences are between lower and higher-status manual workers (laborers have a much higher ratio than craftsmen, operatives, and service workers).

TABLE 2. RATIO OF INVOLUNTARY TO VOLUNTARY FIRST ADMISSIONS BY MAJOR OCCUPATIONAL CATEGORY

Occupational Category	Involuntary Admissions	Voluntary Admissions	Ratio
Professional	116 (144)*	121 (151)	0.95
Farmer/farm manager	64 (286)	44 (194)	1.47
Managerial	64 (83)	60 (78)	1.06
Clerical	43 (117)	53 (144)	0.81
Sales	83 (211)	95 (242)	0.87
Craftsmen	324 (156)	241 (116)	1.34
Operatives	209 (196)	156 (146)	1.34
Service	124 (411)	108 (358)	1.15
Farm laborer	82 (559)	20 (136)	4.11
Laborer, nonfarm and nonmine	839 (1,847)	426 (938)	1.97

* Figure in parenthesis is rate per 100,000. Source of figures for population base: U.S. Bureau of the Census 1962, table 121.

A disadvantage of using major census categories, of course, is that most categories contain several occupations that are different in a number of aspects. However, the categories of farmer/farm manager and farm worker are more homogeneous; both are largely rural (which allows for the control for urban-rural differences to some extent).

The social and economic disadvantages for farm workers are clearly greater than for farmers or for any other major occupational group.[48] They have the lowest income of any major occupation in Washington (and in the nation as a whole); also, seasonal employment means that

---

[48] Rushing, Class, Culture, and Alienation.

they are unemployed for considerable periods of time. Their low life chances generally—low education, poor housing, high mortality, and inadequate medical care—have been documented in numerous studies.[49] The low level of social supports is also indicated for Washington farm workers and is reflected in level of community integration, rates of social participation, and community visibility.[50] Furthermore, most farm workers are constantly concerned with finding their next job. Frequent moving and "day-to-day, hand-to-mouth" survival allow little time for activities that can build stable and viable social supports.

Moreover, their political power is weak or nonexistent; they are denied unemployment compensation and other social-security benefits, and until recently were not covered by minimum-wage legislation. In addition, there have been few legislative efforts to strengthen their unionization (as was done for industrial labor; e.g., the Wagner Act). Society certainly has not provided economic supports for them as it has for farmers. Their limited resources lead us to expect an unusually high involuntary/voluntary *ratio* of hospitalization for this group. Since, however, they are not well-integrated in their communities,[51] we can expect a relatively low hospitalization *rate*. While farm workers may have little power and resources to resist coercive hospitalization, their low visibility makes hospitalization less frequent than might be expected on the basis of their socioeconomic level alone.[52]

Results conform to these expectations (see Table 2). In contrast to nonfarm laborers, whose ratio (1.97) is next highest, the farm workers' ratio is 4.11 while the ratio for farmers is only 1.47. On the other hand, the overall hospitalization rates for farm workers (559 involuntary; 136 voluntary) are considerably lower than the rate for nonfarm laborers (1,847; 938). Thus it appears that socioeconomic status and community isolation interact to produce relatively low rates but high ratios of involuntary/voluntary hospitalization.

Marital Status

Our hypothesis that the ratio will be highest for the single, next for the disrupted-estranged, and lowest for the married, is upheld (Table 3).

TABLE 3. RATIO OF INVOLUNTARY TO VOLUNTARY FIRST ADMISSIONS BY MARITAL STATUS

Marital Status	Involuntary Admissions	Voluntary Admissions	Ratio
Married	929 (158)*	796 (136)	1.17
Disrupted-estranged	502 (1,087)	343 (742)	1.46
Single	798 (853)	344 (368)	2.32

* Figure in parenthesis is rate per 100,000. Source of figures for population base: *U.S. Bureau of the Census 1962*, Table 105.

Since the difference between the single and the disrupted-estranged is greater than that between the disrupted-estranged and the married, it is clear that individuals with social supports originating in the husband-wife relationship (even if the marriage is no longer intact) have resources resembling those of persons with intact marriages. Thus, insofar as their resources tend to mediate the societal reaction, the disrupted-estranged do not occupy a midpoint between the others. Therefore, results parallel the differences observed for socioeconomic status in which the ratio for stratum V is much higher than the ratios for the other strata.

Interaction of Socioeconomic and Marital Status

Analysis of the involuntary/voluntary ratio simultaneously by socioeconomic and marital status (Table 4) reveals that the effects of socioeconomic status vary considerably by marital status.[53] For the married, the only clear difference is between stratum V and the other four; but for the single, the rate rises steadily as occupational status declines, with rates for adjacent

---

[49] *Ibid.*
[50] *Ibid.*
[51] *Ibid.*
[52] Community isolation probably has two effects. As noted, it may contribute to a low hospitalization rate. It may also contribute to a high ratio. A person with few community ties will have fewer resources to utilize (i.e., persons to turn to) in time of need than a person with many community ties. The specific effect of community isolation on the involuntary/voluntary ratio will be examined below.

[53] Rates per 100,000 cannot be given for socioeconomic-marital status groups, since the census does not report population figures for occupations cross-classified by marital status.

TABLE 4. RATIO OF INVOLUNTARY TO VOLUNTARY FIRST
ADMISSIONS BY SOCIOECONOMIC STRATA
AND MARITAL STATUS

Socioeconomic Strata	Married	Disrupted-Estranged	Single	N
I	0.87	1.29	1.11	(194)
II	0.86	0.78	1.43	(603)
III	1.17	1.16	2.26	(631)
IV	0.98	1.85	2.33	(520)
V	1.60	2.11	3.34	(1,167)
N	1,486	737	(892)	(3,115)

strata being about the same except for the slight increase from stratum III to stratum IV. Among the disrupted-estranged, the ratios rise regularly to stratum V, except that the ratio for stratum I is unusually high.

The results reveal that the ratio consistently increases from the married to the single only within the two lowest strata; the ratio for the single is higher than for the other two for strata II and III, with no apparent relationship for stratum I.

The effects of each status variable depend somewhat on the values of the other. The effects of each appear to be greatest when the values of the other are lowest, and weakest when the values of the other are highest. Socioeconomic status has less effect for the married than for the other two marital statuses; the only difference among the married is between the lowest level and the other four. At the same time, the effects of marital status tend to increase in magnitude and consistency as socioeconomic status decreases. These patterns suggest, therefore, that regardless of low resources in one status variable, high resources in another may effectively prevent coercive institutionalization proceedings. Nevertheless, the general pattern is that high resources of both status variables produce low ratios of involuntary to voluntary admissions (upper left-hand portion of Table 4), while low resources in both variables produce the highest ratios (lowest right-hand portion of Table 4).

Interaction of Occupational and Marital Status

If the effect of one status-resource variable is especially strong when the value of another is low, a particularly strong effect of marital status

should be evident among farm laborers because socioeconomic resources are so low for this group. Ratios are presented by marital status, for farm workers, nonfarm laborers, and farmers/farm managers in Table 5.[54] The effects of marital status among farm workers are indeed strong; the ratio for the single is more than double that for the disrupted-estranged, and over 3.5 times the ratio of the married.

TABLE 5. RATIO OF INVOLUNTARY TO VOLUNTARY FIRST
ADMISSIONS BY MARITAL STATUS FOR FARMERS/FARM
MANAGERS, NONFARM AND NONMINING
LABORERS, AND FARM WORKERS

Occupational Category	Married	Disrupted-Estranged	Single
Farmer/farm managers	1.07	1.29	3.00
Nonfarm and non-mining laborers	1.37	2.04	2.89
Farm workers	2.10	3.25	7.67

Since farm workers live in relative isolation in the community, it is not possible to know whether the usually strong effect of marital status is due to the interaction of marital status with socioeconomic status, or to the interaction of marital status with community isolation. Community isolation may contribute to a high ratio as well as to a relatively low hospitalization rate. A person without a network of community relations is less able than one with such a network to obtain support from other persons during periods of crisis.[55] Also, limited contact—especially with "respectable" members of the community—makes it less probable that others will testify to his sound mental status, his good standing, and the harmless nature of his behavior to himself and the community. Community isolation, no less than socioeconomic status

[54] Ratios by marital status for all major census occupational categories show no particular pattern. Farmers/farm managers and laborers, nonfarm and nonmining, are included with farm workers in Table 5 in order to compare farm workers with a higher socioeconomic rural group and a group that approximates it in terms of socioeconomic status, but which probably differs in terms of community isolation.
[55] The significance of this for farm workers is exemplified by the statement of one farm worker, in response to a question concerning the thing he most feared about the future: "Not having enough to eat, enough (money) coming in, and having *nobody to go to for help.*" A more extensive analysis is presented in Rushing, *Class, Culture, and Alienation.*

and marital status, is an important factor in the level of resources available to an individual. It is probable, therefore, that the strong effect of marital status among farm workers may represent an interaction of marital status with community isolation, as well as with low socioeconomic status.

Inspection of the ratios for farmers/farm managers throws some light on the question, since they also live in relative isolation. The ratio for single farmers/farm managers is also substantially higher than that for the married or for disrupted-estranged farmers/farm managers. When the ratios for the two rural occupations, by marital status, are compared with those for nonfarm laborers, an interactive effect between community isolation and marital status is indicated—that is, the relative difference between the ratios for the single and each of the other two marital statuses is considerably higher for both farmers and farm workers, than for nonfarm workers. Thus community isolation appears to be a significant contingency in coercive hospitalization.[56]

---

[56] This is not to say that persons with limited resources or who are weakly integrated in the community are more apt to be "railroaded" into mental hospitals, however. The extent to which individuals are in fact "railroaded" is an unanswered question; Kutner ("The Illusion of Due Process") implies that significant numbers of patients are "railroaded," although Rock et al. ("Hospitalization and Discharge of the Mentally Ill," p. 235) and others (Klots et al., *Mental Illness and Due Process*, pp. 195–96) seriously question it. If "railroading" means that petitioners or other court participants want to have the defendant hospitalized although they do not believe hospitalization is necessary for his welfare, findings of this study do not bear on the issue. They indicate only that persons are most apt to be hospitalized involuntarily when their social and economic resources for defending themselves are limited. Thsi does not show, or even imply, that persons against whom a defendant must defend himself are not motivated by a concern for this welfare.

CONCLUSION

A person's social and economic resources and degree of community integration appear to be significant contingencies in the tendency to hospitalize. Results provide rather consistent support for the societal-reaction perspective on deviant behavior.

At the same time, these results do not invalidate behavior pathology approaches to mental illness and hospitalization. We have dealt only with different types of societal reactions and pathways to the hospital; no measures of behavior pathology are included in the analysis. Consequently, no claim can be made that societal reactions are relatively more important than behavior pathology in the initiation of court proceedings and in court dispositions. Our findings indicate only that family, occupational-economic, and community status appear to be important contingencies in the way patients enter state mental hospitals. It would be valuable to learn if behavior pathology and societal reaction interact, and of their relative influence.[57]

---

[57] This paper received serious criticism from Gove and Howell subsequent to its original publication. See Walter Gove and Patrick Howell, "Individual Resources and Mental Hospitalization: A Comparison and Evaluation of the Societal Reaction and Psychiatric Perspectives," *American Sociological Review* 39 (February, 1974), pp. 86–100. Gove and Howell's criticism is based on a misinterpretation of what this study was designed to show and what it claims to show. They believe the study is a *comparison* of a psychiatric approach to mental illness, which stipulates that persons are in mental hospitals because they are sick, and a societal reaction perspective, which contends that persons are in mental hospitals only because of the societal reaction. (*Ibid.*, esp. pp. 87, 94). It is explicit in the conclusion section, at the beginning, and elsewhere in the paper, that this is *not* what this study purports to do. It is an investigation of sociological contingencies in the societal reaction, not a comparison of psychiatric and societal reaction factors in hospitalization.

B. SOCIAL RELATIONS AND PROCESS

The two selections in this section illuminate the social relationships and processes that can occur at two stages in the life of a mental patient, the prepatient phase when the individual's mental status is being legally established and the patient phase during the period of actual hospitalization.

The first phase is investigated by Thomas J. Scheff who examines the behavior of court appointed psychiatrists involved in sanity hearings. He argues that, rather than being professional judgments that are independent of nonprofessional judgments, the diagnoses of court affiliated psychiatrists seldom depart from lay "diagnoses." Sanity hearings are usually initiated by a relative, friend, or law enforcement official, who (presumably) suspects the individual of being insane. Despite the ignorance of a layman and the variety of motives that may instigate a referral, psychiatrists seldom disagree with lay opinion. The psychiatrist's diagnosis is rarely based on an adequate examination of the patient but is largely controlled by the presumption that the conception held by the referring party is correct. Hence lay suspicion of mental illness may lead, in a rather routine manner, to an individual's being given the *legal* status of insane.

As in most organizations, individuals (patients) in mental hospitals are classified by certain categories. One obvious classification is the psychiatric diagnosis. Belknap, in "The Mental Patient in the Hospital Ward System," describes two additional classifications. One derives from institutional patient-management problems and the other from ward-management problems. The former classifies patients according to age, sex, race, and behavior patterns, while the latter classifies them according to their ability to work. The ward-management system is intertwined with the hospital authority and power structures that allow attendants considerably more authority and power over patients than they are officially supposed to have. Because professional personnel, particularly doctors, are scarce, patients' relations with hospital staff are largely limited to attendants. The attendant's power derives from his ability to grant and suspend privileges and from his ability to administer punishment. This gives him virtually complete power over patients, who have almost no way to counter such power. While this situation may have negative consequences for the psychiatric welfare of patients, the maintenance of order within the hospital would be difficult, if not impossible, without it.

COURT RELATIONS AND PSYCHIATRIC SCREENING OF PATIENTS
THOMAS J. SCHEFF

The case for making the societal reaction to deviance a major independent variable in studies of deviant behavior has been succinctly stated by Kitsuse:

> "A sociological theory of deviance must focus specifically upon the interactions which not only define behaviors as deviant but also organize and activate the application of sanctions by individuals, groups, or agencies. For in modern society, the socially significant differentiation of deviants from the non-deviant population is increasingly contingent upon circumstances of situation, place, social and personal biography, and the bureaucratically organized activities of agencies of control."[1]

In the case of mental disorder, psychiatric diagnosis is one of the crucial steps which "orga-

Reprinted with permission of author and publisher, from "The Societal Reaction to Deviance: Ascriptive Elements in the Psychiatric Screening of Mental Patients in a Midwestern State," *Social Problems* 11 (Spring, 1964), pp. 401–13. This report is part of a larger study, made possible by a grant from the Advisory Mental Health Committee of Midwestern State. By prior agreement, the state in which the study was conducted is not identified in publications.

[1] John I. Kitsuse, "Societal Reaction to Deviant Behavior: Problems of Theory and Method," *Social Problems* 9 (Winter, 1962), pp. 247–57.

nizes and activates" the societal reaction, since the state is legally empowered to segregate and isolate those persons whom psychiatrists find to be committable because of mental illness.

Recently, however, it has been argued that mental illness may be more usefully considered to be a social status than a disease, since the symptoms of mental illness are vaguely defined and widely distributed, and the definition of behavior as symptomatic of mental illness is usually dependent upon social rather than medical contingencies.[2] Furthermore, the argument continues, the status of the mental patient is more often an ascribed status, with conditions for status entry external to the patient, than an achieved status with conditions for status entry dependent upon the patient's own behavior. According to this argument, the societal reaction is a fundamentally important variable in all stages of a deviant career.

The actual usefulness of a theory of mental disorder based on the societal reaction is largely an empirical question: to what extent is entry to the status of mental patient independent of the behavior or "condition" of the patient? The present paper will explore this question for one phase of the societal reaction: the legal screening of persons alleged to be mentally ill. This screening represents the official phase of the societal reaction, which occurs after the alleged deviance has been called to the attention of the community by a complainant. This report will make no reference to the initial deviance or other situation which resulted in the complaint, but will deal entirely with procedures used by the courts after the complaint has occurred.

The purpose of the description that follows is to determine the extent of uncertainty that exists concerning new patients' qualifications for involuntary confinement in a mental hospital, and the reactions of the courts to this type of uncertainty. The data presented here indicate that, in the face of uncertainty, there is a strong presumption of illness by the court and the court psychiatrists.[3] In the discussion that follows the

presentation of findings, some of the causes, consequences and implications of the presumption of illness are suggested.

The data upon which this report is based were drawn from psychiatrists' ratings of a sample of patients newly admitted to the public mental hospitals in a Midwestern state, official court records, interviews with court officials and psychiatrists, and our observations of psychiatric examinations in four courts. The psychiatrists' ratings of new patients will be considered first.

In order to obtain a rough measure of the incoming patient's qualifications for involuntary confinement, a survey of newly admitted patients was conducted with the cooperation of the hospital psychiatrists. All psychiatrists who made admission examinations in the three large mental hospitals in the state filled out a questionnaire for the first ten consecutive patients they examined in the month of June, 1962. A total of 223 questionnaires were returned by the 25 admission psychiatrists. Although these returns do not constitute a probability sample of all new patients admitted during the year, there were no obvious biases in the drawing of the sample. For this reason, this group of patients will be taken to be typical of the newly admitted patients in Midwestern State.

The two principal legal grounds for involuntary confinement in the United States are the police power of the state (the state's right to protect itself from dangerous persons) and *parens patriae* (the state's right to assist those persons who, because of their own incapacity, may not be able to assist themselves.)[4] As a measure of the first ground, the potential dangerousness of the patient, the questionnaire contained this item: "In your opinion, if this patient were released at the present time, is it likely he would harm himself or others?" The psychiatrists were given six options, ranging from Very Likely to Very Unlikely. Their responses were: Very Likely, 5 percent; Likely, 4 percent; Somewhat Likely, 14 percent; Somewhat Unlikely, 20 percent; Unlikely, 37 percent; Very Unlikely, 18 percent. Three patients were not rated (1 percent).

As a measure of the second ground, *parens*

---

[2] Edwin M. Lemert, *Social Pathology* (New York: McGraw-Hill, 1951); Erving Goffman, *Asylums* (Chicago: Aldine, 1962).

[3] For a more general discussion of the presumption of illness in medicine, and some of its possible causes and consequences, see the author's "Decision Rules, Types of Error and Their Consequences in Medical Diagnosis," *Behavioral Science* 8 (April, 1963), pp. 97–107.

[4] Hugh Allen Ross, "Commitment of the Mentally Ill: Problems of Law and Policy," *Michigan Law Review* 57 (May, 1959), pp. 945–1018.

patriae, the questionnaire contained the item: "Based on your observations of the patient's behavior, his present degree of mental impairment is: None.......... Minimal........ Mild.. .... Moderate........ Severe........." The psychiatrists' responses were: None, 2 percent; Minimal, 12 percent; Mild, 25 percent; Moderate, 42 percent; Severe, 17 percent. Three patients were not rated (1 percent).

To be clearly qualified for involuntary confinement, a patient should be rated as likely to harm self or others (Very Likely, Likely, or Somewhat Likely) and/or as Severely Mentally Impaired. However, voluntary patients should be excluded from this analysis, since the court is not required to assess their qualifications for confinement. Excluding the 59 voluntary admissions (26 percent of the sample) leaves a sample of 164 involuntary confined patients. Of these patients, 10 were rated as meeting both qualifications for involuntary confinement, 21 were rated as being severely mentally impaired, but not dangerous, 28 were rated as dangerous but not severely mentally impaired, and 102 were rated as neither dangerous nor severely mentally impaired. (Three patients were not rated.)

According to these ratings, there is considerable uncertainty connected with the screening of newly admitted involuntary patients in the state, since a substantial majority (63 percent) of the patients did not clearly meet the statutory requirements for involuntary confinement. How does the agency responsible for assessing the qualifications for confinement, the court, react in the large numbers of cases involving uncertainty?

On the one hand, the legal rulings on this point by higher courts are quite clear. They have repeatedly held that there should be a presumption of sanity. The burden of proof of insanity is to be on the petitioners, there must be a preponderance of evidence, and the evidence should be of a "clear and unexceptionable" nature.[5]

On the other hand, existing studies suggest that there is a presumption of illness by mental health officials. In a discussion of the "discrediting" of patients by the hospital staff, based on observations at St. Elizabeth's Hospital, Washington, D.C., Goffman states:

> [The patient's case record] is apparently not regularly used to record occasions when the patient showed capacity to cope honorably and effectively with difficult life situations. Nor is the case record typically used to provide a rough average or sampling of his past conduct. [Rather, it extracts] from his whole life course a list of those incidents that have or might have had "symptomatic" significance.... I think that most of the information gathered in case records is quite true, although it might seem also to be true that almost anyone's life course could yield up enough denigrating facts to provide grounds for the record's justification of commitment.[6]

Mechanic makes a similar statement in his discussion of two large mental hospitals located in an urban area in California:

> In the crowded state or county hospitals, which is the most typical situation, the psychiatrist does not have sufficient time to make a very complete psychiatric diagnosis, nor do his psychiatric tools provide him with the equipment for an expeditious screening of the patient....
>
> In the two mental hospitals studied over a period of three months, the investigator never observed a case where the psychiatrist advised the patient that he did not need treatment. Rather, all persons who appeared at the hospital were absorbed into the patient population regardless of their ability to function adequately outside the hospital.[7]

A comment by Brown suggests that it is a fairly general understanding among mental health workers that state mental hospitals in the U.S. accept all comers.[8]

Kutner, describing commitment procedures in Chicago in 1962, also reports a strong presumption of illness by the staff of the Cook County Mental Health Clinic:

> Certificates are signed as a matter of course by staff physicians after little or no examination.... The so-called examinations are made on an assembly-line basis, often being completed in two or

---

[5] This is the typical phrasing in cases in the *Dicennial Legal Digest,* found under the heading "Mental Illness."

[6] Goffman, *Asylums,* pp. 155, 159.
[7] David Mechanic, "Some Factors in Identifying and Defining Mental Illness," *Mental Hygiene* 46 (January, 1962), pp. 66–75.
[8] Esther Lucile Brown, *Newer Dimensions of Patient Care,* Part I (New York: Russell Sage, 1961), p. 60, fn.

three minutes, and never taking more than ten minutes. Although psychiatrists agree that it is practically impossible to determine a person's sanity on the basis of such a short and hurried interview, the doctors recommend confinement in 77 percent of the cases. It appears in practice that the alleged-mentally-ill is presumed to be insane and bears the burden of proving his sanity in the few minutes allotted to him. . . .[9]

These citations suggest that mental health officials handle uncertainty by presuming illness. To ascertain if the presumption of illness occurred in Midwestern State, intensive observations of screening procedures were conducted in the four courts with the largest volume of mental cases in the state. These courts were located in the two most populous cities in the state. Before giving the results of these observations, it is necessary to describe the steps in the legal procedures for hospitalization and commitment.

STEPS IN THE SCREENING OF PERSONS ALLEGED TO BE MENTALLY ILL

The process of screening can be visualized as containing five steps in Midwestern State:

1. The application for judicial inquiry, made by three citizens. This application is heard by deputy clerks in two of the courts (C and D), by a court reporter in the third court, and by a court commissioner in the fourth court.

2. The intake examination, conducted by a hospital psychiatrist.

3. The psychiatric examination, conducted by two psychiatrists appointed by the court.

4. The interview of the patient by the guardian *ad litem,* a lawyer appointed in three of the courts to represent the patient. (Court A did not use guardians *ad litem.*)

5. The judicial hearing, conducted by a judge.

These five steps take place roughly in the order listed, although in many cases (those cases designated as emergencies) step No. 2, the intake examination, may occur before step No. 1. Steps No. 1 and No. 2 usually take place on the same day or the day after hospitalization. Steps

No. 3, No. 4, and No. 5 usually take place within a week of hospitalization. (In courts C and D, however, the judicial hearing is held only once a month.)

This series of steps would seem to provide ample opportunity for the presumption of health, and a thorough assessment, therefore, of the patient's qualifications for involuntary confinement, since there are five separate points at which discharge could occur. According to our findings, however, these procedures usually do not serve the function of screening out persons who do not meet statutory requirements. At most of these decision points, in most of the courts, retention of the patient in the hospital was virtually automatic. A notable exception to this pattern was found in one of the three state hospitals; this hospital attempted to use step No. 2, the intake examination, as a screening point to discharge patients that the superintendent described as "illegitimate," i.e., patients who do not qualify for involuntary confinement.[10] In the other two hospitals, however, this examination was perfunctory and virtually never resulted in a finding of health and a recommendation of discharge. In a similar manner, the other steps were largely ceremonial in character. For example, in court B, we observed twenty-two judicial hearings, all of which were conducted perfunctorily and with lightning rapidity. (The mean time of these hearings was 1.6 minutes.) The judge asked each patient two or three routine questions. Whatever the patient answered, however, the judge always ended the hearings and retained the patient in the hospital.

What appeared to be the key role in justifying these procedures was played by step No. 3, the examination by the court-appointed psychiatrists. In our informal discussions of screening with the judges and other court officials, these officials made it clear that although the statutes give the court the responsibility for the decision to confine or release persons alleged to be mentally ill, they would rarely if ever take the re-

---

[9] Luis Kutner, "The Illusion of Due Process in Commitment Proceedings," *Northwestern University Law Review* 57 (Sept. 1962), pp. 383–99.

[10] Other exceptions occurred as follows: the deputy clerks in courts C and D appeared to exercise some discretion in turning away applications they considered improper or incomplete, at step No. 1; the judge in Court D appeared also to perform some screening at step No. 5. For further description of these exceptions see "Rural-Urban Differences in the Judicial Screening of the Mentally Ill in a Midwestern State."

sponsibility for releasing a mental patient without a medical recommendation to that effect. The question which is crucial, therefore, for the entire screening process is whether or not the court-appointed psychiatric examiners presume illness. The remainder of the paper will consider this question.

Our observations of 116 judicial hearings raised the question of the adequacy of the psychiatric examination. Eighty-six of the hearings failed to establish that the patients were "mentally ill" (according to the criteria stated by the judges in interviews).[11] Indeed, the behavior and responses of 48 of the patients at the hearings seemed completely unexceptionable. Yet the psychiatric examiners had not recommended the release of a single one of these patients. Examining the court records of 80 additional cases, there was still not a single recommendation for release.

Although the recommendation for treatment of 196 out of 196 consecutive cases strongly suggests that the psychiatric examiners were presuming illness, particularly when we observed 48 of these patients to be responding appropriately, it is conceivable that this is not the case. The observer for this study was not a psychiatrist (he was a first year graduate student in social work) and it is possible that he could have missed evidence of disorder which a psychiatrist might have seen. It was therefore arranged for the observer to be present at a series of psychiatric examinations, in order to determine whether the examinations appeared to be merely formalities or whether, on the other hand, through careful examination and interrogation, the psychiatrists were able to establish illness even in patients whose appearances and responses were not obviously disordered. The observer was instructed to note the examiner's procedures, the criteria they appeared to use in arriving at their decision, and their reaction to uncertainty.

Each of the courts discussed here employs the services of a panel of physicians as medical examiners. The physicians are paid a flat fee of ten dollars per examination, and are usually assigned from three to five patients for each trip to the hospital. In court A, most of the examinations are performed by two psychiatrists, who went to the hospital once a week, seeing from five to ten patients a trip. In courts B, C and D, a panel of local physicians was used. These courts seek to arrange the examinations so that one of the examiners is a psychiatrist, the other a general practitioner. Court B has a list of four such pairs, and appoints each pair for a month at a time. Courts C and D have a similar list, apparently with some of the same names as court B.

To obtain physicians who were representative of the panel used in these courts, we arranged to observe the examinations of the two psychiatrists employed by court A, and one of the four pairs of physicians used in court B, one a psychiatrist, the other a general practitioner. We observed 13 examinations in court A and 13 examinations in court B. The judges in courts C and D refused to give us the names of the physicians on their panels, and we were unable to observe examinations in these courts. (The judge in court D stated that he did not want these physicians harassed in their work, since it was difficult to obtain their services even under the best of circumstances.) In addition to observing the examinations by four psychiatrists, three other psychiatrists used by these courts were interviewed.

The medical examiners followed two lines of questioning. One line was to inquire about the circumstances which led to the patient's hospitalization, the other was to ask standard questions to test the patient's orientation and his capacity for abstract thinking by asking him the date, the President, Governor, proverbs, and problems requiring arithmetic calculation. These questions were often asked very rapidly, and the patient was usually allowed only a brief time to answer.

It should be noted that the psychiatrists in these courts had access to the patient's record (which usually contained the Application for Judicial Inquiry and the hospital chart notes on the patient's behavior), and that several of the psychiatrists stated that they almost always familiarized themselves with this record before making the examination. To the extent that they were familiar with the patient's circumstances from such outside information, it is possible that the psychiatrists were basing their diagnoses of

---

[11] In interviews with the judges, the following criteria were named: Appropriateness of behavior and speech, understanding of the situation, and orientation.

illness less on the rapid and peremptory examination than on this other information. Although this was true to some extent, the importance of the record can easily be exaggerated, both because of the deficiencies in the typical record, and because of the way it is usually utilized by the examiners.

The deficiences of the typical record were easily discerned in the approximately one hundred applications and hospital charts which the author read. Both the applications and charts were extremely brief and sometimes garbled. Moreover, in some of the cases where the author and interviewer were familiar with the circumstances involved in the hospitalization, it was not clear that the complainant's testimony was any more accurate than the version presented by the patient. Often the original complaint was so paraphrased and condensed that the application seemed to have little meaning.

The attitude of the examiners toward the record was such that even in those cases where the record was ample, it often did not figure prominently in their decision. Disparaging remarks about the quality and usefulness of the record were made by several of the psychiatrists. One of the examiners was apologetic about his use of the record, giving us the impression that he thought that a good psychiatrist would not need to resort to any information outside his own personal examination of the patient. A casual attitude toward the record was openly displayed in 6 of the 26 examinations we observed. In these 6 examinations, the psychiatrist could not (or in 3 cases, did not bother to) locate the record and conducted the examination without it, with one psychiatrist making it a point of pride that he could easily diagnose most cases "blind."

In his observations of the examinations, the interviewer was instructed to rate how well the patient responded by noting his behavior during the interview, whether he answered the orientation and concept questions correctly, and whether he denied and explained the allegations which resulted in his hospitalization. If the patient's behavior during the interview obviously departed from conventional social standards (e.g., in one case the patient refused to speak), if he answered the orientation questions incorrectly, or if he did not deny and explain the

petitioners' allegations, the case was rated as meeting the statutory requirements for hospitalization. Of the 26 examinations observed, eight were rated as Criteria Met.

If, on the other hand, the patient's behavior was appropriate, his answers correct, and he denied and explained the petitioners' allegations, the interviewer rated the case as not meeting the statutory criteria. Of the 26 cases, seven were rated as Criteria Not Met. Finally, if the examination was inconclusive, but the interviewer felt that more extensive investigation might have established that the criteria were met, he rated the cases as Criteria Possibly Met. Of the 26 examined, 11 were rated in this way. The interviewer's instructions were that whenever he was in doubt he should avoid using the rating Criteria Not Met.

Even giving the examiners the benefit of the doubt, the interviewer's ratings were that in a substantial majority of the cases he observed, the examination failed to establish that the statutory criteria were met. The relationship between the examiners' recommendations and the interviewer's ratings are shown in the following table.

TABLE 1. OBSERVER'S RATINGS AND EXAMINERS' RECOMMENDATIONS

Observer's Ratings	Criteria Met	Criteria Possibly Met	Criteria Not Met	Total
Examiners' recommendations				
Commitment	7	9	2	18
30-day observation	1	2	3	6
Release	0	0	2	2
Total	8	11	7	26

The interviewer's ratings suggest that the examinations established that the statutory criteria were met in only eight cases, but the examiners recommended that the patient be retained in the hospital in 24 cases, leaving 16 cases which the interviewer rated as uncertain, and in which retention was recommended by the examiners. The observer also rated the patient's expressed desires regarding staying in the hospital, and the time taken by the examination. The ratings of the patient's desire concerning staying or leaving the hospital were: Leave, 14 cases; Indifferent, 1 case; Stay, 9 cases; and Not Ascertained, 2 cases. In only one of the 14 cases in which the patient wished to leave was the interviewer's rating Criteria Met.

The interviews ranged in length from five minutes to 17 minutes, with the mean time being 10.2 minutes. Most of the interviews were hurried, with the questions of the examiners coming so rapidly that the examiner often interrupted the patient, or one examiner interrupted the other. All of the examiners seemed quite hurried. One psychiatrist, after stating in an interview (before we observed his examinations) that he usually took about thirty minutes, stated:

> "It's not remunerative. I'm taking a hell of a cut. I can't spend 45 minutes with a patient. I don't have the time, it doesn't pay."

In the examinations that we observed, this physician actually spent 8, 10, 5, 8, 8, 7, 17, and 11 minutes with the patients, or an average of 9.2 minutes.

In these short time periods, it is virtually impossible for the examiner to extend his investigation beyond the standard orientation questions, and a short discussion of the circumstances which brought the patient to the hospital. In those cases where the patient answered the orientation questions correctly, behaved appropriately, and explained his presence at the hospital satisfactorily, the examiners did not attempt to assess the reliability of the petitioner's complaints, or to probe further into the patient's answers. Given the fact that in most of these instances the examiners were faced with borderline cases, that they took little time in the examinations, and that they usually recommended commitment, we can only conclude that their decisions were based largely on a presumption of illness. Supplementary observations reported by the interviewer support this conclusion.

After each examination, the observer asked the examiner to explain the criteria he used in arriving at his decision. The observer also had access to the examiner's official report, so that he could compare what the examiner said about the case with the record of what actually occurred during the interview. This supplementary information supports the conclusion that the examiner's decisions are based on the presumption

of illness, and sheds light on the manner in which these decisions are reached:

1. The "evidence" upon which the examiners based their decision to retain often seemed arbitrary.

2. In some cases, the decision to retain was made even when no evidence could be found.

3. Some of the psychiatrists' remarks suggest prejudgment of the cases.

4. Many of the examinations were characterized by carelessness and haste. The first question, concerning the arbitrariness of the psychiatric evidence, will now be considered.

In the weighing of the patient's responses during the interview, the physician appeared not to give the patient credit for the large number of correct answers he gave. In the typical interview, the examiner might ask the patient fifteen or twenty questions: the date, time, place, who is President, Governor, etc., what is 11x10, 11x11, etc., explain "Don't put all your eggs in one basket," "A rolling stone gathers no moss," etc. The examiners appeared to feel that a wrong answer established lack of orientation, even when it was preceded by a series of correct answers. In other words, the examiners do not establish any standard score on the orientation questions, which woud give an objective picture of the degree to which the patient answered the questions correctly, but seem at times to search until they find an incorrect answer.

For those questions which were answered incorrectly, it was not always clear whether the incorrect answers were due to the patient's "mental illness," or to the time pressure in the interview, the patient's lack of education, or other causes. Some of the questions used to establish orientation were sufficiently difficult that persons not mentally ill might have difficulty with them. Thus one of the examiners always asked, in a rapid-fire manner: "What year is it? What year was it seven years ago? Seventeen years before that?" etc. Only two of the five patients who were asked this series of questions were able to answer it correctly. However, it is a moot question whether a higher percentage of persons in a household survey would be able to do any better. To my knowledge, none of the orientation questions that are used have been checked in a normal population.

Finally, the interpretations of some of the evidence as showing mental illness seemed capricious. Thus one of the patients, when asked, "In what way are a banana, an orange, and an apple alike?" answered, "They are all something to eat." This answer was used by the examiner in explaining his recommendation to commit. The observer had noted that the patient's behavior and responses seemed appropriate and asked why the recommendation to commit had been made. The doctor stated that her behavior had been bizarre (possibly referring to her alleged promiscuity), her affect inappropriate ("When she talked about being pregnant, it was without feeling,") and with regard to the question above:

> She wasn't able to say a banana and an orange were fruit. She couldn't take it one step further, she had to say it was something to eat.

In other words, this psychiatrist was suggesting that the patient manifested concreteness in her thinking, which is held to be a symptom of mental illness. Yet in her other answers to classification questions, and to proverb interpretations, concreteness was not apparent, suggesting that the examiner's application of this test was arbitrary. In another case, the physician stated that he thought the patient was suspicious and distrustful, because he had asked about the possibility of being represented by counsel at the judicial hearing. The observer felt that these and other similar interpretations might possibly be correct, but that further investigation of the supposedly incorrect responses would be needed to establish that they were manifestations of disorientation.

In several cases where even this type of evidence was not available, the examiners still recommended retention in the hospital. Thus, one examiner, employed by court A stated that he had recommended 30-day observation for a patient whom he had thought *not* to be mentally ill, on the grounds that the patient, a young man, could not get along with his parents, and "might get into trouble." This examiner went on to say:

> We always take the conservative side (commitment or observation). Suppose a patient should commit suicide. We always make the conservative decision. I had rather play it safe. There's no harm in doing it that way.

It appeared to the observer that "playing safe" meant that even in those cases where the examination established nothing, the psychiatrists did not consider recommending release. Thus in one case the examination had established that the patient had a very good memory, was oriented and spoke quietly and seriously. The observer recorded his discussion with the physician after examination as follows:

> When the doctor told me he was recommending commitment for this patient too (he had also recommended commitment in the two examinations held earlier that day) he laughed because he could see what my next question was going to be. He said, "I already recommended the release of two patients this month." This sounded like it was the maximum amount the way he said it.

Apparently this examiner felt that he had a very limited quota on the number of patients he could recommend for release (less than two percent of those examined).

The language used by these physicians tends to intimate that mental illness was found, even when reporting the opposite. Thus in one case the recommendation stated: "No gross evidence of delusions or hallucinations." This statement is misleading, since not only was there no gross evidence, there was not any evidence, not even the slightest suggestion of delusions or hallucinations, brought out by the interview.

These remarks suggest that the examiners prejudge the cases they examine. Several further comments indicate prejudgment. One physician stated that he thought that most crimes of violence were committed by patients released too early from mental hospitals. (This is an erroneous belief.)[12] He went on to say that he thought that all mental patients should be kept in the hospital at least three months, indicating prejudgment concerning his examinations. Another physician, after a very short interview (8 minutes), told the observer:

---

[12] The rate of crimes of violence, or any crime, appears to be less among ex-mental patients than in the general population. Henry Brill and Benjamin Maltzberg, "Statistical Report Based on the Arrest Record of 5354 Ex-patients Released from New York State Mental Hospitals During the Period 1946–48." Mimeo available from the authors; Louis H. Cohen and Henry Freeman, "How Dangerous to the Community Are State Hospital Patients?", *Connecticut State Medical Journal* 9 (Sept., 1945), pp. 697–700; Donald W. Hastings, "Follow-up Results in Psychiatric Illness," *American Journal of Psychiatry* 118 (June 1962), pp. 1078–86.

On the schizophrenics, I don't bother asking them more questions when I can see they're schizophrenic because *I know what they are going to say*. You could talk to them another half hour and not learn any more.

Another physician, finally, contrasted cases in which the patient's family or others initiated hospitalization ("petition cases," the great majority of cases) with those cases initiated by the court.

The petition cases are pretty *automatic*. If the patient's own family wants to get rid of him you know there is something wrong.

The lack of care which characterized the examinations is evident in the forms on which the examiners make their recommendations. On most of these forms, whole sections have been left unanswered. Others are answered in a peremptory and uninformative way. For example, in the section entitled Physical Examination, the question is asked: "Have you made a physical examination of the patient? State fully what is the present physical condition." A typical answer is "Yes. Fair.", or, "Is apparently in good health." Since in none of the examinations we observed was the patient actually physically examined, these answers appear to be mere guesses. One of the examiners used regularly in court B, to the question "On what subject or in what way is derangement now manifested?" always wrote in "Is mentally ill." The omissions, and the almost flippant brevity of these forms, together with the arbitrariness, lack of evidence, and prejudicial character of the examinations, discussed above, all support the observer's conclusion that, except in very unusual cases, the psychiatric examiner's recommendation to retain the patient is virtually automatic.

Lest it be thought that these results are unique to a particularly backward Midwestern State, it should be pointed out that this state is noted for its progressive psychiatric practices. It will be recalled that a number of the psychiatrists employed by the court as examiners had finished their psychiatric residencies, which is not always the case in many other states. A still common practice in other states is to employ, as members of the "Lunacy Panel," partially retired physicians with no psychiatric training whatever. This was the case in Stockton, California, in 1959,

where the author observed hundreds of hearings at which these physicians were present. It may be indicative of some of the larger issues underlying the question of civil commitment that, in these hearings, the physicians played very little part; the judge controlled the questioning of the relatives and patients, and the hearings were often a model of impartial and thorough investigation.

DISCUSSION

Ratings of the qualifications for involuntary confinement of patients newly admitted to the public mental hospitals in a Midwestern state, together with observations of judicial hearings and psychiatric examinations by the observer connected with the present study, both suggest that the decision as to the mental condition of a majority of the patients is an uncertain one. The fact that the courts seldom release patients, and the perfunctory manner in which the legal and medical procedures are carried out, suggest that the judicial decision to retain patients in the hospital for treatment is routine and largely based on the presumption of illness. Three reasons for this presumption will be discussed: financial, ideological, and political.

Our discussions with the examiners indicated that one reason that they perform biased "examinations" is that their rate of pay is determined by the length of time spent with the patient. In recommending retention, the examiners are refraining from interrupting the hospitalization and commitment procedures already in progress, and thereby allowing someone else, usually the hospital, to make the effective decision to release or commit. In order to recommend release, however, they would have to build a case showing why these procedures should be interrupted. Building such a case would take much more time than is presently expended by the examiners, thereby reducing their rate of pay.

A more fundamental reason for the presumption of illness by the examiners, and perhaps the reason why this practice is allowed by the courts, is the interpretation of current psychiatric doctrine by the examiners and court officials. These officials make a number of assumptions, which are now thought to be of doubtful validity:

1. The condition of mentally ill persons deteriorates rapidly without psychiatric assistance.

2. Effective psychiatric treatments exist for most mental illnesses.

3. Unlike surgery, there are no risks involved in involuntary psychiatric treatment: it either helps or is neutral, it can't hurt.

4. Exposing a prospective mental patient to questioning, cross-examination, and other screening procedures exposes him to the unnecessary stigma of trial-like procedures, and may do further damage to his mental condition.

5. There is an element of danger to self or others in most mental illness. It is better to risk unnecessary hospitalization than the harm the patient might do himself or others.

Many psychiatrists and others now argue that none of these assumptions are necessarily correct.

1. The assumption that psychiatric disorders usually get worse without treatment rests on very little other than evidence of an anecdotal character. There is just as much evidence that most acute psychological and emotional upsets are self-terminating.[13]

2. It is still not clear, according to systematic studies evaluating psychotherapy, drugs, etc., that most psychiatric interventions are any more effective, on the average, than no treatment at all.[14]

3 There is very good evidence that involuntary hospitalization and social isolation may affect the patient's life: his job, his family affairs, etc. There is some evidence that too hasty exposure to psychiatric treatment may convince the patient that he is "sick," prolonging what might have been an otherwise transitory episode.[15]

4. This assumption is correct, as far as it goes. But it is misleading because it fails to consider what occurs when the patient who does not wish to be hospitalized is forcibly treated. Such patients often become extremely indignant and angry, particularly in the case, as often happens, when they are deceived into coming to the hospital on some pretext.

5. The element of danger is usually exaggerated both in amount and degree. In the psychiatric survey of new patients in state mental hospitals, danger to self or others was mentioned in about a fourth of the cases. Furthermore, in those cases where danger is mentioned, it is not always clear that the risks involved are greater than those encountered in ordinary social life. This issue has been discussed by Ross, an attorney:

> A truck driver with a mild neurosis who is "accident prone" is probably a greater danger to society than most psychotics; yet, he will not be committed for treatment, even if he would be benefited. The community expects a certain amount of dangerous activity. I suspect that as a class, drinking drivers are a greater danger than the mentally ill, and yet the drivers are tolerated or punished with small fines rather than indeterminate imprisonment.[16]

From our observations of the medical examinations and other commitment procedures, we formed a very strong impression that the doctrines of danger to self or others, early treatment, and the avoidance of stigma were invoked partly because the officials believed them to be true, and partly because they provided convenient justification for a preexisting policy of summary action, minimal investigation, avoidance of responsibility and, after the patient is in the hospital, indecisiveness and delay.

The policy of presuming illness is probably both cause and effect of political pressure on the court from the community. The judge, an elected official, runs the risk of being more heavily penalized for erroneously releasing than for errorouly retaining patients. Since the judge personally appoints the panel of psychiatrists to serve as examiners, he can easily transmit the community pressure to them, by failing to reappoint a psychiatrist whose examinations were inconveniently thorough.

Some of the implications of these findings for the sociology of deviant behavior will be briefly

---

[13] For a review of epidemiological studies of mental disorder see Richard J. Plunkett and John E. Gordon, *Epidemiology and Mental Illness* (New York: Basic Books, 1960). Most of these studies suggest that at any given point in time, psychiatrists find a substantial proportion of persons in normal populations to be "mentally ill." One interpretation of this finding is that much of the deviance detected in these studies is self-limiting.

[14] For an assessment of the evidence regarding the effectiveness of electroshock, drugs, psychotherapy, and other psychiatric treatments, see H. J. Eysenck, *Handbook of Abnormal Psychology* (New York: Basic Books, 1961), Part III.

[15] For examples from military psychiatry, see Albert J. Glass, "Psychotherapy in the Combat Zone," in *Symposium on Stress* (Washington, D.C., Army Medical Service Graduate School, 1953), and B. L. Bushard, "The U.S. Army's Mental Hygiene Consultation Service," in *Symposium on Preventive and Social Psychiatry,* 15–17, April 1957 (Washington, D.C.: Walter Reed Army Institute of Research), pp. 431–43. For a discussion of essentially the same problem in the context of a civilian mental hospital, cf. Kai T. Erikson, "Patient Role and Social Uncertainty—A Dilemma of the Mentally Ill," *Psychiatry* 20 (August 1957), pp. 263–75.

---

[16] Ross "Commitment of the Mentally Ill," p. 962.

summarized. The discussion above, of the reasons that the psychiatrists tend to presume illness, suggests that the motivations of the key decision-makers in the screening process may be significant in determining the extent and direction of the societal reaction. In the case of psychiatric screening of persons alleged to be mentally ill, the social differentiation of the deviant from the non-deviant population appears to be materially affected by the financial, ideological, and political position of the psychiatrists, who are in this instance the key agents of social control.

Under these circumstances, the character of the societal reaction appears to undergo a marked change from the pattern of denial which occurs in the community. The official societal reaction appears to reverse the presumption of normality reported by the Cummings as a characteristic of informal societal reaction, and instead exaggerates both the amount and degree of deviance.[17] Thus, one extremely important contingency influencing the severity of the societal reaction may be whether or not the original deviance comes to official notice. This paper suggests that in the area of mental disorder, perhaps in contrast to other areas of deviant behavior, if the official societal reaction is invoked, for whatever reason, social differentiation of the deviant from the non-deviant population will usually occur.

CONCLUSION

This paper has described the screening of patients who were admitted to public mental hospitals in early June, 1962, in a Midwestern state. The data presented here suggest that the screening is usually perfunctory, and that in the crucial screening examination by the court-appointed psychiatrists, there is a presumption of illness. Since most court decisions appear to hinge on the recommendation of these psychiatrists, there appears to be a large element of status ascription in the official societal reaction to persons alleged to be mentally ill, as exemplified by the court's actions. This finding points to the importance of lay definitions of mental illness in the community, since the "diagnosis" of mental illness by laymen in the community initiates the official societal reaction, and to the necessity of analyzing social processes connected with the recognition and reaction to the deviant behavior that is called mental illness in our society.

---

[17] Elaine Cumming and John Cumming, *Closed Ranks* (Cambridge, Mass.: Harvard University Press, 1957), p. 102; for further discussion of the bipolarization of the societal reaction into denial and labeling, see the author's "The Role of the Mentally Ill and the Dynamics of Mental Disorder: A Research Framework," *Sociometry* 26 (December, 1963), pp. 436–53.

THE MENTAL PATIENT IN THE HOSPITAL WARD SYSTEM

IVAN BELKNAP

PATIENT CLASSIFICATION AND THE SOCIAL STRUCTURE OF THE HOSPITAL WARD SYSTEM

In Southern State Hospital there are actually three classification schemes for patients. The first

---

Reprinted as abridged from *Human Problems of a State Mental Hospital* by Ivan Belknap (pp. 123, 128–31, 146–47, 151–53 and 164–71; excerpts from pages 124, 125, 132, 145, 148, 150, 154, and 163; and Figure 5, p. 149). Copyright © 1956, McGraw-Hill Book Company, Inc. Used by permission of McGraw-Hill Book Company and the author.

is the scientific one employed in records and formal staff presentation. The second is the institutional classification, or patient-management system. The third is the informal system of patient classification used by the ward attendants and physicians in their daily work with the patients. The first and second systems are both official systems, although they are essentially unrelated to each other. The third system is unofficial and unacknowledged but is in fact closely integrated with the second system. In the over-all organization of Southern State Hospital, the second system seems to work at least in part as an intermediate or coupling system between the medical-psychiatric function of the hospital and the custodial-maintenance function.

Learning how to integrate the three systems is the first task which the new physician faces in Southern State Hospital as he takes up his duties on the wards. His textbooks and academic and residency training have usually centered around the conceptions of the official record diagnoses. In the state hospital institutional classification he often encounters something new as far as much of his formal training goes.

The clinical psychiatry in which the physician has been trained has developed mainly in private practice, specialized psychiatric research, and small psychopathic hospitals, usually attached to medical schools in America and Europe. Its categories are derived from, and assume, intimate personal knowledge of the patient. Institutional psychiatry, of the kind represented in state hospitals, has developed largely in these state hospitals and seems to represent in many respects an altogether different kind of growth.[1] When the types of classification used in state hospitals are compared with the categories of the revised nomenclature of the American Psychiatric Association, the differences in origin and effect of the two types of classification are quite striking.[2] The institutional system is essentially an operational device for the management of large numbers of patients from the point of view of their relation to an administrative organization. The

APA classification is just as clearly the beginning of a scientific taxonomy developed by and for research and individual practice in psychiatry. . . .

Historically, the institutional classification scheme used in the hospital was developed before the present system of psychiatric classification; it represents a pattern for the institutional management of incoming patients in terms of age, sex, and behavior patterns, rather than a scientific nosology. Many of these institutional categories cut across the official psychiatric diagnoses, as, for example, when one patient will be formally diagnosed as an agitated psychoneurotic, another as an excited paranoid schizophrenic, another as a manic-depressive in a strong manic phase. Informally, all three may be classified as "disturbed" or "excited" and treated accordingly.

One of the peculiarities of procedure in Southern State Hospital is that the institutional classification and diagnostic system seems to be far more important in the care, treatment, and discharge of patients than the official classification. Yet, the professional personnel must report and speak in terms of the official classification, while they and their subordinates are required to manage the patients and do most of the practical work of the hospital in terms of the institutional ward systems. This situation leads to a great deal of confusion, since the formal administrative action of the hospital proceeds in terms of quite deceptive labels. The official diagnostic terms must be used in the statistical reporting of the hospital, so that records kept of patients often reflect little of what is being done for them except to people who know what the formal terms actually mean in the institutional classification scheme. The phrase "continuous-treatment," applied to a patient in Southern State Hospital, almost always means in the institutional classification that he is receiving no psychiatric treatment at all. The diagnosis of schizophrenia in one of its subtypes in the APA classification may apply to a patient in almost any category of the institutional classification.

This situation is further complicated by the third classification used on the wards. The ward classification is completely unofficial in Southern State Hospital. It is keyed to the institutional classification but has an altogether different structure and execution from that implied in the

---

[1] See the analyses of William Bryan in *Administrative Psychiatry* (New York: W. W. Norton & Company, 1936), and of Maurice Grimes in *When Minds Go Wrong* (Chicago: published by the author, 1951).

[2] Compare the categories used in *Diagnostic and Statistical Manual* (Washington, D.C.: American Psychiatric Association, 1952) with those used by Bryan and Grimes in the works cited in Note 1. Both Bryan and Grimes were technically trained psychiatrists, but they employed a different frame of reference when discussing procedure with hospital patients. There is of course very little doubt that behind these two types of classification a deeper problem exists: the relation of psychiatry to two types of clientele—one dependent, institutionalized, and of relatively lower social status; the other independent, uninstitutionalized, and of relatively higher status. Redlich points out the powerful effects of social definitions, over which neither psychiatrist nor patient has explicit control, in developing a somewhat coercive definition of "adjustment" as "normal" for the first of these groups, and a more permissive one of creativity, spontaneity, and fulfillment of potential for the latter. See F. C. Redlich, "The Concept of Normality," *American Journal of Psychotherapy* 6 (July, 1952), pp. 551–76. See also Leslie Schaffer and Jerome K. Myers. "Psychotherapy and Social Stratification," *Psychiatry* 17 (February, 1954), pp. 83–93.

institutional system. The ward classification distributes the patients in terms of their manageability and occupational utility on the ward and in the hospital work. Just as the APA categories may describe little of the patient's position in the hospital's institutional classification, the latter may give little information about the patient's status on the ward.

Our study of the composition of the wards in the hospital in relation to the two official classifications of the hospital showed that neither of these two classifications was employed in any apparent functional way in determining the composition of any one of the wards. Patients are distributed throughout most of the wards without much homogeneity even in the institutional classification. Young persons are placed with senile persons, and wards which are predominantly made up of psychiatrically deteriorated mental patients frequently house a group of patients who are comparatively in much better condition. On the male white ward in which many senile cases are kept, 10 percent of the ward is made up of new admissions or convalescent cases. In terms of the official psychiatric classifications, comparatively light cases, some of them diagnosed as mild behavior disorders, are found scattered among stuporous catatonic schizophrenics, badly deteriorated hebephrenic schizophrenics, advanced cases of paresis, and the mentally deficient with psychoses.

This mixture of patients is of course contrary to the logic of any modern school of psychiatry, and it means in substance that little if any systematic group therapy or occupational or industrial therapy can be set up on the natural administrative unit of the ward in the hospital. At the same time this mixture of patients exposes the severely ill, mild, and intermediate mental patients to uncontrolled interactive relationships with one another, while it makes integrated professional treatment programs for the group impossible.

It was during our efforts to find some explanation for this mixture of patients that we began to see some of the elements of the hospital's third classification and assignment system. This system had been mentioned indirectly, and we had been given several hints about it by people we interviewed; but the subject seemed taboo at

this level. When we began to spend time on the wards, and when some of our observers on the wards gained the confidence of the attendants, however, the general pattern of the third system emerged as the most important and most thoroughly consistent of the hospital's classification and assignment procedures.

We had been told (as we usually were with any problem we brought up) that the mixture of patients on the ward was the result of the hospital's chronic understaffing and lack of space. This answer explained overcrowding in the hospital generally, but it did not explain the mixture. In pursuing the question further we found that in nearly every case the patients in reasonably good mental condition always seemed to do the housekeeping work on their wards. They also cleaned up after the patients who soiled, and they bathed and dressed and toileted the patients who needed these services.

In due course of time it became clear that the mild mental cases on all the wards were part of a definite work system of patients who performed most of the work of the wards under the supervision of the attendants. This work group was maintained without regard for the logic of the two official classifications, because such a group was necessary in the operation of the wards for the hospital as a whole. Once we had this clue, it was easy to see that it was the admixture of definite proportions of lucid patients in most of the wards for work purposes which produced what at first had appeared as a rather chaotic mixture of patient types.

When we suggested this explanation for the mixture to our informants for verification, they admitted that it was true and told us at first that this arrangement of working patients on the wards is a practical necessity for ward management, since the population of the hospital is badly distended and personnel in poor supply. But as we became more familiar with the wards, we found that this was only a partial explanation of the arrangement. The use of patient labor is tied in with the ward status system, and has many purposes and functions which are not simply the result of overcrowding of patients and small attendant staff. On the wards it serves as much to focus a definite system of patient management as it does to get physical work done. It is in this area of management that the hospital's informal or third classification system centers.

The organization of ward work defines a particular status for the attendant and a set of patients' working statuses underneath him; and these statuses in turn determine the position of all patients on the ward. The principle of this system, as we saw it, was that the ward attendant must give orders in the ward which will be obeyed. If his authority fails with the patients, there are no further levels of authority until the ward physician is reached. For most people, one element in authority is symbolized by supervisory rather than servile activities, and for this reason, although his job specifications require it, the attendant cannot clean up after patients.

In developing at this point a supervisory role which is not formally defined in his job, the attendant also creates the third classification system of the hospital. This system had developed far back in the hospital's history as a device which supported the authority of the attendant through his ability to determine privileges for the patients in return for work in the hospital and for obedience. And the patients in the working group serve the attendant in many ways that go beyond housekeeping. Some of them are lieutenants, spies, helpers with food service, and with minor therapy. As a group they appear to be essential in the present operation of the hospital.

It is this third classification system, necessary in the management of the ward, more than any other feature which produces the peculiar distribution of patients. A sufficient number of patients in the privileged, or working, status must be present to do ward housekeeping and provide the necessary authority pattern by which the attendant operates the ward. This is accomplished by assigning, if necessary, the needed proportions of the "right" sort of patient to wards which may be made up of badly deteriorated psychotic and senile individuals. The effect of this practice is of course that of altering the second, or institutional, classification scheme to conform to the requirements of ward organization set by the third system.

As will be shown below in the more detailed treatment of ward organization and social control, the social organization of attendants and patients has many other effects than those on classification and assignment. It is enough to point out here that the effects of living with deteriorated patients are obviously not those desired by modern psychiatry for treatment of the patients who are closer to normality and capable of maintaining good contact with reality. And it is also evidently not a desirable professional situation when the physician in charge must go along with the requirements of ward management and housekeeping without primary reference to desirable courses of therapy for the patients. . . .

All three of these systems serve historically developed purposes and interests inside and outside the hospital, and each of the systems contributes in certain ways to each of the others. Although there are conflicts between the systems, they seem to be accommodated to each other, in the sense that elimination of one of them would require many changes in each of the others.

Most of the reforms proposed in the numerous investigations of Southern State Hospital in the years since its foundation have made the crucial mistake of concentrating their proposals on the two formally acknowledged systems, without taking account of the third, except perhaps as a flaw in the hospital. Yet an acquaintance with all levels of Southern State Hospital's operation makes it certain that the third, or ward, system is in an operational sense just as important in the hospital's stability and in its effect on patients as the other two. It is the ward system which deals with the Southern State patient on a daily basis, defines his behavior, carries out the daily supervision of his treatment, both physical and psychiatric, sees that he is fed, protects him from injury, provides a sanitary and orderly environment and most of whatever personal consideration, entertainment, or recreation is possible for him. These things done by the ward system obviously should have high priority in any organization for mental patients.

The formal organization of the wards shows the formal authority line in ward management as operating downward from the Clinical Director (level I) through the Director of Nursing Service (level II), the general-duty registered nurses (level II), the attendant supervisors (level III), and ending in the ward charge attendants (level III). The charge is chief of the attendants on all shifts on the ward.[3]

For Southern State Hospital this is a relatively new arrangement and replaces, or rather attempts to replace, an older authority line which ran from the Superintendent through the ward physician and directly to the charge attendant by way of the attendant supervisor. At the time of our study the older authority line was the one employed in practice, since operating procedure on the wards was not adjusted in any way to the use of registered nurses. The occasional presence of the nurse on the ward as a supervisor split the authority line from the physician to the charge attendant without contributing in any tangible way to the psychiatric job of either. This arrangement was causing a good deal of friction during all the time of our study. It was apparent that the hospital either should have had enough nurses to replace all the attendants or should not have attempted their employment on the wards at all. As it was, however, the problem was largely solved by the fact that the registered nurses were scarce and expensive (by hospital standards) and were used more appropriately in terms of their medical qualifications in the hospital's specific therapies (electroshock, insulin therapy) and in the two infirmaries. The nurses' oversight of the wards was something of a fiction.

As an administrative structure, the actual authority line between the ward physician and charge attendant is an oddity. The formal job definitions rigidly limit the range of decision of the charge attendant to minor nursing and housekeeping duties, and his pay is adjusted to this limitation. The attendant supervisors, who are placed in the formal line between the physician and the charge attendant, seldom perform (and seldom could perform, since there are only two of them) regular supervisory duties in ward operations. The formal functions of the supervisors seem to be restricted in practice to serving as staff clerks to the ward physicians for routine administration, including supplies, reports, and personnel and patient assignment.[4]

The professional and subprofessional personnel in level II, like the supervisors, are essential staff people with reference to the physician's line to the wards, without any defined line functions. Thus the formal line function of the physician runs directly to the charge attendant with no intervening delegated formal steps of responsible execution and supervision. The average physician's line and staff structure is shown in Figure 1, below, on the conservative assumption that he will be responsible for four wards, averaging sixty-six patients each.

Administratively the official position of the ward physician is that of an executive whose accountability embraces 296 people, since his line runs directly to each individual patient. Properly speaking, in administrative terms, the ward physician does not have a span of control in any official sense. This is because, in terms of formal job definitions, the charge attendants are not actually foremen or supervisors but rather orderlies and helpers in dealing with the patients on the ward. Formally, the physician's span of control in Figure 1 is a span of performance.

This formal definition of executive responsibility at the work level of the hospital would indicate a severe problem to any experienced administrator. When executive authority of any kind is diffused in this manner, no social system can accomplish any type of work at all. In the eighteen wards of Southern State Hospital which we analyzed, however, the informal organization of the hospital had long since closed and organized this gap in executive control by establishing a well-understood social organization for both attendants and patients.

In effect, this organization redefined the span of control of the ward physician to include, taking Figure 1, as an example, the twelve charge attendants as something approaching area supervisors or administrative assistants to the physician and to include the attendants as foremen in

---

[3] In theory each shift of attendants is under a Charge Attendant, but all three shifts are usually supervised by one of the senior charge attendants, who is the informal supervisor of the ward (and, at times, of two or three wards). The chief charge is usually the first day-charge, who informally controls all shifts. He is almost without exception the attendant best acquainted with the ward physician, who usually makes his rounds during the day-man's shift. In Southern State Hospital the third, or night, shift is generally supposed to have at least two attendants on duty with the charge, but turnover and shortage of personnel often reduce this shift, as they often reduce the other shifts, to one man.

[4] See Chapter Three of Ivan Belknap, *Human Problems of a State Mental Hospital* (McGraw-Hill Book Company, 1956).

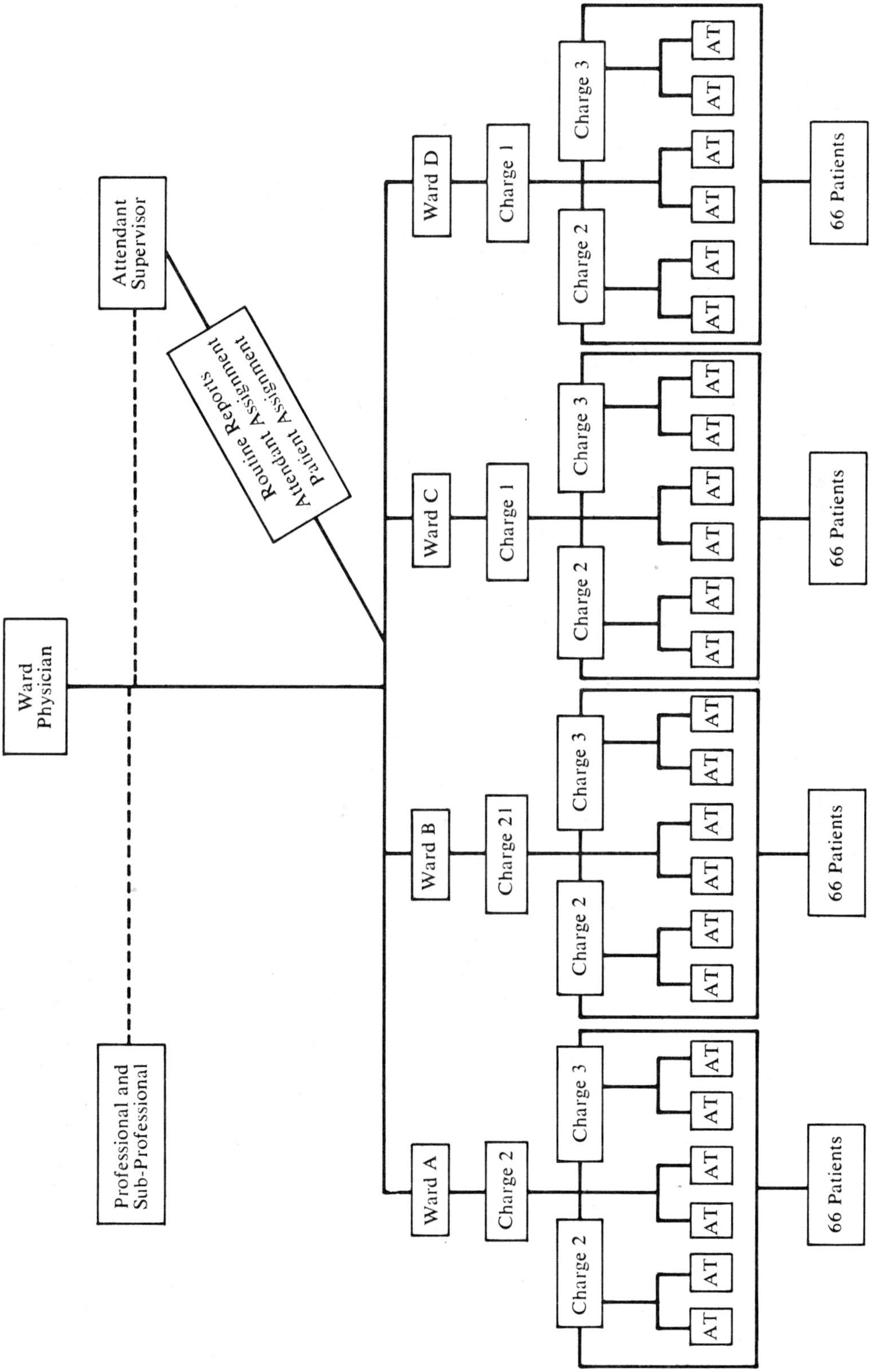

FIGURE 1. SPAN OF CONTROL OF AN AVERAGE SOUTHERN STATE HOSPITAL WARD PHYSICIAN

direct charge of the patients. This organization, in administrative terms, inserted two levels of supervision between the physician and the patient and thus permitted a practically inoperable system to operate, at least in a certain way. . . .

The informal organization of the wards is maintained and transmitted in its essentials by a core of about 18 percent of the attendants. The annual turnover rate of this group is less than 1 percent, as compared with 83 percent for the remaining 82 percent of the attendants. Seven out of ten of this core live on the hospital grounds, and six out of ten are married to other attendants employed in the hospital. Two out of each ten men in the core had fathers or mothers who had been employed in Southern State Hospital or other state hospitals. The median length of hospital employment for this core is 12 years, as compared with the median length of employment for ward physicians of 1.5 years, and a median tenure for the hospital superintendents of 2.6 years.[5] The core of attendants had completed a median of 8 years of school. The core employees hold most of the charge and supervisory positions in level III, although a few of them are ward attendants. In the direct work of Southern State Hospital with its patients, these core attendants are almost the only career employees in the medical part of the hospital.

FUNCTION OF PATIENT CLASSIFICATION

The main function of the informal organization on the wards for the attendant is to set up a system which permits him to adjust personally the requirements of psychiatric treatment, as represented by the hospital's formal classification on the one hand, with the requirements of daily patient management on the other. This adjustment involves a definite organization of interpersonal relations between the attendant and his fellow attendants, between the attendants and the members of the two upper administrative

levels, and between the attendants and the patients.

The system includes patterns of expected behavior and ideas for the attendants in relation to patients and to the upper-level professionals in the hospital. These patterns are justified by an ideology centering around the attendant's functions in the hospital, and the entire system is held together with considerable solidarity, or ingroup feeling, against patients and the professionals, who are outgroups. The system is a complete social organization, with an ideology and a tradition at least seventy years old. It can be considered as a type of culture in the hospital, with its own functionaries, legends, and justifications.

Toward the hospital patients on the wards, the attendants' system operates primarily as a set of behavior controls, backed up by a system of rewards and punishments. Toward the professionals in the hospital, and particularly toward the physicians, the attendants' culture operates both cooperatively and defensively. Among the attendants themselves the system of organization is maintained by informal but organized training and by the regular elimination of attendants who do not conform to the roles defined for them.

In our material on ward organization a number of general points seem to stand out. One of the major points is that the hospital's formal organization has defined an impossible span of control for the ward physician. Essentially this means that the hospital's formal organization has avoided the problem of defining daily patient management and supervision on the ward and left a gap which had to be filled in the hospital's operation. The attendant's functions have not been delegated to him at all but have grown up by default.

The second major point is related to the first. The formal system of the hospital defines the attendant and pays him more or less as equivalent to a general hospital orderly. But because of the administrative gap, the attendants in Southern State Hospital have always had far more important nursing responsibilities than those of any general hospital orderly. This mixture of low status and serious responsibility is resented by every one of the old attendants to whom we talked, and it is immediately sensed and resented

---

[5] The only positions in the hospital with comparable average length of service were some of the business office positions, many of which were filled with former attendants who had risen to them over relatively long periods. The route into the business side of the hospital is almost the only line of promotion we could find for the attendant.

by most new employees. It was obviously blocking and inhibiting creative activity for most attendants and had in fact become a definite part of the negative attitude toward the upper levels and any innovations which we found characteristic in the wards. In the ideology of the attendants about their jobs, this situation was translated into statements like the following, taken from our case records:

This place would go to pieces if it weren't for the attendants. But we never get any credit or recognition.

The doctor spends 5 minutes a day on my ward and doesn't know one patient from the other. But if I try to tell him anything he puts his foot in my mouth.

I've worked here 20 years, and I've learned a good deal about mental cases and helped a few of them. But the doctor always takes the credit for anything good, and I get the blame for anything that goes wrong.

That bunch in the front office [the level I and II personnel] sit around on their ————s all day and read reports and write letters and diagnose the cases at long range, but we're the boys who have to handle the problems.

Statements of this sort are part of what the new attendant hears almost as soon as he comes on the ward, and they are given freely to investigators who show any sympathy.

A third major point on the attendant's ward organization is that he is in fact faced with an extremely difficult and unpleasant job, with many potential personality strains. To the person who has never made more than a conducted tour of a state hospital this point needs special emphasis. The state hospital must take all kinds of patients, from the seriously to the mildly ill. Many of the patients have troublesome chronic physical ailments, and among these are many partially debilitated senile persons. Incontinence, both of feces and urine, is a characteristic symptom or phase in several types of mental illness. Behavior of the various patients on the wards of the state mental hospitals almost always runs the scale from hyperactivity to complete listlessness. With any large number of mental patients, there is always the risk of dangerous violence at unpredictable times. And the average number of

patients on most of the Southern State Hospital wards is near eighty.

Familiarity with the daily environment of the attendant demonstrates very quickly that the individual working in this atmosphere must make adjustments not required of people in more ordinary occupations. The attendant does not even escape this atmosphere periodically and retire to an office, as do even professionals closely associated with treatment. He must live with it for his entire shift.

In making his adjustment to his job, the attendant's first need is obviously for order and control of his ward environment, and, secondly, for some psychological support while he performs his job. The in-group of attendants with its culture meets both these needs and is probably essential, both in helping the individual attendant organize his work and in maintaining his personality balance. . . .

In the experienced attendant's classification, the patients in Southern State Hospital are divided into three groups: (1) the cooperative patients, to be given the most privileges, who may be used for work in the ward, for helping with other patients, for surveillance of patients, and for protection; (2) the neutral patients, who may be given limited privileges, and who are generally neither cooperative nor uncooperative; (3) the uncooperative group, who have no privileges, and who may be potentially dangerous or disturbing.

From among the first group the attendant draws his assistants and helpers, without whom ward management would be impossible. This assistance is not provided in the hospital's formal organization, but, according to the attendants' belief, the average hospital ward would be completely unmanageable without it. By using his social position, the attendant is able to make it worth while for this group of patients to obey his orders and keep him informed. These patients aid him in the management of the neutral group, and they protect him from and enable him to handle the patients in the uncooperative group, as he finds this necessary.

The authority of the attendant in the operation of his control system is backed up by both positive and negative power. This power is an essential element in his control of the ward. He can give patient privileges, and he can punish the patient. The privileges consist of having the best job, better rooms and beds, minor luxuries like coffee on the ward, a little more privacy than the average patient, going outside the ward without supervision, having more access than the average patient to the attendant's companionship or to professional personnel like the physicians, and enjoying such intangible but vital things as being treated with personal kindness and respect.

The punishments which can be applied by the ward attendant are suspension of all privileges, psychological mistreatment, such as ridicule, vicious ribbing, moderate and sometimes severe corporal punishment, or the threat of such punishment, locking up the patient in an isolated room, denial or distortion of access to the professional personnel, threatening to put, or putting, the patient on the list for electroshock therapy, transfer of the patient to undesirable wards, and regular assignment of the patient to unpleasant tasks such as cleaning up after the soilers.

This working system of patient classification we have represented as three sublevels of patient status, each accompanied by a pattern of privileges or penalties. As the patient experiences the hospital, it is as a member of one of these three groups, as defined by the attendants on the wards:

1. Patients with special and outside privileges
2. Patients with limited privileges
3. Patients without privileges

The privilege classifications are part of the attendants' control system, but to the patient they are primarily definitions of what he does in the hospital, including definitions of his relations to the attendants, to the other patients in his particular status, and to the patients below or above this status.

The system is by no means evident to casual visitors to the wards. Interview material suggests strongly that it is not thoroughly understood by many of the professionals in level II. The system does not stand out clearly until the observer has spent enough time on the wards and gained enough intimacy with the patient-attendant organization to see the connections which actually exist between isolated examples of behavior. And such access is almost impossible for anyone in the upper levels of the hospital. Inquiry or observation by these line superiors does occur, but it is so limited by the diffuse administrative control span and personnel shortage and turnover in the upper level that it produces no visible results in the form of knowledge in level II. Such inquiry usually only increases mutual suspicion between the members of the two systems.

Once the characteristic patterns of the patient organization are understood, it is easy to see that all these patterns have great significance in determining the effect of the hospital on the patient. In the long run, only those formal medical orders which can be applied without any general disturbance of the ward social system will be put into effect, a fact which often reduces or even eliminates the physician as a factor in the experience of the patient. In a time sense, the attendant always has close to 24 hours' advantage of any of the upper-level personnel. The hierarchy of patient status establishes a system of relations among the patients themselves which may have many treatment effects uninfluenced by professional control; one of the most obvious of these is that the upper group of patients monopolizes access to the attendant (and thus to the doctor), to recreation on the ward, and much recreational therapy activity in the hospital. This group maintains the monopoly vigorously by sarcasm, ridicule, physical threats, and sometimes physical punishment directed against lower-status trespassers. This exclusion is also at times an exclusion from a group which the lower-status patient desires to join. Many of these lower-status patients are of course in much greater need of attention from the attendant and physician than are the members of the upper group, and this exclusion blocks their mobility into a position where they can secure such attention.

In general, patients with special or outside privileges are distributed throughout most of the different wards in the hospital. There seems to be a tendency for them to cluster, however, on certain wards, one of which, male Ward 14, has the status of an "open" ward, where patients are free to come and go almost at will. Generally speaking, the special-privilege patients can go unattended about the grounds and can go to work or to the canteen at will. Much of the hospital's housekeeping and maintenance work is done by them, and although they are not forced to do this work, most of them apparently prefer to work. Within this top group there seem to be two subdivisions, the first with almost unrestricted privileges, the second enjoying these privileges but in a probationary status. The group is not psychiatrically homogeneous, either in professional or institutional terms. It includes a few patients in almost every psychiatric classification, and a large number of patients (the institutional cures) who are regarded as probable lifelong residents of the hospital. Mixed with these last, however, are a number of patients who are considered convalescent and expected to leave the hospital within a year or less. Since these convalescent patients are also present in the group below the privileged patients, the latter cannot be regarded as made up entirely of patients who are convalescents.

The next lower group of patients, those with limited privileges, consists largely of patients who are candidates for the top group or whose condition has stabilized into a mildly cooperative or predictably neutral balance. These patients cannot leave the ward at will but must always be supervised and leave the ward only at scheduled times. Their privileges are confined to the negative one of being subjected to a minimum of the control techniques of the attendants,[6] and to the opportunity to get away from the ward at appropriate times. This last may seem a small privilege to the outsider, but it is of great importance to the patient, who must otherwise remain shut up in a ward which is almost always oppressive and dismal. The trips outside for the second group may be to the canteen, to church, or to hospital recreation. In all these cases, the patients are accompanied and supervised by attendants; occasionally by designated therapy personnel.

The third group of patients, those without privileges, are strictly custodial inmates, whose position is even more circumscribed than that of most penitentiary prisoners. These patients may receive visitors and may be permitted to leave the ward on special and irregular occasions. This group is quite heterogeneous on a psychiatric or any other basis. It includes patients who are almost completely stuporous, some who are clearly mentally deficient, some who are passive and listless, senile and deteriorated largely through physical aging, some who are frequently disturbed, and some who are nearly always uncooperative. Of these a few are potentially dangerous to the attendant or to other patients, and some of them are given to occasional or regular incontinence. Other patients have hallucinatory or delusional symptoms which force them to nag or pester anyone who will listen, and many who will not. Members of this last group, very frequent on the wards we observed, are often subjected to treatment by both attendants and other patients which is little short of brutal. After observing the cumulative effect of this nagging and pestering on the human beings exposed to it hour after hour on a daily basis, we were able to understand some of the reasons for this treatment. But the effect of the natural defensive reaction on the part of attendants and fellow patients was of course that of closing for these patients an avenue which a trained psychiatrist could have used for treatment.

But among the patients without privileges there is another group—the newly admitted patients—who are there because there has not been sufficient time for them to be placed in the ward system by the attendants and other patients. Their status is indeterminate for the time being. Subject to a variety of intricate interactional processes on the ward, the newly admitted patients will ultimately be classified in one of the other two general patient statuses or remain permanently in the group without privileges.

The interactional processes which determine the movement of the new patients into more or less permanent hospital categories are not generally highly visible, but they operate constantly. The patient placed in this lower group will have different experiences in different wards, depending on the way the attendants manage the ward, the type of patients in the other two groups, the patient's own social or ethnic background, and his own configuration of personality or psychiatric symptoms at the time of commitment. In general, however, he runs considerable risk of

[6] There is considerable negative control by upper patient group members of this second group. Since the upper group monopolizes most of the ward privileges, conformity by the second-group members is necessary if they want any of these privileges. Members of this second group who rise to the first actually seem to do so through the judgment of the upper group of patients rather than through the judgment of attendants or physicians.

being typed and permanently placed in the thinking of the upper patients and attendants in terms of his initial symptomatology and social background. If this does occur, and if the judgment is adverse to his progress, he has an additional problem beyond that of overcoming his illness. The additional problem is one of finding ways to get around the various sanctions of the ward social system which tend to keep him isolated from medical attention and from fairly normal social interaction, and under authoritarian management of both upper patient groups and attendants.

The over-all pattern in which this variable process of early ward patient classification occurs is a relatively simple one from the administrative point of view. The chief focus of the attendant system is on maintenance of order in the ward. The patient systems below the attendants function to bring about the same focus. To the attendant and the members of the upper patient systems, those actions on the part of the new patient which show probability that his mental condition will not lead to unpredictable outbursts of anger or fits of excitement are regarded as signs that he is potentially a good patient. The patient who dutifully executes the orders of the attendant and cooperates as indicated with members of the upper patient group is likely to become a candidate after a few weeks for the limited privilege group. He can now leave the ward under supervision for special occasions. If he continues to show this sort of improvement, he ultimately qualifies for the top group of patients.

In this top group of privileged patients, the patient has a new and gratifying status—one which approaches at times that accorded to normal persons. But the new status is subject to controls by the attendant which are as stringent as those elsewhere. If the patient breaks the working rules of this upper group—becomes insubordinate, forces too much intimacy on the attendants, shows disturbance—whether justified or not, he can be disqualified instantly and sent back down to the lower groups. This is not usually done directly by the attendant but requires official action by the ward physician, since it involves suspension of privileges.

In the usual case of this kind, such things as impudence, insubordination, and excessive familiarity are translated into more or less professional terms, such as "disturbed" or "excited," and presented by the attendant to the physician as a medical status report. The doctor must then officially revoke or modify the patient's privileges on the ward or work out a transfer to another ward where the patient has to begin all over to work up from the lowest group. A "good" doctor in the attendants' culture is one who does not raise too many questions about these translated medical terms.

In summary, as the ward system seems to work generally in Southern State Hospital, there is good reason to believe that this system, rather than formal hospital operating procedures and directives, is what usually prescribes the treatment a particular patient will be receiving at a particular time. Direct individual attention to most of the patients by the professional staff seemed to be the exception rather than the rule; and even such attention as did appear to be individual often was filtered in administration and evaluation through the ward system. Professional functions were largely those of administration. In general, the physician, nurse, psychologist, and social worker had to depend on the attendant for continuous information about the patients. Most of the treatment of the patients in the wards we studied was dictated by the status they came to occupy in the organization of patient status under the attendants in the ward.

C. CONSEQUENCES

In this section we will examine the differential consequences of hospitalization for the patient, depending on social characteristics of the patient. The first two selections investigate differences in hospital length of stay, and the third investigates differences in rehospitalization.

Just as the assumption that an individual's mental status primarily determines whether he is hospitalized has been questioned, so the assumption that a patient's mental status determines when he is released is in doubt. In "The Psychiatric Patient's Family and Length of Hospitalization," James R. Greenley shows that a family's desire (or lack thereof) to receive a patient back home is a crucial factor in a patient's release. He shows that this factor has an influence independent of other factors, including the patient's psychiatric status, the degree to which he is harmful to himself and others, and the nature of his behavior. Indeed, results suggest that when the family's wishes about the patient's release are in conflict with the psychiatrist's opinions, the former take precedence.

The next selection compares the length of stay for patients who are admitted voluntarily or involuntarily who have different marital and class statuses. Results show that patients who are involuntarily committed are apt to have a far longer hospital stay than patients who volunteer for admission, even when the patient's level of impairment and marital and social class statuses are controlled. Results also show that the influence of impairment, social class, and marital status on length of stay varies depending on patient legal status. Hence, the effects of mental, marital, and class statuses are specified with respect to legal status.

In the final selection, Robert Maisel investigates whether social (family and work) status, rather than the psychiatric normality-abnormality of behavior, is the crucial factor in rehospitalization of former mental patients. He finds that while the "abnormals" are more apt than the "normals" to be hospitalized, the individual's work status is a more important factor and is independent of behavior pathology. He also notes that family setting is also associated with rehospitalization, and that the influence of work status varies depending on family setting. Accordingly, family setting is a significant situational factor that influences the role of work status. The last two selections, then, reveal that factors associated with the consequences of mental hospitalization must be specified with respect to other conditions.

THE PSYCHIATRIC PATIENT'S FAMILY AND LENGTH OF HOSPITALIZATION

JAMES R. GREENLEY

This paper examines the relationship between families' desires for the release or retention of psychiatric inpatients and actual lengths of hospitalization. Correlates of length of hospitalization are sought because the length of treatment is often taken as a measure of the effectiveness of the therapeutic attempt, because long periods of hospitalization are felt to undesirably "institutionalize" patients, and because the size of the patient population and thus the cost of care are

Reprinted with permission of the author and the American Sociological Association, from *Journal of Health and Social Behavior* 13 (March, 1972), pp. 25–37.

as dependent on length of stay as upon the number of admissions. This attempt at explaining various lengths of hospitalization focuses on the impact a patient's family may have on his length of stay. The actions and attitudes of families have an effect on such diverse aspects of the psychiatric treatment experience as the timing of the initial identification and hospitalization,[1] the choice of a patient's placement in the community,[2] and the chances for and time of rehospitalization.[3] And it has long been recognized that family members may play a crucial role in the etiology, treatment, and recovery of the patient. Therefore, we will explore the extent to which family desires explain length of hospitalization and evaluate several explanations for our findings.

Numerous observers suggest that the presence of relatives who do not desire a loved one released can delay the release.[4] A few imply that a family who wishes to speed a release can do it.[5] Yet all these arguments are largely speculations based on the observation that what families want to happen often occurs. While researchers suggest that family attitudes may serve to lengthen or shorten a patient's stay in the hospital, none actually report this to be the case.

Some argue for a causal link between family desires and discharge timing. For instance, family interest in release may aid the patient's recovery.[6] Negative attitudes on the part of the family may deprive the psychiatrist of an adequate placement for the patient in the community. Even if the family is influential in the release decision, it is not clear why this may be. On the other hand, the desires of the family may be only spuriously related to length of hospitalization. A family may desire release and the release may occur because of several factors long thought to be determinants of discharge decisions.

From a medical perspective, estimates of the type and severity of a patient's psychopathology should be useful indicators of when a patient will be released. However, the literature relevant to the medical explanation of length of hospitalization is seemingly inconsistent. As would be expected, clinical observers have argued that the timing of discharge depends on the type and severity of the patient's illness,[7] and it has been shown that those diagnostic categories signifying more severe impairment, e.g. schizophrenia and organic disturbances, are associated with longer hospital stays.[8] Yet actual observations of clinical teams in one study indicated that only in rare instances did discharge decisions relate to psychopathology.[9] Similarly, a small study of schizophrenics could not distinguish those discharged from those retained on the basis of mental status examinations or observations of ward behavior.[10] And three studies, including the one just cited, employed psychiatric rating devices but did not find that those patients who tested as more psychiatrically impaired stayed longer.[11] Thus while psychiatric estimates of diagnoses are found to be related to length of hospitaliza-

[1] Marion Yarrow, Charlotte Schwartz, Harriet Murphy, and Leila Deasy, "The Psychological Meaning of Mental Illness in the Family," *Journal of Social Issues* 11, No. 4, pp. 12–24.

[2] O. G. Simmons, J. A. Davis, and K. Spenser, "Interpersonal Strains in Release from a Mental Hospital," *Social Problems* 26 (July, 1956), pp. 21–28.

[3] Howard E. Freeman and Ozzie G. Simmons, *The Mental Patient Comes Home* (New York: John Wiley, 1963).

[4] A. B. Hollingshead and F. C. Redlich, *Social Class and Mental Illness* (New York: John Wiley, 1958), p. 343; Thomas Scheff, "Legitimate, Transitional, and Illegitimate Mental Patients in a Midwestern State," *American Journal of Psychiatry* 120 (September, 1963), pp. 267–69; Jerome K. Myers and Bertram H. Roberts, *Family and Class Dynamics in Mental Illness* (New York: John Wiley, 1964), p. 217; and Daniel Levinson and Eugene Gallagher, *Patienthood in the Mental Hospital—An Analysis of Role, Personality. and Social Structure* (Boston: Houghton Mifflin, 1964), p. 42.

[5] Joan Sall, William W. Vosburgh, and Abby Silverman, "Psychiatric Patients and Extended Visits: A Survey of Research Findings," *Journal of Health and Human Behavior* 7 (March, 1966), pp. 20–28.

[6] Shirley Jacobson and G. L. Klerman, "Interpersonal Dynamics of Hospitalized Depressed Patients' Home Visits," *Journal of Marriage and the Family* 28 (February, 1966), pp. 94–102; Myers and Roberts, *Family and Class Dynamics;* and H. W. Dunham and S. K. Weinberg, *The Culture of the State Mental Hospital* (Detroit: Wayne State University Press, 1960).

[7] Stanley M. Kaplan and George C. Curtis, "Reactions of Medical Patients to Discharge or Threat of Discharge from a Psychosomatic Unit of a General Hospital," in M. Greenblatt, D. Levinson, and G. Klerman, eds., *Mental Patients in Transition* (Springfield, Illinois: Charles C. Thomas, 1961), pp. 8–12.

[8] Hollingshead and Redlich, *Social Class and Mental Illness,* p. 297.

[9] Sall et al., "Psychiatric Patients and Extended Visits," p. 22.

[10] Dexter Bullard, Jr., and Barbara R. Hoffman, "Factors Influencing the Discharge of Chronic Schizophrenia Patients," in *Research Conference on Therapeutic Community, Manhattan State Hospital, Wards Island, New York, 1959* (Springfield, Illinois: Charles C. Thomas, 1960).

[11] Robert B. Ellsworth and William H. Clayton, "Measure of Improvement in Mental Illness," *Journal of Consulting Psychology* 23 (February, 1959), pp. 15–20; John R. Barry and Samuel C. Fulkerson, "Chronicity and the Prediction of Duration and Outcome of Hospitalization from Capacity Measures," *Psychiatric Quarterly* 40 (January, 1966), pp. 104–21; and Bullard and Hoffman, "Factors Influencing the Discharge of Chronic Schizophrenia Patients."

tion, estimates of impairment based on other measures are not. Yet even if psychopathology were not related to length of hospitalization, the psychiatrist's evaluation of the patient's behavior may influence his decision to release and also, when it is conveyed to the family, bring them to desire release at a certain time.

Psychiatric institutions are often seen as "social control" as well as medical facilities.[12] As such, mental health professionals supposedly base their release decisions on whether or not the consequences would threaten the community.[13] There is considerable speculation in the literature that patients may be kept hospitalized when their behavior cannot be adequately controlled, such as through outpatient care[14] or through placement with a family which agrees to assume responsibility.[15] Yet there is no careful research linking past or present harmfulness or dangerousness to length of hospitalization. Nevertheless because the dangerous patient may remain longer due to the fearful family's refusal to accept him back into the home, the patient's dangerousness to himself or to others requires examination in this study of family influence.

SETTING AND METHOD

One six-ward "unit" of a large New England state mental hospital, a unit serving a specified geographical area, provides the site for this research. The psychiatric staff of this unit includes: (1) consulting psychiatrists from both the community and a local prestigious eastern university who supervise residents and handle intake and disposition staffings, (2) resident psychiatrists, most of whom are foreign born and trained, and (3) non-psychiatrically trained M.D.'s who are often in administrative positions and typically have been working with psychiatric patients for

years. All three of these categories are represented in the interviews with and observations of the psychiatrists described below. This hospital is by reputation neither exceptionally good nor very poor in the quality of patient care given. The staff is conscientious (even though normally harassed by an overly large patient load) and generally views the hospital with pride.

This research involved gathering material from the patient, his psychiatrist, and his family during the hospitalization. Extensive informal observations were made of contacts between these psychiatrists and their patients. In addition, structured interviews were sought from the patients, families, and psychiatrists involved in 125 consecutive psychiatric admissions from a New England city of about 140,000 plus virtually all its suburbs. The "cases" chosen for study were consecutive admissions between May and September, 1969, 21 to 65 years old, and not primarily suffering from drug addiction, alcoholism, or senility. Interviews were obtained with the psychiatrist and the patient, with few exceptions, during the first week of the patient's hospitalization. After three weeks of the patient's hospitalization, the patient and his psychiatrist were reinterviewed and, at this time, the patient's family was also interviewed. Interviews were obtained before the patient was released from the hospital. The patient's hospital record was also searched for further relevant information.

While certain persons refused to be interviewed in particular cases (refusal rate for the various populations ranged from 0 percent to 11 percent), many cases were lost when psychiatrists, regardless of whom their patients were, refused to participate in the research (39 percent of the initial interviews with the psychiatrists were not obtained for this reason). Because each interview schedule administered resulted in a different completion rate, various maximum numbers of cases were available for and used in different statistical analyses Tests were done individually for each schedule to determine if the completed cases differed from the 125 originally selected admissions on the following characteristics: sex, age, marital status, religion, occupation, education, social class, and previous admission to a psychiatric hospital. The categories of the control variables used in this study are as follows: Age: 21–30, 31–40, 41–50, 51–65; Race: White, Negro (3 of the 125 cases

[12] Jerome K. Myers and Lee Bean, *A Decade Later: A Follow-up of Social Class and Mental Illness* (New York: John Wiley, 1968).

[13] Ronald Leifer, *In the Name of Mental Health* (New York: Science House, 1969), and Orville G. Grim and Stanton Wheeler, *Socialization After Childhood: Two Essays* (New York: John Wiley, 1967).

[14] Peter Weiss, Jacqueline Macaulay, and Allen Pincus, "Geographic Factors and the Release of Patients from State Mental Hospitals," *American Journal of Psychiatry* 123 (October, 1966), pp. 408–12.

[15] Dunham and Weinberg, *The Culture of the State Mental Hospital*

were eliminated from this analysis because they were Puerto Rican); Religion: Protestant, Catholic (11 of the 125 cases were dropped from this analysis because they listed themselves as "none," "Jewish" or "other"); Marital Status: married, single, divorced or widowed or separated; Education: less than 7 years, 7–9 years, 10–12 years, some college, completed college, graduate work done; Occupation: seven categories used as given in A. B. Hollingshead's *Two Factor Index of Social Position;* Social Class: five categories used as computed by A. B. Hollingshead's *Two Factor Index of Social Position.* Chi-square goodness of fit tests employed demonstrated that in no instance did any completed group of cases differ significantly from what would have been expected on the basis of the original 125 cases.

The major dependent variable, the outcome of the release decision, is measured behaviorally, in terms of when the patient actually left the hospital, rather than based on a report or opinion concerning what decision was made. Patients left the hospital in five relatively distinct groups. The first group, the "Rapid Exit Group," consists of those patients leaving at or very near the time of their "intake staffing." The intake staffing is a formal 15 to 30-minute review of the patient's condition conducted by a senior consulting psychiatrist heading a team of psychiatric residents, nurses, social workers, aides, and auxiliary personnel (occupational therapists, music therapists, etc.). Those patients leaving after the intake staffing, but before a "review" staffing is scheduled, form a distinct group to be called the "Attenuated Stay Group." The third group are those patients who are released from the hospital near the time of their review staffing (21 to 36 days from admission). These patients, being proportionately the most numerous, are called the "Modal Stay Group." The fourth group, the "Extended Stay Group," are those patients leaving the hospital between 37 and 100 days from admission, i.e. clearly after the period of their review staffing but before the staff begins to lose hope and interest in them. After 100 days of hospitalization the probability is 3 to 1 that a patient will remain over 200 days. This last patient group, experiencing a sharply reduced chance of exit, is called the "Long Stay Group." Only by treating length of hospitalization in terms of these five ordered groups can the real-

ities of this hospital's organization and staff attitudes be taken into account.

RESULTS

First the desires of the patient's family for release or retention will be examined to see if they are related to the length of the patient's hospitalization. Interviews with members of the patient's family were conducted in their homes in order to minimize the chance that the family member would attempt to please the hospital staff with his response. The "closest relative," as defined by the patient, was interviewed. They were 42 percent spouses, 4 percent children, 40 percent parents, and 13 percent other relatives, mainly siblings. One friend of a patient was interviewed. In addition it was made clear that the interviewer was not on the hospital staff and that the family member's responses would not be made available to the hospital staff. During these interviews family members were asked straightforwardly whether they wished their relative to remain hospitalized or not. Generally their responses were direct and unequivocal; in only 5 of 80 cases (6 percent) could the family's response be considered "neutral," "undecided," or "ambivalent." These five cases were scored as being neither definitely in favor of nor against release but as somewhere between these extremes. The expressed desires of the family, classified in this way, are strongly associated with the time each patient remained in the hospital, as shown in Table 1. This relationship remains statistically significant and substantial in each category of the following control variables: age, sex, race, religion, marital status, education, occupation, and social class. The desires of the patient's family are highly related to the length of the patient's hospitalization.

Second, other factors traditionally thought influential in release decisions are inspected to see if they can help explain this strong relationship between family desires and length of hospitalization. These are the patient's psychiatric symptoms, his dangerousness to himself or others, and professional judgments of his condition and needs. Initially we will examine the manner in which each of these itself relates to length of hospitalization.

TABLE 1. FAMILY DESIRES AND LENGTH
OF HOSPITALIZATION

| | Family Desires | | |
Exit Group	Family Wants Patient Released	Family is Neutral or Ambivalent	Family Wants Patient Retained
	% (N)	% (N)	% (N)
Rapid exit group	32(5)	0(0)	2(1)
Attenuated stay group	31(5)	80(4)	7(4)
Modal stay group	25(4)	20(1)	29(17)
Extended stay group	6(1)	0(0)	30(18)
Long stay group	6(1)	0(0)	32(19)
Total	100%	100%	100%

Gamma = .78, p < .001, N = 80

The patient's psychiatric symptoms are evaluated with a psycho-biological symptom based scale. In this scale, twenty questions, e.g. "Do you have loss of appetite?" and "Have you ever had spells of dizziness?", are asked the respondant whose mental health is to be rated. The questions are given in Myers and Bean[16] and are essentially those used by Gurin, Veroff, and

Feld[17] in their national study of mental health. These questions were chosen for this scale from a large pool of questions because responses to them most closely correlated with clinical evaluations of the respondant's mental health. Generally if a person answers as "never" having had the symptom he is given four points, if he says he "hardly ever" has the symptom he gets three points, if he responds that he "sometimes" has the symptom he receives two points, and if he has the symptom "many times" he is given one point. These points are summed over the twenty questions into a total score ranging from 20 to 80. The scale scores attempt to distinguish between groups of persons that psychiatrists would evaluate as either impaired or unimpaired. See Myers and Bean[18] for a more extended discussion of the history and use of this device.

The scores on this measure of psychiatric impairment are unrelated, even in the more severe range of symptomatology, to the timing of the patient's hospital exit. (See Chart 1) While it is tempting to conclude that the patient's psychopathological behavior is not a significant factor in his move from patient to ex-patient status, it is quite possible that this scale can not readily distinguish between the degrees of pathology in this type of population. When used in a com-

[16] Myers and Bean, *A Decade Later*, pp. 238–40.

[17] Gerald Gurin, Joseph Veroff, and Sheilfa Feld, *Americans View Their Mental Health* (New York: Basic Books, 1960).
[18] Myers and Bean, *A Decade Later*.

CHART 1. LENGTH OF HOSPITALIZATION ASSOCIATED WITH PSYCHIATRIC IMPAIRMENT, DANGEROUSNESS, AND PROFESSIONAL JUDGMENT VARIABLES

Independent Variable	Length of Hospitalization		
	Gamma	Level of Significance	N
Psychiatric symptomatology			
Psycho-biological symptom score	.01	NS*	103
Dangerousness			
Assaultive, destructive, and homicidal tendencies	.10	NS	125
Suicidal tendencies	−.32	†	125
Psychiatrist's judgment			
Psychiatric impairment	.44	‡	62
Potential dangerousness	.05	NS	59
Need of hospitalization	.53	§	63

* NS indicates p > .05.
† p ≤ .05.
‡ p < .01.
§ p < .001.

munity population, researchers have argued and presented data showing that this type of symptom checklist is a crude though valid and useful tool for distinguishing the psychiatrically impaired from the unimpaired.[19] And one study of a similar scale even compared new admissions to a psychiatric hospital with patients on "pre-discharge wards," finding as would be expected that the new admissions registered more severely impaired.[20] Yet there is no evidence that this symptom-based scale can distinguish degrees of psychiatric impairment in a group of recently hospitalized mental patients. Because patients in this study, being newly admitted psychiatric inpatients, are relatively severely disturbed, this scale may not validly distinguish between them. Jackson[21] suggests ranges of scores on this measure roughly corresponding to those persons needing inpatient psychiatric treatment, those needing outpatient treatment, and those needing no treatment at all. The percentages of the study group scoring in each of these ranges is 80 percent, 19 percent and 1 percent respectively. This is not to mention several other problems this type of scale may have.[22] Psychiatric impairment may be associated with length of hospitalization even though this scale cannot adequately measure it. Nevertheless, for purposes here we will view this scale score not as a measure of overall psychiatric impairment but as an indication of the number of patient reported psycho-biological symptoms.

Aside from symptomatology, a patient who is dangerous to himself or to others may be hospitalized longer. Initial identification of a symptom-laden person as mentally ill may often depend on whether or not he is dangerous.[23] And if

dangerousness similarly contributes to continued designation of the patient as ill, he may remain hospitalized longer. Furthermore, a dangerous patient may be retained longer simply because the hospital's task is to some extent to protect the community from such persons.[24] As a patient dangerous to others is very different than one who is only a threat to himself, each of these cases requires separate treatment.

A patient's danger to others is measured here by whether he is assaultive, destructive, or homicidal. On the basis of behavior both during and before hospitalization, each patient is listed in the hospital records as either being or not being "assaultive," "destructive," or "homicidal." Reference to a patient's being one of these refers to it being stated as such in the hospital records. Employing hospital records, despite their notorious reputation, is probably useful in assessing these patient characteristics. If a patient is not assaultive, destructive, or homicidal, it is unlikely he would be recorded as such. And if he had a history of this type of behavior, especially homicidal behavior, it is reasonable to assume that in most cases such information would find itself into the records. Yet whether a patient is recorded as possessing none, one, two, or all three of these behavior patterns is essentially unrelated to the length of his hospitalization as shown in Chart 1. There is only a slight tendency for patients dangerous to others to remain longer. These findings are somewhat surprising in the face of consistent claims by psychiatrists that release depends relatively heavily on the patient's dangerousness.[25]

Suicidal behavior is the form of dangerousness to self that is often given as a reason for initial hospitalization and continued hospitalization. Thus suicidal patients are examined to see if they remain hospitalized longer. A patient is considered to be suicidal if registered as such in the hospital records. The hospital staff is motivated to keep somewhat accurate records of this due to the possibilities and consequences of a patient actually commiting suicide while at the hospital. Yet despite the numerous times that suicidal tendencies are given by psychiatrists as reasons

[19] L. Srole, T. S. Langner, S. T. Michael, M. K. Opler, and T. A. C. Rennie, *Mental Health in the Metropolis: The Midtown Manhattan Study*, Volume 1 (New York: McGraw-Hill Book Company, 1962); Lloyd H. Rogler and A. B. Hollingshead, *Trapped: Families and Schizophrenia* (New York: John Wiley, 1965).

[20] Jerome Manis, Milton Brawer, Chester L. Hunt, and Leonard Kershner, "Validating a Mental Health Scale," *American Sociological Review,* 28 (February, 1963), pp. 108–16.

[21] Elton Jackson, "Status Consistency and Symptoms of Stress," *American Sociological Review* 27 (August, 1962), pp. 469–80.

[22] Bruce P. Dohrenwend and Barbara Snell Dohrenwend, *Social Status and Psychological Disorder: A Causal Inquiry* (New York: Wiley-Interscience, 1969).

[23] Elaine Cumming and John Cumming, *Closed Ranks* (Cambridge, Mass.: Harvard University Press, 1957).

[24] Leifer, *In the Name of Health.*

[25] Louis Weinstein, "Real and Ideal Discharge Criteria," *Mental Hospitals* 15 (December, 1964), pp. 680–83.

for denying release, patients listed in the records as suicidal leave significantly earlier, as shown in Chart 1. As might be expected, suicidal patients exit sooner as a group because they tend to be concentrated in those diagnostic categories (the neuroses and transient situational disturbances) with shorter average hospitalizations. The negative relationship between suicidal behavior and length of hospitalization disappears within diagnostic groups. Yet, even within diagnostic groups, the suicidal patient tends to remain no longer than the non-suicidal patient. Danger to self, measured in this manner, does not appear as a factor helping explain why some patients exit sooner than others.

According to the psychiatric version of the medical model as described by Goffman,[26] the psychiatrist is the expert who makes treatment-related decisions such as when to release a patient. The psychiatrist uses much more information in his recommendation about discharge than simply the patient's psycho-biological symptoms and types of his dangerous tendencies. He judges the totality of the relevant information, evaluating the meanings of various patterns of pathological signs and symptoms. Thus we will review the psychiatrist's more global estimates of both the patient's psychiatric impairment and his potential for dangerous behavior, plus an inclusive assessment by the psychiatrist of how much the patient needs hospitalization.

In order to obtain a professional evaluation of each patient's psychiatric impairment, each patient's psychiatrist was asked during the private interview, "How psychiatrically impaired is this patient now?" Six response categories were supplied ranging from "very severely impaired" to "no visible impairment." It is admittedly difficult to tell what factors were most determinant of the psychiatrist's responses. Comments made by psychiatrists at the time of their response indicated they took into account, among other things, prognosis, diagnoses, present behavior, past behavior, and availability of treatment. Yet these comments give no indication which factors were more salient in the minds of the psychiatrists. In any event, their responses are strongly

related to the timing of the patient's exit, as shown in Chart 1, with those patients rated most impaired remaining longer. While this relationship is notably weaker than the association between family desires and length of hospitalization, it must be remembered that the responses to this impairment question may be based on factors different than those influencing the psychiatrist's decision to release the patient.

A second question was asked each patient's psychiatrist: Is this patient potentially harmful to himself or others? Five response categories were supplied ranging from "definitely yes" to "definitely not." This question is concerned not only with the patient's past behavior, as were the other measures of dangerousness, but also with future behavior. What the patient will do is possibly more important in the decision to release than are his past actions. Yet even with this further consideration, length of hospitalization is not found associated with whether the psychiatrist views the patient as harmful or not. Thus dangerousness of the patient, whether measured in terms of past behavior or a professional prediction of future behavior, is not associated with the timing of the patient's release.

Finally, psychiatrists were asked how much each of their patients was in need of further hospitalization, and they were again given five ordered response categories. This question allowed the therapist to jointly assess both considerations of psychopathology and dangerousness. Furthermore it allowed him to incorporate in his judgment such diverse factors as availability of a placement in the community and ability of the hospital to care for or help the patient. And, as would be expected, those patients seen as most in need of further hospitalization remain hospitalized longer (again, see Chart 1). Yet this relationship is much weaker than that between length of hospitalization and family desires.

Family desires are thus more strongly associated with length of hospitalization than are the measures of psychiatric symptomatology, dangerousness, or professional judgment used here. Family wishes may be only spuriously related to length of hospitalization. The family may desire further hospitalization only because the patient's psychiatrist has recommended it and the patient may remain because of the psychiatrist's de-

[26] Erving Goffman, *Asylums: Essays on the Social Situation of Mental Patients and Other Inmates* (Garden City, N.Y.: Anchor Books, 1961).

cision. Therefore, the family desires and length of hospitalization relationship is examined controlling for the above indicators of symptomatology, dangerousness, and professional judgment. As shown in Chart, 2 in no case does the control

CHART 2. LENGTH OF HOSPITALIZATION AND FAMILY DESIRES RELATIONSHIP CONTROLLED BY PSYCHOPATHOLOGY, DANGEROUSNESS AND PSYCHIATRIST'S JUDGMENTS

	Length of Hospitalization and Family Desires	
	Gamma	N
Zero Order Relationship	.78	80
Control Variables	Partial Gammas	N
Psychiatric symptomatology Psycho-biological symptom score	.95	72
Dangerousness Assaultive, destructive, and homicidal tendencies	.76	80
Suicidal tendencies	.85	80
Psychiatrist's judgments Psychiatric impairment	.74	42
Potential dangerousness	.60	40
Need of hospitalization	.87	42

variable appear to account for any substantial part of the relationship. None of the partial Gammas differ significantly at the .05 level from the zero order Gamma. Thus despite the influence of psycho-biological symptoms, dangerousness, and psychiatrist's evaluations, family desires appear to have a strong impact on the timing of the patient's exit.

Thus, it is suggested that a family may be able to have an exit occur in the face of opposition by the psychiatrist. In an initial test of this possibility, those crucial cases are examined where the psychiatrist and family disagree over the timing of the patient's release. The desires of the psychiatrists for release or retention are themselves strongly associated with length of hospitalization (Gamma $= +.58$, p $< .001$, N $= 79$). In those cases (9) where these psychiatrists' wishes unequivocally differ from the wishes of the family, the timing of exits most closely corresponds to the family's desires (Gamma $= +.81$, p $< .01$, N $= 9$). Where the family wants

the patient to remain but the psychiatrist wishes the patient discharged, in 3 cases the patient remains beyond the Modal Group and in only 1 case does he leave before it. But where the family wants the patient discharged and the psychiatrist wishes the patient to remain, 2 patients leave before the Modal Group and none after it. The family appears able to secure the patient's release or retention even when the patient's psychiatrist wishes otherwise.

Furthermore, those cases are examined where the family wishes a discharge decision presumably not indicated by the patient's pathology. Family influence may be more apparent than real if release occurs to the family's pleasure only for patients neither extremely pathological nor impairment free. If families have a real impact on the discharge decision, then even patients rated severely ill would leave relatively early if the family desired it, and patients with little pathology would remain hospitalized if the family desired that. While only six such cases occur in this sample, the tendency is for family desires to be the stronger factor (Gamma $= +.20$, NS, N $= 6$).

It is possible that we' have not in fact controlled for several dimensions, but rather that these independent variables are highly intercorrelated themselves. The matrix of gammas shown in Chart 3 allows assessment of this possibility.

The psycho-biological symptom score is not found significantly related to any of the other independent variables measuring psychiatric impairment. This may mean that the symptom score is not an adequate indicator of psychopathology, at least in this group of relatively severely disturbed persons. On the other hand, it may simply be measuring a different dimension of psychopathology. Assessments and desires of the psychiatrist and family are also not significantly associated with this psychobiological symptom score. This suggests that neither the family nor psychiatrist is primarily concerned with these symptoms in regards to release.

Two indicators which may be in large part measuring the same underlying dimension are the psychiatrist's estimate of the patient's psychiatric impairment and his estimate of the patient's need for further hospitalization. These two variables are associated more closely than

CHART 3. INTERCORRELATION MATRIX OF GAMMAS AMONG THE INDEPENDENT VARIABLES

Variables	1	2	3	4	5	6	7
1. Psycho-biological symptom score							
2. Assaultive, destructive, and homicidal behavior	.07 (100) NS						
3. Suicidal tendencies	.15 (100) NS	.02 (125) NS					
4. Psychiatric impairment	.14 (51) NS	−.31 (63) *	−.40 (63) †				
5. Potential dangerousness	.04 (60) NS	.41 (60) †	.43 (60) †	.24 (63) NS			
6. Need of hospitalization	.18 (52) NS	.35 (63) *	−.34 (63) *	.61 (62) ‡	.19 (60) NS		
7. Family desires	−.05 (69) NS	−.007 (80) NS	−.54 (80) †	.27 (30) NS	.42 (40) †	.56 (42) ‡	

Note: N in parentheses.
* indicates p ≤ .05.
† indicates p < .01.
‡ indicates p < .001.
NS indicates p ≥ .05.

are any two other independent variables. Furthermore, these two variables are associated with each of the other variables in a similar manner, with one exception. Assaultive, destructive, and homicidal patients are seen as in need of more hospitalization, but as less psychiatrically impaired. The psychiatrist may not only estimate need for hospitalization by keying on those factors which lead to his estimate of psychiatric impairment, but also take into account tendencies toward violent behavior. This difference probably warrants our dealing with these two variables as indicators of at least some different underlying factors.

Three variables measure dimensions of the patient's dangerousness, i.e., the patient's suicidal tendencies, the patient's assaultive, destructive and homicidal tendencies, and the psychiatrist's overall estimate of his dangerousness. Suicidal behaviors are not significantly related to assaultive, destructive and homicidal behaviors. Yet both are significantly related to the psychia-

trist's judgment of the dangerousness, presumably because both are taken into account by the psychiatrist making the determination. Thus the psychiatrist's estimates of dangerousness probably combine measures of dangerousness to self and others, as was desired and expected. These three ratings of dangerousness measure some dimension not presently in the psychiatrist's ratings of psychiatric impairment. Suicidal as well as assaultive, destructive, and homicidal tendencies are negatively related to the psychiatrists' impairment ratings. This may occur because dangerous characteristics tend to be concentrated among patients in diagnostic categories considered less serious (the personality disorders, neuroses, and transient situational disturbances). Even so, the psychiatrist's assessment of potential dangerousness bears a slight positive relationship to his estimate of impairment. The judgment of potential dangerousness may to some extent take into account the overall psychiatric condition of the patient, too. Thus while these measures of dangerousness to some extent tap the same dimensions, they are clearly individuated sufficiently to necessitate separate inspection.

Finally, family desires are essentially unrelated to past assaultive, destructive, and homicidal acts on the part of the patient. Few patients are so threatening to the family that dangerousness in itself becomes the determining factor (only 9 percent of the sample studied had even one of these characteristics). The patient dangerous to others is likely to be less disordered in other respects; when weighed jointly with these other factors, in the vast majority of cases, dangerousness may be a relatively unimportant consideration. Furthermore, families appear to more often want patients released who have made suicide attempts. Many "suicidal" patients do not really intend to kill themselves but rather desire to communicate their distress to others. And many suicide attempts appear to establish, at least temporarily, some communication of the patient's plight, and patients as a result often reciprocate by stating that they will not attempt suicide again. Because suicide attempts function this way, they are often actions of patients who exhibit relatively benign pathological patterns. As a result, families of suicidal patients are more likely to want them released. Family desires are probably related positively to all of the psychiatrist's evaluations because families and psychiatrists weigh many factors similarly in making their decisions.

None of the above findings in itself suggests any mechanism linking family desires and length of hospitalization. It has been suggested that positive family attitudes toward release may aid recovery and this recovery leads to earlier release. To examine this proposition, a measure of relative patient improvement was devised by comparing the psychiatrist's original impairment estimate with one he made three weeks later. The psychiatrist's second estimate of impairment is subtracted from his first estimate (the response categories being numbered from one to six). The resulting "improvement" score, ranging from -5 to $+5$, is used with the original impairment estimate employed as a control variable in each instance reported. This is done because the more impaired a patient was initially the more he

could and the more likely he did improve according to this measure. There is no relationship between family desires and patient improvement measured in this manner. From the families' point of view, patients reported as "better now" than when they were hospitalized are only slightly more likely to be wanted home (Gamma $= +.11$, n.s. $N = 47$). The basic argument is sometimes elaborated as follows: Families who wish their patient's return home often visit the patient and this visiting, being ameliorative, speeds release.[27] Yet families in this study who reported visiting their patient more often are no more likely to have their patient seen by the psychiatrist as improved (Gamma $= -.09$, NS, $N = 49$). No evidence could be found suggesting that family attitudes accelerate release by speeding recovery.

Direct family pressure on the psychiatrist is a possible reason family desires may come to pass. Families may be able to pressure a psychiatrist into granting a release or keeping a patient. To explore this possibility, psychiatrists placed each patient's family through a series of four questions into one of four ordered categories. First are those families whose patient's psychiatrist did not even know whether the family wished release or retention of the patient. Second are those families whose desires are known to the psychiatrist but who never confronted the psychiatrist with these desires. Third are those families who went out of their way to explicitly tell the psychiatrist what they wanted. Fourth are those families who made the psychiatrist feel "pushed" by the family to decide in favor of release or retention. This variable is not associated with how long a patient remains hospitalized, (Gamma $= +.01$, NS, $N = 33$) and more importantly, patients are not significantly more likely to leave in one of the more extreme exit groups when the psychiatrist feels the family is more aggressively "pushing" for release or retention (Gamma $= +.11$, NS, $N = 33$). Thus

[27] George Brown, "Social Factors Influencing the Length of Hospital Stay of Schizophrenic Patients," *British Medical Journal*, 2 (December, 1959), pp. 1300–02; Dunham and Weinberg, *The Culture of the State Mental Hospital*, pp. 151–52; and Arnold J. Marx and Arnold M. Ludwig, "Resurrection of the Family of the Chronic Schizophrenic: Clinical and Ethical Dilemmas," *American Journal of Psychotherapy* 23 (January, 1969), pp. 37–52.

family desires are probably not associated with length of hospitalization simply because some families actively use what power and influence they have to effect a decision to their liking.

DISCUSSION

Our major finding is that the desires of mental patients' families are strongly related to how long patients remain hospitalized. Evidence is presented that this relationship is not spurious; other variables traditionally thought to influence release decisions are not determining both length of hospitalization and family desires. Neither is the relationship due to differential patient improvement or overt pressure placed on the psychiatrist by the family. Unfortunately the interview evidence itself does not adequately suggest a mechanism by which family desires and length of hospitalization are linked.

Informal observations of family-psychiatrist interaction do indicate that family desires may be closely related to the timing of discharge because psychiatrists consider family wishes very seriously when making release decisions. There are several possible reasons that psychiatrists in this inpatient setting may be influenced by the families' preferences. First, the psychiatrist is much more likely to successfully place the patient in the home if the family supports his return. The family who wants the patient released is likely to be supportive and to help the patient reintegrate into the community; the reluctant family may undermine the plans of the psychiatrist, exacerbate the patient's symptoms, and drive the patient back to the hospital. Rational planning of treatment decisions, such as discharge, may demand seriously taking into account the desires of the family. Second and possibly more important, the psychiatrist may follow the wishes of the family to avoid a range of possible family actions. At one extreme, the family may use the judicial system in seeking release or further retention. The psychiatrist may wish to avoid a hearing or other courtroom processes because they have a damaging impact on the patient or consume a considerable amount of his time and effort. The therapist may prefer to discharge the patient "Against Medical Advice" or

to hold a patient while seeking a non-family placement in the community. Families may also place psychiatrists in awkward positions by taking their questions and demands to unit chiefs, department heads, or superintendents of the institutions involved. Institutional leaders both expect and easily tolerate a few such complaints. Yet if such complaints multiply beyond a scattered few, these leaders may come to question not the assertive families but the accused psychiatrists. This may give a family considerable leverage of which even it is unaware. Most commonly, a family's persistent questions and demands constitute a significant nuisance to the psychiatrist himself. In the state hospital studied, the work load was so heavy that a moderately interested and aggressive family could cause a substantial and disruptive drain on the psychiatrist's available time and energy. Under the pressure of too many patients, the psychiatrist appears to welcome the family which wishes to remove the patient from the hospital and the responsibility for him from the psychiatrist. On the other hand, if the family resists the patient's return, the over-worked psychiatrist often redirects his limited energies toward patients whose return to the community seems more likely, thus continuing the hospitalization of the unwanted patient. Finally, the psychiatrist may seek to please the family because he feels it to be as much his client as is the patient himself. The family is often the complainant, the patient often only its symptom.

In general, psychiatrists may follow family wishes as a means to cope with the exigencies of their jobs. Their response to family desires may be one means of stretching limited resources into maximum patient care. It may also signify that psychiatric hospitals give high priority to avoiding complaints from its nonpatient community. Unfortunately, a mental hospital which simply avoids stirring waves of public protest is often seen as adequate. In order to best serve and protect the institution, himself, and his patients, the psychiatrist may bow to the wishes of the patients' families. This view does not assume that families in any sense make decisions. The psychiatrist decides when the patient will leave, often without the active participation of the family. Nevertheless, family desires may be even larger determinants of length of hospitalization than the psychiatrists' own preferences. Investigations are needed to determine if this is in fact the link between family desires and length of hospitalization.

These findings suggest that an exploration of the origins of family desires would be useful. The above results do indicate family desires may be less dependent on the patient's psychopathology or potential dangerousness than on other factors. Our interviews with family members reveal that family wishes are typically based on factors beyond the knowledge and even interest of the hospital staff. Relatively few families have their relative's health as their primary concern. They may want the patient retained or released for a wide variety of reasons including: availability of housing; plans to move to a new home or state; the timing of a vacation; the loss or gain of income from job, welfare agency, disability payments, or relatives; the need for help with childcare; fear of being attacked; pressure on the part of municipal authorities; consequences for a coming court appearance; loneliness; guilt; shame; past experiences with mental hospitals; and a death in the family. Because family desires appear important in release timing, it would be useful to empirically explore those factors leading to various family attitudes toward release. At the same time, further assessment is needed of the impact of other variables such as social class, marital status, and race.

Whatever the determinants of family wishes concerning release, the therapist needs to be aware of their potential impact on his desires and the eventual outcome. For rational therapy decisions to be made, such as when to discharge a patient, the crucial role of family preferences needs to be made overt. Unseen and unrecognized pressures often are largely unmanageable, having consequences, benign or not, which cannot be sought or avoided. Making them conscious factors may facilitate their manipulation through treatment strategies, such as how to approach a family. Thus psychiatrists may benefit from a fuller consciousness of the nature and extent of the impact of patients' families on their decisions.

Finally, the finding that family desires are closely related to the timing of release may support, in a way, the societal reaction view of mental illness. Proponents of this view argue in part that whether a person is treated as mentally ill is largely dependent on the judgments of nonprofessionals.[28] Whether these nonprofessionals base their reactions to a person, such as hospitalizing him, on the basis of professionally recognized signs of pathology or not, their reaction is thought to elicit further "pathological" behavior from the person. In this study of return to the community, the desires of the family are seen to be highly related to whether a patient is discharged. His behavior and judged psychopathology appear much less important. Release may actually and symbolically signify that the patient is expected no longer to behave as if mentally ill; these changed expectations may draw the patient into more normal forms of behavior. Societal reaction proponents note, in support of such hypotheses, that nonprofessionals often are the first to identify who is "mentally ill," that the behavior patterns of those hospitalized are not categorically different from the behaviors of many of those left in the community, and that the professionals do not themselves decide who is and is not to be hospitalized. In a similar manner, this research on exit from the psychiatric hospital indicates that nonprofessionals have much to do with when the release occurs, that the released can only partially be distinguished from those retained on the basis of measures of pathological behavior, and that the psychiatrist's evaluations are less important in the decision to release than are the family's desires. Yet whether the discharge decision is made by nonprofessionals on nonprofessional grounds is a question which requires further examination of the causal relationship between family desires and length of hospitalization. At the very least, this research adds to a growing body of data indicating that families play a major role in deciding the course of a patient's treatment career.

---

[28] Walter R. Gove, "Societal Reaction as an Explanation of Mental Illness: An Evaluation," *American Sociological Review* 35 (October, 1970), pp. 373–84.

THE STATUS RESOURCE HYPOTHESIS AND LENGTH OF MENTAL HOSPITALIZATION

WILLIAM A. RUSHING AND JACK ESCO

The process of mental hospitalization continues to be the subject of much debate. Gove argues that persons who enter mental hospitals have serious mental impairments.[1] Transition to the status of mental patient is considered the result of a psychiatric condition. Scheff, on the other hand, considers this a much too narrow view of the process by which mental patient status is generated.[2] Mental illness, in and of itself, is not a sufficient condition to explain mental hospitalization; on occasion mental illness is not even a *necessary* condition. Not all persons diagnosable as mentally ill are hospitalized, and it is possible for perfectly sane people to be hospitalized. Scheff argues that an explanation of the process of mental hospitalization should be sought in nonpsychiatric factors.

We believe that decisions made subsequent to hospital admission may also be influenced by nonpsychiatric factors. For example, in the previous paper, Greenley shows that family desires influence timing of discharge regardless of patient's mental status.[3] Simmons, Davis, and Spencer present data that show that discharge decisions are determined more by the power of individual patients and their families than by purely medical considerations.[4] In addition, evidence shows that length of hospital stay varies according to type of admission process.[5] In the present paper, we shall investigate the relationship between length of hospitalization and three status attributes of mental patients. Our basic hypothesis is that the social resources inherent in or associated with the social status of a patient are significant nonpsychiatric factors affecting length of hospitalization.

The hypothesis is similar to one presented earlier, which states that societal reactions in the hospitalization process vary depending on the prepatient's marital and class resources.[6] Thus, as is the case in areas other than mental hospitalization, the behavior of others toward an individual is shaped by the individual's status. Our hypothesis here is, generally, that the behavior of psychiatrists and other hospital personnel toward mental patients is partly a function of the status resources of mental patients and, specifically, that the timing of discharges is associated with patient marital, class, and admission (legal) statuses. Note, however, that we do not argue that degree of illness (or the attributed degree of illness) is of no consequence in length of hospital stay; evidence for this is inconsistent (see p. 437 above). Our argument is only that the social status of a patient is important regardless of degree of illness.

Most data are for all 21 to 64-year-old male first admissions who had been admitted to and discharged from the three state hospitals in Washington between 1955 and 1965. These data will be supplemented with comparable data for patients from Tennessee.

Prepared especially for this volume.

[1] See Walter R. Gove, "Societal Reaction as an Explanation of Mental Illness: An Evaluation," *American Sociological Review* 35 (October, 1970), pp. 873–84, and "Who Is Hospitalized? A Critical Review of Some Sociological Studies of Mental Illness," *Journal of Health and Social Behavior* 10 (December, 1970), pp. 294–303.

[2] For Scheff's most recent statement, see Thomas J. Scheff, "The Labelling Theory of Mental Illness," *American Sociological Review* 39 (June, 1974), pp. 444–52. See also his *Being Mentally Ill* (Chicago: Aldine, 1966) and pp. 412–22 above.

[3] See pp. 433–44 above.

[4] Ozzie G. Simmons, James A. Davis, and Katherine Spencer, "Interpersonal Strains in Release from a Mental Hospital," in Stephan P. Spitzer and Norman K. Denzin, *The Mental Patient: Studies in the Sociology of Deviance* (New York: McGraw-Hill, 1968), pp. 376–84.

[5] Richard D. Morgan and Leonard B. Cook, "Relationship of Methods of Admission to Length of Stay in State Hospitals," *Public Health Reports* 78 (July, 1963), pp. 619–29.

MARITAL STATUS AND CLASS STATUS

The social resource hypothesis contends that social resources are highest for the married and lowest for the single with the disrupted-estranged (separated, divorced and widowed) in between.[7] It therefore predicts that single patients would have the longest length of stay and married patients the shortest. Comparison of the median

[6] See pp. 403–5 above.

[7] See p. 404 above.

number of days each group stays in the hospital is consistent with the hypothesis.

Single	Disrupted-Estranged	Married
108.4	71.4	61.4
(N = 1,142)	(N = 845)	(N = 1,725)

Although we have no data on specific processes that influence discharge decisions, several processes may be involved. Hospital staff may think that a patient's status and his accompanying resources are important factors to consider in discharge decisions because they are thought to facilitate post-hospital functioning. It is also probable that the greater the patient's social resources the greater his ability to prevent hospital officials from keeping him in the hospital. The processes described by Greenley may be involved. Greenley discovers that length of hospitalization is inversely related to how much the families want patients released.[8] Single patients are least apt to have families who want them back or to influence hospital officials to terminate their stay. Married patients are more apt to have intact families who want patients returned; families may view the return of adult male patients as especially beneficial since these patients are apt to be the primary breadwinners for families. Disrupted-estranged patients are in between the two situations. Although patients in this latter group are not as likely as the married to have intact families, in many instances they will have children, in-laws, relatives, and friends that are the result of marriage, all of whom may express an interest in having the patient discharged. Also, estranged-disrupted patients may remain the chief breadwinners for their families; this may be true for divorced or separated males even when children are living with the estranged wife. Consequently, we would expect the length of stay for the disrupted-estranged group to be shorter than for the single but longer than for the married. Results are consistent with this expectation.

The class status of a patient is based on Duncan's transformed NORC values for all census occupations. Five class strata are defined as in previous analysis; they are indicated by numbers I through V, with the low number indicating high class status.[9] Patients with higher status are more apt to have social and economic resources that may be utilized in obtaining release. Families of patients with higher status, and hence more income, can probably afford visits to the hospital, which may be a factor in discharge decisions of hospital staff. Hospital staff may be more willing to discharge higher-status patients simply because greater economic resources are believed to facilitate post-hospital functioning and because higher-status patients are more apt to continue treatment in out-patient agencies.[10] Also, higher-status patients are more apt to have family members and other persons in the community concerned with their welfare and, hence, persons who show an interest in having patients released; these persons may actually exert pressure in an effort to get them released.[11] Conse-

---

[8] See pp. 433–44 above.

[9] See pp. 396–97. The five strata are defined as follows: I = 76 and above; II = 66–75; III = 56–65; IV = 46–55; and V = 45 and below.

[10] This idea has been suggested by Jerome K. Myers and Lee L. Bean, A Decade Later: A Follow-up of "Social Class and Mental Illness" (New York: John Wiley, 1968), p. 145. They do find that higher-status patients are more apt to receive outpatient care subsequent to discharge from the hospital. Ibid., p. 83. However, they do not show that this difference actually enters into staff decisions to discharge. In fact they suggest a number of factors are involved in class differences in discharge rates. They believe that the professionals in hospitals are more likely to "give up" on lower-class patients, to consider them as "poorer risks," and to "have more negative attitudes toward lower-status persons." Ibid., p. 83. Also, staff attitudes "may be influenced by other community authorities such as social workers and police who regard lower-class patients as problems and question the wisdom of discharging them. The spoken, or unspoken, questions that recur are: 'Why bother us with these crocks? Why don't you keep them locked up where they belong?' Such attitudes may have an effect on staff members who become increasingly reluctant to discharge lower-class patients a second or third time." Ibid., p. 84. Myers and Bean comments here are with respect to patients who have been rehospitalized after having been discharged. However, it is clear from their comments that their view of staff attitudes is not limited to patients who have been hospitalized more than once. Ibid., pp. 83–84.

[11] In discussing patients who are readmitted to the hospital, Myers and Bean state: "the lower-class patient's family is less likely to accept the patient back home. These families sometimes do not have adequate facilities at home to care for the patient and because of different values they are less willing than upper-class families to accept back into their midst a member who has been hospitalized for mental illness. . . . Once a [lower-class] patient is hospitalized, . . . he is no longer a burden on the rest of the family. As time goes on, the family displays less and less interest in him." Myers and Bean, A Decade Later, p. 84. Myers and Roberts state that more lower-class than higher-class "patients felt neglected by their families and believed their families did not want them to return home. The patients might have desired to leave the institution but had no place to go. Apparently, many [lower-] class patients had to remain hospitalized simply because their families would not accept them back home." Jerome K. Myers and Bertram H. Roberts, Family and Class Dynamics in Mental Illness (John Wiley, 1959), p. 217.

quently, length of stay should decrease from the lowest class to the highest. The median number of days of hospitalization is given for each class stratum below and is consistent with the hypothesis.[12]

V	IV	III	II	I
94.9	72.4	59.1	57.7	56.0
(N = 1,180)	(N = 530)	(N = 635)	(N = 608)	(N = 196)

Occupational Differences

In an earlier paper,[13] we observed differences in specific occupations among levels of social and economic resources. In particular we noted that the resources of farm workers were extremely low, much lower than those of any other major occupational group. Moreover, community supports for farm workers as well as their political power are most limited. We hypothesized that because their resources were so low, court commitments would be much more frequent than voluntary admissions for this group. Results were consistent with this prediction.

We have argued here that social resources in-

fluence how long one stays in the mental hospital. If this hypothesis is true, we would expect a much longer length of stay for farm workers than any other occupational group. Examination indicates that this is the case. Median number of hospital days for farm workers is 135 days, which is far above that for the next highest groups (90.0 and 86.8 for service workers and nonfarm, nonmining laborers). The median length of stay for farmers is less than half that for farm workers (58.9 days). In light of the very limited resources of farm workers, such results are precisely what the social resource hypothesis predicts.

INTERACTION OF SOCIAL CLASS AND MARITAL STATUS

Table 1 gives the median number of days of hospitalization for patients cross-classified by social class and marital status. For all three marital status groups the length of hospitalization is generally longer for patients from the lower end of the class scale than for patients toward the upper end. The effects are not uniform, however. They are most pronounced for the single, with the length of stay decreasing sharply from stratum V to stratum IV after which the decline is gradual but continuous. There is no clear trend for the married except that the length of stay is shorter for patients toward the lower end of the scale than it is for patients toward the upper end. The pattern for the disrupted-estranged resembles that for the single except for class I, in which the length of stay is unusually high.

Looking at the effects of marital status, in all

---

[12] Our hypothesis and findings are consistent with the results of the study and review of Kahn, Pollack and Fink. They found that the influence of class status on length of stay varies with the type of treatment found in different institutional settings. In psychoanalytically oriented private hospitals and clinics, patients with higher class status (indicated by education) tend to remain in treatment for a longer period. In state mental hospitals, on the other hand, where the treatment modality is likely to be somatic and custodial, higher class status is associated with a shorter length of stay. See Robert Kahn, Max Pollack, and Max Fink, "Sociopsychologic Aspects of Psychiatric Treatment in a Voluntary Mental Hospital," *Archives of General Psychiatry* 1 (December, 1969), pp. 565–74. In each setting, the least desirable treatment is accorded the lower-status patients.

[13] See pp. 403–11 above.

TABLE 1. MEDIAN HOSPITAL STAY FOR PATIENTS BY SOCIAL CLASS AND MARITAL STATUS

Marital Status	Social Class				
	V	IV	III	II	I
Married	63.9 (448)*	69.2 (246)	61.4 (369)	61.6 (326)	53.6 (99)
Disrupted-estranged	90.9 (255)	73.0 (134)	46.1 (140)	43.8 (153)	83.5 (55)
Single	153.3 (464)	109.3 (140)	88.3 (124)	85.7 (124)	67.5 (40)

* Figure in parenthesis is N.

but one stratum (stratum I), the length of stay is highest for single patients, and in three out of five strata, the length of stay is shortest for married patients. The effects of marital status are most pronounced for patients from stratum V. though they are clearly present for stratum IV patients as well. Thus, effects of marital status are strongest at the lower end of the class structure.

Such results indicate that when patient resources are extremely low as a result of either marital or class status, the effects of the remaining status are most pronounced. This pattern is almost identical to the pattern we observed for involuntary/voluntary admissions.[14] It suggests that the same general principle may operate after the patient is in the hospital that operates prior to his admission. Just as patient status resources influence the actions of others toward an individual in the admission process, they influence decisions authorities make regarding his discharge after he has been admitted.

Severity of Impairment as an Explanation

We observed in an earlier paper that the mental hospitalization rate is inversely related to social class and that this is possibly due to an inverse relationship between mental illness and social class.[15] This would not necessarily account for class differences in length of hospitalization, however. Just because the lower class has a higher proportion of persons who are hospitalized (and presumably mentally ill) does not mean that lower-class persons who are hospitalized are, on the average, any sicker than persons from higher-class backgrounds. A high rate for a group does not necessarily mean a high level of impairment in that group.

It has been suggested, however, that level of impairment is inversely associated with class status as well as with marital status. In a sample of 258 admissions to a state hospital from Snohomish County in Washington, Gove and Howell report that the assessed severity of symptoms is inversely related to marital resources and is higher for patients with income of less than $4,000 than for patients above this level. They

mention that one other study reports a similar finding for marital status and that four other studies indicate that the severity of illness may be negatively related to patient class status.[16] Therefore, an alternative interpretation to the status resource hypothesis might be that social status is associated with length of stay only because the level of psychiatric impairment is correlated with social status; thus, the level of psychiatric impairment would determine length of stay. According to this argument status resources have no effect on their own but are mediated by level of psychiatric impairment. Consequently, control for a possible correlate (level of impairment) of status resources would cause the relationship between status resources and length of hospitalization to disappear.

In the absence of data on level of impairment we are unable to discount this interpretation entirely. Several problems are associated with such an interpretation, however. The results of studies that Gove and Howell cite as providing evidence for an inverse relationship between psychiatric impairment and class and marital status are less than compelling. This is especially true with respect to persons admitted to state mental hospitals. The results of each of the studies will be reviewed.

First, Turner et al. show that the relationship between class status and severity of impairment varies depending on the type of patient or source of treatment (state hospital patient, private psychiatric patient, etc).[17] Since the patients in our study are from state hospitals, the relevant results of Turner's study are those for state hospital patients. Turner et al. report that for state hospital admissions in their study, only one of two measures of social class is significantly related to level of impairment, and in this one instance it

---

[14] See p. 408 above.
[15] See pp. 401–2.

[16] Walter R. Gove and Patrick Howell, "Individual Resources and Mental Hospitalization: A Comparison and Evaluation of the Societal Reaction and Psychiatric Perspectives," *American Sociological Review* 39 (February, 1974), pp. 91–92, 98. The studies cited are as follows: Myers and Roberts, *Family and Class Dynamics in Mental Illness;* Richard I. Shader, Michael H. Ebert, and Jerold S. Harmatz, "Langner's Psychiatric Impairment Scale: A Short Screening Device," *American Journal of Psychiatry* 128 (November, 1971), pp. 596–601; and R. Jay Turner, Joann Raymond, Lawrence J. Zabo, and James Diamond, "Field Survey Methods in Psychiatry: The Effects of Sampling Strategy Upon Findings in Research on Schizophrenia," *Journal of Health and Social Behavior* 10 (December, 1969), pp. 289–97; Myers and Bean, *A Decade Later.*
[17] Turner et al., "Field Survey Methods in Psychiatry."

is not even clear that the relationship is negative.[18] Another study, by Myers and Roberts, is based on just 50 treated patients from New Haven, Connecticut. There was no effort to determine whether patients from one class were more severely impaired than patients from another; focus instead was on identifying class differences in social and psychological patterns in the development of schizophrenia and psychoneurosis. The study reported class differences in the etiology of these disorders, but it did not report that schizophrenics or psychoneurotics in the lower class were more (or less) severely impaired than schizophrenics or psychoneurotics in the higher class.[19] Another study also took place in New Haven and is a follow-up of ten years later of patients in Hollingshead and Redlich's original study of *Social Class and Mental Illness*. It includes both former hospital patients and former clinic patients. For the former hospital patients, the authors report that psychiatric impairment and class status are *positively* rather than negatively related.[20] Although their results for samples of former *clinic* patients and matched controls do show that level of psychiatric impairment is inversely related to class status,[21] it is the finding for former *hospital* patients that is most relevant.

In addition, Myers and Bean report that hospital discharge rates between 1950 and 1960 are inversely related to class status even after several social and psychiatric variables are controlled.[22] This of course is consistent with our hypothesis. The last study cited by Gove and Howell is based on 243 applicants for outpatient evaluation at the walk-in service of the Massachusetts Mental Health Center.[23] These patients were administered the 22-item Langner Psychiatric Impairment Scale, and results showed that severity of impairment was inversely related to class status. In light of the findings of Turner et al., it is questionable whether these findings are relevant to the present study. The persons involved in the study are applicants for outpatient treatment and, according to Turner et al., the relationship between impairment and class status for this type population may differ from the relationship for persons admitted to state hospitals. In addition, the Langner scale is a questionable measurement. The scale may serve best to detect persons "with physical discomfort and lack of fulfillment." While it may be a reasonably good index of neurosis and psychosomatic orientations, its value for scaling level of psychotic behavior appears to be most limited.[24] We note that neurotics and persons with psychosomatic disorders are not the types of persons who qualify for admission to state mental hospitals; these hospitals are for the *insane*. Although insanity is a legal rather than psychological term, psychosis is the nearest psychiatric equivalent.

Only the study by Gove and Howell suggests that there is an inverse relationship between class status and severity of psychiatric impairment among patients in state mental hospitals. Their distinction between class statuses is quite gross and is based on what mental patients report on their income. The distinction is between patients with over and under $4,000 reported annual income. Consequently, their comparison, at best, is between poverty and nonpoverty patients rather than between several class levels. Moreover, all of their patients are from one county in Wash-

[18] Turner et al., state "no general gradient could be observed" for the relationship between class status and impairment level for state hospital patients. *Ibid.*, p. 295.

[19] Myers and Roberts, *Family and Class Dynamics in Mental Illness.* However, this study does report class differences in prominent symptoms, *ibid.*, pp. 286–87. This is the basis for Gove and Howell's belief that the study suggests that lower-class patients are more severely impaired.

[20] Myers and Bean state, "compared to their matched controls, former upper and middle-class patients are less well-adjusted than patients at other class levels" and "the higher the class, the greater the degree of psychiatric impairment." Myers and Bean, *A Decade Later,* pp. 133–42.

[21] *Ibid.*, pp. 132–43. In their review Gove and Howell cite neither of these results. Their focus, instead, is on class differences in types of symptoms as reported by Myers and Bean, with the more severe symptoms inversely related to social class. Myers and Bean report that "anxiety, depression, obsessions, compulsions and phobias" are directly related to social class and "memory or orientation disturbances, disorganized thought process, delusions and hallucinations, aggressive verbal behavior and aggressive behavior" are inversely related to social class. *Ibid.*, pp. 90–91. The apparent contradiction with other class relationships stems from the fact that the reference to patterns of symptoms is for patients who have been rehospitalized. Even so, it is not clear that it is severity of psychiatric impairment that leads to rehospitalization. Myers and Bean believe that the major factor may be a higher level of aggressive behavior in the lower classes, so that the lower-status individual's "symptoms are more likely than those characteristics of higher-status persons to come to the attention of community authorities who will rehospitalize him" even if the family doesn't. *Ibid.*, p. 92.

[22] *Ibid.*, pp. 80–82, 224. See footnote 11 for Myers' and Bean's suggestion as to the reasons for such a relationship.

[23] Shader, Ebert and Harmatz, "Langner's Psychiatric Impairment Scale."

[24] David L. Muller, "Discussion," *American Journal of Psychiatry* 128 (November, 1971), p. 601.

ington; this raises questions as to the generality of their results.

In summary, one must conclude that a negative relationship between class status and level of psychiatric impairment for persons who are admitted to state mental hospitals has not been demonstrated. Indeed, when the equivocal and contradictory results of all studies are considered, little can be concluded as to the relationship between class status and illness severity for hospitalized and formerly hospitalized patients. Certainly when all the evidence is considered, there is little empirical basis for assuming that lower-class patients are more severely impaired than higher class patients, and the assumption of an inverse relationship between marital resources and level of impairment can be based on results from only two studies.[25] Consequently, to attribute our finding of a relationship between length of hospitalization and status resources, especially class resources, to status differences in severity of psychiatric impairment would be most questionable.

On the other hand, there are compelling reasons for believing that our results for marital and class status are, in fact, due to level of status resources available. First, in the analysis below, findings for type of admission and length of stay are consistent with the status resource hypothesis even when level of impairment is controlled. Second, the interaction effects between type of admission and both class and marital status are consistent with the status resource hypothesis; as will be noted, these effects appear to be beyond the purview of hypotheses based on the assumption that level of impairment is inversely related to status resources and directly related to hospitalization. We will examine the relationship for type of admission and length of stay controlling for level of impairment first.

TYPE OF ADMISSION AND LEVEL OF IMPAIRMENT

Those who believe that patients are in mental hospitals because of serious mental disorders do not appreciate the significance of the distinction between voluntary and involuntary patients. Gove and Howell contend that, according to "the psychiatric perspective," the distinction is "relatively unimportant" and "is believed to have little effect on the patient or his subsequent progress." Yet they also state that they themselves "do not wish to imply that the distinction is not unimportant, but only that it is unclear how such a distinction should be treated."[26] But from a sociological perspective, the meaning of the distinction is clear since a very definite and unambiguous *legal status* is conferred by virtue of type of admission. Most hospital personnel, and certainly those responsible for discharging patients, know the patient's legal status. We suggest that the way patients are admitted to hospitals influences the way hospital staff behave toward them.[27] The hospital has the legal right to retain involuntary patients until they believe they should be released, whereas they must release voluntary patients within twelve days after written request from the patient or his guardian, provided the request is not made within the first eighteen days. In effect this means that voluntary patients are normally committed to at least a thirty-day period of hospitalization whereas involuntary patients are committed for an indeterminate period. Our hypothesis is that this is an important contingency in patient length of stay. How long a patient is in the hospital is influenced by the constraints patient legal status presents to hospital staff.

Data are consistent with the hypothesis. A total of 86.0 percent of all voluntary admissions in Washington hospitals were released within

---

[25] The two studies are Turner et al., "Field Survey Methods in Psychiatry," and Gove and Howell, "Individual Resources and Mental Hospitalization."

[26] Gove and Howell, "Individual Resources and Mental Hospitalization," pp. 87–88. In this article it is not always clear whether Gove and Howell are stating their own position or whether they are presenting the position of what they call "the psychiatric perspective." However, since Gove believes his assessment of the evidence supports the psychiatric perspective and rejects the societal reaction perspective (see footnote 1 above), he seems to identify his position with that of the psychiatric perspective.

[27] The statement is consistent with research on staff attitudes toward involuntary and voluntary patients. One study found that hospital staff tended to regard involuntary patients less favorably than voluntary patients. Involuntary patients were felt to be unwilling to acknowledge their mental illness, the value of psychiatric treatment, or the importance of compliance with staff demands. They were therefore seen as unlikely to fulfill staff expectations of proper illness behavior. See Norman K. Denzin and Stephen P. Spitzer, "Paths to the Mental Hospital and Staff Predictions of Patient Role Behavior," *Journal of Health and Social Behavior* 7 (Winter, 1966), pp. 265–71.

ninety days, in comparison to only 38.1 percent for involuntary admissions; virtually all voluntary patients (99.2 percent) were released within one year, but only 64.5 percent of involuntary patients were. The difference in median number of days is extreme.

Involuntary	Voluntary
171.1	24.6

The data indicate that patient progress (at least in terms of length of stay) is affected by type of admission, and substantially so.

Because of the custodial and sometimes punitive nature of most state mental hospitals,[28] it is reasonable to assume that a high percentage of patients, even voluntarily admitted patients, want out of the hospital soon after they enter. It is probable, therefore, that a large proportion of voluntary patients are released within thirty days because their legal status changes at the end of thirty days rather than because so many show dramatic improvement at this time. On the other hand, involuntary patients are not legally able to effect release upon demand; their median length of stay is much greater than that of voluntary patients accordingly. Results suggest that legal status creates constraints on hospital personnel which influence the timing of discharge decisions.

These differences could conceivably be due to severity of illness; that is, involuntary patients may have a longer length of stay because they are more severely ill than the voluntary patients, as some contend.[29] Since no estimates of severity of illness are available for patients from Washington, we are unable to report the relationship between types of admission and length of stay with severity of illness controlled. A measure of

illness severity is available for another patient population, however.

These patients are all 21 to 64-year-old male first admissions to the six Tennessee state mental hospitals who began and completed their hospitalization during the ten-year period, 1956 through 1965. Demographically the Tennessee patients are equivalent to Washington patients. There are a total of 5,177 Tennessee patients.

Upon admission, persons admitted to Tennessee hospitals were rated by members of the hospital staff as either mildly, moderately or severely impaired.[30] In a number of instances (slightly over 25 percent) no rating is given, presumably because the patient's condition was too ambiguous to permit a judgment. These will be included along with the three groups for which a judgment is reported, since the status resource hypothesis anticipates differences within this category depending on patient admission status.

First, under the assumption that illness status determines discharge decisions, a direct relationship between assessed severity of impairment and length of stay would be expected. Results below are consistent with this, although it is not clear from this hypothesis why the not reported category would have a longer length of stay than the mild and moderate categories.

Mild	Moderate	Severe	Not Reported
38.8	50.4	88.1	54.3
(N = 1,150)	(N = 1,556)	(N = 1,168)	(N = 1,303)

It is also not clear that this relationship is in fact a function of *actual* impairment. The measure of impairment level is one of *attributed* severity and we do not know to what extent the assessments made by personnel in Tennessee hospitals correlate with patients' "true" levels of impairment. But regardless of this ambiguity, it is clear that the impairment assessment is a *staff definition of patient condition*. It is likely that this definition will influence subsequent staff behavior toward patients, specifically, how long

[28] For one example, see Ivan Belknap, pp. 422–32 above. For a discussion of the patient's constitutional "right to treatment" and the denial of this right for most patients in state mental hospitals ("if you are a patient in a public mental hospital, you are almost certainly not receiving adequate treatment"), see Bruce Ennis and Loren Siegel, *The Rights of Mental Patients: The Basic ACLU Guide to Mental Patients' Rights* (New York: Avon Books, 1973), pp. 49–50.

[29] See Norman Barr, "Voluntary Imprisonment: Its Usefulness in the Rehabilitation of Criminal Offenders," *American Journal of Psychiatry* 124 (March, 1967), pp. 170–78; Allen T. Klots et al., *Mental Illness and Due Process: Report and Recommendations on Admissions to Mental Hospitals under New York Law* (Ithaca: Cornell University Press, 1962), p. 59; and Gove and Howell, "Individual Resources and Mental Hospitalization," pp. 87–88.

[30] On the original scale there are five degrees of impairment: none, minimal, mild, moderate, and severe. To give three groups of approximately equal numbers, we have combined the first three levels into one category.

staff attempt to keep patients in the hospital.[31] But if this definition were the sole criterion and the type of admission were of no significance, then we would expect no difference in length of stay between voluntary and involuntary admissions for patients with the same degree of attributed impairment. As Table 2 shows, this is not the case. The length of stay for involuntary patients is greater than that of voluntary patients for each impairment level.[32] Even among patients whose level of impairment is not recorded, the length of stay is considerably higher for the involuntary group. These results indicate that patient legal status is a significant factor in patient discharge. Its effects on length of stay are apparent even when level of assessed impairment is controlled. This supports the status resource hypothesis.

Interaction of Admission Status and Level of Impairment

Staff attempts to keep patients in the hospital are probably weakest when patients are defined as mildly impaired, strongest when they are defined as severely impaired. It is when this staff behavioral force is weakest that patient legal status is least important. Patients who are believed to be mildly impaired are apt to be released in a relatively short time regardless of their legal status; for these patients, the advantages of being admitted voluntarily are probably not great. On the other hand, for patients who are defined as more severely ill, voluntary admission status, which gives patients a legal basis for demanding release, may effectively prevent hospital staff from retaining them in the hospital against their wishes. According to this reasoning, differences in length of stay between voluntary and involuntary patients should be least for patients who are defined as mildly impaired and greatest for patients who are defined as severely impaired. Results in Table 2 are consistent wtih this reasoning. Whereas length of stay is only 22 percent higher for involuntary patients in the mild category (42.0 days versus 35.7 days), it is 120 percent higher for patients in the severe category (93.5 days versus 42.5 days). Therefore, the effect of legal status on length of hospitalization depends to some extent on how sick the staff think the patients are.[33]

At the same time, staff definition of impairment influences length of stay for both voluntary and involuntary patients. This influence varies, however, and is considerably stronger for involuntary patients. For voluntary patients, the severely impaired group stays only slightly longer than those in either the mild or moderate categories (42.5 days versus 35.7 and 34.1 days), and for whatever the reason, the not reported category stays longer than the severe category (43.2 days). For involuntary patients, differences in length of stay are considerably greater and they increase continuously from mild to severe. We are therefore drawn to this conclusion: it is when staff behavior is least constrained (for involuntary patients) that the effects of attributed illness are strongest. Apparently it is when hospital officials have greatest legal control over patients that discharge decisions are most apt to be consistent with staff definition of patient mental status. Staff definitions are most forceful when they have the support of the law.

---

[31] To illustrate, several investigators had themselves admitted to twelve mental hospitals in different parts of the country. Each investigator had no known psychiatric impairment, but his simulation of symptoms led to a diagnosis of schizophrenia in all but one instance. All twelve pseudopatients had great difficulty in convincing the staff that they were sane and in getting discharged from the hospital. In one instance the length of stay was fifty-two days—this for a perfectly sane person! Since these persons were not psychiatrically impaired, it seems obvious that they were retained in the hospital only because they were defined as impaired. Hence, regardless of actual impairment, staff definition of patient impairment is an important factor in length of hospital stay. See David L. Rosenshan, "On Being Sane in Insane Places," *Science* 179 (January, 1973), pp. 250–58.

[32] Comparison of length of stay for Washington and Tennessee shows that most Washington patients stay much longer than most Tennessee patients. This in itself undoubtedly reflects social, legal, and economic differences between the states and hospital systems rather than psychiatric factors. It is not likely that Washington patients are so much sicker than Tennessee patients as to require such a longer period of hospitalization.

[33] The test for the effect of legal status is probably a most conservative one. This is because the assessment of patient mental status may have been influenced by the way patients are admitted. Considering that many psychiatric professionals consider involuntary patients to be more severely ill (see Barr, "Voluntary Imprisonment"; Klots et al., *Mental Illness and Due Process;* and Gove and Howell, "Individual Resources and Mental Hospitalization," pp. 87–88) and to view them in less favorable terms than voluntary patients (see Denzin and Spitzer, "Paths to the Mental Hospital"), it is not unreasonable to believe that the physicians' assessments of patients in Tennessee hospitals were influenced by their knowledge of patient admission status. It is probable, therefore, that to some degree (perhaps to a substantial degree), control for assessed impairment also controls for type of admission.

TABLE 2. MEDIAN HOSPITAL STAY FOR PATIENTS BY ILLNESS IMPAIRMENT
AND TYPE OF COMMITMENT

Type of Commitment	Illness Impairment			
	Mild	Moderate	Severe	Not Recorded
Involuntary	42.0	60.4	93.5	60.5
	(698)*	(1095)	(1034)	(1051)
Voluntary	35.7	34.1	42.5	43.2
	(452)	(461)	(134)	(252)

* Figure in parenthesis is N.

In summary, then, results provide consistent evidence that type of admission has important consequences for length of hospitalization and that this effect is not due to the fact that involuntary patients are more severely ill than voluntary patients. Patient legal status has effects in its own right.

INTERACTION OF LEGAL STATUS AND CLASS STATUS

We observed above that since we have no way to control for severity of impairment for Washington patients, interpretation based on the assumption that class status and impairment are inversely related cannot be discounted altogether. However, if class resources have effects that are independent of impairment, specific interaction effects would be expected between legal status and class status. Since voluntary patients have the legal right to leave the hospital after 30 days if they wish to do so, class status resources are not needed to obtain release. This is not true for court committed patients. Consequently, a relationship between class status and length of stay would be expected for involuntary patients but not for voluntary patients.

Results in Table 3 are consistent with this reasoning. There is no relationship for voluntary patients, whereas length of stay systematically decreases from the lowest class status to the highest for involuntary patients. The influence of class status varies depending on legal status, as predicted. We interpret this to be due to the fact that legal differences modify the effects of class status. When there are no legal constraints on a patient's leaving the hospital, the influence of class status in effecting release is minimal or nonexistent, whereas the influence is considerable when legal constraints do exist.

Let us assume, however, that severity of illness is inversely related to social class. Then, if illness severity were the only or primary factor in length of hospitalization, we would expect an inverse relationship for voluntary patients. As we see from Table 3, no such relationship exists.

INTERACTION OF LEGAL STATUS AND MARITAL STATUS

A similar type of interaction exists between admission status and marital status. Table 4 gives the median length of stay by marital status separately for voluntary and involuntary admissions. Length of stay among involuntary patients is longest for the status group with the fewest social resources, but no differences of any significance exist for voluntary patients. As with the effects of social class, the effects of marital status are modified by patient legal status. When the patient's legal status is such that staff actions toward him are restrained (as in voluntary admissions after 30 days), the patient is free to leave the hospital and no relationship exists between length of hospitalization and differences in marital status resources. But when the patient's legal status is such that official actions are not so restrained, a relationship does exist. Table 4 suggests, as does Table 3, the following conclusion: under conditions where patients legal resources are limited (involuntary confinement), other social resources are needed to obtain release from the hospital and length of stay is directly and consistently related to the amount of resources normally associated with the status occupied by the patient outside the hospital.

TABLE 3. MEDIAN NUMBER OF HOSPITAL DAYS BY TYPE OF ADMISSION AND SOCIAL CLASS

Admission Status	Social Class				
	V	IV	III	II	I
Involuntary	214.0 (815)*	185.3 (313)	157.8 (361)	160.9 (295)	135.0 (99)
Voluntary	25.0 (365)	24.7 (216)	22.7 (274)	25.7 (313)	26.5 (97)

* Figure in parenthesis is N.

This would appear to be far more plausible than an interpretation based on the assumption that severity of impairment is inversely related to status resources.

TABLE 4. MEDIAN NUMBER OF HOSPITAL DAYS BY TYPE OF ADMISSION AND MARITAL STATUS

Admission Status	Marital Status		
	Single	Disrupted-Estranged	Married
Involuntary	197.5 (771)*	147.7 (491)	145.4 (929)
Voluntary	26.9 (336)	23.6 (343)	24.6 (797)

* Figure in parenthesis is N.

Indeed, results in Table 4 actually suggest that such an impairment explanation is not a valid interpretation of the findings for marital status. If it were, we would expect differences between the three groups for voluntary as well as involuntary patients in length of stay. As Table 4 shows, the length of stay for voluntary patients does not differ significantly among the three marital status groups. For involuntary patients, single patients have the longest stay, and although the differences between the disrupted-estranged and married in Table 4 is slight, it is in the direction predicted by the status resource hypothesis.

CONCLUSION

Since we were unable to control for assessed mental impairment for the Washington patients, we cannot state without qualification how staff assessment influenced the results for Washington patients. But to attempt explanation of those findings in terms of psychiatric factors would require very questionable assumptions.

One might attempt to account for the Washington results by assuming that severity of illness is inversely related to level of status resources. The assumption of such a relationship may be warranted in one instance since we found that for Tennessee patients the level of *attributed* impairment is higher for involuntary patients. But this does not account for the effect of type of admission on length of stay. When attributed illness is controlled, the relationship between type of admission and length of stay remains. Controlling attributed illness severity does not eliminate the effects of legal status. There is no reason to expect that results for Washington patients would be any different.

As for marital status and class status, each may be inversely related to level of impairment, although we have seen that the evidence is not very conclusive. Even so, the strength of the relationships would have to be quite high to assure that control for mental impairment would cause the relationships for marital and class status to disappear. As we have seen, although assessed mental impairment is correlated with legal status, control for mental impairment does not eliminate the effects of legal status. Also, the status resource hypothesis provides a plausible basis for predicting the interactive effects between type of admission and level of impairment, class resources, and marital resources. Such effects are not plausibly explained by an assumption concerning level of impairment.

Results supporting the status resource hypothesis for length of hospitalization are what one would expect from the data for admissions. The latter findings show that the more undesirable form of mental hospital admission (involuntary admission) was inversely related to the patients' marital and class resources.[34] Results in this paper show that social resources are related to the disadvantages acquired through involuntary admission, and we infer that this relationship is a result of patient status resources exerting an influence on hospital staff behavior toward patients. Such findings and inferences are consistent with other studies which have found that an individual's status attributes have a significant impact on the way he is treated in various settings in society.[35]

All things considered, it would be most diffi-

cult to explain our findings except in terms of the status resource hypothesis. True, at least some and perhaps all of the patients in the two state systems were mentally impaired (even by the narrowest of definitions). Also, we have observed that staff assessment is a factor in length of stay. And we observed that the effects of legal status varied depending on staff assessment of patient impairment. But legal status continues to have an independent effect, and the evidence consistently supports the view that marital and social class positions also have effects that do not depend on differences in severity of illness. Our argument is neither that mental hospital patients are not mentally impaired (though we do wonder about the percentage who actually are impaired and the extent of impairment) nor that level of impairment does not influence length of stay. We do argue, however, that the relationships reported here are the result of sociological factors and not psychiatric factors.

[34] See pp. 403–11 above.
[35] The differential treatment of individuals according to their social status has been documented for a variety of settings. In addition to mental institutions (see Kahn, Pollack, and Fink, "Sociopsychologic Aspects of Psychiatric Treatment"), differences have been observed in the court and in court outcomes [see Theodore G. Chiricos, Philip D. Jackson, and Gordon P. Waldo, "Inequality in the Imposition of a Criminal Label," *Social Problems* 19 (Spring, 1972), pp. 553–71; Richard D. Schwartz and Jerome H. Skolnick, "Two Studies of Legal Stigma," *Social Problems* 10 (Fall, 1962), pp. 133–42; and David Sudnow, "Normal Crimes: Sociological Features of the Penal Code in a Public Defender Office," *Social Problems* 13 (Winter, 1965), pp. 255–74]. Study of patient treatment in emergency rooms of general hospitals reveals the same thing. See David Sudnow, *Passing On: The Social Organization of Dying* (Englewood Cliffs: Prentice-Hall, 1967), pp. 100–109. This study is especially interesting. Sudnow observed that staff treatment of persons brought to the emergency room in critical condition (and hence possibly "dead on arrival") varied according to staff perceptions of the individual's "social worth." The crucial variables seemed to be patient age, appearance and "moral character." Given similar physiomedical conditions, young,

well dressed, sober persons received a greater range of treatment efforts and received them more promptly than did those who were older, shabbily dressed or drunk. These do not exhaust the examples that could be given of the role social status plays in the way individuals are treated by others as many others exist in the research literature. But they are sufficient to note that our observations for mental hospital patients are specific aspects of a more general phenomenon. Considering the generality of the phenomenon, it would be most surprising indeed if social status did not influence the timing of discharge decisions for mental patients.

THE EX-MENTAL PATIENT AND REHOSPITALIZATION: SOME RESEARCH FINDINGS

ROBERT MAISEL

Recent efforts to reduce the distance that separates mental patients from the rest of society have helped focus attention on a more broadly sociological view of mental disorder. Speedier discharges, encouragement of home visits, establishment of out-patient clinics (often in general hospitals), and health insurance for mental disabilities, have tended to break down barriers which separated inmates of mental hospitals from their communities. (Such developments are

partially responsible for the rise of interest in the sociological, rather than purely psychological, problems of the discharged mental patient seeking to regain a stable position within the community.[1]) At the same time, studies devoted

Reprinted with permission of the author and The Society for the Study of Social Problems, from *Social Problems* 15 (Summer, 1967), pp. 18–24.

[1] Recent surveys of the most prominent problems and topics of the sociology of mental illness may be found in: John Clausen, *Sociology and the Field of Mental Health* (New York: Russell Sage Foundation, 1956); John Clausen, "The Sociology of Mental Illness" in Robert K. Merton, Leonard Broom, and Leonard S. Cottrell, Jr., editors, *Sociology Today* (New York: Basic Books, Inc., 1959); Howard E. Freeman, Sol Levine, and Leo G. Reeder, editors, *Handbook of Medical Sociology* (Englewood Cliffs, N.J.: Prentice-Hall, 1963).

to the experiences of the ex-mental patient tend to maintain the traditional individualistic focus of psychiatry, that is, on indications and expressions of mental pathology either in the ex-patient or in members of his family.[2] These studies reflect concern for the efficacy of hospital treatment programs as related to the unfolding course of mental illness. Further, they often implicitly assume that rehospitalization is merely a function of the recurrence of the ex-patient's illness, a consequence of "relapse." In general, the problems of social adjustment are absorbed into psychiatric evaluations of mental health or illness.

There is reason to suspect that the rejection of ex-mental patients as expressed by rehospitalization involves issues which transcend the psychiatric formulations of their problems as mental illness. Research in the sociology of deviance has made us aware of the additional difficulties mental patients face as degraded persons subject to penalties for having behaved in socially disapproved ways.[3] Apart from the problems caused by social stigmatization, ex-patients also are "homecomers" who are especially vulnerable to unique difficulties of social adjustment.[4] Finally, there is empirical evidence that problems associated with commonly recognized social factors, such as marital status, employment record, and family composition are positively related to rehospitalization.[5] These considerations encourage, if not demand, closer exploration of the social-structural as well as the sociopsychological context within which rehospitalization occurs.

THE STUDY

The present study proposes to examine some of the processes which underlie the social adjustment of discharged mental patients on return to the community. It explores two related questions: (1) what kinds of ex-patient behavior are typically associated with their rehospitalization? (2) what considerations influence the family's decision to rehospitalize an ex-patient?

The data on which this paper is based were gathered by the author between June, 1960 and January, 1962, using a select sample of New Haven, Connecticut residents who had been in a State or Veteran's Administration mental hospital prior to the onset of the study. The main source of information was provided by lengthy interviews with family members of these ex-patients, supplemented by hospital records and material from an earlier survey. The ex-patients selected for study met the following criteria: white adult males, ages 17–60, diagnosed as psychotic without organic impairment who were discharged into the community at least once within the period December 1, 1950–June 1, 1960. There was sufficient information to retain 60 of the 73 ex-patients chosen for inclusion in the original sample. (Three families refused to be interviewed and 10 ex-patients could not be located.) Of these 60 ex-patients, 51 had been discharged by 1953.

[2] In the medical and psychiatric literature, rates of recidivism are generally analyzed with reference to hospital practices; e.g., diagnosis, various types of treatments, length of stay, prognosis, and the like. The implication is, clearly, that social adjustment is a secondary consideration for understanding rehospitalization. As examples of the general tendency to overlook, or to treat casually, community response to mental illness, see the following studies: N. Q. Brill and G. Beebe, *A Follow-up Study of War Neuroses* (V.A. Medical Monograph, January 22, 1955): Benjamin Balinski, "Factors in the Vocational Adjustment of Schizophrenics after Mental Hospital Discharge," *Journal of Clinical Psychology* 3 (October, 1947); R. Israel and N. Johnson, "Schizophrenic Discharge and Readmission Rates," *American Journal of Psychiatry* 112 (1955–56); Jay Hoffman, Ernest Parsons and Margaret Hagen, "Post-Hospital Adaptation of Selected Groups of Patients with Dementia Praecox," *Journal of Nervous and Mental Disease* 93 (June, 1941); Charles Rupp and Elizabeth Fletcher, "A Five to Ten Year Follow-up Study of 641 Schizophrenic Cases," *American Journal of Psychiatry* 96 (January, 1940); Thomas Rennie, "Follow-up Study of 500 Patients with Schizophrenia Admitted to the Hospital from 1913 to 1923," *Archives of Neurology and Psychiatry* 42 (November, 1939); R. Williams and R. Walker, "Schizophrenics at Time of Discharge," *AMA Archives of General Psychiatry* 4 (January, 1961).

[3] Lemert seems to have been the first to note that the mentally ill are popularly defined not by their actions (however bizarre) but their incarceration in a state mental hospital. See Edwin M. Lemert, *Social Pathology* (New York: McGraw-Hill, 1951). This insight has been elaborated further by Erving Goffman, *Asylum* (Garden City, N.Y.: Anchor Books, 1961), and Kai T. Erikson, "Patient Role and Social Uncertainty: A Dilemma of the Mentally Ill," *Psychiatry* 20 (August, 1957).

[4] Alfred Scheutz, "The Homecomer," *Collected Papers*, Volume II (The Hague: Martinus Nijhoff, 1964).

[5] Howard Freeman and Ozzie Simmons, *The Mental Patient Comes Home* (New York: John Wiley, 1963); George Brown, "Experiences of Discharged Chronic Schizophrenic Patients in Various Types of Living Groups," *Milbank Memorial Fund Quarterly* 37 (April, 1959); Leta M. Adler, "Patients of a State Mental Hospital: The Outcome of Their Hospitalization," in Arnold Rose, editor, *Mental Health and Mental Disorder* (New York: W. W. Norton Co., 1955); Enid Mills, *Living with Mental Illness* (London: Routledge and Kegan Paul, 1962); Mark Lefton, Shirley Angrist, Simon Dinitz, and Benjamin Pasamanick, "Social Class, Expectations and Performances of Mental Patients," *American Journal of Sociology* 68 (July, 1962).

FINDINGS

It is commonly assumed that bizarre or abnormal behavior manifested by ex-patients precipitates their rehospitalization. To investigate this assumption, relatives were asked to report on the behavior of patients while out of the hospital. A check-list of behavior items, similar but shorter than the one used by Freeman and Simmons in their research,[6] was used to classify the responses. These items were divided into two groups. The first group, called "major symptoms," included items such as attempted suicide and incontinent behavior which are usually regarded by common sense and professional opinion as evidence for severe mental disturbance. The second group ("minor symptoms") were those generally considered less indicative of mental disturbance, e.g., "stays by himself." In the discussion which follows, patients will be called "abnormal" if they are reported to have exhibited one or more major symptoms or at least five minor ones. Otherwise, they will be designated as "normal." This procedure enabled us to discriminate in a rough fashion between the "poor" and "good" performers in our patient group.[7]

Nineteen of the 40 patients for whom information on reported behavior was available[8] were scored as "abnormal"; 10 of these patients manifested 2 or more major symptoms while 7 more had 1 major symptom. Those considered abnormal also exceeded the normal group in the number of minor symptoms reported, showing a mean of 2.4 symptoms per person as against 1.4 per person in the normal group.

How is the reported severity of symptoms related to rehospitalization? During the one year period following the post-1950 discharge date, 28 percent of those rated as "abnormal," as compared with 14 percent of those rated as "normal," were rehospitalized. This distribution conforms to what might be expected from a purely psychiatric point of view. However, the percentage of "abnormals" remaining in the community (72 percent) is strikingly high. Comparable percentages for those with severe psychiatric impairment who have managed to avoid rehospitalization have been reported by Brown (30 percent), Freeman and Simmons (45.5 percent), and Fuller (32 percent).[9] These findings suggest that symptomatic behavior only partially explains the social rejection of mental patients underlying decisions to rehospitalize. Types of "performances" other than "abnormal" may be of equal or greater importance for convincing others that an ex-patient needs further hospitalization. One possibility is that acceptance or rejection stems more from the ex-patient's current *social* status than from his *diagnostic* status. The two terms are by no means generically similar. A person's ability to maintain his position in society depends upon adequate performance in several crucial, social roles, which in no way precludes personality difficulties or even erratic behavior.[10]

Social adequacy indicated by income-producing work was singled out for analysis on the assumption that this particular role performance is crucial for maintaining the status of an adult male in our society. Work record originally was recorded in three categories: (1) regular work, (2) part-time work, irregular work, or income from a source other than a job (e.g., pension, welfare payments), and (3) no work or other source of income. An initial inspection of "failure" (rehospitalization) rates in these categories discloses that even those with partial incomes have a failure rate no greater than regular workers, and much lower than non-workers. Nine of

---

[6] Freeman and Simmons, *Mental Patient Comes Home*, p. 229.

[7] There is no attempt to tap "mental illness" with the behavior items listed above. The point is, rather, to explore kinds of behavior which are popularly thought to be symptoms of mental illness. Our rating of "abnormal" hopefully refers to peculiarities of behavior which are popularly thought to be symptoms of mental illness. Our rating of "abnormal" hopefully refers to peculiarities of behavior which are considered sure signs of derangement and therefore causes of hospitalization. Again, we wish to examine the belief that peculiar behavior is the necessary and sufficient condition for hospitalization, rather than establishing sociological criteria of mental health or sickness.

[8] Of the twenty ex-patients for whom behavior ratings were unavailable, nine lived alone, interviews with four relatives could not be completed, and the whereabouts of seven ex-patients could not be ascertained. Information gathered on social background factors, work status, and hospital readmissions (if any) is utilized for some of our tabulations.

[9] George Brown, "Experiences of Discharged Chronic Schizophrenic Patients," p. 117; Freeman and Simmons, *Mental Patient Comes Home*, p. 66; Raymond Fuller, "What Happens to Mental Patients after Discharge from the Hospital," *Psychiatric Quarterly* 9 (1940).

[10] The terms status, role, and personality, as used here, follow the distinctions established by Talcott Parsons, *The Social System* (Glencoe, Ill.: The Free Press, 1951). Thomas H. Marshall, *Sociology at the Crossroads* (London: Heinemann, 1963), has clarified the usage of these standard sociological terms.

the ten patients in the intermediate work category were not rehospitalized. This suggests that ex-patients with some independent income, however derived, resemble workers rather than non-workers in socially significant respects. Consequently, in the following tabulations the intermediate and regular work categories were combined.[11]

In Table 1 the relationship between work and rehospitalization is examined. Sixty-one percent of the ex-patients worked or had some source of

income in the first year following discharge from a mental hospital. During this period, 89 percent of the workers as compared with only 48 percent of the non-workers managed to remain in the community.

Table 2 shows the relationship between work and rehospitalization by family setting. Subjects who lived with their parents tended to be the poorest performers and of all non-workers were rehospitalized most frequently. Of the 24 patients living with parents, 16 (67 percent) did not work and only one of these avoided rehospitalization.

It is evident that while work, as defined here, proves to be an excellent predictor of "success," the nature of this relationship needs close examination. How, for example, is work functionally related to abnormal behavior? The inability to work may well be a measure of the degree of psychic impairment which is present. This possibility is examined in Table 3 where work and rehospitalization are compared with abnormality (as assessed by the criteria for abnormal and normal behavior stated earlier).

Examination of the data presented in Table 3 discloses that work remains highly associated with success, and non-work with failure, irrespective of behavior rating. The association

[11] That working even part-time influences successful adjustment is a finding corroborated by other studies. George Brown, "Expriences of Discharged Chronic Schizophrenic Patients," p. 119), found that ex-patients who hald jobs for at least 6 of 12 months while out of the hospital had a relapse rate of only 3 percent as compared with the total patient rate of 32 percent. Fifty-seven percent of those who did not work were rehospitalized. Freeman and Simmons (*Mental Patient Comes Home*, pp. 49–50) report that "At the end of the year, about 60 percent of the 'successful' males were gainfully employed. In comparison, only 35 percent of those who failed were employed at the time of their rehospitalization." It can also be estimated from the data given in their tables that 24 percent of the workers, as compared with 50 percent of the nonworkers, were rehospitalized. (In using an omnibus category for all those with some independent income this study departs somewhat from the usual practice of defining work as "gainful employment" [either part or full time] and the usual intention of assessing work as a measure of social performance. If the focus, however, is on rehospitalization [and such is typically the case] then our findings suggest that "work" be construed more broadly to mean economic self-sufficiency and be related to the question of personal independence.)

TABLE 1. WORK RECORD AND REHOSPITALIZATION AFTER ONE YEAR

	Not Rehospitalized	Rehospitalized	Total
Patient worked	33	4	37
Patient did not work	11	12	23
Total	44	16	n = 60

Value of $X^2 = 8.72$, significant at the .01 level.

TABLE 2. REHOSPITALIZATION AFTER ONE YEAR, BY WORK RECORD AND FAMILY SETTING

Patient Lived With:	Work Record	No.	Percent Rehospitalized
Parents	Worked	8	13%
(n = 24)	Did not work	16	63%
Wives	Worked	12	17%
(n = 15)	Did not work	3	33%
Siblings	Worked	10	0%
(n = 14)	Did not work	4	25%
Alone	Worked	7	14%
(n = 7)	Did not work	0	

TABLE 3. REHOSPITALIZATION AFTER ONE YEAR, BY WORK RECORD AND BEHAVIOR RATING

Behavior Rating	Work Record	No.	Percent Rehospitalized
Normal	Worked	15	7%
(n = 21)	Not worked	6	83%
Abnormal	Worked	10	0%
(n = 19)	Not worked	9	78%

Value of X^2 = 1.50, n.s.

between work status and ability to avoid hospitalization tends not to vary greatly with "symptomatic" behavior. Those who work usually remain in the community; those who do not work are commonly rehospitalized. It should also be noted that those who were rated "normal" are more likely to work than those rated "abnormal."

Clearly, such operationally defined terms as "work," "social adjustment," and "aberrant behavior" are merely rough indicators of a complex social reality. The positive association between work and successful adjustment found here raises additional questions. Does non-work, for example, cause an erosion of authority and status for a male ex-patient within the family, giving other members grounds for eventual rejection?[12] Certain observations tend to support this hypothesis. Non-working ex-patients living with insolvent families have higher failure rates than ex-patients from solvent families (i.e., those with other breadwinners or sources of income). Our data indicate that reduction in family income (often due to illness or retirement of the chief breadwinner) precipitates rehospitalization for a non-working patient. This circumstance is especially characteristic of failures from parental homes in which are found the highest percentage of non-workers.

A related issue is the extent to which a non-working ex-patient is a "nuisance," trying heavily the patience and good will of relatives. Parents may be old, infirm, and living on reduced incomes. Wives may have to work, hire baby sitters for young children, and worry about leaving their husbands alone at home. Brown has suggested that friction may occur between an ex-patient and various family members merely because he remains in the home, rather than away during the day at work.[13]

SUMMARY AND CONCLUSION

The importance of work for an ex-mental patient implies that protection of status (if not its enhancement) through having an income gives him leverage in combating the forces threatening to dislodge him from the community. Dependence upon others purchases security, but only in the short-run,[14] often at the sacrifice of freedom. Strain is placed on their good will and tolerance. Ex-patients with little bargaining power and reduced status within the family also are vulnerable to unilateral decisions made by others. Power-conscious terms are the most realistic vocabulary for describing their situation, because rehospitalization rarely occurs without a battle of wills, conflicts of interest, appeals to status, authority, and the ultimate political weapon, the use of force.[15]

In suggesting the functional value of work for the ex-patient we have not touched on the reasons underlying his successful or unsuccessful vocational adjustment. Until recently, there has

[12] Parallel to the loss of self-esteem felt by unemployed men generally, see Bohan Zawadski and Paul Lazarsfeld, "The Psychological Consequences of Unemployment," *Journal of Social Psychology* 6 (1935); E. Wight Bakke, *The Unemployed Man* (London: Nisbet and Co., 1933); Sebastian de Grazia, *The Political Community* (Chicago: University of Chicago Press, 1948); Mirra Komarovsky, *The Unemployed Man and His Family* (New York: Dryden Press, 1940).

[13] George Brown, "Experiences of Discharged Chronic Schizophrenic Patients."
[14] Data gathered for this study, but not reported here, show that non-working ex-patients tend to avoid rehospitalization *only* for short periods of time. This trend is not discernible in follow-up studies which use short time spans (usually six months to one year) to gauge patterns of rehospitalization.
[15] See Thomas Szasz, *The Myth of Mental Illness* (New York: Harper Hoebel, 1963); F. Lindman and D. McIntyre, Jr., editors, *The Mentally Disabled and the Law* (Chicago: University of Chicago Press, 1961).

been little interest or information on this topic, though it has often been assumed that many ex-patients are unemployable because of residual mental disabilities. Yet, these same patients often may have worked steadily and usefully within the hospital. A sociologically realistic view would stress the exigencies faced by an ex-patient in finding and keeping a job, as well as the stigmatizing responses of potential employ-ers, atrophying of job skills, and the loss of con-fidence and self-respect that hospitalization in-evitably produces.[16] These problems are not peculiar to mental patients. They are shared by Negroes, the aged, and workers who have be-come "technologically unemployable." This per-spective puts the experiences of an ex-patient in a larger social context, in company with others who suffer common social disadvantages.

---

[16] This possibility has been suggested by Dorothy Miller in several papers. See especially Dorothy Miller and William Dawson, "Effects of Stigma on Re-employment of Ex-mental patients," *Mental Hygiene,* 49 (April, 1965).

CHAPTER TEN

SUICIDE

On the basis of official statistics for the United States, about eleven persons in one-hundred thousand committed suicide in 1970. Thus, in terms of numbers, not very many persons were involved. At the same time, projecting this rate for the entire world with its three billion population, the number of persons committing suicide yearly would be about 300,000. And the actual number of suicides may be considerably higher because the rates in most other countries may be higher than in the United States.

Nevertheless, in terms of *rates,* the frequency of suicide is low in comparison to most forms of deviance. Despite this, students of human behavior have shown a long and persistent interest in the topic. This interest probably stems from the fact that, from one point of view, suicide represents the most extreme form of behavior one can express. Sociologically it represents the individual's deliberate self-exclusion from society. As we shall see below, this action appears to be preceded by a particular process in society, specifically, by a pattern in which the individual is excluded by society.

A. ANTECEDENTS AND DETERMINANTS

Probably the most famous theoretical and empirical analysis of the causes of suicide is Emile Durkheim's study at the turn of the century.[1] Durkheim was concerned with the social causes of suicide, and postulated four types of suicide differentiated by their causes. The different types were called egoistic, altruistic, anomic, and fatalistic suicide.

Egoistic suicides occur due to weak group integration. Durkheim observed that Protestants have higher suicide rates than Catholics; that

---

[1] Emile Durkheim, *Suicide,* trans. by John A. Spaulding and George Simpson (Glencoe: The Free Press, 1951).

single persons have higher rates than married persons; that members of small families have higher rates than members of larger families; and that suicide decreases during political crises. Durkheim argued that all these differences are due to differences in group integration.

Protestantism places greater emphasis on free inquiry, has fewer group ceremonies and rituals, and makes greater appeals to individual conscience than Catholicism. Protestant religious tradition, collective beliefs, and practices are less structured and less steadfast. Hence, Protestants are not as strongly integrated in group religious life as Catholics. Married persons and members of large families have more beliefs and sentiments shared in common than single people and members of small families; so the "collective states" binding the former to a group life are stronger. Finally, during political crises (for example, war, revolution) collective sentiments are aroused and strengthened, patriotic feelings are stimulated, and there is greater concentration of activities toward a single social end than during political stability. Social integration is intensified, and society experiences a drop in suicide rates accordingly.

Durkheim gave several reasons why weak group integration causes suicide. Weakly integrated individuals are suicide prone because they have little beyond themselves to live for. Also, they are less apt to receive moral support from others in a time of personal crisis. Moreover, because group control over individual conduct decreases when integration is weak, group norms and moral appeals against self-destruction may go unheeded by a weakly-integrated individual.

There is considerable evidence supporting Durkheim's general thesis, which states that weak social ties contribute to suicide. Results from a number of subsequent investigations reveal that suicide victims are apt to have suffered serious disruptions in their social relations, often occurring just prior to the suicide. In comparison to non-suicidal individuals, suicide victims more often lived alone, came from broken homes, were estranged from their families, experienced frictions with loved ones (spouse, children, sibling, lover), or suffered the recent death of a loved one.[2]

Durkheim argued that suicide may also stem from excessive integration. He observed that in some societies suicide is expected and preferred under certain conditions. He believed it to be particularly common in non-literate societies during periods of illness and after the death of a master or husband. Durkheim observed also that suicide is more frequent among military personnel than among civilians. He argued that in both non-literate and military societies, the individual's wishes are subordinate to group objectives and individuals are almost completely controlled by group life. Consequently, when group norms require suicide, the individual is obliged to comply: "The weight of society is thus brought to bear on [the individual] to lead him to destroy himself."[3] This manner of suicide thus

---

[2] See pp. 467–68 below.
[3] Durkheim, *Suicide*, p. 254.

occurs only when individuals are so strongly integrated in a society that they cannot escape its force. Durkheim called it *altruistic* suicide.

Anomic suicide occurs when society's regulation of individual aspirations is weakened. This occurs during periods of social disruption, as in periods of economic depression or prosperity. During these periods, persons encounter a rapid drop or rise in economic status. Drops in status necessitate the lowering of aspirations and goals to meet the means of achievement. Rapid rises, on the other hand, may lead to unlimited aspirations that can never be achieved. In both cases, society's control over aspirations may be weakened. The resulting frustrations may produce suicide.

The final form of suicide is called *fatalistic* suicide, which occurs when both ambitions and alternative courses of action towards ambitions are blocked. In this case, there is excessive regulation of both ends and means, such as with slaves, persons living in extreme poverty, and inmates of institutions such as prisons and mental institutions. Fatalistic suicide occurs among groups who are severely oppressed. Durkheim gave only passing comment to this type, feeling that it was so infrequent that it deserved little consideration.[4]

Despite the variety of suicides postulated by Durkheim, he focusses primarily on one thing in all four types: suicide is a function of social arrangements and conditions that are external to the individual. The selections on antecedents and determinants use a variation of Durkheim's focus. In "Disrupted Social Relations and Suicide," the editor presents evidence that suicide is a result of disrupted social relations and, in a sense, a form of egoistic suicide. The results of a large number of studies reveal that persons who commit suicide have engaged in types of behavior and have experienced events that frequently result in disrupted social relations. (Additional evidence on suicide among widowed persons also shows that suicide is more likely if there are no alternative social relations through which the widowed can find social support.[5]) He further notes that his evidence is consistent with research findings for death in general, that persons who suffer the loss of a spouse, parent, child, or sibling are far more apt to die during the next few months than persons who did not suffer such a loss. Therefore, suicide as a consequence of disrupted social relations may be a special case in the more general phenomenon of death.

In the next selection, "The Situational Contexts and the Relationship of Alcholism and Mental Illness to Suicide," the editor examines differences in the relationship between suicide and two other forms of deviant behavior (alcoholism and mental illness). He finds that the relationship between alcoholism and suicide exists among whites and males but not

---

[4] *Ibid.*, p. 276, n. 25.
[5] See E. Wilbur Bock, "Aging and Suicide: The Significance of Marital, Kinship, and Alternative Relations," *The Family Coordinator* 21 (January, 1972), pp. 71–79. See also E. Wilbur Bock and Irving L. Webber, "Suicide among the Elderly: Isolating Widowhood and Mitigating Alternatives," *Journal of Marriage and the Family* 31 (February, 1972), pp. 24–31.

among blacks and females, which distinction he attributes to differences in societal reaction—for example, black alcoholics are not as apt to be ostracized and rejected by family and friends as the white alcoholic. Additional findings show that former mental patients are most apt to commit suicide during periods in which their relations with others are most problematic.

DEVIANCE, DISRUPTED SOCIAL RELATIONS, INTERPERSONAL CONTEXTS, AND SUICIDE

WILLIAM RUSHING

This paper deals with the relationship between suicide and other forms of deviance. In writing it my first objective is to review and assess the evidence concerning the relationship of suicide to mental illness, alcoholism, homicide, drug addiction, and economic failure. A second objective is to present a conceptual framework within which all of these relationships may be expressed. Most theoretical formulations of the relationship between deviance and suicide view both as either the manifestation of personality trends or of forces of social structure. The formulation to be presented in this paper, on the other hand, views the relationship in terms of interpersonal dynamics. Interpersonal disruptions and disturbances are viewed as intervening links between norm violation and suicide. Rather than suicide and deviance being the result of a "common cause," suicide is viewed as a consequence of interpersonal processes which deviant behavior tends to initiate.

The review of the evidence is largely, though not exclusively, limited to studies of individual suicide, in contrast to studies of population rates. It is important to keep this in mind because the theoretical formulation to be presented refers to individual suicide. Since correlations based on observations of individuals are not necessarily consistent with correlations between rates,[1] the

use of theories of individual suicide to explain suicide rates (and vice versa) may be questioned. The units of reference in this paper, therefore, are individuals rather than populations. Futhermore, although the similarity between successful and unsuccessful suicide attempts is suggested in the evidence reviewed by Wilkins,[2] the present analysis is largely limited to successful suicide. If Wilkins' claim is subsequently validated, the analysis here will of course apply to unsuccessful attempters and victims alike.

DEVIANCE AND SUICIDE: THE EVIDENCE[3]

One of the most striking findings of suicide research is the finding that suicide tends to be preceded by deviant behavior. At least five forms of deviance have been found to be associated with suicide.

Mental Illness and Suicide

Investigations of the relationship between mental illness and suicide fall into three categories.

One, a large number of studies are based on the *ex post facto* diagnosis of suicide victims. Such diagnoses are derived from information

Portions of this paper first appeared in "Deviance, Interpersonal Relations and Suicide," *Human Relations* 22 (1969), pp. 61–75, and are reprinted with permission of the Plenum Publishing Corporation.

[1] W. Robinson, "Ecological Correlations and the Behavior of Individuals," *American Sociological Review* 15 (1950), pp. 351–57.

[2] J. Wilkins, "Suicidal Behavior," *American Sociological Review* 32 (1967), pp. 286–98.

[3] This section draws heavily on Rushing's review, "Individual Behavior and Suicide," in J. Gibbs, ed., *Suicide* (New York: Harper and Row, 1967).

gleaned from official records (e.g., death certificates, court records), personal documents (e.g., diaries, suicide notes) and statements by informants (e.g., relatives, friends and work associates). These investigations report from 53 to 100 percent of victims were mentally ill (see Table 1).

TABLE 1. PERCENTAGES OF SUICIDES DIAGNOSED AS MENTALLY ILL

Reference*	Post Factum Diagnosis	Diagnosis, Institutionalization, or Reference to Mental Illness Prior to Death
Dublin & Bunzel	53	
Tuckman & Lavell	68	
Seager & Flood	85	30
Yessler, Gibbs & Becker	86	
Robins et al.	94	
Dorpat & Ripley	100	
Cavan		16–12.5†
Temoch, Pugh & MacMahon		12.5
Weiss		21
Schmid		21
Vail		22
Gardner, Boku & Mack		36

* See references at the end of this paper.
† For Males and Females respectively.

A second type of study classifies victims as mentally ill if they are known to have received psychiatric care, to have been institutionalized, or if there is specific reference to mental illness in official records on the victim (e.g. death certificate). These studies differ from the first in that the victim was classified as mentally ill *prior* to the act of suicide. Results in Table 1 show that from 12 to 36 percent of victims may be classified as mentally ill. Although these percentages are lower than figures based on *post factum* diagnoses (compare columns 1 and 2 in Table 1), they are probably much higher than for the general population. This is indicated by two studies which show that, in comparison to the general population, the suicide rate among former mental patients is about four and nine times as high for males and females respectively.[4]

A third type of study is a follow-up to determine how many mental patients subsequently commit suicide. There has been one such study. Pokorny tabulates the number of first admission discharges from the Houston Veterans Administration Hospital between the years 1949 and 1963 who had committed suicide by 1964.[5] The result is a minimal figure, since suicide information was not available in all cases and because the follow-up period for patients released during the later years was necessarily short. Nonetheless, the suicide rate among ex-mental patients is still seven times higher than the age adjusted rate for the general population.

In summary, results indicate that mental illness and suicide are closely related. Some results may be questioned, to be sure. Problems of definition and reliable psychiatric diagnosis are well known. When these difficulties are combined with those inherent in *post factum* diagnoses based on indirect evidence, the precise validity of some of the reported findings is most questionable. Nevertheless, the evidence is clear from the last two types of studies that a disproportionate number of persons who were at least defined and treated as mental patients do commit suicide.

Alcoholism and Suicide

Alcoholism may be even more closely associated with suicide than mental illness. Alcoholism-suicide studies are of two types.

In one, drinking histories of suicide victims are studied. Several such studies report that approximately 30 percent of all victims were alcoholic, and figures for *all* studies fluctuate between 6 and 31 percent (see Table 2). The alcoholism rate for the general population has been estimated at about 4 percent.[6] Follow-up studies of alcoholics constitute the other type of study. Several studies from different countries report that from 2 to 21 percent of alcoholics

---

[4] I. P. James and S. Levine, "Suicide Following Discharge from Psychiatric Hospital," *Archives of General Psychiatry* 10 (1964), pp. 43–46; and A. A. Temoch, T. F. Pugh, and B. MacMahon, "Suicide Rates among Current and Former Mental Patients," *Journal of Nervous and Mental Disease* 138 (1964), pp. 124–30.

[5] A. D. Pokorny, "Suicide Rates in Various Psychiatric Disorders," *Journal of Nervous and Mental Disease* 139 (1964), pp. 499–506.

[6] M. Keller, "The Definition of Alcoholism and the Estimation of Its Prevalence," in D. Pittman and C. Snyder, eds., *Society, Culture and Drinking Patterns* (New York: John Wiley, 1962), p. 326.

TABLE 2. PERCENTAGE OF ALCOHOLICS WHO COMMIT
SUICIDE AND PERCENTAGE OF SUICIDE VICTIMS
ADJUDGED TO HAVE BEEN ALCOHOLIC

Reference*	Alcoholics Who Commit Suicide	Suicides Adjudged to be Alcoholic
Ritson	2	
Kendell & Staton	5	
Kessel & Grossman†	7	
Kessel & Grossman†	8	
Lemere	8	
Norvig & Neilsen	11	
Gabriel	20	
Dahlgren	21	
Sainsbury		6
Schmid		10
Tuckman & Lavell		10
Yessler, Gibbs & Becker		10
Pitts & Winokur		10
Robins, et al.		23‡
Dahlgren		30§
Palola, Dorpat & Larson		31§

* See References at the end of this paper.
† Results from 2 separate studies reported.
‡ This figure of 23 percent is for the total number of suicides in the sample; if only cases are included in which the evidence is complete enough to allow a diagnosis, the percentage is 28 percent.
§ This figure includes several studies which report approximately 30 percent.

subsequently commit suicide (see Table 2).[7] Only about .011 percent of the general population in both the United States and United Kingdom do so in a given year.[8]

As with mental illness, alcoholism is not easy to define in precise terms. There is no universal agreement as to what it involves. Consequently, many suicide victims who are classified as alcoholic may not have been alcoholic. On the other hand, however, some who were not so classified probably should have been. In any case, follow-ups reveal that individuals who have been defined as alcoholic and treated as such tend to commit suicide in disproportionate numbers.

[7] Differences in percentages reported are due at least in part to differences in length of follow-up. This presents something of a problem insofar as comparison with the suicide rate for the general population is concerned, since the population rate is reported for all persons for one year. This rate would no doubt be higher if all adults living at time 1 were followed for a period of years to time 2, and the number of suicides committed among this cohort recorded. Still, the figures would be much lower than those reported in Table 2.

[8] J. P. Gibbs, "Suicide," in R. Merton and R. Nisbet, eds., *Contemporary Social Problems,* rev. ed., (New York: Harcourt, Brace and World, 1966).

Homicide and Suicide

Three studies of suicide victims have revealed that 5, 4, and 0.8 percent of the cases were preceded by homicide. (See Table 3.) Even the last

TABLE 3. PERCENTAGES OF SUICIDE VICTIMS WHO
COMMITTED MURDER AND PERCENTAGE OF MURDERERS
AND MURDER SUSPECTS WHO COMMITTED SUICIDE

Reference*	Suicide Victims Who Murdered	Murderers and Murder Suspects Who Suicided
Schmid	0.8	
Dorpat	4	
Cavan	5	
Durret and Stromquist		2
Wolfgang		4
Illinois Crime Survey		4
Guttmacher		6
Dublin & Bunzel		9
Morris & Blom-Cooper		30

* See references at the end of this paper.

figure is 160 times higher than the homicide rate for the general U.S. population. Reversing the procedure, studies of murderers and murder suspects in different cities, states and regions in the United States reveal that from 2 to 9 percent subsequently commit suicide. For England, the figure for the period, 1900–1959, is approximately 30 percent (See Table 3).

Drug Addiction and Suicide

Death and cause of death are reported for 1,272 British heroin addicts who became addicted between 1947 and 1966 and who died within this period. A total of 8 committed suicide and seven others "died from an overdose of some drug, other than the one to which they were currently addicted, in circumstances suggesting suicidal intent."[9] On a percentage basis, this is 1.3 percent of all addicts (suicide constituted 23.3 percent of all deaths), so that, on the average, about 68 per 100,000 committed suicide each year. On this basis, the suicide rate among drug addicts is

[9] T. H. Bewley, O. Ban-Arie, and I. P. James, "Morbidity and Mortality from Heroin Dependence," *British Medical Journal* (March 23, 1968), p. 725.

more than six times higher than in the general population.

Economic Failure and Suicide

Inasmuch as downward mobility, unemployment and financial failure constitute deviations from the normative ideal, they may be considered forms of deviance.

For years 1928–1930, a study of Minneapolis suicides reports that a substantial proportion— 20 percent—were unemployed or experiencing "financial troubles" at the time of death, although comparable figures for the general Minneapolis population are not given.[10] Data from studies in New Orleans, London, and Philadelphia, however, reveal that the number of victims who were either unemployed, working irregularly, or working at part-time jobs is disproportionately high.[11] The New Orleans study also reports that victims were more apt to be downwardly mobile than a control group of nonsuicides.[12] In addition, statistics for England show an unusually high suicide rate for persons who are classified as "unoccupied."[13] Finally, three studies reveal that the unemployed and suicide population rates are directly related.[14]

In conclusion, the relationship of suicide to mental illness, alcoholism, homicide, drug addiction, and economic failure can hardly be questioned. To be sure, many suicide victims were neither mentally ill, excessive drinkers, homicides, drug addicts, nor economic failures. In addition, some of the findings may be questioned—especially those based on the *post factum* diagnosis of mental illness and alcoholism. Nonetheless, an assessment of the evidence leads to one 'inescapable conclusion: many and perhaps most acts of suicide were preceded by deviance or by social processes in which the victims were defined as deviant.[15] Furthermore, an unknown number of victims were undoubtedly prostitutes,[16] homosexuals, and criminals of various types. The conclusion, therefore, that suicide is frequently preceded by deviance is beyond dispute. Only the question concerning the causal dynamics of this relationship remains. Before presenting a theoretical formulation in this respect, the interpersonal context of suicide will be analyzed.

THE INTERPERSONAL CONTEXT OF SUICIDE

Most theories of suicide emphasize one of two types of causal factors: psychological and intrapsychic processes or the forces of social structure. Psychologists and psychoanalysts have emphasized personality types, death instincts, and suicide trends and tendencies as factors which lead to suicide[17] while sociologists have stressed the impact of urbanization, social disorganization, external restraints, and social integration.[18] Such polar emphases have caused the interpersonal aspects of suicide to be largely ignored.[19] This is not to say that anyone denies their importance. However, the determining factors of suicide are usually considered to be bio-psychic or psychological forces which drive the individual from within, or macrosociological forces which push him from without. In neither case are links between the victim's act and the micro-

---

[10] C. Schmid, "Suicide in Minneapolis, Minnesota: 1928–32," *American Journal of Sociology* 49 (1933), p. 47.

[11] W. Breed, "Occupational Mobility and Suicide," *American Sociological Review* 28 (1963), pp. 179–88; P. Sainsbury, *Suicide in London* (London: Chapman and Hall, 1955); and J. Tuckman and M. Lavle, "Study of Suicide in Philadelphia," *Public Health Reports* 53 (1959), pp. 547–53.

[12] Breed, "Occupational Mobility and Suicide."

[13] L. Dublin, *Suicide: A Sociological and Statistical Study* (New York: Ronald Press, 1963), p. 62.

[14] B. MacMahon, S. Johnson, and T. F. Pugh, "Relation of Suicide Rates to Social Relations," *Public Health Reports* 78 (1963), pp. 285–94; and D. Swinscow, "Some Suicide Statistics," *British Medical Journal* 1 (1951), pp. 1417–22.

[15] Apparently Malinowski thought that among the Trobriand Islanders, deviance in some form was always associated with suicide. For instance, he states that in suicide, "there is always some sin, crime or passionate outburst to expiate, whether a breach of exogamous rules, or adultery, or an unjust injury done, or an attempt to escape one's obligations. . . ." B. Malinowski, *Crime and Custom in Savage Society* (Paterson, N.J.: Littlefield, Adams and Co., 1962).

[16] Harold Greenwald in *The Call Girl* (New York: Ballantine Books, 1958) reports that fifteen of twenty girls studied by him made at least one suicide attempt. It is not known, however, to what extent Greenwald's sample is a representative sample of prostitutes or even call girls.

[17] K. Menninger, *Man Against Himself* (New York: Harcourt, Brace and Co., 1938).

[18] Gibbs, "Suicide."

[19] This is less true of Henry and Short's theory of "external restraints" than the other sociological theories, since "external restraints" refer to the restraints imposed by the behavior and expectations of others. A. Henry and J. Short, Jr., *Suicide and Homicide* (Glencoe, Ill.: Free Press, 1954).

sociological features of his interpersonal relations made explicit or considered crucial in the conceptualization. Nevertheless, research evidence indicates that the victim's interpersonal relations may be crucial.

Several studies report that suicide tends to be preceded by the loss of or friction with persons with whom the victim has engaged in frequent and intense interaction—for example, mates and relatives.[20] The phenomenon has been observed for entire societies[21] as well as for specific groups within society, such as students at the University of California, Berkeley.[22] And a study of suicide notes reveals that in a majority of cases the problem being "resolved" by suicide is of an interpersonal nature.[23]

A large number of studies show the same thing for attempted suicide.[24] Such findings are consistent with statements of unsuccessful attempters. Results from two investigations based on interviews with attempters reveal that more than 50 percent in one and 37 percent in the other claim that disruptions in social relations were precipitating factors in their suicidal behavior.[25] Of course, the accuracy of such verbal statements may be questioned, as can the similarity of motives involved in unsuccessful suicide attempts and completed suicides. It is significant, however, that the attempters' stated beliefs and the objective facts of suicide coincide. *Loss in social interaction,* actual or threatened, appears to be an important antecedent of suicide. It is within the framework of this result that the de-

viance-suicide relationship is to be interpreted.

Another relevant finding is that suicide victims tend to have been "social isolates." In two studies, 27 and 20 percent of victims lived alone, in comparison to one report that only 7 percent of the general population do so.[26] Also, Breed has reported that in comparison to a control group of non-suicides, suicides have about half as many friends and participate socially about half as much, as indicated by visiting patterns and church attendance;[27] and Seiden reports that University of California suicide students are socially withdrawn.[28] However, these investigations do not indicate whether the relative social isolation is a pattern of long duration or whether it represents recent interaction loss.

THEORY AND INTERPRETATION

Most theories of the relationship between deviance and suicide view both to be the result of the same "cause"—either a component of personality or a force of social structure. Menninger's theory[29] that alcoholism and suicide are manifestations of the death instinct is particularly well known, while social structure theories have emphasized the impact of macrosociological forces such as urbanization and social disorganization.[30] Theoretical perspectives on the deviance-suicide relationship are not exhausted by such "common cause" interpretations, however. It is also possible, and altogether plausible, that deviance itself may lead to suicide. It may do so because of the interpersonal consequences it tends to have; the effects of deviance may be a special case of the effects of interaction loss. The deviant is apt to be stigmatized, socially rejected, and hence to suffer the loss of significant social relations. The process may be seen in Malinowski's classic description of suicide by a Trobriand youth.

[20] W. Breed, "Suicide and Loss of Social Interaction," in E. Shneidman, ed., *Essays in Self Destruction* (New York: McGraw-Hill, 1967); T. Dorpat, J. Jackson, and H. Ripley, "Broken Homes and Attempted and Completed Suicides," *Archives of General Psychiatry* 12 (1965), pp. 213–16; E. Reitman, "On Predictability of Suicide," *Journal of Mental Science* 88 (1942), pp. 580–82; and Gibbs, "Suicide," pp. 304–5.

[21] J. O. Hoskins et al., "A High Incidence of Suicide in a Preliterate Primitive Society," *Psychiatry* 32 (1969), pp. 200–10.

[22] R. H. Seiden, "Campus Tragedy: A Study of Student Suicide," *Journal of Abnormal Psychology* 72 (1966), pp. 389–99.

[23] J. Jacobs, "A Phenomenological Study of Suicide Notes," *Social Problems* 15 (1967), pp. 60–72.

[24] See review in Rushing, "Individual Behavior and Suicide."

[25] E. Robins, E. Schmidt, and P. O'Neal, "Some Interrelations of Social Factors and Clinical Diagnosis of Attempted Suicide," *American Journal of Psychiatry* 114 (1957), pp. 222, 224; and M. Moore, "Cases of Attempted Suicide in a General Hospital: A Problem in Social and Psychological Medicine," *New England Journal of Medicine* 217 (1937), p. 295.

[26] N. Farberow and E. Shneidman, *The Cry for Help* (New York: McGraw-Hill, 1957), and Sainsbury, *Suicide in London.*

[27] Breed, "Suicide and Loss in Social Interaction."

[28] Seiden, "Campus Tragedy."

[29] Menninger, *Man Against Himself.*

[30] M. Clinard, *Sociology of Deviant Behavior* (New York: Holt, Rinehart and Winston, 1963); and M. Elliott and F. Merrill, *Social Disorganization,* 4th ed., (New York: Harper and Row, 1961).

One day an outbreak of wailing and a great commotion told me that a death had occurred somewhere in the neighborhood. I was informed that Kima'i, a young lad of my acquaintance of sixteen or so, had fallen from a coco-nut palm and killed himself. . . .

Only much later was I able to discover the real meaning of these events: the boy had committed suicide. The truth was that he had broken the rules of exogamy, the partner in his crime being his maternal cousin, the daughter of his mother's sister. This had been known and generally disapproved of, but nothing was done until the girl's discarded lover, who had wanted to marry her and who felt personally injured, took the initiative. This rival threatened first to use black magic against the guilty youth, but this had not much effect. Then one evening he insulted the culprit in public—accusing him in the hearing of the whole community of incest and hurling at him certain expressions intolerable to a native.

For this there was only one remedy; only one means of escape remained to the unfortunate youth. . . .[31]

Such descriptions, of course, are only isolated illustrations of the postulated mediating interpersonal dynamics of deviance and suicide; they obviously do not constitute systematic investigations of such events. Needed are longitudinal studies in which the reaction to deviance is systematically observed. Deviants need to be identified, the social reaction to them must be described, and the resulting suicidal/nonsuicidal behavior will have to be determined. Such studies have not been conducted. Nonetheless, several studies reveal that types of deviance found to be associated with suicide do tend to have the kinds of interpersonal consequences that have been postulated.

Alcoholism

Excessive prolonged drinking is apt to involve the drinker in a number of additional deviant and irresponsible acts, such as public drunkenness sex indiscretions, and occupational difficulties. Such matters may be embarrassing and status threatening to the drinker's relatives and friends. As a result, the drinker may be rejected and excluded from social relations that are important to him. The McCords, in their longitudinal study of alcoholics state:

the alcoholics were social outcasts. They found it extremely difficult to hold regular jobs, and economically they failed to provide for their families. . . . The alcoholic's almost continuous state of intoxication naturally interferes with many other aspects of his life. His occupational efficiency falters, he loses his role as the "rock" of the family, his image of himself as an independent male is undermined in various ways. The evidence indicates that he is usually a social outcast. . . .[32]

The drinker's family may be particularly damaged and threatened by the drinker's behavior; its reaction may be especially severe. Jackson reports the following.

[Finally], the family gives up trying to understand the alcoholic. They do not care if the neighbors know about the drinking. The children are told that their father is a drunk. They are no longer required to show him affection or respect. The myth that father still has an important status in the family is dropped when he no longer supports them, is imprisoned, caught in infidelity, or disappears for long periods of time. . . . The alcoholic's status is gradually downgraded when he does not fulfill family and cultural expectations and as other family members assume his traditional roles in order to keep the unit as a whole functioning. Indeed, the alcoholic's major role in some families appears to be that of a spur to the solidarity of the rest of the family who react against him.[33]

Hence, alcoholism appears to have the kinds of interpersonal consequences that are frequently antecedent to suicide. Even Menninger's view of alcoholism and suicide considers interpersonal disturbances and interaction loss as intervening links between alcoholism and suicide.

Sooner or later . . . most alcoholics get themselves into a hopeless impasse. They *lose all their friends,* they *estrange their wives,* they drive their *parents* to *repudiate them.* . . . I don't know what usually happens after that. Naturally the psychiatrist sees only a small proportion of them. We know that some land in jail, some in the asylum, and that some *commit suicide.* (Emphasis supplied.)[34]

The difference in Menninger's formulation and the one presented here is that Menninger does

[31] Malinowski, *Crime and Custom in Savage Society,* p. 78.

[32] W. McCord and J. McCord, *Origins of Alcoholism* (Stanford: Stanford University Press, 1960), pp. 126, 156.
[33] J. Jackson, "Alcoholism and the Family," in Pittman and Snyder, *Society, Culture, and Drinking Patterns,* pp. 485, 488.
[34] *Ibid.,* p. 165.

not consider the social reaction as having an effect in its own right. According to him, the social response can be nothing more than an external event that "triggers" a psychological disposition to suicide. If it had not been a negative reaction to excessive drinking that led to suicide, it would have been something else, because suicide, as well as alcoholism, is an expression of a deeply ingrained personality trend which originated in childhood.[35] Of course, one may turn the matter around: if the interpersonal consequences are severe enough, suicide will be the result regardless of the composition of one's personality structure. More plausible, however, is the hypothesis that interpersonal disruptions have more disastrous consequences for some personality types than for others. What these personality differences may be, however, is for future research to say.

Drug Addiction

Although few studies have been conducted on societal reaction to drug addicts and former drug addicts, we know that the societal image of drug addicts is quite negative. Drug addicts are a despised group and a large proportion of crimes are attributed to them. It is believed that drug addiction tends to be permanent—"once a junkie, always a junkie"—which probably adds to the stigma and ostracism of being a known drug addict. In addition, the fear that loved ones, especially children, will become addicted looms large in the minds of many persons. For these reasons, the avoidance and rejection of persons addicted to drugs would be expected. Although the overall evidence for this is meager, studies by Ray and Waldorf are consistent with this thesis.[36]

Economic Failure

A number of studies have described the disastrous interpersonal and psychological consequences of unemployment. The unemployed's family authority and status as husband and father are undermined; his relations with work associates, friends, and neighbors are disrupted; his rate of social participation decreases; his morale and emotional stability drop; and his self-confidence and self-respect take a turn for the worse.[37] Such findings suggest that unemployment and economic failure are related to suicide for the reasons postulated. This interpretation is quite clear in Breed's conclusion concerning New Orleans suicides.

> . . . when a man—one of our suicides—is fired, or not rehired, or when a businessman continually fails to show a profit, these actions may result in encounters with others eventuating in a sense of "shame." On telling his wife the news, or facing colleagues and co-workers in the community, the fact of his inadequate work performance may be reflected in their eyes and lodged in the actor's self-awareness.[38]

Factors leading to suicide are clearly viewed as interpersonal consequences of economic failure.

The effects of unemployment may be particularly severe when combined with other forms of deviance, such as alcoholism or mental illness. In a study of excessive male drinkers who had attempted suicide, for example, 80 percent are reported to have had "unsatisfactory work records," 50 percent were unemployed or "off work," and 54 percent were downwardly mobile from their childhood status.[39] Different forms of deviance may thus interact to make suicide more probable than if only one form of deviance occurred.

Mental Illness

The symptoms of mental illness—bizarre, aggressive, irrational behavior—are apt to create interpersonal disturbances and thus lead to interaction loss. In addition, it is commonly be-

---

[35] *Ibid.*, pp. 18, 23, 47, and 82.

[36] Marsh Ray, pp. 383–90 of this volume, and Dan Waldorf, "Life Without Heroin: Some Social Adjustments During Long-Term Periods of Voluntary Abstention," *Social Problems* 18 (Fall, 1970), pp. 228–43.

[37] E. Bakke, *The Unemployed Man* (New York: E. P. Dutton, 1935), pp. 72–73, 156–62, 195–97, and 246–48; P. Eisenberg and P. Lazarsfeld, "The Psychological Effect of Unemployment," *Psychological Bulletin* 35 (1939), pp. 358–90; M. Komarovsky, *The Unemployed Man and His Family* (New York: The Dryden Press, 1940); H. Pope, "Economic Deprivation and Social Participation in a Group of Middle-Class Factory Workers," *Social Problems* 11 (1964), pp. 290–300; and N. Morse and R. Weiss, "The Function and Meaning of Work and the Job," *American Sociological Review* 20 (1955), pp. 191–98.

[38] Breed, "Occupational Mobility and Suicide."

[39] I. Batchelar, "Alcoholism and Attempted Suicide," *Journal of Mental Science* 100 (1954), p. 454.

lieved, and there is some empirical evidence to support the belief, that social rejection is a probable consequence of institutionalization. Such reactions, therefore, may be mediating links in the mental illness-suicide relationship. See pp. 479–80 below.

Homicide

There are two aspects of homicide that are particularly relevant for the present analysis. First, investigations in several countries reveal that a very high proportion of homicides are committed against relatives, friends, and other primary-group associates.[40] It is probable, therefore, that many suicides which follow homicide are preceded by the permanent loss of a significant social relation. Findings on homicide-suicide indicate that this is so. In his study of homicide, Wolfgang reports that in 96 percent of all homicide-suicides (N = 26), the homicide victim was either a relative or a paramour of the offender. By comparison, for homicides *not* followed by suicide, relatives and paramours comprised only one-third of the victim-offender relationships.[41] It is thus clear that suicide following homicide is preceded by the loss of a significant social relation in a disproportionate number of cases.

The second aspect of homicide concerns the social reaction to it. The *general societal* reaction, as represented in type of punishment, is extremely severe. In addition to this, because many murders are directed against primary-group members, rejection by the remaining primary-group associates must be virtually complete. Thus, homicide has precisely the kinds of interpersonal consequences that would be expected to precede suicide.[42]

---

[40] H. Bullock, "Urban Homicide in Theory and Practice," *Journal of Criminal Law, Criminology and Police Science* 45 (1955), p. 572; E. Driver, "Interaction and Criminal Homicide in India," *Social Forces* 40 (1961), p. 156; W. East, *Medical Aspects of Crimes* (London: J and A Churchill, 1939), p. 309; K. Svalastoga, "Homicide and Social Contact in Denmark," *American Journal of Sociology* 62 (1956), p. 40; H. Von Tentig, *The Criminal and His Victim* (New Haven, Conn.: Yale University Press, 1948), p. 392; M. Wolfgang, "An Analysis of Homicide-Suicide," *Journal of Clinical and Experimental Psychopathology* 19 (1958), pp. 212–13.

[41] M. Wolfgang, *Patterns of Criminal Homicide* (Philadelphia: University of Pennsylvania Press, 1958).

[42] It is interesting that suicide as a cause of death among murderers is more frequent than execution when executions were permitted. See Wolfgang, *Patterns of Criminal Homicide*.

Summary

To summarize, a review of the evidence shows that suicide is associated with disruptions in social relations and with loss in social interaction. Research also reveals that suicide is apt to be preceded by deviant behavior, and that deviant behavior frequently causes disruptions and loss of social relations. It is postulated, therefore, that deviance and suicide are related, at least partly, because of the interpersonal consequences that deviance tends to have. Such consequences frequently take the form of social rejection, ostracism and stigma.

The analysis may be summarized with three empirically based propositions and one hypothesis derived from these propositions:

Proposition 1. Suicide is directly related to loss in social interaction.

Proposition 2. Suicide is directly related to deviance.

Proposition 3. Deviance is directly related to loss in social interaction.

Hypothesis   Suicide and deviance are related because loss in social interaction is a consequence of deviance and an antecedent of suicide.

The hypothesis states, in essence, that when loss in social interaction is controlled, the deviance-suicide relationship will disappear or at least it will be significantly reduced in magnitude.

FURTHER CONSIDERATIONS

Several points about the theory should be noted. It obviously conforms to a sequential model of deviance rather than a simultaneous model, as these have been characterized by Becker.[43] Rather than viewing suicide and other forms of deviance as correlated at a point in time, a sequence is assumed. Emphasis is placed on the social reaction to deviance, and suicide is viewed as a component of the social process in which the reaction is involved. However, the theory does not assume that deviance is defined only in

---

[43] H. Becker, *Outsiders* (New York: The Free Press of Glencoe, 1963), pp. 22–25.

terms of its consequences. Instead, it views such consequences as etiologically related to another form of deviance—suicide. In this sense, the social reaction is viewed as determinant, not as definer.

The validity of the hypothesis, of course, remains to be tested. As noted previously, systematic longitudinal investigations of deviants are needed. Nonetheless, the validity of the propositions from which the hypothesis is derived has been rather conclusively demonstrated; the hypothesis is derived from empirical fact rather than theoretical postulates and assumptions.[44] Consequently, there is more evidence to support the theory than can be found for other theories of suicide.

As a general phenomenon, interaction loss refers to loss of social relations for any reason whatever—death, marital discord, or deviance. It may well be, however, that loss due to different causes should be kept conceptually distinct. Although they may produce similar effects (i.e., all may tend to precipitate suicide), they may do so for different reasons. The subjective experiences of loss due to death and loss due to social rejection are undoubtedly different. However, because distinctions in types of interaction loss are apt to imply corresponding psychological distinctions, about which little is known, we have chosen not to distinguish between types of interaction loss in this paper. The attempt instead has been to construct an interpersonal theory which would be both consistent with the facts of suicide and suggest additional lines of investigation. As it stands, the theory does not indicate *why* interaction loss should lead to suicide.

Finally, the relationship between death and loss of social relations may not be limited to death due to suicide. Studies have shown that the death rate among survivors (spouse and relatives) of the deceased is higher than for comparable groups in the population. Young, Benjamin and Wallis report that the death rate for widowers during the first six months of widowerhood is 40 percent higher than the death rate for married males of comparable ages.[45] In a more extensive study, Reese and Lutkins compare the death rates for two separate groups in an entire community in England.[46] One group consists of close relatives (spouse, parent, child, or sibling) of individuals who died in the community over a six-year period following January 1, 1960. Each deceased individual is matched with another individual from the community with respect to age, sex and marital status; the relatives of these latter individuals constitute the "control" group. Reese and Lutkins report that during the first year, 4.76 percent of the bereaved close relatives died in comparison to 0.68 percent in the control group. The difference between the two groups in death rate decreased over time, which is consistent with the finding of Young, Benjamin and Wallis for widowers. The results are not limited to widowhood, however; when widowed people are excluded from the analysis, 3.21 percent of the bereaved group died during the first year in comparison to only 0.58 percent of the control group.

The specific factors involved are not clear. Common infection, common environment, and lack of care (a male spouse may become malnourished when he no longer has his wife to look after him) may be involved in subsequent death. Such factors are probably more likely to exist for older and widowed persons; we have seen, however, that the relationship exists for the nonwidowed, and indeed, that it exists indepently of age, sex, and marital status. Moreover, the risks of subsequent death are less if the relative dies in the home than if he dies in the hospital or even in other settings outside the home.[47] Presumably, infections would be most apt to exist when deaths occur in the home. Another interpretation is that the loss of social relationships is itself a causal factor in death, since grief and bereavement may precipitate changes in the endocrine and central nervous system.[48]

But regardless of the precise mechanisms involved, death in general, not just suicide in par-

---

[44] Most theories of suicide are constructed through another method, with the hypothesis to be tested being derived from a series of untested (and sometimes, perhaps, untestable) postulates. For one example of such a theory, see J. P. Gibbs and W. T. Martin, *Status Integration and Suicide* (Eugene, Ore.: University of Oregon Books, 1965).

[45] M. Young, B. Benjamin, and C. Wallis, "The Mortality of Widowers," *The Lancet*, August 31, 1963, pp. 454–56.
[46] W. Reese and S. Lutkins, "Mortality of Bereavement," British Medical Journal, October 7, 1967, pp. 13–16.
[47] *Ibid.*
[48] Young, Benjamin, and Wallis, "The Mortality of Widowers."

ticular, is associated with changes in one's social environment. Therefore, the relationship between disruptions in social relations and suicide may be a special case of a more general relationship. This is not to say, of course, that the specific causes of suicide are the same as those involved in deaths that are attributable to physiological processes. Yet we see another resemblance between homicide and suicide. As noted earlier Robins observes that the high homicide risk group—young black males—is also characterized by a high risk of death in general (see pp. 183–85 above). Similarly, persons who have a high suicide risk (that is, those who suffer serious disruptions in primary group relations) tend also to have an unusually high death rate from all causes.

TABLE REFERENCES

Cavan, R.
1927   *Suicide.* Chicago: The University of Chicago Press, pp. 112, 254.

Dahlgren, K.
1945   *On Suicide and Attempted Suicide—A Psychiatrical and Statistical Investigation.* Sweden: Lund.

Dorpat, T.
1966   "Suicide in Murderers." *Psychiatry Digest,* pp. 51–55.

Dorpat, T., and Ripley, H.
1960   "A Study of Suicide in the Seattle Area." *Comprehensive Psychiatry,* 1, pp. 349–59.

Dublin, L., and Bunzel, B.
1933   *To Be or Not to Be.* New York: Harrison Smith and R. Haas, p. 300.

Durret, M., and Stromquist, M.
1925   "Preventing Violent Death." *Survey,* 59, p. 437.

Gabriel, E.
1935   *Zeitschrift für Neurologie und Psychiatrie,* 153, p. 384.

Gardner, E., Boku, A., and Mack, M.
1964   "Suicide and Psychiatric Care in the Aging." *Archives of General Psychiatry,* 10, pp. 547–53.

Guttmacher, M.
1960   *The Mind of the Murderer.* New York: Farrar, Straus and Cudahy, p. 9. (Based on statistics reported in Twentieth Annual Report of the Department of Post Mortem Examiners of the State of Maryland.)

Kendell, R., and M. Stanton
1966   "The Fate of Untreated Alcoholics." *Quarterly Journal of Studies on Alcohol,* 27, pp. 30–41.

Kessel, N., and Grossman, G.
1961   "Studies in Alcoholics." *British Medical Journal,* pp. 1671–72.

Lemere, F.
1953   "What Happens to Alcoholics." *American Journal of Psychiatry,* 109, p. 675.

Morris, T., and Blom-Cooper, L.
1967   "Homicide in England," in M. Wolfgang, ed., *Studies in Homicide.* New York: Harper and Row, p. 31.

Norvig, J., and Neilsen, B.
1953   "A Follow-up Study of 221 Alcoholic Addicts in Denmark." *Quarterly Journal of Psychiatry,* 109, pp. 633–42.

Palola, E., Dorpat, T., and Larson, W.
1962   "Alcoholism and Suicidal Behavior," in D. Pittman and C. Snyder, eds., *Society, Culture, and Drinking Patterns.* New York: John Wiley, pp. 511–34.

Pitts, F. N., and Winokur, G.
1964   "Affective Disorders III: Diagnostic Correlates and the Incidence of Suicide." *Journal of Nervous and Mental Disease,* 139, pp. 176–81.

Ritson, E.
1968   "Suicide Amongst Alcoholics." *British*

Journal of Medical Psychology, 41, pp. 235–42.

Robins, E., et al.
1959   "Some Clinical Observations in the Prevention of Suicide Based on a Study of 134 Successful (Completed) Suicides." *American Journal of Public Health*, 49, pp. 888–99.

Sainsbury, P.
1955   *Suicide in London*. London: Chapman and Hall.

Schmid, C.
1933   "Suicide in Minneapolis, Minnesota: 1928–32." *American Journal of Sociology*, 49, p. 47, Table X.

Seager, C., and Flood, R.
1965   "Suicide in Bristol." *British Journal of Psychiatry*, 111, pp. 919–32.

Temoch, A. A., Pugh, T. F., and MacMahon, B.
1964   "Suicide Rates Among Current and Former Mental Patients." *Journal of Nervous and Mental Disease*, 138, pp. 124–30.

The Illinois Crime Survey
1929   Chicago: Association for Criminal Justice and the Chicago Crime Commission, p. 612.

Tuckman, J., and Lavel, M.
1959   "Study of Suicide in Philadelphia." *Public Health Reports*, 53, pp. 547–53.

Vail, D.
1959   "Suicide and Mental Responsibility." *American Journal of Psychiatry*, 115, p. 1007.

Weiss, J.
1954   "Suicide: An Epidemiologic Analysis." *Psychiatric Quarterly*, 28, pp. 243–44.

Wolfgang, M.
1958   *Patterns of Criminal Homicide*. Philadelphia: University of Pennsylvania Press.

Yessler, P., Gibbs, J., and Becker, H.
1961   "On the Communication of Suicidal Ideas: II. Some Medical Considerations." *Archives of General Psychiatry*, 5, pp. 12–29.

SITUATIONAL CONTEXTS AND THE RELATIONSHIP OF ALCOHOLISM AND MENTAL ILLNESS TO SUICIDE

WILLIAM A. RUSHING

As noted in the previous paper, the investigation of the causal effect of societal reactions on suicide ideally requires longitudinal studies. Persons who commit deviance would be studied over time and societal reactions would be observed. Deviants who are reacted to harshly would be expected to have a higher suicide rate than those who are tolerated and accepted despite their actions. Numerous problems would be associated with such studies, and observation of a number of deviants over a period of time would be very expensive. It would be desirable to observe and compare "secret deviants"[1] with officially labelled deviants in terms of the societal reaction, but since "secret deviants" are unknown to society (and to most sociologists), the identification and study of such persons would be most difficult. In addition, a large number of deviants would

Portions of this paper first appeared in "Suicide and the Interaction of Alcoholism (Liver Cirrhosis) with the Social Situation," *Quarterly Journal of Studies on Alcohol* 30 (March, 1969), pp. 90–113, and are reprinted with permission of the Center for Alcohol Studies.

[1] H. Becker, *Outsiders*, (New York: The Free Press of Glencoe, 1963).

probably have to be studied. This is so because, despite the comparatively high suicide rate for some groups, such as alcoholics and former mental patients, only a small proportion of all alcoholics and former mental patients commit suicide.[2] Consequently a large number of individuals would have to be studied before a sufficient number of suicides were involved to permit reliable conclusions.

There is, however, another way to investigate the hypothesis. One may determine whether the magnitude of the relationship between deviant behavior and suicide varies depending on different conditions as these conditions relate to differences in the societal reaction to deviant individuals. The process is sometimes called specification of a relationship[3] or the analysis of statistical interaction effects.[4] The effects of variable X (deviant behavior) on variable Y (suicide) are said to be interactive rather than additive if they vary depending on variable Z (condition which reflects the nature of the societal reaction). In this paper we will report differences in the relationship between alcoholism and suicide and mental hospitalization and suicide depending on the social context.

ALCOHOLISM AND SUICIDE

Data and Measures

Data for both suicide and alcoholism are based on official U.S.A. statistics.[5] Following the procedure used in most studies, rates of alcoholism are based on cirrhosis of the liver death rates. Terris' analysis,[6] in particular, indicates that ex-

cessive drinking and liver cirrhosis mortality are closely related. Obviously, however, if subsequent research should show that this is not the case, the findings will contribute only to knowledge of the effect of liver cirrhosis on suicide.

In addition to questions which may surround the specific assumption of the cirrhosis-alcoholism relationship, there are the usual doubts concerning the validity of official statistics in general. Although official statistics on deviant behavior have been and continue to be used in sociological research, their validity remains in doubt. Problems associated with suicide statistics have been discussed by Gibbs[7] and need not be repeated here; suffice it to say that as much evidence supports their accuracy as challenges it. Even less is known about the accuracy of statistics on liver cirrhosis. As will be noted below, however, both measures give results similar to results of other studies of suicide and alcoholism, and that lends confidence in their validity.

Specification of the Relationship by Sex and Race

The relationship between the two rates will be examined separately for sex and race (whites and non-whites). As will be suggested below, sexual and racial differences are associated with differences in the reaction to alcoholic drinking.

Sex. The suicide rate of men is considerably higher than that of women.[8] Except for indications from cirrhosis rate, however, there is no evidence concerning sex differences in alcoholism, although more men drink than women.[9] Results of the present investigation are consistent with these findings. The average annual rate of suicide and liver cirrhosis mortality per 100,000 persons in the period 1949–1951 was 17.3 and 12.4 in men, and 6.5 and 4.9 in women. To determine the effect of sex on the cirrhosis-suicide relationship, correlations (ρ) were computed for age groups, separately for men and women. Since alcoholism and liver cirrhosis due to excessive drinking can occur only after sev-

[2] See pp. 464–65 above.

[3] See pp. 19–25 above. See also H. Hyman, *Survey Design and Analysis* (New York: Free Press, 1955).

[4] H. Blalock, "Theory Building and the Statistical Concept of Interaction," *American Sociological Review* 30 (1965), pp. 374–80.

[5] U.S. Department of Health, Education and Welfare, Public Health Service, National Office of Vital Statistics, "Mortality from Selected Causes by Marital Status, United States, 1949–51." *Vital Statistics—Special Reports*, 39 (Washington: D.C.: U.S. Government Printing Office, 1956), pp. 418–19, 426–27; and U.S. Department of Health, Education and Welfare, Public Health Service, National Office of Vital Statistics, "Mortality by Occupation and Cause of Death among Men 20 to 64 years of Age: United States, 1950." *Vital Statistics—Special Reports*, 63 (Washington, D.C.: U.S. Government Printing Office, 1963).

[6] M. Terris, "Epidemiology of Cirrhosis of the Liver; National Mortality Data," *American Journal of Public Health* 57 (1967), pp. 2076–88.

[7] J. Gibbs, "Suicide," in R. Merton and R. Nisbet, ed., *Contemporary Social Problems*, 2nd. ed. (New York: Harcourt, Brace and World, 1966).

[8] *Ibid.*, p. 293.

[9] R. Straus, "Alcohol and Alcohol Drinking," in Merton and Nisbet, *Contemporary Social Problems*.

eral years of consistent heavy drinking, only groups above 34 years of age were included in the analysis (Table 1). The results show that ρ is 1.00 for men, —.01 for women. The association between alcoholism and suicide is clearly stronger for men.

TABLE 1. ALCOHOLISM RATE* AND SUICIDE RATE IN SEVEN AGE GROUPS,† BY SEX

Age Class (years)	Men Alcoholism	Suicide	Women Alcoholism	Suicide
35–44	12.0	21.1	7.2	7.5
45–54	26.6	30.8	13.0	9.5
55–59	37.3	39.5	15.8	10.0
60–64	42.2	45.0	18.1	9.9
65–69	46.7	47.7	18.9	9.9
70–74	47.5	50.4	22.8	8.6
75+	49.4	56.8	29.2	7.7

Source: U.S. Department of Health, Education and Welfare, "Mortality from Selected Causes by Marital Status, United States, 1949–51," *Vital Statistics Special Reports*, 39 (Washington, D.C.: U.S. Government Printing Office, 1956), pp. 418–19, 426–27.
  * Cirrhosis of liver death rate. See text for explanation.
  † See text for explanation.

Probably little significance should be attached to the absolute magnitude of either of these correlations; neither may be a precise estimate of the true correlation. Since the units of analysis are age populations, and because the rates are not standardized for age, the extent to which the correlations reflect the effects of age cannot be estimated. Also, there is undoubtedly some error in the two measures. At the same time, however, there is no reason for assuming that these problems are greater in one sex than in the other. The differences in the two ρ's cannot be attributed to such problems of measurement. The findings seem to indicate, therefore, that the effects of alcoholism and sex interact.

Race. Analysis of alcoholism and suicide by race is based on rates, standardized for age (SMRS), for 9 of the 11 major U.S. Census occupational categories,[10] for White and non-white men aged 20 to 64 (Table 2). Since

Negroes constitute 95 percent of all non-White men in the experienced labor force and all non-White employed men, the White–non-White difference will be interpreted as a White–Black difference.

Cirrhosis and suicide SMRS are given in the vital statistics publication only if the death of at least 20 incumbents is attributed to cirrhosis and suicide. Consequently in several instances SMRS are not reported and had to be computed. These cases are noted in Table 2.

TABLE 2. STANDARD MORTALITY RATES (SMR) FOR ALCOHOLISM* AND SUICIDE IN NINE OCCUPATIONAL CATEGORIES, BY RACE

	Whites Alcoholism	Suicide	Non-Whites Alcoholism	Suicide
Professional	91	90	72†	60†
Managerial	112	96	97†	63†
Clerical	101	72	59†	64†
Sales	109	103	51†	83†
Craftsmen	94	104	55	43
Operatives	101	96	58	38
Private household workers	16†	0	100†	20†
Service	196	126	131	27
Laborers, except farm and mine	164	151	124	63

Source: U.S. Department of Health, Education and Welfare, "Mortality by Occupation and Cause of Death among Men 20 to 40 Years of Age: United States, 1950," *Vital Statistics—Special Reports* 63 (Washington, D.C.: U.S. Government Printing Office, 1963), pp. 104–33.
  * Cirrhosis of liver death rate. See text for explanation.
  † Standard mortality rate not given in vital statistics publication because frequency is less than 20. Rate based on author's computations.

Except among "private household workers," Whites have higher rates of both suicide and cirrhosis than non-Whites in all occupational categories. These results are consistent with other evidence of White–Black differences in suicide in the U.S.A.[11]

Studies of racial differences in alcoholism have produced inconsistent results. A major difficulty with most of these studies, however, is that they are based on selective populations, such as mental patients and holders of insurance policies.[12]

---

[10] SMRs are actually available for 10 occupational categories, with the rates of "farmers and farm managers" and "farm laborers and farm foremen" combined in one category, "farmers and farm laborers." However, since these two groups are so different with respect to so many things, the category "farmers and farm laborers" was excluded from the analysis.

---

[11] Gibbs, "Suicide," pp. 300–01.
[12] M. Sterne, "Drinking Patterns and Alcoholism among American Negroes," in D. Pittman and C. Snyder, ed., *Alcoholism* (New York: Harper and Row, 1967).

The results in Table 2 reveal a wide racial difference in the cirrhosis-suicide relationship: for Whites, ρ is .73, for Blacks, —.43. Since there are fewer than 20 cases of cirrhosis mortality and suicide among both White and Black "private household workers," this category was eliminated. This had little effect on the results: ρ is .65 for Whites and —.34 for Blacks.

As with sex, the correlations may not be accurate estimates of the true association in either race (although SMRS eliminate any error that might be due to the uncontrolled effects of age). The correlations are based on groups rather than individuals, and group correlations are almost always larger than individual correlations. Nevertheless, the differences are too great to dismiss. The evidence clearly indicates that the effects of alcoholism (or liver cirrhosis) interact with sex and race.

DISCUSSION

The process of specifying a result is important because it may reveal that generalizations concerning the nature of a relationship should be qualified. In this way conditions under which the postulated causes of a phenomenon are operative may be identified. Explanations of the alcoholism–suicide relationship have focussed on urbanization, social disorganization, personality and the social reaction to alcoholism.[13] For any of these explanations to be true, the effects of the variable in question should differ by sex and race. The first three explanations can probably be dismissed. There is little basis for believing that the effects of urbanization, social disorganization and personality differences of the type postulated should vary by sex and race. It is possible, of course, that Blacks may be exposed to socially disorganized conditions more than Whites. However, if social disorganization contributes to alcoholism and suicide, the Negro rates should be higher than those of Whites. As we have seen, this is not the case with suicide, and it may not be with alcoholism. Consequently, the following discussion will be restricted to the social-reaction hypothesis.

Sex. The social-reaction hypothesis postulates that disruptions in social relations (e.g., social ostracism and social rejection) are frequent consequences of alcoholism, and that this may precipitate suicide. According to the hypothesis, then, disruptions in ongoing social relations should be less severe and frequent for women alcoholics than for men alcoholics. Although there has been no systematic comparison of the reactions to men and women alcoholics, there are indications that the social reactions to women are less severe.

First, alcoholism in women probably has fewer and less severe adverse economic consequences for others. Studies of men alcoholics reveal that between 25 and 35 percent are unemployed;[14] other studies indicate that unemployment may be a precipitating factor in rejection by relatives and friends.[15] The proportion of women alcoholics who lose their jobs is undoubtedly much lower since fewer women perform full-time occupational roles. Consequently, the punitive social reactions which result when the family's economic welfare is threatened are undoubtedly much less frequent and severe for women, and women are also less likely to suffer disruptions in the social relations connected with work as a result of losing an occupational role.

In addition, the woman's functioning in her major roles—as mother and spouse—may not be as seriously undermined by excessive drinking.

[13] See p. 467 above.

[14] R. Straus and S. Bacon, "Alcoholism and Social Stability: A Study of Occupational Integration in 2,023 Male Clinic Patients," *Quarterly Journal of Studies on Alcohol* 12 (1951), pp. 231–60; B. Chodorkoff, H. Krystal, J. Nunn, and R. Wittenberg, "Employment Characteristics of Hospitalized Alcoholics," *Quarterly Journal of Studies on Alcohol* 22 (1961), pp. 106–10. S. Warkov, S. Bacon, and A. Hawkins, "Social Correlates of Industrial Problem Drinking, *Quarterly Journal of Studies on Alcohol* 18 (1957), pp. 388–404. A study of alcoholics in a private hospital in Seattle reported only 3.4 percent unemployed. W. M. Wellman, M. A. Maxwell and P. O'Hollaren, "Private Hospital Alcoholics Patients and the Changing Conception of the 'Typical' Alcoholic," *Quarterly Journal of Studies on Alcohol* 18 (1957), pp. 388–404. However, since 41 percent were officials, managers and owners, and 42 percent were self-employed, the alcoholics in this study were predominantly of high socioeconomic status.

[15] W. McCord, J. McCord, and J. Gudeman, *Origins of Alcoholism* (Stanford: Stanford University Press, 1960); J. Jackson, "Alcoholism and the Family," in D. Pittman and C. Snyder, eds., *Society, Culture, and Drinking Patterns* (New York: John Wiley, 1962), chapter 27; S. Bacon, "Alcoholics Do Not Drink," *Annals of American Academy of Political and Social Science* 315 (1958), pp. 55–64; and M. Clinard, *Sociology of Deviant Behavior*, rev. ed. (New York: Holt, Rinehart and Company, 1963).

Women alcoholics, more than men, do their drinking alone, presumably in the home.[16] This is consistent with the belief held by some that "plateau drinking"—imbibing small amounts, often wine, at frequent intervals during the day —is more common among women alcoholics.[17] Since such drinking may be "sufficient to dull the edges of reality but not enough to hamper . . . functioning seriously,"[18] women alcoholics may create fewer hardships and inconveniences for others, and experience fewer strains in their interpersonal relations, than men do.

Drinking in the home may have another significant consequence—it keeps the visibility of drinking behavior low. Consequently, women alcoholics are less likely to come to community attention or to be a source of embarrassment and status threat to their relatives and friends. On the basis of her comparison of women and men alcoholics, Lisansky[19] concluded that many women alcoholics are able to keep "out of public view and out of difficulty in the community. They are not 'public nuisances.' They are rather, in a sense, the 'respectable' women alcoholics. It may well be that this group constitutes the major proportion of the population of women alcoholics."

Lisansky's study also showed that women alcoholics were less likely to be arrested or committed to mental hospitals than were men. More than just the application of the "double standard" is probably involved here. True, in most forms of deviance women are less likely to be publicly embarrassed, humiliated, and punished; they are treated with more tolerance and sympathy and tend to be forgiven. The same is probably true in the case of excessive drinking.[20] But aside from this, as the woman alcoholic probably generates fewer and less severe problems in the lives of other people, she is less likely to be ostracized by the community or to experience disruptions in her family and friendship ties. And, of course, disruptions in occupational relations are also less probable. Therefore, the association between suicide and alcoholism should be weaker in women, as the results show.

Race. Ostensibly in regard to the societal reaction to deviant behavior, the Black's position vis-à-vis Whites is the opposite of that of women vis-à-vis men. Reactions to Black deviance are usually more punitive than reactions to White deviance; and compared to Whites, Blacks are more likely to be arrested, convicted and sentenced. However, it is not disruptions in relations with public officials (e.g., police, court officials, etc.) that appear to contribute to suicide. Instead, it is the loss of intimate social relations—loss of, rejection by, or friction with, spouse, siblings, children, lover, friends.[21] If the social-reaction hypothesis is correct, such interpersonal disruptions should be more frequent in the lives of White than Black men alcoholics.

The existing evidence does suggest that Blacks, especially lower-class Blacks, are quite tolerant and permissive of deviant and aggressive behavior; evidence presented by Drake and Cayton,[22] Dollard,[23] Lewis,[24] and Short and Strodtbeck[25] all suggest that this is the case. Furthermore, observations by Drake and Cayton and by Short and Strodtbeck indicate that in lower-class Black urban ghettos, deviant behavior (e.g., drug use, sexual conduct) is interwoven with "non-deviant" conduct, to form one overall "normal" pattern. For example, in their comparison of White and Black lower-class communities in Chicago, Short and Strodtbeck concluded that in the latter, adolescent deviance "is more a part of a total life pattern in which delinquent behaviors are not as likely to create disjunctures with other types of behavior," that "delinquency tends not to be clearly differentiated from nondelinquent behavior."[26]

---

[16] E. Lisansky, "Alcoholism in Women: Social and Psychological Concomitants, I. Social History Data," *Quarterly Journal of Studies on Alcohol* 18 (1957), pp. 588–623.

[17] *Ibid.*

[18] *Ibid.*

[19] *Ibid.*

[20] There are those who assert, however, that in the case of alcoholism the double standard works in reverse, although no evidence is offered. For example, Lolli states that "the whip of the law hits (the woman alcoholic) more frequently and more painfully than it does the male addictive drinker." See G. Lolli, *Social Drinking* (Cleveland: World Publishing Co., 1960), p. 261. As noted above Lisansky's findings suggest the opposite.

[21] W. Rushing, "Individual Behavior and Suicide," in J. Gibbs, ed., *Suicide* (New York: Harper and Row, 1967).

[22] S. Drake and H. Cayton, *Black Metropolis* (New York: Harper and Row, 1962), Chapter 20.

[23] J. Dollard, *Caste and Class in a Southern Town* (New York: Doubleday, 1957), Chapter 15.

[24] H. Lewis, *Blackways of Kent* (Chapel Hill N.C.: University of North Carolina Press, 1955).

[25] J. Short, Jr., and F. Strodtbeck, *Gang Delinquency and Group Process,* Chicago: University of Chicago Press, 1965), pp. 36, 106.

[26] *Ibid.,* p. 106.

If these observations are valid, it suggests that Blacks are more likely to accept alcoholism as "normal" than are Whites. Since excessive drinking creates fewer disjunctures with other types of actions, it probably creates fewer serious permanent disruptions in a Black man's ongoing social relations. As a result, the association of suicide with alcoholism should be less among Blacks. This hypothesis is consistent with the finding that the cirrhosis–suicide relationship is higher among Whites than among Blacks.[27]

Nevertheless, the interpretation should be accepted cautiously. Our findings are based on group correlations while the theory argues that the probability of suicide among individual alcoholics differs depending on the social reaction. The present data do not allow us to know the social reaction to specific individuals. We do not know, for example, whether the social reaction to White men alcoholics who committed suicide was harsher than the social reaction to White men alcoholics who did not. Still, the evidence for group differences is consistent with theoretical expectations. (It is also consistent with Vitols' observations about differences between White and Black alcoholics.[28] He reports that there is greater tolerance of alcoholic behavior by Black families and communities, particularly in low socioeconomic areas. Black alcoholics are less apt to be referred to mental facilities for alcoholism, and when they are, they are more accepting of hospitalization and even of being placed in jail than their White counterparts. In addition, according to Vitols, alcoholic drinking is not as apt to be accompanied by emotional trauma and family disruptions among Blacks as

among Whites, and feelings of guilt are less apt to be associated with drinking among Blacks. Vitols also observes that there are "less suicidal ruminations and suicidal attempts in the Negro than in the white" alcoholic.[29] These differences are believed to stem from differences between the White and Black communities in the acceptance of deviant behavior, including alcoholic drinking. Whites react to alcoholic drinkers more violently and deal with such drinkers more harshly.)

MENTAL ILLNESS AND SUICIDE

According to our formulation, it is not mental illness that is significant in suicide, but the way people respond to persons who have been designated as "mentally ill." Evidence from several types of studies indicates that the relationship between being mentally ill and suicide varies depending on the reaction of others.

First, evidence indicates that the suicide rate among former mental patients is highest during the period immediately following release from the hospital, and decreases steadily thereafter.[30] It is probable that the period immediately following release is the time at which social avoidance, rejection, and interactional difficulties are apt to be most severe. Thus, a plausible explanation for this finding is that mental illness is most apt to result in suicide when the response from others is most negative. Once this interpersonal crisis passes, the probability of suicide decreases.

There is also evidence that interpersonal processes are associated with the suicide rate of patients even during periods of treatment. One study reports that the suicide rate in one hospital fluctuated with the amount of personnel and patient turnover in the hospital.[31] The occurrence of suicide, therefore, is "related to events which dispose toward unstable social environments."[32] (The finding has important implica-

---

[27] The hypothesis does not explain the negative correlation for Blacks, however. Two comments about this finding may be made. First, for Blacks, more than for Whites, alcoholism and suicide may be alternative responses to a similar life situation; consequently, alcoholism may lessen the probability of suicide. Such an explanation would be consistent with the assumption that both alcoholism and suicide are responses to the frustration, tension and oppression associated with an extremely low socioeconomic life situation. Hence alcohol may be a palliative for Blacks that makes life seem worth living. Without alcohol, life may be more intolerable and suicide more probable. Second, however, as previously noted, the absolute magnitude of the two correlations may contain error. Perhaps the true correlation for Blacks is closer to zero. In any case, in this paper little significance is attached to the absolute magnitude of the correlations, but only to the difference between them.

[28] M. Vitols, "Culture Patterns of Drinking in Negro and White Alcoholics," *Diseases of the Nervous System* 29 (1968), pp. 391–94.

[29] *Ibid.*, p. 394.

[30] A. Pokorny, "Suicide Rates in Various Psychiatric Disorders," *Journal of Nervous and Mental Disease* 139 (1964), pp. 499–506, and A. Temoch, T. Pugh, R. MacMahon, "Suicide Rates among Current and Former Mental Patients," *Journal of Nervous and Mental Disease* 138 (1964), pp 124–30.

[31] M. Kahne, "Suicides in Mental Hospitals: A Study of the Effects of Personnel and Patient Turnover," *Journal of Health and Social Behavior* 9 (1968), pp. 255–66.

[32] *Ibid*, p. 257.

tions for how hospitals should respond to suicide attempts. Specifically, it calls attention to the problem of overreacting by hiring more personnel or reassigning hospital personnel to wards on which suicidal behavior has been most prevalent. This may increase the relative number of strangers, make the environment more unstable, and thus aggravate the situation.[33]) Although this study shows that suicide is associated with the character of social relationships in an institution and probably with interpersonal difficulties, it does not reveal that it is associated with the type of rejecting behavior that is frequently associated with deviant behavior. Another study does report such a relationship, however. In a study of 32 suicides covering a ten-year history in one psychiatric clinic, retrospective analysis of the circumstances of each suicide suggests that in *every* case the suicide was preceded by the rejecting behavior of the therapist who was treating the patient. Thus in some instances for patients undergoing psychiatric treatment, the rejecting behavior by the psychiatrist may be an important contributing factor in suicide.[34]

In summary, then, the relationship between mental illness and suicide is not a simple one in which suicide is just another manifestation of mental pathology. Such pathology may be involved, but as with alcoholism, it is the nature of the socal environment in which the pathology exists (or is perceived to exist) that may be the crucial factor.

---

[33] *Ibid.,* p. 264.

[34] V. Bloom, "An Analysis of Suicide at a Training Center," *American Journal of Psychiatry* 123 (1967), pp. 918–25.

B. SOCIAL RELATIONS AND PROCESS

Suicide differs from many forms of deviance since its expression requires no interaction with others. Nevertheless, most pre-suicides appear to be compelled to inform others of their intention. An investigation by Eli Robins and associates, reported in "The Communication of Suicidal Intent," reveals that more than two-thirds of all suicide victims are known to have informed others of their intent. In most instances, recipients of these communications are spouses, relatives, and friends. The recipients, in turn, face the dilemma of feeling both responsible for the individual but helpless to do anything for him. The authors describe ways in which people react to this dilemma. Thus, although the act of suicide itself does not usually involve interaction between the victim and others, a particular pattern of interaction between the victim and the intimate associate appears to precede it.

THE COMMUNICATION OF SUICIDAL INTENT:

A Study of 134 Consecutive Cases of Successful (Completed) Suicide

ELI ROBINS, M.D.,[1] SEYMOUR GASSNER, M.D.,[2] JACK KAYES, M.D.,[3]
ROBERT H. WILKINSON, JR., M.D.,[4] AND GEORGE E. MURPHY, M.D.

There are many phenomena related to successful (completed) suicide that cannot be studied adequately by statistical methods from coroners' records, by individual case reports, or by obtaining only hospital records of suicides who may have been hospitalized sometime prior to their deaths. The communication of suicidal intent is one such phenomenon. One method of investigating such phenomena is the study of a consecutive series of successful suicides a short time after their suicidal acts, through systematic interviews with relatives, in-laws, friends, job associates, physicians and others.[5] By means of such interviews we have obtained information concerning the expression of suicidal intent by persons who recently committed suicide. In the present report certain findings concerning suicidal communication will be described: (1) The ways in which these persons communicated their suicidal intentions, whether by a direct statement or by indirect allusions to their imminent deaths. (2) The frequency and chronology, as related to the time of suicide, of such communications. (3) To whom the communications were made. (4) The relationships between communication or failure to communicate, and sex, age, clinical diagnosis, marital state, occupation, education, whether a suicide note was written, and whether the person was living alone or not. The relationships of these findings to certain other aspects of successful suicide will also be discussed.

METHOD

In the one-year period between May 15, 1956, and May 15, 1957, the coroners of the City of St. Louis and of St. Louis County[6] returned a verdict of suicide in the deaths of 134 persons. In 119 of these cases we have held a primary interview with close relatives or friends within a few weeks to a few months after the suicide. The relatives refused an interview in 13 cases and 2 suicides were transients in St. Louis. In addition to the primary interview, interviews were obtained with other relatives, friends, job associates, clergymen, landladies, bartenders, nurses, attorneys, policemen, and physicians. A total of 305 interviews were done, including ancillary interviews of the 15 persons for whom no primary interview was obtained. General and mental hospital records, Social Service Exchange and police records were also examined.

The primary interview was a systematic open-ended interview which lasted an average of over 2 hours. This interview covered past and present medical and psychiatric history, personal and social history, and details of the successful suicide and the events which led up to it. The following items were particularly noted: (1) The ways of communicating suicidal intent. (2) The frequency of such communication. (3) To whom communicated. (4) Interval between the communication and the suicide. (5) Frequency of

Reprinted with permission of author and publisher, from the *American Journal of Psychiatry* 115 (1959), pp. 724–33. Footnotes have been renumbered. Read at the 114th annual meeting of The American Psychiatric Association, San Francisco, California, May 12–16, 1958.

[1] From the Department of Psychiatry and Neurology, Washington University School of Medicine, St. Louis, Mo.

[2] Part of this work was done during the tenure of a Medical Student Research Fellowship, United States Public Health Service.

[3] Part of this work was done during the tenure of a Lederle Laboratories—Washington University Medical Student Research Fellowship.

[4] See footnote 2.

[5] This method of studying suicide is not a new one. Over 30 years ago Serin [S. Serin, *Presse Medicine* 2 (1926), p. 1404, and *Annales Medico-Psychologie* 84 (1926), p. 356] studied suicides and attempted suicides in Paris by interviews with relatives and others. Since her reports did not separate attempted from successful suicide, it is difficult to interpret her results. It is also not clear whether a consecutive series was studied (she obtained the names from newspapers) or whether a systematic interview was used. So far as the authors are aware, this is probably the first study in which a consecutive series was systematically interviewed.

[6] We wish to thank the coroners for the City of St. Louis (Patrick J. Taylor) and for St. Louis County (Arnold J. Willmann and Raymond I. Harris) and their staffs (Mary Alice Quinn, Mildred B. Saemann, and Rose Marie Algarda) without whose cooperation this study would not have been possible.

repeated expression of suicidal ideas. (6) Content of suicide notes and to whom addressed. (7) Prior suicide attempts, number of circumstances. (8) Medical and psychiatric care given these patients. These items were systematically asked for, and additional information was also obtained in the "free" portion of the interview where the respondent gave a description of the person, his illness, and the circumstances of the suicidal act. The interview also contained items designed to elicit the history and symptoms, if present, of the psychoses, psychoneuroses, sociopathic personality disturbances (psychopathic personality, chronic alcoholism, drug addiction), and homosexuality. The clinical diagnostic criteria used will be described in another publication. Statistical methods used have been described.[7]

RESULTS

Kinds of Communication of Suicidal Ideas. The most striking finding was that over two-thirds (69 percent) of the entire group communicated their suicidal ideas (Table 1). The ways of communicating these ideas were highly varied, requiring 26 categories[8] to group the responses of the 134 persons (Table 1). The most frequent manner was a direct and specific statement of the intent to commit suicide (41 percent of the entire group). There were, however, many other ways of communicating suicidal ideas. Examples presented below suggest the variety of communications of individual persons.

Manic-depressive depression group. (1) 64-year-old man. Frequently said that he wanted to die, that his family would be better off when he was dead, and that he was going to commit suicide. He threatened to drink a solution of Drano. He began to fear that he would hurt himself and was taken to the hospital by his wife. (2) 58-year-old man. He said he would be better off dead. He put his affairs in his wife's name. On being told he was

going to the hospital, he said, "I know I'm not coming back."[9] He spoke frequently of doing the "Dutch" act and often went through a pantomime of shooting himself in the head, saying, "If I had a gun I'd do it myself." He made two suicide attempts in the 8 weeks preceding his successful suicide. (3) 59-year-old woman. She spoke frequently of wanting to die, of fearing that she would kill herself, and of wanting to jump in the river. Shortly before her suicide she frequently said, "If I don't get better, I'm going to stick my head in the oven." She did indeed finally commit suicide by putting her head in an oven in a closed room. (4) 42-year-old woman. The night before her suicide, while combing her 16-year-old daughter's hair, she suddenly (and quite uncharacteristically) asked, "What would you do without me?" Her husband stated that on the morning of the day of her suicide she was sweeter and more attentive than ever before, "She kissed me better than she ever had before."

Chronic alcoholic group. (1) 37-year-old man. The night before his suicide he told his friends in a tavern that they would see his death notice in the newspapers on Thursday. This actually happened, since he borrowed a gun from his brother-in-law on Wednesday and shot himself that evening. (2) 37-year-old man. This man spoke repeatedly of wanting to die, or being better off dead, and of his family being better off if he were dead. He told his 6-year-old child that he was going to kill himself. His anguished and pathetic communications to his current wife ("Mommy, I'm going to have to go away." "Mommy, where are you going to bury me?" "Mommy, I won't be here in the morning. I'm going to die tonight." "Oh, Mommy, come and sleep with me this one night more, and hold me tight, I'm so afraid.") contrasted with his bitter telephone statement to his ex-wife ("Come out and see my grave sometime"). On the day of his suicide he took a religious medallion with him (which he had never done before). Just before his suicide, he called the mother of his ex-wife and told her to burn a candle for him. (3) 56-year-old woman. She wondered, to her son and relatives, how quick death by hanging would be. A week before her death she said, "If things don't change in a week, I am going to hang myself by November 25." However, she did not wait until the 25th, but hanged herself on November 23. (4) 34-year-old woman. She spoke of killing herself on many occasions. On the day of her suicide, she said to her husband, "This is the last time I will see you." She committed suicide 2 hours later.

Miscellaneous group. (1) 45-year-old man, dying from carcinoma of the lung. On the day before

---

[7] James J. Murtell, Eli Robins and Mandel E. Cohen, "Observations on Clinical Aspects of Hysteria," *Journal American Medical Association* 146 (July 7, 1951), pp. 902–909.

[8] These 26 ways include 25 which were direct verbal references to suicide and death or to the possibility of imminent death, and 1 which was non-verbal, a suicide attempt. The occurrence, for example, of feelings and expressions of depression, of hopelessness, of illness, and of so being a burden will be considered later in the paper.

---

[9] The quoted statements throughout the paper are verbatim quotes from interviews.

TABLE 1. KINDS OF COMMUNICATION OF SUICIDAL IDEAS IN PERSONS WHO HAVE COMMITTED SUICIDE

Manner of Communication	Men N = 103 %	Women N = 31 %	Total Group N = 134 %*
Statement of intent to commit suicide	41	42	41
Better off dead; tired of living	26	16	24
Desire to die	23	19	22
Suicide attempts	19	32	22
References to methods of committing suicide	20	10	18
Dire predictions†	17	13	16
Statement that his family would be better off if he were dead	15	6	12
References to dying before or with spouse	7	3	6
Putting affairs in order, or planning to	6	3	5
Can't take it any longer; no other way out	3	3	3
References to burial or to grave	4	0	3
Statement of not being afraid, or being afraid, to die	3	0	3
Talk about suicides of other people	3	3	3
The game is over; this is the end	2	3	2
Insistent that spouse not buy new things for him	2	0	1
Called old friends whom not spoken to in 10 years	1	3	1
Miscellaneous‡	7	13	8
Total communicating at least 1 suicidal idea	68	74	69
No communication of suicidal ideas	32	26	31

* The percentages total more than 100 percent because some persons used more than 1 kind of communication.

† These included such statements as, "I won't be here tomorrow"; "You'll find a dead man in the street"; "I am going to get off the face of the earth"; "Don't be surprised if you find I walked into the water"; "I know I'm not coming back (from the hospital)"; "Some day you'll find me dead"; "Buddy, goodbye now, you don't know how you're going to find me"; "This is your last kiss"; "I'll never leave alive"; "This is the last time I will see you"; "By that time it will be too late (when physician referred her to a psychiatrist)"; "You won't see me again except in a hearse"; "I won't be here Thursday"; "If something happens to me, don't be surprised."

‡ These included such statements and actions as, "I'm going to throw everything in your lap (to son)"; "I will not die a lingering death"; "I'm ready to go"; "You'd better watch me, I'm not responsible for what I do"; "Wait, George, (to dead friend) don't get too far ahead; I'll be coming soon"; asked daughter night before suicide, "What would you do without me?"; phoned ex-wife's mother and asked her to burn a candle for him; repeatedly went through a pantomine of shooting himself (without a gun in his hand).

his suicide he spoke aloud to a friend who had died in 1950. "Wait, George, don't get too far ahead, I'll be coming soon." On the night before his suicide he pleaded with his wife, "I saw your (deceased) father, and I could take you to him if you want to go." The wife refused. (2) 62-year-old man with an undiagnosed psychiatric illness. A year prior to his suicide he suggested that he and his wife commit suicide together. On the afternoon of his suicide, he turned as he was leaving his place of business and, with a flamboyant gesture, said to his employees, "Goodbye, everybody!" (One of these employees who had been with him 20 years said that he had never before said goodbye when leaving in the afternoon.) (3) 31-year-old man with an undiagnosed psychiatric illness. During the 9 months preceding his suicide he spoke repeatedly of wanting to die and of committing suicide. On one occasion he pointed a gun at his wife and threatened to kill her and himself. On another occasion he held a knife to his bare chest and taunted his wife, saying, "I wonder how it would feel." On a third occasion he took his wife down to the basement, put a rope around a beam, made a hangman's noose, put his head in it and said to his wife, "I

wonder how it would feel." (4) 62-year-old woman, dying of lymphosarcoma. During the 3 weeks prior to her suicide she had repeatedly said, "I'm through. I'm whipped. This is the end. I can't take it any longer." During the final week she added, "I will not die a lingering death." On the morning of her suicide, she kissed her husband goodbye as he was leaving for work and said to him, "Darling, this is your last kiss." She committed suicide later that morning.

As these examples and the data in Table 1 show, the communicated suicidal ideas covered a wide range of explicit statements and of (inferred) emotional states. Most of the statements showed preoccupation with suicide, with methods of committing suicide, and with death. It was striking that in the vast majority of instances the relatives and friends did not regard these communications as efforts to manipulate the environment by playing on the emotions of the hearers. Instances of taunts (subject 3 in the miscellaneous group above) were rare. A small minority (5 percent of the total number of communications) appeared to be bitter and hostile. The majority were considered as expressions of anguish, hopelessness, and defeat, and the wish to disappear ("I am going to get off the face of the earth." "You'll never see me again").

Men and women did not differ significantly in the frequency of suicidal communication (Table 1).

Other Features of the Communication of Suicidal Ideas

In addition to analyzing the content of the suicidal ideas and the proportion of persons expressing them, other features, including frequency, time of expression, and to whom expressed, were studied (Table 2). Almost two-thirds (65 percent) of the persons used more than one type of expression. The mean number of ways per person of expressing suicidal ideas was 3.2. In the majority of instances, expressions of suicidal ideas were diverse even for individual persons. The ideas were communicated, on the average, to 2 different groups (footnote, Table 2); and in two-thirds (67 percent) of instances the communications were repeated. Thus, not only did the communications occur in a high proportion of cases but they tended to be multiple, repeated, and expressed to a number of different persons.

A question arises whether these communications were of long standing or reflected only a current preoccupation with suicide and death. In almost three-quarters of the persons (73 percent) these ideas had been expressed for less than 1 year and in 43 percent for less than 3 months. Of the remaining 27 percent, 13 percent of those who had expressed these ideas prior to 1 year ago had shown an increase in the frequency of the communications within 1 year. Therefore, 86 percent of the persons who were

TABLE 2. SOME FEATURES OF THE COMMUNICATION OF SUICIDAL IDEAS

	Men N = 70	Women N = 23	Total Group N = 93
Kinds of suicidal ideas			
Mean number per person	3.4	2.6	3.2
Proportion of persons with > 1 way of communication (%)	68	57	65
Maximum number in any 1 person	12	7	12
To whom expressed			
Spouse (%)	65	43	60
Relatives, including in-laws (%)	50	57	51
Friends (%)	34	39	35
Job associates (%)	5	4	5
Physicians (%)	13	35	18
Others: ministers, police, landlady (%)	5	4	5
Mean number per person*	1.8	1.9	1.8
Repeated vs. infrequent expression			
Repeatedly (%)	66	70	67
Once or at most a few times (%)	34	30	33
Time of first expression of suicidal ideas			
Within 1 year of suicide† (%)	74	70	73
More than 1 year, with an increase within 1 year (%)	10	22	13
More than 1 year, without an increase within 1 year (%)	16	8	14
Considered a genuine warning by respondents			
Genuine (%)	69	87	73
Not genuine‡ (%)	31	13	27

* This number is *not* the mean number of *individuals* to whom the suicidal person communicated his intent, but is the number of different *groups* of individuals to whom a suicidal communication was made. (Only the category spouse necessarily refers to a single individual.)

† It is striking that 39 percent of the men and 52 percent of the women (43 percent of the total group) first expressed suicidal ideas within 3 months of the time of their suicides.

‡ Scored as "not genuine" if there were occasional instances when the person to whom suicidal idea was expressed felt it was a threat and that it did not signify a real intent to commit suicide. It was scored this way even if there were other times when the statement of suicidal intent was considered genuine.

reported to have expressed suicidal ideas had recently expressed them for the first time or had shown a recent intensification of these ideas.

Since all these persons had in fact committed suicide, one might expect respondents retrospectively to change their opinions as to whether the threat of suicide had been genuine. It was of interest, however, that one-quarter of the respondents still reported that they thought that at times the suicidal ruminations had not been genuine (Table 2). There were others who felt that the communications were genuine but were nevertheless irritated and angered by them.

In Table 2 the only difference between men and women which was statistically significant (significance ratio, 2.27) was the greater proportion of women who communicated suicidal ideas to their physicians. This may be a reflection of the fact that a greater proportion of the women than of the men were seen by physicians for their psychiatric symptoms within a year prior to their suicides.

Relation of Communication of Suicidal Ideas to Clinical Diagnosis

For purposes of the present report, the suicides have been divided into 3 groups by clinical diagnosis: Manic-depressive depression,[10] chronic alcoholism, and a miscellaneous group. (See Table 3). No significant differences were found between the groups as to the number who communicated suicidal ideas. A comparison of the 3 groups with respect to the variables in Table 2 shows that the chronic alcoholics significantly more frequently expressed a greater variety of suicidal ideas than the other 2 groups (means: alcoholics 4.2, manic-depressive depressions 3.1, and miscellaneous group 2.5). There were no differences among the diagnostic groups with regard to whom the ideas were expressed, to whether the expression was repeated, and to the

time of first expressing these ideas. The suicidal communications of the chronic alcoholics were considered to be not genuine (see footnote to Table 2 for definition) in 46 percent, of the miscellaneous group in 25 percent, and of the manic-depressive group in 17 percent. The difference between the alcoholic and manic-depressive groups was statistically significant (significance ratio, 2.52).

More of the chronic alcoholics made the specific statement of intent to commit suicide than did the manic-depressives (significance ratio, 1.92) or the miscellaneous group (significance ratio, 2.41) (Table 4). Since in Table 3, the chronic alcoholic group also had the highest proportion who communicated suicidal ideas (although not statistically significant), there may be a real but slight tendency for the chronic alcoholics to be more communicative in this respect.

Relations of Communication of Suicidal Ideas to Selected Social Variables (Table 5)

Sex, age, marital state, socioeconomic status, religion, and whether living alone or not did not significantly affect the proportion of suicides who communicated their suicidal ideas.

Relation of the Communication of Suicidal Ideas to the Leaving of a Suicide Note

Of the 93 persons who had communicated their suicidal ideas, 37 percent left a suicide note; of the 41 persons who did not communicate their suicidal ideas, 27 percent left a note. Therefore, there was no significant relationship between prior communication of suicidal ideas and leaving a suicide note.

Psychiatric and Medical Care

The direct communication of suicidal ideas and of preoccupation with death has been discussed. The question arises whether these were isolated statements and actions in persons who gave no clear evidence of being clinically ill. From the diagnoses presented in Table 3 it is evident that only 3 persons, all men, could be considered clinically well. In the remainder of the suicides (131 persons), there was little or no question of

---

[10] This diagnostic term is used to include also psychotic depressive reaction and involutional melancholia. The relations between the diagnoses of manic-depressive depression and neurotic depressive reaction will be discussed in another paper. Here it should be pointed out that there was no patient who had *only* a phobic, anxiety, obsessive, or conversion reaction. It is the belief of the authors that what is ordinarily called neurotic depressive reaction, *in the absence of a preexisting clinically evident neurotic disorder*, is a manic-depressive (or psychotic) depression without delusions or grossly apparent psychomotor retardation.

TABLE 3. COMMUNICATION OF SUICIDAL IDEAS: DIAGNOSTIC GROUPS

Diagnostic Group	Number and Proportion Communicating by Any Means (see Table 1)					
	Men		Women		Total	
	No.	%	No.	%	No.	%
Manic-depressive depression*	29	69	12	67	41	68
Chronic alcoholism†	20	74	4	+	24	77
Miscellaneous illnesses‡	21	62	7	+	28	67
Total	70	68	23	74	93	69

* 42 men and 18 women.
† 27 men and 4 women.
‡ 34 men and 9 women, including, among the men, 4 chronic brain syndromes, 3 schizophrenics, 1 drug addict, 17 undiagnosed psychiatric illnesses, 3 insufficient information for diagnosis, 3 with terminal medical illness, and 3 who apparently were clinically well; and, among the women, 1 chronic brain syndrome, 2 terminal medical illnesses, 1 conversion reaction associated with drug addiction, 3 undiagnosed psychiatric illnesses, and 2 insufficient information for diagnosis.
+ Percentages not calculated, less than 10 women in each group.

the presence of either a terminal medical illness or a psychiatric illness, even though a clear-cut diagnosis could not always be made in the latter group. People in whom a clear-cut diagnosis could not be made were considered psychiatrically ill if they had a multiplicity of psychiatric symptoms or disturbances in behavior. In the manic-depressive group, the symptoms and behavior disturbances were usually of only a few months' duration, whereas, in the chronic alcoholics, the disturbances were of at least 5 years' and more frequently of over 10 years' duration. In the vast majority of instances, therefore, the suicidal ideas and the eventual suicide were the accompaniments and culmination of an obvious and severe psychiatric disturbance. The respondents knew the suicides were clinically ill not only because they directly communicated suicidal ideas but also because they had other symptoms—for example, depression, loss of interest, joylessness, anorexia, weight loss, insomnia, job disability, delusions, and excessive alcoholic intake with its consequences. These perceptions of the respondents are supported by the findings that within the year preceding the suicide, over 50 percent of the group had had medical or psychiatric care for psychiatric disease, including approximately one-fifth who had seen a psychiatrist and some of whom had been in a psychiatric hospital. It is noteworthy that an uncomplicated "neurosis" (anxiety reaction, conversion reaction, or obsessive-compulsive reaction) did not occur in any person in the study. Communication of the possibility of suicide, therefore, involves not only the direct allusions to suicidal ideas by the suicidal person but also the awareness on the part of the respondent that this is not an "ordinary kind of nervousness" (a quote from a respondent) even in a severe form, but that there has been a recent *change* in the person or that his uncontrolled alcoholism has got him into serious difficulties.

DISCUSSION

Methodological Considerations

This is probably the first study of an unselected series of suicides in which relatives and other

TABLE 4. SPECIFIC STATEMENT OF INTENT TO COMMIT SUICIDE: DIAGNOSTIC GROUPS

	Men		Women		Total Group	
	No.	%*	No.	%*	No.	%*
Manic-depressive depression	18	43	5	28	23	38
Chronic alcoholism	15	56	4	+	19	59
Miscellaneous illnesses	9	26	4	+	13	31
	42	41	13	42	55	41

* Percentages based on total diagnostic groups, not just those persons communicating suicidal ideas.
+ Percentages not calculated, less than 10 women in each group.

TABLE 5. THE RELATION OF THE COMMUNICATION OF
SUICIDAL IDEAS TO SELECTED SOCIAL VARIABLES

Social Variables	Proportion Who Communicated Suicidal Ideas %
Sex	
Men (N = 103)	68
Women (N = 31)	74
Age	
<44 (N = 36)	75
44–59 (N = 45)	67
>59 (N = 53)	70
Marital State	
Married (N = 83)	69
Not married (N = 51)*	74
Religion	
Protestant (N = 60)	67
Catholic (N = 30)	73
Jewish (N = 6)	†
None (N = 20)	75
Other members of household	
Immediate family (N = 90)	70
Other relatives (N = 13)‡	69
None (living alone) (N = 30)	73
Income (annual)	
<$3000 (N = 28)	71
$3000–$5000 (N = 43)	70
>$5000 (N = 24)	50
Education	
8 grades or less (N = 59)	76
>8 grades (N = 45)	64
Occupation	
Lower status (N = 52)§	66
Higher status (N = 72)§	69

* Not married includes never married, divorced, separated, and widowed.
† Percentage not calculated; N is less than 10.
‡ Includes 2 persons living with friends.
§ Lower status—lower than skilled workers; higher status—skilled workers or higher. Housewives' occupational statuses were classified according to their husbands' occupations.

relevant persons were systematically interviewed shortly after the suicide. As to the validity of these respondents' reports, we can only point out that the descriptions of the illnesses from which the suicides suffered were detailed and coherent enough to allow a specific diagnosis to be made in 82 percent of the cases, although the diagnostic features of these illnesses were unknown to the respondents. This suggests that the respondents were reasonably accurate observers of these phenomena. The whole problem of the validity of psychiatric histories taken from rela-

tives or even from patients themselves is a largely neglected area in psychiatric investigation.

There are certain hiatuses in our knowledge of the suicides which are inevitable when the ill person himself is not examined. These, however, do not seem especially important for the purposes of the present paper. With regard to communication, the recipient of the communication is as integral a part of the communication process as is the communicator, and it may be as valuable to interview the recipient as it is to interview the communicators. In fact, it is our impression that we received a more extensive, lucid, and verbatim report from the respondents about the communication of suicidal ideas than it is possible to obtain from suicidal patients themselves.

It should be emphasized that the reports of suicidal communications, although strikingly frequent in these persons, probably represent only a minimal figure. It is likely that at least some of the 31 percent of the suicides whom we report as having not made a suicidal communication actually had made such communication to someone who was not interviewed or had made one to the respondent interviewed which he subsequently forgot or did not tell us.

Communication of Suicidal Ideas

Our most striking finding was that two-thirds of the persons who commit suicide communicate their suicidal ideas and preoccupation with imminent death prior to the suicidal act. Persons who talk about suicide may, therefore, very well commit it. In the majority of instances these communications are repeatedly verbalized, diverse in content, and expressed to many different persons. In three-quarters of the suicides who communicated their suicidal ideas, their expression is of recent onset and is *not* found in the persons' usual behavior. The vast majority of these persons were clinically ill prior to their suicides, and half of them had received medical or psychiatric care for their psychiatric illness. There were, therefore, 2 factors involved in communication of suicidal ideas: the direct expression of such ideas, and the perception by the relatives, physicians, and often by the suicidal person himself that he was ill, or at least very different from his usual self.

Analysis of the Results as a System of Communication

We were greatly aided in this analysis by the formal description of the process of communication by Hovland and his colleagues.[11] The study of communication requires the investigation and analysis of 4 factors: (1) The one who makes the communication, that is, the suicidal person. (2) The content of the communication. (3) The audience responding to the communication (relatives, friends, job associates, physicians, and others). (4) The responses made by the audience.

1. The communicator. Since these persons committed suicide, it must be accepted that they wanted to die. Perhaps the most easily understood behavior would have been for the person to decide to kill himself and to do so without any communication. Since this did not happen in the majority of instances, what are some of the possible explanations? There are at least 4. The first 3 possibilities imply a specific purpose in making the suicidal communication. First, the person is ambivalent about dying, both wanting and not wanting to, or being afraid of dying. His communications may be considered as a means of bringing his plight to the attention of others so that they can help him. Second, the communications may reflect the desire to warn the audience of what the communicator is about to do and, therefore, in some way prepare them for his death so that it will be less of a shock. Third, even though he wished to die, the communications are also meant as taunts or threats. A possible subcategory would consist of his hostile use of the communications without a genuine desire to die. This subcategory probably occurred only once in this series, since only one of these deaths appeared to be accidental resulting from a spurious suicide attempt. The fourth possibility contrasts with the first 3 in that it does *not* imply a specific purpose. The nature and consequences of the illnesses from which these persons suffer might be such that the person becomes so preoccupied with ideas of suicide and death that he is merely expressing the content of his thoughts,

rather than trying to achieve any particular goals through his suicidal communications. In analyzing our data (see especially Table 1) we have the impression that all 4 explanations are relevant in some cases, but that the fourth possibility is the most common reason for the expression of suicidal ideas.

2. The content of the communication. The contents have been described in detail. The outstanding characteristic is that they probably tended to produce anxiety and arouse fear in the respondents.

3. The audience. The chief characteristics of the audience relevant to the present analysis are: whether those who received the suicidal communications desired the death of the communicator, were indifferent to it, or were distressed by it. As far as could be ascertained from our interviews, only a very small minority of the respondents appeared to desire or welcome the death of the suicidal person, or to be indifferent. The indifference did not appear to be complete; the suicide was at least unwelcome and unpleasant to this group. By far the largest number of respondents were genuinely distressed and upset by the suicidal death.

4. Responses of the audience. The majority of the respondents expressed a feeling of marked tension. They were being repeatedly warned of the possible or even probable occurrence of a dire event about which they could do nothing definitive. They did not feel able either to prevent the suicidal act or to ameliorate the psychiatric illnesses. Nor had they been able to turn total responsibility for the person over to anyone else. Although half of the suicidal persons had been seen by a physician, only 6 percent were in a hospital at the time of their suicides. In the majority of the remaining cases, therefore, the respondent felt some degree of responsibility for the suicidal person prior to and at the time of the suicide.

What then are the ways in which the respondents attempted to deal with this dilemma? Their attempts will be analyzed in accordance with the discussion of Hovland, Janis, and Kelley[12] concerning audience response to what they term fear-arousing appeals. The work of these authors

---

[11] Carl L. Hovland, "Social Communication," *Proceedings of the American Philosophical Society* 92 (November 12, 1948), pp. 371–75.

[12] *Ibid.*

is based on an experimental situation in which the communicator was, for the most part, directly threatening the audience with pain, cancer, etc., if they did not take care of their teeth properly. In spite of the marked differences between this experimental situation and the present study, many aspects of their analysis are nevertheless applicable. Like their respondents, our respondents tended to deal with the dilemma in 3 ways:[13] (1) By changing their original attitudes toward the communication itself; (2) By changing their attitudes to the communicator; (3) By changing their perceptions of their own roles in this situation.

Changes toward the communication itself included the following: The outright rejection of a fear-arousing communication, when after the first rush of dismay and alarm, the respondents began to regard the possibility of suicide as improbable ("I thought he didn't really mean it." "I didn't think it would happen.") or, if possible, then perhaps at some remote time ("He might do it but not now. Maybe if he gets worse."). Since it was usual for the suicidal person to communicate his suicidal ideas repeatedly and over a period of time, the respondents began to discount their seriousness because of their frequent repetition with no suicidal action having been taken ("She had been saying it for so long I became more used to it"; "He'd said it so many times, I just began to hope it would never happen."). Finally, we have the impression that a very high level of anxiety in the respondent acted directly in some fashion to reduce his panicky and severely distressful reactions to the suicidal communication ("I just got worn out with the constant worry.").

Changes in attitudes towards the suicidal person included the following: After the initial shock and belief that the suicidal person might commit suicide, the respondent would cease to believe that the suicide would happen because,

"He had never talked or acted this way before. It just wasn't him. He couldn't do something like that." Related to the preceding response was the belief initially that the person was ill and as a result he might commit suicide. This would then change to the idea that he was ill but not sick enough to commit suicide ("He's sick but he's not that much 'off'; he won't do it. He's just not himself."). In other instances the respondents became so angry and irritated at the suicidal person's repeatedly making them anxious and distressed ("I got so mad at her constantly talking about it (suicide and death) that I just didn't listen.") that they rejected the significance of the communication. Finally, a mixture of anger and outright disbelief occurred when the suicidal person taunted the respondent with his suicidal communications.

Changes in the respondents' perceptions of their own roles: It was our impression that initially the critical considerations here were whether the respondent had little or no idea of what to do for the suicidal persons or whether he believed he should see a psychiatrist or other physician. In the cases where a psychiatrist or other physician had examined the suicidal person and had not hospitalized him or had hospitalized him only briefly, the respondents were left with the problem of a communicator who was in part their responsibility and for whom they knew nothing definitive to do. As a result, the original picture of themselves as being helpful and effective in getting the suicidal person to a physician was changed and they were left with an insoluble problem. It should be pointed out that there is a lack of realistic information concerning what a respondent should do when confronted with this kind of situation. This is due to a lack of knowledge of the medical profession and not only of the respondents. No clear-cut information is available to physicians or to the public as to what should be done in this situation. A very real dilemma, therefore, confronts the respondent.

[13] It must be emphasized that we do not have systematic data concerning the respondents' ways of dealing with this dilemma. Not only were these sorts of questions not asked systematically in the questionnaire but also close questioning of the respondents concerning their own feelings or actions tended to break up the interview. The ways to be described in which respondents dealt with this dilemma, therefore, will represent examples where we have clear evidence that at least a few of the respondents used this technique. This area of audience responses appears to be a fruitful one for further research on the nature of suicide.

SUMMARY

1. A study of the communication of suicidal ideas by 134 consecutive suicides has been done by means of systematic interviews with family, in-laws, friends, job associates, physicians, min-

isters, and others a short time after the suicide.

2. Two striking findings were that over two-thirds (69 percent) of the suicides had communicated suicidal ideas and that 41 percent had specifically stated they intended to commit suicide. In the majority of instances, the suicidal communications were of recent onset (months), repeatedly verbalized, and expressed to many persons.

3. Another striking finding was that 98 percent of these persons were probably clinically ill prior to their suicides.

4. The frequency of expression of suicidal ideas was not significantly related to age, sex, marital state, religion, whether living alone or not, clinical diagnosis, occupational status, income, or education. Chronic alcoholics had a somewhat greater tendency than the other diagnostic groups to make the specific statement that they intended to commit suicide.

5. The communication of suicidal ideas was analyzed as a general system of communication with reference to experimental psychological studies.

C. CONSEQUENCES

Only a few of the many studies of suicide have been concerned with the consequences of suicide. Two of the most provocative of these studies are reported in this section.

The first, "Suicide Attempts and the Social Response," by Arthur L. Kobler and Ezra Stotland, examines the consequences of attempted suicide rather than suicide per se. According to some formulations, since many who commit suicide make at least one attempt prior to the successful act, an expected consequence of attempted suicide is successful suicide. This view is dependent on the idea that suicide is a trait of the individual, so that both attempted and successful suicides are considered expressions of suicidal tendencies of individuals. Kobler and Stotland argue, however, that the consequences of attempted suicide vary, that the probability of one who attempts suicide subsequently taking his life depends on the response of others. These authors believe that most attemptees view their situations as hopeless (e.g., because of financial difficulties) and that the suicide attempt is a plea for help. If others react helpfully (e.g., by getting the jobless attemptee a job) and indicate that the situation is not hopeless, future attempts tend not to be repeated. However, if others deny that the attempt was made or if they also view the situation as hopeless, they confirm the attemptee's belief. Suicide may result. Thus, the societal reaction to the communication of intent may generate additional suicidal consequences. This analysis has significant implications for the way hospital personnel react to persons who have been hospitalized for attempting suicide, as Kobler and Stotland note toward the end of their paper.

In the next selection, "Children's Disturbed Reactions to Parent Suicide," Albert C. Cain and Irene Fast examine some of the interpersonal consequences of suicide. Their results indicate that the psychological consequences for children of a parent committing suicide may be extremely traumatic. Parent suicide may lead to deep feelings of guilt in children and to distorted communication between children and others, especially the surviving parent. Since Cain and Fast's findings are based on a group of children who had been referred to treatment agencies, one must hesitate before generalizing their findings in relation to all children of suicides. But regardless of that, their findings are relevant to a significant philosophical issue. Some persons feel that individuals have the right to take their life if they wish and that society should not attempt to deprive individuals of that right.[1] Others deny that an individual has such a right. Such denial is explicit when others prevent individuals from killing themselves and when others commit suicidal individuals to institutions for treatment. Mental health professionals who treat suicidal patients and try to show their patients that life is worth living deny that individuals have this right, although their treatment is viewed as an effort to help the individual and not as an attempt to deprive him of a civil right. Although Cain and Fast do not confront the issue of rights, their paper contains the type of data that discussion of this issue must consider. Should the right, assuming its existence, of an individual to take his own life be denied because the expression of that right infringes on the psychological welfare of others?

---

[1] Thomas Szasz, Address at the International Conference on Suicide Prevention (London, September 27–28, 1969).

SUICIDE ATTEMPTS AND THE SOCIAL RESPONSE

ARTHUR L. KOBLER AND EZRA STOTLAND

We have characterized our approach to emotional disturbance, and particularly to suicide, as psychosocial, as including environmental as well as intrapsychic factors. Our conception views suicidal attempts and verbal or other communications of suicidal intent as efforts, however misdirected, to solve problems of living, as frantic pleas for help and hope from other people: help in solving the problems, and hope that they can be solved. Whether the individual then actually commits suicide—and this is our central concern—seems to depend in large part on the nature of the response by other people to his plea. If the response to the plea is hopeless and helpless, suicide is more likely to occur. It is our conviction that an implicit or explicit fear or expectation of suicide is most often communicated by a hopeless, helpless response and that this communication is important in facilitating suicide.

Our approach is opposed to the view that suicide-proneness is per se a sickness, existing as an autonomous force within the individual. Seeking the answer within the individual is one of the oldest and most consistently used frames of reference for understanding suicide. Before the era of modern science, explanations sometimes were derived from demonology, the belief in a supernatural being who entered the body and soul of the victim, driving him inevitably to suicide. Sometimes this search within the person led to the condemnation of the suicide as a self-willed sinner violating the Sixth Commandment. But even more recently, the search within the person has led to a conception of suicide as the outcome of a mysterious "sickness" within the person. This approach to suicide is implicit in the popular medical and psychological view that suicide proneness in a person is to be identified as soon as possible. Individuals so identified are viewed as being driven toward actual suicide unless the drive is alleviated through treatment. This concept of drive toward self-murder has

Reprinted with permission of author and publisher from *The End of Hope* (Glencoe: The Free Press, 1964), pp. 1–18. Footnotes have been renumbered.

been most pointedly formulated by Lindemann,[1] who endowed it with the name "hypereridism," defined as a "morbid state of hostile tension leading to suicide." This approach sometimes utilizes Freud's theory of a death-instinct, the striving of all living beings toward a state of nothingness. For example, Menninger[2] describes the suicidal person as one who desires to kill, to be killed, and to die. Related versions of this approach postulate the complex process of the individual's incorporating a beloved but rejecting person into his own psyche, then destroying himself in order to destroy the beloved person and to punish himself in the same act.

Some have questioned this recent view as a pseudo-scientific version of the prescientific explanation of a devil as the cause of mental illness. Szasz[3] states,

> The notion of mental illness provides an amoral and impersonal "thing" (an "illness") as an explanation for *problems in living*. We may recall in this connection that not so long ago it was devils and witches who were held responsible for man's problems in social living. The belief in mental illness, as something other than man's trouble in getting along with his fellow men, is the proper heir to the belief in demonology and witchcraft. Mental illness exists or is "real" in exactly the same sense in which witches existed or were "real."

Implicit in this "illness" point of view is the expectation that one can predict suicide on the basis of symptoms emanating from the person. In medical tradition and in medical actuality, symptoms generally permit a diagnosis which implies the course of an illness. But what are considered to be the symptoms predictive of suicide? Psychoanalysis has emphasized the importance of conditions of depression. In addition, Zilboorg quotes Freud as saying: "It is remarkable that, in contradistinction to depressions, the compulsive neurotic never makes a suicidal attempt; he gives the impression of being immune

against the danger of suicide, more so than the hysteric."[4] Zilboorg comments,

> Patients with other than typical depressions are likely to commit suicide, and in the light of present day clinical experience Freud would not subscribe to his original statement that neurotic patients, particularly those with obsessional (compulsive) neuroses, appear to be immune to suicidal impulses.

He adds,

> Evidently there is no single clinical entity recognized in psychiatry that is immune to the suicidal drive.... While the fundamental mechanism which was described by Freud as characteristic of depressions is met in all instances of apparent depression, in some cases of suicide it is not possible to demonstrate that this mechanism is the only determining factor brought into full play in the act. Moreover, as has already been stated, the clinician observes a number of patients displaying the operation of this mechanism without the suicidal drive being either directly present or effectively operative when present. Hence, the presence or apparent absence of this mechanism cannot well serve as a reliable diagnostic or prognostic criteria.

Most studies of suicide have focussed upon the presence of depression in the people who attempt or actually commit suicide. The presence of depressive symptoms must, however, be distinguished from the psychiatric diagnosis of depression. Levy and Southcombe,[5] for example, found that in a state mental hospital "depression seemed to be at work" in 55 percent of the patients who committed suicide, but only 10 percent had had a *diagnosis* of depression. Diagnoses of depression vary, depending upon many other aspects of the situation. In some cases, depression is a symptomatic diagnosis having little to do with the dynamic mechanisms implicit in psychoanalytic diagnoses. In some settings, those who tend to treat patients with electric shock will more often make a diagnosis of depression than those who tend to treat patients with psychotherapy, if only because the former view

[1] E. Lindemann, in E. Stengel and Nancy G. Cook, *Attempted Suicide: Its Social Significance and Effects* (London: Chapman-Hall, 1958).

[2] K. A. Menninger, *Man Against Himself* (New York: Harcourt, Brace, 1938).

[3] T. S. Szasz, "The Myth of Mental Illness," *American Psychologist* 15 (1960), pp. 113–18.

[4] G. Zilboorg, "Differential Diagnostic Types of Suicide," *Archives of Neurology and Psychiatry* 35 (1936), pp. 270–91.

[5] S. Levy and R. Southcombe, "Suicide in a State Hospital for the Mentally Ill," *Journal of Nervous and Mental Disease* 117 (1953), pp. 504–14.

electric shock as helpful to depressed patients. Dorpat[6], in his recent study of suicide in Seattle, noted that "all patients in this group had evidence of depression." Of 114 suicides, however, he gave only 19 a diagnosis of psychotic depression. Dorpat's attitude toward depression seemed to be important in his finding that all had symptoms of depression. He notes: "The examiners were especially assiduous in obtaining a history of depression." One might comment that assiduousness is scarcely required. It is commonplace to assume that those who commit suicide are uncommonly unhappy; and severe unhappiness is itself a depressive symptom. With "assiduousness," how can one not find evidence of depression in suicides?

Must we not ask the question this way as well: how many of those who are depressed, or who have depressive symptoms, later commit suicide? We do not have direct data on which to base an answer, but there is evidence that the number may be surprisingly small. For example, Stengel and Cook[7] report that in England and Wales, from 1920 to 1947, the average number of suicides per year in mental hospitals was one for every 2000 beds. Since many depressed patients would be in a mental hospital population, it appears in this connection, again, that depression is of small value in diagnosing the "suicide-prone" person.

What seems necessary, if depressive symptoms are to have any predictive significance for suicide, is that they must have an unequivocal meaning and indicate a distinct set of dynamics, directed specifically toward suicide. The literature on depression in suicide does not, thus far, reveal the presence of such a distinct set of dynamics.

Within this view of suicide as an illness, attempted suicide has also been seen as a precursor of actual suicide. There are many studies demonstrating that those who have attempted suicide are not, in fact, special suicide risks. In a series of five-year follow-up studies of several hundred persons who had attempted suicide, Stengel and

Cook[8] found that less than 4 percent later suicided. Batchelor and Napier[9] found that 2 percent of those who had attempted suicide had killed themselves within a year. Hove[10] found that 4.8 percent had committed suicide in two to three years. Most impressively, Ringel[11] at the University of Vienna Hospital reports that of 2,879 patients seen because of attempted suicide in 1948, 1949, and 1950, only one had committed suicide by August 1951. While Ringel felt that the surprisingly small number of suicides was largely due to the treatment and attention offered, we feel that such results generally are not a consequence of intensive individual psychotherapy. On the contrary, as we will indicate later, in some situations where intensive treatment is carried out, the actual suicide rate may be considerably higher.

One may explore the extent to which suicide-attempts are predictive of actual suicide by asking: how many of those who actually commit suicide had previously attempted suicide? Studies of actual suicides have reported that 14 to 33 percent of their subjects had made previous suicide attempts.[12] Or, to put it the other way, no previous attempts were discovered in from 67 to 86 percent of the actual suicides. Although these data are not totally reliable, it seems clear that if previous attempts are used as an indicator of suicide-proneness, most of the actual suicides would remain unpredicted. Thus, an examination of attempted suicide confronts us with two issues which argue against the importance of autonomous self-destructive impulses in the motivation of the suicidal act. These are, say Stengel and Cook,[13] "the comparatively very small proportion of persons who having made suicidal attempts, finally kill themselves, even among those who frequently react with suicidal attempts to stressful situations; and the corresponding fact that among the suicides only a minority have attempted suicide before."

[6] T. L. Dorpat and H. S. Ripley, "A Study of Suicide in the Seattle Area," *Comprehensive Psychiatry* 1 (1960), pp. 349–59.

[7] Stengel and Cook, *Attempted Suicide*.

[8] *Ibid.*

[9] I. R. C. Batchelor and Margaret B. Napier, "The Sequelae and Short-Term Prognosis of Attempted Suicide," *Journal of Neurology, Neurosurgery and Psychiatry* 17 (1954), pp. 261–66.

[10] H. Hove, in Stengel and Cook, *Attempted Suicide*.

[11] E. Ringel, *Der Selbstmord* (Vienna: Maudrich, 1952).

[12] Dorpat and Ripley, "A Study of Suicide in the Seattle Area," and Stengel and Cook, *Attempted Suicide*.

[13] Stengel and Cook, *Attempted Suicide*.

Clinicians may point out that many depressed people are not viewed as suicidal, nor are those whose suicide attempts are evaluated to be gestures. Few, however, would doubt that a "serious" or "severe" attempt implies the acute danger of actual suicide.

One effective study of severe suicidal attempts —done in England by Stengel and Cook[14]—was based on a four- to five-year follow-up of a group of cases which they had classified into degrees of dangerousness, in terms of damage to the individual and an evaluation of intent. They report two pertinent findings: (1) "No grading for seriousness of large groups of suicidal acts can be really satisfactory. . . . Clearly the degree of danger to life is not a reliable measure of seriousness of intent." (2) "At this stage of research, no prognostic inference can be made in individual cases from the degree of dangerousness and intent of a particular attempt." And it should be recalled that in the studies of actual suicides, previous attempts ranged from 14 to 33 percent. In all these studies anything that had the character of an attempt, whether gesture or serious, was so categorized. Thus, the number of those who had made severe attempts prior to actual suicide was relatively small.

It seems, then, that the popular and apparently reasonable indicators of potential suicide— depression, suicide attempt, and serious suicide attempt—do not stand up under examination. None of them seems to be effective in predicting suicide—in identifying the potentially suicidal individual.

Accordingly we conclude that the attempt to approach the understanding of suicide through the concept of a suicidal drive, a tendency toward suicide existing autonomously within the individual, has not proven fruitful. In our introduction we described our approach to emotional disturbance as field-theoretical and psychosocial. Emotional disturbance, we have suggested, cannot be understood except in terms of the field of which the disturbed individual is a part. Much of the data presented in the literature suggest that such a frame of reference may be considerably more fruitful in understanding attempted and actual suicide.

We view suicide attempts as frantic generalized cries for help. Stengel and Cook,[15] who studied many people who attempted suicide, state, ". . . in our society every suicidal warning or attempt has an appeal function whatever the mental state in which it is made." Shneidman and Farberow[16] state, "prevention of suicide lies in answering the individual's cry for help." Rubenstein, Moses, and Lidz[17] summarized their study on attempted suicide with the statement, "we have come to regard attempted suicide not as an effort to die but rather as a communication to others in an effort to improve one's life."

The appeal nature of the attempted suicide is indicated by the fact that most often the person makes the attempt with an expectation and hope of being rescued. Jensen and Petty[18] found that those who attempt suicide almost invariably have a fantasy of being rescued. Stengel and Cook[19] found this fantasy relatively realistic; people often make a suicide attempt in situations in which they have a good chance of being rescued. Rubenstein et al.,[20] described "a characteristic sequence of events":

> The patient was involved in a struggle with the persons important to him and sought a modification of their attitudes or a specific change in his relationships with them. After a crisis was reached in this struggle, the patient sought to effect these changes through a suicide attempt. These changes sought were sometimes described directly by the patient. At other times the patient was not conscious of his seeking these changes, or he denied them, but they were clearly revealed in his behavior. Patients sometimes told of seeking such changes prior to their suicide attempt, of seeking them through the attempt, and by still other means afterward. . . . We often found that a crisis had been reached in a struggle between the patient and the same person toward whom the attempt was directed.

Attempted suicide is a loud cry for help—and almost invariably people hear and respond. Sten-

[14] *Ibid.*

[15] *Ibid.*

[16] E. Shneidman and N. Farberow, *Clues to Suicide* (New York: McGraw-Hill, 1957).

[17] R. Rubenstein, R. Moses, and T. Lidz, "On Attempted Suicide," *AMA Archives of Neurology and Psychiatry* 79 (1958), pp. 103–12.

[18] V. W. Jensen and T. A. Petty, "The Fantasy of Being Rescued in Suicide," *Psychoanalytic Quarterly* 27 (1958), pp. 327–39.

[19] Stengel and Cook, *Attempted Suicide.*

[20] Rubenstein, Moses and Lidz, "On Attempted Suicide."

gel and Cook[21] report that the attempts often lead to significant changes in the person's life through the intervention of other people, such as would come about through medical and psychiatric care, as well as to changes in the relationship with "a special person." Rubenstein et al.,[22] report that in 34 of 44 cases of attempted suicide "desired effects" were clearly brought about through the attempt. They add, "we regard these 34 attempts as successful in the sense that desired changes in the life situation of the patients occurred as a consequence of the attempt. . . ." Moss and Hamilton[23] stated, in evaluating factors in recovery after suicide attempts,

> Success in recovered cases was most often attributable to the therapist's active intervention in the patient's home environment. . . . We found consistently that recovery requires a major change in the life situation. Only three recovered patients returned to the same environment in which the illness arose without fundamental changes in the employment situation or personal relationships.
>
> The most common changes, in order of frequency, were (a) changes in occupation or retirement; (b) significant improvement in the marital relationship; (c) emancipation from domineering and restricting parents; (d) breaking of unsuitable engagements; (e) changes in psychosexual orientation . . .; (f) divorce of immature and sadistic mates . . . and marriage . . .; (g) significant widening of social contacts, recreations, and hobbies.

The therapeutic effectiveness of a positive change in environment is further attested to by the fact that few of those persons whose suicide attempts are followed by such change repeat the attempt. Stengel and Cook[24] found that no more than 17 percent attempted suicide again within five years. Furthermore, as suggested by the data presented, these persons rarely subsequently commit suicide.

How do we understand these results? Actual changes in the individual's life situation mean that change is possible—that the world is not overwhelmingly and absolutely unchangeable, that hope is possible and warranted. The active re-

sponse to the individual's plea demonstrates that he can hope. Furthermore, the concern in the response to the plea communicates the value and significance of the person—as one who is worthy of having hope, as one who deserves concern and active effort.

Our argument suggests that those who follow suicide attempts with actual suicide have made efforts, directly or indirectly, to elicit help from significant others in their world; and have received in response a hopeless expectation of suicide, a helpless answer. The evidence indeed supports this view. The vast majority of persons who commit suicide have told other people about their plans. Dorpat and Ripley[25] reported that 83 percent of 114 actual suicides had previously communicated, one-third by suicide attempts. Robins, Gassner, Kayes, Wilkinson, and Murphy[26] found that 69 percent of 134 similar cases so communicated, 29 percent by attempts. Although these researchers were diligent in tracing down the people with whom the person had contact before his suicide to learn of possible communications of suicidal intent made to them, it is obvious that these percentages cannot fully represent that total number of such communications. Furthermore, both these researchers found that the communications were often made to several different people. Dorpat[27] states, "the data indicate that people who commit suicide usually communicate their intention prior to the act and that they do so to different people and in different ways." Robins et al.,[28] state,

> The mean number of ways per person of expressing suicidal ideas was 3.2. In the majority of instances, expressions of suicidal ideas were diverse even for individual persons. The ideas were communicated, on the average, to two different groups; and in two-thirds (67 percent) of instances the communications were repeated. Thus, not only did the communications occur in a high proportion of cases but they tended to be multiple, repeated, and expressed to a number of different persons.

---

[21] Stengel and Cook, *Attempted Suicide.*
[22] Rubenstein, Moses and Lidz, "On Attempted Suicide."
[23] L. M. Moss and D. M. Hamilton, "Psychotherapy of the Suicidal Patient" in Schneidman and Farberow, *Clues to Suicide.*
[24] Stengel and Cook, *Attempted Suicide.*

[25] Dorpat and Ripley, "A Study of Suicide in the Seattle Area."
[26] E. Robins et al., "The Communication of Suicidal Intent: A Study of 234 Consecutive Cases of Successful (Completed) Suicide," pp. 481–90 of this volume.
[27] Dorpat and Ripley, "A Study of Suicide in the Seattle Area."
[28] Robins et al., "Communication of Suicidal Intent."

They also add that "86 percent of the persons who were reported to have expressed suicidal ideas had recently expressed them for the first time or had shown recent intensification of these ideas." It is clear then that those who actually committed suicide had previously communicated regarding suicide.

The data also support our second contention that the response to the suicidal communication of those who later committed suicide was generally characterized by hopelessness and helplessness. Robins et al.,[29] in discussing the reactions of the important people in the environment to those who committed suicide, report,

> The chief characteristics of the audience relevant to the present analysis are: whether those who received the suicidal communications desired the death of the communicator, were indifferent to it, or were distressed by it. As far as could be ascertained from our interviews, only a very small minority of the respondents appeared to desire or welcome the death of the suicidal person, or to be indifferent. The indifference did not appear to be complete; the suicide was at least unwelcome and unpleasant to this group. By far the largest number of respondents were genuinely distressed and upset by the suicidal death. . . . The majority of the respondents expressed a feeling of marked tension. They were being repeatedly warned of the possible or even probable occurrence of a dire event about which they could do nothing definitive. They did not feel able either to prevent the suicidal act or to ameliorate the psychiatric illness. Nor had they been able to turn total responsibility for the person over to anyone else.

They describe the respondents as denying and rejecting the fear-arousing communications; as denying the possibility of real suicide; or, lastly, "they rejected the significance of the communication."

> It was our impression that initially the critical considerations here were whether the respondent had little or no idea of what to do for the suicidal person or whether he believed he should see a psychiatrist or other physician. In the cases where a psychiatrist or other physician had examined the suicidal person and had not hospitalized him or had hospitalized him only briefly, the respondents were left with the problem of a communicator who was in part their responsibility and for whom they knew nothing definitive to do. As a result, the original picture of themselves as being helpful and effective in getting the suicidal person to a physician was changed and they were left with an insoluble problem. It should be pointed out that there is a lack of realistic information concerning what a respondent should do when confronted with this kind of situation. This is due to a lack of knowledge of the medical profession and not only of the respondents. No clear-cut information is available to physicians or to the public as to what should be done in this situation. A very real dilemma, therefore, confronts the respondent.

Thus the respondents to those people who did actually commit suicide were characterized as distressed, upset, using denial, and feeling helpless. (Obviously, the results were influenced by the fact that the study was done after the suicides had occurred.)

These findings present a sharp contrast to the quality of the responses reported by Rubenstein and his collaborators[30] in cases where suicide was attempted but did not eventually occur. They attempted to assess the immediate reactions of others to the patient and to the attempt. They distinguished three major immediate responses: "(1) concerned and sympathetic, (2) calm and relatively indifferent, and (3) punitive and counteraggressive." They state,

> These immediate responses are of importance in dealing with suicide attempts because of the indications they offer of whether or not a given attempt will be followed by desired change in the patient's life situation, and hence of whether or not the needs which brought about the attempt will continue to operate.

> In 22 of the 35 attempts where the "desired effect" was achieved, the immediate response shown by at least one important person was concern and sympathy. . . . Of the only two cases in which a "desired effect" was discernible but not achieved, the response elicited was consistently calm and indifferent in one and consistently punitive and counteraggressive in the other.

These studies suggest that when the response to attempted suicide was positive and active, only a small percentage (two or three percent) subsequently committed suicide. Conversely,

---

[29] *Ibid.*

[30] Rubenstein, Moses and Lidz, "On Attempted Suicide."

there are strong indications that actual suicide follows upon a helpless, fearful response to communication of suicide intent. Two clinical examples with markedly different consequences seem to support our point of view. Wilmer[31] used none of the "traditional measures" in dealing with suicide in his therapeutic community, "though over 10 percent of our patients had made bona fide suicidal attempts prior to their admission and the risk was probably present in 25 percent of the total patient sample." He states,

> The practice of writing "suicidal precautions" orders on patients' charts, it seems to me, is sometimes a "buck-passing" device that is not only ineffectual but has some very unfortunate results. If the staff is made to feel responsible for what the psychiatrist himself cannot prevent, their anxiety mounts. The doctor goes home. They are left with the orders, the responsibility, and the patient. They tensely watch him and follow him about, thereby isolating him from the patient community as a specially dangerous case; then, at the least provocation, they medicate and seclude him, primarily to protect or "cover" themselves.

> Under these circumstances, the staff's fear becomes a disruptive element which can seriously interfere with care of the patient. Moreover, this fear communicates itself to the patient. If we expect that he is going to attempt suicide, our expectation is communicated to him by the elaborate precautions we are taking. This only increases the chances that he will do so. On the other hand, the firm expectation that he will not commit suicide can also be communicated to the patient, and can have an effect that will considerably reduce the risk.

In his ten-month experiment, two patients made suicide attempts and neither could be described as serious or well-planned.

An illustration of the outcome of a helpless, fearful response is found in a paper by Moss and Hamilton.[32] They viewed their patients—people who had attempted suicide—with the expectation that they would actually suicide unless they received therapy specifically directed to the elimination of the suicidal drive. They state: "Since in our series [of cases] only seriously sui-

cidal patients were selected, therapy was often life-saving." While treating their patients with intensive psychotherapy, they expected a recurrence of suicidal impulses. "The reactivation phase must be anticipated. The patient and his relatives must be adequately warned and prepared for a return of suicidal urges and symptoms." Thus, their expectations were explicit. Their results were as follows. "Fifty percent of our cases were considered recovered and 20 percent much improved. . . . Four patients remained unimproved and permanently hospitalized. Eleven died by suicide." That is, 22 percent of their total group actually committed suicide [22,000 per 100,000], a figure strikingly higher than any other report on follow-up of persons hospitalized as a consequence of suicidal attempts.

Our view is that the expectation of suicide and feelings of hopelessness and helplessness are facilitative of actual suicide. The expectations of Moss and Hamilton, as they appear in their statements, were clear; the relatives were warned of the suicidal danger. It is noteworthy here that "four-fifths of reactivations occurred while the patient was on a day or overnight visit." Further, "the characteristic reactivation of the suicidal drive in over 90 percent of the patients . . . occurred when the patient was considered markedly improved and had the opportunity to come into contact once more with the environment in which the illness began." We suggest that the families, faced with the warning that their relatives were intense suicidal risks, felt hopeless and helpless and expected suicide to occur. The relatively high suicide rate in Moss and Hamilton's group may be a consequence of the communication of the therapist's fears and expectations.[33]

It is striking in this context to find that in discussing factors in recovery, Moss and Hamilton report the crucial significance of "fundamental changes in the employment situation or personal relationships." This emphasis on changes in the individual's life-space seems inconsistent

[31] H. A. Wilmer, *Social Psychiatry in Action* (Springfield, Ill.: C. C. Thomas, 1958).

[32] Moss and Hamilton, "Psychotherapy of the Suicidal Patient."

[33] Moss and Hamilton (*ibid.*) argue that their high rate was a consequence of the very seriousness of the previous attempts of these persons. Yet Stengel and Cook, who attempted to predict suicide from the seriousness of the attempt, found that they were unable to do so. Likewise, Rubenstein, Moses and Lidz ("On Attempted Suicide") feel that seriousness of intent to kill oneself cannot be judged from the danger involved in the suicide attempt.

with their general "illness" approach and their emphasis on individual psychotherapy as necessary to prevent suicide. In fact, their detailed study and the conclusions quoted earlier can be seen as strongly supporting our view that when positive changes are made in the field—in the world of the disturbed individual—actual suicide does not occur.

Sociological studies suggest that actual suicide tends to occur when there is a process in which negative changes occur in the individual's field, leading to a decrease of hope. Durkheim,[34] in his classic discussion of suicide, interpreted "egoistic suicide" as an outcome of that loss of meaning in life which results from disintegration of the individual's relations with other persons and with social groups.

Henry and Short[35] give figures on suicide as it is related to periods of economic depression—which would affect most profoundly, one might reasonably assume, the social roles of those whose lives are most affected by fluctuations in the business cycle. This assumption is supported by their findings which show that the rate of suicide among males (who lose jobs) goes up more in depression periods than does the suicide rate for females; that persons living in higher rental areas (who may have to leave them) show more increase in suicide rate during depression than those in lower rental areas (who cannot leave their area); that white persons (who have more stable social roles in normal times) increase their rate of suiciding during depressions more than do Negroes. Other findings similarly support the connection between suicide and the loss of some significant aspect of life. The high rate among widows, widowers, and divorcees has been long and repeatedly noted. Older persons, especially those who have been separated from their families, have a high rate.[36] Persons who have recently fallen into poverty have a high rate,[37] as do the newly unemployed.

It is interesting that Sainsbury[38] finds that low income per se does not lead to a high rate of suicide, except for the poverty-stricken; many of the working class persons in this study lived in highly socially integrated and very stable communities. Sainsbury points out that in studies such as Cavan's,[39] which showed high suicide rates in the disorganized and poor sections of the city, the high rates may reflect instability rather than poverty.

These data strongly suggest that suicide and preoccupation with suicide are more likely to occur in response to a new experience involving the loss of a stable role. Suicide, then, is not made more likely solely by what may objectively be expected to be an "intolerable situation" but by a new set of circumstances which destroys the individual's entire sense of adequacy for dealing with the world as he knows and views it. The intolerability has to be viewed subjectively and not "objectively."

The experience, then, of an individual pushed to the point of making a suicidal communication is one of feeling that his life situation has become impossible. His identity has been undermined; his self-esteem sinks. In their review of the literature on suicide from 1945 to 1956, Vitanza, Church, and Offenkrantz[40] find that one of the few points upon which researchers generally agree is that suicidal persons have self-derogatory feelings, feelings of worthlessness and self-hatred. Andics,[41] in a study of 100 persons who attempted suicide, found them to have feelings of unworthiness as well as a sense of meaninglessness.

Threatened with the loss of purpose and hope, and feeling as a consequence that life is empty, what can such people do? Obviously, they can seek new bases for hope. They are most likely to seek it in their relationships with others, since these relationships provided them with adequate and hopeful social roles in the past. It is noteworthy that persons with low self-esteem tend to depend upon others for guidance and to be more responsive to their expectations.[42] The work re-

[34] E. Durkheim, *Suicide* (Glencoe, Ill.: The Free Press, 1951).

[35] A. F. Henry and J. F. Short, *Suicide and Homicide* (Glencoe, Ill.: The Free Press, 1954).

[36] Batchelor and Napier, "Sequelae and Short-Term Prognosis."

[37] P. Sainsbury, *Suicide in London* (London: Chapman-Hall, 1955).

[38] *Ibid.*

[39] Ruth S. Cavan, *Suicide* (Chicago: University of Chicago Press, 1926).

[40] A. Vitanza, E. Church, and W. Offenkrantz, "Suicide: A Review of the Literature, 1945–1956," *International Record of Medicine* 170 (1957), pp. 678–83, 697–99.

[41] M. von Andics, *Suicide and the Meaning of Life* (London: 1947).

[42] E. Stotland et al., "The Effects of Group Expectations and Self-Esteem upon Self-Evaluation," *Journal of Abnormal and Social Psychology* 54 (1957), pp. 55–63.

ported by Janis and his co-workers[43] suggests that persons of low self-esteem are more persuasible than persons of high self-esteem. Furthermore, Janis et al., report that mental patients generally, with their low sense of adequacy, are more persuasible than "normal people." Therefore, when people in such a state appeal to others, the response provided them will have important, and sometimes crucial, effects. Crucial are the attitudes and expectations of important people in the troubled individual's world: family members, treatment personnel, etc. It is this aspect of our view which seems to offer an important clue to the "why" of suicide as a solution, as contrasted with, let us say, the development of a psychosis.

In our view, when the disturbed individual seeks an organizing principle or purpose he will be guided to a great extent by his interpretation of the expectations of people significant to him in his world. How others identify him seems crucial. If the potential suicide is responded to with an expectation that he will commit suicide, his suicide will be facilitated. He grasps at the suicidal identity, and achieves a kind of equanimity and stability of behavior. Many clinicians have noted that patients act in an organized fashion, seem to be getting better, seem to be calmed, prior to a suicidal act. It is putative that when depressed patients organize they are in most danger of suicide. This phenomenon was noted in the Moss and Hamilton study, as pointed out above. In such cases, people often deliberately and thoughtfully go about preparing for the end. Stengel and Cook[44] have noted that they may even buy a plot in a cemetery and make wills at this time. In this somewhat bizarre fashion, life achieves a new goal: its own end.

It is also significant that when the clear purpose to commit suicide is grasped, the suicide is often done away from possible interference from other people. Stengel and Cook, and others, have found that most actual suicides are committed in isolation, in sharp contrast to attempted suicides, which are enacted in a social setting providing for rescue. Although in such cases the individual may be physically isolated, it is noteworthy that he is seldom socially indifferent. We refer here to the argument developed earlier, that those who commit suicide have made many prior communications of their intent. And many write suicide notes, which suggests again that they are not socially indifferent.

How is it possible that an individual comes to grasp an identity which inflicts upon him the ultimate punishment? The soundest basis for our total view of this problem seems to be offered by the theoretical formulations of Erik Erikson. Referring to adolescents, in whom he feels the state of identity diffusion is most often seen (although it is also seen in others in periods of emotional disability, and particularly when the identity is made diffuse through the recent or sudden loss of stability in the social world), Erikson[45] notes the "act through which society 'identifies' its young members and thus contributes to their developing identity."

> If, for simplicity's sake, or in order to accommodate ingrown habits of law or psychiatry, they diagnose and treat as criminal, as a constitutional misfit, as a derelict doomed by his upbringing, or —indeed—as a deranged patient, a young person who, for reasons of personal or social marginality, is close to choosing a negative identity, *that young person may well put his energy into becoming exactly what the careless and fearful community expects him to be—and make a total job of it.* [Italics ours.]

It is our view that "society" can play a similar role with regard to suicide. Some desperately troubled, "marginal" individuals communicate explicitly—and we do not know why—their consideration of the alternative of suicide; others do not. Nevertheless, "society's" expectations are crucial in defining the choice of identity.

The case studies which follow, and which are described in detail, seem to us to supply dramatic illustration of the above point of view. Four patients killed themselves within six months—an epidemic of suicide—in a hospital where only one suicide had occurred since its opening nine years earlier. This group of people all came to the hospital with expectations of being helped. Some were actively considering suicide among other alternatives. In our view, the hospital and its personnel had the potential

---

[43] I. L. Janis et al., *Personality and Persuasibility* (New Haven: Yale University Press, 1959).
[44] Stengel and Cook, *Attempted Suicide.*

[45] E. H. Erikson, "Identity and the Life Cycle," *Psychological Issues* 1 (1959).

of providing a crucial source of expectation and identification. At the time when these patients were admitted to the hospital, the hospital staff's self-confidence was slowly deteriorating. The hospital and its personnel in this situation were incapable of providing the disturbed individuals with new goals, new social roles, new identities.

In their hopeless and helpless state, and finding no meaning in life, the patients struggled still more desperately for purpose. As will be seen, what was offered in the environment of the hospital—in the disintegrating social atmosphere—was the expectation, the fear of suicide. The patients grasped at it as an identity.

CHILDREN'S DISTURBED REACTIONS TO PARENT SUICIDE

ALBERT C. CAIN and IRENE FAST

Increasing attention to the problem of suicide has been evidenced recently by an upsurge in research and theoretical writing, more forthright presentations in the mass media, and the inception of suicide prevention centers.[1] Amidst this, one of the striking gaps in the advance toward a comprehensive sociopsychological study of suicide is in our awareness of children's involvement in a parent's suicide, and in our understanding of the psychological impact of parent suicide upon a young child. In most of the suicide literature, case reports implicitly assume no relevance of the suicide's children to the suicide. Theoretical writings consistently omit such considerations. Comprehensive epidemiologic studies often even omit questions as to whether the married suicide had children. Similarly, many suicide prevention projects apparently ignore the suicide's young children and fail to include any form of preventive work with the children of the attempted suicide or the child survivors of a "successful" suicide.

Whatever the sources of this paucity of awareness and investigation, the matter is surely one of neglect if not denial. The potential patholog-

ical impact of parent suicide upon a child is an obvious matter; it is suggested by the general findings of personality distortions readily stemming from childhood bereavement, and is occasionally boldly visible among those who attempt suicides identical in virtually all respects to their parent's suicide.[2] The cases reported here clearly if less dramatically demonstrate children's multifaceted involvement in a parental suicide. Even assaying only the external events surrounding parent suicide in these cases, the findings include: suicides occurring in the context of family battles focused upon a child, with the child acutely aware of this background to the suicide; suicides directly "precipitated" by the child, most typically by his misbehavior; suicides in which the child was given the responsibility of watching over the potential suicide and stopping any suicidal attempt; instances where a child was aware of a parent's preparations for the suicidal act but told no one; suicides where the body had been found by the child, and indeed cases where the surviving parent obviously knew of the forthcoming suicide, made no effort to stop it, but sent the child to "check if Mom's all right," and grotesque instances in which suicidal parents had their child unwittingly assist them in the suicide.

Proceeding beyond such indications of children's involvement in parental suicide, this study represents an initial clinical exploration of the

Reprinted with permission of the authors and the American Association of Orthopsychiatry, from *American Journal of Orthopsychiatry* 36 (1966), pp. 873–80. Copyright © 1966 by *The American Journal of Orthopsychiatry*.

[1] E. R. Ellis and G. N. Allen, *Traitor Within: Our Suicide Problem* (New York: Doubleday and Company, 1961); N. L. Farberow and E. S. Shneidman, eds., *The Cry for Help* (New York: McGraw-Hill, 1961); and Irene Fast and A. Cain, "Disturbances in Parent-Child Relationships Following Bereavement" (unpublished paper, presented at the 1963 annual meeting of the American Psychological Association).

[2] Such identical parent-child suicides once were considered illustrations of the hereditary nature of suicide.

psychological impact of parent suicide upon children. It is ' ased on the case materials of 45 *disturbed* chilu.en, one of whose parents had committed suicide.[3] The children, ranging in age from 4 to 14 years old, had almost all been seen for diagnostic evaluation and/or treatment in child guidance settings. The materials of the study consisted of the typical data from outpatient evaluations (usually though not always including a developmental history, psychiatric interviews, diagnostic testing and referral materials), plus therapy notes from outpatient treatment if initiated, and in nine cases the additional materials from inpatient treatment.

While the focus of this report will be upon some frequently encountered dimensions and patterns of disturbed reactions to parent suicide, each child's response, of course, was in important ways individual, embedded within his unique personality structure. And the very suicidal acts had distinctive features, each with its impact on the child. It should also be clear that such data as school records, prior evaluations, and extended clinical contact demonstrated that the severe psychopathology found in these children is by no means to be traced solely to the direct impact of the parent suicide and the highly pathogenic chain of events it frequently sets in motion.

Lastly, these children each had to cope with many of the psychological stresses and burdens typical of parent loss: their surviving parent's shock, grief, preoccupied withdrawal, guilt and blaming; their own heightened separation problems and deep sense of loss; misconceptions and fears of death; irrational guilts; anger over desertion; distorted intertwining of the bereavement reactions of the child and the surviving parent; realignments of family dynamics necessitated by the loss; stressful changes made in basic living arrangements; revival or heightening of intrapsychic conflicts and the related problems of the one-parent family.[4] Insofar as possible the following observations are restricted to

those relevant to parent *suicide as such,*[5] rather than with general characteristics of childhood bereavement.[6] Definitive assessment of the unique impact of parent suicide ultimately will require supplementing such clinical qualitative investigations with quantitative comparative studies involving groups of children who have experienced different forms of parent loss.

THE CLINICAL SAMPLE

The nature of this study's data permits little meaningful statistical analysis. Cases were seen from a few days to more than 10 years after the parent's suicide at a number of clinics with different recording practices by various staff members. The clinical material (often from closed cases) ranged from brief diagnostic evaluations to detailed notes of intensive psychotherapy. In the sample there were 32 boys and 13 girls. There were approximately twice as many fathers as mothers among the parent suicides. The age of the children at the time of the suicide: 15 percent under 3 years old; 30 percent between 3 and 6 years old; 40 percent between 6 and 12 years old; 15 percent over 12 years old. The mean period between the parent suicide and psychiatric referral was slightly over four years. It is perhaps worth briefly noting that along a number of dimensions, this group of children was not appreciably different from one of the major clinic's general population in sex ratio, nature of referral sources, age at referral, or range of disorders.

The children ranged widely in the severity of their psychopathology, from relatively mild neurotic conditions to psychoses. What is most striking is that even with conservative diagnostic

---

[3] Note that these were *all* disturbed children, permitting us minimal opportunity for studying more adaptive, integrative responses to parent suicide—and suggesting caution in the generalization of our findings.

[4] P. B. Neubauer, "The One-Parent Child and His Oedipal Development," *Psychoanalytic Study of the Child* 15 (New York: International University Press, 1960).

[5] Some of the differences in impact from other forms of bereavement are implicit in the very nature of the suicide's act: its abruptness, deliberateness, lack of inevitability; its implicit accusation and overt rejection of the suicide's objects; the virtual impossibility (by contrast with death from natural causes or accidents) of excluding psychic considerations and interpersonal events as causative factors; also, the unique stresses upon the bereaved following a suicide, and the community's tendency to avoid or blame rather than support the suicide's survivors.

[6] B. Arthur and M. L. Kemme, "Bereavement in Childhood," *Journal of Child Psychology and Psychiatry* 5 (1964); A. Cain and Irene Fast, "The Legacy of Suicide: Some Post-Suicide Patterns of the Suicide's Spouse," *Psychiatry* 39 (1966); and Irene Fast and A. Cain, "Disturbances in Parent-Child Relationship Following Bereavement."

assessment, 11 of the 45 children must be considered unquestionably psychotic (vs. only four psychoses in a *roughly* comparable nonsuicide group of 45 childhood bereavement cases). Whether contrasted with childhood psychosis incidence figures from the general population or from the Children's Psychiatric Hospital where the majority of these children were seen, the incidence of psychotic conditions in this parent suicide group was many times that of the more general group of disturbed children—a tribute not only to the impact of the suicide but of course also the pathological presuicide family background.

The symptom pictures of the children covered a broad spectrum, including psychosomatic disorders, obesity, running away, delinquency, fetishism, and encopresis, along with characterological problems, classical neurotic disorders and psychotic conditions. Perhaps the most meaningful division of these children into clinical subgroups would include two major groups, composing approximately 60 percent of the total sample: those children whose disorders were of a minimally veiled depressive nature (typically sad, guilt-laden, withdrawn, fearful, inhibited) and those with more alloplastic object-loss reactions, especially seen in the more angry, truculent, defiant child, whose plentiful aggressive behavior often seemed poorly organized and almost objectless in nature.

Turning from a brief, necessarily sketchy characterization of the sample, this report deals exclusively with two crucial facets of disturbed reactions to parent suicide, namely, the role of guilt and distortions of communication. While the forms of these distortions varied considerably, dependent upon a myriad of factors (preexistent personality of child and surviving parent, nature of the suicide and the child's relationship to it, the child's age, etc.), their presence was pervasive and often quite blatant.

THE ROLE OF GUILT

The child's guilts related to his parent's suicide were generally so intense that the superego distortions were readily visible in the child's psychopathology: overt in open, even insistent statements of guilt and self-recrimination, or

prominent in a wide variety of pathological forms, including depression, masochistic character formations, guilt-laden obsessive ideation, character structures based on rebellion against an externalized superego, rampant self-destructiveness, and reaction-formated suffocating passivity, inhibition, undoing, and ultragoodness.

Particularly striking were the multiple sources and foci of these guilts. In part, they inevitably derived from typical preexisting sources of hostile wishes toward the suicided parent. These hostile impulses and fantasies were seen as fulfilled by and responsible for the parent's death. Such hostile wishes stemmed from customary sources in parent-child interaction, varied from totally unconscious to quite open anger and in some instances had been unfortunately heightened just prior to the suicide by otherwise transient resentments such as a refusal to give the child a two-wheeler. But quite aside from these typical sources of children's guilt in the face of parent loss, there were numerous special wellsprings. Where the parent's suicide was the outgrowth of a long-standing depressive character structure or condition, the depressive parent often had long exercised his expertise at making his children (as well as his spouse) feel guilty about and partially responsible for his sadness and despair—all the more so, then, for his suicide. Where the parent had been severely disturbed, especially in borderline or highly agitated conditions, often the child had been warned by his other parent or the family physician that he was "upsetting Mom," that he was "driving her crazy," that he must be very quiet and not argue or upset her "even if she does do funny things sometimes." Thus a large burden of responsibility was placed on the child. Even more devastating were those cases where the parent's repeated histrionic suicide threats and gestures had eventually driven the frightened but increasingly exasperated child to the point of consciously angrily wishing that the parent would "go ahead and do it."

Specific incidents immediately preceding the suicide, especially incidents involving some form of misbehavior on the child's part, were quite frequently seen by the child as having *caused* his parent's suicide. Coming home late from the playground, a bad report card, another fight with the boy next door, and even "getting another bad cold" were all stated as the cause of the parent's committing suicide. Single, partial precipitating events (if that) were confused with causes. The confusion and guilt-distorted perception of these events involved more than just the child's guilt, concretization, distorted conceptions of causality and naivete regarding psychic realities. The suicidal parent in a number of cases openly had reacted with rage and anguish as though these incidents *were* the causes, at least the last straw, and shortly thereafter committed suicide. The surviving spouse also was likely to focus upon such a preceding incident in his or her understanding of the suicide, often needing such an explanation if not an external object to blame.

Aside from specific incidents prior to the suicide, the children often felt they were primarily responsible for the general background events and feelings that led to the suicide. That is, the child was convinced that it was his basic badness or his father's disappointment in him that bred unhappiness and ultimately suicide; or he blamed himself for a good share of the marriage difficulties, for consistently siding against the suicidal parent in arguments, for "costing too much" amidst financial troubles, and he especially recalled parental arguments about himself.

Another constellation of guilts frequently encountered centered around the suicidal act. These children felt they should have stopped it and somehow saved their parent. Some plagued themselves with feeling it wouldn't have happened if they had been home instead of at camp or at the playground or at a friend's house. Others fiercely condemned themselves for not having told someone about previous suicidal attempts or preparations for the suicide. In some instances the children hadn't initially understood what they saw of earlier attempts or preparations, or were too frightened to talk about them, or had been sworn to secrecy, or had been rebuffed before when they tried to tell. Particularly guilt-inducing were those instances where the child had been asked to watch over a potentially suicidal parent, to "call Daddy right away at the office if Mommy seems real upset," or "make sure you watch and go with her if she goes down into the basement." This enormous burden was transformed into equally intense guilt when the child failed to give a warning or to stop the suicide. Similarly, some children

found grounds for blaming themselves for not getting help soon enough: for not running quickly enough, not knowing who to call, not opening the windows or being able to drag their parent's body out of a gas-filled room. The ferocity of their guilt was fully attested by their absolute *insistence,* in the face of therapists' interpretations and reality confrontations, that it was their fault.

In addition to preexisting sources of guilt and those forming the psychological context of the suicide, distortions of affects and interpersonal relations following the suicide were further contributants to these children's guilts. There is general recognition of the guilts bred by a child's partial (usually unconscious) satisfaction at the "vanquishing" of his parental rival, and over the increasing instinctual temptations and role-aggrandizement triggered by the death of a same-sex parent. There is also recognition of the child's rage, amidst parent-loss, over what he often simultaneously perceives as desertion by the dead parent. This was much heightened by the more direct, irrefutable sense of deliberate rejection of the world—and its objects—communicated by the suicide. Yet the consequent rage-filled fantasies directed against the suicide were essentially unacceptable, for they poured into earlier angers against the suicidal parent which were seen as responsible for his death, and they collided with defensive needs to idealize the dead parent. The result was that these later bitter angers exacerbated the earlier guilts over anger directed against the suicided parent.

Brief mention is required here of the profound impact of an individual's suicide upon his spouse.[7] The marital partners of the suicide, in addition to the particularly intense guilt and shame typically engendered by their spouse's suicide, have a series of often extremely trying contacts with the police, the coroner's office, and insurance representatives. They usually find in their extended family, neighbors and community not the emotional support and practical assistance usually offered the bereaved, but rather ambivalent avoidance, flurries of gossip and downright accusations. The following describes only one of the many effects the surviving par-

---

[7] Neubauer, "One-Parent Child and His Oedipal Development."

ent's guilts, social embarrassment, and other distorted postsuicide bereavement reactions were found to have upon these children.

DISTORTIONS OF COMMUNICATION

In all but a few cases, the surviving parents (to an extent difficult to imagine) avoided directly communicating with their children about the suicide. This was not a matter of small hesitations, evasions or sudden hushes when the child entered a room. Some examples will illustrate the intensity of the parents' need to block off communication in this realm. A father was pressed by relatives to tell his sons the truth about their mother's death, but he totally refused. When his sons joined the group and *themselves* told their father they knew their mother had killed herself, he first refused to listen, and then refused in any way to corroborate their accurate account of her suicide. A number of these mothers reported they repeatedly prayed that their children would never ask them about their father's death. Another patient insisted he would proceed with an outpatient evaluation only if no mention of the maternal suicide were made either to the child or the referral sources, neither of whom knew. During the evaluation it became clear that both the child and referral sources were fully aware of the suicide. Some parents would not discuss the matter in the face of their children's insistent demands. Most children, though, seem to have quickly received the parent's basic message in subtler fashion. Their parents later stated in all innocence and with obvious relief that "they never asked."

The distortions of communication between surviving parent and children were even more profound. In about one-quarter of these cases the child had directly witnessed some aspect of the suicide, only to have the surviving parent within a few hours or days tell him (and insist upon his overtly accepting) that the death was *not* a suicide, but due to an illness or accident. A boy who watched his father kill himself with a shotgun was told later that night by his mother that his father died of a heart attack. A girl who discovered her father's body hanging in a closet was told he died in a car accident. And two brothers who found their mother with her wrists

slit were told she had drowned while swimming. Efforts by the children to assert the reality of their senses in these instances were derogated, shamed, or met with statements that they had confused it all with a TV program or bad dream. Another type of gross confusion was not infrequently introduced when the surviving parent gave the child different accounts of the death at different times, or when a parent's statement differed blatantly from the versions presented by grandparents, schoolmates, neighbors, or a minister.

Most of these children received in many forms the message, even the threat, that they should *not tell* and they *should not know* about the suicide and that knowing and telling about it was dangerous. Maids, laundresses, housekeepers were discharged "because they knew." The family often precipitously moved to another community where people "wouldn't know." Visits from relatives who talked about the death were actively avoided, as was contact with many friends or previous business associates "who knew." The implications were not lost upon the children.

The pathogenic elements stemming from this context were not solely based on the loss of opportunities to cathart, to relieve guilts, to have reality corrections placed upon fantasies around the parental death, or on the unnecessarily ominous, shame-filled qualities implied by the death's mysteriousness. In many cases knowing became dangerous only as related to the suicide, but in others it spread to learning and knowing in general, and played a major role in learning disabilities and conditions of pseudostupidity which emerged after the suicide. With others, following the suicide there was a sudden onset and maintenance of various inhibitions of speech: stammers, stutters, transient elective mutism and a general reticence to speak.

In only a few of the older children was there an open, angry distrust of their surviving parent, focused upon the parent's obvious lies, evasions and unwillingness to confront with them the realities of their parent's death. More typical of the most fully studied parent-suicide children was their significant distrust of the reality of their own experiences. This was not distrust in a paranoid sense, nor obsessive doubt, nor a psychotic disturbance of reality testing: rather it might be described as a disturbance of the *reality sense*—a tendency to find experiences vaguely unreal, to doubt or disbelieve much of what they're told, and to have a troubling uneasiness about many of our everyday certainties —difficulties which appeared in good part attributable to the prolonged, confused twisting of reality around their parent's suicide.

Two major dimensions of disturbance (of guilt and communication) have been traced in these children: there is more to be said from our clinical data and a great deal more to be explored regarding the multifaceted impact of parent suicide. But the purpose of this paper will be fulfilled if it stimulates greater awareness of the involvement of the suicide's child in the events surrounding a suicide, recognition of the severely pathogenic potential parent suicide has for a child, and sensitization of clinicians to some major aspects of disturbance prominent in the child's reactions and crucial for preventive or therapeutic interventions.

NAME INDEX

Page numbers in italics indicate selections in this volume.

SUBJECT INDEX

Aggression, socialization of, 169–72

Alcohol, as medicine, 308; for religious purposes, 303–7; substitutes for, 309

Alcoholism, among American Indians, 301, 304; antecedents and determinants of, 290–91; and bottle groups, 310, 318–24; and effect on children, 334–36; consequences of, 325; cultural differences in rates of, 299–310; among the Irish, 301–2, 307–8; among the Jews, 304–7; in marriage, 311–15; among Moslems, 304; among Negro men, 326–34; and norms, 292–98; among occupational groups, 309; social relations in, 310; and suicide, 465–66, 469–70, 474–79; theory of causes of, 290–91

Altruistic suicide, 461–63

American Psychiatric Association, nomenclature of, 423

Anomic suicide, 461, 463

Approaches to deviant behavior, biological, 16; economic, 16; psychological, 16; sociological, 15–29

Armed robbery, arrest strategy in, 116; functional differentiation and group structure in, 118–20; minimum essentials of, 120–21; skills in, 122–23; social organization of, 111–23; styles in, 122–23

Authority, and corruption of guards in prisons, 224–29; by default, 227–28; by friendship, 226–27; by reciprocity, 227

"Bar-hustler," 254

"Bell-shaped curve," 3–4

"Binging," 13

Bisexuality, 233

Black Bourgeoisie, 360

"Bonaroos," 207

Bondsmen and attorneys, burgler's relation to, 129–30

Bottle groups, 310, 318–24; "chiseling" in, 322; formation of, 318–20; group processes of, 318; psych-group functions of, 320–22; selection criteria in, 322–23; socio-group functions of, 318–20; "treating" in, 322

Burglers, external relations of, 123–30. *See also* Tipster, Fence, Bondsmen and attorneys

"Butch," 249–54

"Call-boy," 254

"Cats," 355–63, characteristics of, 356–57; drug use of, 356–63; as social types, 357–58

"Chiseler," 13

Circumcision, 305

Cirrhosis of liver mortality, as measure of alcoholism, 475–77

Commitment, in mental illness, 403–11; and court proceedings, 406–7; initiation process of, 405–6; involuntary, 403–4; social and economic factors of, 408–11; voluntary, 403–4

Convict culture. *See* Prison subculture

Copping community, 364–70; dealer's role in, 368–69; social structure of, 364–68; treatability characteristics of, 368–69

Crime, 92–157; antecedents and determinants of, 94–95; and armed robbery, 113–23; consequences of, 136–38; and the "new" and "old" criminal, 131–36; and police and violence, 138–44; property, 102–10; public concern about, 92–93; rate, 93–94; social relations in, 111–13; and unemployment, 96–102

Crime rate, 93–94

Criminal homicide, alcohol and, 164–65; defined, 161–62; methods of, 163–64; and race, sex, and age, 162–63; sociological analysis of, 160–68; victim-offender relationship of, 165; victim precipitated, 165–66

Delinquent commitment, 39–44

Delinquent gangs, critique of sociological interpretation of, 45–58; the classical view of, 46–49; Cloward and Ohlin's theory of, 55–58; Cohen's theory of, 49–50; and interaction with family variables, 58–63; Miller's theory of, 51–55, as "near groups," 65–71. *See also* Juvenile delinquency

Demeanor, 83–84

Detached gang worker, 68

Printed in U.S.A.

DATE DUE
DATE DE RETOUR

MAR 2 5 1982	APR 0 8 1991	
DEC 1 4 1982	APR 1 7 198	
JAN 2 4 1983	NOV 2 5 1992	
FEB 7 1983	DEC 0 8	
FEB 2 2 1983		
MAR 8 1983	APR 0 1 1993	
MAR 2 2 1983	NOV 1 5 1994	
NOV 2 9 1983	DEC 0 6 1994	
DEC 1 3 1983	NOV 2 4 1994	
APR 1 2 1986	MAY 1 5 1996	
MAR 1 4 1988	MAY 2 6 1997	
DEC 0 1 1989	NOV 2 5 1997	
MAR 1 6 1990	DEC 0 8 1997	
MAR 2 0 1990		
APR 0 5 1990		
NOV 1 6 1990		
DEC 0 7 1990		

LOWE-MARTIN No. 1137